CLARIN in the Low Countries

Edited by
Jan Odijk and Arjan van Hessen

]u[

ubiquity press
London

Published by
Ubiquity Press Ltd.
6 Osborn Street, Unit 2N
London E1 6TD
www.ubiquitypress.com

First published 2017

Cover design by Amber MacKay
Cover art by Manuchi / Pixabay
Licensed under Creative Commons CC0

Printed in the UK by Lightning Source Ltd.
Print and digital versions typeset by diacriTech.

ISBN (Hardback): 978-1-911529-24-8
ISBN (PDF): 978-1-911529-25-5
ISBN (EPUB): 978-1-911529-26-2
ISBN (Mobi): 978-1-911529-27-9

DOI: https://doi.org/10.5334/bbi

The full text of this book has been peer-reviewed to ensure high academic standards. For full
review policies, see http://www.ubiquitypress.com/

Suggested citation:
Odijk, J. and van Hessen, A. (eds.) *CLARIN in the Low Countries*.
London: Ubiquity Press. DOI: https://doi.org/10.5334/bbi.
License: CC-BY 4.0

To read the free, open access version of this
book online, visit https://doi.org/10.5334/bbi
or scan this QR code with your mobile device:

Contents

Acknowledgements

The parts of this research conducted in the Netherlands result from the CLARIN-NL research programme (project number 184.021.003), which is partly financed by the Netherlands Organisation for Scientific Research (NWO).

The parts of this research conducted in Flanders were partly financed by the Flemish government's Department of Economy, Science and Innovation (EWI).

Competing interests

The editors declare that they have no competing interests in publishing this book.

Foreword

Butterflies have the typical four-stage insect life cycle. Winged adults lay eggs on the food plant on which their larvae, known as caterpillars, will feed. The caterpillars grow, sometimes very rapidly, and when fully developed, pupate in a chrysalis. When metamorphosis is complete, the pupal skin splits, the adult insect climbs out, and after its wings have expanded and dried, it flies off.

This quote from Wikipedia (November 2016) is in many ways applicable to the genesis of CLARIN: the project started out as a bottom-up initiative by a number of visionary researchers (the 'winged adults'), who developed their ideas (the 'eggs'), which were successfully submitted to the ESFRI Roadmap, after which funding from the European Commission gave the basis for the CLARIN Preparatory Phase project (the 'fast growing caterpillar' coming out of the eggs), followed by a brief transition phase (the 'pupal stage'), after which CLARIN ERIC was formally established and took off (the butterfly unfolding its beautiful wings for the whole world!).

The whole process took from autumn 2005 until 29 February 2012, the day CLARIN ERIC was born. What is interesting about this is that, although at all stages many people from other countries made very significant contributions, much of the whole process actually took place in the Low Countries. It is therefore not surprising that CLARIN ERIC is hosted by the Dutch Ministry of Education, Culture and Research, and that its Head Office is hosted by Utrecht University.

From the very beginning the Netherlands has played a leading role in CLARIN, in close collaboration with Germany, through the Max Planck Institute for Psycholinguistics, based in Nijmegen (NL) but part of the German Max Planck Gesellschaft as an important trait d'union.

I can say without any hesitation that the activities conducted in the Low Countries have had a very strong influence on the development and expansion of CLARIN. We were very fortunate that the Dutch CLARIN consortium was set up at a very early stage of the Preparatory Phase, which meant that it could serve as a test bed for the infrastructure as a whole and act as an example for countries joining in later. This latter role became even stronger when Flanders joined in and worked together with the Dutch CLARIN consortium on a very close basis.

I hope that this book will show the achievements of the joint Dutch–Flemish effort and that it will serve as an important source of inspiration for parties within and outside the Low Countries for the further development of CLARIN.

Let the world enjoy the beauty of the butterfly that CLARIN has created, with the Dutch–Flemish team in a prominent and instrumental role!

Steven Krauwer
CLARIN ERIC Executive Director 2012–2015.

Preface

The book before you provides a sample of the results of the CLARIN activities in the Netherlands and Flanders.

The CLARIN-NL project ran in the Netherlands from 2009 through to 2015, and launched more than 50 subprojects covering a wide range of scientific disciplines and topics, each focused on making contributions to the CLARIN research infrastructure.

The scale of the CLARIN activities in Flanders was much smaller, and these activities were made possible by the close cooperation between the Netherlands and Flanders for research on the Dutch language, which they have in common, continuing earlier programmes of cooperation to strengthen the Dutch language and support for it though language technology.

The results of the CLARIN-NL project were made possible only by the hard work of many individuals, who, unfortunately, we cannot all mention by name. First of all, we express our gratitude to Steven Krauwer and Peter Wittenburg: they are the visionary 'winged adults' that created CLARIN and got it on the ESFRI Roadmap, a *sine qua non* for any national CLARIN project. They also played an important role in setting up the CLARIN-NL project in the Netherlands.

Next, we would like to thank the members of the CLARIN-NL Board and of the CLARIN National Advisory Panel, and our fellow members of the CLARIN Executive Board. We gratefully acknowledge the hard work that was excellently carried out by the International Advisory Panel in reviewing and ranking tens of project proposals over multiple years and their important role in the CLARIN-NL Interim Evaluation:

- Koenraad De Smedt (University of Bergen)
- Scott Farrar (University of Washington)
- Jan Hajič (Charles University in Prague)
- Erhard Hinrichs (Eberhard Karls University Tübingen)
- David Hoover (New York University)
- Clifford Lynch (Coalition for Networked Information)
- Harold Short (King's College London)
- Benjamin T'sou (City University of Hong Kong)
- Hugo Van hamme (ESAT, KU Leuven)
- Tamás Váradi (Hungarian Academy of Sciences)

We also would like to express our gratitude to the CLARIN-NL project secretaries, Erica Renckens, Jolien Scholten, and Arwin van der Zwan: without them it would have been impossible to manage the CLARIN-NL project.

And we extend our gratitude to the project participants, who designed and constructed the research infrastructure and filled it with curated data and software. There were over 200 unique project participants, several of which are present in this book as authors.

We thank all people who contributed to this book: first, the authors. Second, the reviewers of each chapter: all chapters of this book were reviewed by at least two and often by three independent reviewers; their names can be found in the List of Reviewers section.

Finally, we are indebted to the staff at Ubiquity Press for their help in producing this Open Access book.

The CLARIN activities in the Netherlands and Flanders started relatively early, when CLARIN in Europe was still carrying out its preparatory project, and far ahead of most other countries. We sincerely hope that this book may inspire its readers and contribute to a better CLARIN infrastructure overall and in individual countries, many of which have only just started or are yet to start their work on CLARIN.

Utrecht, The Netherlands,
Jan Odijk
Arjan van Hessen

List of Reviewers

Yvonne Adesam (University of Gothenburg)

Haithem Afli (ADAPT Centre, Dublin City University)

Liesbeth Augustinus (KU Leuven)

Sjef Barbiers (Leiden University)

Hans Bennis (Meertens Institute)

Adrian Bingham (University of Sheffield)

Gosse Bouma (Rijksuniversiteit Groningen)

António Branco (University of Lisbon)

Adrienne Bruyn (Utrecht University)

Jesse de Does (IVDNT)

Karina van Dalen-Oskam (Huygens ING)

Koenraad De Smedt (University of Bergen)

Matej Ďurčo (ICLTT Vienna)

Tomaž Erjavec (Jožef Stefan Institute)

Bronwen Evans (UCL)

Lenz Furrer (University of Zurich)

Eva Hajičová (Charles University Prague)

Henk van den Heuvel (Radboud University Nijmegen)

Gary Holton (University of Hawai'i)

Veronique Hoste (Ghent University)

Nancy Ide (Vassar College)

Bart Jongejan (Copenhagen University)

Dagmar Jung (University of Zurich)

Ans van Kemenade (Radboud University Nijmegen)

Marc Kemps-Snijders (Meertens Institute)

Daniël de Kok (University of Tübingen)

Emanuele Lapponi (University of Oslo)

Ruta Marcinkeviciene (Vytautas Magnus University)

John McCrae (National University of Ireland, Galway)

Paul Meurer (Aksis, Unifob, University of Bergen)

Monica Monachini (ILC-CNR)

Karlheinz Mörth (Austrian Academy of Sciences)

Jauco Noordzij (Huygens ING)

Antje Orgassa (Hogeschool van Arnhem en Nijmegen)

Henk Pander Maat (Utrecht University)

Rūta Petrauskaitę (Vytautas Magnus University)

Maciej Piasecki (Wrocław University of Technology)

Stelios Piperidis (Institute for Language and Speech Processing (ILSP), Athens)

Nicoline van der Sijs (Meertens Institute)

Kiril Simov (Linguistic Modelling Laboratory, IICT-BAS)

Pavel Smrž (Brno University of Technology)

Maria Sukhareva (Goethe University Frankfurt)

Thorsten Trippel (University of Tübingen)

Frank Van Eynde (University of Leuven)

Pierre Van Hecke (University of Leuven)

Dieter Van Uytvanck (CLARIN ERIC)

Erik Velldal (Oslo University)

Christophe Verbruggen (Ghent University)

Andreas Witt (Institut für Deutsche Sprache)

Martin Wynne (University of Oxford)

Joost Zwarts (Utrecht University)

CHAPTER 1

CLARIN in the Low Countries: Introduction

Jan Odijk and Arjan van Hessen

UiL-OTS, Utrecht University

j.odijk@uu.nl, A.J.vanHessen@uu.nl

ABSTRACT

In this chapter we introduce the notion of research infrastructure, CLARIN as a research infrastructure for the Humanities and Social Sciences, the CLARIN projects carried out in the Low Countries (the Netherlands and Flanders), and some closely related projects in the Netherlands. We end with a description of the structure of this book.

1.1 Introduction

This book describes the results of activities undertaken to construct the CLARIN research infrastructure in the Low Countries (CLARIN-LC), i.e., in the Netherlands and in Flanders (the Dutch-speaking part of Belgium).

The activities in the Netherlands were carried out mainly through the CLARIN-NL project, a national project for the design, construction, and exploitation of the Netherlands part of the European-wide CLARIN infrastructure. Through a proposal for joint activities on CLARIN between the Netherlands and Flanders for the (shared) Dutch language, it was possible to obtain some (small) funds for work on CLARIN in Flanders. Results of the close collaboration of the CLARIN communities in the Netherlands and Flanders, as well as results of independent activities of the Flanders CLARIN community, are included in this book.

In this chapter, we will provide some basic information on the background and history (section 1.2) of CLARIN, and its basic characteristics (section 1.3). In section 1.4 we describe the CLARIN projects in the Netherlands and in Flanders, as well as some independent but closely related projects. We sketch the structure of this book in section 1.5.

How to cite this book chapter:

Odijk, J and van Hessen, A. 2017. CLARIN in the Low Countries: Introduction. In: Odijk, J and van Hessen, A. (eds.) *CLARIN in the Low Countries*, Pp. 1–9. London: Ubiquity Press. DOI: https://doi.org/10.5334/bbi.1. License: CC-BY 4.0

1.2   CLARIN: Historical Background

CLARIN Europe   CLARIN is an acronym for *Common Language Resources and Technologies Infrastructure*. A proposal for CLARIN was submitted and accepted for inclusion in the 2006 ESFRI Roadmap.[1] A proposal for a CLARIN Preparatory Project coordinated by Utrecht University (CLARIN-PP, 2008–2011) was submitted and received funding from the European Commission.

Since February 2012 CLARIN is coordinated by CLARIN ERIC, hosted by the Netherlands. An *ERIC (European Research Infrastructure Consortium)* is a legal entity at the European level specifically set up for European research infrastructures. An ERIC has countries or intergovernmental organisations as its members. CLARIN ERIC has 19 members (Austria, Bulgaria, the Czech Republic, Denmark, the Dutch Language Union, Estonia, Finland, Germany, Greece, Hungary, Italy, Latvia, Lithuania, the Netherlands, Norway, Poland, Portugal, Slovenia, and Sweden), with the UK as an observer, and the number of members is growing.[2] Each ERIC member commits to paying the ERIC yearly fee and to contributing to the CLARIN infrastructure by setting up national projects to this end.

CLARIN in the Netherlands   In the Netherlands the national CLARIN project was called *CLARIN-NL*. It ran from 2009 through 2015. Though the CLARIN-NL project finished in 2015, funding was obtained for two projects to continue and extend the work on infrastructures for the Humanities: CLARIAH-SEED (2013–2014), and CLARIAH-CORE (2015–2018).

CLARIN in Flanders   In Flanders, the activities for CLARIN were funded from 2010 through 2012, in part thanks to a close collaboration with CLARIN in the Netherlands. Independently funded projects also made several contributions to CLARIN.

1.3   The CLARIN Infrastructure

The CLARIN infrastructure (from now on simply *CLARIN*) is a **research infrastructure** for **Humanities researchers** who work with **digital language resources**. We will explain each of the bold-faced terms.

Infrastructure refers to (usually large-scale) basic physical and organisational resources, structures and services needed for the operation of a society or enterprise.[3] Familiar examples are railway networks (Figure 1.1), road networks, electricity networks, but also (on a smaller scale) Eduroam[4], which provides world-wide wireless internet facilities through higher and further education organisations.

A **research infrastructure** is an infrastructure intended for carrying out research, i.e., facilities, resources and related services used by the scientific community to conduct top-level research. Famous examples are the European Extremely Large Telescope (E-ELT) in Chile (Figure 1.2) and the CERN Large Hadron Collider.

---

[1] ESFRI is an acronym for European Strategy Forum on Research Infrastructures (http://www.esfri.eu/).

[2] This is the situation on 15 November 2016. See https://www.clarin.eu/content/participating-consortia for an up-to-date overview.

[3] This description is an adaptation of the description from English-language Wikipedia (http://en.wikipedia.org/wiki/Infrastructure).

[4] We will provide hyperlinks in the text but usually not show the URL. People reading this chapter electronically can directly click on such links. People who read this chapter on paper do not want to copy the URLs by hand anyway, so they will turn to the electronic version if they want to follow a link.

Figure 1.1: Dutch Railway Network (picture from Wikipedia).

Humanities researchers include linguists, historians (including art historians), literary scholars, philosophers, religion scholars, and others, as well as political science researchers, who are usually considered part of the Social Sciences.[5]

Digital language resources includes both data and software. They include a wide spectrum of digital data types:

- Data in natural language (texts, lexicons, grammars, etc.)
- Databases about natural language (typological databases, dialect databases, lexical databases, etc.)
- Audio-visual data containing (written, spoken, signed) language (e.g. pictures of manuscripts, audiovisual data for language description, descriptions of sign language, interviews, radio and TV programmes, etc.)

As for software, digital language resources include software dedicated to browsing and searching in digital language data (e.g. software to search in a linguistically annotated text corpus), as well

---

[5] CLARIN at the European scale is intended for the Humanities *and* the Social Sciences, but the Netherlands has focused on the Humanities.

Figure 1.2: European Extremely Large Telescope in Chile (source: Wikipedia).

as software to analyse, enrich, process, and visualise digital language data, (e.g., a parser, which enriches each sentence in a text corpus with a syntactic structure). We will often use the term *resource* as shorthand for *digital language resource*.

CLARIN is intended for **language** in various functions, including:

- As an object of inquiry
- As a carrier of cultural content
- As a means of communication
- As a component of identity

Though the creation of data for research certainly is part of creating a research infrastructure, CLARIN-LC has **not** created any new data. It has mainly adapted existing data and software to make them compliant with CLARIN-requirements and interoperable, and it has created new user-friendly software for searching, analysing and visualising data.

CLARIN is not one big physical installation on a single location such as the CERN Large Hadron Collider or the Chile Large Telescope. On the contrary, CLARIN is

- a **distributed** infrastructure, which has been implemented as a network of **CLARIN centres**. A CLARIN centre is a centre that is certified as such and provides CLARIN services. The Netherlands has several such centres. These will be discussed in more detail in chapters 3 and 4.
- a **virtual** infrastructure, which provides services electronically (via the internet). Every user can use CLARIN from any location where (s)he has access to internet.[6]

Many applications have been developed that enable searching, enriching, analysing or visualising huge amounts of data. These applications are web applications, so that no software needs to be downloaded or installed on the local computer of a researcher. The data that the applications apply to are stored on servers at CLARIN centres, so that no data need to be downloaded and stored locally. This is important, because the huge size of the relevant data makes storing them locally

---

[6] Though CLARIN also makes available software that operates locally on a single computer. This is necessary in some cases where internet access is absent or limited.

increasingly more difficult. Many applications have been developed in CLARIN with multiple user-interfaces, ranging from very user-friendly interfaces intended for novice users to expert interfaces which offer full functionality but require expert knowledge, and many intermediate forms. In many search applications, queries formulated through a simple interface can also be seen in the more complex interfaces, so that more complex queries can be built up incrementally, starting with a relatively simple query in a simple interface, and extended and refined in one of the more advanced interfaces. In this way CLARIN makes many more data accessible to researchers than ever before, and the researchers can actually use the data thanks to the dedicated user interfaces of the web applications that apply to these data. We will see many examples of such applications in the book parts II through IV.

The CLARIN infrastructure is still under construction, is highly incomplete, and is fragile in some respects. The development of the infrastructure also differs dramatically from country to country. Some countries started their national projects rather early (e.g. Germany, the Czech Republic and the Netherlands), but others only recently joined CLARIN ERIC and are still to start their national project. Budgets also differ significantly from country to country, which also determines the amount of work that can be done.

Many parts of the CLARIN infrastructure can already be used. In fact, it is already used for carrying out research, and yielded scientific articles. Concrete examples are the articles in the Lingua Special Issue on CLARIN (Odijk, 2016b), the PhD thesis (Augustinus, 2015), which crucially uses GrETEL (see chapter 22), and the PhD thesis (Hansen-Morath, 2016), which crucially uses Gabmap (Leinonen et al., 2016).

1.4   Projects in CLARIN-LC

In the Netherlands, the CLARIN-NL project ran from 2009 through 2015. It will be described in more detail in section 1.4.1. The project in Flanders is described in section 1.4.2. There are also several independent but related projects in the Netherlands, which will be described in section 1.4.3.

1.4.1   The CLARIN-NL project

The CLARIN-NL project received a funding of approximately 9 million euros for the period from 2009 through 2015 from the Netherlands Organisation for Scientific Research (NWO) roadmap for large-scale research infrastructures.

The CLARIN-NL project had a mixed set-up. On the one hand, a top-down approach was taken to implement essential functionality for the Netherlands part of the CLARIN infrastructure, for setting up the network of CLARIN centres, and for contributions to the central CLARIN infrastructure. Projects for these activities were defined and were assigned to relevant experts in the field selected by the CLARIN-NL Board. Originally two big projects were defined for this purpose, but in later stages multiple additional (usually relatively small) projects turned out to be necessary due to new developments, lacking functionality, increased use of certain services which required coordination, support for newly developed software, etc. More than 21% of the total budget was spent on these top-down activities.

On the other hand, a more bottom-up approach was taken for populating the infrastructure with data and software services. Here a small consortium consisting of one or more Humanities researchers and a CLARIN centre could make a proposal for the curation of existing data (i.e., for making them CLARIN-compatible) and/or for creating or updating a software application for browsing, searching, enriching, annotating, analysing and/or visualising data. The submitted proposals were evaluated by independent national and international experts, and the best-scoring project proposals were awarded funding. Four calls for such projects were launched. This approach has been very successful in that it offered much opportunity to react to emerging problems, bring in more partners, increase the coverage of Humanities disciplines in CLARIN, and to react to ideas and proposals coming from our prospective users. Almost 46.9 % of the total budget was spent on these activities.[7]

Though CLARIN was initiated by the linguistics and language technology communities, it was always the intention to make it an infrastructure for the Humanities more generally, and even to include the Social Sciences: it is intended for all Humanities researchers that work with language. The CLARIN-NL project was quite successful in involving other disciplines from the Humanities.[8] There were projects on history, linguistics, literary studies, religion studies, media studies, archaeology, political studies, and philosophy, covering quite a broad spectrum of the Humanities.

Of these, linguistics was most dominant, and covered linguistic subfields such as dialect studies, discourse studies, historical linguistics, first-language acquisition, language attrition, language documentation, language typology, lexicography and lexicology, morphology, phonetics, second-language acquisition, semantics, sign language and syntax. History was also prominently present with projects on subfields such as the history of the Second World War, mediaeval studies, naval history, oral history and parliamentary history. In the domain of literary studies there were projects on Arthurian novels, emblem studies, literary reception, mediaeval studies, and songs. For many more details, we refer to Odijk (2016a).

We summarise here the major achievements of the CLARIN-NL project, and indicate where more details on these achievements can be found in this book:

- CLARIN-NL created the Netherlands part of the CLARIN infrastructure with five centres, four of which are certified CLARIN centres (chapter 4);
- CLARIN-NL has incorporated a wide range of data and dedicated software applications into the CLARIN infrastructure, enabling their use by a much larger community than before CLARIN-NL (parts II, III and IV);
- CLARIN-NL has raised wide awareness of the existence and importance of the CLARIN infrastructure within the Humanities researcher community in the Netherlands;
- The CLARIN infrastructure and the data and software applications contained in it are actually used in research, and its use is increasing (see section 1.3 for some examples);
- CLARIN-NL has a clear focus on language but covers a large spectrum within the Humanities (see above, and part IV);
- Big steps have been taken in improving interoperability of data and software, both on the syntactic and the semantic level (chapters 5, 6 and 7);
- Through CLARIN-NL, the Netherlands have played a leading role in CLARIN at the European level and promoted international cooperation (this chapter).

Of course, there is still room for significant improvement. We list the major issues:

- There is as yet no business model that makes the CLARIN infrastructure sustainable, i.e. so that it can continue to exist without occasional funding through the National ESFRI Roadmap funds;
- Interoperability of software and data still requires a lot of improvements, not only in the Netherlands but also in the whole CLARIN infrastructure;

---

[7] This also includes the CLARIN expertise centres on data curation and historical resources.
[8] But it intentionally did not focus on the Social Sciences except for some closely related disciplines, e.g. political sciences, which are, in terms of infrastructural needs, very close to the study of history.

- Visibility of the resources (e.g. via the CLARIN Virtual Language Observatory) must be significantly improved;
- The creation of common CMDI metadata must be made much simpler;
- More sophisticated options for searching through distributed content must be created.

Fortunately, significant amounts of funding were obtained for successor projects (CLARIAH-SEED, CLARIAH-CORE), in which these (and other) issues can be addressed.

1.4.2   CLARIN in Flanders

It was difficult to obtain funding for work on CLARIN in Flanders. Fortunately, by focusing on cooperation between the Netherlands and Flanders, in particular with regard to the shared language (Dutch), funds were obtained for some work in Flanders. The activities in Flanders consisted of two parts:

- Close collaboration with the Netherlands on turning natural language processing tools that were developed earlier (inter alia in the joint Netherlands-Flanders STEVIN project; Spyns and Odijk, 2013) into web services and integrating them in a workflow system. The results of this TTNWW project are described in chapter 7.
- A number of small projects carried out fully in Flanders, in particular on syntactic search (see chapter 22), stylistics (see chapter 16), and tools for extraction of pregnancy and ideological context from speeches.

These projects were carried out successfully, and some results were extended in independently financed projects (e.g., the GrETEL application resulting from the project on syntactic search).

1.4.3   Related Projects

There were other projects in the Netherlands that were independent of CLARIN-NL but played a role in CLARIN-NL: the CKKC-project, Nederlab, and Taalportaal.

The CKCC project (Circulation of Knowledge and Learned Practices in the 17th-century Dutch Republic) was an independently financed project. It aimed to build an application to browse and analyse around 20,000 letters that were written by and sent to 17th century scholars who lived in the Dutch Republic, as well as to enable visualisations of geographical, time-based, social network and co-citation inquiries. It was selected in the CLARIN-EU call for Humanities and Social Sciences projects as the project proposal that '[would] best demonstrate the use of LRT and would show the potential of a research infrastructure in the Humanities' (CLARIN Newsletter 6, p. 3).[9] It has received funding from CLARIN-NL to apply language technology in the project (esp. part of speech tagging) and to make their results CLARIN-compatible. The results of the project are described in Part IV, chapter 26.

The Nederlab project is an independently funded project that aims to provide data and tools for the longitudinal study of the Dutch language and culture. It has also been supported financially by CLARIN-NL and has been set up as the second (virtual) CLARIN-NL centre of expertise, more specifically on data and tools for the study of the Dutch language and culture across time. Within the Nederlab project large amounts of historical data are curated, and their metadata created or curated. A dedicated search application has been constructed to search in the data, their metadata and in annotations on these data on multiple tiers. A first version of the Nederlab application was demonstrated at the CLARIN-NL final event (March 2015), and extended versions that incorporate

---

[9] https://www.clarin.eu/sites/default/files/cnl06_web.pdf.

parts of the multitier annotation search facilities at various workshops in 2015. Development of the full dataset and search application is ongoing, and the project will, when it is finished, bring huge amounts of historical Dutch text corpora and a dedicated search application into the CLARIN infrastructure.

The Taalportaal project is an independently financed project that aims to create a comprehensive and authoritative scientific digital grammar, the *Taalportaal* (Language Portal), which is an interactive knowledge base about the three languages Dutch, Frisian, and Afrikaans. It covers syntax, morphology and phonology. From the Taalportaal links are made to language resources such as annotated text corpora and lexical databases. CLARIN-NL has supported a project to create such links with ready-made queries to illustrate the description of specific constructions with actual examples from richly annotated corpora. The results of this project are described in chapter 24.

1.5   Structure of this book

This book starts with two introductory chapters (of which the current chapter is one). They are followed by multiple chapters grouped into 4 parts, each dealing with a specific topic and addressing a specific user group. Each part starts with an introductory chapter that sketches the background, and relates the individual chapters to each other and to the CLARIN infrastructure as a whole.

Chapter 2 provides a more detailed overview of the CLARIN infrastructure and explains how it can benefit a researcher.

In Part I, the technical infrastructure is described: the technical facilities that are needed to implement the functionality described in chapter 2, as well as their organisation as a network of CLARIN centres.

The remaining parts deal with specific data and software that CLARIN has been populated with in CLARIN-LC.

Part II deals with linguistics: data and applications that may benefit research into linguistics. Given the linguistic roots of the CLARIN infrastructure, data and applications for linguistics are of course prominently represented. In fact, one subdiscipline of linguistics, syntax, was so well represented that a special book part is dedicated to it: Part III deals with data and applications for syntactic research.

Part IV covers data and application from other disciplines than linguistics.
The book structure is summarised here:

Introduction (this chapter)
The CLARIN Infrastructure in the Low Countries (chapter 2)
Part I The Technical Infrastructure (chapters 3 through 8)
Part II Infrastructure for Linguistics (chapters 9 through 16)
Part III Infrastructure for Syntax (chapters 17 through 24)
Part IV Infrastructure for Other Humanities Disciplines (chapters 25 through 32)

Acknowledgements

This work was financed by CLARIN-NL and CLARIAH.

References

Augustinus, Liesbeth (2015), *Complement Raising and Cluster Formation in Dutch: A Treebank-supported Investigation*, Phd thesis, KU Leuven, Leuven.

Hansen-Morath, Sandra (2016), *Regionale und soziolinguistische Variation im alemannischen Dreiländereck – Quantitative Studien zum Dialektwandel*, Phd thesis, Albert-Ludwigs-Universität, Freiburg.

Leinonen, Therese, Çağrı Çöltekin, and John Nerbonne (2016), Using Gabmap, *Lingua* **178**, pp. 71–83. Linguistic Research in the CLARIN Infrastructure. http://www.sciencedirect.com/science/article/pii/S0024384115000315.

Odijk, Jan (2016a), CLARIN-NL final report, *CLARIN-NL report*, Utrecht University, Utrecht, The Netherlands. http://www.clarin.nl/sites/default/files/CLARIN%20NL%20Final%20Report%202016-06-08%20FINAL.pdf.

Odijk, Jan (2016b), Linguistic research using CLARIN, *Lingua* **178**, pp. 1–4. Linguistic Research in the CLARIN Infrastructure, http://dspace.library.uu.nl/handle/1874/339377. http://www.sciencedirect.com/science/article/pii/S0024384116300237.

Spyns, Peter and Jan Odijk (2013), Essential speech and language technology for Dutch. Results by the STEVIN-programme. (on-line ISBN:) 978-3-642-30910-6. http://link.springer.com/book/10.1007/978-3-642-30910-6/page/1.

CHAPTER 2

The CLARIN infrastructure in the Low Countries

Jan Odijk

UiL-OTS, Utrecht University

j.odijk@uu.nl

ABSTRACT

In this chapter I will describe what the CLARIN infrastructure is and how it can be used, with a focus on the Low Countries (and especially the Netherlands) part of the CLARIN infrastructure. I aim to explain how a Humanities researcher can use the CLARIN infrastructure. I describe the basic functionality that CLARIN aims to offer, including searching for data and software, applying software to data, and storing data and software resulting from research.

2.1   Introduction

In this chapter I will describe what the CLARIN infrastructure is and how it can be used, with a focus on the Low Countries (and especially the Netherlands) part of the CLARIN infrastructure. I aim to explain how a Humanities researcher can use the CLARIN infrastructure.[1]

The CLARIN infrastructure aims to offer services so that a researcher

- can find all data and software relevant for the research;
- can apply the software to the data without any technical background or ad-hoc adaptations;
- can store data and software resulting from the research;

and the researcher should be able to access all this functionality via a single portal.

---

[1] There is a series of presentations covering the major contents of this chapter. See http://www.clarin.nl/node/1959.

How to cite this book chapter:
Odijk, J. 2017. The CLARIN infrastructure in the Low Countries. In: Odijk, J and van Hessen, A. (eds.) *CLARIN in the Low Countries*, Pp. 11–30. London: Ubiquity Press. DOI: https://doi.org/10.5334/bbi.2. License: CC-BY 4.0

I will discuss each of these aspects in the sections to follow: finding data and software in section 2.2, applying software to the data in section 2.3, storing data and software in the CLARIN infrastructure in section 2.4, and the portal in section 2.5. I will end with concluding remarks (section 2.6).

2.2   Finding Data and Software

An essential function offered by CLARIN is the possibility to find resources (data and software) that might be relevant to one's research. That is in itself not a trivial task, but it is especially difficult because of the distributed character of the CLARIN infrastructure. How can one find data and software that are distributed over multiple CLARIN centres? Of course, access is possible via the internet, but, as is well-known, web pages and URLs regularly change or even disappear over time: how can it be guaranteed that a link to data is still there tomorrow? Searching via Google will not work, because even if it finds all relevant results, it will also find too many irrelevant search results, and it will not be easy and will be a lot of work to select the relevant ones.

CLARIN offers this functionality of finding relevant resources as follows. First, it offers descriptions of all resources (such descriptions are known as *metadata*). Such *metadata*[2] are made in the *CMDI* format (Broeder et al., 2010). *CMDI* stands for *Component-based Metadata Infrastructure*, and it offers a flexible format for representing descriptions of resources. CMDI prescribes the format of the metadata but not their contents: these are determined by the data provider. I will go deeper into CMDI in section 2.4.

Second, the resources and their CMDI-descriptions are stored on servers of CLARIN centres. The CMDI-descriptions are made available to the outside world via a specific protocol, the *OAI-PMH* protocol (*Open Archives Initiative - Protocol for Metadata Harvesting*).[3]

Third, all metadata records are referred to via *persistent identifiers (PIDs)*, i.e identifiers that are guaranteed to exist and correctly refer persistently. The resources themselves are accessible through the metadata.

Fourth, CLARIN offers browsers and search engines to browse and search for resources via their CMDI metadata. Such browsers and search engines operate on a database of CMDI metadata located on a server of a specific CLARIN centre that acts as a metadata service provider. This database is filled and regularly updated[4] by 'metadata harvesting', i.e. an automatic process of collecting all metadata records made available by the various CLARIN centres (using the OAI-PMH protocol) and storing them in a single database.

Currently, CLARIN offers two browsers and search engines to search for resources via their metadata, viz. the *Virtual Language Observatory (VLO)*, which will be discussed in section 3.6.1, and the *Meertens CLARIN Metadata Search Engine*, which will be discussed in section 2.2.2.

Which resources can one currently find in the CLARIN infrastructure? There are several. First, there are the data and software owned by the CLARIN centres themselves (e.g. the Corpus Gysseling and associated search engine at INT). Second, there are the data and software hosted by a CLARIN centre but originating from a researcher from another research organisation (e.g., the FESLI data and search engine at Meertens). Third, there are CLARIN centres of a special type (called *CLARIN-NL Data Providers* or Type D CLARIN centres[5]), which distribute data independently of (and long before) CLARIN, but have made provisions to give access to the data that

---

2 Though I prefer the use of the term *resource description* instead of *metadata* for the reasons sketched in Odijk and van Hessen (2011:100), I will use the term *metadata* in this book.

3 Lagoze et al. (2002)

4 See http://www.clarin.eu/faq/when-metadata-vlo-harvested for the update schedule for one such search engine, the *Virtual Language Observatory*.

5 This type of CLARIN centre is currently only found in the Netherlands.

are relevant to Humanities researchers in a CLARIN-compatible manner (via CMDI metadata). Examples are the National Library, the Netherlands Institute for Sound and Vision and Utrecht University Library (see chapter 4 for more details).

2.2.1   *Virtual Language Observatory*

The Virtual Language Observatory (VLO) offers facilities for browsing and searching in CMDI metadata. Once the desired metadata have been found, links to the actual resources (data and software) enable researchers to make use of the resources in their research.

The VLO enables a user to do a keyword (string) search for keywords that occur in the metadata. When one types in a keyword, the VLO provides suggestions for keywords that occur in the metadata (query completion): for example, if one starts typing *tree*, one gets suggestions such as *treetagger*, *trees*, and *treebank*. In addition to keyword search, the VLO offers *faceted browsing*: one can select values for a range of facets such as *language, collection, resource type, country, modality, genre, subject, format, organisation, national project, keyword* and *data provider*. For example, if one has selected *treebank* as a keyword, one can narrow down the search results to treebanks for the Dutch language by selecting *Dutch* in the *language* facet, yielding the 15 metadata records for Dutch treebanks in the VLO at the time of writing (November 2016). The VLO currently gives access to around 900K metadata records, and this number is expected to grow considerably in the coming years.[6] One can find the data dealt with in the CLARIN-NL project, as well as the data provided by the Dutch Language Union via the HLT-Agency (TST-Centrale), currently hosted by the certified CLARIN centre INT. For more information on finding data through the VLO, I refer to Van Uytvanck (2014).

2.2.2   *Meertens CLARIN Metadata Search*

The Meertens CLARIN Metadata Search Engine (Zhang et al., 2012) offers an alternative way to find resources through metadata. This search engine operates in principle on the same metadata as the VLO: the metadata harvested for the VLO. But snapshots from the metadata harvested for the VLO are taken at specific intervals, so there may be a difference between what is visible via the Meertens Metadata Search and the VLO.[7]

The Meertens CLARIN Metadata Search Engine also offers keyword (string) search, and it offers query completion but now on all keywords that occur in the metadata. It also indicates in which metadata element the keyword occurs and how often. This helps in selecting the desired or most relevant metadata records. For example, after typing in the character sequence *pe*, suggested keywords starting with this character sequence are immediately shown, e.g., *period*, in combination with the information of how often it occurs (403 times at the time of writing) in the *description* element of the metadata element *time coverage* (see left top corner of Figure 2.1).

---

[6]   The count of the number of metadata records was done in November 2016. However, this number does not say very much, because different providers of metadata may have different views on the granularity of the metadata: in some cases a metadata record describes just one small piece of text (e.g. a newspaper article or a song), in other cases it describes a full collection of newspaper articles for a whole year of a specific newspaper. Finding a good balance between the optimal granularity in function of the main purpose of the VLO (finding relevant research resources) will be a major challenge in the coming years.

[7]   And in the meantime (November 2016) even these snapshots are not taken anymore, so that one finds much less data here than via the VLO.

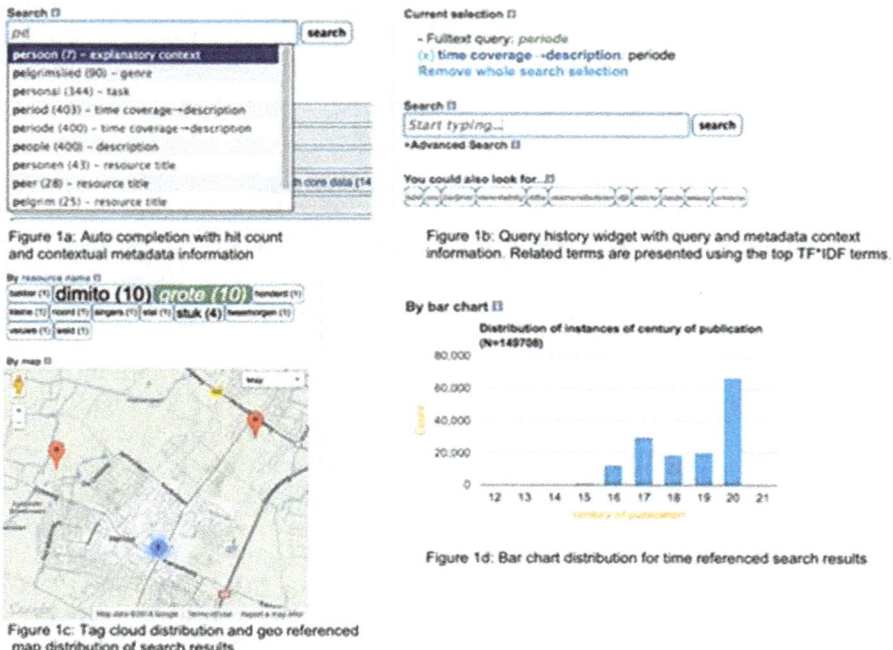

Figure 1a: Auto completion with hit count and contextual metadata information

Figure 1b: Query history widget with query and metadata context information. Related terms are presented using the top TF*IDF terms.

Figure 1c: Tag cloud distribution and geo referenced map distribution of search results

Figure 1d: Bar chart distribution for time referenced search results

Figure 2.1: Meertens CLARIN Metadata Search Interface.

The interface also makes suggestions for other searches (see under *You could also look for...* in the mid right part of Figure 2.1). Keywords suggested there form the most important keywords related to the query based on the TF-IDF statistics.[8]

When a query has run, the search selection is automatically stored, so that a user can refine the search within the current collection. There is also an option to remove the whole search selection.

The interface offers different overviews of the retrieved results, inter alia a dynamic word cloud of the aggregated content within the metadata element (see mid left part of figure 2.1), and it offers different visualisations of the aggregated search features: resources for which a geo-reference is available are displayed on a map (see left bottom part of Figure 2.1), and there are editable charts for displaying the date ranges of documents (see right bottom part of Figure 2.1).

Finally, it recommends related resources (see Figure 2.2) by providing links to related metadata records and a snippet of the first recommended metadata record.

2.3   Applying Software to Data

There is a lot of software in the CLARIN infrastructure that can be applied to data. Even if we restrict attention to the Netherlands, there are too many to describe them all here in any detail. Instead, we will briefly describe what *types* of tools and services CLARIN currently contains, give a few concrete examples with a short description and a pointer to the CLARIN-NL portal, and mostly refer to other parts of this book where the application is described in more detail, or to other literature.

---

8   A numerical statistic that is intended to reflect how important a word is to a document in a collection or corpus (Salton et al., 1975).

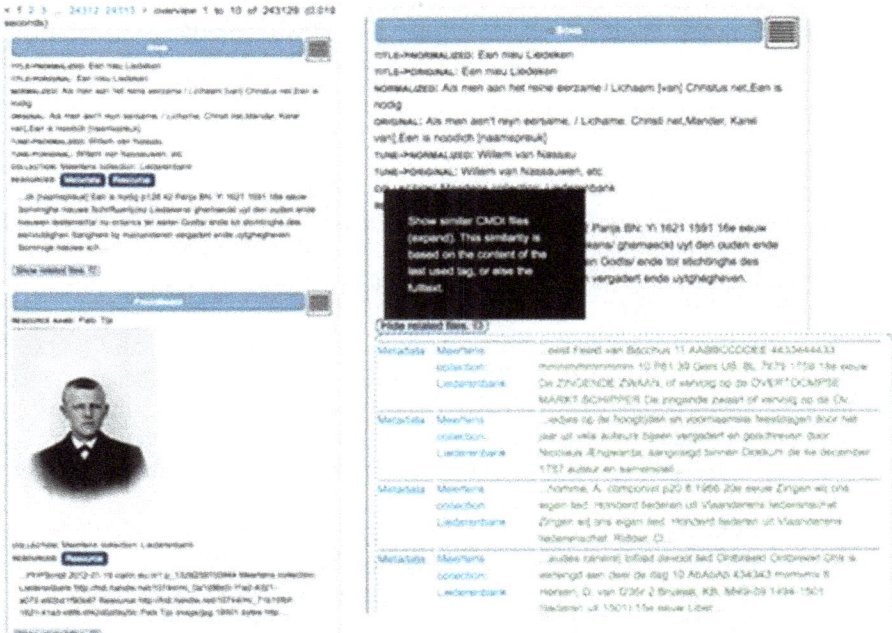

Figure 2a: Customized views different CMDI profiles displaying relevant profile information

Figure 2b: Recommendation list of related results

Figure 2.2: Meertens CLARIN Metadata Search Interface: recommended resources.

The tools and services can be found most easily via the CLARIN-NL portal, under Services.

Three major classes of applications and services will be discussed: searching in data (section 2.3.1), annotation and related tools (section 2.3.2), and processing data (section 2.3.3).

2.3.1   Searching in Data

Federated Content Search is a technique in which a single query can be launched to search *through* multiple resources that are stored in a different locations and that may each have their own particular format. A limited form of federated content search is possible in data via the CLARIN-D Federated Content Search graphical user interface (FCS). This federated content search is limited in two respects: first, it currently only enables string (keyword) search, and second, it only applies to a limited number of resources in the CLARIN infrastructure.[9]

There are also many search engines that apply to specific resources only. They include search engines for searching *in* a wide variety of resources covering a wide variety of disciplines, including literary research, historical research, religion research, media research and social research. See part IV, chapter 25 for a more detailed overview of these search applications and the other chapters in part IV for a detailed description of selected search applications.

Not surprisingly, search for linguistic properties is prominently present, e.g. through search in typological databases, in text corpora, and in lexical resources. Some applications focus on the

---

[9]   At the time of writing (November 2016) one could search in resources from at least CLARIN-NL (though only in data at MPI), CLARIN-D, LINDAT (CLARIN-CZ) and CLARIN Poland. See https://centres.clarin.eu/fcs for a full overview of the current endpoints.

analysis of language variation. The scientific grammar of Dutch in the *Taalportaal* contains links to these search applications. This is described in more detail in part II (for linguistics) and in part III (for syntax).

2.3.2   Annotation and Related Tools

A number of tools focus on annotating resources, i.e. enriching them with new information. They include a web service AAM-LR for annotating where in an audio file there is speech (instead of other sounds), and identifying who is speaking in the parts containing speech (diarisation). Many improvements were made in ELAN and ANNEX, tools for the creation of complex annotations on video and audio resources, and in some closely related tools. In the SignLinC project it was made possible to link lexical databases and annotated corpora of signed language in these tools. The ColTime project extended ELAN and ANNEX with a referencing and note exchanging system. The EXILSEA project enhanced these tools for users of different languages with multilingual features. The MultiCon project enhanced ELAN and ANNEX with multilayer visualisation of multilayer collocates. TQE is a web application for evaluating the quality of phonetic transcriptions of speech files.

Several of the tools for automatic enrichment (described in section 2.3.3) can also be used for annotation purposes. They can bootstrap the annotation by automatically enriching a resource with annotations, followed by manual verification and correction. The FLAT application described in chapter 6 is an application for manual verification and correction of annotations on text corpora encoded in the FoLiA format, and the ELAN and ANNEX tools mentioned above can be used for annotating multimedia resources.

2.3.3   Processing Data

Tools for processing data include a tool for orthographic normalisation (TICClops), which is also embedded in a workflow for converting digital images into textual resources in TEI[10] format (@PhilosTEI, see chapter 32); a tool chain and methodology for converting legacy data sets in the area of maritime history (DSS); an application to analyse writing style (Stylene, see chapter 16)); and a set of web services for format conversions between a variety of formats for textual resources (OpenConvert).

It also includes tools for tokenising, lemmatising, part of speech tagging (Adelheid) and parsing (INPOLDER) of mediaeval Dutch. This functionality is also offered for modern Dutch, together with tools for assigning semantic roles and co-reference relations, and for identifying and analysing named entities. In addition, there are tools for the automatic orthographic transcription of the speech in audio files. Most of these have been implemented as web services or as workflows of web services, in particular in the TTNWW application (see chapter 7). PaQu (see chapter 23) invokes the Alpino parser to parse text corpora and makes the resulting treebank available for search and analysis.

2.4   Storing Data and Software in CLARIN

If a researcher has a resource or is going to create one, e.g. in the context of a research project, he/she can store this resource in the CLARIN infrastructure, and every researcher is strongly recommended to do so. Of course, the resource must meet the CLARIN requirements before it can enter the CLARIN infrastructure.

---

[10] TEI (Text Encoding Initiative) is a widely used standard for encoding textual resources and is supported by CLARIN.

I will first discuss why it makes sense to store one's resource in CLARIN (section 2.4.1). Next, I will describe how one should store a resource in CLARIN, initially focusing on new resources. In storing a resource in CLARIN, two parties are involved: the resource provider (usually a researcher or research group that has created a resource), and a CLARIN centre. I will describe the responsibilities of the resource provider (section 2.4.3) and the responsibilities of the CLARIN centre (section 2.4.4), initially for new resources. Finally, I will discuss what has to be done for resources that already exist (section 2.4.5).

2.4.1   Why Should One Store One's Resource in CLARIN?

The first question that arises when one has a resource is: why store it in the CLARIN infrastructure? Well, there are many reasons. I summarise them here:

Benefits to the researcher A very important reason is that the researcher may benefit from doing so: if one makes one's resource ready for storage in CLARIN, one has to put the data in a CLARIN-supported format. As a consequence, one may easily make use of existing software and data in CLARIN, so that one's data or software can be produced more efficiently, with better quality and/or with more features. One may also use CLARIN tools such as search engines, analysis tools, and visualisation tools on one's resources, so that the resource can be used immediately in research. And when one's resource is in the CLARIN infrastructure, one can be sure it is stored safely, always easily findable and accessible in ways that respect any legal or ethical restrictions, and one does not have to worry about these data in a world where software updates and upgrades are frequent so that resources can become obsolete in a very short period of time. It often happens that researchers change research topics and do not need research data created in an earlier project in the next one. However, when one does need one's resource in a later stage, one does not have to worry where it is, and whether the medium it is stored on is still working: one can be sure to find it and get access to it via CLARIN.

Benefits to others A second reason is that others may benefit from one's resource. There are always unexpected uses of research data, immediately or only years or even decades later. CLARIN ensures that all researchers have access to the resources used in or resulting from research. Furthermore, making one's resource available via CLARIN fits in well with the general scientific attitude of openness. Most resources are produced with public money, so it is important that the whole society can benefit from these resources.[11]

Better science There are also reasons of integrity: we have recently encountered several scandals in the Netherlands where faked data were used in research. Making resources openly available via CLARIN will reduce the risks of such fraud. More generally, science progresses by being open to criticism, and verification and replication of research results are important instruments to make progress in science and are essential for the proper conduct of science: visibility and accessibility of one's research data and software is essential for that, and CLARIN provides ideal facilities for this.

Better publications Since openness about research data and results is an essential ingredient for the proper conduct of science, more and more scientific journals are beginning to require that one publishes one's research data and software, so that the results are verifiable and replicable. For the same reasons, funding agencies are also beginning to require an explicit data management plan, so that data produced in a research project do not get lost after the research project has finished[12] and are available for verification and replication purposes.[13]

---

[11] Here is a clip by DANS on the importance of data sharing (in Dutch).
[12] Which, unfortunately, has happened a lot in the past.
[13] See for example, for the Netherlands, NWO (2014:19, article 30).

Benefits to the researcher's institution Increasingly, evaluation of research units includes requirements on data management and integrity. For example, the Standard Evaluation Protocol (SEP) 2015-2021 by VSNU, KNAW and NWO (VSNU et al., 2014) states that the assessment committee 'is interested in how the unit deals with research data, data management and integrity' (p. 9) and the self-evaluation should describe 'how the unit deals with and stores raw and processed data' (p. 23). Each research unit wants to meet such evaluation requirements and will therefore most likely require that every researcher deals carefully with data: CLARIN offers the facilities for this.

2.4.2 How to Store Resources in CLARIN

If one's research is expected to lead to new resources, it is important to immediately start taking into account that they will be stored in the CLARIN infrastructure. Ideally, one starts with this before any data or software have been produced. If part or all of one's resources have already been produced, see section 2.4.5.

Two parties are involved in storing resources in CLARIN: the resource provider, and a CLARIN centre. Both parties have responsibilities when a resource has to be stored in CLARIN. We describe these responsibilities in separate sections: the responsibilities of the resource provider in section 2.4.3, the responsibilities of the CLARIN centre in section 2.4.4.

It is important for a resource provider to contact a CLARIN centre as soon as possible. The CLARIN centre will be able to help with preparing the resource for incorporation in CLARIN, and the resource must be stored at a CLARIN centre for it to become part of the CLARIN infrastructure.

CLARIN centres come in different types.[14] The type relevant in this context is type B.

The Netherlands has multiple Type B CLARIN centres. They include the Meertens Institute (Amsterdam), the Language Archive (TLA) of the Max Planck Institute for Psycholinguistics (MPI, Nijmegen), Huygens ING Institute (The Hague), and the Institute for the Dutch Language (INT, Leiden).[15] These centres are certified CLARIN centres, which provides confidence that one's data are safely stored there in a CLARIN-compatible way. The Data Archiving and Networked Services (DANS, The Hague) is not certified as a CLARIN centre yet, but is also a reliable data centre. Which one to choose? Well, that depends on the type of resource one has and its primary intended research use. The CLARIN Portal provides information about the various centres and the types of resources they are most suited for. See chapter 4 for more details.

2.4.3 The Resource Provider

The first thing to do is to define clearly what the resource is going to be. Once this is clear, one can select a CLARIN centre, and contact this centre.[16] Next, one has to ensure that legal and ethical issues do not prevent incorporation of the resource in the CLARIN infrastructure and making it available to other researchers. There are several ways of doing this, depending on the type of resource. If the owner of the resource is a third party, the resource provider will have to obtain explicit permission for this through some licence agreement. If subjects participate in a resource creation project, one will have to ask them explicit permission to use the resource in the CLARIN infrastructure. The CLARIN centre can help with this, and there are templates for licence agreements, as well as a licence category calculator on the European CLARIN website. Together with the centre, the resource provider will have to ensure that ethical issues (mostly privacy issues), where they arise, are properly dealt with.

---

[14] This document contains an overview of the different types of CLARIN centres.
[15] Formerly the Institute for Dutch Lexicography (INL).
[16] Contact information for CLARIN centres can be found here.

We will discuss the tasks of the resource provider, initially focusing on data. We dedicate a separate paragraph to the case where one's resource is software.

CLARIN-recommended formats The resource provider has to determine a CLARIN-recommended format for the resource. A list of CLARIN-recommended formats, protocols, etc., can be found here. It is strongly recommended to consult the CLARIN centre on this issue, or to ask help from the CLARIN-NL helpdesk (`helpdesk@clarin.nl`). Since we are in the area of research, it is possible that the resource is of a completely new type, for which no CLARIN-recommended format exists. It is also possible that none of the CLARIN-recommended formats can accommodate all elements of the resource, even though the resource is not of a completely novel type. In all these cases, one has to consult the CLARIN-NL helpdesk first before continuing.

Metadata One or more descriptions must be made of one's resource. These metadata must be in CMDI-format. CMDI (Component MetaData Infrastructure) provides a model for metadata, and a format for them. It also provides tools to make metadata records. CMDI metadata are written in XML (eXtensible Markup Language). CMDI does not in any way prescribe the contents of the metadata. That is completely up to the resource provider (though CMDI helps researchers in several ways to create correct and 'useful' metadata).

CMDI metadata are structured in accordance with a *profile*. A profile describes which elements can or must be used in a metadata record. Metadata elements are XML elements, consisting of a *name*, a *value* in accordance with a *value scheme*, and a (possibly empty) set of attribute-value pairs. The definition of a CMDI element is illustrated in (1):

(1) **Element:**   ResourceName
     Value scheme: string
     Attribute-Value Pairs

   ConceptLink: `http://hdl.handle.net/11459/CCR_C-2544_3626545e-a21d-058c-ebfd-241c0464e7e5`
   Number of occurrences: 1 - unbounded
   Multilingual: yes

It describes a metadata element called *Resourcename*, of type *string*, that must occur once but can occur multiple times. The contents can be in multiple languages. We discuss the *ConceptLink* below. Often, a group of such elements naturally belong together, e.g., because they describe a particular aspect of a resource together. One can group such elements in a metadata *component*. This enables one to treat such a collection of metadata elements as a unit. Metadata components consist of a combination of components and metadata elements. An example CMDI component is illustrated in (2):

(2) **Name: Location**
     Description: Component for describing a certain location (address, region, country, continent)
     Composed of:

   Element: Address

   Value scheme: string
   Attribute-Value pairs

   ConceptLink: `http://hdl.handle.net/11459/CCR_C-2528_1eaf4da1-64cc-71fc-1622-bb5bfd6e52c9`
   Number of occurrences: 0 - 1
   Multilingual: no

> **Element:**   Region
>
> >**Value scheme:**   string
> >**Attribute-Value pairs**
> >
> > >**ConceptLink:**   `http://hdl.handle.net/11459/CCR_C-2533_fa6e1812-`
> > >`e29b-3cf6-e15a-50aa34b9be68`
> > >**Number of occurrences:**   0 - 1
> > >**Multilingual:**   no
>
> **Component:**   Country [0 - 1]
> **Component:**   Continent [0 - 1]

This component consists of two optional CMDI-elements (*Address* and *Region*), followed by two optional components (*Country* and *Continent*).

A profile consists of a combination of components and elements. A (partial) profile description is illustrated in (3):

> (3)   **Name:**   LexicalResourceProfile-DLU
> **Description:**   a profile for describing a lexical resource
> **Components**
>
> >**Component:**   GeneralInfo-DLU [1 - 1]
> >**Component:**   Access [1 - 1]
> >**Component:**   Project [0 - 1]
> >**Component:**   Creation [0 - 1]
> >**Component:**   SubjectLanguages [1 - 1]
> >
> >...

It gives the name of the profile, a short decription, and a list of components that it consists of and whether these are obligatory [1 - 1], optional [0 - 1], or iterating ([0 - unbounded] or [1 - unbounded]).

This component-based system provides high flexibility: *the resource provider* determines the contents of the descriptions for the resource by defining his/her own profiles, components, and elements. CMDI helps the resource provider with this in a variety of ways:

- A list of existing profiles and components enables one to reuse what has already been made by others: it thus saves work, and one can profit from work done by others.
- A profile and component editor [login required] enables one to create one's own profiles and components if existing profiles and components are not suited.
- Metadata editors enable one to create descriptions for resources in accordance with the selected profile in an easy and user-friendly manner. One such metadata editor is Arbil; an alternative is COMEDI (Lyse et al., 2015), developed by CLARIN Norway (CLARINO).

The flexibility offered by CMDI also has some drawbacks. One has to be aware that a major purpose of metadata is the discovery of the resources by others. It is therefore important to include information that characterises this resource and distinguishes it from other resources. It is therefore also highly recommended to use certain components that contain important metadata elements one is likely to overlook if one has to make one's profile from scratch (e.g. the GeneralInfo component, which contains elements for general information about the resource, e.g., its name, title, the time coverage of the data, etc.). One should also be aware of the fact that certain properties that are 'obvious' to one researcher are not obvious to other researchers and must therefore be included in a proper metadata record. For example, several researchers that only work with the Dutch language omitted an indication of the language of the resource in a first version of their metadata record. The same holds for the *resource type* element, which was omitted by researchers who mainly work with text corpora. The profile name (e.g. TreebankProfile) does not itself end up in the metadata record, so any information implicitly encoded in this way (i.e., that it describes a resource of type *treebank*) must be made explicit by a metadata element. It is also important to give one's resource a name: that makes referring to it much easier. And each resource should be given an explicit version number from the start: otherwise it will become very difficult to know later which version is intended.

Reusing existing profiles and components is essential for getting better metadata, since one does not have to reinvent the wheel. It is strongly advised to follow an introductory course on CMDI before making CMDI metadata.

Explicit semantics   The flexibility of CMDI has other consequences as well. In rigid metadata schemes (e.g. a CSV format), the position of an element determines its interpretation, and in certain schemes (e.g http://dublincore.org/) the names of elements and their values are prescribed. But with CMDI, one can choose one's own profiles, components and metadata elements, give metadata elements any name one likes, and also choose the labels for the values of these elements. But then how does another researcher or a computer program 'know' what is meant?

The flexibility offered by CMDI is possible only if the semantics of the metadata elements is made explicit . The CLARIN infrastructure must 'know' what is meant with the metadata elements, otherwise it cannot use faceted browsing in the VLO or the Meertens Metadata Search Engine.

Explicit semantics for a resource or metadata record is obtained by explicitly linking each element and its possible values in the resource or metadata record to an element of a CLARIN-recognised concept or data category registry. The most prominent registry for this purpose in CLARIN until 2014 was ISOcat (Kemps-Snijders et al., 2010). ISOcat describes data categories and their properties, such as a name and definition (in multiple languages), a unique persistent identifier, the thematic domain it belongs to, and some other properties.

ISOcat was the primary semantic interoperability registry in CLARIN, but it was not the only one. For certain types of information ISOcat is not particularly suited (e.g. for names of organisations in all their variants); for others independent registries exist and are maintained (e.g., for language codes: ISO639-3, maintained by ISO). In order to use such other registries in addition to ISOcat in a transparent manner, the CLAVAS Vocabulary Service has been set up as an interface to data category registries and vocabularies. CLAVAS is dealt with in chapter 5.

In 2014, it was decided to switch to a different system, the so-called CLARIN Concept Registry (CCR) (see chapter 4). CCR is a concept registry according to the W3C SKOS recommendation (Schuurman et al., 2016). It has not really played a big role in the CLARIN-NL project, but it will be important in the CLARIAH-CORE successor project.

The values after *Concept Link* in the CMDI element descriptions in (1) and (2) are URLs that provide the link to a concept in the CCR. The concept referred to in (1) is represented in CCR as indicated in (4):

(4)   **class**   Concept
     status   approved
     prefLabel@en   resource name
     definition@en   A short name to identify the language resource. (source: CLARIN)
     notation   resourceName
     changeNote   This concept is based on the ISOcat data category: http://www.isocat.org/
       datcat/DC-2544
     inScheme   Metadata

inSkosCollection Metadata
textCorpusProfile UCPH
uri `http://hdl.handle.net/11459/CCR_C-2544_3626545e-a21d-058c-ebfd-241c0464e7e5`
license Creative Commons Attribution (CC BY) (use the uri above for the attribution)

In order to really use the registries and tools offered effectively, one has to attend dedicated tutorials on CMDI and semantic interoperability through CCR and CLAVAS. These have been and will be regularly organised in the Netherlands. Usually, the CLARIN centre can help researchers in creating the CMDI metadata and the explicit semantics that it requires.

Operational format v. exchange/archive format In several cases, data come in two versions: a version intended for exchange and for long term preservation (exchange/archive format), and a version that is actually used in services (operational format). A concrete example is a lexicon: a CLARIN-supported format for lexicons is the Lexical Markup Framework (LMF). LMF-compatible text formats often make use of XML, and these are excellently suited for exchange of data and for long term preservation (storage in an archive). However, this format is less suited for actual use by a service. For example, a simple search program will usually operate unacceptably slowly if it has to work directly with the LMF textual format. Typically, the data have to be transformed into different formats, enriched with indexes, etc., for such a search service to operate in an acceptable way. This creates the problem that it must be ensured that the operational format version and the exchange format version remain consistent. This requires explicit versioning, and ideally the operational format version is derived from the exchange format version in a fully automated manner. The CLARIN centres can make recommendations on how to deal with such issues.

Software The resource may be software. Software comes in many varieties. First, software may run locally on a single desktop, or over the web. Second, software may have a user interface for specialists (e.g. a command-line interface), or an interface specifically designed for a specific user community (an *application*), or it may have an interface to other software (a (software) *service*).

Software intended for the CLARIN user community must of course have a dedicated interface. It preferably works over the web so that no software needs to be downloaded and installed. Such software thus typically comes in the form of a *web application*. For certain cases (e.g., language documentation field work), there is no or very limited internet availability, and a web application is not so useful: for such cases *desktop applications* are more suited.[17]

It is good practice to separate the program that implements the interface from the backend software that provides the core functionality of the application. This backend may contain a single software program, but it might also contain multiple programs that work together to provide the application's functionality. These programs communicate with one another and therefore they are (software) *services*. For services that work over the web there are special protocols to make this communication possible. The ones supported in CLARIN are SOAP and REST. If a researcher has a desktop program, (s)he will often want to turn it into a web service in the CLARIN context. For this purpose, a special piece of software has been developed, called Computational Linguistics Application Mediator (CLAM), which turns one's desktop software into a web service using the REST protocol (van Gompel (2014); see also chapter 6 and chapter 7). Though CLAM creates a web service, it actually also creates a simple web interface (hence a web application), but that is not necessarily the best interface for the targeted user group.

---

[17] There may be other considerations to prefer desktop over web applications. For example, web interfaces are generally quite primitive and generally slow; if a sophisticated and/or fast operating interface is required, a desktop might be preferable. Ideally of course, one single interface operates both over the web and locally, and uses synchronisation/replication mechanisms to keep the local version and the version on the server in sync.

A piece of software is a resource, and therefore there must be a metadata record for each piece of software.[18] A CMDI profile for the description of software exists and is further being refined (Westerhout and Odijk, 2013).[19]

This concludes the section on the tasks of the resource provider. We now turn to the CLARIN centre.

2.4.4   Services Offered by the CLARIN Centre

The CLARIN centre assists the resource provider with his/her tasks. The centres have experience with CMDI, with semantic interoperability, with IPR and ethical issues, and with CLARIN-supported formats and protocols, so they can advise the resource provider in such matters.

Storing the resources   The CLARIN centre stores the resource provider's resource in its repository. Some centres use special software for this; e.g., LAMUS is used by MPI/The Language Archive, and the DANS EASY archiving system also offers deposition facilities that can be used by users.

Metadata harvesting   The centre makes the resource available and accessible in the CLARIN infrastructure for other researchers. This is done through the metadata of the resource. The centre makes the metadata of the resource available for harvesting by others through OAI-PMH.[20] Links to the actual resource are included in the metadata, and the metadata are assigned a persistent identifier (PID, see section 2.2).

Persistent Identifiers   Each centre runs or uses services for the issuing, assignment and resolution of persistent identifiers, i.e., systems that issue a persistent identifier (PID) when requested and associate it to a precise location, and that, given a PID, determine the precise location of the associated resource or metadata. See chapter 3 for more details on this.

Legal and ethical restrictions   The centre makes provisions for legal and ethical restrictions, so that only persons who are allowed to get access actually get access to resources that have such restrictions. CLARIN aims to make the resources available as openly and with as little restrictions as possible. However, there are resources with legal and/or ethical restrictions, and therefore it is sometimes not possible to access such resources directly. The restrictions can lead to various consequences: (1) a login may be required; (2) approving special usage conditions may be required; or (3) signing a separate (paper) licence agreement may be required.

Logging in   Hiding resources behind a login is intended, in the CLARIN context, to ensure that the user is an academic researcher, or has otherwise received special permission to access the relevant resources. There are also other reasons why login is sometimes necessary or desirable. For example, certain centres preserve data for a user that has uploaded the data to apply a service to it, as well as the data that result from this service. In such a case only this researcher (or the research team (s)he belongs to) should see and be able to manipulate these data, and this researcher does not want to be bothered by data that belong to other researchers or research groups. Logging in is an essential ingredient to achieve this. Certain services require a lot of computational resources, and the CLARIN centre where such a service runs wants to monitor its usage and to control the computational resources made available to a user. Again, this requires logging in.

Logging in in the CLARIN infrastructure is not an obvious thing. The CLARIN infrastructure is a distributed infrastructure, so how can it be avoided that the user has to log in again each time a resource happens to be located at a different centre? How can it be avoided that the user has to

---

[18] The term 'metadata' sounds somewhat odd for descriptions of software.

[19] Its ID in the CLARIN component registry is clarin.eu:cr1:p_1342181139640, but it has not been published yet.

[20] Open Archives Initiative Protocol for Metadata Harvesting (Lagoze et al., 2002).

remember many different user names and passwords? And from the CLARIN centres' perspective, how can it be avoided that each CLARIN centre has to securely store user names, passwords and possibly other privacy-sensitive information?

Systems that take care of login and related matters are called *Authentication and Authorisation Infrastructures (AAI)*: they *authenticate* a user (determine who the user is) and *authorise* the user to do some things but not others. The AAI-system used in CLARIN is SAML-based Federated Identity Management (FIM), with Shibboleth as the most popular software implementation, and it avoids the problems mentioned above.[21]

It works as follows:

- When a user logs in (for example, to edit a CMDI component in the CLARIN Component Registry, which requires login, see Figure 2.3), the user is directed to a login with the user's own institute. See Figure 2.4.
- The user then logs in with the user's institute's user name and password. See Figure 2.5.
- If the login is successful, the institute server confirms that the user is a trusted person, and the user can enter this part of the CLARIN infrastructure. See Figure 2.6.
- If the user now goes to another part of the CLARIN infrastructure that requires login (e.g the Adelheid web application), this other part 'knows' that the user is already logged in, so the user does not have to log in again: therefore this is called *Single Sign On (SSO)*. See Figure 2.7.

Logging out is not so well-defined in this Single Sign On system. If the user has logged in to a CLARIN service, and then goes to a second one (where no login is needed because the system 'knows' that the user is logged in), the user can try to log out of the first service, but then (s)he is still logged in to the second service. So if the user now goes to the first service again, (s)he does

Figure 2.3: The user wants to login in the CLARIN Component Registry.

---

[21] CLARIN only makes use of the authentication part.

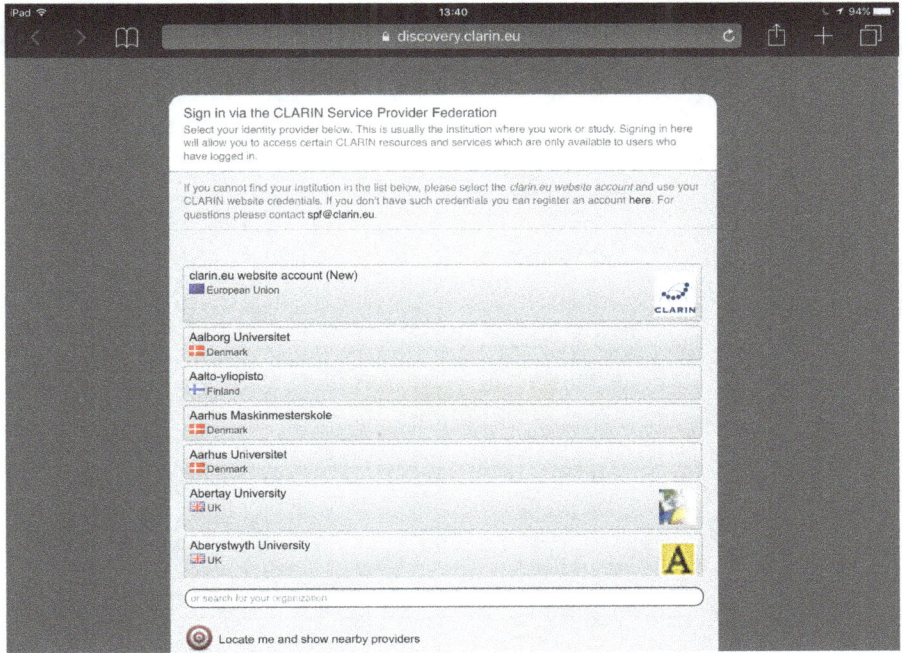

Figure 2.4: The user is redirected to a login via the user's own institute.

not have to login despite having logged out, because it is a 'Single Sign On' system. Logout can only be achieved by closing all CLARIN services, and closing the browser(s) the user used to access the CLARIN services.

Long Term Preservation   Finally, the CLARIN centre ensures long term preservation of the user's resource: it makes sure that it is still accessible after 10 or 20 years or longer. Centres have made special provisions in order to become certified as CLARIN centre. Sometimes they take care of long term preservation themselves (e.g., DANS), but most centres outsource it to specialised centres (e.g the MPI/TLA outsources it to the long term preservation services of the Max Planck Gesellschaft). In any case, each centre must have a clear procedure in place for ensuring long term preservation, and work according to this procedure. This is one of the ingredients of the Data Seal of Approval (DSA), which each centre must be awarded if it is to become a certified CLARIN centre.[22] All candidate CLARIN centres in the Netherlands have been awarded the Data Seal of Approval[23] and most are CLARIN-certified centres.[24]

2.4.5   Existing Resources

If a researcher already has a resource, or has partially created it, the things that have to be done are basically the same as when one starts with a new resource. However, since the researcher already has selected a format for his/her resource, and possibly also for the associated metadata, the resource probably has to be adapted to the requirements of CLARIN (this is called *resource curation*). Again,

---

[22] This DSA consists of 16 guidelines for the curation of data, 3 of which apply to the data producer (i.e., the researcher), and 3 to the data consumer (that is, also the researcher), so it is well worth reading. The remaining 10 guidelines apply to the centre.

[23] See https://www.datasealofapproval.org/en/community/.

[24] See http://www.clarin.eu/content/certified-centres.

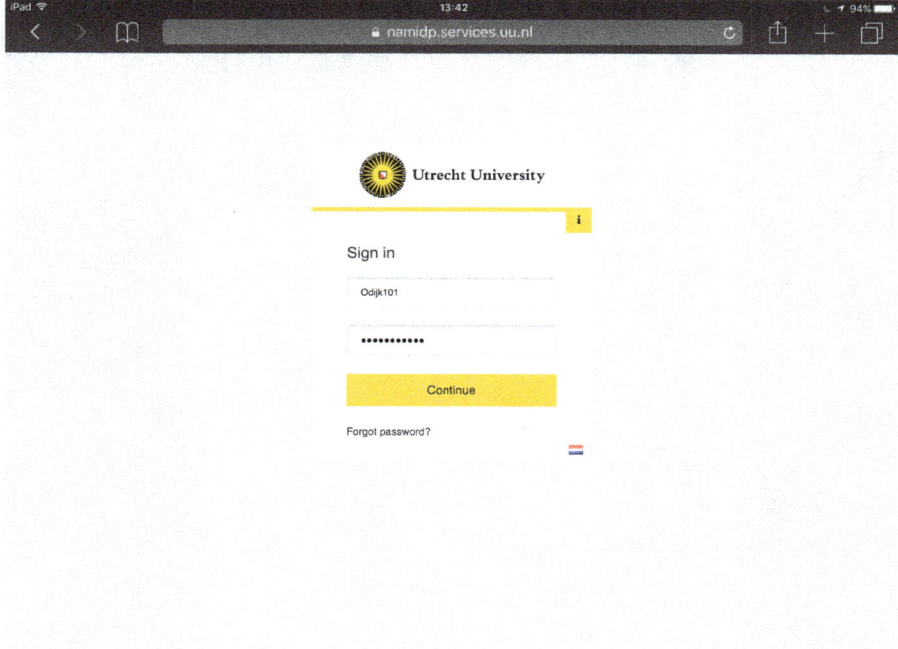

Figure 2.5: The user logs in with his/her institute's user name and password.

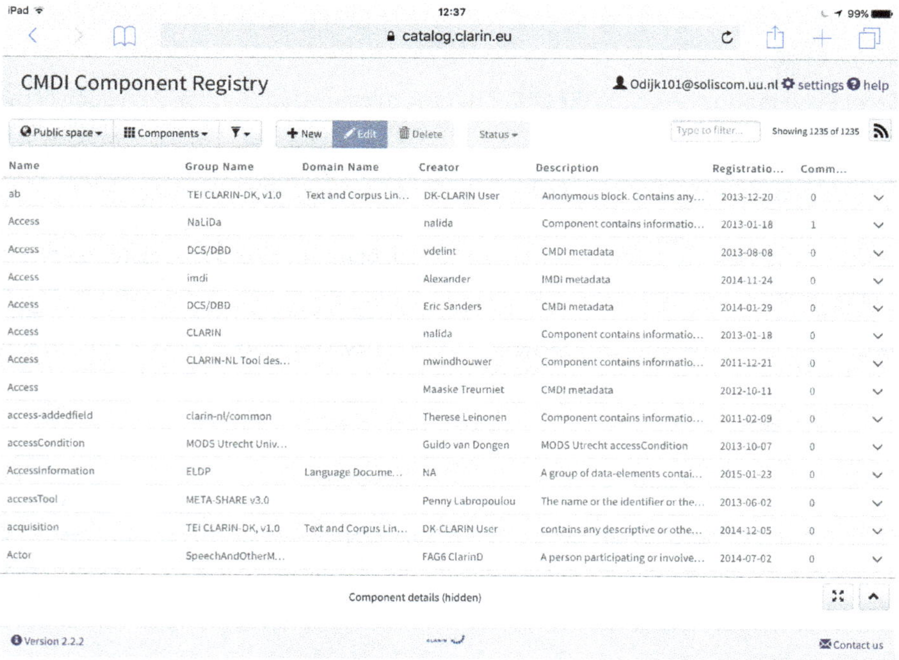

Figure 2.6: The user gets access to the application.

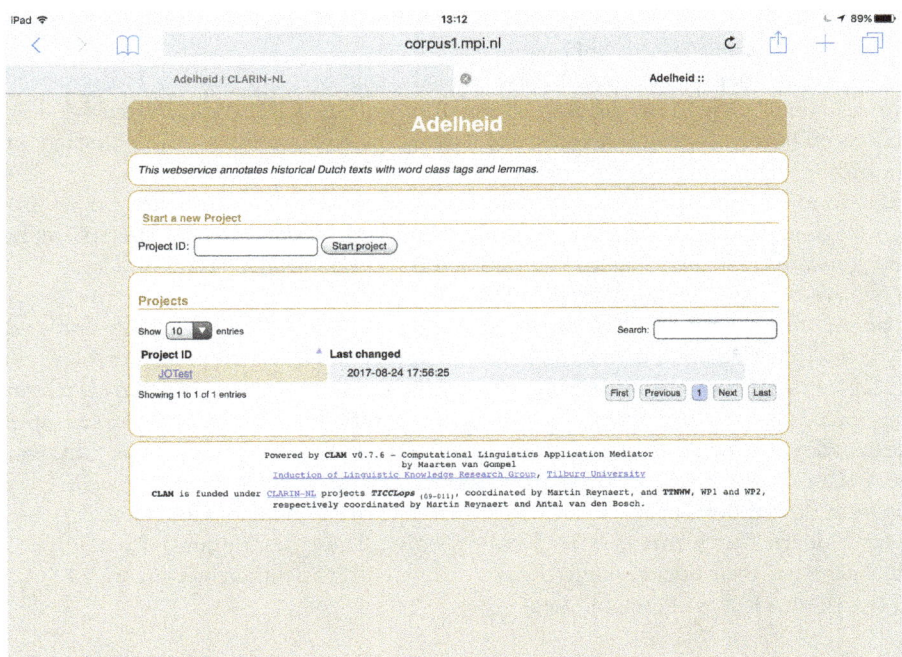

Figure 2.7: Other CLARIN services (e.g., the Adelheid application), wherever they are located, now 'know' that the researcher is a trusted user, and no further login is needed.

it is very important to contact a CLARIN centre as early as possible, because centres may be able to help with this. If the format of the resource is sufficiently formalised, it may be possible to convert it automatically into a CLARIN-compatible format. The same is true for metadata: if they are in a sufficiently formalised notation, it may be possible to convert them automatically into a CMDI format.

The CLARIN-NL project has financed many such resource curation projects. It has also set up a Data Curation Service: a team of specialists dedicated to the curation of important data for Humanities researchers.

The curated resources include many of the data for which search and analysis applications that we mentioned earlier have been made, so these will be mentioned again in the overview given here. But they also include data that have just been curated, i.e. put into CLARIN-recommended formats, associated with CMDI metadata, where metadata are associated with PIDs, and the data stored in a CLARIN-certified centre. The types of data again cover many disciplines: within linguistics, language acquisition data, language variation data, lexical data, language documentation data, and other text corpora; for other disciplines, data for historical research, for literary research, and for religion research. They also include data from the CLARIN data providers that cover many different disciplines. See parts II, III and IV for concrete examples.

In the CLARIAH successor project, such resource curation activities have been continued, and researchers can suggest resources to be curated by the data curation service.

2.5   Portal

It is convenient for users if they do not have to remember a lot of URLs or other identifiers to get access to the functionality offered by CLARIN. For this reason, a portal has been set up for CLARIN. The idea is that from this portal all functionality offered by CLARIN can be accessed.

The Europe-wide CLARIN portal, which only features a selection of everything that CLARIN has to offer, can be found via this link.

The CLARIN portal gives access to the Virtual Language Observatory (see section 3.6.1), featured resources, showcases, general information on CLARIN, CLARIN-related blogs, and instructions on how to deposit resources, and it offers the opportunity to search through multiple corpora with one query (federated search).

In addition to the Europe-wide portal, national CLARIN portals are also being created.[25] These will also make it possible to access all CLARIN functionality but will put special emphasis on data and software created nationally. The national CLARIN portal for the Low Countries can be accessed via the `http://portal.clarin.nl` URL.

This portal offers an introductory page; an overview of Dutch CLARIN centres; and a selection of tools to find relevant resources through their metadata and to search in data themselves (`http://portal.clarin.nl/node/4218`), an inventory of tools and services with faceted search on facets such as *resource type*, relevant *scientific discipline, tool functionality*, and others. For example, if one is interested in *syntax*, one can select that value for the facet *research discipline*; if, within syntax, one is more specifically interested in *parsing*, one can select this value for the facet *toolTask*: one then ends up with descriptions of the INPOLDER parser for 13th-century Dutch and for the *Alpino* parser for Modern Dutch that is offered via *TTNWW*. These descriptions also contain links to the actual services, their documentation and demonstration scenarios (see Figure 2.8). A similar faceted search interface is offered for data.

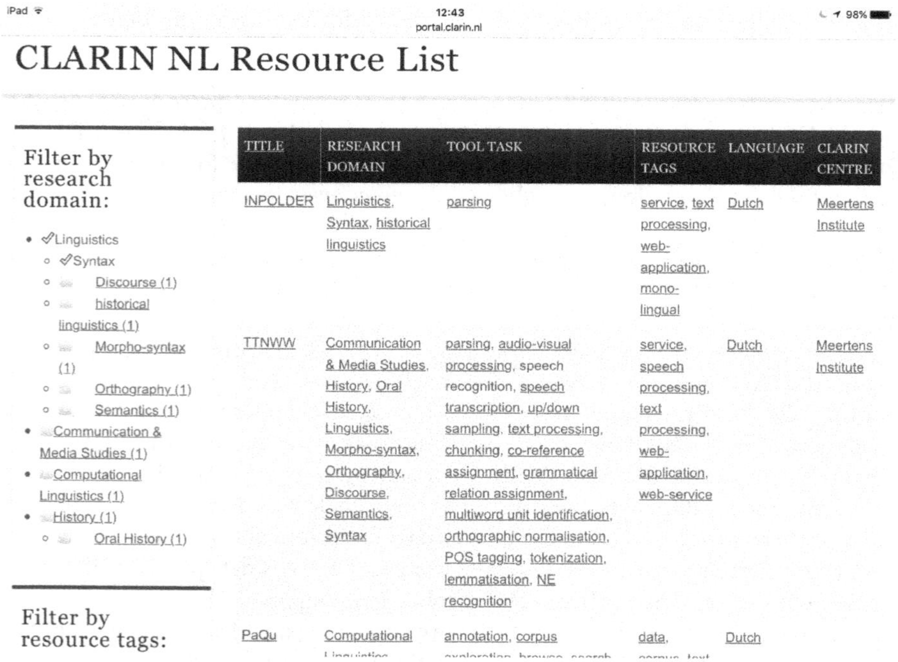

Figure 2.8: Selection of services via faceted browsing in the Dutch portal.

It is not a problem that there are multiple portals, which each focuses on different aspects of the CLARIN infrastructure. However, it is essential that all functionality in CLARIN can be reached from each portal. And at least one portal, the CLARIN ERIC portal, should contain links to all other portals.

The portal also offers a section called CLARIN recipes to get concrete guidelines in a range of matters, such as standards, issues related to intellectual property rights, how to cite data, and frequently asked questions, as well as a range of educational packages and other educational material.

2.6   Concluding Remarks

I have briefly described what functionality CLARIN aims to offer, and what is available at this point in the Low Countries. Though these descriptions can serve to get a first global picture of CLARIN, additional documentation must be read and/or courses attended for really ensuring optimal use of the functionality offered. I refer to the CLARIN, CLARIN Portal and CLARIAH websites for additional sources, for educational and training events, and for educational packages that can be used in the curricula of Humanities students.

In the course of the discussion of the functionality offered by CLARIN, I have referred to many more detailed descriptions of specific functionality that will be discussed in other chapters of this book.

It must be clear from this chapter that the CLARIN infrastructure already has a lot to offer to Humanities researchers. In fact, it is already used for carrying out research, as was already pointed out in chapter 1, section 1.3. However, there is also still a lot to do: many parts of CLARIN are incomplete, fragile, and sometimes just prototypes instead of stable services, and for many aspects further improvements and extensions are desired or required both in terms of the functionality offered and in terms of user-friendliness. These form important challenges for the near future. In the Netherlands, the CLARIAH project, which continues the Netherlands' contributions to the design and construction of the CLARIN and DARIAH infrastructures starting in 2015, has taken up these challenges.

Acknowledgements

This work was financed by CLARIN-NL and CLARIAH.

References

Broeder, D., M. Kemps-Snijders, D. Van Uytvanck, M. Windhouwer, P. Withers, P. Wittenburg, and C. Zinn (2010), A data category registry- and component-based metadata framework, in Calzolari, N., B. Maegaard, J. Mariani, J. Odijk, K. Choukri, S. Piperidis, M. Rosner, and D. Tapias, editors, *Proceedings of the Seventh International Conference on Language Resources and Evaluation (LREC 2010)*, European Language Resources Association (ELRA), Valetta, Malta, pp. 43–47.

Kemps-Snijders, M., M.A. Windhouwer, and S.E. Wright (2010), Principles of ISOcat, a data category registry, Presentation at the RELISH workshop Rendering endangered languages lexicons interoperable through standards harmonization Workshop on Lexicon Tools and Lexicon Standards, Nijmegen, The Netherlands, August 4-5, 2010. http://www.mpi.nl/research/research-projects/language-archiving-technology/events/relish-workshop/program/ISOcat.pptx.

Lagoze, Carl, Herbert Van de Sompel, Michael Nelson, and Simeon Warner (2002), The Open Archives Initiative Protocol for Metadata Harvesting. Protocol version 2.0 of 2002-06-14, *Technical report*, Open Archives Initiative. https://www.openarchives.org/OAI/openarchivesprotocol.html.

Lyse, Gunn Inger, Paul Meurer, and Koenraad De Smedt (2015), COMEDI: A component metadata editor, in Odijk, Jan, editor, *Selected Papers from the CLARIN 2014 Conference, October 24-25*

2014, Soesterberg, the Netherlands, number 116 in *Linköping Electronic Conference Proceedings*, CLARIN, Linköping University Electronic Press, Linköping, Sweden, pp. 82–98. http://www.ep.liu.se/ecp/article.asp?issue=116&article=008&volume=.

NWO (2014), *NWO Subsidieregeling 1 Mei 2011 (Versie juli 2014)*, NWO, The Hague. http://www.nwo.nl/documents/nwo/juridisch/regeling-subsidieverlening-nwo.

Odijk, Jan and Arjan van Hessen (2011), Sharing resources in CLARIN-NL, *Proceedings of the Language Resources, Technology and Services in the Sharing Paradigm workshop at IJCNLP 2011*, IJCNLP 2012, Chiang Mai, Thailand, pp. 98–106. http://www.clarin.nl/sites/default/files/restore/CLARIN-NLijcnlp2011_110811.pdf.

Salton, G., A. Wong, and C. S. Yang (1975), A vector space model for automatic indexing, *Commun. ACM* **18** (11), pp. 613–620, ACM, New York, NY, USA. http://doi.acm.org/10.1145/361219.361220.

Schuurman, Ineke, Menzo Windhouwer, Oddrun Ohren, and Daniel Zeman (2016), CLARIN Concept Registry: The New Semantic Registry, *in* Smedt, Koenraad De, editor, *Selected Papers from the CLARIN Annual Conference 2015, October 14{16, 2015, Wroclaw, Poland*, number 123 in *Linköping Electronic Conference Proceedings*, CLARIN, Linköping University Electronic Press, Linköping, Sweden, pp. 62–70. http://www.ep.liu.se/ecp/article.asp?issue=123&article=004.

van Gompel, Maarten (2014), CLAM: Computational Linguistics Application Mediator. Documentation.version 0.9.12 - revision 1.1, *Language and Speech Technology Technical Report Series LST-14-02*, Radboud Centre for Language Studies, Radboud University Nijmegen, Nijmegen. http://www.clarin.nl/sites/default/files/clam_manual_2.pdf.

Van Uytvanck, Dieter (2014), How can I find resources using CLARIN?, Presentation held at the *Using CLARIN for Digital Research* tutorial workshop at the *2014 Digital Humanities Conference*, Lausanne, Switzerland. https://www.clarin.eu/sites/default/files/CLARIN-dvu-dh2014_VLO.pdf.

VSNU, KNAW, and NWO (2014), *Standard Evaluation Protocol 2015-2021: Protocol for Research Assessments in the Netherlands*, KNAW, Amsterdam. https://www.knaw.nl/nl/actueel/publicaties/standard-evaluation-protocol-2015-2021.

Westerhout, Eline and Jan Odijk (2013), Metadata for tools: creating a CMDI profile for tools, Presentation held at CLIN 2013, Enschede, the Netherlands. http://www.clarin.nl/sites/default/files/13CLIN.pdf.

Zhang, Junte, Marc Kemps-Snijders, and Hans Bennis (2012), The CMDI MI search engine: Access to language resources and tools using heterogeneous metadata schemas, *in* Zaphiris, P. et al., editor, *Proceedings of Theoretic and Practice Digital Libraries Conference (TPDL 2012)*, Vol. 7489, Springer, Berlin / Heidelberg, pp. 492–495. http://www.clarin.nl/system/files/Zhang_tpdl2012.pdf.

PART I

Technical Infrastructure

CHAPTER 3

Introduction to the CLARIN Technical Infrastructure

Jan Odijk

UiL-OTS, Utrecht University, j.odijk@uu.nl

ABSTRACT

This chapter provides an introduction to the design of the CLARIN technical infrastructure, with a focus on the Netherlands part. It provides a basic introduction to the techniques behind PIDs, CMDI-metadata, authentication and authorisation (AAI), semantic interoperability related to CMDI-metadata, and search. Search covers searching for data through metadata with the VLO and the Meertens metadata search application, as well as federated content search activities in the Netherlands. The chapter ends with an introduction to the chapters of Part I on the technical infrastructure of CLARIN.

3.1 Introduction

This chapter serves as an introduction to Part I of this book, which covers CLARIN's technical infrastructure, and it also provides an introduction to the design of this technical infrastructure, with a focus on the Netherlands part. I will try to explain what has to be done behind the scenes to make the CLARIN infrastructure in the Netherlands work. For many aspects, a more detailed description is required than can be given in this chapter. For these, I refer to other chapters in Part I of this book.

CLARIN-NL is probably best known among humanities researchers in the Netherlands for the data curation and demonstrator projects,[1] in which humanities researchers, in close

---

[1] http://www.clarin.nl/node/281.

How to cite this book chapter:
Odijk, J. 2017. Introduction to the CLARIN Technical Infrastructure. In: Odijk, J and van Hessen, A. (eds.) *CLARIN in the Low Countries*, Pp. 33–44. London: Ubiquity Press. DOI: https://doi.org/10.5334/bbi.3.
License: CC-BY 4.0

cooperation with computer scientists and CLARIN centres, adapt their research resources to the requirements of CLARIN (*curation*), and/or create user-friendly applications to browse, search or analyse research data (*demonstrators*). The focus of the current part of this book (Part I) will be on aspects of the CLARIN-NL project which have been less visible to the outside world but have been crucial for a working CLARIN infrastructure. The relevant work has been carried out in subprojects that focused on the design and construction of the CLARIN infrastructure in the Netherlands. The two most important and largest subprojects were:

IIP (*Infrastructure Implementation Project*), which has implemented the basic functionality of the CLARIN infrastructure in the Dutch CLARIN centres. It will be described in more detail in chapter 4.

S&D (*Search & Develop*), which has developed a metadata search application and worked on federated content search. Its results will be described in section 3.6.2 and section 3.6.3.

They were complemented by a whole range of smaller subprojects that we will not all mention here. See http://www.clarin.nl/node/281 for more details on these projects. Some of these projects will be mentioned in the course of this chapter and some have their own chapter in this part of the book.

The construction of the Netherlands part of the CLARIN infrastructure requires a whole range of activities. I mention them here and indicate where they will be discussed. Some are discussed in this chapter, others in other chapters of this part of the book (Part I).

- Setting up a network of certified CLARIN centres and contributions to a variety of Type A services and registries, e.g. applications and registries for supporting the creation of CMDI metadata (see chapter 4).
- Setting up a Persistent Identifier (PID) infrastructure (see section 3.2 and chapter 4).
- Providing and testing metadata profiles and components (see section 3.3 and chapter 4).
- Setting up a CLARIN-compatible Authentication and Authorisation Infrastructure (AAI) (see section 3.4 and chapter 4).
- Contributions to further development and maintenance of facilities for semantic interoperability (see section 3.5 and chapter 4).
- Setting up a metadata search and browse application (see section 3.6.2).
- Setting up a Federated Content search application (see section 3.6.3).
- Setting up a CLARIN-NL Portal (see section 3.7).

In addition, the Low Countries collaborated in setting up a system for organising language technology web services in a workflow system (TTNWW), which will be discussed in chapter 7.

3.2   Persistent Identifiers

Locations on the internet are usually specified by means of a Universal Resource Locator (URL), such as http://www.clarin.nl. It is well-known that URLs often simply disappear, or change name. This happens because the URLs are usually created and maintained by a particular project (which is temporary by nature), or by a particular organisation (which tends to be more stable but nevertheless is not immune to changes). URLs often also reflect the internal structure of an organisation, and that is surely less stable than the organisation itself.

In CLARIN we need a way to refer to objects on the internet that is more stable than using URLs. *Persistent identifiers* offer that functionality. A *persistent identifier (PID)* is no more than an identifier, and does not bring very much by itself. A crucial ingredient for persistent identifiers to serve their role is (1) an organisation that holds itself responsible for the PIDs it assigns, and

(2) a software system that supports this organisation in the creation (issuing), the assignment, the maintenance and the resolution of PIDs.

A persistent identifier is an identifier, ideally without any internal structure or semantics. It is is created and issued by a PID-service organisation. It is issued to the organisation that requested the PID and considers itself responsible for it.[2] A newly created PID must be unique. A PID is associated with a URL by the requesting organisation (PID assignment), and this relation is stored in a PID resolution system. The PID will never change. Of course, the URL it is associated with may change, or disappear, but it is the responsibility of the organisation that assigned the PID to ensure that the PID will continue to refer to the same object through some other URL. Of course, an organisation can ensure this only for URLs that it controls itself.

In the CLARIN infrastructure, each metadata record[3] is assigned a PID. In this way, a user or software program that wants to use a specific resource can simply refer to the PID assigned to its associated metadata and never has to change this reference anymore. The PID resolution system will resolve the PID, i.e., in the context of accessing web resources, replace it by its associated URL, and transfer the user or the software to the metadata record, and, through this metadata record, to the resource itself.

CLARIN requires the use of the Handle System PID-technology. An example of a Handle PID is *10032/12824827a77b9602cc66840a62aedf43*. The uniqueness of each PID is guaranteed because each issuer has its own prefix (10032 in this example), and the PID-system guarantees the assignment of a unique new identifier within the system. Having a PID preceded by the prefix `http://hdl.handle.net/` turns it into a URL. By clicking on it, it brings the user to the PID, which is resolved and leads the user to the metadata record it is associated with.

Chapter 4 will describe in more detail how the various centres in the Netherlands dealt with PIDs, their assignment, and their resolution.

3.3   CMDI Metadata

Metadata play a crucial role in CLARIN in offering services for finding data and software. Metadata in CLARIN must be in CMDI-format. CLARIN-NL made many contributions to the CLARIN CMDI infrastructure.

In order to make sure that profiles for frequently occurring resource types were available before a large set of data curation projects were in need of them, early in the CLARIN-NL project the *Metadata* subproject created and tested profiles for text corpora, lexical resources and speech corpora, and for a number of specific other resources in the Netherlands. This was done initially only for data, but not for software. Originally, very few metadata for software were made in CLARIN-NL, but in 2011 a Metadata for Tools (MD4T) subproject was started up to create a profile for software. This profile was developed by testing it against five pieces of software curated in CLARIN-NL. It is currently being refined and applied to all software curated or created in CLARIN-NL.

It must be possible to make new metadata or adapt existing ones using the profiles and components defined in the Component Registry. To that end, an existing metadata editor, Arbil, was adapted so that it could work with the profiles and components defined in the Component Registry. The IIP project contributed to this adaptation.

CMDI offers, through its flexibility, many advantages, but this flexibility also has some drawbacks. Flexibility is needed when there are good reasons to deviate from what others have done, but may be a burden for cases where there are deviations because of lack of knowledge of what has been done before. It is therefore essential that a Component Registry exist so that reuse of profiles

---

[2]   The issuing organisation and the requesting organisation can be identical, but this need not be the case.
[3]   Usually a resource itself is assigned a PID as well, though this is not required.

and components can be maximised, and unnecessary errors or omissions can be avoided. It also provides researchers with the opportunity to inspect resource profiles, which may make them aware of properties that may be 'obvious' to them but not to the whole CLARIN research community.

The Component Registry was created and is in use, but it quickly became clear that it was not easy to find components and profiles that could be relevant to one's resource, since the registry consists, in essence, of a flat list of profiles and components, and advanced search facilities are lacking. As a consequence, new users started creating their own profiles and components, which actually increased the problem of finding potentially relevant profiles and components. The lack of a clear versioning strategy also increased the problem.[4]

In 2014, a project has indeed been started up to investigate how the quality of existing and new metadata can be improved, how reuse of existing profiles and components can be increased, and how profiles relate to one another. It resulted in a report on a strategy for metadata quality (Kemps-Snijders, 2014). The problem is not unique to the Netherlands. Austria has reported it as well, and has developed a tool, the SMC-browser, to investigate the relations between profiles and components (Ďurčo and Windhouwer, 2014). The CLARIAH-CORE successor project will address these issues as well.

3.4   AAI

If a user wants to get access to CLARIN data or services, CLARIN must, for certain data and services, identify who the user is (*authentication*) and determine what the user is allowed to do (*authorisation*). Systems that take care of this are therefore called *Authentication and Authorisation Infrastructures (AAI)*. Both aspects will be discussed in separate sections.

3.4.1   Authentication

In chapter 2 we saw that it is in some cases necessary or desirable to authenticate a user, i.e to determine who the user is. Authentication is usually done by requiring login.

Logging in in the CLARIN infrastructure is not an obvious thing, as we described in chapter 2. We repeat here the major problems: the CLARIN infrastructure is a distributed infrastructure, spread out over all of Europe (and beyond), so how can it be avoided that the user has to login again each time a resource happens to be located at a different centre? How can it be avoided that the user has to remember many different user names and passwords? And from the CLARIN centres' perspective, how can it be avoided that each CLARIN centre has to securely store user names, passwords and possibly other privacy-sensitive information for a user community as large as the CLARIN one? Clearly, it does not scale to have every centre use a separate identity store.

The basic idea behind the solution adopted in CLARIN is that a user, when (s)he logs in, is redirected to his/her own organisation (which acts as an identity provider), logs in there with the user name and password of the organisation, and, when this is successful, the organisation communicates to CLARIN that this is a trusted user, who can be given access to CLARIN data and services. Since every user is directed to his/her own identity provider, this type of system is called Federated Identity Management (FIM).

We describe here globally how this works and what has to be done for it to make it work. The work that had to be done here has been carried out in the context of the IIP project (unless stated otherwise) and is described in chapter 4.

---

[4]   For example, at a certain point there were three different components called *GeneralInfo* created by user *nalida*, and it was totally unclear how they were related. Currently (November 2016) there is fortunately only one (but many components with the same name by other users).

When a user tries to log in on a CLARIN service, (s)he must be directed to a login at his/her own institute. For this to work, a number of things are required, which are partly administrative and partly technical in nature.

- First, a *Service Provider Federation (SPF)* must be set up: this is a federation of centres that offer software services. CLARIN set up its own CLARIN SPF. This was done by CLARIN-PP.
- Second, an agreement must be made between this CLARIN SPF and the National Research and Education Network (NREN), i.e. SURFnet in the Netherlands and Belnet in Flanders, so that the CLARIN SPF is recognised by the NREN, and a trust relation is created between these parties.[5]
- Third, the centre where the data reside or the service runs must be a member of the CLARIN SPF, and thus be bound by the agreement between the CLARIN SPF and SURFnet. This is necessary, because the user must be sure that (s)he is indeed using a CLARIN service, and not some unknown service that might abuse the situation or implicitly charge costs to the user or his/her institute. All CLARIN centres in the Netherlands are members of the CLARIN SPF.
- Fourth, the organisation of which the user is an employee or student must enable the usage by its employees/students of services offered by members of the CLARIN SPF. The Netherlands has a so-called opt-in system: no service can be used by a member of an organisation unless explicit permission has been given for it by this organisation.[6]
Requiring explicit permission for each service offered by CLARIN is not feasible, and not scalable. Fortunately, it was agreed with SURFnet that an organisation could give a single permission for the use of the whole set of CLARIN services.
- Fifth, the CLARIN centre where the data reside or the server runs must implement a running version of Shibboleth (or similar software), and ensure that access to the data or service always leads to the shibboleth system, so that the credentials of the user can be checked. SURFnet offers services in this respect through SURFconext. However, this service is by default accessible for researchers from the Netherlands only, which is too limited in the CLARIN context, which aims to provide access to all European researchers (and even wider). Making FIM available in the European CLARIN context requires some additional configuration and administrative actions.
- Sixth, the system must determine somehow, when a user logs in, to which organisation the user has to be redirected. The system does not know this, and therefore has to ask the user. A simple way to achieve this is to present the user with a list of all organisations, so that the user can make the selection.[7] But since hundreds of organisations will be in that list, doing only this is not really user-friendly.[8] Therefore additional systems are used. In particular, systems are used that put the organisations that are geographically close to the user at the top of the list: it does this by determining the user's geographical location, e.g. using HTML5 Geo Location. If the user is working at his/her institute, it will most probably end up in the top of the list,[9] and the user does not have to search through the whole list with hundreds of entries. Of course, this will not work when the user works at a different location. But these systems also make it possible to remember choices a user made earlier, e.g. via cookies on the user's computer. So the user's

---

[5]   And similarly in other countries with their local NRENs. Otherwise, Dutch researchers cannot get access to services outside of the Netherlands, and foreign researchers cannot get access to services in the Netherlands.

[6]   The alternative is opt-out: each service can be used by default unless an organisation explicitly excludes its use.

[7]   Most centres use Discojuice for this purpose, but some use other systems.

[8]   Having the user type in the name of the organisation is also not user-friendly, and it will not be easy to make it work since usually many different variants of an organisation's name are in use, and very few people know the official name of their organisation (and the official names tend to be long, so are difficult to type without errors).

[9]   Not necessarily at the top, since the accuracy of geolocation systems may differ depending on the equipment one works on.

institute will be in the top of the list even if the user works from a different location, provided the user works on the same computer.

When the user is redirected to his/her own institute, (s)he can login with his/her institute's user name and password. If the login is successful, the institute server confirms that the user is a trusted person, and (s)he can enter this part of the CLARIN infrastructure.

If a logged-in user now goes to another part of the CLARIN infrastructure that requires login, this other part 'knows' that this user is already logged in and a trusted user, so (the user does not have to do this again. In this way, *Single Sign On (SSO)* is implemented.

All this requires a lot of communication between various systems. AAI in CLARIN uses SAML[10] Version 2.0 for this and it is therefore called SAML-based (or SAML2-based) FIM.

3.4.2   Authorisation

Authorisation means determining what a logged in user is allowed to do. For example, in some applications some users are only permitted to view certain data, while others are also allowed to edit them, and again others are also allowed to delete them. Though CLARIN imposes no requirements here, CLARIN centres must of course ensure proper use of their resources, so they must make provisions for such cases.

In services and applications, authorisation is usually dealt with at the service or application level, and there is no role for CLARIN. For data, all users have the same rights for aspects such as viewing, downloading, editing and deleting: all metadata can be viewed and downloaded by all users, most resources can be viewed (often through a specific application) by all users, and some resources can be downloaded by all users. Editing and deleting is only allowed for managers of the data at the CLARIN centre.

A special case concerns legal and ethical restrictions. Each CLARIN centre must make provisions for this, so that only persons who are allowed to get access to resources that have such restrictions actually get access to them, and to ensure that researchers use resources in the way they are allowed to use them. Restrictions related to the Creative Commons licensing conditions must be explicitly marked in the metadata and are visualised in the VLO with the Creative Commons 'laundry tags' to inform the users of their rights and obligations. CLARIN aims to make available the resources as openly and with as little restrictions as possible. However, there are and always will be resources with legal and/or ethical restrictions, and therefore it is sometimes not possible to access such resources directly. The restrictions can lead to various consequences: (1) a login may be required; (2) approving special usage conditions may be required; or (3) signing a special licence agreement may be required.

Some CLARIN centres in the Netherlands have special provisions to deal with such matters, e.g. the MPI/TLA. For example, one option is to show a user a text with usage conditions, but let the user access the data without reading this text. A second option shows such text but requires confirmation by the user that the text has been read and agreed to. A third option is to require explicit permission from the data provider for usage of the data according to a specific licence agreement (this is the case for, for example, the IPROSLA dataset, which requires special provisions to protect the privacy of the participants, who come from the (small) sign language using community in the Netherlands). Other centres have arranged such matters by providing access to such data in limited ways. For example, most text corpora at INL can only be accessed via specific search interfaces, and after login. Export of the results of the search queries is highly limited. Downloading these text corpora is simply not possible.

---

[10] Security Assertion Markup Language.

3.5   Semantic Interoperability

The flexibility of CMDI is only possible if the semantics of the metadata elements is made explicit. Explicit semantics for a resource or metadata is obtained by explicitly linking each element and its possible values in the resource and the metadata to an element of a CLARIN-recognised concept or data category registry. The most prominent registry for semantic interoperability in CLARIN until 2014 was ISOcat (Kemps-Snijders et al., 2010). Its design and construction was initiated in combination with the ISO initiated ISO TC37 (Terminology and Other Language and Content Resources) technical committee, but a large part of the construction, and the main part of the maintenance since 2009 was carried out in the context of the CLARIN-NL IIP project.

ISOcat offers a registry for data categories in accordance with the ISO 12620 standard, a web application for browsing, searching and editing, and a web service for communication with other programs.

ISOcat is basically just a flat list of data categories.[11] Finding an existing data category that might be relevant is therefore quite difficult. For example, if one searches for a data category for *grammatical relation*, one will not find one with this name. Perhaps one will find the data category *grammatical function* because of its alphabetical closeness, but how is one ever going to find that ISOcat also contains a data category for *syntacticFunction* (Odijk, 2009: 12)? One can only find these by manually going through the whole list of data categories. In part because of this, reuse of data categories has been minimal, and ISOcat has seen a proliferation of near-identical data categories. This is one of the reasons why it is desirable to be able to specify relations between data categories. Relations between data categories can be used to group data categories by various criteria, which will make searching for related data categories easier, and will make it possible to consider different categories (such as *grammatical function* and *syntacticFunction*[12]) as identical or near-identical. This can be done in a special registry, called RELcat (which, however, never got beyond α-version status).

It is sometimes necessary or convenient to know more about the internal structure of a resource. For that purpose, the registry SCHEMAcat (α-version) has been set up. For example, the *de facto* standard for PoS-tags for Dutch (Van Eynde, 2004) is well-structured in accordance with a clearly defined syntax, which, however, is specific for this tag set. For example, a tag for nouns takes the form:

- tag = 'N ', '(', NTYPE, ', ', GETAL, ', ', GRAAD, ', ', GENUS, ', ', NAAMVAL,')

where the upper-case labels between the brackets are non-terminals (corresponding to attributes and/or the types of the possible values of an attribute) that can be rewritten into terminals corresponding to the values of the attributes.

Since the syntax of such tags is idiosyncratic, standard programs (that expect e.g. XML syntax) will consider such tags as unanalysable values. But we want to associate parts of these tags to ISOcat data categories, e.g. the attribute *NTYPE* to http://www.isocat.org/datcat/DC-4908, and the value *soortnaam* to http://www.isocat.org/datcat/DC-4910. SCHEMAcat makes the syntax of these tags explicit so that ISOcat data categories can be assigned to parts of the tag.

Finally, ISOcat may be the primary registry for semantic interoperability in CLARIN, but it is not the only one. For certain types of information, ISOcat is not particularly suited (e.g. for names of organisations in all their variants); for others independent registries exist and are maintained (e.g. for language codes: ISO639-3, maintained by SIL for ISO). In order to use such other registries in

---

[11] There is a little bit of hierarchy in it through so-called complex categories which basically group a limited set of simple types, and there is a division of the data categories by thematic domain, but this is by far not enough for efficiently finding closely related data categories.

[12] And the category with name *syntactic function*.

a transparent manner, the CLAVAS Vocabulary Service has been set up (by the CLAVAS project) as an interface to other data category registries and vocabularies, and as a service to store data categories not dealt with elsewhere. The CLARIN Vocabulary Service is described in more detail in chapter 5

In 2013, CLARIN switched from ISOcat to the CLARIN Concept Registry (CCR; see chapter 4 for the background. CCR is a concept registry according to the W3C SKOS recommendation (Schuurman et al., 2016) and is hosted by the Meertens Institute. It has not really played a role in CLARIN-LC, but it will be important in CLARIAH-CORE.

3.6   Search

If there is a CMDI metadata record for each resource, and if the metadata can be referred to via a PID (and the resource itself via the metadata), combined with harvesting facilities through OAI-PMH, everything is in place to create functionality for browsing and searching for resources.

This functionality requires a browsing and/or search engine in combination with a web interface. Such engines operate on a database of CMDI metadata located on a server of a CLARIN centre that offers essential infrastructure services (a so-called Type A centre), which is filled and regularly updated by metadata harvesting, as will be described below.

CLARIN offers the *Virtual Language Observatory (VLO)* as a browser and search application to search for resources via their metadata. It will be discussed in section 3.6.1. CLARIN-NL developed the *Meertens CLARIN Metadata Search Application*, which will be discussed in section 3.6.2.

Services offered by CLARIN centres in the Netherlands can also be found by faceted search in the CLARIN-NL portal. This will be discussed in section 3.7.

3.6.1   VLO

As described in chapter 2, the Virtual Language Observatory (VLO) offers facilities for browsing and searching in CMDI metadata. It enables a user to do a string search for keywords that occur in the metadata, and it offers faceted browsing.

In order to make this functionality possible, the Type A centre that hosts the VLO regularly gathers the metadata of all CLARIN centres in one central database. This process is called *metadata harvesting*, and it is done through the OAI-PMH protocol. This has to be done regularly,[13] since new metadata will regularly appear at each CLARIN centre.[14]

The 'harvesting' software run by a Type A centre must 'know' where the metadata of each centre can be found. This is one of the reasons why the CLARIN centre registry has been set up.[15] A registry is a central database that enables one to store and maintain information, and it provides facilities to extract information from it. The centre registry has an entry for each CLARIN centre with information about this CLARIN centre (inter alia, the server where the metadata are made available through OAI-PMH, its *OAI-PMH end points*).

The centre registry has been developed by CLARIN-D, and each Dutch CLARIN centre has entered the required information about itself there. Here are views on the centre registry, and here is an overview of the OAI-PMH end points.

---

[13] See http://www.clarin.eu/faq/when-metadata-vlo-harvested for the harvesting update schedule for the *Virtual Language Observatory* (see section 3.6.1).

[14] Currently, only the MPI / TLA does such regular harvesting. The Meertens Institute only occasionally took a snapshot of the metadata harvested by MPI / TLA for its CLARIN search engine.

[15] See http://www.clarin.eu/blog/central-role-centre-registry for other reasons why the centre registry is important in the CLARIN infrastructure.

3.6.2   Meertens CLARIN Metadata Search

The functionality of the Meertens CLARIN Metadata Search application was described in chapter 2, section 2.2.

This metadata search application has been created taking into account the diversity of the CMDI metadata descriptions and descriptive metadata elements. Harmonisation of the metadata fields using ISOcat concepts has proven to be possible and an automated ingest procedure for CMDI metadata files has been realised. The set up has been tested against all available CMDI profiles from the CLARIN EU community.

The metadata search application still exists, but it is not maintained or operated. No new metadata are harvested, so the current application contains only metadata from several years back. Development and operation of this application was stopped because it was intended as the initial step for federated content search, but development of the Dutch federated content search was stopped as well, as described in section 3.6.3.

The metadata search application has also been used as part of the Nederlab project, though a new design of the interface tuned to the intended Nederlab users was created.

3.6.3   Federated Content Search

Most CLARIN centres maintain dedicated search applications at the level of individual resources. However, these search interfaces are often not directly accessible through web service interfaces and display a large variety of query languages and implementation details. For a research infrastructure such as CLARIN that aims to offer an integrated search facility to make these unrelated and partly overlapping content search engines available to the research community, a general perspective of these content search engines must be developed.

Federated Content Search (FCS) is a technique that may serve this purpose: FCS enables a user to enter a single query, which is sent to multiple search engines at different CLARIN centres, each of which enables search in a specific resource with its own idiosyncratic structure and format.

FCS basically works as follows: the user wants to make a query. Of course, such a query must be formulated in some language. Federated Search in CLARIN uses the Contextual Query Language (CQL)[16] for this purpose.

This query has to be sent to each search engine at the CLARIN centres via some protocol. The protocol used is based on the Search Retrieval via URL (SRU) protocol, which was originally developed in the library world for federated metadata search and was extended by CLARIN to cover textual content search.[17] A so-called *end point* was created for each search engine which can receive queries via the SRU protocol and translate a CQL query into a query suited for the search engine. The results of the query are of course in the format provided by the search engine. These results must therefore be translated by the end points to a common result format. Such a result format has been defined, and it is extensible. With the results from the different search engines all in a common format, they can be put together (aggregated) and presented to the user.

In order to test the approach, each CLARIN centre involved in the S&D project had to set up some end points, and they did: DANS for the Lieffering CQL Searchable database (Eighteenth-Century Music and theatre advertisements from the 's-Gravenhaagsche Courant and Gazette de La Haye), INL for the Corpus Gysseling and for the Brieven als Buit corpus (17th and 18th century

---

[16] Not to be confused with the Corpus Query Processing Language, which is sometimes also abbreviated as CQL and is also highly relevant in the CLARIN context.

[17] See the discussion paper Federated Content Search for a description of the approach to federated search in CLARIN.

Dutch letters), MPI for the TROVA Search engine,[18] and Meertens for MIMORE (Morphosyntactic variations in Dutch dialects).[19]

The S&D project aimed to provide a combined metadata/content search solution to the end users. Through this, end users can search a central metadata catalogue and at the same time have the possibility to search through the content located at the participating CLARIN centres. To provide a single point of access to end users the CMDI metadata search engine described in section 3.6.2 was to be combined with the content search end points. For this purpose, the content search end points may be added to the metadata specification of individual resources to indicate the availability of a content search end point for this resource.

When such a content search engine is available for a specific resource, it should be made accessible through the Meertens metadata search engine, which is able to detect the availability of such a service and integrates an additional widget to the user interface allowing end users to search the underlying resources directly.[20]

Both CLARIN-NL and the German national CLARIN project *D-SPIN* have adopted the CLARIN SRU/CQL protocol as a joint specification for content search end point implementations. However, some noteworthy differences between the approaches of the two projects exist. While development of a metadata search engine was part of the Dutch CLARIN-NL project, the German D-SPIN project chose only to implement individual content search end points. No effort was made to provide an integrated search solution for resources and their metadata in this project. Instead, an aggregator called CLARIN-D Federated Content Search was developed for distributing the content search query over a number of content search engines and displaying the results. Content search end points have to be registered as part of the centres' registry thus connecting content search engines to organisations rather than resources. Since organisations usually maintain specialised content search engines for various resources this makes it difficult if not impossible to focus the content search on only a limited number of resources of interest. The CLARIN-NL approach uses the metadata to specify the content search engine end point instead, and thus establishes a relation between the content search engine and a resource. This should be more efficient, since organisations usually maintain multiple content search end points for different resources. By registering content search end points in the centres' registry this option is lost. It is also technically possible to combine all end points in an aggregator, as was done in the D-SPIN project, by extracting all unique end points specifications from the CMDI documents. Although an aggregator was realised as a proof of concept, implementation during the project was not pursued any further awaiting convergence at the European level concerning the registration of end points (centres' registry versus metadata). For the moment, CLARIN-NL has decided to follow the German approach, since there appears to be a critical mass of adoption of this approach within CLARIN. Although, as far as we can see, there is no reason why the Dutch approach cannot be taken as well, activities in this area stopped and the attention of the relevant researchers was shifted to Nederlab.

A limited form of federated content search is possible in data via the CLARIN-D Federated Content Search graphical user interface (FCS). This federated content search is limited in two respects: first, it currently only enables string (keyword) search, and second, it only applies to a limited number of resources in the CLARIN infrastructure. It returns search hits in the form of a *KeyWord In Context (KWIC)* list. At the time of writing one could search in resources at least from CLARIN-NL, CLARIN-D, LINDAT (CLARIN-CZ) and CLARIN Poland. See https://centres.clarin.eu/fcs for a full overview of the current end points. Work on federated content search is continuing, and

---

[18] TROVA itself searches at MPI / TLA in multiple corpora, which may be in a wide range of different formats.

[19] Which itself provides access to three databases of Dutch dialects: the Dynamic Syntactic Atlas of the Dutch Dialects, the Diversity in Dutch DP Design database, and the Goeman, Taeldeman, van Reenen Project database

[20] The VLO also allows to search for data connected to federated content search only. Selecting this option reduces the number of metadata records (at the time of measuring (2014) to around 63,000 records, or about 10% of the total).

work is underway to formulate queries in the Corpus Query Processing (CQP) language (Evert and The OCWB Development Team, 2010), both at the European level and at the Dutch national level (CLARIAH-CORE project).

The CMDI search engine technology developed in the CLARIN-NL S&D project has found practical application in a number of subsequent projects, including the Nederlab project and Dutch Songs Online. Although these projects take an aggregated content search approach (i.e. content is stored centrally as part of the index) rather than a federated content search approach, the technological foundation in these projects is largely the same. The results of the S&D project thus demonstrate a practical applicability beyond the CLARIN domain and continue to be developed for more advanced use cases.

3.7   Portal

The functionality of the CLARIN-NL portal was described in chapter 2, section 2.5. It has been implemented as a straightforward website using the Drupal content management system. CLARIN-compatible login has been created here as well.

For the faceted browsing and searching in data and software, small taxonomies for the facet values were created. Having the freedom of experimenting with the relevant values in a working faceted browser without being penalised for not being compatible with existing defined values sets was a big advantage. However, with these taxonomies relatively stable now, we should work on including them into the CCR, and to derive the faceted browsing and search interfaces automatically from CMDI-descriptions of the relevant data and software, since it will be inefficient to maintain the faceted browsing and search on the portal directly. Deriving the faceted browsing and search from CMDI-descriptions for data and software is indeed being worked on in the CLARIAH-CORE successor project.

3.8   Concluding Remarks

I have provided an introduction to the major technical requirements that the CLARIN infrastructure must meet. In this chapter I described requirements and CLARIN solutions for persistent identifiers, for metadata, for authentication and authorisation, and for semantic interoperability. I described the options offered for search for data through VLO and the Meertens Metadata Search engine, and for federated content search, how they were implemented, and what problems were encountered in implementing them. And finally, we described the implementation of the CLARIN-NL portal.

The remainder of Part I is structured as follows. In chapter 4, a description is given of the construction of the CLARIN infrastructure in the Low Countries (mainly the Netherlands). It deals with the set-up of the network of CLARIN centres and their certification as CLARIN centres, with the set-up of essential infrastructure services, with the contributions by the Netherlands to several central CLARIN registries and services, and with how data and software have been made available to researchers via the CLARIN centres.

Chapter 5 deals with the CLARIN vocabulary service CLAVAS, a SKOS-based knowledge system to provide integrated access to a variety of managed vocabularies (copied from other knowledge sources), so that CLARIN users can transparently use concepts and data categories from each of them.

Chapter 6 deals with the FoLiA-format: a format that emerged out of the CLARIN-NL project and a range of other projects as a *de facto* standard for annotated textual resources. It discusses the format, the design principles behind the format, and the tools that accompany the format, e.g. for validation, editing, conversion, search and visualisation of documents in FoLiA-format.

Chapter 7 describes the TTNWW workflow system for web services: through this system a whole range of natural language processing tools for the Dutch language created in earlier projects were turned into web services and combined in workflows, so that any humanities researcher can enrich data in a very user-friendly manner with automatically created annotations such as lemmas, part-of-speech codes, syntactic structures, named entity annotations, etc. TTNWW covers not only textual data but also audio data, which can be enriched with automatically generated orthographic transcriptions.

Chapter 8 describes a bridge between CMDI-metadata and Linked Open Data. CMDI is the *de facto* standard with CLARIN for metadata. However, its use outside of CLARIN is very limited. In order to make the CMDI-metadata also available to the Linked Open Data community, a bridge has been made to convert CMDI-metadata into Linked Open Data in the Resource Description Format (RDF).

Acknowledgements

This work was financed by CLARIN-NL and CLARIAH.

References

Evert, Stefan and The OCWB Development Team (2010), The IMS Open Corpus Workbench (CWB): CQP Query Language Tutorial, *Ocwb report*, IMS, Stuttgart. http://cwb.sourceforge.net/files/CQP_Tutorial/.

Kemps-Snijders, M., M.A. Windhouwer, and S.E. Wright (2010), Principles of ISOcat, a data category registry, Presentation at the RELISH workshop Rendering endangered languages lexicons interoperable through standards harmonization – Workshop on Lexicon Tools and Lexicon Standards, Nijmegen, The Netherlands, August 4-5, 2010. http://www.mpi.nl/research/research-projects/language-archiving-technology/events/relish-workshop/program/ISOcat.pptx.

Kemps-Snijders, Marc (2014), Metadata quality assurance for CLARIN, *Clarin report*, CLARIN-NL / Meertens Institute, Utrecht / Amsterdam. http://www.clarin.nl/sites/default/files/The%20Metadata%20Quality%20Assurance-final.pdf.

Odijk, Jan (2009), Data categories and ISOCAT: some remarks from a simple linguist, Presentation given at FLaReNet/CLARIN Standards Workshop, Helsinki. http://www.csc.fi/english/pages/neeri09/workshop/materials/odijk.pdf.

Schuurman, Ineke, Menzo Windhouwer, Oddrun Ohren, and Daniel Zeman (2016), CLARIN Concept Registry: The New Semantic Registry, *in* De Smedt, Koenraad, editor, *Selected Papers from the CLARIN Annual Conference 2015, October 14–16, 2015, Wroclaw, Poland*, number 123 in *Linköping Electronic Conference Proceedings*, CLARIN, Linköping University Electronic Press, Linköping, Sweden, pp. 62–70. http://www.ep.liu.se/ecp/article.asp?issue=123&article=004.

Van Eynde, Frank (2004), Part of speech tagging en lemmatisering van het Corpus Gesproken Nederlands, *CGN report*, Centrum voor Computerlinguïstiek, KU Leuven, Leuven, Belgium. http://www.ccl.kuleuven.be/Papers/POSmanual_febr2004.pdf.

Ďurčo, Matej and Menzo Windhouwer (2014), The CMD cloud, *in* Calzolari, Nicoletta, Khalid Choukri, Thierry Declerck, Hrafn Loftsson, Bente Maegaard, Joseph Mariani, Asuncion Moreno, Jan Odijk, and Stelios Piperidis, editors, *Proceedings of the Ninth International Conference on Language Resources and Evaluation (LREC'14)*, European Language Resources Association (ELRA), Reykjavik, Iceland, pp. 687–690.

CHAPTER 4

Building CLARIN Infrastructure in the Netherlands

Daan Broeder[1,a], Jan Theo Bakker[b], Marco van der Laan[c], Marc Kemps-Snijders[d], Menzo Windhouwer[e], Marjan Grootveld[f]

[a]Meertens Institute, daan.broeder@meertens.knaw.nl, [b]INL, JanTheo.Bakker@inl.nl, [c]INL, Marco.vanderLaan@inl.nl, [d]Meertens Institute, marc.kemps.snijders@meertens.knaw.nl, [e]Meertens Institute, menzo.windhouwer@meertens.knaw.nl, [f]DANS, marjan.grootveld@dans.knaw.nl

ABSTRACT

In 2011 the Dutch national CLARIN project started the Infrastructure Implementation Project (IIP) as one of the means to build a national CLARIN infrastructure based on a network of CLARIN centres and to contribute to the CLARIN EU-wide effort. The IIP resulted in the certification of four CLARIN centres in the Netherlands and the provisioning of many Dutch language resources and services.

4.1 Introduction

The CLARIN Research Infrastructure is being created by a coordinated effort of many national projects and initiatives to provide an interoperable research infrastructure for the Humanities and Social Sciences on a European scale (T. Varadi et al., 2008). CLARIN has been on the ESFRI roadmap[2] since 2008 and was granted ERIC status in February 2012. CLARIN ERIC coordinates the interoperability and consistency of the infrastructure and the different national contributions through committees and task forces, although the national projects have freedom to choose their contributions to the EU infrastructure and in arranging the integration of CLARIN infrastructure with their national research projects.

---

[1] Daan Broeder and Menzo Windhouwer were both employed at the Max Planck Institute for Psycholinguistics (MPI) and involved in the CLARIN-NL project during the IIP; Daan Broeder was the IIP project coordinator.

[2] See http://cordis.europa.eu/esfri/roadmap.htm (accessed 14 January 2016).

How to cite this book chapter:

Broeder, D, Theo Bakker, J, van der Laan, M, Kemps-Snijders, M, Windhouwer, M and Grootveld, M. 2017. Building CLARIN Infrastructure in the Netherlands. In: Odijk, J and van Hessen, A. (eds.) *CLARIN in the Low Countries*, Pp. 45–59. London: Ubiquity Press. DOI: https://doi.org/10.5334/bbi.4. License: CC-BY 4.0

Two major projects were defined in CLARIN-NL to provide basic infrastructure services: the Infrastructure Implementation Project (IIP) and the Search and Development (S&D) project. The results of the S&D project were described in chapter 3 (see also Zhang et al., 2012); the IIP project will be described in this chapter.

The IIP was intended to create the Dutch part of the CLARIN technical infrastructure, and also provided resources to the CLARIN centres to adapt their internal workflow and infrastructure to CLARIN requirements.

Adoption of this technical infrastructure by the candidate CLARIN centres must culminate in:

- their certification as a CLARIN B centre[3]
- making their resources and services available in a CLARIN-compatible way

This chapter describes how this adoption was achieved. It is structured as follows: in section 4.2 we describe the background for the CLARIN infrastructure construction. In section 4.3 we discuss the set-up of the network of CLARIN centres in the Netherlands and their certification as CLARIN centres. In section 4.4 we describe how the essential infrastructure services were set up. Section 4.5 describes how data and software services were made available by the CLARIN centres. Section 4.6 deals with their contributions to central infrastructure registries and services. We end the chapter in section 4.7 with conclusions and recommendations.

4.2   CLARIN-NL Infrastructure Building Background

The design and prototyping of the CLARIN technical infrastructure had already begun during the CLARIN preparatory phase (2008–2011), in collaboration with a number of European partners (T. Varadi et al., 2008), and the basic technical ambitions and the infrastructure design remain largely valid to this day.

The basic CLARIN technical infrastructure can be broken down into a number of key areas:

- Metadata to find resources by using the Component Metadata Infrastructure (CMDI).
- Semantic interoperability by using central semantic registry services to provide semantic interoperability for concepts used within metadata and annotations.
- Persistent Identifiers (PIDs) to identify resources and to provide options to refer to multiple copies of a resource and handle migrations in a transparent manner.
- Orchestration of web services to provide a workflow system for Language Technology (LT).
- Authentication and Authorisation Infrastructure (AAI) framework using SAML2 Identity Management for user identification and authorisation to provide a domain where researchers have a single identity and can use Single Sign On (SSO) for all CLARIN services.
- Recommended CLARIN formats for Language Resources (LRs).

This technical infrastructure should be supported and populated by a large set of European centres that provide language data and technology.

CLARIN ERIC and the many CLARIN committees and task-forces created a framework for discussing and certifying interoperability requirements. This culminated in a system of requirements for CLARIN centre types and an accompanying certification process.

Every national CLARIN project is expected to support a number[4] of certified CLARIN centres publishing useful LR data and LT services for the community. In addition, some contributions

---

[3]   See https://www.clarin.eu/content/centres (accessed 14 January 2016) for an explanation of CLARIN centres and the assessment procedure.

[4]   Currently every national CLARIN project should at least have one type B centre.

to the development and maintenance of central CLARIN infrastructure services are expected. In the following sections, we describe how, in this context, the IIP implemented the CLARIN infrastructure for the Netherlands and the contributions of CLARIN-NL to the CLARIN EU infrastructure.

4.3   A Network of CLARIN Centres

One of the main purposes of the IIP was the preparation of first four, and later five, organisations to become certified CLARIN centres. Such centres are instrumental in the provisioning of data and services in a standardised, CLARIN-compatible way; the collaboration between centres makes such provisioning more easily transferable and thus sustainable.

CLARIN centres come in different types[5]. For the Netherlands, three types are relevant: type A, type B, and type D centres.

4.3.1   Type B Centres

Type B centres offer online services and harvestable metadata that are accessible in a CLARIN-compatible manner, and they provide fully integrated CLARIN-conformant services.

The Netherlands started with four Type-B candidate centres; at a later stage one more (Huygens ING) joined. These candidate centres differ in the kind of resources that they are interested in, usually as a function of their research interests. The following is a list the Dutch Type B CLARIN centres and characterises the resource types they are most interested in:

- The Meertens Institute (MI) holds resources relevant for the study of the function, meaning and coherence of cultural expressions; and resources relevant for the structural, dialectological and sociolinguistic study of language variation within the Dutch language.
- The Institute for Dutch Lexicology (INL) provides resources and services that are relevant to the lexicological study of the Dutch language; and resources relevant for research in and development of language and speech technology.
- The Max Planck Institute for Psycholinguistics (MPI/The Language Archive) houses resources related to the study of the psychological, social and biological foundations of language; documentation of endangered languages; resources for sign languages; phonetic resources for the study of phone perception; speech error databases; and also tools for creating and annotating resources.
- Data Archiving and Networked Services (DANS) provides archiving services and access to a broad classification of research data in the fields of humanities, such as oral history, archaeology, geospatial sciences and behavioural and social sciences.
- The Huygens ING Institute (HI) holds resources related to the study of the history and literature of the Netherlands.

Most centres provide not only data but also software services.[6] DANS, however, commonly favours the provision of data only. For type B centres a certification procedure was set up in CLARIN. A centre can become a certified CLARIN centre if it meets the following requirements:

1. it must offer metadata for the centres' resources in the format used by the Component Metadata Infrastructure (CMDI; Broeder et al., 2010)

---

[5] See https://www.clarin.eu/content/centres, accessed Jan 14, 2016 for an explanation of CLARIN centers and the center assessment procedure.

[6] Such centres are sometimes called B+ centres, but this is not an official term

2. it must issue Persistent Identifiers (PIDs) for metadata and resources

3. it must have implemented SAML2-based Federated Identity Management (FIM) for user identification and authentication when accessing protected resources

4. it must offer resources in CLARIN-recommended formats

5. it must comply with the Data Seal of Approval (DSA)[7]

Optionally a centre can also make available one or more endpoints that are compatible with the approach adopted for Federated Content Search in CLARIN.

We will discuss the various requirements for certification one by one:

4.3.1.1   CMDI (Metadata) Resource Descriptions

Each CLARIN centre publishes many CMDI-metadata records, predominantly metadata for the centre's own resources, but in part metadata from external researchers who deposit their resources at the centre, or resource descriptions from the CLARIN-NL Data Curation Service (DCS; see chapter 2, section 2.4.5).

The resource descriptions must be made public, otherwise nobody will know of the resources' existence: each CLARIN centre makes its resource descriptions available through a publicly accessible service using the OAI-PMH protocol (*Open Archives Initiative - Protocol for Metadata Harvesting*; Lagoze et al., 2002), which allows other programmes to harvest the metadata records in an easy way.

4.3.1.2   Persistent Identification of Resources (PIDs)

Each Netherlands CLARIN centre has set up a PID-system for the creation, the assignment, the maintenance and the resolution of persistent identifiers. Initially, any working system of PIDs was allowed, but in a later phase CLARIN required the use of the Handle System: each CLARIN centre in the Netherlands now uses the Handle System for the assignment and resolution of persistent identifiers.[8]

4.3.1.3   Authentication and Authorisation

CLARIN requires the use of SAML2 Identity Management for user identification and authentication. This provides a unified domain where researchers have a single identity and can use Single Sign On (SSO) for all CLARIN services.

To enable this in the Netherlands each CLARIN centre that hosts protected data or services must be a member of the CLARIN Service Provider Federation (SPF) and the Dutch academic and higher education Identity Federation SURFconext. Such legal contracts with national Identity Federations are necessary, because the users must be sure that they are indeed using an approved service, and not some unknown service that might abuse users' personal information or implicitly charge costs to users or their institutes. All CLARIN centres in the Netherlands are also members of the CLARIN SPF, which takes care of inter-federating the different national Identity Federations with regards to CLARIN services, so that Dutch users may access CLARIN services of other European CLARIN centres and vice versa.

To make SAML2-based FIM possible, in addition to joining the federations, every centre has to deploy Shibboleth middleware (or similar software), and ensure that access to the protected data or service always leads to the Shibboleth system: this middleware enables the provisioning

---

[7] http://www.datasealofapproval.org/en/ (accessed 14 January 2016).

[8] DANS originally only used its own URN:NBN resolver; however the choice of URN:NBN is no longer CLARIN compatible, and only services based on the Handle System technology such as EPIC or DOI/DataCite are now accepted. DANS now also uses DOIs.

and checking of user credentials at the user's home organisation. SURFsara, which hosts the Dutch National Research and Education network (NREN) organisation, offers administration of FIM services through the SURFconext federation; however, this service is by default a national service, connecting only users and services from Dutch organisations. This is too limited in the CLARIN context, which aims to provide access to all European researchers (and even wider). Making FIM available in a European CLARIN context requires some extra configuration and administrative actions. Some centres ran into this problem, and DANS still needs to make final adjustments.

To enable the interfederation function of the CLARIN SPF, the administrators of the identity stores from the user home organisations (e.g. universities and research organisations) need to give permissions for their students and employees to use CLARIN services. To this end, SURFconext made a request to all their members to allow SURFconext to pass through user information to CLARIN service providers.[9] However, the response to this request was minimal: only a few organisations gave permission. In order to improve the situation, a new strategy was followed. Firstly, a documentation package was prepared to explain exactly what was involved and what type of information would be conveyed to CLARIN service providers. It included a letter by the general director of NWO, in which each organisation was requested to grant permission for usage of the CLARIN services. It referred to the original letter sent by SURFconext. It also included a link to a tool to test, after permission was given, whether the technical implementation of this permission actually worked correctly. Secondly, for each organisation, a prominent researcher (mostly a full professor) active in CLARIN was approached for assistance. The idea was that a request from a prominent researcher from inside the organisation might have more success than a general request from SURFconext, and might more easily lead to follow-up, face-to-face contacts, etc. The package contained a model letter that the prominent researcher had to adapt slightly to his/her own organisation, but that described exactly what the request was, and what it involved. This approach was indeed more successful, though in some cases it still took quite some time before the permission was given and the technical measures were taken and tested. Currently, all CLARIN-NL partners have given permission to their employees and students to use the CLARIN services.

The same package has been sent to our colleagues in Flanders, and it has been successfully used there as well, since at least some universities in Flanders (e.g. Ghent University and KU Leuven) have access to the CLARIN services through the CLARIN AAI system. This was especially important for the INL, which, by its very mission, serves both the Netherlands and Flanders, and has most of its corpus and lexicon search engines behind a login.

With respect to authorisation, CLARIN does not make any requirements regarding the use of a specific system or technology. However, CLARIN does require the hosting centre to make all the legal and ethical requirements for using a specific resource or service explicit.[10] Some CLARIN centres in the Netherlands have special provisions to deal with such matters, e.g. The Language Archive unit of the Max Planck Institute for Psycholinguistics (MPI/TLA). For example, one option is to show users a text describing usage conditions, but letting users access the data without reading this text. In a second option, such a text is shown but confirmation by users that they have read the text and agree to it is required.[11] A third option is to require explicit permission from the data provider for usage of the data according to a specific licence agreement (this is the case for, for example, the IPROSLA data set, which requires special provisions to protect the privacy of the participants, who come from the (small) sign-language-using community in the

---

[9] SURFconext, the Dutch Identity Federation has a 'star' architecture so the technical configuration of such permissions can be done solely by SURFconext itself. In other countries with a different Identity Federation architecture, the Identity Providers must make such adaptations themselves.

[10] Currently CLARIN has developed a simple classification system for such licences: see https://www.clarin.eu/content/license-categories

[11] See https://www.eff.org/wp/clicks-bind-ways-users-agree-online-terms-service for clickwrap and browsewrap agreements.

Netherlands). Most other centres have arranged such matters by providing access to such data in limited ways. For example, most text corpora at INL can only be accessed via specific search interfaces, and after login. Export of the results of the search queries is highly limited. Downloading these text corpora is simply not possible.

4.3.1.4   Resources in CLARIN-Recommended Formats

Each CLARIN centre makes resources available in a CLARIN-compatible manner, as was described in detail in chapter 2 (sections 2.2 and 2.4.5). A note of concern is that multiple lists of recommended formats are circulating within CLARIN, and as of today no authorative list has been presented yet. This problem and other issues with respect to standardisation are the domain of the CLARIN standards committee.

4.3.1.5   Data Seal of Approval

CLARIN centres must store data and software. To that end, each CLARIN centre has to set up a repository. Different repository systems exist, and CLARIN does not prescribe which system has to be used. Many centres use an open source repository platform, such as the Fedora Commons repository[12] or DSpace, and some have developed their own software, for instance LAMUS/LAT, developed by the MPI (Broeder et al., 2006).

The CLARIN centre registry contains information on the repository systems used by the various CLARIN centres. Currently each Dutch CLARIN centre uses a different system: DANS uses its own EASY system, which is built on Fedora Commons; INL uses DSpace; MPI/TLA uses LAT; and Huygens ING and the Meertens Institute use their own systems.

Some centres use special software so that users can store resources in the repository; for example, MPI/TLA's LAT and the DANS EASY archiving system offer deposition facilities. Storing resources in the repository must be supported by special software, since it is not an easy matter. Typically PIDs are assigned at this stage, usually to a large set of resources: a PID must be generated for the resource, it must be associated with the resource location and it must be added to the resource description, which now can be finalised and gets its own PID. Provisions for legal or ethical access and usage restrictions must be taken care of. Finally the resource itself must be stored on a server that is accessible from outside of the CLARIN centre, and its description must be put on a location where it can be harvested by the OAI-PMH protocol.

Each CLARIN centre must ensure the long-term preservation of the resources; CLARIN centres have to make special provisions for this. Sometimes they take care of long-term preservation themselves (e.g. DANS), but most centres outsource it to specialised centres (e.g. the MPI/TLA outsources it to the long-term preservation services of the Max Planck Gesellschaft). In any case, each CLARIN centre must have a clear procedure in place for managing its data and for ensuring long-term preservation, and must work according to this procedure. Each CLARIN centre must be awarded a DSA it is to become a certified CLARIN centre. The DSA guidelines[13] are elaborations of a small number of criteria that data must meet: the data can be found on the Internet; the data are accessible (clear rights and licences); the data are in a usable format; the data are reliable; and the data are identified in a unique and persistent way so that they can be referred to.

All candidate CLARIN centres in the Netherlands have now been awarded the DSA. Initially some Dutch candidate centres perceived the DSA requirements as unclear or too difficult and beyond their ambitions. This was unexpected, based on information from other national CLARIN projects and the fact that the archives of MPI and DANS had already received the DSA. The main

---

[12] Fedora stands for 'Flexible Extensible Digital Object Repository Architecture'.
[13] See https://www.datasealofapproval.org/en/community/, in particular guidelines 6,7 and 8.

issue turned out to be insufficient clarity as to the extent to which the DSA requirements at that time also allowed centres to outsource the required persistent archiving functions to other organisations. Information meetings on certification topics organised by the CLARIN ERIC did not resolve this issue – this caused some delays. As a positive side effect of this it can be mentioned that in the current version of the DSA it has been made explicit that all guidelines can be outsourced (as long as the outsource partner has a DSA or better level of trust certification).

4.3.1.6   Evaluation of the Certification Process

At the start of the IIP, the full CLARIN certification procedure as it stands now was not yet in place beyond the requirement to obtain the DSA. However, formal certification was always seen as one of the major targets to achieve. Though a lot of preparatory work could be done before, focused activities on certification started only when the requirements were fully clear and these were adopted in the IIP work plan.

The speed and final level of implementation and enabling of the specific CLARIN infrastructure technologies varied across the different candidate centres. This was in part due to their different histories: some of them were already involved in earlier infrastructure projects – e.g. DAM-LR (Broeder et al., 2008) or the EU-funded CLARIN-Preparatory Phase project – and two prospective CLARIN centres had also already acquired the DSA.

The first CLARIN-NL centre that obtained its CLARIN certification was the MPI, as it was also part of the German CLARIN-D project that started the certification process as soon as initial certification procedures were in place. This enabled the MPI to provide advice and hands-on help to the other Dutch centres in their preparations for certification. The other CLARIN-NL centres passed certification at different moments. Challenges encountered varied from problems with configuration requirements for joining the CLARIN SPF to problems regarding the full integration of required services with already existing ones, such as authentication and authorisation. Currently (in December 2015) only DANS is still not fully certified as a type B CLARIN centre. One of the reasons is that DANS needs to satisfy multiple groups of customers outside the direct CLARIN domain and thus has problems committing to CLARIN service requirements, for which it already has existing (CLARIN-incompatible) services in place.

Another concern raised by the candidate centres was the changes of CLARIN certification requirements during the run of the IIP project without clear communication. Although in a developing infrastructure such changes are unavoidable, it became clear that the existing communication channels did not always reach all involved parties, and improvements have been made to communicate all relevant information from the CLARIN committees directly to the (candidate) centres.

4.3.1.7   Stability

The set-up of the CLARIN infrastructure as a network of CLARIN centres is intended to create a flexible and robust infrastructure. During the CLARIN-NL project this network was put to the test on several occasions.

First, the HLT Agency (TST-Centrale) was split off from the INL and turned into the CLARIN centre of the Dutch Language Union. This resulted in a lot of additional work to implement the split and created a situation where the HLT Agency had to start from scratch again in becoming a certified CLARIN centre. The HLT Agency worked towards this goal, but, because of financial problems at the Dutch Language Union, the necessary staff could not be made available, and most available employees started looking for other opportunities, reducing the staff even further. Fortunately, the HLT Agency did create CMDI metadata for the data that it manages, and these can be found via the Virtual Language Observatory (VLO). Recently, the data of the HLT Agency also went back to INL.

At the same time, there were managerial problems at INL, and the future of the INL was reassessed. It was clear that a large restructuring was going to take place. This created a lot of uncertainty among the INL staff, which was not optimal. Fortunately, that period is now over, and INL is turning into the Institute for the Dutch Language (INT) and plays a full role in the CLARIN-NL successor project CLARIAH.

Most problematic, however, was the decision of the MPI management to stop its activities as a CLARIN A-centre, and minimise its activities as a CLARIN B-Centre to the level of what was contractually required by its participation in the German CLARIN-D project. This required several adaptations. We concentrate here on the consequences for the Dutch B-centres (for the consequence related to the type A services, see section 4.3.3). MPI decided that the archiving system and workflow used was too complex for their smaller role, so an activity was set to design and construct a simpler version. This has been done in the context of The Language Archive collaboration (TLA), a consortium of MPI, DANS and the Meertens Institute. It resulted in a new CLARIN-compatible repository system called Fedora Language Archiving Technology (FLAT; Windhouwer et al., 2016). Testing the use of FLAT for depositing the results of some previous CLARIN data curation projects at the Meertens Institute was financed by CLARIN-NL (the MDF project).

In addition, it was concluded that it might be beneficial to have important resources available at multiple centres, and an action was started to ensure that resources hosted by MPI are also hosted by other CLARIN centres in the Netherlands. Nevertheless, the reduction of the activities by MPI also means that there is no natural centre for specific types of language data, especially if they concern languages other than the Dutch language (both INL/INT and the Meertens Institute focus on the Dutch language).

4.3.2   Type D Centres

The missions of resource-providing centres vary, and in many cases such centres need to satisfy multiple groups of customers outside the direct CLARIN domain and thus cannot commit themselves exclusively to CLARIN requirements. To address this issue, CLARIN-NL introduced the NL-specific CLARIN data providers centre type D[14] for centres not exclusively focusing on typical CLARIN resources or services.

CLARIN centres of this special type (called CLARIN-NL Data Providers or Type D CLARIN centres[15]) distribute data independently of CLARIN (and have been doing this long before its establishment), but have made provisions to give access to the data that are relevant to humanities researchers in a CLARIN-compatible manner (via CMDI resource descriptions). These CLARIN centres include organisations that, by their very mission, make available large amounts of data. Currently the Type D centres are:

- Koninklijke Bibliotheek (KB)[16] for digital books, articles, newspapers.
- Digitale Bibliotheek voor de Nederlandse Letteren (DBNL; now included within KB)[17] for literary works.
- Nederlands Instituut voor Beeld & Geluid (NIBG)[18] for audio-visual data (especially TV and radio programmes).
- Utrechtse Universiteitsbibliotheek (UBU)[19] for digital books and articles.

---

[14] See http://www.clarin.nl/sites/default/files/restore/New%20Centre%20Types%2011060.pdf and http://www.clarin.nl/node/130 (accessed 14 January 2016).
[15] This type of CLARIN centre is distinguished from others only in the Netherlands.
[16] National Library.
[17] Digital Library for Dutch Literature, which merged with KB in 2014.
[18] Netherlands Institute for Sound and Vision.
[19] Utrecht University Library.

Since many of the data provided by these organisations are highly relevant to humanities researchers, these data should be available via the CLARIN infrastructure – and they already are, for NIBG and for UBU, or will soon be (for KB).[20]

Although the CLARIN Data Providers were subsidised in separate CLARIN subprojects, the IIP supported these efforts, e.g. with the development of suitable CMDI metadata schema. Such smaller consultancy services were also rendered by the IIP to the CLARIN-NL curation and demonstrator projects and to other CLARIN-NL projects, e.g. the DCS.

4.3.3   Type A Centres

Type A centres offer core, essential infrastructure services; for example, the MPI/TLA hosts[21] the VLO (see section 4.6.3), and carries out the necessary harvesting of resource descriptions. A list of essential services is available via CLARIN.[22]

Only the MPI/TLA and the Meertens Institute offer type A services (in addition to the type B services they offer) in the CLARIN-NL project. MPI/TLA offer many type A services, and the Meertens Institute a few; for example, the Meertens Institute hosts the CLARIN Concept Registry (CCR; see section 4.6.2) and CLAVAS (see chapter 5).

CLARIN-NL contributed to these core infrastructural services, which was quite natural since MPI was involved in building and managing many of these services. CLARIN-NL also contributed significantly to registries and services for CMDI metadata, e.g. the CMDI registry, the Arbil metadata editor, the VLO and the CLARIN discovery services (see section 4.6).

An official certification procedure for type A services only became available in 2016, long after the end of the IIP; but the concept of a CLARIN type A centre existed since the start of CLARIN, and CLARIN-NL, through the IIP, contributed considerably to the maintenance and further development of these core services.

4.4   IIP Strategy for Technical Infrastructure Adoption by Centres

4.4.1   Knowledge Exchange and Consultancy

To build a technical infrastructure as used by CLARIN, it is crucial that the different centres have expert staff available and that there be lines of communication and information and training possibilities to keep their knowledge up-to-date.

During the run of the IIP, many meetings and workshops were held to discuss technical infrastructure aspects necessary for CLARIN certification and interoperability with the CLARIN infrastructure. Prior to the certification round at the end of 2013, direct consultancy by the previously certified[23] MPI CLARIN centre was provided to other centres, as also happened for the second round in April 2014.

4.4.2   CLARIN-NL Infrastructure Work in a European and Historical Context

Both MPI and INL had been involved in the DAM-LR EU project, which pioneered technical solutions that would become part and parcel of the CLARIN infrastructure, such as SAML-based

---

[20] The number of metadata records available from KB is so huge that it requires modifying the VLO.

[21] Because of the MPI's changed CLARIN ambitions the VLO service has been moved and is currenty under the direct responsibility of the CLARIN ERIC.

[22] See http://www.clarin.eu/content/services for a list of such essential infrastructure services.

[23] As mentioned earlier, MPI had already been certified in the certification round for the centres in the German CLARIN project.

FIM and PIDs based on the Handle System (HS). Within INL, the DAM-LR work was carried out by the Dutch-Flemish HLT Agency, then hosted at the INL. Both INL and MPI had an operational Handle System server installation and knew about the effort required for administrating this. From the earlier experiences with SAML-based FIM a concern arose over the increasing complexity of the managed metadata and the policing of the authentication system for every provided service. This was solved by centralising the SAML2 service on a web server that acts as a 'reverse proxy' and where all Shibboleth configuration takes place and then publishing all to-be-protected services via this proxy. This solution was implemented both at MPI and INL.

CLARIN requires the use of CMDI metadata for Language Resources and Language Technology services, which differs from the approach to metadata in DAM-LR. IIP supported the CMDI development, which was already initiated during the CLARIN EU preparatory phase (CLARIN-PP), and had already resulted in creating the necessary software components at the MPI (see section 4.6). The applicability of the CMDI approach to a variety of resources stored in the candidate CLARIN centres was first tested in a small project (De Vriend et al., 2013).

As a PID solution, most CLARIN centres chose, based on their experiences in DAM-LR, either to provide their own instance of the Handle System or to use Handle System PID services provided by EPIC (this was the case the Meertens Institute, for instance). In the Netherlands, EPIC handle services are delivered by SURFsara.[24]

To realise the CLARIN AAI objectives, it was necessary for all CLARIN-NL centres to join the CLARIN EU SPF, which, as mentioned before, implied that the centres also join the Dutch Identity Federation SURFconext. The MPI provided support to adopt the necessary technological knowledge and coordination with SURFconext and other EU AAI organisations. Although current AAI solutions provide satisfactory authentication and authorisation procedures for accessing web-applications, the necessary AAI infrastructure for the orchestration of web-services was only tested on a small scale and never fully deployed (Blumtritt et al., 2015). This hampered the further development of more advanced use cases where services authenticate on behalf of the user to perform advanced types of analysis.

With respect to the development of a flexible workflow system for Language Technology, no convergence was achieved at the CLARIN EU level and, as mentioned above, a suitable stable AAI technology for such a system was lacking, although prototypes were successfully tested. The CLARIN-NL TTNWW project delivered a functional workflow system based on a number of fixed recipes (see chapter 7).

With respect to LR format standards especially, the IIP based itself on the work done in the CLARIN EU preparatory phase, extending the accepted set of CLARIN-allowed data formats with the new 'Folia' annotation format used widely in the Low Countries (see Van Gompel et al., 2013; and chapter 6).

4.5   Populating the CLARIN Infrastructure

With centre certification, a second aspect of the centre build-up activities has been making the centres' data accessible and available in the CLARIN infrastructure. Partly this was covered by the requirement that all results of (other) CLARIN projects should be provided in a CLARIN-compatible way, but it was also expected that, as part of the IIP, centres would transform already existing data sets into CLARIN-compatible ones.

---

[24] See https://www.surf.nl/en/services-and-products/data-persistent-identifier/index.html (accessed 14 January 2016).

Continuous work was performed by the candidate centres to make their resources available. The result of this work can be found on the CLARIN-NL portal,[25] which shows all the corpora and services that were created in CLARIN-NL and that can now be accessed in a CLARIN-compatible manner, or by using the VLO CLARIN metadata catalogue[26] or CLARIN centre portal pages such as the INL CLARIN Portal.[27]

A complication in this process for the INL centre was the split-off of their TST-centrale (Dutch-Flemish HLT Agency) partner, which is currently the candidate CLARIN centre for the Dutch Language Union. Also, although this occurred after the official end of the IIP, the MPI centre decided to scale down its efforts in infrastructure building and provisioning projects. Such events prove very challenging for infrastructures such as CLARIN that depend on centres as stable components of the infrastructure for providing essential data and services. With respect to the provisioning of services, we have been able to partially overcome such changes by involving other centres or moving services to other centres or to CLARIN ERIC. With respect to data provisioning, sustainability very much depends on the possibility to make copies available – this is not always easily possible in view of copyright and licence issues.

4.6   Contributions to Central CLARIN Registries and Services

An important requirement for a functioning CLARIN infrastructure is the availability of certain specific *central* registries and services. The IIP made important contributions to this. These registries and services mainly concern the CLARIN Component Metadata Infrastructure registry and registries for managing semantics, as well as registries used in CLARIN data and central services that are needed for using FIM for authentication to CLARIN services. The European scope requires that these services and registries also be available EU-wide, and they should thus be considered a major contribution to the EU CLARIN infrastructure.

In the IIP, MPI was assigned the task of developing and maintaining the registries and services. MPI had already started developing prototypes within the CLARIN EU preparatory phase and was well positioned to coordinate with the other national projects, especially CLARIN-D, in which it also participated. The German CLARIN project also provided considerable support to the development and maintenance of these registries and services.

The relevant registries and services are:

- *The CMDI Component Registry and Editor.* A web-based tool[28] that allows researchers and data scientists to reuse and create new (CMDI) metadata profiles to create metadata records.
- *The ISOcat Data Category Registry (DCR) and later the CLARIN Concept Registry (CCR).* Registries providing semantic interoperability for concepts used within metadata and annotations.
- *VLO, the Virtual Language Observatory.* A faceted browser that shows all the metadata records available within the CMDI domain. This service includes the metadata-harvesting infrastructure.
- *Arbil*[29]. A metadata editor that users can use to create CMDI metadata records
- *The CLARIN Discovery Service and the CLARIN Identity Provider for users without an academic institute affiliation (homeless).*

---

[25] The CLARIN NL portal can be found at: http://portal.clarin.nl/clarin-data-list-fs
[26] https://vlo.clarin.eu/search?8& fq=nationalProject:CLARIN-NL
[27] https://portal.clarin.inl.nl
[28] https://www.clarin.eu/cmdi
[29] http://tla.mpi.nl/tools/tla-tools/arbil/

Of these we will discuss the CMDI Component Registry; ISOcat and the CCR; and the VLO in more detail.

4.6.1   *CMDI Component Registry*

Apart from the continuous support and improvements to the stability and performance of the CMDI Component Registry, its functionality was also extended in the IIP. Since Component Registry content management is required not only for CLARIN-NL but also for other CLARIN EU projects, coordination and close collaboration was required. A matter of concern is that projects occasionally choose to create or modify their metadata schema outside of the Component Registry. This can lead to incompatible metadata, a matter that is not always noticed immediately since the central metadata-harvesting process does not check the records thoroughly enough. This is currently addressed by the CLARIN ERIC CMDI and the Metadata Curation task forces.

Another matter of concern connected to the metadata records produced for CLARIN is the sometimes questionable quality of these records, both in semantic correctness and in suitability of the created schema for a particular type of data. This is not a matter that can be solved by technological means, but one that needs to be addressed by curation of the schema and community review. Having metadata content quality managers, as is planned, will be a good step forward.[30]

4.6.2   *ISOcat and the CCR*

In 2009 the ISOcat DCR (Broeder et al., 2014) went into production as a joint effort between ISO TC 37 and CLARIN. Within the IIP, ISOcat has been extended to better fit into the developing CLARIN infrastructure. The most salient additions are the implementation of FIM for ISOcat, the interoperability with the CLARIN CLAVAS vocabulary service (see chapter 5) and the supporting of community recommendations gathered by the CLARIN ISOcat content manager. In 2013 there was an extensive evaluation of the problems encountered and of both ISO TC 37's and CLARIN's uptake of ISOcat. In a joint meeting of these two major user communities at the end of 2013, the extent of overlap of the requirements of both communities was further assessed. As a result CLARIN and ISO TC 37 developments were further decoupled. It was decided that the design and implementation of a successor to ISOcat would need to be based on a simpler data model focused on concept specifications and on a workflow that is more geared towards community agreement, rather than towards an official ISO standardisation process ISO 12620. Since the MPI CLARIN centre has also expressed its desire to lessen its responsibility towards external infrastructures, CLARIN has switched to the CLARIN Concept Registry (CCR), which is based on OpenSKOS[31] and hosted by the Meertens Institute. A successful migration at the start of 2015 proved to be a showcase of a successful transfer of software, data and responsibilities between centres.

The IIP supported the ISOcat coordinator and various CLARIN projects through tutorials, workshops, question-answering and help with regard to the import/export of data category specifications.

4.6.3   *VLO*

The Virtual Language Observatory (Van Uytvanck et al., 2012) is the CLARIN EU-wide metadata catalogue that harvests all CLARIN-compatible metadata. The IIP contributed to the development of this application, which serves the whole CLARIN EU community. Much effort was made to make

---

[30] In the new CLARIAH-core project extra efforts will also be spent on metadata quality issues.
[31] http://openskos.org/

the VLO more stable and to make it work with the semantic mappings provided by the ISOcat and CCR registries. Related to the VLO is the metadata-harvesting process itself, which occasionally requires intensive communication with the metadata providers when problems occur.

4.6.4   Further CLARIN EU Collaboration

The IIP also contributed to the CLARIN EU task forces and committees: these are CLARIN ERIC coordinated groups to discuss and further the different CLARIN infrastructure components. The IIP contributed to the CLARIN metadata task force, the CLARIN AAI task force, the CLARIN Standards Committee and the CLARIN Centre Assessment Committee.

4.7   Conclusions and Recommendations

In this section we describe achievements and hopeful beginnings, but also some lessons learned that should be taken up by future projects such as the continuation of CLARIN-NL within the more broadly scoped CLARIAH CORE project.

First of all, four CLARIN centres were certified during the CLARIN-NL project, and the centres built up a critical mass of expertise enabling them to participate in the next phases of (also European) infrastructure construction and exploitation. At the beginning of the project, most of this expertise was only available at MPI and INL, but this was successfully transferred to the new CLARIN centres, and, additionally, in discussions with the new CLARIN D-type centres we exchanged expertise with library partners (such as KB and UBU) and Cultural Heritage institutes (such as Sound and Vision).

Secondly, although the direct funding came from outside the IIP, the IIP has succeeded in offering opportunities for a wide range of humanities researchers to familiarise themselves with typical research infrastructure services such as aggregated metadata catalogues, persistent identifiers etc.

The CLARIN-NL project was also very successful since it enabled all centres involved to gain knowledge and expertise about the different aspects of research infrastructures and the technical and organisational challenges involved in providing data and services in new ways not always immediately related to a centre's own research groups or customer base.

On an organisational level we have seen that the need for sustainability cannot be addressed by relying on the CLARIN centre model only. The model has to be augmented by some capable central agency able to step in (if even temporarily) and take care of essential central services; alternatively, suitable incentives for CLARIN centres to take over orphaned services must be put in place. Of course, such services must be built from the beginning as 'transferable' services, e.g. with no hidden local dependencies and built on open software. The new requirements for CLARIN A-type services cover such aspects. During and just after the IIP we saw that the performance of two Dutch CLARIN centres (MPI and INL) was compromised by the changing goals of their organisations. Fortunately, it was possible to transfer essential services largely to the direct care of CLARIN ERIC and to the Meertens Institute, but it proved very difficult to find CLARIN centres (even outside the Netherlands) prepared to take over responsibility for such services. In this respect, the CLARIN-NL landscape proved vulnerable.

An interesting issue is the relative difficulty with which the Dutch candidate CLARIN centres were certified compared to the experiences in the German project. This can maybe partly be explained by the fact that the German centres initially[32] were certified earlier (with somewhat lighter requirements). However, in the Netherlands the motivation to adopt CLARIN requirements

---

[32] However, in a new (re)certification wave three years after the initial certification, with more heavier requirements, the German centres also proved successful.

often seemed less pronounced and the discussions to reach a consensus and to agree to implement CLARIN centre requirements took much time and effort. Since the candidate centres all agreed to the CLARIN goals, this could be an issue of internal institute strategy alignment, or of a need for a more specific CLARIN argumentation at all necessary organisational levels in the Dutch context. But we should also add that the CLARIN centre requirements were under development, and it was felt that this development process was outside the direct influence of those involved. In this respect, increased participation and the need to foster more support for CLARIN requirements and policies from those needed to implement and work with them is a strong recommendation.

In the case of centres with a more heterogeneous mission, it is less certain that all CLARIN centre requirements can be taken up with sufficient priority. The CLARIN-NL project planning itself was targeted towards centre organisations mainly concerned with language data, where the CLARIN scope aligns with a large part of the existing activities. For centres with a broader or more heterogeneous mission, however, special road maps may be needed if their CLARIN participation at a high level is required or desired. It is matter of political consideration how much effort and resources should be invested. A different CLARIN centre classification, such as C, K or D, should also be considered in such cases.

References

J. Blumtritt, W. Elbers, M. Hinrichs, W. Qiu, T. Goosen, M. Sallé, M. Windhouwer. User Delegation in the CLARIN Infrastructure. In J. Odijk (ed.), *Selected Papers from the CLARIN 2014 Conference.* Linköping Electronic Conference Proceedings, August, 2015.

D. Broeder, M. Kemps-Snijders, D. Van Uytvanck, M. Windhouwer, P. Withers, P. Wittenburg, and C. Zinn. A data category registry- and component-based metadata framework. In N. Calzolari, B. Maegaard, J. Mariani, J. Odijk, K. Choukri, S. Piperidis, M. Rosner, and D. Tapias, editors, *Proceedings of the Seventh International Conference on Language Resources and Evaluation* (LREC 2010) , pages 43–47, Valetta, Malta, 2010. European Language Resources Association (ELRA).

D. Broeder, D. Nathan, S. Strömqvist, S., & R. van Veenendaal. Building a federation of Language Resource Repositories; the DAM-LR project and its continuation within CLARIN. In *Proceedings of the Sixth International Conference on Language Resources and Evaluation* (LREC 2008), European Language Resources Association (ELRA), Marrakech, Morocco, May 28–30, 2008.

Broeder, D., Claus, A., Offenga, F., Skiba, R., Trilsbeek, P., & Wittenburg, P. (2006). LAMUS: The Language Archive Management and Upload System. In Proceedings of the 5th International Conference on Language Resources and Evaluation (LREC 2006) (pp. 2291–2294).

D. Broeder, I. Schuurman, M. Windhouwer. Experiences with the ISOcat Data Category Registry. In *Proceedings of the Ninth International Conference on Language Resources and Evaluation* (LREC 2014), European Language Resources Association (ELRA), Reykjavik, Iceland, May 28–30, 2014.

F. de Vriend, D. Broeder, G. Depoorter, L. van Eerten, D. van Uytvanck. Creating & testing CLARIN metadata components. *Language Resources and Evaluation.* 2013. Vol 47, 1315–1326.

ISO 12620:2009. *Terminology and other language and content resources – Specification of data categories and management of a Data Category Registry for language resources.* International Organization for Standardization, Geneve, Switzerland, December, 2009.

Carl Lagoze, Herbert Van de Sompel, Michael Nelson, and Simeon Warner. The Open Archives Initiative Protocol for Metadata Harvesting. Protocol version 2.0 of 2002-06-14. Technical report, Open Archives Initiative, 2002. https://www.openarchives.org/OAI/openarchivesprotocol. html.

M. van Gompel, M. Reynaert. Folia: A practical XML Format for Linguistic Annotation – a descriptive and comparative study. In Computational Linguistics in the Netherlands Journal 3, 2013.

D. van Uytvanck, H. Stehouwer, L. Lampen. Semantic metadata mapping in practice: The Virtual Language Observatory. In *Proceedings of the Eight International Conference on Language Resources and Evaluation* (LREC 2012), European Language Resources Association (ELRA), Istanbul, Turkey, May 23–25, 2012.

T. Váradi, S. Krauwer, P. Wittenburg, M. Wynn, K. Koskenniemi. CLARIN: Common Language Resource and Technology. In *Proceedings of the Sixth International Conference on Language Resources and Evaluation* (LREC 2008), European Language Resources Association (ELRA), Marrakech, Morocco, May 28–30, 2008.

M. Windhouwer, M. Kemps-Snijders, P. Trilsbeek, A. Moreira, B. van der Veen, G. Silva, D. von Rhein. FLAT: constructing a CLARIN compatible home for language resources. In *Proceedings of the Tenth International Conference on Language Resources and Evaluation* (LREC 2016), European Language Resources Association (ELRA), Portorož, Slovenia, May 23–28, 2016.

J. Zhang, M. Kemps-Snijders, H. Bennis. The CMDI MI Search Engine: Access to language resources and tools using heterogeneous metadata schemas. *Theory and Practice of Digital Libraries*. Springer Berlin Heidelberg, 2012. 492–495.

CHAPTER 5

CLAVAS: A CLARIN Vocabulary and Alignment Service

Hennie Brugman

Meertens Institute, Amsterdam, Netherlands
hennie.brugman@meertens.knaw.nl

ABSTRACT

The CLARIN Vocabulary and Alignment Service (CLAVAS) project started as an attempt to address problems that occurred with the use of the CLARIN ISOcat repository to deal with vocabularies used for value ranges in CMDI metadata elements and attributes. CLAVAS objectives were easier maintenance of vocabularies and new ways to exploit these vocabularies in end user tools; the underlying aims were the improvement of metadata quality and the reduction of concept proliferation in the ISOcat repository.

Also, during the project three specific vocabularies were processed and made available via the newly created CLAVAS service platform. We present and evaluate CLAVAS in relation to the family of semantic registries that together played a role in CLARIN: ISOcat, OpenSKOS and the CLARIN Concept Registry. We discuss developments that occurred after the end of the CLAVAS project period, especially the discontinuation of ISOcat as a CLARIN service and the subsequent roles of OpenSKOS and CLAVAS.

5.1 Introduction

Central in CLARIN is work on the standardisation, creation and exploitation of metadata for linguistic resources. Many metadata records were produced, collected and published in IMDI, and have been subsequently in CMDI (Broeder et al., 2012). However, over the course of CLARIN more and more problems with the quality of this metadata became apparent (Broeder et al., 2014). One category of problems had to do with the interpretation of metadata fields and values. Although

How to cite this book chapter:

Brugman, H. 2017. CLAVAS: A CLARIN Vocabulary and Alignment Service. In: Odijk, J and van Hessen, A. (eds.) *CLARIN in the Low Countries*, Pp. 61–69. London: Ubiquity Press. DOI: https://doi.org/10.5334/bbi.5. License: CC-BY 4.0

guidelines and technical means were provided to document, publish and share the semantics of resource descriptions, in practice this did not lead to standardisation and reuse, but to proliferation of often underspecified semantic descriptions.

CLARIN provided the ISOcat Data Category Service as a central registry for the meaning of resource descriptions (Windhouwer et al., 2010). ISOcat combined two purposes: on the one hand it aimed for complex and precise semantic specifications of data categories, with community standardisation as the long-term purpose; on the other hand it supported registration of more volatile and project-specific ranges of values (e.g. lists of genres). For both types of data categories it used the same open update policy, in which everybody is allowed to add their own data categories.

In the meantime, the CATCHPlus project[1] developed OpenSKOS (Brugman and Lindeman, 2012). OpenSKOS is a repository service platform that offers uniform and standardised ways to publish, manage and retrieve vocabulary data in forms that can be used for various usage scenarios, e.g. during metadata creation (e.g. pick lists with autocompletion) or during metadata curation (e.g. search for preferred labels, given some alternative label).

The name 'OpenSKOS' refers to:

- A *standard* format. The OpenSKOS service uses the W3C SKOS[2] recommendation (Miles and Bechhofer, 2009) as its data model.
- An *architecture*. The platform supports multiple nodes that can exchange vocabulary data using the OAI-PMH harvesting protocol.
- An *Application Programming Interface*. This API offers functionality for creating and maintaining SKOS vocabularies.
- A Linked Data endpoint. Vocabulary data in an OpenSKOS node can be addressed with resolvable HTTP links or queried using the SPARQL query language. Links both within and across vocabularies are supported.
- A *publication* platform.
- A platform for *creation and maintenance* of vocabularies.
- A user community promoting the use of *Open licences* for vocabulary data.

Unlike ISOcat, OpenSKOS uses a simple data model with deliberately imprecise semantics. Its main purpose is easy and flexible management, publication and reuse of vocabularies used for resource description. It has no ambition to standardise concepts within communities, other than de-facto, by shared usage. OpenSKOS itself allows an open update strategy, like ISOcat does, in the sense that if no specific restrictions are applied OpenSKOS vocabularies can be freely uploaded and modified.

Where the ISOcat approach seemed especially suitable to define and publish core domain concepts, such as often-used fields in metadata specifications, OpenSKOS seemed the better choice for dealing with the second type of concepts, that is the ranges of values used to fill those fields. The CLARIN-NL CLARIN Vocabulary and Alignment Service (CLAVAS) project was started as a best-of-both-worlds effort to combine the two concept registry systems, where each system dealt with the type of concepts that was best supported by its design.

The CLAVAS[3] project extends CATCHPlus' OpenSKOS platform with CLARIN-specific components: first, it publishes three vocabularies required by the CLARIN community and it offers tools to keep those vocabularies synchronised with their sources. Second, it offers an interactive web application that can be used to curate existing vocabularies or to create new ones from scratch

---

[1] www.catchplus.nl
[2] http://www.w3.org/TR/skos-primer/
[3] https://openskos.meertens.knaw.nl/clavas/

(the OpenSKOS Editor). And third, it aims for implementation of usage scenarios where main-stream CLARIN tools (like Arbil[4]) use vocabularies directly via the OpenSKOS RESTful API.

This chapter starts with a presentation of the history, design objectives, description and comparison of both ISOcat and OpenSKOS semantic registries. In subsequent sections we present the CLAVAS project, its objectives, components and architecture, we evaluate its results and we present lessons learned.

Currently, CLAVAS usage is the proposed solution for utilising external vocabularies at the operational level in the CMDI 1.2 specification (CLARIN CMDI Taskforce, 2014) and therefore still is part of the CLARIN landscape of semantic registries: we thus also describe the state of this landscape and recent developments.

5.2   ISOcat and OpenSKOS

As said in the introduction, CLAVAS started as an attempt to combine two existing semantic registry systems, ISOcat and OpenSKOS, thereby exploiting the strengths of each of the two approaches. In Table 5.1 a direct comparison between the two initial systems on a number of specific aspects is given.

	ISOcat	OpenSKOS
data model	• (ISO) data category-based • accurate semantics	• (SKOS) concept-based • simplified semantics
relations between concepts in vocabularies included	no	yes
linking of concepts across vocabularies supported	no	yes
update strategy	open	open
main objectives	• community standards, reference vocabularies • documentation • reuse of vocabularies	• publish and reuse vocabularies • cross-link/align vocabularies • easy in, easy out • many alternatives for input and output • practical applications by humans and machines
input	• manual via GUI	• manual via GUI • RDF file upload • harvesting using OAI-PMH • via RESTful API
output	• user interface • RESTful API	• user interface • RESTful API • OAI-PMH data provider • browsable html pages
standards	ISO TC37 DCR; 12620	W3C SKOS

Table 5.1: Comparison of ISOcat and OpenSKOS.

---

[4] https://tla.mpi.nl/tools/tla-tools/arbil/

Concerning the data models used, ISOcat uses data categories, with Complex Data Categories representing properties of items and Simple Data Categories representing atomic elements to be included in the value set of Complex Data Categories (Schuurman et al., 2015). ISOcat does not contain relations between Data Categories. OpenSKOS has a simpler model, and uses SKOS as its data model. The SKOS (and OpenSKOS) model includes relations between concepts, as well as properties of these concepts to model alignment between concepts in different vocabularies (SKOS ConceptSchemes).

Concerning input and output options, the OpenSKOS design objectives have a stronger focus on supporting a wide range of practical applications, both by humans and by machines, such as online term suggestion using autocompletion in the context of (metadata editing) tools.

5.3   The CLAVAS Project

In this section we first present the CLAVAS components and architecture and then discuss the vocabulary data involved in the project.

5.3.1   Components and Architecture

Figure 5.1 shows an architectural overview of the CLAVAS building blocks. The figure represents a data flow, starting from sources of vocabulary data (left) and ending with the CLAVAS semantic repository (right). The blue parts are the parts developed by the CLAVAS project. We chose three different source vocabularies to import into this repository: ISO 639-3 language codes,[5]

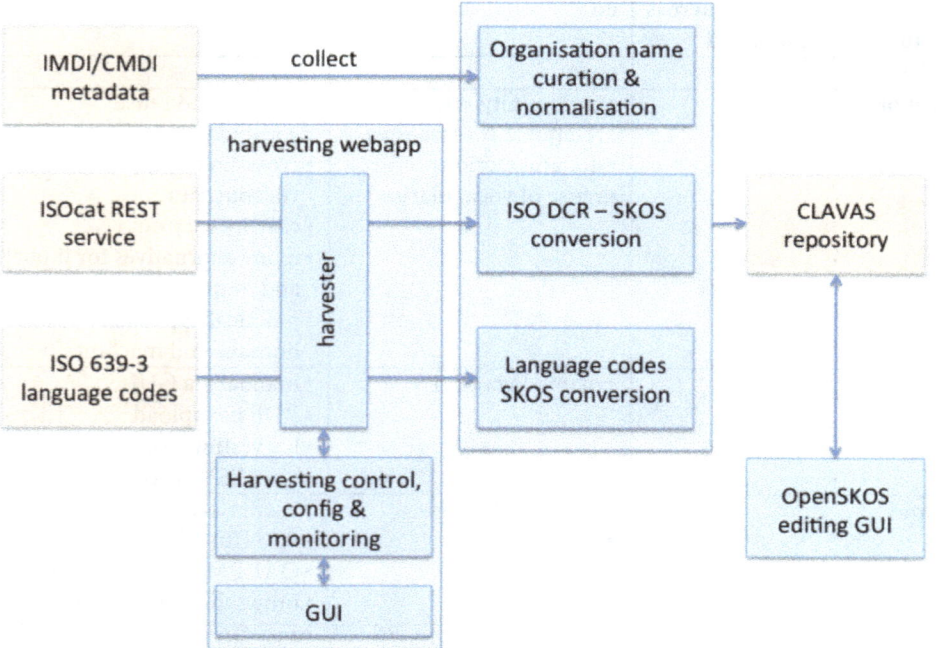

Figure 5.1: CLAVAS architectural overview.

---

[5] http://www-01.sil.org/iso639-3/

organisation names, and ISOcat closed and Simple Data Categories.[6] These vocabularies differed with respect to quality at the start of the project, transport protocol and import pipeline. Two of the import pipelines were fully automated; the third involved manual curation. Import pipelines can be controlled via a dedicated harvesting web application. Once imported in CLAVAS, all vocabularies can be manually inspected and curated with the help of a specialised vocabulary curation web application, the OpenSKOS Editor.

5.3.1.1   Updating Vocabularies

A simple web application was built and integrated in the CLAVAS OpenSKOS site. This web application has three tabs, one for each of the CLAVAS vocabularies. The two that can be periodically updated have a facility to modify download paths for the source information and a download button; the RDF file that is created and downloaded is suitable to upload to an OpenSKOS instance. Sources for the web application as well as for all converters are available from the CLAVAS GitHub repository.

5.3.1.2   OpenSKOS Vocabulary Editor

CLAVAS requirements with respect to the vocabulary editor were relatively simple: the presence of the functionality to curate simple, unstructured lists of concepts was sufficient. However, the Netherlands Institute for Sound and Vision contributed to the OpenSKOS project by providing a full-blown thesaurus editing environment, including support for simple workflows. The Open-SKOS Editor was built by Picturae as an integrated extension of the OpenSKOS software stack and was made available under open source licence via the CATCHPlus OpenSKOS GitHub repository. The OpenSKOS Editor was tested and applied during the CLAVAS project, and is currently part of the CLAVAS service.

5.3.2   Three Vocabularies

5.3.2.1   ISO 639-3

ISO 639-3 language codes can be downloaded/harvested by the CLAVAS harvesting web application. The download location (at SIL) of the source files can be modified if it changes in the future. The source files are parsed and converted to an SKOS RDF/XML file that is uploaded and subsequently published by the CLAVAS OpenSKOS instance. The core of the conversion module is a script that can also be used as a standalone tool. The script is available as part of the CLAVAS open source distribution on GitHub.[7]

5.3.2.2   ISOcat

Closed and simple data categories can be harvested directly from ISOcat as RDF/XML; this function was made available for CLAVAS by MPI/TLA. The CLAVAS harvesting web app does some necessary post-processing on the ISOcat SKOS RDF/XML data. The resulting SKOS is uploaded to and made available from the CLAVAS OpenSKOS site.

5.3.2.3   Organisation Names

Organisation names used in CLARIN IMDI and CMDI metadata are diverse and are very domain-specific (for example, several linguistics departments at universities all over the world). Because no

---

[6] http://www.isocat.org/
[7] https://github.com/hennie/CLAVAS

existing vocabulary resource was found that covered the full range of organisation names actually used in the CLARIN VLO, it was decided to start a manual curation project. This project was undertaken by the Nijmegen-based Data Curation Service, in close collaboration with CLAVAS. The process was as follows: all organisation name instances were extracted from the VLO. Two manual passes bundled spelling variations of organisation names and identified the preferred spelling. A tabular text format was used to store this information;remarks and editorial notes were also recorded. The intermediate results were automatically processed and converted to SKOS. The conversion process also extracted hierarchical structure where possible. Conversion errors were kept separate in the form of a set of SKOS Concepts that needed further curation. The converted result was evaluated using the search and browse facilities of the OpenSKOS Editor. In a final manual pass the OpenSKOS Editor was used to fix the Concepts. In the process, the OpenSKOS Editor was also evaluated with respect to usability for CLARIN vocabulary curation tasks. As with previous vocabularies, the Organization Names vocabulary was published on the CLAVAS OpenSKOS site.

5.4   Evaluation of Results

5.4.1   Evaluation Criteria

At the beginning of CLAVAS we explicitly formulated success factors from the perspectives of all types of stakeholders for the CLAVAS service to be developed. We first present our initial evaluation criteria and subsequently discuss how far they were met in the results of the CLAVAS project.

Our initial evaluation criteria were as follows:

Researchers creating and maintaining metadata:

- Will produce better-quality metadata with less effort.
- Will be able to use vocabularies that are outside the scope of ISO DCR (e.g. long lists of names, or vocabularies from the cultural heritage domain).
- Will have seamless access to vocabulary information in the context of their metadata editing environment.
- Will have easy ways (such as autocompletion) to select from available terms.
- Will be able to find terms on the basis of alternative labels or closest match.
- Will be able to contribute terms that are missing from a vocabulary (if that is allowed for the vocabulary in question).

Collection users

- Will experience better precision and recall when searching metadata.
- Will be able to involve vocabularies when formulating queries.

Collection managers curating metadata

- Will be able to check existing metadata values against some vocabulary. The system should be able to provide them with matching terms or closest matching candidates.
- Will be able to do vocabulary curation when they are working on metadata curation.

Vocabulary curators

- Will be able to easily check if a suitable term already exists in some vocabulary (e.g. by searching for it on the basis of one of its alternative labels and inspecting notes or definitions).

CLAVAS content managers

- Will be able to set parameters of harvesting or update processes and have control over these processes. The harvesting process will be so clear, reliable and stable that it will be easy to (re)run it, even if this (re)run is done only once a year.

Builders of tools and services

- Will be able to integrate vocabulary support in their tools and services easily.

5.4.2   Actual Realisation of These Criteria

Although the CLAVAS service is up-and-running and all planned components are in place, not much use is made of CLAVAS: the most probable reason for this is that CLAVAS benefits will become apparent only after integration of CLAVAS services into other tools, which has not happened yet. Another reason may be related to the potential lack of usefulness (for ISO language codes and the – somewhat ad hoc – republished version of ISOcat data categories) and quality (for organisation names) of the vocabularies currently published by CLAVAS. In more detail, these are the evaluations of the service per group of stakeholders:

For metadata editors:

- It is too early to make any claims about improved metadata quality. A necessary step to take is the integration of the use of CLAVAS/OpenSKOS in tools like Arbil. In general, CLAVAS supports open vocabularies that are not suited for ISOcat, it offers autocompletion and easy, fine-grained search on the basis of all SKOS attributes, and it contains the basic functionality to allow suggestion of missing concepts by metadata editors.

For collection users and metadata managers:

- It is too early to make any claims relevant to these stakeholders here.

For vocabulary curators:

- The criteria are met. Curation with OpenSKOS was tested by the CLARIN-NL Data Curation Service and found satisfactory.

For CLAVAS content managers:

- Periodic updates of ISO 639-3 and ISOcat vocabularies are possible and easy to perform. The Organization Names vocabulary is bootstrapped from the VLO and can be curated manually using the OpenSKOS Editor.

For tool builders:

- The RESTful API is freely available for builders of tools and services.

5.5   Current State and Future Work

Although CLAVAS was not widely adopted by the CLARIN community in terms of actual usage, this is different for the underlying OpenSKOS platform, which is used by several organisations and projects across Europe, both in the domain of linguistic resources and in the description of cultural heritage collections.

Schuurman et al. (2015) describes why and how the ISOcat semantic registry was phased out and replaced by a new CLARIN Concept Registry (CCR) based on OpenSKOS. The main aims of this migration were to reduce complexity and the proliferation of concepts by adopting a simpler data model, new tooling and revised, stricter maintenance procedures that include editorial supervision.

For the new CCR several new components were developed by the Meertens Institute: support for persistent identifiers (handles), Shibboleth-based authentication, support for skos:Collections in the OpenSKOS data model and interactive web access via a new faceted browser.

Both CCR and CLAVAS are now based on the same data model (SKOS) and the same service platform (OpenSKOS). Furthermore, usage of CLAVAS as a service platform to provide open or closed vocabularies as value domains for CMDI elements and attributes is part of the CMDI 1.2 specification (CLARIN CMDI Taskforce, 2014). Thus it can be expected that CLAVAS will play a bigger role in the CLARIN community in the near future.

Currently, there are new developments going on in the OpenSKOS community, which, in addition to CLARIN, includes a number of large cultural heritage institutions and companies in the Netherlands and Europe. One of them, the Netherlands Institute for Sound and Vision, together with Picturae, is developing a new version of OpenSKOS. The new version contains an RDF triple store. It supports SKOS XL as data model and provides a SPARQL endpoint to its users. For this updated OpenSKOS the Meertens Institute is currently extending the API to cover the complete OpenSKOS data model, and is building a new faceted browser on top of that.

5.6   Conclusions

CLAVAS succeeded in delivering a service platform for the provision and manual curation of vocabularies for value domains in CMDI. However, the service is currently not widely used. The main reason for this most likely is that CLAVAS, being mostly middle-ware, hardly offers functionality directly targeted at end users. Built-in support from tools (e.g. Arbil) may help improve on this situation.

CMDI and CMDI vocabularies are evolving towards RDF and Linked Open Data. For example, a recent development is CMDI2RDF, a CLARIAH[8] activity that is going to provide CMDI metadata as RDF. CLAVAS and OpenSKOS, being SKOS- and therefore RDF-based, nicely fit into this development.

CLAVAS is part of the wider range of OpenSKOS applications, and is the component where CLARIN may benefit the most from contributions of other OpenSKOS users. Especially, well-curated and extensive vocabularies from the cultural heritage domain may turn out to be very useful for linguistic and digital humanities applications as well.

Acknowledgements

Work on CLAVAS was funded by CLARIN-NL. OpenSKOS was produced by the CATCHPlus project, which was funded by NWO as part of the CATCH programme. We thank the Netherlands Institute for Sound and Vision and Picturae for their collaboration and for funding parts of OpenSKOS.

---

[8] http://www.clariah.nl/

References

Broeder, D., Windhouwer, M., van Uytvanck, D., Goosen, T., & Trippel, T. (2012). *CMDI: a Component Metadata Infrastructure.* Proceedings of LREC Workshop Describing LRs with Metadata: Towards Flexibility and Interoperability in the Documentation of LR. Istanbul, Turkey.

Broeder, D., Schuurman, I. & Windhouwer, M. (2014). *Experiences with the ISOcat Data Category Registry.* Proceedings of the Ninth International Conference on Language Resources and Evaluation (LREC 2014), Reykjavik, Iceland.

Brugman, H. & Lindeman, M. (2012). *Publishing and Exploiting Vocabularies using the OpenSKOS Repository Service.* Istanbul, Describing Language Resources with Metadata workshop at LREC2012.

CLARIN CMDI Taskforce (2014). *CMDI 1.2 changes - executive summary.* Technical Report CE 2014-0318, CLARIN ERIC, Utrecht, The Netherlands, April 2014.

ISO 12620:2009. *Specification of data categories and management of a Data Category Registry for language resources.* International Organization for Standardization, Geneve.

Miles, A., Bechhofer, S. (2009). *SKOS Simple Knowledge Organisation System Reference.* W3C Recommendation 18 August 2009.

Schuurman, I., Windhouwer, M., Ohren, O. & Zeman, D. (2015). *CLARIN Concept Registry: the new semantic registry.* At the CLARIN Annual Conference. Wroclaw, Poland, October 15–17, 2015.

Windhouwer, M.A., Wright, S.E., Kemps-Snijders, M. (2010). *Referencing ISOcat data categories.* In proceedings of the LRT standards workshop (LREC 2010), Malta, May 18, 2010.

CHAPTER 6

FoLiA in Practice: The Infrastructure of a Linguistic Annotation Format

Maarten van Gompel[a,c], Ko van der Sloot[a,c], Martin Reynaert[a,b,c] and Antal van den Bosch[c]

[a]Centre for Language and Speech Technology, Radboud University, [b]Tilburg Centre for Cognition and Communication, Tilburg University, [c]Centre for Language Studies, Radboud University

ABSTRACT

We present an overview of the software and data infrastructure for FoLiA, a **Fo**rmat for Linguistic Annotation developed within the scope of the CLARIN-NL project and other projects. FoLiA aims to provide a single unified file format accommodating a wide variety of linguistic annotation types, preventing the proliferation of different formats for different annotation types. FoLiA is being developed in a bottom-up and practice-driven fashion. We have invested mainly in the creation of a rich infrastructure of tools that enable developers and end-users to work with the format. This work will present the current state of this infrastructure.

6.1   Introduction

CLARIN's aim is to deliver an infrastructure for researchers that work with language data and tools. This is impossible without agreeing on standards with regard to data formats. Standardisation is an important prerequisite for good interoperability between the many language tools that have emerged within and outside of the scope of the CLARIN project, and to ensure the various datasets released are usable in practice.

In the field, however, we often encounter an abundance of ad-hoc formats. We define ad-hoc formats to be data formats that are characterised by most of the following traits:

- They are only used once, often by one specific tool or for just one specific purpose;
- They are poorly formalised or not formalised at all, i.e. there is a lack of a formal schema and semantics;

How to cite this book chapter:
van Gompel, M, van der Sloot, K, Reynaert, M and van den Bosch, A. 2017. FoLiA in Practice: The Infrastructure of a Linguistic Annotation Format. In: Odijk, J and van Hessen, A. (eds.) *CLARIN in the Low Countries*, Pp. 71–81. London: Ubiquity Press. DOI: https://doi.org/10.5334/bbi.6. License: CC-BY 4.0

• They are poorly documented;
• They are often rigid and hard to extend.

The use of such ad-hoc formats can be considered the opposite of proper standardisation and is to be avoided in any large infrastructure project.

CLARIN adheres to the following principles when it comes to standardisation:

• Open standards are preferred over proprietary standards;
• Formats and protocols should be:

  • well documented

  • verifiable

  • proven (being used in practice);

• Text-based formats are (where possible) preferred over binary formats.

Fortunately, there are various initiatives for standardisation resulting in annotation formats that transcend the ad-hoc level, each with their own merit, and ours being of one of them. At the onset of CLARIN-NL, however, the Dutch and Flemish Natural Language Processing (NLP) community lacked such a proper standard with respect to linguistically annotated text, and ad-hoc formats were prevalent in the field. In the scope of CLARIN-NL project TTNWW (see chapter 7), the NWO project DutchSemCor, and the STEVIN project SoNaR, FoLiA (Format for Linguistic Annotation) was developed as a solution to accommodate the representational needs of these projects.

The aim of FoLiA is to provide a practical standard, following a generic paradigm, for the linguistic annotation of primarily written text. For this purpose, a wide variety of linguistic annotation types is supported.

In the current chapter, we intend to focus on the *practical* nature of the format, or rather, on the infrastructure that is built around the format, the software that supports it, and the ways in which it has been put to use in CLARIN and beyond. Section 6.3 will explain the philosophy behind FoLiA and its infrastructure.

Earlier work (van Gompel and Reynaert, 2013) addresses the motivation for the creation of FoLiA. In summary, FoLiA sprung from a limited corpus format used in the Dutch and Flemish NLP communities (Apperloo, 2006), at a time and place where a more comprehensive format was needed for various corpora and tools in development. Existing solutions often did not sufficiently meet the needs at the time, were not mature yet, or were simply not well known.

FoLiA currently represents one of various possible solutions. We claim that its merit is best decided on its practical usability with respect to the user's specific purpose. Focus on the practical dimension, i.e. the availability of hands-on tools and libraries, was in fact a key reason for the creation of yet another format. The tools, libraries and existing FoLiA-delivered corpora described in the current work are intended to help people assess whether it is an appropriate solution for their tasks.

The aforementioned work (van Gompel and Reynaert, 2013) presents a comparison with similar initiatives such as the D-Spin Text Corpus Format (TCF), PAULA XML, XCES, as well as with more abstract frameworks such as LAF (Linguistic Annotation Format) and comprehensive text-encoding formats such as TEI. In summary, the prior study observes that rather than a format, LAF (Ide and Romary, 2004) is an abstract framework which offers a greater level of abstraction and genericness than FoLiA, whereas FoLiA is more specific and aims at the practical level. This makes FoLiA more readily adoptable in software tools. In the comparison with TEI (Burnard and Bauman, 2007), it was observed that TEI is very extensive and specific when it comes to encoding text structure, but FoLiA is more specific when it comes to linguistic annotation types, for which TEI only offers more abstract solutions. TEI is very extensive and therefore fairly complex;

schemas may come in various flavours, as elements can be adapted by users in many ways. FoLiA offers one single specific solution instead, the format is a given, and the flexibility to customise is deliberately limited to the data categories or tagsets, in the form of set definitions. Initiatives such as TCF (Heid et al., 2010), PAULA XML (Zeldes et al., 2013), and also NAF (Fokkens et al., 2014) are more similar to FoLiA, as they are less abstract and provide practical usability in software. Differences come down to paradigm choices, sustainability, tool availability and documentation maturity, and especially to variation in coverage of available linguistic annotation types and text structure elements.

Full documentation of FoLiA is available elsewhere (van Gompel, 2014). It offers a reference guide to all elements and attributes that FoLiA defines. A brief summary of key features will be repeated in Section 6.2. Section 6.4 subsequently presents the currently available software infrastructure for FoLiA. Section 6.5 presents some corpora that have been delivered in FoLiA.

6.2   Overview

FoLiA is an XML-based format and defines specific XML elements for *structure annotation* (e.g. paragraphs, sentences, word tokens, lists, figures, etc.) and *linguistic annotation* (e.g. part-of-speech, dependency relations, syntax, named entities, etc.). FoLiA makes use of a combination of inline and stand-off annotation, making proper use of the hierarchical nature of XML and facilitating the job for parsers where possible. FoLiA does not define any linguistic categories; the format is fully language and tagset independent as tagsets are defined separately in *FoLiA Set Definitions* by users and never prescribed by FoLiA itself. These tagsets can in turn be related to data category registries. Validation can proceed on a shallow level, against a RelaxNG schema, as well as on a deep level which validates the used tagsets against the set definition files.

The sets are at the core of the FoLiA paradigm; annotation elements take a generic attribute named 'class'. These *classes* pertain to a set and are defined by whatever set definition the user decides to use. The set definition defines all allowed classes and allows for links with data category registries for formal semantic closure.

Other generic attributes besides 'class' are attributes to denote the annotator of a particular annotation, the annotator type (human or machine), the confidence level of the annotation, the time of the annotation, and more.

FoLiA also allows for various types of *higher-order annotation*, such as the ability to include alternative annotations, as well as extensive support for corrections on annotations. Moreover, there is the possibility to link other modalities, such as imagery or audio fragments of speech, to structural elements. So, even though FoLiA is primarily a format to annotate text documents, speech transcripts are supported as well.

For metadata CLARIN-NL was committed to the CMDI standard (Broeder et al., 2011). Although FoLiA has simple native support for metadata, we see no sense in reinventing the wheel and FoLiA is ideally used in combination with an external metadata format such as CMDI whenever extensive metadata is desired. A reference to the metadata file can be made in the header of the FoLiA document.

The FoLiA paradigm laid out here is schematically illustrated in Figure 6.1 (van Gompel, 2014). A more in-depth treatise is beyond the scope of this current chapter.

6.3   Our philosophy

Recalling the CLARIN principle that a format should be proven and used in practice, FoLiA has been designed in a bottom-up manner taking especially this principle to heart. Our focus is to solve real problems people face in the field with regards to their linguistic representation needs, and to

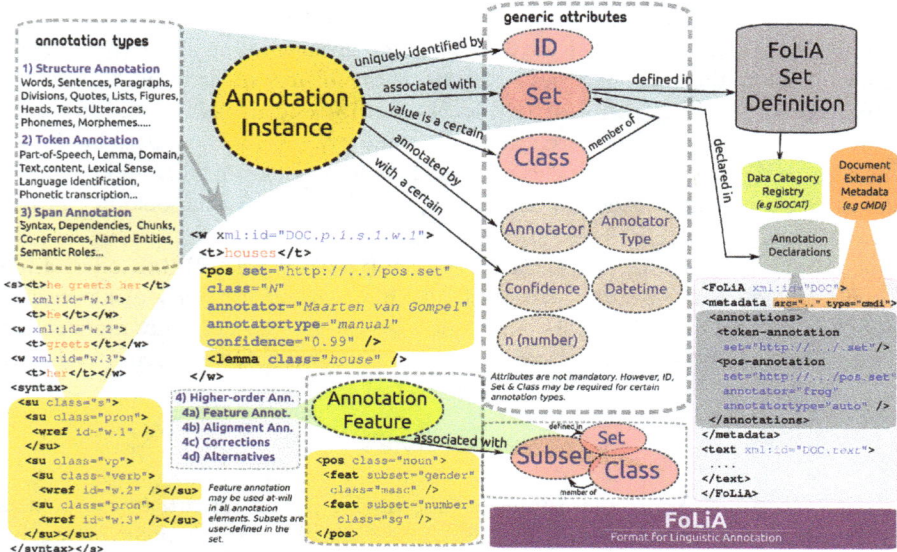

Figure 6.1: A schematic overview of the most important aspects of the FoLiA paradigm, including XML examples (van Gompel, 2014).

do so in a generic manner. The ambition is to deliver a single unified file format that can effectively handle a multitude of annotation needs in a generic way. The main motivation is to prevent the need to switch formats whenever an extra annotation type is introduced, and to prevent the scenario in which a plethora of different formats are used for different annotation types.

It is nevertheless always conceivable that a user's particular need is not yet covered by the latest version of FoLiA; in such cases we gladly hear from the user and expand FoLiA where necessary, in collaboration with the user. The development of FoLiA has already proceeded for several years in such a collaborative workflow, and various annotation types have been added in close contact with end-users both from within CLARIN and from beyond.

In our philosophy, the creation of a file format is useless if an infrastructure of tools to work with said format is not simultaneously created. This has therefore been our main focus over the years and will be the subject of the next section.

6.4   Software Infrastructure

When we speak of a FoLiA software infrastructure we refer to a published set of software, from whatever sources and for whatever architecture, that enable people to work with FoLiA. Such an infrastructure in simple terms encompasses anything that can either process or deliver the data in the format. We can subdivide it into the following components:

1. programming libraries;
2. tools for validation;
3. tools for conversion from and to other formats;
4. tools for visualisation;
5. tools for searching/querying;
6. editing tools and

7. special-purpose tools; i.e. specialised tools that use the format but are not necessarily focused on it. In the case of FoLiA, this includes Natural Language Processing or Information Retrieval tools that use the format as input and/or output.

The programming libraries and tools that are purely designed to visualise, manipulate, or convert the format in basic ways can be considered part of a *core layer* of the infrastructure, whereas the special-purpose tools can be considered to constitute an outer layer.

As FoLiA is an XML-based format, the rich and well-established XML infrastructure is open to its users as well. In fact, almost all FoLiA tools effectively rely on the existing software infrastructure available for XML.

It is possible to not use any of the FoLiA-specific tools and use the infrastructure offered by XML directly. For instance, one can use XPath to query a FoLiA document and XSL to transform it. To do so effectively, however, the user/developer needs to be more familiar with the intricacies of FoLiA than when using a tool from the FoLiA infrastructure that abstracts over this for the benefit of the user/developer.

Many of the tools of the core layer are available as command-line tools and are bundled in two software packages: there is a Python-based **FoLiA Tools** package[1] and a **FoLiA Utilities** package[2] consisting of tools written in C++. Both are built on the respective libraries. There is some overlap in tools, but each also offers distinct tools the other does not. It is therefore recommended to install both.

These packages, and all other tools pertaining to the FoLiA infrastructure which have been developed at Radboud University, are bundled in our **LaMachine** distribution.[3] LaMachine greatly facilitates installation of this software and is a recommended starting point if you work with FoLiA. It is available as a Virtual Machine, a Docker package or a local compilation & installation script.

We subscribe strongly to the CLARIN principle that standards should be open and place a similar requirement on the infrastructure components we build.

6.4.1   Programming Libraries

At the heart of the FoLiA infrastructure are the *programming libraries* that enable developers to work with documents in the format in their software. We ourselves offer libraries for both Python and for C++.

Python is a widely popular high-level programming language in the academic world, and the NLP world in particular. The Python library for FoLiA enables developers to quickly integrate support for FoLiA in their scripts. The library is part of the larger **PyNLPl** library[4] and is also available from the Python Package Index.[5] It is extensively documented and comes with tutorials for users.

The Python library suffers from the performance drawback that any high-level interpreted language has. Whenever faster processing is required, or integration in high-performance tools is desired, **libfolia**,[6] the FoLiA library for C++, offers a better solution. The library is modelled after the Python library, so both are similarly structured, employ a similar syntax and the respective authors try their best to keep the libraries in sync.

---

[1]   https://pypi.python.org/pypi/FoLiA-tools
[2]   https://github.com/LanguageMachines/foliautils
[3]   https://proycon.github.io/LaMachine/
[4]   https://github.com/proycon/pynlpl
[5]   https://pypi.python.org/pypi/PyNLPl
[6]   https://github.com/languagemachines/libfolia

A third popular language in the field is Java, but no Java-based FoLiA library is available yet to our knowledge. There are a number of Java-based tools in the FoLiA infrastructure that have nevertheless been developed without a common underlying FoLiA library.

6.4.2   *Validation*

We already touched upon the notion of shallow and deep validation. FoLiA's syntax is formalised in a RelaxNG schema, and shallow validation can therefore be done using any XML validator with support for RelaxNG.

The tools **foliavalidator** and **folialint**[7] also perform shallow validation, and their usage is strongly recommended, or should even be considered mandatory, for anybody producing FoLiA documents. Moreover, the former tool can optionally perform deep validation as well, i.e. it can validate the used classes against the set definitions.

6.4.3   *Conversion*

The FoLiA tools and utilities collections contain tools for the conversion from and to various different other formats:

* Conversion to plaintext
* Conversion to HTML
* Conversion to simple columned data or to CSV
* Conversion from/to reStructuredText[8]
* Conversion from/to DCOI XML format (Apperloo, 2006)
* Conversion from the Alpino XML format (Bouma et al., 2000)
* Conversion from ALTO XML format[9]
* Conversion from hOCR HTML format (Breuel, 2007)
* Conversion from PAGE XML format[10]

Conversions may be limited by the source or target format. Conversion to FoLiA's predecessor DCOI XML, for instance, is only possible for the subset of elements that DCOI supports. Similarly, conversion to reStructuredText is limited to text, its structure and markup, and does not include linguistic annotations.

Besides the in-house developed FoLiA tools, third parties also make available converters from or to FoLiA. A notable case is **OpenConvert**,[11] developed by the former Institute for Dutch Lexicology (INL), now Institute for the Dutch Language (INT), which can convert from TEI, plaintext, ALTO, Microsoft Word, and HTML to FoLiA.

6.4.4   *Visualisation*

An XSL stylesheet is available to visualise FoLiA documents. It renders documents and unobtrusively pops up with annotation information when hovering over structural items such as words. A major advantage is that this form of visualisation can be conducted entirely client-side in nearly every web browser. The **folia2html** conversion tool also employs the same stylesheet.

---

7   Part of respectively **FoLiA Tools** and **FoLiA Utilities**
8   http://docutils.sourceforge.net/rst.html
9   http://www.loc.gov/standards/alto/
10 http://www.primaresearch.org/tools
11 https://github.com/INL/OpenConvert

6.4.5   Searching

Tools for searching and querying FoLiA documents can be divided into two categories:

1. In-document search and
2. Document retrieval systems / corpus search tools.

At a low level, in-document search can be conducted with the command-line tool **foliaquery**, part of the FoLiA tools. This tool reads one or more FoLiA documents in memory (sequentially), executes a search query, and presents the matching results. This, however, is not a solution that scales to large numbers of documents as it takes a fair amount of time and memory to process a document.

Full document retrieval systems do not rely on such costly real-time processing of the FoLiA documents, but construct smart indices from the original documents and operate on these indices. The corpus retrieval engine **BlackLab**[12], based on Apache Lucene, and the front-end **WhiteLab** (Reynaert et al., 2014) (see chapter 19) are examples of this. WhiteLab was developed in the CLARIN-NL project OpenSoNaR[13], and can operate on FoLiA documents, as does BlackLab. So far, these engines typically only supported a simpler subset of the annotation types supported by FoLiA, such as Part-of-Speech tags and lemmas. At the time of writing, there is collaboration, and some competition, between the various developers in the Netherlands to support span annotation types such as dependency relations, syntax and named entities. Another FoLiA-capable search and retrieval system called Multi-Tier Annotation Search (**MTAS**) has been promised by the Meertens Institute, and builds upon Solr and Lucene. It is being developed in the scope of the Nederlab project (Brugman et al., 2016) and the CLARIAH project. This system, however, is still in early stages of development and has not been released yet.

As FoLiA is a highly expressive format, the need arose for a query language tuned specifically to the idiosyncrasies of FoLiA. Although FoLiA can be perfectly searched with XPath, formulating a robust query is not always trivial and may require more in-depth knowledge of FoLiA. The *FoLiA Query Language* (FQL) was designed as a higher-level query language, covering all of FoLiA, to make querying FoLiA documents easier. FQL is implemented alongside the FoLiA Python library in **PyNLPl**. It is documented as part of the FoLiA documentation (van Gompel, 2014).

FQL is a new and expressive query language specifically attuned to the FoLiA paradigm. People in the field are likely more accustomed to the simpler and established query languages such as CQL, the *Corpus Query Language* (Christ, 1994), developed at the Corpora and Lexicons group, IMS, at the University of Stuttgart in the early 1990s. For this reason, **PyNLPl** includes a library that converts CQL to the more expressive but verbose FQL. The low-level query tool makes use of both these libraries. In the next section we will discuss FQL further and introduce higher-level tools in the FoLiA infrastructure that make use of it.

6.4.6   Editing

FQL has been designed in such a way that it is not just a language for passive querying, but a language that allows active manipulation of FoLiA documents. In other words, FQL is to FoLiA as SQL is to relational database tables. Therefore, the **foliaquery** command-line tool and the FQL library it relies on can be used not just to passively retrieve information, but also to actively edit documents.

---

[12] https://github.com/INL/BlackLab
[13] https://github.com/TiCCSoftware/WhiteLab

A FoLiA document server[14] has been constructed as a back-end for the editing of FoLiA documents. It is implemented as a RESTful webservice, with a simple human-interface to manually enter queries, and takes care of on-demand loading and unloading of documents in memory and serialising them to disk. It maintains a browsable document repository, which features **git** version control support.

Neither the command-line tool nor the document server offers an interface adequate for human end-users to easily work with. To provide such an environment, we have been developing the **FoLiA Linguistic Annotation Tool (FLAT)**[15]. It is a modern web-application that offers an interface for the visualisation and editing of FoLiA documents. Under the hood, user-interface interactions are translated to FQL queries and communicated to the aforementioned FoLiA document server. The motivation for the creation of FLAT, as opposed to the adaption of existing web annotation environments, was the desire for a solution that seamlessly integrates with FoLiA and adopts the same paradigm. Different design choices implied it would be easier to build this from the ground up.

Although not yet supporting all of FoLiA at the current stage, **FLAT** has already been used successfully in several annotation projects with student assistants at Radboud University. Further development of FLAT is planned for the CLARIN-NL successor project CLARIAH, with the aim of providing a mature editing environment covering all of FoLiA. FLAT is intended to be deployed as a platform for crowd-sourcing annotation tasks in CLARIAH and other projects.[16]

6.4.7   Special-purpose tools

The previous sections discussed tools that can be considered part of the core layer. In this section we will discuss the outer layer of tools; these are tools that either take FoLiA as their input or deliver it as their output to perform a specific and specialised task, usually an NLP (annotation) task. It is a most essential layer to the infrastructure and consists of tools such as:

- **Ucto**[17] – An advanced rule-based tokeniser and sentence-splitter for a variety of languages. Supports FoLiA input and output. Can be used to bootstrap plaintext to tokenised FoLiA (van Gompel et al., 2012).
- **Frog**[18] – An NLP suite for Dutch, implementing tokenisation (through Ucto), Part-of-Speech tagging, Lemmatisation, Dependency Parsing, Named Entity Recognition, Shallow Parsing and Morphological Analysis. Supports FoLiA input and output.
- **CLAM**[19] – Turns command-line NLP tools into RESTful webservices with an interface for human end-users. It integrates the FoLiA viewer to visualise FoLiA documents. (van Gompel, 2012)
- **TICCL**[20] – Text-Induced Corpus Clean-up (Reynaert, 2010). Supports FoLiA input and output. Used in the CLARIN-NL projects TICCLops[21] and @PhilosTEI[22] (Reynaert, 2014), see chapter 32.

---

[14] https://github.com/proycon/foliadocserve
[15] https://github.com/proycon/flat
[16] The PARSEME project for example, http://typo.uni-konstanz.de/parseme/, has recently adopted FLAT for the annotation of Multi-Word Expressions
[17] https://languagemachines.github.io/ucto
[18] https://languagemachines.github.io/frog
[19] https://proycon.github.io/clam
[20] https://github.com/martinreynaert/TICCL
[21] Available in the CLARIN infrastructure at: http://ticclops.clarin.inl.nl/ticclops/
[22] Available in the CLARIN infrastructure at: http://ticclops.clarin.inl.nl/philostei/

- **Cesax**[23] – A co-reference editor for syntactically annotated XML corpora. Supports FoLiA import and output through conversion.
- **T-Scan**[24] – A Dutch text analytics tool for readability prediction (Pander Maat et al., 2014).
- **Colibri Core**[25] – A tool for the computation of corpus statistics on n-grams and skipgrams in a quick and memory-efficient way. It can import FoLiA documents, which it subsequently compresses to an internal optimised binary format.
- **Gecco**[26] – Generic Environment for Context-Aware Correction of Orthography: A spelling correction engine fully based on FoLiA. Powers *Valkuil.net* and soon also *Fowlt.net*.
- **FoLiA-langcat**[27] – Performs language detection, built on TextCat[28]. Part of the FoLiA utilities.
- **FoLiA-stats**[29] – Performs simple n-gram statistics on FoLiA documents. Part of the FoLiA utilities.
- **PaQu**[30] – A web application for the analysis of Dutch texts based on dependency parses computed using Alpino (Bouma et al., 2000). PaQu supports FoLiA input (see chapter 23).

6.5   Data Infrastructure

A format's usefulness is not just determined by the tools available, but also by the data sets delivered in the format. The following corpora are currently delivered in FoLiA:

- **Basilex** – The Basilex corpus collects Dutch written language by children, and contains about 11.5 million words. It includes lexical semantic sense annotation (Tellings et al., 2014).
- **DutchSemCor** – The DutchSemCor project delivered a Dutch corpus annotated with lexical semantic senses. Part of the annotation was manual, and a part was tagged automatically with a Word Sense Disambiguation system trained on the manual part. The corpus is based on SoNaR, as well as extra sources (Görög and Vossen, 2010).
- **VU-DNC** – A diachronic Dutch newspaper corpus (2 million tokens) with annotations of subjectivity. Provides a gold standard for OCRed newspapers published in 1950. (Vis et al., 2012)
- **SoNaR-500** – The STEVIN project SoNaR delivered a 540 million word corpus of written Dutch (including Flemish) from numerous sources. The corpus is annotated with Part-of-Speech tags, lemmas, and named entities (Oostdijk et al., 2013).
- **Nederlab** – The Nederlab project attempts to collect all digitised texts relevant to the history of Dutch language, culture and heritage (circa 800 – present) in one user-friendly and tool-enriched open access web interface[31] (Brugman et al., 2016).

In addition to corpora, the data part of the infrastructure also consists of a growing number of Set Definitions.[32]

---

[23] http://erwinkomen.ruhosting.nl/software/Cesax/
[24] https://github.com/proycon/tscan
[25] https://proycon.github.io/colibri-core
[26] https://github.com/proycon/gecco
[27] https://github.com/LanguageMachines/foliautils
[28] http://odur.let.rug.nl/~vannoord/TextCat/
[29] Also part of the FoLiA Utilities
[30] https://github.com/rug-compling/paqu
[31] http://www.nederlab.nl/onderzoeksportaal/
[32] https://github.com/proycon/folia/tree/master/setdefinitions

6.6   Conclusion

In this chapter we have described the rich infrastructure that has been developed around the Format for Linguistic Annotation (FoLiA). We emphasised the need for a practical and proven format, in line with CLARIN's standardisation principles, and hence placed the focus for this chapter on the software and data infrastructure. A more extensive overview of FoLiA itself and of the motivation for its inception was presented in earlier work (van Gompel and Reynaert, 2013).

Continued efforts in the CLARIN-NL successor project CLARIAH ensure that the developments on the infrastructure surrounding FoLiA will continue in the foreseeable future. FoLiA XML is the pivot format in the project 'Philosophical Integrator of Computational and Corpus Libraries', or PICCL, (Reynaert et al., 2015) which is part of CLARIAH.

Acknowledgements

We gratefully acknowledge the funding provided by CLARIN-NL and its successor CLARIAH in a range of projects. Martin Reynaert further acknowledges being funded by NWO in the Nederlab project.

References

Wilko Apperloo. 2006. XML basisformaat D-Coi: Voorstel XML formaat presentational markup. Technical report, Polderland Language and Speech Technology.

Gosse Bouma, Gertjan van Noord, and Rob Malouf. 2000. Alpino: Wide-coverage Computational Analysis of Dutch. In Walter Daelemans, Khalil Sima'an, Jorn Veenstra, and Jakub Zavrel, editors, *CLIN*, volume 37 of *Language and Computers - Studies in Practical Linguistics*, pages 45–59. Rodopi.

Thomas Breuel. 2007. The hOCR Microformat for OCR Workflow and Results. In *Proceedings of the Ninth International Conference on Document Analysis and Recognition*, volume 2, pages 1063–1067. IEEE Computer Society.

Daan Broeder, Oliver Schonefeld, Thorsten Trippel, Dieter Van Uytvanck, and Andreas Witt. 2011. A pragmatic approach to XML interoperability – the Component Metadata Infrastructure (CMDI). In *Balisage: The Markup Conference 2011*, volume 7.

Hennie Brugman, Martin Reynaert, Nicoline van der Sijs, René van Stipriaan, Erik Tjong Kim Sang, and Antal van den Bosch. 2016. Nederlab: Towards a single portal and research environment for diachronic Dutch text corpora. In Nicoletta Calzolari et al., editor, *Proceedings of the Tenth International Language Resources and Evaluation Conference (LREC-2016)*, Portorož, Slovenia. ELRA.

Lou Burnard and Syd Bauman, editors, 2007. *TEI P5: Guidelines for Electronic Text Encoding and Interchange*. Text Encoding Initiative Consortium.

Christ, Oliver (1994) A modular and flexible architecture for an integrated corpus query system. *Proceedings of COMPLEX'94: 3rd Conference on Computational Lexicography and Text Research*. Budapest, Hungary. pp. 23–32.

Antske Fokkens, Aitor Soroa, Zuhaitz Beloki, German Rigan, Willem Robert van Hage, and Piek Vossen. 2014. NAF: The NLP annotation format. Technical report.

Attila Görög and Piek Vossen. 2010. Computer assisted semantic annotation in the DutchSem-Cor project. In *Proceedings of the Seventh International Conference on Language Resources and Evaluation, LREC-2010*, pages 1220–1226, Valletta, Malta.

Ulrich Heid, Helmut Schmid, Kerstin Eckart, and Erhard Hinrichs. 2010. A Corpus Representation Format for Linguistic Web Services: The D-SPIN Text Corpus Format and its Relationship with

ISO Standards. In Nicoletta Calzolari, Khalid Choukri, Bente Maegaard, Joseph Mariani, Jan Odijk, Stelios Piperidis, Mike Rosner, and Daniel Tapias, editors, *Proceedings of the Seventh International Conference on Language Resources and Evaluation (LREC'10)*, Valletta, Malta, May. European Language Resources Association (ELRA).

Nancy Ide and Laurent Romary. 2004. International standard for a linguistic annotation framework. *Natural Language Engineering*, 10(3-4):211–225.

Nelleke Oostdijk, Martin Reynaert, Véronique Hoste, and Ineke Schuurman. 2013. The construction of a 500-million-word reference corpus of contemporary written Dutch. In *Essential Speech and Language Technology for Dutch: Results by the STEVIN-programme*, chapter 13. Springer Verlag.

Henk Pander Maat, Rogier Kraf, Antal van den Bosch, Nick Dekker, Maarten van Gompel, Suzanne Kleijn, Ted Sanders, and Ko van der Sloot. 2014. T-Scan: a new tool for analyzing Dutch text. *Computational Linguistics in the Netherlands Journal*, 4.

Martin Reynaert, Matje van de Camp, and Menno van Zaanen. 2014. OpenSoNaR: user-driven development of the SoNaR corpus interfaces. In *Proceedings of COLING 2014: System Demonstrations*, pages 124–128, Dublin, Ireland. Dublin City University and Association for Computational Linguistics.

Martin Reynaert, Maarten van Gompel, Ko van der Sloot, and Antal van den Bosch. 2015. PICCL: Philosophical Integrator of Computational and Corpus Libraries. In *Proceedings of CLARIN Annual Conference 2015 – Book of Abstracts*, pages 75–79, Wrocław, Poland. CLARIN ERIC.

Martin Reynaert. 2010. Character confusion versus focus word-based correction of spelling and OCR variants in corpora. *International Journal on Document Analysis and Recognition*, 14: 173–187. DOI: 10.1007/s10032-010-0133-5.

Martin Reynaert. 2014. Synergy of Nederlab and @PhilosTEI: diachronic and multilingual Text-Induced Corpus Clean-up. In *Proceedings of the Ninth International Language Resources and Evaluation Conference (LREC'14)*, Reykjavik, Iceland. ELRA.

Agnes Tellings, Micha Hulsbosch, Anne Vermeer, and Antal van den Bosch. 2014. Basilex: an 11.5 million words corpus of Dutch texts written for children. *Computational Linguistics in the Netherlands Journal*, 4:191–208, 12/2014.

Maarten van Gompel and Martin Reynaert. 2013. FoLiA: A practical XML Format for Linguistic Annotation - a descriptive and comparative study. *Computational Linguistics in the Netherlands Journal*, 3.

Maarten van Gompel, Ko van der Sloot, and Antal van den Bosch. 2012. Ucto: Unicode Tokeniser. Reference Guide. Technical report, Tilburg Centre for Cognition and Communication, Tilburg University and Radboud Centre for Language Studies, Radboud University Nijmegen.

Maarten van Gompel. 2012. CLAM: Computational Linguistics Application Mediator. Documentation. Technical report, Tilburg Centre for Cognition and Communication, Tilburg University and Radboud Centre for Language Studies, Radboud University Nijmegen.

Maarten van Gompel. 2014. FoLiA: Format for Linguistic Annotation. Documentation. Technical report, Radboud University Nijmegen.

Kirsten Vis, José Sanders, and Wilbert Spooren. 2012. Diachronic changes in subjectivity and stance – A corpus linguistic study of Dutch news texts. *Discourse, Context & Media*, 1(2–3): 95–102. The view from here, there and nowhere: discursive approaches to journalistic stance.

Amir Zeldes, Florian Zipser, and Arne Neumann. 2013. PAULA XML Documentation. Rapport de recherche, Institut für Deutsche Sprache und Linguistik - IDSL , INRIA Saclay - Ile de France, Universität Potsdam.

CHAPTER 7

TTNWW to the Rescue: No Need to Know How to Handle Tools and Resources

Marc Kemps-Snijders[a], Ineke Schuurman[b], Walter Daelemans[c],
Kris Demuynck[d], Brecht Desplanques[d], Véronique Hoste[d],
Marijn Huijbregts[e], Jean-Pierre Martens[d], Hans Paulussen[b],
Joris Pelemans[b], Martin Reynaert[e,g], Vincent Vandeghinste[b],
Antal van den Bosch[e], Henk van den Heuvel[e], Maarten van Gompel[e],
Gertjan van Noord[f] and Patrick Wambacq[b]

[a]Meertens Instituut Amsterdam, [b]KU Leuven, [c]Universiteit Antwerpen, [d]Universiteit Gent,
[e]Radboud Universiteit Nijmegen, [f]Universiteit Groningen, [g]Tilburg University

ABSTRACT

'But I don't know how to work with [name of tool or resource]' is something one often hears
when researchers in Human and Social Sciences (HSS) are confronted with language technology, be it written or spoken, tools or resources. The TTNWW project shows that these
researchers do not need to be experts in language or speech technology, or to know all kinds
of details about the tools involved. In principle they only need to make clear what they want
to achieve.

In this chapter we describe a series of tools that are already available as a webservice. Details
are not presented — interested readers are referred to the papers mentioned in the References
and to the TTNWW website.

7.1 Introduction

The idea behind the Flemish/Dutch CLARIN project TTNWW[1] ('TST Tools voor het Nederlands
als Webservices in een Workflow', or 'NLP Tools for Dutch as Web services in a Workflow') was that
many end users of resources and tools offered by CLARIN will not know how to use them, just as
they will not know where they are located. With respect to the location, the CLARIN policy is that
the Human and Social Sciences (HSS) researcher does not need to know this as the infrastructure
will take care of that: the only thing the user needs to do is to indicate what (s)he is interested in.

---

[1] https://dev.clarin.nl/node/1964.

How to cite this book chapter:
Kemps-Snijders, M, Schuurman, I, Daelemans, W, Demuynck, K, Desplanques, B, Hoste, V, Huijbregts, M,
Martens, J-P, Paulussen, H, Pelemans, J, Reynaert, M, Vandeghinste, V, van den Bosch, A, van den Heuvel,
H, van Gompel, M, van Noord, G and Wambacq, P. 2017. TTNWW to the Rescue: No Need to Know
How to Handle Tools and Resources. In: Odijk, J and van Hessen, A. (eds.) *CLARIN in the Low Countries*,
Pp. 83–93. London: Ubiquity Press. DOI: https://doi.org/10.5334/bbi.7. License: CC-BY 4.0

The same should hold for the use of tools and resources: users do not need to know which (other) tools are to be used in order to obtain the data one is looking for. Once more, the infrastructure has to take care of that.

For the Dutch language TTNWW served as a pilot project, trying to provide this service for a whole range of existing resources (both text and speech) and tools. The envisaged end users in TTNWW were researchers in social history, literary onomastics and archaeology. Of course, the web service can also be useful for researchers in other domains, such as linguistics, media, political sciences, communication technology, and sociology. Currently, the requirements are that the resources be in Dutch (spoken or written).[2]

Once resources have been handled by (some of) the services described below, it becomes much easier for researchers to find the data they are looking for, especially for audio resources where the gain of time can be tremendous, that is if something be found at all without the data being transcribed. Suppose one needs data about 'lead paint', nowadays considered hazardous but commonly used in the past. In metadata such a concept will only be mentioned when the document is about lead paint, not when artists are discussed and remarks about the paint they commonly used are made in passing. A specific document about, say, Rembrandt could easily escape notice, while it contains just the data one is looking for. When the transcription and the original resource are time-synchronous, the user can listen to the parts of the resource (s)he is interested in. In originally written documents it is easier to find such data once a resource is available in machine-readable format, but even in such cases the gain of time can be huge as one can search in a much more goal-oriented manner.

As shown in Figure 7.1, two main types of input are possible in TTNWW: written or spoken. The transcribed audio resources can be used as such, or they can be inserted in the pipeline for written texts.

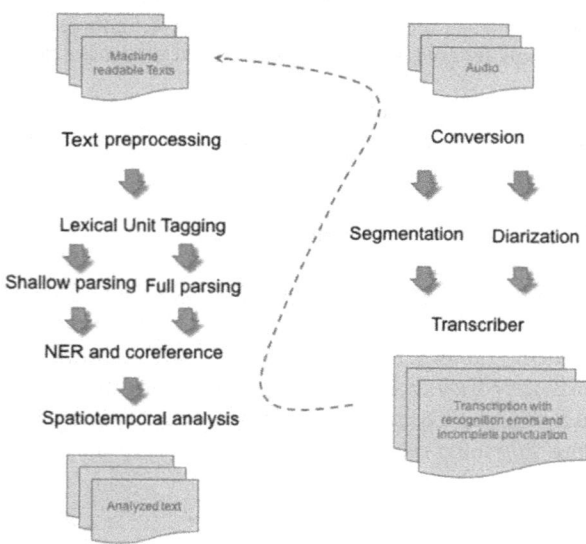

Figure 7.1: Architecture of TTNWW.

---

[2] But see the section on Alignment.

In the following sections we will first discuss the workflow for written texts, followed by the workflow for audio recordings. In the remainder of the chapter the TTNWW web service will be explained.

7.1.1   Formats and Web Service Support

Some necessary conditions for building a text workflow based on existing linguistic tools are that the tools need to be able to communicate and that they need to share a particular text annotation format rich enough to accommodate all the components in the workflow. FoLiA (Format for Linguistic Annotation), cf. van Gompel and Reynaert (2013), was explicitly developed to this end in the scope of both TTNWW and other projects. The format proposes a flexible and generic paradigm over a wide variety of linguistic annotation types. FoLiA aims at practical usage, and the focus has been on the development of a rich infrastructure of tools to work with the format. Although many of the tools employed in the TTNWW project have adopted FoLiA either as input or output format, it should also be noted that other formats have been used as well — most notably the Alpino XML format for syntactic processing, but also other formats for more complex annotation structures. This emphasises the need for more convergence amongst these formats. In this respect FoLiA aims to provide a single comprehensive solution supporting a multitude of annotation types, and its ongoing development offers the possibility to extend it towards any annotation layers not provided yet. Such extensions can be informed by similar initiatives in this area such as the German Text Corpus Format (TCF) or the NLP Annotation Format (NAF); these may also provide alternatives in their own right, and the availability of good converters is therefore desirable for projects such as TTNWW. On a more practical level, interoperability should also address more ordinary issues, such as common tokenisation methods, to provide the opportunity to truly interrelate different annotation layers.

For linguistic enrichment to be effective in the web services/workflow paradigm, most already existing command-line tools had to be transformed to web services. In fact, the road towards this had already been paved in the prior CLARIN-NL (Odijk, 2010) demonstrator project TICCLops (Reynaert, 2014b), which not only turned an existing spelling correction system into a web application and service, but in fact delivered a generic solution for turning linguistic applications with a command-line interface into web applications and RESTful services.

The generic solution to turning any linguistic application into a web application/service, the Computational Linguistics Application Mediator, or CLAM (van Gompel, 2014; van Gompel and Reynaert, 2014),[3] was readily adopted by the TTNWW consortium to prepare their own linguistic applications for integration into the TTNWW workflow.

7.2   Text

7.2.1   Text Preprocessing

As a primary input TTNWW accepts digital texts that are either 'born digital' or the result of a digitisation process. To reduce the amount of Optical Character Recognition (OCR) noise in digitised texts TTNWW offers a corpus clean-up tool. The spelling and OCR post-correction system Text-Induced Corpus Clean-up (TICCL) was turned into the 'online processing system' TICCLops.[4] The approach is based on anagram hashing, which was first fully described and evaluated on English and Dutch in Reynaert (2005). In Reynaert (2010) it was applied to OCR post-correction of large

---

[3] Also available as Open Source software (via https://proycon.github.io/clam/).

[4] http://www.clarin.nl/node/70#TICCLops.

corpora. Two efficient modi operandi for obtaining the same end result, i.e. the set of vocabulary neighbours differing up to a specified number of characters, were presented. In a naive implementation based only on edit or Levenshtein distance (LD), each and every item in the vocabulary has to be compared to every other item. Anagram hashing typically reduces the number of comparisons required by several orders of magnitude, depending on the size of the vocabulary involved. Automatic correction of the Early Dutch Books Online corpus, which has a vocabulary of nearly 20 million items, is described in Reynaert (2014a).

7.2.2   Linguistic and Semantic Layers in TTNWW

To understand a text, key information can be inferred from the linguistic structure apparent in and across the sentences of the text. To determine who does what, to whom, when, where, why, and how, it is vital that the syntactic roles of words and word groups be identified, that entities be properly detected, and that different references to the same entities be linked.

TTNWW offers a number of tools that automatically identify this information. Of the following tools, tools 1 to 3 were developed and integrated into Frog, an Open Source natural language processing toolkit for the Dutch language[5] (van den Bosch et al., 2007). Almost all tools were integrated into TTNWW through the web service shell software package CLAM. We briefly discuss the tools independently:

1. Part-of-speech tagging and lemmatisation: identifying the syntactic roles of individual word-forms (e.g. 'paints' in 'Rembrandt used lead white paints for flesh tones' is a plural noun), and linking these wordforms to their standard dictionary lemma ('paint, noun'). The particular machine learning approach to part-of-speech tagging adopted for TTNWW, MBT (memory-based tagger), was originally introduced by Daelemans et al. (1996). Frog lemmatizes words and also performs a morphological analysis using a machine learning approach introduced in van den Bosch and Daelemans (1999).

2. Chunking: grouping words into syntactic phrases (e.g. 'lead white paints' and 'flesh tones' are noun phrases). Chunking can be used for different purposes, for example for identifying salient units in term extraction ('flesh tones' makes more sense as a term than 'flesh' or 'tones' individually) and for identifying the units for answering the 'who did what to whom...' questions ('Rembrandt' is the subject who 'used' 'lead white paints' as an object). The chunking approach in TTNWW, also based on the use of machine learning algorithms, was introduced by Daelemans et al. (1999). As training material, the Lassy Small Corpus was used, which is a syntactic treebank; tree structures from Lassy were converted into chunks with a rule-based script, and a memory-based tagger was trained on the chunked sentences.

3. Named entity recognition (NER): identifying proper names as names of people ('Rembrandt'), places, organisations, or other types of entities. For the system delivered for TTNWW, the developers experimented with a classifier ensemble in which a genetic algorithm was used for the weighted voting of the output of different classifiers (see Desmet and Hoste (2013) for more information). Since it performed equally well as the meta-learning approach, we opted for a single classifier based on the conditional random fields algorithm (Lafferty et al., 2001) as final NER classifier, which was delivered as a CLAM web service.

4. Coreference resolution: linking references to the same entities. For instance, if 'Rembrandt' is later referred to as 'He', the latter pronominal reference should be linked to Rembrandt

---

[5] Downloadable from http://languagemachines.github.io/frog/.

and not to any other entity mentioned in the text. For TTNWW, an existing mention-pair approach to coreference resolution (Hoste, 2005; de Clercq et al., 2011) which was further refined in the framework of the STEVIN projects COREA (Hendrickx et al., 2012) and SoNaR (Oostdijk et al., 2008; Schuurman et al., 2009; Oostdijk et al., 2012; Reynaert et al., 2012), was adapted to the pipeline of tools developed in the other work packages in TTNWW (e.g. the construction of markables was derived from Alpino output, cf. below). The resulting system was delivered as a CLAM web service.

5. Automated syntactic analysis is made available as a web service, by providing an interface to the Alpino parser for Dutch. Researchers can upload their texts to a web service which takes care of the required preprocessing, and takes care of running the Alpino parser. The result, syntactic dependency structures in the standard format developed in CGN (Schuurman et al., 2003), D-Coi (van Noord et al., 2006) and Lassy (van Noord et al., 2012), is made available to researchers in a simple XML format. Named entity recognition and classification, part-of-speech tagging and lemmatisation is integrated in the output of the parser.

   The underlying Alpino parser (van Noord, 2006; de Kok et al., 2011) is the de-facto standard syntactic parser for Dutch. It is a stochastic attribute value grammar where a hand-written grammar and lexicon for Dutch is coupled with a maximum entropy statistical disambiguation component. The parser is fairly accurate, with labeled dependency accuracy of around 90% on newspaper text. The speed of the parser varies with sentence length and ambiguity, but is about 2 seconds per sentence on average for typical newspaper text on standard hardware.

6. Spatiotemporal analysis: the STEx-tool (SpatioTemporal Expressions) for spatiotemporal analysis used in TTNWW enables researchers to deal with *incomplete* information and to analyze geospatial and temporal information the way the *intended* reader would have interpreted it, taking into account the relevant temporal and cultural information (using the metadata coming with the resource).

   Information presented in a text is never complete (Schuurman, 2007). What is meant is solvable by knowing where (and when) a text appeared originally. This information is stored in the metadata coming with a resource (Schuurman and Vandeghinste, 2010, 2011). In 'Hij doet opgravingen in het Turkse Sagalassos' (E: 'He is excavating in Sagalassos in Turkey'. De Morgen, 22-10-2011), 'Sagalassos' would be annotated as being situated in the Asian part of Turkey, where in 2011 the province of Antalya was located, Sagalassos having coordinates '37.678,30.519'. It was part of the region of Pisidia, and existed more or less from 10,000 BC until 600 AD. As input, STEx uses fully parsed sentences as provided by Alpino (cf. above).

7.2.3   Alignment

Alignment is a little bit of an outsider in the TTNWW project, as it is the only task involving another language than Dutch. Within the STEVIN project DPC (Dutch Parallel Corpus) an alignment tool chain was developed to arrive at a high-quality, sentence-aligned parallel corpus for the language pairs Dutch-English and Dutch-French, with Dutch as the central language (Paulussen et al., 2012). Within TTNWW this task included creating a web service for the alignment and the annotation of parallel texts (Dutch and English). The constraints of the alignment task involved a number of challenges not encountered elsewhere in TTNWW, due to the fact that more than one language is involved. The existing flow of the web service tool supposes the processing of just one input file (or a set of similar input files using the same processing chain), whereas an alignment task requires at least two input files. For the time being, the alignment service in TTNWW opts for a provisional solution.

7.2.4   Additions and Some Use Cases

Several other tools can be added, for example dealing with sentiment analysis, summarisation, semantic role labelling, information extraction, etc. TTNWW is designed to enable further extensions.

Some of the tools described above have been put to practice in large-scale follow-up projects. TICCL, for example, has been used as a standard preprocessing step in the Nederlab project (Brugman et al., 2016) for the Early Dutch Books Online corpus (Reynaert, 2016). Work in the Nederlab project also involves POS tagging using Frog to produce linguistically annotated corpora. Alpino is used in a broad range of projects; for HSS GrETEL (Augustinus et al., 2013), and Poly-GrETEL (Augustinus et al., 2016) are especially relevant, making it much easier to search in treebanks.

7.3   Speech

7.3.1   Tools Included in TTNWW

Speech recognition software provides HSS researchers with the possibility to transform audio signals into machine readable text formats. The speech recognition output could be reused as input for the text analysis processes, provided that the recognition rate is sufficiently high. Speech recognition systems are complex pieces of software requiring a fair amount of expertise to install and maintain. To make life easier for HSS users several web services were incorporated in TTNWW in which submitted audio files are automatically transcribed or where related tasks are performed. Several of these web services have been combined, resulting into ready-to-use workflows available to the HSS end user, see (Pelemans et al., 2012). Speech recognition web services are based on the SPRAAK software, see Demuynck et al. (2008).

1. Converter: extracts or converts speech files to the required .wav format for the Transcriber web service from a variety of other formats, including MP3 and video. This service is described in more detail in Pelemans et al. (2014).

2. Segmentation: within the TTNWW project, an audio segmentation tool was further improved and was made available via an easily accessible web service through CLAM. The provided audio segmentation tool first analyses the audio to find intervals which contain foreground speech without long interruptions, a process called speech/non-speech segmentation. Next, the speech intervals are divided into shorter segments uttered by a single speaker (speaker segmentation), and the speech fragments belonging to the same speaker are grouped (speaker clustering). These steps basically solve the "who-speaks-when" problem. Finally, the system identifies the language being spoken by each speaker (Dutch vs non-Dutch), enriches every audio fragment with extra non-verbal meta-information (e.g. is this music or telephone speech or dialect speech etc.), and detects the gender of every speaker. See Desplanques and Martens (2013), Desplanques et al. (2015), and Desplanques et al. (2014).

3. Diarisation: automatic speaker diarisation is the task of automatically determining: "who spoke when". On reception of an audio file, the web service labels each speaker in the recording ("SPK01", "SPK02", etc), it finds all speech segments and it assigns a speaker label to each segment. The result of the web service can be used as a preprocessing step in most state-of-the-art automatic speech recognition systems. The system is described in Hain et al. (2010) and Wooters and Huijbregts (2008).

4. Dutch Transcriber: uploads and transcribes Dutch broadcast news style of speech. Users have to answer some questions about the audio input so that the best recognition models are

chosen from a set of existing ones. More information on the transcription service may be found in Pelemans et al. (2014).

7.3.2   Additions and Some Use Cases

In addition to the services described above, several other useful speech services have been made available. Due to their experimental character they have not been incorporated into standard workflows for the TTNWW project. Some end users may however find some of them useful for their purposes. They are available as CLAM-enabled services and can be found on the www.spraak.org/webservice website. These include the

1. Dutch phoneme recogniser: this recogniser returns a phonetic transcription for the given audio input.

2. Grapheme to Phoneme Converter (g2p): this web service takes a list of (orthographic) Dutch words and returns a phonetic transcription for each of them.

3. Dutch speech and text aligner: takes as its input both an audio file and a text file and tries to align them. The output file contains the same words as the input, but with added timing information for every word. Optionally a speech segmentation file can also be given that contains speech/non-speech, male/female and speaker ID information as obtained from the speech segmenter described above.

These web services have already been put to use by several HSS users as demonstrated by some use cases:

- A test dataset of nine interviews from the KDC (Catholic Documentation Centre) at RU Nijmegen was prepared to be processed by the TTNWW speech chain. The interviews (total duration of 22.5 hours) were a small subset of the KomMissieMemoires series (KMM 873-880). All interviews obtained a CMDI metadata file which followed the OralHistoryDans profile (see https://catalog.clarin.eu/ds/ComponentRegistry) used in van den Heuvel et al. (2012).
- Currently, about 50 users have registered for the SPRAAK-based web services. Many users of the services want to check the potential performance of speech recognition on their specific task (often interview transcription and transcription of broadcast material) and find this a fast and flexible way to achieve this.
- Some applications and projects need existing tools, and instead of installing and maintaining these locally, prefer to call them over the web, as a RESTful service. One such example is the STON project (about semi-automated subtitling based on speech recognition), where a g2p converter is needed to provide phonetic transcriptions when new words are entered in the lexicon of the subtitling application, cf. Verwimp et al. (2016).

7.4   Web Services and Workflows

7.4.1   Web Service Delivery

All linguistic processing modules were required to be made available as web services. Web service deployment allows for a single service to be used by more non-technical users by lowering the barriers of installation and maintenance requirements. However, most modules had been constructed as command line tools as a result of previous projects. CLAM, (cf. Section 7.1.1), allows any command line tool to be wrapped as a web service — only parameters, input formats and output formats need to be described. Many of TTNWW's web services have been constructed in this manner. To facilitate transfer of web services from technology providers to CLARIN centres, providers were requested to deliver services as fully installed virtual images. This reduces the installation overhead for CLARIN centres and ensures that web services are delivered according to the technology provider's recommended operating system. Images were deployed in an OpenNebula High Performance Cloud environment made available by SURFsara through a parallel project.

7.4.2   Combining Web Services in a Workflow

Depending upon the end user's requirements towards the desired linguistic annotation output, web services may need to be combined into pipelines. For example, to obtain coreference annotations the process entails tagging of textual input through Frog, followed by coreference annotation using the COREA service. To facilitate the full process, rather than just delivering an individual process, web services may be combined into workflows (Kemps-Snijders et al., 2012). In the CLARIN community two approaches were proposed for this. One approach allows end users to construct their own workflows by matching input/output requirements of individual services. Possible service combinations are determined using a generic chaining algorithm. This approach has been used in the WebLicht application (Hinrichs et al., 2010), created as part of the German CLARIN D-SPIN project. An alternative approach is to preconstruct complete workflows and provide these to the end user to perform a specific task. This has the advantage that end users can concentrate on task execution rather than task construction. Given the limited number of services and possible combinations for the available TTNWW services this approach was selected for this project. Incidentally, the WebLicht project now also offers predefined processing chains as an Easy Mode. For TTNWW, Taverna was selected as a workflow construction and execution framework. Upon selection of a specific task, the corresponding workflow definition is sent to a Taverna server monitoring execution and data transfer between contributing annotation services running in the HPC cloud environment. End users are shielded from workflow definitions, web services and execution environment through an easy-to-use user interface allowing them to upload their textual/audio data, to select the annotation task to perform and to collect the results afterwards.

7.5   Related Work

The web services and workflow paradigm has also been adopted by other projects to deliver processing services to the end user community. D-SPIN's WebLicht project mentioned before was an initiative of the German CLARIN community. The Danish CLARIN-DK project (Offersgaard et al., 2013) pursued a similar line with respect to automatic chaining of services into a workflow. The European PANACEA project (Poch et al., 2012), on the other hand, used the Taverna workbench and associated service registry to allow end users to construct and execute workflows in the NLP domain. Another recent service workflow is Galaxy, used by CLARINO[6] and LAPPS[7], amongst others.

7.6   Conclusions and Further Work

The TTNWW project delivers a suite of web services for the Dutch language domain. The CLAM software packaging software was broadly adopted by many teams to turn their shell-oriented software systems into web services. It has been demonstrated in the project that these services can be successfully combined into workflows. The resulting workflows are task-oriented in the sense that

---

[6] http://www.clarin.b.uib.no/about.
[7] http://www.lappsgrid.org/.

a series of web services are combined to deliver a specific end-user-oriented task. End-users only need to select a task and upload their resources, audio or text, after which execution and orchestration of the services is handled by the system. The TTNWW system is currently being revised as part of the ongoing CLARIAH project. Here, a new user workspace based on ownCloud[8] is expected to be added, as well as new features allowing the end user to search the resulting annotation files directly. As far as alignment, (cf. Section 7.2.3), is concerned, future work would involve to split up the original tasks into subtasks (i.e. cleaning, tokenisation and tagging) and to restrict the web service to its main task: i.e. alignment of parallel texts. In this way, the other web services can be used to handle the preparatory tasks, giving more flexibility in the development of tools and in administrating workflows. This will imply that all the other tasks require an extra language flag, so that language-specific modules can be used whenever necessary. Another aspect would consist in adapting the input format to the FoLiA format for input and output, so that the data format matches the requirements of the other tools in the web services chain.

References

L. Augustinus, V. Vandeghinste, I. Schuurman, and F. Van Eynde. 2013. Example-Based Treebank Querying with GrETEL - now also for Spoken Dutch. In *Proceedings of Workshop on Nordic language research infrastructure, NoDaLiDa 2013*, pages 423–428, Oslo, Norway. Linköping University Electronic Press.

L. Augustinus, V. Vandeghinste, and T. Vanallemeersch. 2016. Poly-GrETEL: Cross-Lingual Example-based Querying of Syntactic Constructions. In *Proceedings of LREC'16*, pages 3549–3554, Portorož, Slovenia. ELRA.

H. Brugman, M. Reynaert, N. van der Sijs, R. van Stipriaan, E. Tjong Kim Sang, and A. van den Bosch. 2016. Nederlab: Towards a Single Portal and Research Environment for Diachronic Dutch Text Corpora. In *Proceedings of LREC'16*, pages 1277–1281, Portorož, Slovenia. ELRA.

W. Daelemans, J. Zavrel, P. Berck, and S. Gillis. 1996. MBT: A memory-based part of speech tagger generator. In *Proceedings of 4th Workshop on Very Large Corpora, ACL SIGDAT*, pages 14–27, Copenhagen, Denmark.

W. Daelemans, S. Buchholz, and J. Veenstra. 1999. Memory-Based Shallow Parsing. In *Proceedings of CoNLL-99*, pages 53–60, Bergen, Norway.

O. de Clercq, V. Hoste, and I. Hendrickx. 2011. Cross-Domain Dutch Coreference Resolution. In *Proceedings of RANLP 2011*, pages 186–193, Hissar, Bulgaria.

D. de Kok, B. Plank, and G. van Noord. 2011. Reversible Stochastic Attribute-value Grammars. In *Proceedings of 49th Annual Meeting of ACL*, pages 194–199, Portland, Oregon.

K. Demuynck, J. Roelens, D. Van Compernolle, and P. Wambacq. 2008. SPRAAK : an open source SPeech Recognition and Automatic Annotation Kit. In *Proceedings of Interspeech 2008*, pages 495–498, Brisbane, Australia.

B. Desmet and V. Hoste. 2013. Fine-Grained Dutch Named Entity Recognition. *Language Resources and Evaluation*, 48(2):307–343. Springer.

B. Desplanques and J.-P. Martens. 2013. Model-based speech/non-speech segmentation of a heterogeneous multilingual TV broadcast collection. In *Proceedings of International Symposium on Intelligent Signal Processing and Communication Systems*, pages 55–60, Naha, Japan.

B. Desplanques, K. Demuynck, and J.-P. Martens. 2014. Robust language recognition via adaptive language factor extraction. In *Proceedings of Interspeech 2014*, pages 2160–2164, Singapore, Singapore.

---

[8] https://owncloud.org/.

B. Desplanques, K. Demuynck, and J.-P. Martens. 2015. Factor Analysis for Speaker Segmentation and Improved Speaker Diarization. In *Proceedings of Interspeech 2015*, pages 3081–3085, Dresden, Germany.

T. Hain, L. Burget, J. Dines, P.N. Garner, A. El Hannani, M. Huijbregts, M. Karafiat, M. Lincoln, and V. Wan. 2010. The AMIDA 2009 meeting transcription system. In *Proceedings of Interspeech 2010*, pages 358–361, Makuhari, Japan.

I. Hendrickx, G. Bouma, W. Daelemans, and V. Hoste. 2012. COREA: Coreference Resolution for Extracting Answers for Dutch. In P. Spyns and J. Odijk, editors, *Essential Speech and Language Technology for Dutch*, pages 13–126. Springer.

M. Hinrichs, Th. Zastrow, and E. Hinrichs. 2010. WebLicht: Web-based LRT Services in a Distributed eScience Infrastructure. In *Proceedings of LREC'10*, pages 489–493, Valletta, Malta. ELRA.

V. Hoste. 2005. *Optimization Issues in Machine Learning of Coreference Resolution*. Ph.D. thesis, University of Antwerp.

M. Kemps-Snijders, M. Brouwer, J.P. Kunst, and T. Visser. 2012. Dynamic web service deployment in a cloud environment. In *Proceedings of LREC'12*, pages 2941–2944, Istanbul, Turkey. ELRA.

J. Lafferty, A. McCallum, and F. Pereira. 2001. Conditional random fields: Probabilistic models for segmenting and labeling sequence data. In *Proceedings of 18th International Conference on Machine Learning*, page 282–289, Williamstown, Massachusetts, USA. Morgan Kaufmann.

J. Odijk. 2010. The CLARIN-NL Project. In *Proceedings of LREC'10*, pages 48–53, Valletta, Malta. ELRA.

L. Offersgaard, B. Jongejan, and D. Haltrup Hansen. 2013. CLARIN-DK – status and challenges. In *Proceedings of Workshop on Nordic language research infrastructure, NoDaLiDa 2013*, pages 21–32, Oslo, Norway. Linköping University Electronic Press.

N. Oostdijk, M. Reynaert, P. Monachesi, G. Van Noord, R. Ordelman, I. Schuurman, and V. Vandeghinste. 2008. From D-Coi to SoNaR: a reference corpus for Dutch. In *Proceedings of LREC'08*, pages 1437–1444, Marrakech, Morocco. ELRA.

N. Oostdijk, M. Reynaert, V. Hoste, and I. Schuurman. 2012. The Construction of a 500-million-word Reference Corpus of Contemporary Written Dutch. In P. Spyns and J. Odijk, editors, *Essential Speech and Language Technology for Dutch*, pages 219–247. Springer.

H. Paulussen, L. Macken, W. Vandeweghe, and P. Desmet. 2012. Dutch Parallel Corpus: A balanced parallel corpus for Dutch-English and Dutch-French. In Peter Spyns and Jan Odijk, editors, *Essential Speech and Language Technology for Dutch*, pages 185–199. Springer.

J. Pelemans, K. Demuynck, and P. Wambacq. 2012. Dutch automatic speech recognition on the web: Towards a general purpose system. In *Proceedings of Interspeech 2012*, pages 9–13, Portland, Oregon, USA.

J. Pelemans, K. Demuynck, H. Van hamme, and P. Wambacq. 2014. Speech recognition web services for Dutch. In *Proceedings of LREC'14*, pages 3041–3044, Reykjavik, Iceland. ELRA.

M. Poch, A. Toral, O. Hamon, V. Quochi, and N. Bel. 2012. Towards a User-Friendly Platform for Building Language Resources based on Web Services. In *Proceedings of LREC'12*, pages 1156–1163, Istanbul, Turkey. ELRA.

M. Reynaert, I. Schuurman, V. Hoste, N. Oostdijk, and M. van Gompel. 2012. Beyond SoNaR: towards the facilitation of large corpus building efforts. In *Proceedings of LREC'12*, pages 2897–2904, Istanbul, Turkey. ELRA.

M. Reynaert. 2005. *Text-induced spelling correction*. Ph.D. thesis, Tilburg University.

M. Reynaert. 2010. Character confusion versus focus word-based correction of spelling and OCR variants in corpora. *International Journal on Document Analysis and Recognition*, 14:173–187. DOI: 10.1007/s10032-010-0133-5.

M. Reynaert. 2014a. Synergy of Nederlab and @PhilosTEI: diachronic and multilingual Text-Induced Corpus Clean-up. In *Proceedings of LREC'14*, pages 1224–1230, Reykjavik, Iceland. ELRA.

M. Reynaert. 2014b. TICCLops: Text-Induced Corpus Clean-up as online processing system. In *Proceedings of COLING 2014*, pages 52–56, Dublin, Ireland. Dublin City University and Association for Computational Linguistics.

M. Reynaert. 2016. OCR Post-Correction Evaluation of Early Dutch Books Online – Revisited. In *Proceedings of LREC'16*, Portorož, Slovenia. ELRA.

I. Schuurman and V. Vandeghinste. 2010. Cultural Aspects of Spatiotemporal Analysis in Multilingual Applications. In *Proceedings of LREC'10*, Valletta, Malta. ELRA.

I. Schuurman and V. Vandeghinste. 2011. Spatiotemporal annotation: interaction between standards and other formats. In *Proceedings of IEEE-ICSC Workshop on Semantic Annotation for Computational Linguistic Resources*, Palo Alto, California, USA.

I. Schuurman, M. Schouppe, T. Van der Wouden, and H. Hoekstra. 2003. CGN, an annotated corpus of Spoken Dutch. In *Proceedings of 4th International Workshop on Linguistically Interpreted Corpora, LINC-03*, pages 340–347, Budapest, Hungary.

I. Schuurman, V. Hoste, and P. Monachesi. 2009. Cultivating Trees: Adding Several Semantic Layers to the Lassy Treebank in SoNaR. In *Proceedings of 7th International Workshop on Treebanks and Linguistic Theories*, pages 135–146. LOT Occasional Series. Volume 12. Utrecht.

I. Schuurman. 2007. Which New York, which Monday? The role of background knowledge and intended audience in automatic disambiguation of spatiotemporal expressions. In *Selected Papers of the Seventeenth CLIN Meeting*, pages 191–206. Utrecht: LOT.

A. van den Bosch and W. Daelemans. 1999. Memory-based morphological analysis. In *Proceedings of 37th Annual Meeting of ACL*, page 285–292, San Francisco, California, USA. Morgan Kaufmann.

A. van den Bosch, G.J. Busser, S. Canisius, and W. Daelemans. 2007. An efficient memory-based morphosyntactic tagger and parser for Dutch. In *Selected Papers of the Seventeenth CLIN Meeting*, pages 191–206. Utrecht: LOT.

H. van den Heuvel, E. Sanders, R. Rutten, S. Scagliola, and P. Witkamp. 2012. An Oral History Annotation Tool for INTER-VIEWs. In *Proceedings of LREC'12*, pages 215–218, Istanbul, Turkey. ELRA.

M. van Gompel and M. Reynaert. 2013. FoLiA: A practical XML Format for Linguistic Annotation - a descriptive and comparative study. *Computational Linguistics in the Netherlands Journal*, 3.

M. van Gompel and M. Reynaert. 2014. CLAM: Quickly deploy NLP command-line tools on the web. In *Proceedings of COLING 2014*, pages 71–75, Dublin, Ireland. Dublin City University and Association for Computational Linguistics.

M. van Gompel. 2014. CLAM: Computational Linguistics Application Mediator. Technical report, Nijmegen: Radboud University. Technology Technical Report Series Report Number LST-14-02.

G. van Noord, I. Schuurman, and V. Vandeghinste. 2006. Syntactic Annotation of Large Corpora in STEVIN. In *Proceedings of LREC'06*, pages 1811–1814, Genoa, Italy.

G. van Noord, G. Bouma, F. van Eynde, D. de Kok, J. van der Linde, I. Schuurman, E. Tjong Kim Sang, and V. Vandeghinste. 2012. Large Scale Syntactic Annotation of Written Dutch: Lassy. In Peter Spyns and Jan Odijk, editors, *Essential Speech and Language Technology for Dutch*, pages 147–163. Springer.

G. van Noord. 2006. **At Last Parsing Is Now Operational**. In *TALN 2006 Verbum Ex Machina, Actes De La 13e Conference sur Le Traitement Automatique des Langues naturelles*, pages 20–42, Leuven, Belgium.

L. Verwimp, B. Desplanques, K. Demuynck, J. Pelemans, M. Lycke, and P. Wambacq. 2016. STON: Efficient subtitling in Dutch using state-of-the-art tools. In *Proceedings of Interspeech 2016*, San Francisco, California, USA.

C. Wooters and M. Huijbregts. 2008. The ICSI RT07s speaker diarization system. In *Multimodal Technologies for Perception of Humans*, pages 509–519. Springer.

CHAPTER 8

CMD2RDF: Building a Bridge from CLARIN to Linked Open Data

Menzo Windhouwer[a,1], Eko Indarto[b] and Daan Broeder[a]

[a]Meertens Institute, [b]Data Archiving and Networked Services (DANS)

ABSTRACT

Metadata can be represented in many different ways. CLARIN's Component Metadata Infrastructure (CMDI) uses the eXtensible Markup Language (XML) as the representation format for metadata records. However, the Resource Description Format (RDF) as used by Linked Open Data (LOD) is gaining more popularity. RDF has interesting potential for queries that involve both metadata about and the content of linguistic resources. This chapter describes the implementation of a mapping for records in CMDI from XML to RDF and experiments to assess the potential of this representation.

8.1 Introduction

Metadata has always been a key issue for libraries and archives and thus has a long history (M-Files, 2016). Throughout the ages the physical form and, more recently, the digital representation of metadata has changed, i.e., adapted to the standard current at that time. When the CLARIN preparatory phase started in 2007 the eXtensible Markup Language (XML; Bray et al., 2008) was the current standard. CLARIN's metadata standard as implemented in the Component Metadata Infrastructure (CMDI; Broeder et al., 2012; CLARIN, 2016a) is thus also based on XML as the representation format for metadata. However, the Resource Description Format (RDF; Cyganiak, Wood and Lanthaler, 2014) as used, for example, by the Linguistic Linked Open Data (LLOD) cloud (Chiarcos et al., 2012; LIDER project, 2016) is gaining more popularity. RDF provides an

---

[1] Corresponding author: menzo.windhouwer@meertens.knaw.nl

How to cite this book chapter:
Windhouwer, M, Indarto, E and Broeder, D. 2017. CMD2RDF: Building a Bridge from CLARIN to Linked Open Data. In: Odijk, J and van Hessen, A. (eds.) *CLARIN in the Low Countries*, Pp. 95–103. London: Ubiquity Press. DOI: https://doi.org/10.5334/bbi.8. License: CC-BY 4.0

interesting potential for queries that involve both metadata about and the content of linguistic resources, as both metadata and content can be collected and queried in a set of connected graphs. In the CMD2RDF project CLARIN-NL (2016) CLARIN-NL sponsored the actual implementation of the mapping from Component Metadata (CMD) to RDF, which has been proposed by Durco and Windhouwer (2014a), and the services to provide access to the resulting RDF. This enables the CLARIN community to experiment with RDF representations of the CMD records, and to get a sense of its potential and the opportunities for cross fertilisation with other Linked Data resources like those found in the LLOD cloud

The results of this project are described in the main part of this chapter. The first two sections provide a short summary of both CMDI and the Linked Data paradigm, and the chapter ends with the current status of CMD2RDF and future plans for it.

8.2   The Component Metadata Infrastructure

The basic building blocks of CMDI are, not surprisingly, components. A component focuses on a specific aspect of a (linguistic) resource and groups together metadata elements, which can be used to capture information, and other components. For example, an *address* component contains the elements *street, city* and *country*. This component could be reused by a *contact person* or an *organisation* component. The infrastructure provides a Component Registry for metadata modellers to share and reuse components. The registry is accompanied by an editor, which allows adapting components to specific needs or creating completely new ones. A modeller in the end creates metadata profiles, i.e., a collection of metadata components, targeted at a specific resource type, e.g., a historic text or an audio recording of an endangered language. A CMD profile is a tree-based structure where the nodes are components, from which one is the root of the tree, and the leaves are elements. This tree can be very naturally mapped to XML and thus an XML Schema (XSD; Gao, Sperberg-McQueen and Thompson, 2012) can be used to validate whether a CMD record is compliant with a specific profile. In CLARIN various tools, e.g. online and offline editors, have been developed to create and maintain valid CMD records (also known as metadata descriptions). This core of CMDI, the Component Metadata model, is visualised in Figure 8.1 and has been standardised by ISO *Technical Committee 37* (ISO 24622-1, 2015)

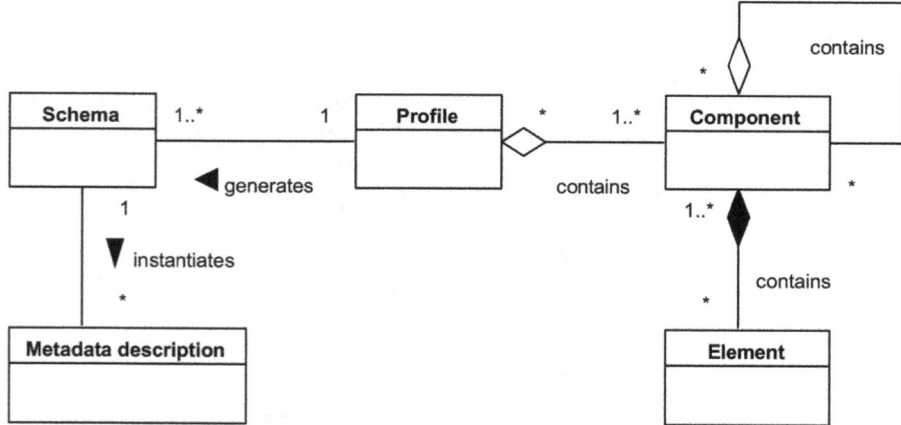

Figure 8.1: Component Metadata model (ISO 24622-1, 2015).

CLARIN centres offer the CMD records they create for harvesting via the Open Archives Initiative's Protocol for Metadata Harvesting (OAI-PMH; Lagoze and Van de Sompel, 2015). Central CLARIN services, like the Virtual Language Observatory (VLO; CLARIN, 2016b), provide access to the full set of harvested CMD records.

8.3   Linked Open Data

Linked Data, open or closed, has become increasingly popular. In this paradigm graphs are constructed out of triples consisting of a subject, a predicate and an object. The object of a triple can be the subject of another triple thus building the graph. All parts of the triple can be identified (nodes, i.e., subjects or objects) or typed (nodes or edges, i.e., predicates) with an Internationalized Resource Identifier (IRI; Dürst and Suignard, 2005), most commonly a Uniform Resource Location (URL; Berners-Lee, Masinter and McCahill, 1994). A coherent vocabulary of types is commonly described in an RDF Schema (RDFS; Brickley and Guha, 2014) or extensions thereof. Many RDF vocabularies (Open Knowledge Foundation, 2016) exist and some are frequently reused. Graphs are linked with each other when they share an IRI. In this way large graphs like the Linked Open Data (LOD) cloud Cyganiak and Jentzsch (2016) and the Linguistic Linked Open Data (LLOD) cloud (LIDER project, 2016) can be identified.

Access to (parts of) these graphs is mostly provided in two ways: 1) as downloads in one or more of the various RDF serialisations, and/or 2) via SPARQL (W3C SPARQL Working Group, 2013) query endpoints. In the latter case the graphs are in general stored in a triple store, i.e., a system for managing (large) sets of triples equivalent to Relational DataBase Management Systems (RDBMS) for structured data.

8.4   The CMD2RDF Bridge

The aim of the CMD2RDF project has been to bring all of the CLARIN CMD record collection to the Linked Data cloud. For this the XML-based records have to be transformed into RDF without loss of information (note that this goal is different from the approach taken by an aggregator like LingHub (McCrae et al. 2015), where only a subset of the information, i.e. in the case of LingHub the set already mapped to Dublin Core (DC; Dublin Core Metadata Initiative 2016) by the OAI-PMH provider, is transformed to RDF). The flexibility of CMDI also means that in such a generic transformation a fixed metadata RDF Schema, like the Data Catalog Vocabulary (DCAT; Maali and Erickson, 2014), is not directly applicable as it would require hand-crafted and maintained mappings to the fixed schema for every CMD profile encountered. But as shown below more generic RDF vocabularies do play a role in transformation. These graphs should also be accessible, either as a download or via a SPARQL endpoint. The next subsections describe the approaches taken to tackle these issues.

8.4.1   The Component Model and RDF

A CMD record is an instance of a CMD profile, which in its turn is an instance of the CMD model. Next to the profile-specific part each record also uses a generic envelope, e.g. to provide information on the resources involved. For all these levels and parts an RDF equivalent has to be created The following description is short, i.e. highlights some issues, the design choices made to resolve them and consists mainly of examples, but Durco and Windhouwer (2014a) gives a full description of the mapping of all these levels and parts.

In the CMD model the main building block, the CMD component naturally corresponds to an RDFS class. A CMD profile can be seen as a specialisation of component, so it is a subclass of the RDFS class for component. It seems natural to map a CMD element to an RDF property. However, a CMD element is more complex than an RDF property, i.e., it can carry additional information in the form of attributes. To be able to retain this information in the mapping a CMD element also has to be mapped to an RDFS class. In RDF, as opposed to XML, the nesting of CMD components or elements in a CMD component needs a predicate. For this the very generic *contains* predicate is introduced. To retain consistency attributes are modelled in a similar way as elements. This results in the following RDF Schema:

```
cmdm:Component a rdfs:Class .
cmdm:Profile rdfs:subClassOf cmdm:Component .
cmdm:Element a rdfs:Class .
cmdm:Attribute a rdfs:Class .

cmdm:contains
    a rdf:Property ;
    rdfs:domain cmdm:Component ;
    rdfs:range cmdm:Component, cmdm:Element .

cmdm:containsAttribute
    a rdf:Property ;
    rdfs:domain cmdm:Component, cmdm:Element ;
    rdfs:range cmdm:Attribute .

cmdm:hasElementValue
    a rdf:Property ;
    rdfs:domain cmdm:Element, rdfs:Literal .

cmdm:hasAttributeValue
    a rdf:Property ;
    rdfs:domain cmdm:Attribute ;
    rdfs:range rdfs:Literal .
```

Based on this mapping of the CMD model a specific component can be transformed into RDF. For example:

```
cmd1:collection
      a cmdm:         Profile ;
      rdfs:label      "collection" .
cmd2:Actor
      a cmdm:         Component ;
      rdfs:label      "Actor" .
cmd2:Actor_Languages
      a               cmdm:Component ;
      rdfs:label      "Languages" .
cmd2:Actor_Languages_Language
      a               cmdm:Element ;
      rdfs:label      "Language" .
```

where the cmd1: and cmd2: prefixes are bound to component-specific IRIs, i.e., the URL to the component specification in the CMDI Component Registry.

A complicating matter is that although a component or element has a unique name among its siblings, within a single component specification a name can very well be ambiguous – so context has to be taken into account. This is done by adding the context to the IRI of a component or element; e.g., cmd2:Actor_Languages_Language represents a *Language* element nested in a *Languages* component which itself is nested in a reusable *Actor* component.[2]

Now that a CMD profile can be transformed into an RDF Schema an actual CMD record can also be transformed. The core of such a record is formed by its instantiation of the component hierarchy allowed by the profile:

```
_:collection1    a              cmd1:collection .
_:actor1         a              cmd2:Actor .
_:languages1     a              cmd2:Actor_Languages .
_:language1      a              cmd2:Actor_Languages_Language .

_:collection1    cmdm:contains              _:actor1 .
_:actor1         cmdm:contains              _:languages1 .
_:languages1     cmdm:contains              _:language1 .
_:language1      cmdm:hasElementValue       "nld" .
```

In this example the hierarchy is instantiated using RDF blank nodes, but the IRI of a record extended with a local unique identifier can also be used.

In a CMD record the profile-specific payload is placed inside a generic CMD envelope, which contains information about the resources involved and metadata about the records themselves, e.g. who has created them and when. This part is also mapped to RDF. And as it is more generic it was possible to reuse existing RDF vocabularies: Dublin Core for the metadata, Open Annotation (OA; W3C Web Annotation Working Group, 2016) for the relation between the profile-specific part and the resources, and the Open Archives Initiative's Object Reuse and Exchange vocabulary (ORE; Open Archives Initiative, 2016) for the relationships of the record with other CMD records.

8.4.2   *From Harvesting CMD to Providing RDF*

Using the RDF mapping described above any CMD record can be transformed. However, to be of actual use the continuously evolving CLARIN-wide collection of CMD records would have to become available in the Linked Data cloud. To achieve this goal the system architecture depicted in Figure 8.2 was implemented in the CMD2RDF project.

CMD records provided by the CLARIN centres are regularly harvested by the CLARIN OAI-PMH harvester. As the harvester currently does not support incremental harvests, and since even if it did all centres would still not necessarily support them, the CMD2RDF conversion pipeline determines which records are new or updated and transforms those into RDF. These RDF records and the RDFS of the components and profiles involved are stored in the Virtuoso triple store (OpenLink Software, 2016). Virtuoso supports a SPARQL endpoint and RESTful access to the RDF graphs, which each correspond to a CMD record. CMD2RDF does put a proxy in front of those to be able to (potentially) control the access, e.g. to prevent too heavy SPARQL queries. The resulting service is available at:

catalog.clarin.eu/ds/cmd2rdf

Another important aspect of the CMD2RDF conversion pipeline is the ability to also enrich the CMD or RDF representations. This makes it possible to introduce links to other datasets, i.e., determine the place of a CMD record in the Linked Open Data cloud and especially in the Linguistic Linked Open Data cloud.

---

[2] This is the only place where the implementation differs from the mapping described in Durco and Windhouwer (2014a): as the dot ('.') has a special meaning in many RDF representations and also in SPARQL its use as a separator for the context turned out to be problematic and was replaced by an underscore ('_').

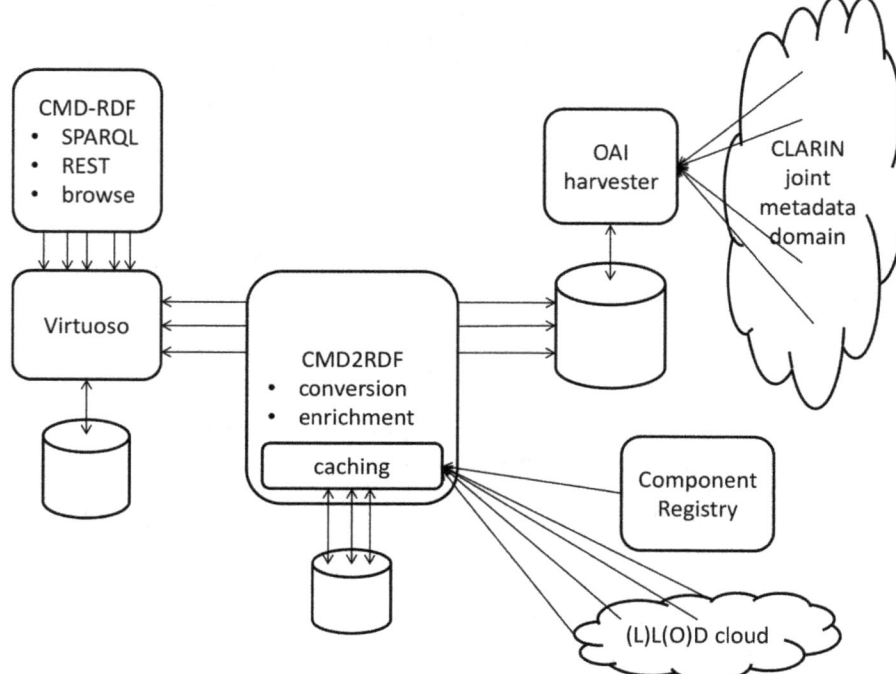

Figure 8.2: The CMD2RDF system architecture (catalog.clarin.eu/ds/cmd2rdf).

8.5   CMD2RDF and LLOD

In the CMD2RDF system architecture CMD records can be enriched with links to other LLOD datasets. The main linking pins for linguistic datasets are of course languages. The most prominent set of language codes is ISO 639:3 (Summer Institute for Linguistics, 2016), which is represented by DBpedia (2016) IRIs in the LOD cloud. Due to the heterogeneous nature of CMDI these codes can appear anywhere in a CMD record. However, due to the semantic network (Durco and Windhouwer, 2014b) that overlays the CLARIN collection of CMD record these places can be identified. Currently CMD2RDF uses the approach used for the VLO facet mapping (Van Uytvanck, Stehouwer and Lampen, 2012) and includes the resulting facets explicitly. To retain the original value next to the IRI identified by the enrichment process the cmdm:hasElementEntity predicate (which gets subclassed by specific enrichments like the VLO facets) was introduced:

```
<hdl:123/456>
    vlo:hasFacetISO6393ElementValue        "nld" ;
    vlo:hasFacetISO6393ElementEntity
        <http://dbpedia.org/resource/ISO_639:nld> .
```

As a showcase the WALS dataset (Dryer and Haspelmath, 2013) was also loaded into Virtuoso. Now SPARQL queries can be issued that involve both CMD records and linguistic content, i.e., WALS. The following query is an example of this:

```
SELECT DISTINCT ?resource ?mimetype ?language ?value
WHERE {
  ?feature dcterms:references wals:9A .
  ?feature dcterms:hasPart/rdfs:label ?value .
  ?feature ^dcterms:isReferencedBy/owl:sameAs ?language
```

```
GRAPH ?g {
  ?cmd vlo:hasFacetISO6393ElementEntity ?language .
  ?cmd oa:hasTarget ?resource .
  ?resource cmdm:hasMimeType ?mimetype .
  }
}
```

This query returns the locations (?resource) of multimedia (?mimetype) resources for languages (?language – from the RDF graph ?g, which represents the CMD record ?cmd) where the WALS contains information (?value) on a typological feature (?feature), i.e., the distribution of the sound η (the velar nasal, which is WALS feature 9A). The example SPARQL queries at catalog.clarin.eu/ds/cmd2rdf include this query so its current result can be inspected there.

Similar queries that cross (multiple times) the boundaries between metadata and content can easily be envisioned. For example, the new Lexicon Model for Ontologies (Ontolex; Cimiano, McCrae and Buitelaar, 2016), which is an RDF-based model, would enable one to query for the word for a concept, e.g., *peace* or *love* in a specific language, and via CMD2RDF time segments in annotated media could be found where this word in uttered. Several lexica are available in Ontolex or its RDF-based predecessors, but the use of RDF for time-based annotations is not so common.

The example query also shows that still quite intimate knowledge of the usage of specific RDF vocabularies by the involved datasets is needed, but this is to be expected for structured queries where one has to know the structure, as opposed to full text or facetted search Writing a SPARQL query like this is a task for a technically savvy and adventurous user, so for the average user easier interfaces will need to be provided. The CMD2RDF service does include a general RDF browser, which allows some basic interaction with the SPARQL endpoint, but for more domain-specific interaction expert user interfaces with more built-in knowledge of the used vocabularies are needed.

8.6   Current Status and Future Plans

For a while the CMD2RDF service has been hosted by the Max Planck Institute for Psycholinguistics, but due to strategic decisions by this CLARIN centre the service had to be moved, and, as a medium-term solution, is now hosted by the Meertens Institute However, the generic CLARIN URL redirect at catalog.clarin.eu/ds/cmd2rdf will take any user to the current host.

In the new Dutch CLARIAH (2016) project, which covers both linguistics and the broader Digital Humanities, there is an agreement to use RDF as a lingua-franca and to merge information obtained from different sources. The CLARIAH approach for the linguistics work package will be based on the CMD Infrastructure for compatibility with CLARIN; however, it will also offer Linked Data via the CMD2RDF service for use by others.

To also enable the discovery and use of interesting resources created within non-linguistic work packages in CLARIAH, an inverse procedure, i.e., RDF2CMD, is required, which if sufficiently scalable, will also make the Linked Data for Language Resources (LR) outside CLARIAH available for CLARIN.

With respect to the procedure to facilitate this transformation of RDF encoded LR metadata the plan is to investigate a number of different strategies. All strategies will start with a PID (Persistent IDentifier) or URI (Uniform Resource Identifier) of a LR and then search from a suitable source, e.g. a SPARQL endpoint, RDF data set, for statements related to this resource. The collected RDF statements are aggregated and processed. The RDF2CMD mapping can then use, for example, the following strategies:

• *Comparison strategy:* the collected RDF is compared to a number of RDF templates that were derived from a set of records, which instantiate recommended CMD profiles. A suitable proximity measure will then select the closest template after which the original CMD profile can be instantiated with the correct values.

• *Building strategy:* the collected RDF is inspected and every triple considered for implying a component or element in a dedicated CMD profile. The generated profile may be unique and can be 'shaved' of linguistically uninteresting non-linguistic adornments.

Minimal functionality should be supporting roundtrip conversion from a CMD record to RDF and back to CMD without loss of information, but the 'perfect' translation from Dublin Core RDF statements to the CMD Dublin Core profile should also be mandatory – a requirement which can be extended to some other popular metadata schemas.

In the proximity measure the semantic registries, e.g. the CLARIN Concept Registry (Schuurman et al., 2016), the Dublin Core metadata elements and terms, and special Linked Data repositories like Schema.org (2016) and sameas.org (2016), will play an important role.

8.7   Conclusion

This first full-fledged implementation of the mapping of Component Metadata to Linked Data already enables powerful queries that cross the line between metadata and content, which is in general prominent in the traditional metadata domain but less so in Linked Data. The future plans outlined will make it possible to more easily switch back and forth between these XML and RDF-based approaches, making the information on language resources available in the CLARIN infrastructure more widely available.

Acknowledgements

The authors would like to thank Matej Durco for the initial work on the mapping from CMD to RDF, which formed the foundation for the CLARIN-NL CMD2RDF project in which we were able to extend this into an actual working system architecture.

References

T. Berners-Lee, L. Masinter and M. McCahill (1994). *Uniform Resource Locators (URL).* IETF. December, 1994.

T. Bray, J. Paoli, C.M. Sperberg-McQueen, E. Maler and F. Yergeau (2008). *Extensible Markup Language (XML) 1.0 (Fifth Edition).* W3C. November 26, 2008.

D. Brickley and R.V. Guha (2014). *RDF Schema 1.1.* W3C. February 25, 2014.

D. Broeder, M. Windhouwer, D. Van Uytvanck, T. Goosen and T. Trippel (2012). CMDI: a Component Metadata Infrastructure. In the *Proceedings of the Metadata 2012 Workshop on Describing Language Resources with Metadata: Towards Flexibility and Interoperability in the Documentation of Language Resources.* LREC 2012. Istanbul, Turkey, May 22, 2012.

C. Chiarcos, S. Hellmann, S. Nordhoff, S. Moran, R. Littauer, J. Eckle-Kohler, I. Gurevych, S. Hartmann, M. Matuschek and C.M. Meyer (2012). *The Open Linguistics Working Group.* LREC 2012. Istanbul, Turkey, May 23–25, 2012.

P. Cimiano, J.P. McCrae and P. Buitelaar (2016). *Lexicon Model for Ontologies: Community Report.* W3C Ontology-Lexicon Community Group. May 10, 2016.

CLARIAH (2016). clariah.nl. Accessed on February 12, 2016.

CLARIN (2016a). *Component Metadata,* www.clarin.eu/cmdi. Accessed on January 18, 2016.

CLARIN (2016b). *Virtual Language Observatory,* vlo.clarin.eu. Accessed on January 18, 2016.

CLARIN-NL (2016). *CMD2RDF data,* portal.clarin.nl/node/4226. Accessed on January 18, 2016.

R. Cyganiak and A. Jentzsch (2016). *The Linking Open Data cloud diagram*, lod-cloud.net. Accessed on January 18, 2016.

R. Cyganiak, D. Wood and M. Lanthaler (2014). *RDF 1.1 Concepts and Abstract Syntax*. W3C. February 25, 2014.

DBpedia (2016). wiki.dbpedia.org. Accessed on January 19, 2016.

M.S. Dryer and M. Haspelmath (eds.) (2013). *The World Atlas of Language Structures Online*. Max Planck Institute for Evolutionary Anthropology. 2013.

Dublin Core Metadata Initiative (2016). dublincore.org. Accessed on February 12, 2016.

M. Durco and M. Windhouwer (2014a). From CLARIN Component Metadata to Linked Open Data. In *Proceedings of the third Workshop on Linked Data in Linguistics: Multilingual Knowledge Resources and Natural Language Processing* (LDL 2014). LREC 2014. Reykjavik, Iceland, May 27, 2014.

M. Durco and M. Windhouwer (2014b). *The CMD Cloud*. LREC 2014. Reykjavik, Iceland, May 28–30, 2014.

M. Dürst and M. Suignard (2005). *Internationalized Resource Identifiers (IRIs)*. IETF. January, 2005.

S. Gao, C.M. Sperberg-McQueen and H.S. Thompson (2012). *W3C XML Schema Definition Language (XSD) 1.1 Part 1: Structures*. W3C. April 5, 2012.

ISO 24622-1 (2015), *Language resource management - Component Metadata Infrastructure (CMDI) - Part 1: The Component Metadata Model*. ISO. January 20, 2015.

C. Lagoze and H. Van de Sompel (2015). *The Open Archives Initiative Protocol for Metadata Harvesting*. OAI, January 8, 2015.

LIDER project (2016). *Linguistic Linked Open Data*, linguistic-lod.org. Accessed on January 18, 2016.

F. Maali and J. Erickson (2014). *Data Catalog Vocabulary* (DCAT). W3C. January 16, 2014.

J.P. McCrae, P. Cimiano, V. Rodriguez-Doncel, D. Vila-Suero, J. Gracia, L. Matteis, R. Navigli, A. Abele, G. Vulcu and P. Buitelaar (2015). Reconciling Heterogeneous Descriptions of Language Resources. *Proceedings of the 4th Workshop on Linked Data in Linguistics: Resources and Applications* (LDL 2015). ACL-IJCNLP 2015. Beijing, China, July, 2015.

M-Files (2016). *The history of Metadata*, m-files.com/en/infographic-the-history-of-metadata. Accessed on January 18, 2016.

Open Archives Initiative (2016). *Object Reuse and Exchange*, www.openarchives.org/ore/. Accessed on February 12, 2016.

Open Knowledge Foundation (2016). *Linked Open Vocabularies*, lov.oknf.org. Accessed on January 19, 2016.

OpenLink Software (2016). *Virtuoso Open-Source Edition*. virtuoso.openlinksw.com/dataspace/doc/dav/wiki/Main/. Accessed on January 19, 2016.

<sameAs> (2016). sameas.org. Accessed on February 12, 2016.

Schema.org (2016). schema.org. Accessed on February 12, 2016.

I. Schuurman, M. Windhouwer, O. Ohren and D. Zeman (2016). CLARIN Concept Registry: the new semantic registry In K. De Smedt (ed.), *Selected Papers from the CLARIN 2015 Conference* Linköping Electronic Conference Proceedings April, 2016.

Summer Institute for Linguistics (2016). *ISO 639-3*, www-01.sil.org/iso639-3/. Accessed on January 19, 2016.

D. Van Uytvanck, H. Stehouwer and L. Lampen (2012). *Semantic metadata mapping in practice: the Virtual Language Observatory*. LREC 2012. Istanbul, Turkey, May 23–25, 2012.

W3C SPARQL Working Group (2013). *SPARQL 1.1 Overview*. W3C. March 21. 2013.

W3C Web Annotation Working Group (2016). www.w3.org/annotation/. W3C. Accessed on January 18, 2016.

PART II

Infrastructure for Linguistics

CHAPTER 9

Infrastructure for Linguistics: Introduction

Jan Odijk

UiL-OTS, Utrecht University

j.odijk@uu.nl

9.1   Introduction

Given its origins in linguistics and language technology, it should come as no surprise that CLARIN-LC created many infrastructural facilities for linguistics. These will be discussed in this part of the book, with the exception of infrastructural facilities for syntax, to which a separate part of this book is dedicated (Part III).

The chapters in this part only partially cover the work done in CLARIN-LC to support linguistic research. I will first provide a brief overall overview of the relevant data and software that resulted from CLARIN-LC (section 9.2), and then summarise the topics of the chapters of this part (section 9.3).

9.2   Work on Linguistics

I have categorised the various datasets and software applications into a number of categories in order to structure the description. This categorisation is in many respects somewhat arbitrary, but nevertheless groups the resources in natural classes. The categories are drawn from different dimensions, and are thus not mutually exclusive. Many datasets and applications can be used for multiple purposes and therefore belong to multiple categories. For this reason, some resources are mentioned under multiple categories.

The categories we distinguish are on the one hand subdisciplines of linguistics, such as *language documentation*, *language variation*, *language acquisition*, *lexicography*, and *discourse and stylistics*; and on the other hand types of software functionality, such as *enrichment*, *annotation* and *search*.

How to cite this book chapter:

Odijk, J. 2017. Infrastructure for Linguistics: Introduction. In: Odijk, J and van Hessen, A. (eds.) *CLARIN in the Low Countries*, Pp. 107–111. London: Ubiquity Press. DOI: https://doi.org/10.5334/bbi.9. License: CC-BY 4.0

Language documentation LAISEANG provides an unrivalled collection of multimedia materials and written documents from 48 languages of Insular South East Asia and West New Guinea (see chapter 10). The Typological Database System (TDS, described in chapter 11), provides the user with integrated access to a collection of independently developed typological databases. NEHOL is a digitally accessible and searchable database of the Dutch-lexifier Creole language Negerhollands or Virgin Islands Dutch Creole, VIDC (see chapter 12).

Language Variation DBD/TCULT: The DBD is a rather substantial collection of data (over 1,500 sessions) from a number of projects and research programmes that were directed at investigating multilingualism and comprises data originating from Dutch, Sranan, Sarnami, Papiamentu, Arabic, Berber and Turkish speakers. The basis of the collection is the data from the TCULT project in which intercultural language contacts in the Dutch city of Utrecht were studied. MIMORE integrates three different but related dialectical databases: DynaSAND (the dynamic syntactic atlas of the Dutch dialects), DiDDD (Diversity in Dutch DP Design) and GTRP (Goeman, Taeldeman, van Reenen Project). The associated MIMORE application enables combined searching in and analysis of these three databases. Barbiers et al. (2016) is an example of research that crucially uses this application. Analysis of data on migration flow between Dutch municipalities via MIGMAP (chapter 29) can be used for analysing language variation within the Netherlands, the influence of one dialect on another, etc. Gabmap (Leinonen et al., 2016) enables a researcher to automatically analyse data of language variation, e.g. varying words for the same concepts, varying pronunciations for the same words, or varying frequencies of syntactic constructions in transcribed conversations. D-LUCEA is a database of speech recordings of native and non-native speakers of English. The recorded speakers are students from an international student community where English is used as lingua franca. These students are being recorded longitudinally throughout their 3-year period on campus (see chapter 15).

Some resources are concerned with variation across time: VU-DNC is a unique diachronic corpus of Dutch newspaper articles from five major Dutch newspapers from 1950/1951 and 2002. Nederlab enables a user to search in all digitised texts relevant for the Dutch national heritage and the history of Dutch language and culture (ca 800 – present).

Language Acquisition COAVA enables a user to search a combination of historical dialect data and first language acquisition data. (Cornips et al., 2016) describe a case study carried out with this application and the underlying datasets. FESLI enables a user to search in the FESLI data, which have been enriched with part of speech tags. These data are from monolingual and bilingual (Dutch - Turkish) children with and without Specific Language Impairment. LESLLA contains speech of 15 low-educated learners of Dutch as a second language. VALID is an open access multimedia archive of language pathology data collected in the Netherlands, primarily on Dutch, with audio files and transcripts. D-LUCEA was mentioned above under *language variation* but it is evidently also relevant to second language acquisition (see chapter 15).

Lexicography Many lexical data have been curated and/or made accessible through user-friendly web applications. They include the Dictionary of the Brabantic Dialects, Part III, General Vocabulary, (WBD); the Dictionary of the Limburgian Dialects, Part III, General Vocabulary (WLD); the Frisian dictionary of WFT-GTB integrated in the language bank and accessible via the language bank web application (see chapter 13); the multiword expression lexical database of DUELME and its associated DuELME web application (Odijk, 2013a;b); the GrNe web application for the classical GrNe Greek-Dutch dictionary (originally for the letter π only, but for an increasing number of letters); and the lexical data of Cornetto, a lexical resource for the Dutch language which combines two resources with different semantic organisations: the *Dutch Wordnet* with its synset organisation and the *Dutch Reference Lexicon* which includes definitions, usage constraints, selectional restrictions, syntactic behaviours, illustrative contexts, etc. The Cornetto data are easily accessible via the dedicated Cornetto web application developed in CLARIN-LC.

Obviously, many search applications described elsewhere in this book, such as OpenSoNaR, AutoSearch, Nederlab, PaQu, GrETEL, CorpusSearchWeb, SHEBANQ, and MIMORE also support lexicography and lexicological research.

Discourse and Stylistics The diachronic VU-DNC corpus of Dutch newspaper articles from five major Dutch newspapers from 1950/1951 and 2002 is annotated not only with part of speech codes but also with discourse annotations. The DiscAn corpus is a collection of subcorpora of the Dutch language specifically created as a corpus annotated at the level of discourse, in particular for coherence relations and discourse connectives.

Stylene is a system for stylometry and readability research on the basis of existing techniques for automatic text analysis and machine learning, and offers a web service that allows researchers in the Humanities and Social Sciences to analyse texts with this system. It is described in more detail in chapter 16.

Enrichment There are many applications and services for enriching data. These include a web application and service for orthographic normalisation (TICClops), which is also embedded in a workflow for converting digital images into textual resources in TEI[1] format (@PhilosTEI, described in more detail in chapter 32)

The TTNWW application, described in chapter 7, provides a wide range of workflows for enriching text corpora with linguistic annotations, among them workflows for tokenisation, lemmatisation, named entity recognition, coreference marking, and marking of semantic roles, as well as workflows for enriching an audio file with an automatically generated orthographic transcription. NameScape enables a researcher to have a text corpus enriched with annotations for named entities.

OpenConvert consists of a set of web services for format conversions between a variety of formats for textual resources, thus enabling a wide variety of formats to be processed by applications such as TTNWW.

Manual annotation A number of applications focus on annotating resources, i.e. manually (or semi-automatically) enriching them with new information. This was described in chapter 2, but is repeated here. Prominent in CLARIN-LC are the ELAN, and ANNEX applications for the creation of complex annotations on video and audio resources. These applications existed before CLARIN-LC but were significantly improved and enhanced in CLARIN-LC. These enhancements include a web service (AAM-LR) for annotating where in an audio file there is speech (instead of other sounds), and identifying who is speaking in the parts containing speech (diarisation). In the SignLinC project it was made possible to link lexical databases and annotated corpora of signed language in these applications. The ColTime project extended ELAN and ANNEX with a referencing and note exchanging system. The EXILSEA project enhanced these applications for users of different languages with multilingual features based on ISOcat. The MultiCon project enhanced ELAN and ANNEX with multilayer visualisation of multilayer collocates. TQE is a web application for evaluating the quality of phonetic transcriptions of speech files.

The FLAT application described in chapter 6 is an application for manual verification and correction of annotations on text corpora encoded in the FoLiA format.

Several of the tools described under *Enrichment* can also be used for annotation purposes. They can bootstrap the annotation by automatically enriching a resource with annotations, followed by manual verification and correction, e.g. through FLAT, ELAN or ANNEX.

---

[1] TEI (Text Encoding Initiative) is a widely used standard for encoding textual resources supported by CLARIN.

Search The search applications OpenSoNaR, AutoSearch, Nederlab, PaQu, GrETEL, CorpusSearchWeb, SHEBANQ, and MIMORE will be described in more detail in part III on infrastructure for syntax, but they can obviously also be used for linguistic research other than syntax, e.g. for lexicography, morphology and semantics, and some even for phonology and phonetics. NameScape enables searching for names and analysing their use in literary works (see chapter 30). Nederlab enables a user to search in all digitised texts relevant for the Dutch national heritage and the history of Dutch language and culture (ca 800 – present).

The Taalportaal is a comprehensive and authoritative digital scientific grammar for Dutch, Frisian, and Afrikaans. In the Taalportaal, links to several search applications were made to provide concrete evidence related to specific constructions described in the Taalportaal. Besides syntax, the links cover morphology and phonology (see chapter 24).

9.3   Contents of Part II: Infrastructure for Linguistics

Part II of this book covers only a small sample of the resources described in section 9.2. For the reader's convenience, we describe the contents of each chapter here:

Chapter 10 describes the LAISEANG collection of multimedia materials and written documents from 48 languages in Insular South East Asia and West New Guinea. The language resources for this collection were gathered by 20 linguists at or in collaboration with Dutch universities over the last 40 years, and were compiled and archived in collaboration with The Language Archive (TLA) at the Max Planck Institute in Nijmegen in accordance with CLARIN standards.

Chapter 11 describes the curation of the Typological Database System (TDS), which provides the user with integrated access to a collection of independently developed typological databases. Curating this independently developed database system was urgently needed to save this valuable resource in a durable, archival environment and convert access to it into a true web service architecture, thus safeguarding future access to the data.

Chapter 12 investigates variation in supra-locative prepositional phrases in two varieties of VIDC, crucially using the NEHOL database curated in CLARIN-LC.

Chapter 13 discusses the use of the WFT dictionary after its integration into the GTB language bank. The authors demonstrate a case of usage for research, and suggests possible improvements and expansions of the online version of the WFT.

Chapter 14 reports on research aiming to determine which language measures are diagnostic indicators of SLI on the basis of narrative data. To that end, morphosyntactic and lexical accuracy and complexity were investigated, crucially using the VALID open access multimedia archive of language pathology data. The authors argues that their results reveal the urgency to have identical, precise protocols in handling and analysing complex data, which is exactly one of the goals of the VALID archive.

Chapter 15 describes the UCU Accent project, and the curation of the resulting D-LUCEA database, which made the recorded speech data and their concomitant metadata widely available to the research community at large. The authors describe some of the research that has been made possible via this project, as well as current plans for applying a similar method for data curation to a new speech accent corpus, *Sprekend Nederland (The Netherlands Speaking)*.

Chapter 16 describes Stylene, which consists of an educational demonstration interface and tools for stylometry (authorship attribution and profiling) and readability research for Dutch. Stylene is again a typical CLARIN result in that it makes advanced computational methods available in a user-friendly manner to researchers from the Humanities and Social Sciences.

Acknowledgements

This work was financed by CLARIN-NL and CLARIAH.

References

Barbiers, Sjef, Marjo van Koppen, Hans Bennis, and Norbert Corver (2016), MIcrocomparative MOrphosyntactic REsearch (MIMORE): Mapping partial grammars of Flemish, Brabantish and Dutch, *Lingua* **178**, pp. 5–31. Linguistic Research in the CLARIN Infrastructure. http://www.sciencedirect.com/science/article/pii/S0024384115002211.

Cornips, Leonie, Jos Swanenberg, Wilbert Heeringa, and Folkert de Vriend (2016), The relationship between first language acquisition and dialect variation: Linking resources from distinct disciplines in a CLARIN-NL project, *Lingua* **178**, pp. 32–45. Linguistic Research in the CLARIN Infrastructure. http://www.sciencedirect.com/science/article/pii/S0024384115002375.

Leinonen, Therese, Çağrı Çöltekin, and John Nerbonne (2016), Using Gabmap, *Lingua* **178**, pp. 71–83. Linguistic Research in the CLARIN Infrastructure. http://www.sciencedirect.com/science/article/pii/S0024384115000315.

Odijk, Jan (2013a), DUELME: Dutch electronic lexicon of multiword expressions, *in* Francopoulo, G., editor, *LMF - Lexical Markup Framework*, ISTE / Wiley, London, UK / Hoboken, US, pp. 133–144.

Odijk, Jan (2013b), Identification and lexical representation of multiword expressions, *in* Spyns, P. and J.E.J.M Odijk, editors, *Essential Speech and Language Technology for Dutch. Results by the STEVIN-programme*, Theory and Applications of Natural Language Processing, Springer, Berlin/Heidelberg, pp. 201–217. http://link.springer.com/content/pdf/10.1007%2F978-3-642-30910-6_12.

CHAPTER 10

Creating a Language Archive of Insular South East Asia and West New Guinea

Marian Klamer, Paul Trilsbeek, Tom Hoogervorst and Chris Haskett

Leiden University, Max Planck Institute for Psycholinguistics, KITLV/Royal Netherlands Institute
of Southeast Asian and Caribbean Studies, MPI Nijmegen

ABSTRACT

The geographical region of Insular South East Asia and New Guinea is well-known as an
area of mega-biodiversity. Less well-known is the extreme linguistic diversity in this area:
over a quarter of the world's 6,000 languages are spoken here. As small minority languages,
most of them will cease to be spoken in the coming few generations. The project described
here ensures the preservation of unique records of languages and the cultures encapsu-
lated by them in the region. The language resources were gathered by twenty linguists at,
or in collaboration with, Dutch universities over the last 40 years, and were compiled and
archived in collaboration with The Language Archive (TLA) at the Max Planck Institute in
Nijmegen. The resulting archive constitutes a collection of multimedia materials and written
documents from 48 languages in Insular South East Asia and West New Guinea. At TLA,
the data was archived according to state-of-the-art standards (TLA holds the Data Seal of
Approval): the component metadata infrastructure CMDI was used; all metadata categories
as well as relevant units of annotation were linked to the ISO data category registry ISOcat.
This guaranteed proper integration of the language resources into the CLARIN framework.
Through the archive, future speaker communities and researchers will be able to extensively
search the materials for answers to their own questions, even if they do not themselves know
the language, and even if the language dies.

10.1 Background of the Project

The geographical region of Insular South East Asia and New Guinea is well-known as an area
of mega-biodiversity. What is less well-known is that its tremendous species diversity correlates

How to cite this book chapter:
Klamer, M, Trilsbeek, P, Hoogervorst, T and Haskett, C. 2017. Creating a Language Archive of Insular South
East Asia and West New Guinea. In: Odijk, J and van Hessen, A. (eds.) *CLARIN in the Low Countries*,
Pp. 113–121. London: Ubiquity Press. DOI: https://doi.org/10.5334/bbi.10. License: CC-BY 4.0

with a rich cultural and linguistic diversity across the area (Gorenflo et al., 2012). But both the biodiversity that supports the humans and all other species in the area and the traditional ethno-linguistic knowledge that helps sustain it are subject to a converging extinction crisis. We are rapidly losing the unique ways of life and the encapsulating languages of peoples in this part of the world.

Over the last 40 years, more than two dozen linguists at, or in collaboration with, Dutch universities collected multimedia materials and written documents from over 50 languages in Insular South East Asia and West New Guinea. However, as these unique records were not digitised and/or archived systematically, they were bound to get lost. The current CLARIN 'Resource Curation' project grew out of the recognition that these unique resources had to be preserved for the future. The initial goal was to archive 52 language resources along with their basic metadata, and make them accessible online. The project ran for 16 months from February 2013 to July 2014 and involved various types of tasks: (i) Collaboration with the linguists who originally collected the resources (and who are not part of this project) to systematically compile their materials and the metadata; (ii) File conversion and digitization; (iii) CMDI profile creation and metadata entry; (iv) Creating an inventory of annotations and the conventions and terminology used in them; (v) Mapping of these with terms in the ISOcat data category registry; (vi) Archiving mappings along with the data sets; (vii) Make the archive accessible online.

Materials that had not yet been digitised were digitised and archived alongside more recent digital collections in accordance with the highest standards and principles as established by The Language Archive at the Max Planck Institute in Nijmegen (Drude et al., 2012).

As a result of this project The Language Archive now contains language resources compiled by twenty linguists over the past 40 years on 48 languages spoken in Insular South East Asia and New Guinea, archived under the name of LAISEANG (Language Archive of Insular South East Asia and New Guinea), see Figure 10.1.

Through this structured digital archive, speaker communities and researchers – be they anthropologists, linguists, historians or researchers from other disciplines – will be able to extensively search the materials for answers to their own questions, even if they do not themselves know the language, and even if the language dies.

10.1.1   Research Question(s)

Research questions that may be (better) addressed using the data of this project include, but are not limited to, the following:

- *Questions relating to language structure, e.g.* What is the structure of a conversation/narrative/-paragraph/sentence/clause/word in language X?
- *Questions relating to language use, e.g.* How do bride-price negotations, religious songs, historical narratives, speeches, etc. function in language X?
- *Questions relating to the history of languages and their speakers, e.g.* Which lexical evidence supports the reconstruction of historical relations between Papuan languages of Timor-Alor-Pantar; or between the Austronesian languages of New Guinea?
- *Questions about the language of particular semantic domains, e.g.* Which numeral systems are employed in group/language X? How does language X express location and motion in space? How does language X encode pronominal reference? What formatives does language X use to express physical sensations or emotional states/experiences?
- *Questions about intonation, prosody, and tone, e.g.* What are the major intonation patterns in language X? How does prosody affect realisation of tone in language X?

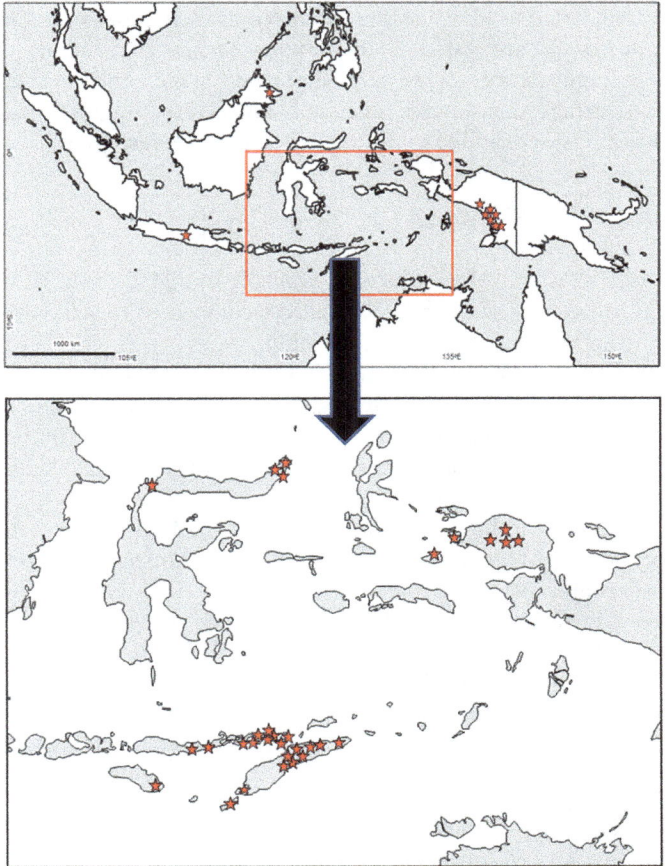

Figure 10.1: Locations of LAISEANG languages in Insular Southeast Asia and New Guinea.

- *Questions relating to comparative folklore, e.g.* What kind of omens are certain species of birds said to hold in ethnolinguistic group X?
- *Questions relating to speech registers and oral literature, e.g.* What are the poetic devices and metaphors used in ritual language? How are songs composed, in terms of tunes and/or texts?
- *Questions from speaker communities, e.g.* How do/did we produce traditional material cultural items such as houses, woven cloth or baskets? How do/did we grow and prepare certain traditional types of food? Which traditional place names are/were used in our region? What kind of mythology or ancestor stories do/did we have?

10.1.2   Research Data

Before the project started we contacted the original collectors of the linguistic data, and almost all emailed their consent for the data they collected to be included. We had to visit some collectors who currently work abroad to collect their data manually and to compile specific details on the content and format of their resources and metadata sets.

As we had anticipated, many different annotation schemes had been used by the collectors. Most of the older materials had handwritten transcriptions and annotations on paper; these paper resources had to be converted to PDF and were archived as such. More recent language resources have often been entered and annotated as Toolbox projects (as files linking texts and lexicon), and various types of linguistic categories were employed for the annotation across the different Toolboxed resources. Where this was possible we mapped these linguistic categories to ISOcat categories; these mappings were added to the archive as separate resources.

10.1.3   Technology

Many of the resources we archived were already available in digital form. However, conversions had to take place in some cases, such that all resources conformed to standards accepted by The Language Archive as suitable for long-term preservation.

The older non-digital recordings we digitised as WAV files included (i) reel-to-reel, (ii) audio cassette tape, and (iii) video cassette tape recordings. A number of cassette tapes that had previously been digitised as MP3 by the original collector had to be digitised again as WAV. Non-digital paper materials, which constitute valuable or unique documents, were scanned into PDF format and also deposited.

The metadata descriptions of the language resources we archived were in a number of different formats: some were available in spreadsheets, some in Word documents, some on paper – and some only in the collector's mind.

For the component metadata infrastructure, we evaluated the existing CMDI profiles in the CLARIN Component Registry and decided that the IMDI CMDI profile (CMDI profile based on the IMDI metadata schema) fitted the needs of the project. In addition to the metadata categories in this profile that had already been linked to the ISO data category registry ISOcat (cf. Kemps-Snijders et al., 2009, among others), the annotation terminology of a number of languages was inventoried and linked to ISOcat as well. The archiving software at TLA automatically assigned a Handle Persistent Identifier to every archived resource and metadata record. It also made all the metadata records available for harvesting via the OAI-PMH protocol. This guaranteed the proper integration of the resources into the CLARIN framework.

10.1.4   Description

Once the resources per language and the metadata were compiled and prepared for archiving, they were put on the server of TLA. Data was structured hierarchically in trees, where each language resource would be assigned one major node in an 'Insular SE Asia & New Guinea' comprehensive corpus. Metadata were entered, and data integrated and organised with the help of the Arbil standalone tool and the LAMUS online tool. The Access Management System (AMS) was used to assign one of four levels of access to any resource or group of resources according to place in the tree structure and/or file type: 1) open, 2) controlled open (where identification and agreement with a code of conduct is necessary), 3) restricted (where individual permission by the researcher or person in charge is required) or 4) closed (to anyone except original researchers/depositors). Except for one resource, the data that were archived in this project are all of level 1: open access.

Annotations in unsupported formats such as DOC were converted to PDF, and were thus treated identically to annotations that are handwritten in (field) notebooks.

We made mappings between the annotation terms used in the data sets and the general ISOcat concept registry for the more recent resources that were already in Toolbox format. In some of these resources, the Leipzig Glossing Rules had been applied, often with an additional set of glossing conventions and labels that only apply to an individual language; the ISOcat data category registry provides a means to clarify the nature of the meaning of such particular glosses.

10.2   Results of the Project

10.2.1   Deliverables and Milestones

A deliverable is a measurable and tangible outcome of a project. They are developed by project team members in alignment with the goals of the project. Milestones are checkpoints throughout the life of the project. They identify when activities have been completed, thus implying that a notable point has been reached in the project. The Appendix contains the list of deliverables and milestones we originally aimed for, in their original order, with the relevant actors. The results are indicated with colour shading, where green deliverables and milestones have been met completely, while red deliverables have not been met. The reasons for not curating some of the resources were of variable nature: some of the resources we originally planned to curate turned out to be untraceable and/or lost, other resources were deemed by the author not yet ready to be archived, or the author decided not to archive them with LAISEANG after all. The list also includes some added deliverables: these resources were added to the archive in the course of the project, or shortly after it.

The LAISEANG archive can be accessed directly at http://hdl.handle.net/1839/00-0000-0000-0018-CB72-4@view. It can also be accessed through The Language Archive (tla.mpi.nl) by clicking on the 'Access the Archive' quick link. In the left-hand panel of the archive there is an alphabetical list of corpora, which includes LAISEANG. As mentioned earlier, except for one, all the resources in the LAISEANG archive are open to everyone.

10.2.2   Lessons Learned

Most of the linguists that contributed their resources were extremely grateful for the opportunity to get their materials digitised and archived in this way, and mentioned that their materials would otherwise never have been curated or archived. Linguistic field researchers typically wish to make their data available for everyone, rather than keep it to themselves. However, our experiences in this project suggest that it is unlikely that their data will be archived unless there is a budget to pay for the time it costs to curate and archive it. In addition, there must be a user-friendly infrastructure to help them actually *do* it, preferably online.

In some cases, we inherited quite large archives with an existing structure that was designed by the collector to archive data and metadata in a logical and transparent way (e.g. the resources on Ma'ya and Matbat, Figure 10.2). It would have been efficient to be able to automatically incorporate such existing structures into the metadata structure, for example by having an option to add resources to Arbil directly from such existing structures, using a kind of 'folder importing' script. At present, Arbil has no such option, so that the original structures unfortunately all got lost.

Another issue that we ran into was that Arbil has been developed as a local tool, originally designed for a single person to archive a single language resource. As a result, Arbil is not a tool to efficiently deal with (i) multiple language resources collected by a single person and archived by several others or (ii) single language resources collected by multiple persons and archived by yet others. Arbil does not offer an online collaborative workspace, which meant that in our project the data sets had to be treated in strict cycles and metadata had to be sent back and forth among the team members responsible for digitisation and metadata collection. It would have been more efficient to allow online collaboration on metadata in a 'Google Docs' manner, such that project members could work simultaneously on the same data sets, and such that authors could look at their own materials and add or correct information if they wished.

One result from this project that may be useful for the future is that we are now able to estimate the costs of curating and archiving a single language resource collected in the field. The size of

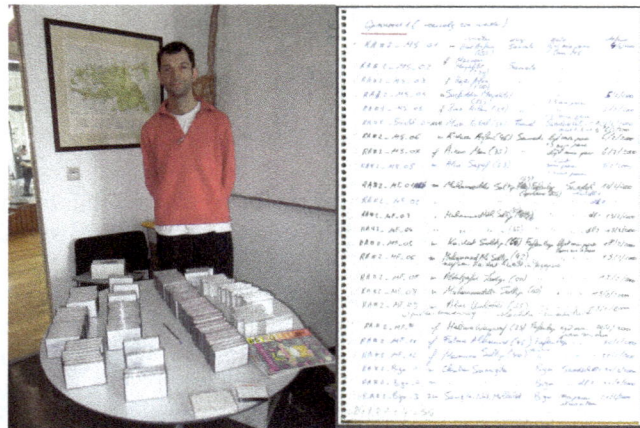

Figure 10.2: Dr. Bert Remijsen with his resources on Ma'ya and Matbat.

the resources for the LAISEANG archive varied enormously: from 30-minute audio recordings to 35-hour video recordings. Some resources were not yet digitised, and/or had no or little organised metadata, while others were completely digitised, with all the metadata organised in spreadsheets. As a result, the time it took to curate and archive an individual resource varied from 4 to 60 hours. With a budget of 73,000 euros and 1,800 work hours we were able to curate and archive 48 language resources. On average, a single language resource thus takes 37.5 hours and costs about 1,500 euros to curate and archive. A project which involves the collection of primary linguistic data should therefore budget *at least* this amount of time and money to prepare the data for archiving. Not included in these figures are the costs that an archive may ask for their services and long-term storage, as in our project this was offered for free by The Language Archive.

References

Drude, S., Broeder, D., Trilsbeek, P., & Wittenburg, P. 2012. The Language Archive: A new hub for language resources. In N. Calzolari (Ed.), Proceedings of LREC 2012: 8th International Conference on Language Resources and Evaluation (pp. 3264–3267). European Language Resources Association (ELRA).

Gorenflo, L.J., S. Romaine, R. A. Mittermeier, K. Walker-Painemillad. 2012. Co-occurrence of linguistic and biological diversity in biodiversity hotspots and high biodiversity wilderness areas. PNAS 109, 21: 8032–8037, doi: 10.1073/pnas.1117511109.

Kemps-Snijders, M., Windhouwer, M., Wittenburg, P., & Wright, S. E. 2009. ISOcat: Remodeling metadata for language resources. International Journal of Metadata, Semantics and Ontologies (IJMSO), 4(4), 261–276. doi:10.1504/IJMSO.2009.029230.

Appendix: Deliverables and Milestones, with actors

FK=František Kratochvíl, MK=Marian Klamer, PT=Paul Trilsbeek, TH=Tom Hoogervorst

Deliverable (D) / Mile-stone (M)	Description	Digital media collected?	Metadata collected by:	Described in Arbil by:	Delivered by:
D	Kambera metadata + data set	yes	MK	MK	MK
D	Teiwa metadata + data set	yes	MK	MK	MK
D	Kaera metadata + data set	yes	MK	MK	MK
D	Alorese metadata + data set	yes	MK	MK	MK
D	Alor Malay metadata + data set	yes	MK	MK	MK
D	Lamaholot metadata + data set	yes	MK	MK	MK
D	Ende metadata + data set	yes	MK	MK	MK
D	Roti metadata + data set	yes	MK	MK	MK
D	Tetun metadata + data set	yes	MK	MK	MK
D	Tokodede metadata + data set	yes	MK	MK	MK
D	Lakalei metadata + data set	yes	MK	MK	MK
D	Kemak metadata + data set	yes	MK	MK	MK
D	Tetun Dili metadata + data set	yes	MK	MK	MK
D	Bunaq metadata + data set	yes	MK	MK	MK
D	Mambai metadata + data set	yes	MK	MK	MK
D	Idate metadata + data set	yes	MK	MK	MK
D	Ambai metadata + data set	yes	MK	MK	MK
D	Abui metadata + data set (by Kratochvíl)	yes	FK	FK & MK	FK
D	Sawila metadata + data set	yes	FK	FK & MK	FK
D	Subo metadata + data set	yes	FK	FK & MK	FK
D	Western Pantar metadata + data set	yes	MK	MK	MK
D	Adang metadata + data set	yes	MK	MK	MK
D	Inanwatan metadata + data set	yes	TH	TH	TH
D	Awyu-Dumut metadata + data set	yes	TH	TH	TH
D	Aghu metadata + data set	no	no	no	
D	Asmat metadata + data set	no	no	no	

(Continued)

D	Wambon metadata + data set	yes (Awyu Dumut)	TH	TH	TH
D	Tsaukambo metadata + data set	no	no	no	
D	Kombai metadata + data set	yes (Awyu Dumut)	TH	TH	TH
D	Citak metadata + data set	no	no	no	
D	Hatam metadata + data set	yes	TH	TH	TH
D	Sougb metadata + data set	yes	TH	TH	TH
D	Mansim metadata + data set	yes	TH	TH	TH
D	Matbat metadata + data set	yes	TH	TH	TH
D	Ma'ya metadata + data set	yes	TH	TH	TH
D	Mpur metadata + data set	no	no	no	
D	Manado Malay metadata + data set	no	no	no	
D	Bantik metadata + data set	no	no	no	
D	Mongondow metadata + data set	no	no	no	
D	Kupang Malay metadata + data set	no	no	no	
D	Javanese metadata + data set	no	no	no	
D	Begak metadata + data set	yes	TH	TH	TH
D	Blagar metadata + data set	yes	TH	TH	TH
D	Fataluku metadata + data set	no	no	no	
D	Bunaq metadata + data set	no	no	no	
D	Kamang metadata + data set	no	no	no	
D	Abui metadata + data set (by Schapper)	no	no	no	
D	Kemak metadata + data set	yes	MK	MK	MK
D	Tokodede metadata + data set	yes	MK	MK	MK
D	Woisika metadata + data set	yes	TH	TH	TH
D	Makasae metadata + data set	yes	TH	TH	TH
D	Dampelas metadata + data set	yes	TH	TH	TH
Added D	Sar metadata + data set	yes	MK	MK	MK
Added D	Klon metadata + data set	yes	MK	MK	MK
Added D	Kafoa metadata + data set	yes	MK	MK	MK
Added D	Kabola metadata + data set	yes	MK	MK	MK
Added D	Kawa metadata + data set	yes	MK	MK	MK

Added D	Hamap metadata + data set	yes	MK	MK	MK
Added D	Biak	yes	TH	TH	TH
Added D	Ambel metadata + data set	yes	TH	TH	TH
Added D	Butleh metadata + data set	yes	TH	TH	TH
Added D	Hewa	yes	TH	TH	TH
D	A synthesis of annotation issues, conventions and how they have been treated in the project, leading to a protocol/procedure for the next six months of the project				
D	Inventory of annotations, conventions and terminology				MK
D	Mapping of resource-specific categories to ISOcat				MK & PT
D	Blagar transcribed, glossed and translated sample				MK
D	Woisika transcribed, glossed and translated sample				
D	Wambon transcribed, glossed and translated sample				
D	Kaera transcribed, glossed and translated sample				MK
D	Pre-final document describing the type of annotation issues and conventions, and the protocol/procedure used in the project to deal with these				
D	Final document describing the type of annotation issues and conventions, and the protocol/procedure used in the project to deal with these				
D	A document describing requirements and desiderata for the CLARIN infrastructure, resulting from the experiences gained through our project				MK
M	1st set of language resources online				PT
M	1st metadata harvesting test				PT
M	Inventory of annotations, conventions and terminology				MK
M	2nd set of language resources online.				PT
M	2nd metadata harvesting test				PT
M	Mapping of resource-specific categories to ISOcat				MK & PT
M	1st sample of annotated texts				MK
M	2nd sample of annotated texts				MK
M	All resources online				PT

CHAPTER 11

Curating the Typological Database System

Menzo Windhouwer[a,1,2], Alexis Dimitriadis[b] and Vesa Akerman[c]

[a]Meertens Institute, [b]Utrecht University, [c]Data Archiving and Networked Services (DANS)

ABSTRACT

The Typological Database System (TDS), which provides integrated access to a dozen independently created typological databases, was launched in 2007. Due to the pace of change in
web technologies, the original software has for some time been edging toward obsolescence.
CLARIN-NL granted funding to the TDS Curator project to migrate this valuable resource
to a more durable platform, archiving the data and converting its interface to a true web
service architecture that can continue to provide interactive access to the data. This chapter
describes the architecture of the new system, and the Integrated Data and Documentation
Format (IDDF) on which it is based.

11.1 Introduction

The Typological Database System (TDS) is a web-based resource that provides integrated access
to a collection of independently created typological databases. Typological databases are used for
research in linguistic typology, 'the study of patterns that occur systematically across languages'
(Croft, 2003), and consulted by linguists and others looking for a high-level, cross-linguistic view
of particular phenomena. Combining several typological databases provides advantages in scale, as
well as the opportunity to look for relations among features. The TDS was developed with support
from NWO grant 380-30-004 / INV-03-12 and from participating universities, and launched in
2007. It provides access to and extended documentation for its component databases, through a
uniform structure and search interface (Dimitriadis et al., 2009). However, web technologies evolve

---

[1] Corresponding author: menzo.windhouwer@meertens.knaw.nl
[2] At the time of the CLARIN-NL TDS Curator project (2011–2012), Menzo Windhouwer was working at the Max Planck
Institute for Psycholinguistics.

How to cite this book chapter:
Windhouwer, M, Dimitriadis, A and Akerman, V. 2017. Curating the Typological Database System. In:
Odijk, J and van Hessen, A. (eds.) *CLARIN in the Low Countries*, Pp. 123–132. London: Ubiquity
Press. DOI: https://doi.org/10.5334/bbi.11. License: CC-BY 4.0

rapidly and thus pose a challenge to software sustainability. Through its Project Call 1, CLARIN-NL granted funding to the TDS Curator project to save the valuable TDS resource in a durable, archival environment and convert access to it into a true web service architecture, thus safeguarding future access to the TDS data.

11.2   The Architecture of the Typological Database System

Figure 11.1 gives a global overview of the TDS architecture. Data from the component databases (at the bottom of the diagram) is pushed through an extensive, manually supervised Extraction, Transformation and Loading (ETL) processing chain and integrated into one data resource, based on knowledge in various knowledge bases (right side of the diagram). The end user interacts with the system to access the data and knowledge bases through its web interface (at the top). The knowledge bases contain all TDS knowledge about the component databases and the linguistic domain. This consists of various interlinked specifications: a set of database-specific ontologies, one global linguistic ontology and (currently) two topic taxonomies. Maintenance of the knowledge base is supported by the TDS Workbench (right) and other custom-built or general-purpose tools, including an ontology editor.

To guarantee continued access to the valuable data integrated into this system, the TDS Curator project addressed three weak spots in the architecture:

1. Although parts of the knowledge base already used W3C recommendations – the Web Ontology Language (OWL; W3C, 2016a) for the linguistic ontology, and the Simple Knowledge Organization System (SKOS; W3C, 2016b) for the topic taxonomies – the core of the system, consisting of the collection of data imported, merged and enriched from the component databases and the database-specific knowledge basis, relies on a proprietary format. This format had already been cleaned up, generalised and formalised as the XML-based Integrated Data and Documentation Format (IDDF; Windhouwer and Dimitriadis, 2008), but IDDF

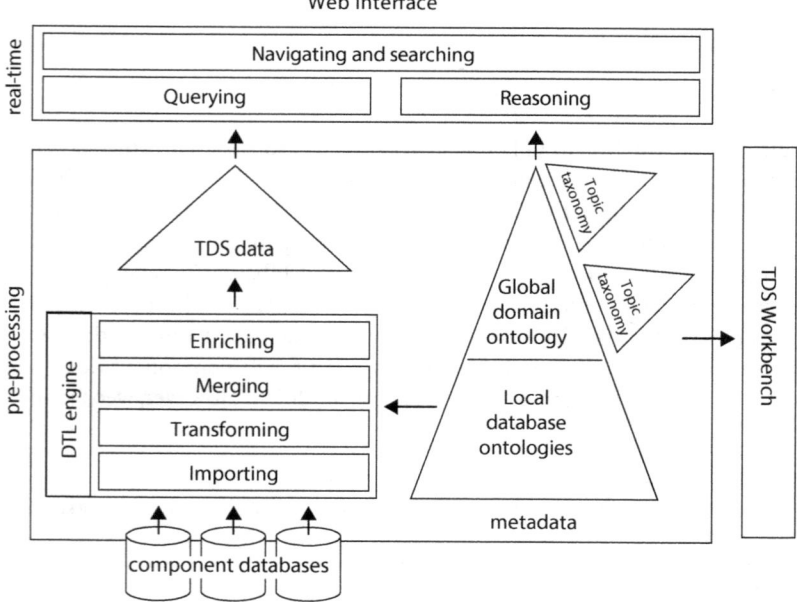

Figure 11.1: The TDS system architecture.

had not actually been implemented in the TDS system architecture. The TDS Curator project transformed the TDS data into the IDDF format, and they are now archived by the Data Archiving and Networked Services (DANS)[3] in their online EASY archiving system.

2. The original TDS engine did not fully implement a client-server architecture, i.e., a clean separation into a back end (the server) and interface components communicating through an explicit Application Programming Interface (API). Instead, features and technical idiosyncrasies of the framework chosen for the interface were deeply interwoven into the ragtag API. In the TDS Curator, an IDDF-driven web API was designed and implemented. This API can potentially be used by other tools besides the current TDS interface.

3. The TDS web interface, which predated HTML5, was based on the Backbase UI framework (Van Emde Boas and Ilinsky, 2009). Unfortunately, this turned out to be a poor technology bet, as support for this framework decreased rapidly and now has completely disappeared. In the TDS Curator project, the interface and the underlying technology have been renewed. However, the world of browser technology remains highly volatile, so unfortunately sustainability problems do remain.

The next sections discuss these problem areas and the implemented solutions in more depth.

11.2.1   Integrated Data Documentation Format

The aim of the TDS project was to integrate a number of typological databases, allowing access to and correlating their information using one uniform interface. The basic technological requirements for this integration are close to the Extraction, Transformation and Loading (ETL) phase in data warehousing. However, a not-so-common need was to add extensive documentation (part of the database-specific knowledge base) to the data and data structures loaded from the component databases. Many of the databases were built over the years by researchers for their own purposes, and had virtually no documentation. The linguistic knowledge designer of the TDS had to solicit this information from these researchers and make it digitally available to the end-users of the TDS (see Figure 11.2). This was done by storing the knowledge in the knowledge base and adding this

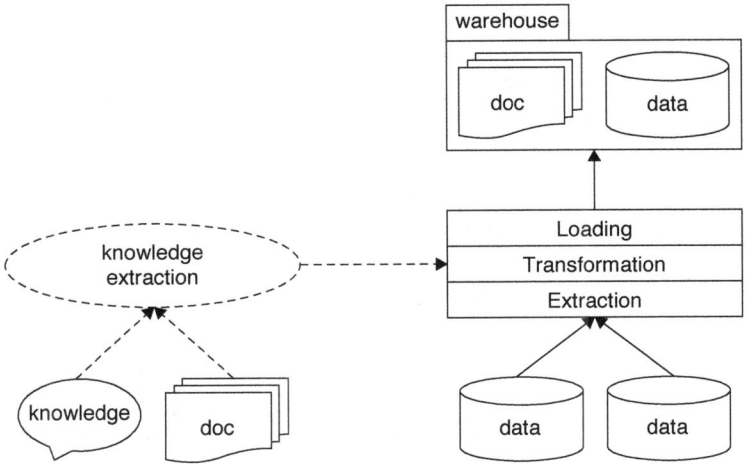

Figure 11.2: Extraction, Transformation and Loading (ETL).

---

[3] DANS was the (candidate) CLARIN centre partner in the project and provides the project's longterm archiving services.

information to the data source in the transformation stage of the ETL phase, resulting in a heavily interconnected combination of data and documentation in the data warehouse.

An IDDF document consists of two major sections: one for the documentation and one for the data. The IDDF schema is expressed in Relax NG (ISO, 2008) and Schematron (ISO, 2006a), both of which are validation languages for XML documents. The hierarchical nature of XML makes it very suitable for IDDF documents. To avoid having to manually overspecify hundreds of data fields and values, and in order to capture some of their interrelationships and higher-level organisation, data fields and values are grouped and documented in so-called semantic contexts. For example, one context contains all the fields related to language identification, while other contexts contain all the fields for particular linguistic phenomena. Data and its documentation will always have to be shown in its semantic context to allow proper interpretation, e.g. to know that this name is the name of a language and not the name of an author of a scientific article. As it is possible to embed a semantic context within another context, a hierarchy, i.e., a tree, of semantic contexts can be built.

Many typological databases consist entirely of information describing languages as a whole (e.g., 'basic word order'); such databases are effectively structured as a single relational table, and can be hierarchically represented by nesting semantic contexts, starting from the root context for *language*. However, more sophisticated typological databases contain data about multiple constructions per language, while other data sources contain information that is not restricted to single languages (e.g., a universal phoneme inventory). This requires more than one hierarchy, i.e., one for languages and one for each of these other entity types, which can refer to each other through foreign/primary key relationships. The data model thus becomes a network of hierarchies. In Figure 11.3 each type of semantic context is represented by a triangle with a specific colour and size. The documentation section describes the types of semantic context, while in the data section they are instantiated – here, the same type can appear multiple times. Relationships between entities are shown by directed edges.

The major aim of the documentation section is to describe the data, which will be stored in the data section. The basic documentation building blocks, to which data will get associated later on, are called *notions*: this term was introduced to make a distinction between the fields and their

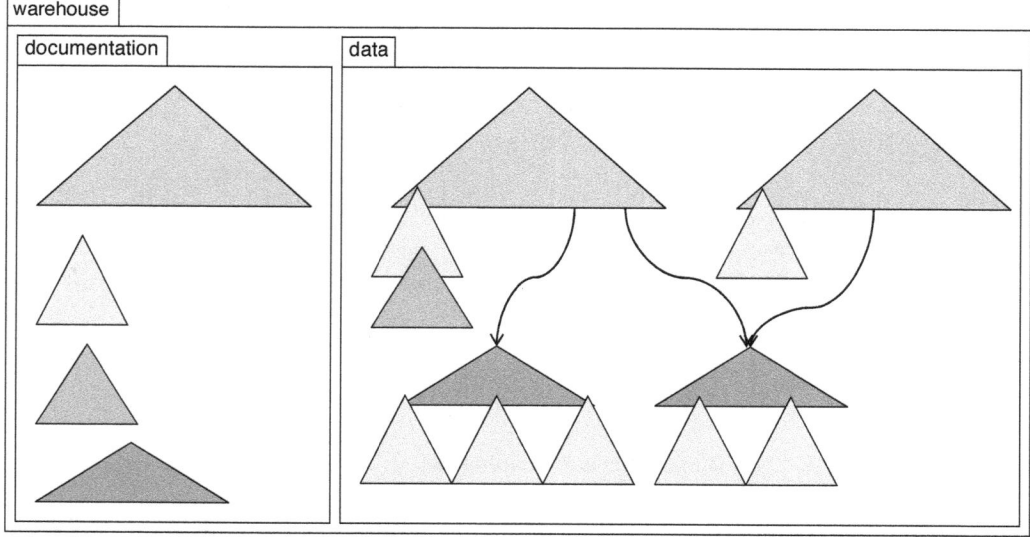

Figure 11.3: Integrated Data and Documentation.

values that get loaded from a component database, on the one hand, and more formal knowledge base building blocks like concepts and topics, on the other hand. Notions are grouped together in small hierarchies, which correspond to the previously introduced semantic contexts. For example, the notions *title*, *name*, *affiliation* and *email* could be grouped together under an *author* notion. Notions that are at the root of such a hierarchy are called *top* notions, i.e., *author* would be a top notion. Semantic contexts are themselves organised into a bigger hierarchy; for example, the author context can be reused in a bibliographic entry semantic context. Notions that are uppermost in these bigger hierarchies are called *root* notions and are required to have a primary key. (By their nature, as mentioned above root notions are also top notions.)

In addition to documenting the data, it is also important to track their provenance. For this, the documentation section defines *scopes*. Each notion belongs to a scope, and only data sources with access to that scope can actually instantiate the notion. On first glance this seems to hinder integration, but actually scopes are nested, and it is allowed that a descendant scope instantiates notions from higher-level scopes. Scopes at the lowest level are tied to one of the actual data sources, while the higher-level scopes express semantic similarity.

```
<iddf:documentation>
    <iddf:scope xml:id="tds">
        <iddf:label>Typological Database System</iddf:label>
        <iddf:scope xml:id="pi">
            <iddf:label>Phoneme Inventories</iddf:label>
            <iddf:scope xml:id="upsid" type="datasource">
                <iddf:label
>UCLA Phonological Segment Inventory</iddf:label>
            </iddf:scope>
        </iddf:scope>
    </iddf:scope>
    <iddf:notion xml:id="n1" scope="tds" name="identification"
      type="top">
        <iddf:label>Language identification</iddf:label>
        <iddf:link rel="datcat"
          href="http://www.isocat.org/datcat/DC-3932"/>
        <iddf:notion scope="tds" name="name">
            <iddf:label>Name</iddf:label>
            <iddf:values datatype="FREE"/>
        </iddf:notion>
    </iddf:notion>
    <iddf:notion scope="tds" name="language" type="root">
        <iddf:label>Language</iddf:label>
        <iddf:description
>One of the world's languages</iddf:description>
        <iddf:keys>
            <iddf:key>
                <iddf:literal>l-iso-tba</iddf:literal>
                <iddf:label>Aikan\~a</iddf:label>
            </iddf:key>
        </iddf:keys>
        <iddf:notion ref="n1"/>
    </iddf:notion>
</iddf:documentation>
```

The example above shows an IDDF documentation section. It declares scopes for TDS, phoneme inventories and the UCLA Phonological Segment Inventory Database (UPSID) data source,[4] and the top notion *identification* which is reused by the root notion *language*. The example also hints at

---

some additional features, which help to extend the coverage of the documentation or make explicit the nature of the data:

- labels and descriptions;
- (key) value enumerations, which can be defined as total or partial;
- links from scopes, notions, (key) values or other documentation elements to (online) resources with further information, e.g. a data category specification or website;
- a hierarchy of relation types, which can be instantiated by links;
- a hierarchy of data types to be used by (key) values, which are in general of a semantic nature, e.g. the 'vernacular tier' of a glossed sentence, and can be used to trigger specific data renderers in the user interface;
- annotations, which can be used in the data section, e.g. to mark the confidence level of a data value or add a comment; and
- associated resources, e.g. an ontology or a taxonomy, which can be referred to by links.

Once notions have been declared, the data section is populated with instances of them, as shown below.

```
<iddf:data xmlns:tds=".../tds" xmlns:pi=".../pi"
  xmlns:sylltyp=".../sylltyp" xmlns:upsid=".../upsid">
    <tds:language key="l-iso-tba" iddf:srcs="upsid">
        <tds:identification>
            <tds:name iddf:src="sylltyp">
                <iddf:value ann="v1" src="sylltyp"
>Wari' (Tubar&#227;o)</iddf:value>
                    <iddf:annotation ann="v1" type="marker"
>UNSURE</iddf:annotation>
            </tds:name>
            <tds:name iddf:src="upsid">Huari</tds:name>
        </tds:identification>
    </tds:language>
</iddf:data>
```

Notice that the schema as defined in the documentation section is very loosely interpreted. For example, IDDF has no facilities to declare the cardinality of the notion *name,* and depending on the actual data loaded from the component databases there can be from zero to many instantiations in the data section. In this example there are two names, one ('Wari' (Tubarão)') provided by SyllTyp (Syllable Typology Database) and the other ('Huari') by the UPSID database. The only mandatory information is provenance information and keys for root notions. Some information can be expressed in multiple ways, so a canonical form is defined. This form can be created for any IDDF document and simplifies the development of tools, i.e., the tools can use the canonical path to this information and disregard the alternative paths.

Finally, validation of IDDF documents consists of two phases, implemented with the help of Relax NG, Schematron, NVDL (ISO, 2006b) and XSLT (W3C, 2007):

1. validate the documentation section against the general IDDF RELAX NG + Schematron schema;

2. validate the data section against the document-specific IDDF RELAX NG + Schematron schema created by a transformation to make explicit the schema implied by the documentation section.

The resulting XML-based IDDF provides a rich container for the collected semi-structured data and their documentation. An IDDF document is sufficiently self-describing to support data use and integrity checks, even without the software infrastructure described in this chapter.

In the TDS Curator project the ETL tool chain was left intact, i.e., the tool chain still generates the TDS internal format, with the resulting integrated data source then converted into IDDF.

11.2.2   An IDDF-based Application Programming Interface

The TDS interface is browser-based: the user's web browser interacts via HTTP with the back-end server. The back-end server provides access to IDDF documents, so it is natural to base the client-server interaction, the API, on concepts natural to IDDF. The following methods are provided by the API:

IDDF collection
documents()
    Gets all IDDF documents stored in the system, and their description.
IDDF documentation section
annotation(file, ann)
    Gets the definition of a specific annotation.
annotations(file)
    Gets the definitions of all annotations.
context(file, notion, keys=no, values=no, desc=no)
    Gets the definition of a specific semantic context identified by the top notion.
context-links(file, notion)
    Gets all the semantic contexts that refer to a specific top notion.
datatype(file, datatype)
    Gets the definition of a specific data type.
datatypes(file)
    Gets the definition of all data types.
fulltext-filter(file, notion, text, labels=no)
    Gets matches of the given text within the context of a specific root notion.
fulltext-search(file, text, labels=no)
    Gets notions which match the given text.
key(file, notion, key)
    Gets the definition of a specific key value of a specific notion.
keys(file, notion, random=25)
    Gets the definitions of all key values of a specific notion.
links(file)
    Gets an overview of all links between semantic contexts.
notion(file, notion, keys=no, values=no, desc=no)
    Gets the definition of a specific notion.
relation(file, rel)
    Gets the definition of a specific relation.
relations(file)
    Gets the definition of all relations.
root-links(file, notion)
    Gets the notions that refer to a specific root notion.
roots(file)
    Gets all the root notions.
roots-links(file)
    Get the notions that refer to a root notion.
scope(file, scope)
    Get the definition of a specific scope.

scopes(file)

Get the definition of all scopes.

value(file, notion, value)

Get the definition of a specific value of a specific notion.

values(file, notion, random=25)

Get the definition of all values of a specific notion.

IDDF data section

context-instance(file, id, labels=no, deep=no)

Gets a single instance of a specific top notion.

query(file, query, labels=no, pageSize?, startFrom=1)

Query the data section.

root-instances(file, notion, values=no, labels=no, pageSize?, startFrom=1)

Gets all instances of a specific root notion.

The eXist XML database management system (eXist Solutions, 2016) was selected as back-end technology, and the API was implemented using a mixture of XQuery (W3C, 2010) and XSLT. The API uses a Remote Procedure Call (RPC) approach with a single endpoint, i.e., the actual method invoked is specified as a parameter. For example, the first API method is invoked as follows:

```
tds.dans.knaw.nl/tds-services.xql?service=documents
```

11.2.3   A New Web User Interface

The old TDS web interface was deeply intertwined with the old TDS API, so a new web interface was implemented for the new, IDDF-based TDS API. Since HTML5 was still under development and its support in browsers was still immature in 2010, Adobe Flash was selected for the implementation of this front end.[5]

In this new interface, user interaction starts with the selection of an IDDF document to inspect. For inspection, there are two major options: explore the instances using the language browser (see Figure 11.4), or build and execute a query. The query interface follows the three-stage model that the old interface also used:

1. exploration of the notions to find the ones which can help answering the user's question;

2. formulation of the actual query by specifying selection and projection criteria; and

3. execution of the query, followed by the display and inspection of the results.

The new interface lacks some of the more advanced features of the old web interface, e.g. geographical views of result sets and joins between different entity types (roots). This is due to a combination of limited development resources and a desire to avoid features that are particularly likely to stop working over time because of reliance on volatile browser technology or third-party services. Unfortunately, support for Adobe Flash as a client-side technology is also diminishing in favour of HTML5, and there is a possibility the former might disappear soon. But, while the web client may already be approaching the beginning of obsolescence, the clean IDDF-based API created in the TDS Curator project ensures that the server side is isolated, and that less work will be needed when the time comes to create the next, HTML5-based, web interface. However, even when based on HTML5 a state-of-the-art interface also depends on the interactivity provided by JavaScript; and this area is still ridden by browser differences, although less so than in the

---

[5] The Meertens Institute, the project partner who developed the new frontend, has extensive experience with Adobe Flash

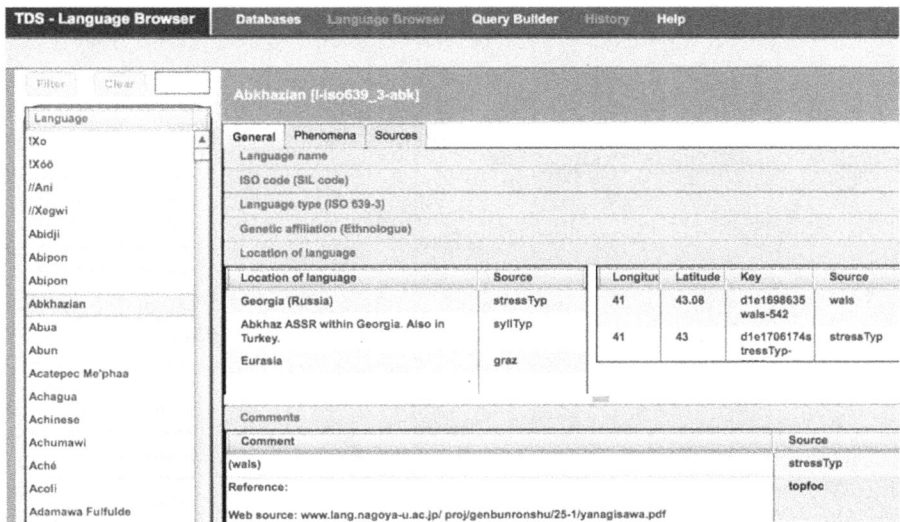

Figure 11.4: The TDS language browser (tds2.dans.knaw.nl).

times of the first TDS interface. Overcoming these differences is hardly achievable for a small-scale development team, so one has to rely on major frameworks. However, the availability and persistence of these frameworks is still largely ruled by hypes, i.e., it remains a challenging problem to select a technology/framework with a long-term horizon.

The approach of the TDS Curator project was to design a generic back-end data structure and API, so that an economy of scale can eventually be achieved through reuse of these components for other resources. Even if changes in browser technology outstrip resources for keeping the TDS web service in operation, the self-documenting format of the IDDF at least preserves and makes available the accumulated data in static, portable form.

11.3   Conclusion

CLARIN-NL's TDS Curator project provided crucial support for the sustainability of this data source. The collected data of the TDS have been safely archived at DANS as a single, integrated IDDF document and in the form of a separate IDDF document for each database. The IDDF-based web service is operational, making it possible to browse and query these documents interactively for the medium-term. Unfortunately the fast cycles of appearance and disappearance of client-side technology are already catching up with the new interface, so that a more sustainable solution is still needed in this area.

In CLARIAH, the successor to the CLARIN-NL project, work is planned to integrate new component databases into the TDS. This will likely involve curation of the tools used in the ETL phase. Work on the web interface is not yet foreseen in CLARIAH.

Another interesting direction for the TDS data is the Linked Data approach. The steadily growing Linguistic Linked Open Data (LLOD) cloud (Chiarcos, Hellmann, Nordhoff et al., 2012; LIDERproject, 2016) already contains many valuable linguistic resources, and the TDS would add typological knowledge to it. While the original TDS project predated the rise of Linked Data technologies, the use of semantic contexts in IDDF resembles the use of components in the Component Metadata Data Infrastructure (CMDI; Broeder, Windhouwer, Van Uytvanck et al., 2012) as used by CLARIN. A successful mapping of CMDI to Linked Data has already been created (see chapter 8), and the patterns learned can most likely be used to map IDDF to Linked Data.

Acknowledgements

The CLARIN-NL TDS Curator project was a collaboration between the University of Utrecht, DANS, the Meertens Institute and the Max Planck Institute for Psycholinguistics. The authors would like to thank these partner institutions and especially their colleagues: Marjan Grootveld, Marc Kemps-Snijders and Rob Zeeman.

References

D. Broeder, M. Windhouwer, D. Van Uytvanck T. Goosen and T. Trippel (2012). CMDI: a Component Metadata Infrastructure. In the *Proceedings of the Metadata 2012 Workshop on Describing Language Resources with Metadata: Towards Flexibility and Interoperability in the Documentation of Language Resources*. LREC 2012 Istanbul, Turkey, May 22, 2012.

C. Chiarcos, S. Hellmann, S. Nordhoff, S. Moran, R. Littauer, J. Eckle-Kohler, I. Gurevych, S. Hartmann, M. Matuschek and C.M. Meyer (2012). *The Open Linguistics Working Group*. LREC 2012. Istanbul, Turkey, May 23-25, 2012.

W. Croft (2003). *Typology and Universals*, 2nd edition. Cambridge University Press, 2003

A. Dimitriadis, M. Windhouwer, A. Saulwick, R. Goedemans and T. Bíró (2009). How to integrate databases without starting a typology war: The Typological Database System. In S. Musgrave, M. Everaert and A. Dimitriadis (eds), *The Use of Databases in Cross-Linguistic Studies*. Mouton de Gruyter, March 2009.

G. van Emde Boas and S. Ilinsky (2009). *Backbase 4 RIA Development*. Packt Publishing, 2009.

eXist Solutions (2016). *eXistdb - The Open Source Native XML Database*. exist-db.org. Accessed on June 15, 2016.

International Organization for Standardization (ISO, 2006a). *Information technology — Document Schema Definition Language (DSDL) — Part 3: Rule-based validation — Schematron*. ISO/IEC 19757-3. Geneva, June 1, 2006.

International Organization for Standardization (ISO, 2006b). *Information technology — Document Schema Definition Language (DSDL) — Part 4: Namespace-based Validation Dispatching Language (NVDL)*. ISO/IEC 19757-4. Geneva, June 1, 2006.

International Organization for Standardization (ISO, 2008). *Information technology — Document Schema Definition Language (DSDL) — Part 2: Regular-grammar-based validation — RELAX NG*. ISO/IEC 19757-2. Geneva, December 15, 2008.

LIDER project (2016). *Linguistic Linked Open Data*, linguistic-lod.org. Accessed on January 18, 2016.

M. Windhouwer and A. Dimitriadis (2008). Sustainable operability: Keeping complex resources alive. In A. Witt, G. Rehm, T. Schmidt, K. Choukri and L. Burnard (eds), Proceedings of the LREC 2008 Workshop *Sustainability of Language Resources and Tools for Natural Language Processing* (SustainableNLP08). Marrakech, Morocco, May 31, 2008.

World Wide Web Consortium (W3C, 2007). M. Kay (ed), *XSL Transformations (XSLT) Version 2.0*. January 23, 2007.

World Wide Web Consortium (W3C, 2010). S. Boag, D. Chamberlin, M.F. Fernández, D. Florescu, J. Robie and J. Siméon (eds), *XQuery 1.0: An XML Query Language (Second Edition)*. December 14, 2010.

World Wide Web Consortium (W3C, 2016a). *Web Ontology* Language (OWL) w3.org/OWL. Accessed on June 15, 2016.

World Wide Web Consortium (W3C, 2016b), *SKOS Simple Knowledge Organization System*. w3.org/skos. Accessed on June 15, 2016.

CHAPTER 12

Variation in Preposition Use in the Virgin Islands Dutch Creole (VIDC) Cluster

Pieter Muysken, Cefas van Rossem and Robbert van Sluijs

Centre for Language Studies, Radboud Universiteit
Corresponding author: p.muysken@let.ru.nl

ABSTRACT

There is a growing consensus that the varieties of Virgin Islands Dutch Creole (VIDC) - often referred to as Negerhollands - should not be viewed as a single language, but rather as a language cluster of related varieties. However, there has been only limited systematic comparison of the varieties in the cluster as to their structural characteristics. We will try to fill this gap in this chapter by charting a specific construction: the supra-locative prepositional phrases in two varieties of VIDC: the 20th century data recorded by Josselin de Jong and the variety in the 18th century religious texts. A systematic search in the VIDC data is possible because of the data base constructed for this language with the support of Clarin-NL. We will try to contrast the feature studied with those found in 17th century Dutch informal writings and in two relevant West-African languages: Akan and Ewegbe. The theoretical model used here derives from the notion of feature pool.

12.1 Introduction

There is a growing consensus that the varieties of Virgin Islands Dutch Creole (VIDC) - often referred to as Negerhollands - should not be viewed as a single language, but rather as a language cluster of related varieties (Muysken 1995; Van Rossem and Van der Voort 1996; Sabino 2012; see also Van Sluijs et al., 2016), which also show considerable internal variation (Van Sluijs 2016). However, there has been only limited systematic comparison of the varieties in the cluster as to their structural characteristics. Building in part on Bakker (2014), we will try to fill this gap in this chapter by charting a specific construction: the supra-locative prepositional phrase of the type *((n)a)bo(no)* 'on' in two varieties of VIDC: the 20th century data recorded by Josselin de Jong (1926), and the

How to cite this book chapter:
Muysken, P, van Rossem, C and van Sluijs, R. 2017. Variation in Preposition Use in the Virgin Islands Dutch Creole (VIDC) Cluster. In: Odijk, J and van Hessen, A. (eds.) *CLARIN in the Low Countries*, Pp. 133–149. London: Ubiquity Press. DOI: https://doi.org/10.5334/bbi.12. License: CC-BY 4.0

variety in the 18th century religious texts. A systematic search in the VIDC data is possible because of the NEHOL data base constructed for this language with the support of Clarin-NL. We will try to contrast the feature studied with those found in 17th century Dutch informal writings and in two relevant West-African languages: Akan and Ewegbe.

The theoretical framework adopted here involves the notion of 'feature pool' (Mufwene 2001). In this framework, creole languages are constructed out of a number of possible features and elements available in the multilingual speech community in which the creole emerged: the so-called feature pool. This framework is interesting for us because the VIDC cluster contains 'layers', corresponding to the various lects in the complex early community and to the various 'authors' of texts. Regarding the variable involved here there exist:

(a)   a 'Dutch' layer of simple prepositions, including *op* 'on' and *boven* 'above';

(b)   an 'Atlantic creole' layer including the general locative preposition *na*;

(c)   West-African substrate patterns which include [NP + LOCATION] and [LOC + NP + LOCATION].

In the extant corpus these layers compete, and have a variable distribution.

In section 12.2 we briefly mention some points in the history of VIDC and briefly discuss the sources. Section 12.3 focuses on the variable: prepositions in VIDC. In section 12.4 Atlantic *na* and possible substrate influence is discussed, and in section 12.5 relevant preposition use in 17th century Dutch. Sections 12.6 and 12.7 present the findings for 18th and 20th century VIDC, followed by some discussion, conclusions and suggestions in section 12.8.

12.2   VIDC: History and Sources

Here we briefly mention some points in the history of VIDC, referring the reader to Van Sluijs (2016) and Van Rossem (2017) for further detail.

12.2.1   History

While St. Thomas was probably inhabited by Arawakan groups since 300 BC, in 1672 the first European settlers arrived at what then became the Danish Antilles. However, many settlers did not come from Denmark, and particularly settlers from Zealand and Flanders were dominant in the new colony, which soon became a plantation colony. In 1673 enslaved Africans started being imported, particularly from Ghana. Around 1700 there must have been a nascent Creole language with Flemish and Zealandic as the main lexifier varieties. Caribbean Dutch functioned as a lingua franca in the colony, and the Moravian missionary community started using the creole. In fact, in 1736 there is the first mention in any Caribbean source of the term *Carriolsche* 'Creole' for the language, as we find the first intentions use VIDC as a missionary language. The language flourished throughout the colony through much of the 18th century, but by 1843 English Creole has largely replaced VIDC.

12.2.2   Documentation and Sources

There is a rich array of 18th century sources, which require, however, considerable philological interpretation (Van Rossem 2017). In 1742 the first printed texts appeared on the island with traces of VIDC, and from that year until 1843 there has been a steady stream of missionary translations into VIDC by the Moravian Brethren and the Danish Lutheran Church. There are also letters of enslaved Africans from the early period, partly in Dutch, partly in VIDC. The first printed grammar of any creole language is also about VIDC and dates from 1770, by J.M. Magens. Oldendorp's (1777) manuscript grammar dates from 1770 as well, and was first printed in a shorter version (the complete version appeared as Oldendorp 2000: 681–724). His dictionary is from 1767/68 (Stein 1996). An anonymous grammar written by Moravian Brethren at the beginning of the 19th century was used by Hesseling (1905). Internationally, VIDC started being studied in 1805 when the historical linguist Rask made a typological comparison of Greenland Inuit and VIDC. In 1871 Van Name compared VIDC to other Caribbean creoles and in 1881/1887 Pontoppidan published his contributions. Hesseling published his anthology of historical sources and 18th century texts in 1905, and in 1922–1923 De Josselin de Jong carried out fieldwork among speakers of whom he thought would be the last ones. However in 1936 Nelson unexpectedly had the opportunity to still compile a word list after interviewing speakers of Dutch Creole, which was used by Reinecke (1937).

In the 1960–80s fragments of the language as remembered by the last speakers were recorded by Sprauve (1976), Adams Graves (1977), and Sabino (1990). The demise of Alice Stevens in 1987 marked the end of the spoken language.

Starting around 1980 and until now 2015, a group initially inspired by the work of Peter Stein and later involving Hans den Besten and Pieter Muysken (who together supervised Hein van der Voort and Cefas van Rossem) started exploring the missionary archives. This led to various book publications (e.g. van der Voort and van Rossem 1996; Stein and van der Voort (1996), and much of the digitalized material was made available electronically via the NEHOL database with the financial and technical support of Clarin-NL through the work of Robbert van Sluijs.

The eighteenth century VIDC texts that were used are given in Table 12.1.

For 17th and 18th century Dutch we used the intercepted letters in Dutch written by seamen and colonists in the 17th and 18th centuries and kept in British National Archives in Kew Gardens

Text	Date	Clarin	Characteristics
Zinzendorf Farewell Letter	1739, 1742	3.1.1	First known text written in VIDC, translation of
Gebeden en Liederen voor die swart Broeder-Gemeenten na S. Thomas, S. Croix en S. Jan.	1765	HERRN65A	First printed hymnbook in VIDC by the Moravian Brethren
Gospel Harmony 321	Around 1773, before 1780	3.2.1_1_35	First 35 sections of translation of S. Lieberkühn's Gospel Harmony by Moravian missionary J. Böhner
Gospel Harmony 322	Around 1780	3.2.1_1_35	First 35 sections of second translation of Gospel Harmony by J. Böhner
Gospel Harmony 3231	Around 1790	3231_1_35	First 35 sections of Gospel Harmony, edited and written by J.C. Auerbach
Gospel Harmony 3232	Around 1795	3232_1_35	First 35 sections of Gospel Harmony, Unfinished manuscript, probably used for printed Gospel Harmony (1833)
Old Testament	Between 1780 and 1785	325	Translation of the Old Testament into VIDC

Table 12.1: 18th century sources used for VIDC.

(Rutten and Van der Wal 2014). For 20th century VIDC we used the recorded fieldwork stories of Jossselin de Jong (1926)

12.3   Prepositions in VIDC

Since this chapter focuses on locative prepositions, we provide some general remarks on locative prepositions and some background information on prepositions in VIDC.

12.3.1   Prepositions in Creoles: Analytical Framework

Following Vandeloise (1991, 1994) and Zribi-Hertz (1984), Zribi-Hertz and Loïc (2015) distinguish +/- configurational locatives to distinguish *à la maison* 'at home' from *dans la maison* 'in the house' in French. Both imply location, but only the second implies configurational location.

A further distinction is between +/- functional locatives (a slightly different distinction is made by Zwarts 1997): I can go to the bank functionally, for typical banking things (e.g. to cash a check) or purely physically, to get nearer a specific building. Functional locatives are typically not configurational. Consider 'I am going home' versus 'I am going to my house'

In this chapter we focus on both configurational, and non-configurational non-functional locative prepositions in VIDC.

12.3.2   Non-locative Prepositions

There are a number of prepositions in VIDC, of which most have Dutch etyma (sometimes homophonous with an English source), with the exception of *te:*, most likely from Portuguese, listed in Table 12.2.

The most striking absent Dutch prepositions, at least in the 20th century materials, are *aan*, which is dative ('to') and sometimes locative ('near') in Dutch, and Dutch *te* 'at'/*tot* 'until'. There are sporadic uses of *aan* in the 18th century missionary texts:

(01) zoo als Hem ha   dot voor yoe **aan** het   Kruis (311)
      like   3SG PST   die for 2SG at   DET.N cross
      'Like He dies for you at the cross.'

(02) En   as   JESus a   wande na <↑die> Galile **aan** Zeekant (321: 23)[1]
      and when Jesus PST walk   LOC DET   Galilea at   sea.side
      'and when Jesus walked near Galilea at the sea side'

However, it is clear in (01) from the use of a non-VIDC neuter determiner that this is a fixed Dutch expression. For (02) the other translations of the same sentence do not have *aan*.[2]

astər/-u	after	< Du achter, E after
fa(n)	of	< Du van
fo	for	< Du voor
gliek, liek	like	< Du gelijk, E like
mi/me:/met	with	< Du met
sondər/-du	without	< Du zonder
te:	until	< Po até

Table 12.2: Non-locative prepositions in 20th century VIDC.

---

[1] For the notational conventions in the examples, see Van Rossem and Van der Voort (1996: XII–XIII).
[2] [322: 23: En as Jesus a wandel **na kant van** die Galilean Zee], [3231: 23: Toen noe Jesus a wandel **bij** die See van Galilea].

12.3.3   Locative Prepositions Without na

A number of locative prepositions, all with Dutch etyma, are formed without *na* in the 20th materials, as listed in Table 12.3.

Some of them, *kan* and *mel/midəl*, correspond to a noun in Dutch. In the 18th century materials, these are combined with *na* and take the preposition *van* 'of', which is a clear indication of their nominal status at the time:

(03)   En   as   Jesus a   wandel **na**   **kant** van   die   Ga=lilean Zee (322: 23)
  and when Jesus PST walk LOC side of   DET Galilean   sea
  'and when Jesus walked at the side of the Galilean sea'

(04)   Em set nabin die   Tempel **na**   **mid=del** van die   Leerar-s   (322: 9)[3]
  3SG sit inside DET Temple LOC midst   of   DET teacher-PL
  'He sits inside the temple in the middle of the teachers.'

12.3.4   Locative Prepositions with na

Finally, there is a class of prepositions that involve the non-configurational locative *na*, which is often claimed to have a Portuguese etymon, the pro-clitic combination *em+a* 'in+DET.F'. Configurational locatives are formed combining this *na* (which can be reduced to *a* or omitted altogether) with a Dutch-etymon preposition, which is generally bisyllabic. See Table 12.4.

In this chapter we will focus exclusively on all forms related to *((n)a)bo(no)* 'on', from this list.

bi	near	< Du bij
de:	through	< Du door
ini	in	< Du in
it (fa)	out of	< Du uit (van)
kan	near, next to	< Du kant 'side'
mel/midəl	in the middle of	< Du middle 'middle'
ron	around	< Du rond

Table 12.3: Locative prepositions without *na*.

na	locative	< ? Po na 'in.DET.F'
((n)a)astə/-u	behind	< Du achter, E after
((n)a)bini	into, inside	< Du binnen
((n)a)biti	outside	< Du buiten
((n)a)bo(no)	on	< Du boven
afo (fa(n))	in front of	< na + Du voor
((n)a) molee	below	< Du omlaag (dialectal)
((n)a)obu	onto, over	< Du over
((n)a)ondə/-u	under	< Du onder

Table 12.4: Locative prepositions with *na*.

---

3   See also [3231: 28 a gooi em **na Meddel** onder sender], where the locative noun is followed by the preposition *onder*, resulting in 'in the midst among them'.

12.4   Atlantic *na* and Possible Substrate Influence

12.4.1   Atlantic na

As shown in (Boretzky 1983: 195) and further argued in detail in Corum (2015), there was a widely used Atlantic creole general locative preposition *na* in use. We find it in Portuguese lexifier creoles such as Principe and Guinée-Bissau, in Papiamentu, in the Surinamese creole cluster, as well as in VIDC. In Haitian, there is a form *nã*, but this may be derived from French *dans* [dã] 'in'. Very likely, the form was part of a number of the pidgins that were used in the Atlantic slave trade.

In the Surinam creole cluster and in VIDC this *na* may be combined with a locative element, as noted above, to mark a configurational locative. This possibility is absent in Papiamentu and in Haitian. However, the location of the locative element varies. It can be post-noun phrase, resulting in [na + NP + X], in Saramaccan and optionally in early Sranan, and pre-noun phrase, resulting in [na + X + NP] both in earlier and later Sranan and in all varieties of VIDC.

12.4.2   Gbe

Gbe adpositional phrases are head-initial, with prepositions preceding their complement (Aboh 2010: 227; see also Ameka 2003)). Aboh assumes a simple structure as in (05b):

(05)   a.   *Kòfi   zé   kwié   xlán   Àsíb*
          Kofi   take-PERF   money   to   Asib

          'Kofi sent money to Asiba'

        b.   [PP [P **xlán**] [DP Àsíbá]]

While prepositions have a verbal origin, the class of locative postpositions has a nominal origin. In inland dialects the possessive marker *fé* is required with them, but in coastal dialects this is absent. Thus the overall pattern is illustrated in (06):

(06)   Akaɖí   le   kpl~ɔ-a   (fé)   ta.me
        lamp   be_at.PRES   table-DEF   (POSS)   above

        'The lamp is above the table.' (Ameka and Essegbey, 2006: 363).

12.4.3   Akan

In Akan the locative preposition (07b) also functions as a locative verb (07a):

(07)   a.   ɔ-wɔ   Eugene
          3sg-be.at   Eugene

          'He is in Eugene.'

        b.   o   hun   no   wɔ   Eugene
          ipl see   3pl   in   Eugene

          'We saw them in Eugene.' (Payne 1997: 87)

As a preposition, it cannot receive person marking.
In addition, there are postpositions to mark a specific configurational location:

(08)   Ntoma   no   sɛn   ahoma   no   **so**
        Cloth   DET   hang   rope   DET   TOP

        'The cloth is/hangs on the clothes line.' (Ofori 2006: 156)

(09) ɛdua   no   si asoredan   no   ho
      tree   DET   sit church.house   DET   SIDE

'The tree is planted by the chapel.' (Owusu et al. 2015: 181)

12.5   Dutch (17/18th c): Letters

We will briefly mention a few aspects of locative preposition usage in Dutch, drawing on the corpus of captured letters.

12.5.1   The Dutch System

The Dutch adpositional system is far too complicated to describe here in any detail. There are at least three categories of elements involved:

- pre- or postpositions (where the latter are often directional in modern Dutch)
- adverbs, which are often morphologically complex (at least diachronically) and contain a *be-* prefix and an *–en* suffix.
- particles of the verb, which can be separated from it as the verb appears in second position

Some examples are given in Table 12.5.

Particles will not be discussed further here (but see Muysken, van der Sluijs and Los, 2017). The adverbs may also be used prepositionally in modern Dutch, as well as functioning as free standing elements.

12.5.2   Naar Boven in 18th Century Dutch

One possibility is that *naar boven* in 18th century Dutch was a model for *na bobo*. It is often used directionally, as in (10) or translocationally, as in (11).

(10) zo dat   wij (…)   genootzaakt   waaren   **na boven**   te   gaan.
      so that we   forced   were   to   go

      'so that we (…) were forced to go upstairs. (to the deck)'
                      (Cape of Good Hope, May 31, 1781) NAAR + BOVEN: 'upstairs'

(11) ons   leger met   den   Prins van orangie (…)   is   **naer boven** int
      our   army with   the   Prince of Orange   is   to above   in.the

      Lant van   keulen om   de   france   daer te doen *ver*huijsen
      Land of   Cologne for the French   there to make move

      'Our army with the Prince of Orange (…) is up in the country of Cologne to make the French move there.' (Hoorn, November 30, 1672)

Pre/postposition	adverb	particle
op/over 'on'	boven 'above'	op-bellen 'phone'
uit 'out'	buiten 'outside'	uit-steken 'stick out'
in 'in'	binnen 'inside'	in-kopen 'to shop'
	beneden 'beneath'	ne(d)er 'down'

Table 12.5: Simplified schematic overview of the Dutch adposition system.

12.5.3   The Preposition op in 18th Century Dutch

The preposition *op* 'on' is frequently used, and may be a very general locative, as in the following two examples:

(12)   Sr. Pieter   Cnoll   Coopman   woonende   in   het
       Sr. P.   C.   merchant   residing   in   the

       Fort **op**   Batavia.
       Fort on   Batavia (Hoorn, 1672)

       'Mr. Pieter Cnoll merchant residing in the Fort in Batavia.'

(13)   Wiens   vader   predicant   is   in   den   classis   van
       whose   father preacher   is   in   the   classis   from

       Alckmaer   tot   Egmont   **op**   zee
       Alkmaar   to   Egmont   on   see   (Hoorn, 1672)

       'whose father is a preacher in the church region from Alkmaar to Egmont aan Zee.'

12.6   VIDC (18th c)

12.6.1   The Earliest Sources

In the materials of Von Zinzendorf (1739) we find standard Dutch examples such as (14), where *boven* is nominal:

(14)   God zegen all met segen van **boven**
       'God bless all with blessing from above.'

However, there are also some much more creole-like data. In the following *na* co-occurs with *op* in the same sentence, recalling the generalized *op* in the 18th century letters:

(15)   Die tyd   mi   a   wes   **na**   Poppo   **op**   Africa
       then   1SG PST   be   LOC   Poppo   on   Africa

       'Then I was in Poppo in Africa.'

In the first printed translation of the VIDC hymns (1765) we find the complex preposition that later became common. Notice this does not mean 'above of' here, but 'on'.

(16)   Mee   joe   Sabbath   **na bovo**   die   Stoel   van   joe   Vader,
       with 2SG   Sabbath   LOC-ABOVE DET   chair of   2SG   Father

       'With/and your Sabbath on the Chair of your Father'

However, we also find the simplex preposition *boven*:

(17)   Noe   Joe   God   **bove**   allemaal, geloofd   **na**   Eewigheid!
       now   2SG   God   above   all   praised   LOC   eternity

       'Now you(r) God above all, praised in eternity!'

12.6.2   VIDC: First Translation of Gospel Harmony (Before 1780)

In the first translation of the Gospel Harmony (around 1773, before 1780) we find productive use of the complex preposition, sometimes used adverbially as a directional, as in (18), sometimes as a true preposition, as in (19) and (20).

(18)   Sender   a   loop   **na-boven**   **na**   Jerusalem
       3PL   PST   go   LOC-above   naar/LOC   Jerusalem

'They went up to Jerusalem.'   German source: *hinauf*

(19)   Ons   Tata   sender   a   ka   bed.aan   **na-boven**   deese   Berg
       1PL   father   3PL   PST   PRF   worship   LOC-above   this   mountain

'Our fathers had worshipped on this mountain.'   German source: *auf*

(20)   maar   a   wees   alltid   Dag   en   Nacht   **na-bovo**   die   Ber=g-en
       but   PST   be   always   day   and night   LOC-above   DET   mountain-PL

'but … was always day and night on the mountains.'

12.6.3   VIDC 18th: op

However, the translations also contain cases of the more Dutch-like preposition *op*. In (21) and (22) it could be part of a fixed Dutch expression:

(21)   Vor   set   ons   Voet[-*t*]   sender   **op**   die   Pad   van   Vrede (321: 5)
       for   put   1PL   foot   3PL   on   DET   path   of   peace

'to put our feet on the path of peace'

(22)   eer   die   Mensch   Soon   sal   sitt   **op**   die   Troon (322: 81)
       before   DET   man   son   FUT   sit   on   DET   throne

'before the Son of Man shall sit on the Throne'

However, in (23) there is an apparent contrast between *op*, which is supra-locative, and the more general locative *na*:

(23)   die   a   see: **Op**   die   Berg-en   (na   Rama)
       DET   PST   say   on   DET   mountain-s   LOC Rama

'He said: in the mountains at Rama.'

In some cases, there appears to be use of *op* as a calque on the German original *auf* in a translation:

(24)   die   a   wees   duis=ter   **op**   die   Afgrond. (325a: 1)
       3SG   PST   COP   dark   on   DET   abyss

'There was darkness above/in the abyss.'   (Finster auf der Tiefe, Luther 1912)

12.6.4   Variation in 18th Century Use of Naboven

There appears to be variation in the use of *naboven* in the 18th century materials. The manuscript for the translation of the Old Testament (325, Job 20: 11), presented alternatives:

(25)   En   leei   met   em   {op|naboven}   die   Stof.
       and   lay   with 3sg   on|LOC.above   DET   dust

'and lay with him on the dust.'

The variation is of two kinds: variation in the forms encountered, and variation in the meaning of the expression. In the Gospel Harmony manuscripts 321 and 322 we find *naboven, na boven, nabovo, na bovo*, and in 3231 and 3232 *naboven* with the alternatives *boven, boven op*.

12.6.5   The Adverb/Preposition Boven in Later Texts

In later texts we also find the use of bare *boven*, possibly under English influence:

(26) Wat   ben   **boven** die,   dat ben van   die   Quaat
      what COP   above   that, that COP from/of DET Evil   (321: 25)

'What is above of it, is from the Evil' (English Gospel Harmony, Lieberkühn 1771: 'cometh of Evil')

(27) Die   Jünger   no\ben   **boven** si   Baas
      DET   disciple NEG\COP   above   3.POSS master (321: 25)

'The disciple is not above his master' (English Gospel Harmony 1771)

(28) en   a   staan **boven** **over** die   Plaats
      and   PST stand above   over   DET   place

'and stood above of the place'   (3231: 7)
(English Gospel Harmony 1771: 'stood over where (…)')

12.6.6   Distribution in Texts in the 18th Century Materials

The distribution of the locative prepositions is presented in Table 12.6.

It is striking that in these materials the most frequent locative marker, by far, is *op*, both locational and directional. The combination *na-boven* and its variants is relatively infrequent, though more frequent in the earlier than in the later translations. Bare *boven* is not frequent, and is sometimes used adverbially. *Bovenop* always has a clear supra-locative interpretation in these materials.

It should be borne in mind that the general locative creole preposition *na* is much more frequent than these alternatives, as shown in Table 12.7:

	locational	*directional*	*adverbial*	*locational*	*directional*	*adverbial*
Before 1780	321			322		
boven	4	-	2	1	-	2
op	21	12	-	23	5	-
bovenop	1	2	-	0	1	-
na bovo, naboven	3	3	-	7	4	-
1790–95	3231			3232		
boven	2	-	2	3	-	4
op	26	9	-	27	10	-
bovenop	2	-	-	2	1	-
na bovo, naboven	1	2	-	2	3	-

Table 12.6: The distribution of the locative prepositions in the 18th century materials.

	All *na*	**#*na*#[4]**	**#*na*# LOC**	**#*na*# DIR**
321 (before 1780)	940	511	109	79
3232 (about 1795)	972	558	34	68

Table 12.7: The occurrence of locative *na* in some of the 18th century materials.

---

4 The # mark spaces is the original manuscript.

The preposition *na* can be both locational and directional. In 3232 locative *na* is often replaced by *in* 'in' or *op* 'on'. The use of *na* should be studied separately because of its multifunctional use and high frequency.

12.6.7   Alternatives in the Texts Used

As pointed out in Van Rossem (2017), an interesting perspective on preposition choice in the 18th century texts is gained from the practice of providing several alternatives, reflecting the struggle of the translators in choosing between different varieties, vernacular creole or more standard, and remaining faithful to the original text. An example is the following:

(29) mi   Tegenparteyder fonk   met s*i*   Oogo {na|op} mi. (325c: Job 16)
      1SG opponent   sparkle with 3SG.POS eye   LOC   1SG

'My adversary sparkles with his eyes upon me.'
(Luther 1912: funkelt mit seinen Augen **auf** mich)

Here the German original has *auf* and the translator is choosing between *op* and *na*[5]

Alternatives found are listed below. All appear only once in the entire Clarin-NEHOL Corpus, unless otherwise indicated.

op|met   op|na
na|op [6]   op|naboven
over|boven   tot|op
op|over   van|op
op|voor [2]   op|van

The preposition *op* is often replaced by *na*, but also by many other prepositions, suggesting its widespread as an all purpose oblique in at least some varieties of 18th century VIDC.

12.7   The 20th Century VIDC Materials

12.7.1   General Overview

The main form in the texts collected by de Josselin de Jong (1926) (although there is considerable variation in the form) is supra-locative preposition(s) *((n)a)bo(no)*, besides the extremely frequent general locative and directional *na*, of course. An example:

(30) mi   ki   ju sit **abo** də stul nou
      1SG see 2SG sit on   DET chair now

'I see you sitting on the chair now.'   (dJdJ 1926:67, Roberts)

Thus we find the following forms, as listed in Table 12.8
In Nelson (1936) only *bo* is found.[6]
There does not appear to be any functional specialization of any of these prepositional form variants. The main contrast with forms with or without preceding *(n)a* (*a* has developed out of *na*)

---

[5] Other examples are 321: 45: JESus a wees alleenig op die Land, en no a ka kom tot sender (na|op die Bood.)] [321: h.3: En Petrus a kik sterk op em met Johannes, en a see: Kik /op|na/ ons.] [325c: 67: En si Gebeenden moet betaal si verborgen S*....* en leei met em {op|naboven} die Stof, where Luther has: und sie werden sich mit ihm **in** die Erde legen.

[6] Den Besten and Van Rossem (2013): 15: *on - bo*, 909: Put something on the table[.+]< /> - Du *th'got bo th' tafl.*, 1127: Wipe your feet on the mat. – *Fek yo fot bo di mat.*, 1129: The fowl (hen) is there on the roof of the house. – *Di hundu bin da bo di hus.*, 1130: It has flown upon the house. –*Ka flik bo di hus*

bo/bu	142	bono	1
abo	8	nabono	5
nabo	2		

Table 12.8: Morpho-phonological variants of *na bono* in the 20th century materials.

is with *na > a. The preposition [a] marks location in a broad sense, and goal in a broad sense, [bo] marks supralocation.[7] A further indication that there is no functional specialization of individual form variants is the finding that they alternate in a wide variety of contexts, including cases where they co-occur idiomatically with specific predicates, such as *wak* 'wait':

(31) bli   da   staan werán lo   wak **bo** Bru   Hon
     stay there stand again IPFV wait on brother dog
     '[he] stopped there again, waiting for Brother Dog'
                                      (dJdJ 1926:51, Roberts) (cf. Du wachten <u>op</u>)

(32) ju   kaa listáá mi   lo   wak **nabono** ju
     2SG PRF let   1SG IPFV wait on   2SG
     'You have kept me waiting for you.'
                                      (dJdJ 1926:25, Prince)

Rather, there is individual variation, since Prince is the only one of De Josselin de Jong's nine informants to use *nabono* and uses it wherever others use *(a)bo*

The items *op* (< Du op) and *abobo* (< Du boven) occur as adverbs as well. Furthermore, *op* can occur as a particle, so that we can double *op*:

(33) Di   kabái a   lep **op op** a   himúl.   *Motion*
     DET horse PST leap up up LOC sky
     'The horse leapt up towards the sky.'   (dJdJ 1926:15, Joshua)

(34) jaa, ju   kaa ho,   wa   də here **abobo** kaa see: *Motion/location*
     yes 2SG PRF hear what DET lord above PRF say
     'Yes, you heard, what the Lord above said'   (dJdJ 1926:52, Roberts)

Note that the two are different in meaning *Op* is always upwards motion/direction; *abobo* can be used for both.

As noted, *op* often occurs as a verb particle, in the case of *dink op* 'remember', 'think of', *op* has fused with the verb and phonologically eroded; but also newly replaced by *bo* 'on':[8]

(35) Ham see, am   nə   kam **dingkóó**.
     3SG   say 3SG NEG can remember
     'He said, he could not remember.'   (dJdJ 1926:18)

(36) di   frou parat a   fraa di   man as am nu kan
     DET woman parrot PST ask DET man if 3SG NEG can
     ding bo weni
     think on when

---

7   Den Besten (letter den Besten, 2 November 1993, see also Den Besten and Van Rossem 2013): "Isabella Sylvester's *bo* in the sense of 'on (the roof of)' and 'upon' in two sentences said by her, however , most probably does not reflect Danish *paa* (*på*). It derives from Dutch *boven* via Creole Dutch *abo/abobo/nabobo*, which consists of the all-purpose locative preposition *na* and *bobo* (from Du. *boven*)."

8   In the 18th century materials *we find dink op na* or *dink op*: [321: 5: en vor dink na si heilig Verbond], [322: 5: en dink op na si heilig Verbond], [3232: 5: en a dink op na Si heilig Verbond].

'The female parrot asked the male one if he could not think of/remember when… '
(dJdJ 1926:41)

12.7.2 Expression of Source:

While the element *na* has many locative uses, it cannot be used as an expression of source by itself. By contrast *fa(n)* can:

(37) Ju   fo   bli   een jaa mi ons fo   ju   nee am<u>fa</u> ons
    2SG   mod   stay   one year with 1PL before 2SG   take 3SG   of   1PL

You must stay with us for one year before you take her from us.'
(dJdJ 1926:14, Joshua)

The combination *fa bo* can mark supralocational source:

(38) Aⁿ   no   kan   kri   di   jung <u>fa boo</u> shi   rigí.
    3SG   NEG   mod   getDET boy   of   on   3s.poss back

'It [a horse] couldn't get the boy from his back.' (dJdJ 1926:15, Joshua)

Finally, there also be an elative meaning added in *(it) fa bo*:

(39) Fo   ma   se   paséé di   wurum kri teki   sinpiwiri,
    COMPL make say   pass DET   worm   get piece aloe.vera

    shini di   hopo a   twee, krou alma di   grun slim it   <u>fa bo</u> di.
    cut   3.INAN open LOC two   scratch all   DET   green slime out of on 3.INAN

'To make the worms go away, get a piece of aloe vera, cut it open in two, scratch all the green slime out of it.'   (dJdJ 1926:66)

12.7.3 Distribution in Texts in the 20th Century Materials

Table 12.9 gives an overview of the distribution in the materials of De Josselin de Jong (1926):

It is clear that the form *op*, which is so common in the 18th century materials, is no longer used as a preposition. Variants of *na bono* are now just about the only forms used. It is clear that the wide variety of morpho-phonological variants of *na bono* is also reflected at the individual level

Table 12.10 presents use of the supra-locative prepositions in dJdJ 1926 per speaker, showing that there was considerable variation (Van Sluijs 2016).

12.8 Discussion, Conclusions and Suggestions for Further Research

The general use of reduced variants of *na bono* in the 20th century materials, to the detriment of *op* and *boven*, which were used with some frequency in the 18th century texts, attests to the strong influence that the Atlantic pidgin and the West African languages had in the genesis of VIDC in its vernacular form used by the descendants of the enslaved Africans. The Atlantic pidgin contributed the general use of *na*, which is pervasive in VIDC, while the West African languages contributed the combination of *na* with a specific location marker to indicate configurational supra-location. The Dutch strong form *boven* and the generalized vernacular Dutch location marker *op* all but disappeared in the 20th century materials, and only survived as adverbs or verb particles

	locational		directional	adverbial	particle
	+ config	− config			
Op	-	-	(2)[9]	1[10]	30[11]
((n)a)bo(no)	35	6	104	-	-
Bobu	-	-	2	-	-
Abobo	-	-	-	9	-

Table 12.9: Distribution of supra-locative prepositions in the 20th century materials.

	bo			*(it) fa bo*	*	*(n)abo*	**		*(na)bono*		*bobu*
	+dir	−dir	−dir	−dir	−dir	+dir	−dir	−dir	+dir	−dir	+dir
		+con	-con	+con	-con		+con	-con		-con	
Joshua	41	8	1	4	1	1	-	-	1	-	-
Prince***	-	-	-	-	-	-	-	-	1	2	-
Testamark	5	3	-	-	-	-	1	-	-	-	-
T'mark/X	1	-	1	1	2	-	-	2	-	-	-
Joseph	1	-	-	-	-	-	-	-	-	-	-
Christian	-	-	-	-	-	-	1	-	-	-	1
Roberts	51	20		1	-	2	2	-	-	-	1

*Joshua uses *fa bo*, Testamark/X and Roberts *it fa bo*
**Testamark and Roberts each use *nabo* once
***Joshua uses *bono*, Prince *nabono*

Table 12.10: Use of the supra-locative prepositions in the 20th century materials per speaker.

Thus, from the available forms in the original feature pool, only a few elements survived as prepositions. It requires detailed analysis to see whether all these forms were really part of the creole in the first place, or simply impositions from European languages by the missionaries, and whether the vernacular Dutch of the Virgin Islands was clearly separate from the creole (Van Rossem 2017).

Even the article length discussion of a singular construction, supra-locative prepositions, barely does justice to the data. Much more needs to be said about the specific meanings conveyed, and the philological interpretation of the material. It would also be useful to consider the other configurational prepositions involving *na* + location. Do they show the same patterns of adaptation and selection as *nabono*?

Casting the net even wider, it would be very interesting to compare the data in VIDC with partly similar, partly different developments in other creole languages, including Berbice Dutch Creole, the Surinam Creole cluster, and Papiamentu.

---

[9]   There are two cases where *op* is indeterminate/ambiguous between being a directional preposition, or a verb particle.

[10] Here, *op* is followed by/co-occurs with a directional AP headed by preposition *a*, and as a whole follows *op* as a verb particle expressing upwards motion. As an adverb, *op* could be said to be some kind of reduplication.

[11] In six of the thirty occurrences of *op* as a verb particle, it expresses upwards motion, just as English 'up' (as in 'he jumped up'). In the other twenty-four occurrences *op* occurs in more or less idiomatic expressions, such as *hou op* 'stop' (< Dutch *hou op* 'stop', lit. hold up), *tu op* 'put away, store' (lit., 'close up'; *tu* 'çlose' < Dutch *toe* 'closed'), *fin op mi* 'encounter' (lit. 'find up with'), and cases where *op* has a destructive meaning, as in *ru op* "wreck up", *skee op* "tear up", *sni op* "cut up", *trample op* "trample up".

Acknowledgements

We are grateful for the comments of the participants in the *The Structure, Emergence and Evolution of Pidgin and Creole Languages* meeting at the University of Amsterdam on December 14, 2015, in particular Enoch Aboh, Adrienne Bruyn, and Anne Zribi-Hertz., and for the anonymous reviews. The NEHOL database has been created in collaboration with the MPI Nijmegen, one of the CLARIN centres in the Netherlands, thanks to the CLARIN-NL-10-010 grant for the NEHOL project (www.clarin.nl/node/162). The NEHOL database is accessible at http://corpus1.mpi.nl/. The metadata and the actual data of the NEHOL database can also be accessed from the CLARIN Virtual Language Observatory: http://catalog.clarin.eu/vlo/search?fq=collection:TLA:+NEHOL

References

Aboh, E 2010 The P route. In G Cinque and L Rizzi (eds.) *Mapping spatial PPs* (The cartography of syntactic structures, 6. New York: Oxford University Press. Pp. 225–260.

Adams Graves, A V 1977 *The present state of Dutch creole of the Virgin Islands*. Ann Arbor, Michigan: University Microfilms.

Ameka, F K 2003. Prepositions and postpositions in Ewe: empirical and theoretical considerations . In A Zibri-Hetz and P Sauzet (eds.) *Typologie des langues d'Afrique et universaux de la grammaire*. Paris: L'Harmattan. Pp. 43–66.

Ameka, F K and J Essegbey. 2006. Elements of the grammar of space in Ewe. In SC Levinson and DP Wilkins (eds.) *Grammars of Space: Explorations in Cognitive Diversity. Cambridge:* Cambridge University Press. Pp. 359–398.

Bakker, P 2014 Three Dutch Creoles in Comparison. *Journal of Germanic Linguistics* 26(3), 191–222.

Besten, H den and C van Rossem. 2013. Diplomatische editie van de Negerhollandse woordenlijsten van Frank G. Nelson. *Tijdschrift voor Nederlandse Taal- en Letterkunde* 130(1). Digital addendum.

Boretzky, N 1983 *Kreolsprachen, Substrate und Sprachwandel* [Creole languages, substrates and language change]. Wiesbaden: Harrasowitz.

Corum, M 2015 *Substrate and adstrate: The origins of spatial semantics in West African Pidgincreoles*. Boston: Mouton de Gruyter.

Hesseling, D C 1905 *Het Negerhollands der Deense Antillen. Bijdrage tot de geschiedenis der Nederlandse taal in Amerika*. Leiden: Sijthoff.

Josselin de Jong, J P B de 1926 *Het huidige Negerhollandsch (teksten en woordenlijst)*. Verhandelingen der Koninklijke Academie van Wetenschappen te Amsterdam, Nieuwe Reeks, Deel 26, no. 1. 124.

Lieberkühn, S 1771 *The Harmony of the four Gospels, or, the history of our Lord and Saviour Jesus Christ (…) English version*. London.

Luther, M 1912 *Die Bibel oder die ganze Heilige Schrift des Alten und Neuen Testaments. Revidierte Fassung der deutschen Übersetzung Martin Luthers*. Stuttgart.

Mufwene, S 2001 *The ecology of language evolution*. Cambridge: Cambridge University Press.

Muysken, P 1995 Studying variation in older texts: Negerhollands. Column for the *Journal of Pidgin and Creole Languages* 10: 335–348.

Muysken, P, R van Sluijs and B Los 2017 Verb particle combinations in Dutch - the lexifier language for several Caribbean creole languages - Papiamentu, and the languages of Surinam: evidence for word order change? Los, B. & P. de Haan (eds.) Word Order Change in Acquisition and Language Contact: Essays in Honour of Ans van Kemenade. Amsterdam: Benjamins.

Nelson, F G 1936 Virgin Island Dutch Creole Word List. Published in Den Besten and Van Rossem (2013).

Ofori, S A 2006 *Topics in Akan grammar*. Doctoral dissertation, Indiana University, Bloomington. University Microfilms.

Oldendorp, C G A 1777 *C.G.A. Oldendorps Geschichte der Mission der evangelischen Brueder auf den caraibischen Inseln S. Thomas, S. Croix und S. Jan*. Herausgegeben durch Johannes Jakob Bossart. Barby, Virgin Islands: Christian Friedrich Laur.

Oldendorp, C G A 2000 *Historie der caribischen Inseln Sanct Thomas, Sanct Crux und Sanct Jan, insbesondere der dasigen Neger und der Mission der evangelischen Brüder under derselben. Erster Teil*. Kommentierte Ausgabe des vollständigen Manuskriptes aus dem Archiv der Evangelischen Brüder-Unität Herrnhut. Ediert von Hartmut Beck, Gudrun Meier, Stephan Palmié, Peter Stein und Horst Ulbricht. [Abhandlungen und Berichte des Staatlichen Museums für Völkerkunde Dresden, Bd. 51 des Gesamtw.: Monographien; 9]. Berlin: VWB, Verlag für Wiss. und Bildung.

Owusu, E, J Agor, A Adade-Yeboah , K Dovlo 2015 Basic Locative Constructions and Simple Clause Structures of English, Akan, and Safaliba. *International Journal of Language and Linguistics* 2(5): 178–191.

Payne, T E 1997 *Describing morphosyntax: a guide for field linguists*. Cambridge: Cambridge University Press.

Reinecke, J E 1937 The Negro Dutch of the Danish Antilles. *Marginal languages: a sociological survey of the creole languages and trade jargons*. Unpublished thesis (PhD), Yale University. Pp. 394–425.

Rossem, C van 2017 The Virgin Islands Dutch Creole Textual Heritage: Philological Perspectives on Authenticity and Audience Design. Unpublished thesis (PhD), Radboud University.

Rossem, C van and H van der Voort (eds) 1996 *Die Creol Taal, 250 Years of Negerhollands Texts*. Amsterdam: Amsterdam University Press.

Rutten, G and M J van der Wal. 2014. *Letters as Loot, A Sociolinguistic Approach to Seventeenth- and Eighteenth-Century Dutch*. Amsterdam/Philadelphia: John Benjamins.

Sabino, R 1990 *Towards a Phonology of Negerhollands: An Analysis of Phonological Variation*. Unpublished thesis (PhD), University of Pennsylvania.

Sabino, R 2012 Language Contact in the *Danish West Indies: Giving Jack His Jacket*. Leiden, NL: Brill.

Sluijs, R van. 2016 Variation and Change in Virgin Islands Dutch Creole: Tense, Modality and Aspect. Unpublished thesis (PhD), Radboud University.

Sluijs, R van, M van den Berg, and P Muysken 2016 Exploring genealogical blends: the Surinamese Creole Cluster and the Virgin Island Dutch Creole Cluster. *Lingua* doi:10.1016/j.lingua.2015.12.004.

Sprauve, GA 1976 Chronological implications of discontinuity in spoken and written Dutch Creole. *New directions in creole studies*. G. Cave, ed. Georgetown: Society for Caribbean Linguistics.

Stein, P 1986 The Documents concerning the Negro-Dutch Language of the Danish Virgin Islands, St. Thomas, St. Croix, and St. John - Negerhollands -, in the Unitäts-Archiv (Archives of the Moravian Brethren) at Herrnhut. A Commented Bibliography. *Papers on Negerhollands, the Dutch Creole of the Virgin Islands. Amsterdam Creole Studies IX*. H. den Besten ed. Amsterdam: Publikaties van het Instituut voor Algemene Taalwetenschap 51, 19–31.

Stein, P and H van der Voort (eds.) 1996 *Christian Georg Andreas OLDENDORP, Criolisches Wörterbuch. Erster zu vermehrender und wo nöthig zu verbessernder Versuch [1767/68], herausgegeben, eingeleitet und mit Anmerkungen versehen von Peter Stein, sowie das anonyme, J.C. KINGO zugeschriebene Vestindisk Glossarium, herausgegeben, eingeleitet und mit Anmerkungen versehen von Hein van der Voort*, Lexicographica, series maior 69. Tübingen: Max Niemeyer Verlag.

Vandeloise, C 1991 *Spatial Prepositions: A Case Study in French*. Chicago: The University of Chicago Press.

Vandeloise, C 1994 Methodology and analyses of the preposition *in*. *Cognitive Linguistics* 5: 157–184.

Zribi-Hertz, A 1984 *Orphan* Prepositions *in French and Concept of Null Pronoun. Bloomington*. IN: Indiana University Linguistics Club.

Zribi-Hertz, A and Loïc, J-L 2015 General Locative Forms in (two) creoles (Haitian, Martinican) (SEEPiCLa), University of Amsterdam, December 14th-15th, 2015.

Zwarts, J 1997 Lexical and functional prepositions. In D Haumann and S J Schierholz, (eds.), *Lexikalische und grammatische Eigenschaften präpositionaler Elemente* Tübingen: Max Niemeyer Verlag. Pp. 1–18.

Digital Sources

http://brievenalsbuit.inl.nl/*The Letters as Loot/ Brieven als Buit corpus*. Leiden University. Compiled by Marijke van der Wal (Programme leader), Gijsbert Rutten, Judith Nobels and Tanja Simons, with the assistance of volunteers of the Leiden-based *Wikiscripta Neerlandica* transcription project, and lemmatised, tagged and provided with search facilities by the Institute for Dutch Lexicology (INL). 2nd release 2015.

http://www.gekaaptebrieven.nl/ Meertens Institute. Compiled by N. van der Sijs (Programme leader), with the assistance of volunteers.

Luther 1912: http://www.bibel-online.net/

Making the Dictionary of the Frisian Language Available in the Dutch Historical Dictionary Portal

Katrien Depuydt[a], Jesse de Does[b], Pieter Duijff[c] and Hindrik Sijens[d]

[a]Dutch Language Institute, katrien.depuydt@ivdnt.org, [b]Dutch Language Institute, jesse.dedoes@ivdnt.org, [c]Fryske Akademy, pduijff@fryske-akademy.nl, [d]Fryske Akademy, hsijens@fryske-akademy.nl

ABSTRACT

The main goal of the Wurdboek fan de Fryske Taal/Woordenboek der Friese taal-Geïntegreerde TaalBank (WFT-GTB) project was to publish the monumental Dictionary of the Frisian Language (Wurdboek fan de Fryske Taal/Woordenboek der Friese taal, WFT) in the CLARIN research infrastructure, according to open, CLARIN-compliant standards. This has been achieved by 1) curation of the dictionary data, resulting in a well-structured TEI-conformant encoding and 2) publication of the dictionary in the Dutch Institute for Lexicology (INL) dictionary portal, together with the main historical dictionaries of Dutch. The project was carried out by two CLARIN partners, the Fryske Akademy (FA) in Leeuwarden and the INL in Leiden.

The dictionary has been online for more than six years now and has served many users, assisting both researchers and general users interested in the Frisian language. In this chapter we look back on the project and discuss the use of the dictionary application by analysing the retrieval application logs and by providing a use case, exemplifying how the dictionary can be used for historical lexicographical research. The chapter concludes with some suggestions for the improvement and enhancement of the online version of the WFT.

13.1 Introduction

Her Majesty Queen Beatrix of the Netherlands launched the online version of the Dictionary of the Frisian Language (Wurdboek fan de Fryske taal/Woordenboek der Friese taal, WFT) on 6 July 2010. The presentation of the online WFT was the final step in the Wurdboek fan 'e Fryske

How to cite this book chapter:

Depuydt, K, de Does, J, Duijff, P and Sijens, H. 2017. Making the Dictionary of the Frisian Language Available in the Dutch Historical Dictionary Portal. In: Odijk, J and van Hessen, A. (eds.) *CLARIN in the Low Countries*, Pp. 151–165. London: Ubiquity Press. DOI: https://doi.org/10.5334/bbi.13. License: CC-BY 4.0

Taal-Geïntegreerde TaalBank (WFT-GTB) project, a project that was supported by CLARIN-NL. The project involved a data curation and a demonstrator project and was carried out by two CLARIN partners, the Fryske Akademy (FA) in Leeuwarden and the Dutch Institute for Lexicology (INL) in Leiden.

The dictionary has been online for more than six years now and has served many users in their research and quest for knowledge about the Frisian language. In this chapter we look back on the project and discuss the use of the dictionary application on the basis of the log files. Furthermore we present a research use case. The chapter concludes with a short outline for improvement and expansion of the online version of the WFT.

13.2   The Dictionary and its Issues

The Dictionary of the Frisian Language is a scholarly, descriptive dictionary of the vocabulary of the Modern West Frisian language from the period 1800–1975. It has its roots in the 19th-century tradition of large dictionaries, and can therefore be compared with the Oxford English Dictionary, the German Dictionary (Deutsches Wörterbuch) and the Dictionary of the Dutch Language (Woordenboek der Nederlandsche Taal).

The dictionary project started in 1938 with the compiling of a corpus, the first volume was published in 1984, and the 25th and final volume was published in 2011. With this dictionary, more than 10,000 pages of lexicographic information about Modern West Frisian is available to the professional linguist and the layperson interested in the Frisian language, a language of about 400,000 speakers, spoken in the Dutch province of Friesland.

The dictionary contains approximately 120,000 lemmas and the entries provide information on the spelling of the headword, its part of speech and its pronunciation. In addition, information is given about the inflexion and etymology of the headword. The semantic section provides the user with information about the meanings of the headwords by means of definitions or translations into Dutch. All the meanings of a word are illustrated by citations, so the user is able to verify the lexicographer's work.

Idiomatic information is given in the idioms section, which contains collocations, proverbs and figurative meanings. The final section of an entry describes compounds and derivatives belonging to the headword.

Five hundred copies have been printed of each volume, and some 400 subscribers received a copy of one volume every year. These subscribers are language enthusiasts and professional linguists, as well as universities and public libraries. The WFT as a paper dictionary has restricted search possibilities; the alphabet is the only means by which the headwords and their descriptions can be accessed. The goal of making the dictionary available online was to enable extensive exploration of the copious linguistic information in the dictionary and to make the dictionary available to a larger audience.

13.3   Integration

Integrating the WFT into the historical dictionary portal of Dutch in the INL was the obvious means of reaching the goal described above and the WFT-GTB project was therefore initiated. The INL dictionary portal describes 15 centuries of Dutch language. It contains four Dutch dictionaries:

- the Dictionary of Old Dutch (Oudnederlands Woordenboek, ONW, ca 500–1200),
- the Dictionary of Early Middle Dutch (Vroegmiddelnederlands Woordenboek, VMNW, 1200–1300),

- the Dictionary of Middle Dutch (Middelnederlandsch Woordenboek, MNW, ca 1250–1550), and
- the Dictionary of the Dutch Language (Woordenboek der Nederlandsche Taal, WNT, ca 1500–1976).

The portal is freely accessible.

The WFT and the Dutch dictionaries were developed in the same lexicographical tradition and integration was feasible because of the similarity in their structures. The advantages of linking the Frisian dictionary with the online Dutch historical dictionaries were many. Connecting the dictionaries enhanced the possibilities for synchronic and diachronic analysis of both languages. To give some examples, the following questions could be researched: which words appear in both languages, and which are specifically Frisian or Dutch? What are the phonological and morphological differences between the two languages? And what is the influence of the Dutch language on Frisian and vice versa? An additional value is that etymological information about Frisian words can be derived from one or more of the Dutch linked dictionaries.

In order to integrate the WFT in the portal, a list of search options had to be drawn up. The starting point was the existing application and the possibilities of the tagged WFT data. Because the WFT and the portal dictionaries are similar both in the information categories they encode and in the dictionary entry structures, the options for searching entries, word senses, quotations, and collocations in the dictionary application are also relevant for increasing the accessibility of the WFT. In fact, it was possible to link most of the information categories in the WFT to the application's existing search options, for example variants of the headword, words in collocations, idioms and proverbs, or languages mentioned in the etymology field.

13.4   Data Curation for the Online WFT

13.4.1   Repair and Optimisation of the Existing Database

The original data for the print edition of the dictionary were stored in a database. Since the early 1990s, this has been a BRS/Search database. BRS/Search is a full-text database and information retrieval system which uses a fully-inverted indexing system to store, locate, and retrieve unstructured data.[1] The only metadata added to a dictionary entry were *Word* and *Desc*, where *Word* refers to the headword of the dictionary entry, and *Desc* to a section devoted to the description of a particular word sense within the full text of the entry. No other information categories were tagged explicitly. The data were stored in Windows cp1252 format and marked with layout codes that were used by scripts to convert the database text to rtf documents. The entries of the dictionary were accessible with a search and input interface and a simple text editor.

Before the data could be added to the portal, mistakes and errors identified in the printed dictionary had to be corrected. The data had to be optimised in other ways as well; for instance, abbreviations such as *Id.* and *ibid.* for same author and same source had to be resolved. In a set of compounds with a common first part, the abbreviation marks had to be expanded. Another job was to verify the consistency of cross-references between entries.

13.4.2   Part-of-Speech Mapping

The part-of-speech information of the headwords needed to be mapped to the tag set used for the Dutch online dictionaries. For instance, a search query for reflexive verbs in the application uses

---

[1] See: https://en.wikipedia.org/wiki/BRS/Search [access date 16 April 2017].

the standardised category label *ww refl.* (werkwoord reflexief, 'reflexive verb') whereas the WFT had the label *v.* (verbum, 'verb') with the addition of the Frisian reflexive pronoun *jin* ('oneself'). Linking the Frisian label to Dutch *ww refl.* enables the simultaneous retrieval of both Frisian and Dutch verbs in this category.

13.4.3   Adding Modern Dutch equivalents

All entries in the integrated Dutch dictionaries are linked to a Modern Dutch headword. Thanks to this link, users have access to the Middle or Old Dutch dictionaries, even if they have no knowledge of older Dutch language stages; for instance, a search query for the Modern Dutch headword PAARD ('horse') will yield forms like *pert* (VMNW) and *peert* (MNW). The same goes for users who do have a command of (Modern) Dutch but no knowledge of Frisian. For them, it may be difficult to search for a Frisian entry in the application; hence, a Modern Dutch headword was added to a Frisian lemma.

Not every Frisian lemma can be linked to a Dutch cognate; for instance, Frisian words like *heit* ('father', Dutch 'vader'), *hynder* ('horse', Dutch 'paard') and *sneon* ('Saturday', Dutch 'zaterdag') do not have a Dutch cognate.

Although Frisian and Dutch are related languages, the differences between them are substantial. One can therefore assume that cognates like Dutch *neus* ('nose') and Frisian *noas* are equivalent; therefore, the Modern Dutch lemma NEUS covers both entries. Both languages also have the word *naad* to mean 'seam'. In the integrated dictionary, Frisian *naad* can thus be mapped to the Modern Dutch equivalent NAAD. Subsequently, all Dutch compounds and derivates with *naad-* can be translated into Frisian in the same way. Yet, another meaning of *naad* in Frisian is 'ridge', which is not recorded for *naad* in the Dutch dictionaries (the Dutch word for this meaning is *nok*). The equivalent of Frisian *naadfoarst* ('ridge tile') would therefore be the non-existent Dutch equivalent NAADVORST. No Dutch, non-Frisian user would use this morphologically correct term to search the dictionaries for the concept 'ridge tile'.

So, when a Frisian lemma has no Dutch equivalent or cognate, another strategy has to be used to find the correct Frisian entry. Since the definitions in the WFT are mostly Dutch synonyms, a user can enter this synonym in the 'definition' search field in the application.

Originally it was planned that only the Frisian lemmas with a known Dutch cognate would be linked to a Modern Dutch lemma, with the intention to show the diachronic similarities and relations between Dutch and Frisian. The assignment of Dutch equivalents to the Frisian headwords was done automatically by selecting the Dutch cognates from the etymology field. When no etymology was known or given, the script searched the field meaning for a one-word definition. Often this resulted in a hit, especially with compound words. It was necessary to check the results of this operating procedure manually.

Through this process about 70% of the Frisian lemmas have been linked to a Modern Dutch headword. On further consideration it is doubtful that only cognates have been linked. Users of the GTB application will find it more beneficial when all Frisian lemmas are linked to a Modern Dutch headword.

13.4.4   Sources and References

It is possible to search the list of citation sources used in the dictionaries. Therefore, a list of sources used in the WFT has been linked to the dictionary. Next to that, a list with references to linguistic literature was created and added to the portal.

13.4.5   Parsing

Writing parsing software in order to tag the logical structure of the dictionary entries caused some difficulties, due to the inconsistencies in the structure. For instance, the etymology section on the heading starts with the label *Etym.* and the etymological information itself consists of references to cognates and equivalents in other languages, or just references to other languages. However, it can also contain morphological information such as *denominatief van noas* ('denominative of nose'), or *dim. van noas* ('diminutive of nose'), or even a cross-reference to another entry: → *nocht* (→ 'companion').

Headword	Field	Etymology
noas	Etym.	→ N. *neus*, D. *Nase*, E. *nose*.
noasje	Etym.:	Fr., Lat.
noaskje I	Etym.:	denominatief van *noas*.
noaskje II	Etym.:	dim. van *noas*?
noflik	Etym.	→ *nocht*.

In order to support specific queries, further analysis was needed to distinguish morphological and etymological information.

13.4.6   Enriching the XML Database with TEI Encoding and Incorporating the Dictionary into the Portal

In order to incorporate the WFT into the portal, the dictionary data had to be converted to the TEI annotation scheme for printed dictionaries. The existing online dictionary application, which is part of the Dutch Language Bank, allows for querying in more than one dictionary simultaneously. At the time the plans were developed, the challenge was not only to give the user optimal access to the dictionary information, but to do so without compromising the uniqueness of each individual dictionary. All Dutch dictionaries were available in digital form, but in a different encoding system and with a different level of encoding. Their structure had similarities, however, with the presence of the headword; the section with linguistic information at entry level; the section with semantic analysis of the headword; and the section with related entries. TEI encoding for printed dictionaries was chosen as a standard because it allows both fine-grained and coarse-grained encoding. Moreover, all encoding needed for the main Dutch historical dictionaries could be converted to TEI without modifying the encoding scheme, which is more than can be said of competing standards like LMF. A basic encoding scheme for the Dutch dictionaries was defined at INL. This scheme defines a minimum level of mandatory encoding for all dictionaries necessary for the integrated retrieval on the dictionary data. Apart from the basic level of encoding which applies to all dictionaries, the additional encoding present in each of the dictionaries has also been converted into TEI. Consequently, there are some retrieval possibilities applicable to all dictionaries, whereas others are applicable to only one, or a smaller group of dictionaries, depending on the level of encoding. The application of the TEI dictionary encoding scheme to the Dutch historical dictionaries is documented in Depuydt (2010).

13.4.7   Interoperability in the CLARIN Research Infrastructure

The WFT dictionary has been integrated into the CLARIN research infrastructure in the following ways:

13.4.7.1   PID, Metadata and Data Category Registry

A PID for the WFT resource has been reserved at http://hdl.handle.net/10032/00-B1C8-4476-53DC-4DED-8. Metadata can be harvested in CMDI and Dublin Core.

The main grammatical part-of-speech categories used in the WFT have been entered into the data category registry.

13.4.7.2 REST Web Service

The dictionary portal retrieval backend is a REST web service. In this way, the dictionary data can be integrated with other applications besides the portal frontend.

The basic use scenario (Figure 13.1) is extremely simple.

The underlying data resources are queried, under the control of a set of control parameters. Results are sent back to the querying client in the form of a result list or an HTML article display.

13.5 The Users

The historical dictionary portal is an often used resource. More than 53 million requests have been sent to the backend engine since it first appeared online in 2007. Since user requests are logged, we can obtain some information about the behaviour of users from these logs.

13.5.1 Robots Versus 'Real' Users.

A first issue in analysing the dictionary usage is that the overwhelming majority of requests do not originate from real users, but from robots such as web indexing spiders. Distinguishing these two categories is not obvious. We have combined two software modules to try to identify the 'bots': Bitwalker user-agent-utils (http://www.bitwalker.eu/software/user-agent-utils) and the perl module HTTP::BrowserDetect, which both rely on the (unwarranted) trustworthiness of the user-agent information sent by the client. Figure 13.2 gives the proportion of bot requests according to these modules.

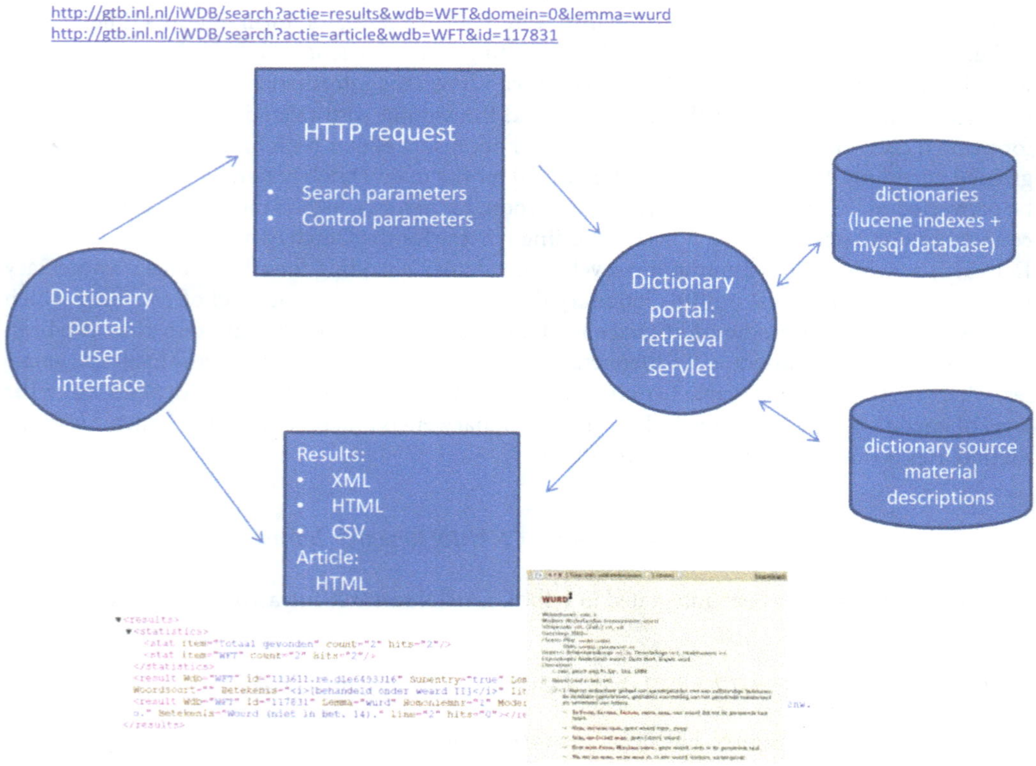

Figure 13.1: Basic use scenario.

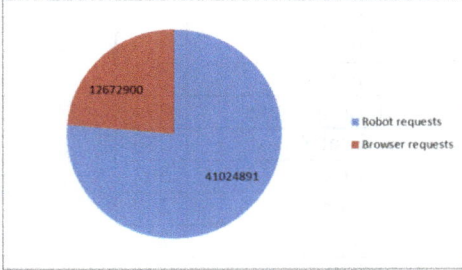

Figure 13.2: Bot requests vs browsers.

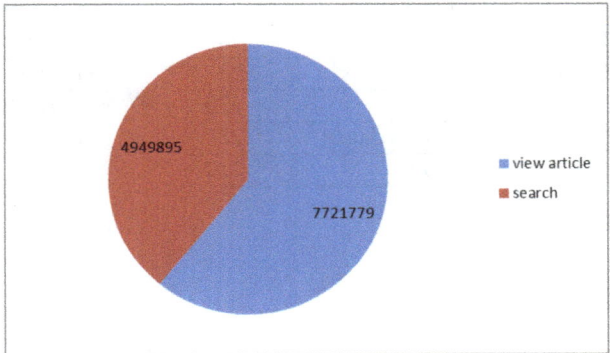

Figure 13.3: Article views vs searches.

13.5.2   WFT Usage

The historical dictionary portal responds to searches by presenting result lists including headword, part of speech and first dictionary sense. In some cases, the user can find the information he/she is looking for in the result lists; however, the user may also jump to article views (cf. Figure 13.3).

13.5.2.1   Article Views

At least 360,196 article views of the WFT can be with some degree of certainty ascribed to real users, and 64,407 different articles have been viewed since 2007.

Most frequently viewed are the lemmas listed in Table 13.1, a lot of which do not have a direct Dutch cognate.

13.5.2.2   Search Requests

The WFT is searchable in combination with the major scholarly dictionaries of Dutch. Hence, it is not obvious how to determine from a search action what the user was really interested in. Analysing the different combinations of dictionaries that have been searched (Figure 13.4 and Table 13.2), the emerging picture is that:

1. Most users do not seem to bother to exclude dictionaries they may not be interested in in their first search; and

2. when not all dictionaries are selected, most users just search a single dictionary (possibly by following links to this option).

omkoal	752
oekedakke	720
pommerant	653
knibbel	603
bargebiten	416
bûter	408
sjampoepel	388
suterich	385
gnob	385
obsternaat	384
njonkelytsen	379
opsokkebalje	367
futsjefinne	354
kloet	346
poppeslok	325
deunsk	320
wurd	316

roppich	303
nuver	300
noflik	295
ramplesant	294
bealch	286
tuike	267
jaan	257
eide	253
jeits	251
hawwe	244
babbelegûchjes	243
kakwangen	242
tuolle	240
frommes	237
heit	230
kattedagen	230
oft	229

gean	226
kapokje	225
tiid	222
tankewol	220
muoike	219
ierappel	216
jeuzel	216
fertuten	215
petiele	213
Fries	210
santjin	209
earrebarre	205
hispel	202
bryk	201
hynder	201

Table 13.1: Frequently viewed entries.

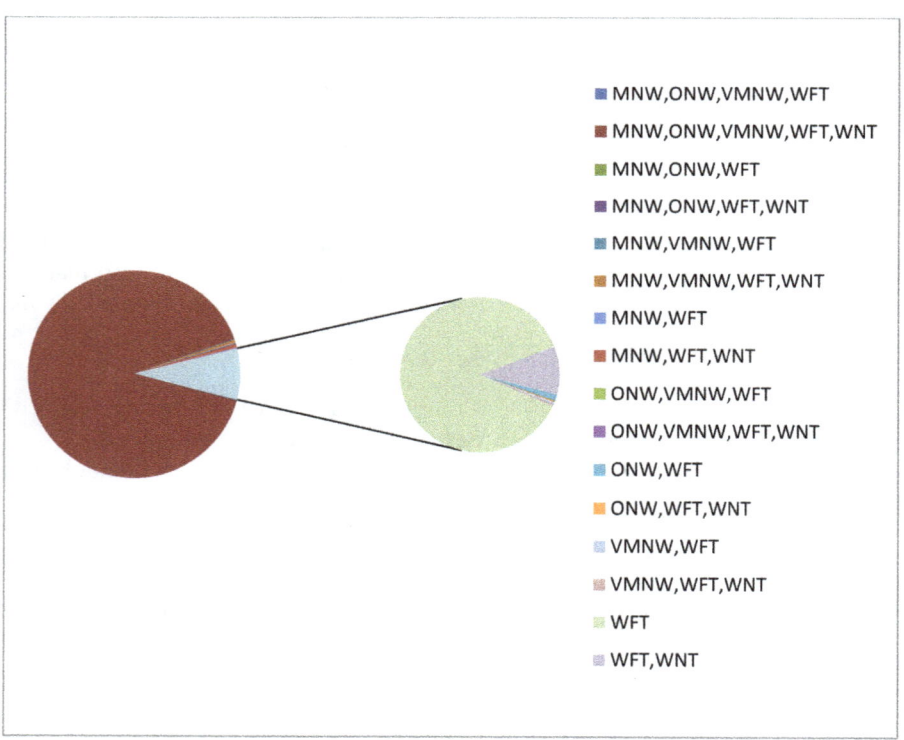

Figure 13.4: Relative frequency of consulted dictionary combinations involving WFT.

MNW,ONW,VMNW,WFT,WNT	1,748,488
WFT	135,462
WFT,WNT	15,318
MNW,WFT,WNT	11,465
MNW,VMNW,WFT,WNT	8,821
MNW,WFT	3,460

Table 13.2: Top consulted dictionary combinations involving WFT.

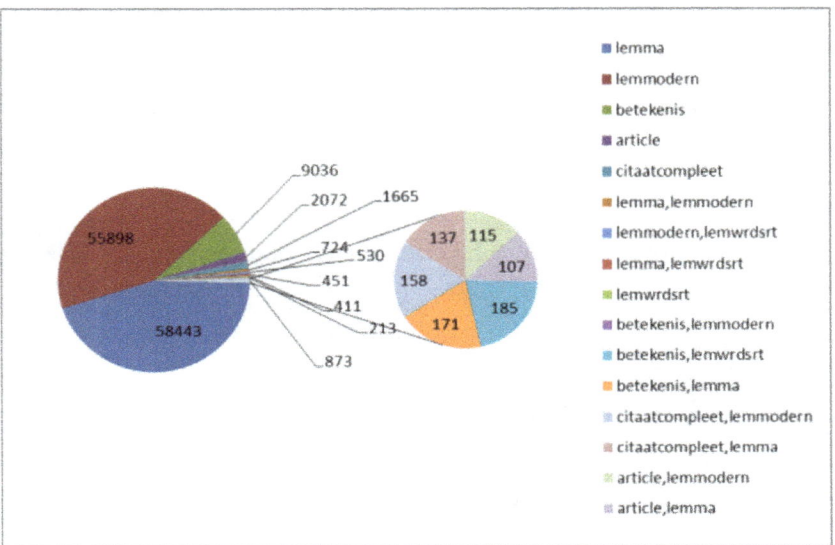

Figure 13.5: Frequency of search field combinations (WFT-only searches).

13.5.2.3   Search Types

The search application has many options (searchable field combinations). As can be seen from Figures 13.5 and 13.6, the overwhelming majority of users search for lemmas, using either the Frisian headword form or the Modern Dutch lemma field.

There is a high proportion of users searching for 'betekenis' in the WFT-only searches, as compared to the WFT-in-combination searches. This probably shows that people are trying to find Frisian equivalents for Dutch words.

It is striking that the many advanced options to explore the corpus of quotations are seldom used. Also, the beautiful set of collocations that has been encoded explicitly appears to be neglected.

13.5.2.4   Search Results

Table 13.3 shows to which extent users find what they look for, as measured through counts of either lemma queries grouped by lemma or ungrouped lemma queries (number of lemma search requests).

Most of these are Dutch words; others are spelling variants (*great, jim*), diminutives (*húske, brochje*) or inflected forms (*is, weagen, hie, froulju*) of existing headwords.

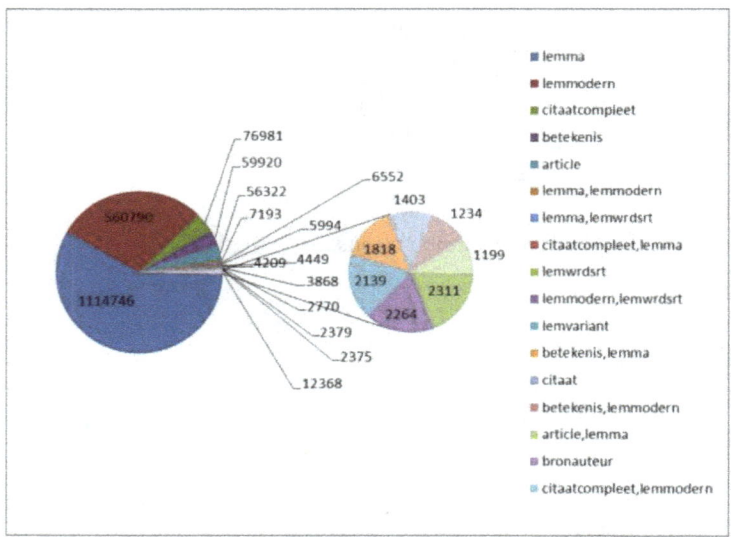

Figure 13.6: Frequency of search field combinations (searches where WFT is selected, possibly with other dictionaries).

Distinct lemma queries (29,893)	Found	20,201
	Not found	9,692
Lemma queries (58,561)	Found	45,972
	Not found	12,589

Table 13.3: Number of successfully or unsucessfully retrieved lemmas.

13.5.3   Usage Through Time

There is a clear decline in the number of users of both WFT and the dictionary portal as a whole from 2014 (Figures 13.7 and 13.8). The main reason for this is that the portal application, developed in 2006, relies on Flash and is thus unsuitable for tablets and phones.

13.6   An Example of Research

Searches in the Frisian lemma field without results (queried more than six times) ate listed in Table 13.4.

In the WFT every dictionary article describes all the meanings of a lemma, and every meaning is illustrated with citations, if available, for the complete described period (from 1800 until 1975). Accordingly, the dictionary can function as a source to shed light on the development of Frisian words and word variants. Using the search functions in the dictionary portal and the citations in the WFT, we wanted to investigate the historical development of Frisian word forms. The portal is a better tool than the paper dictionary for this type of research, since searching the paper dictionary is limited to looking up articles. We illustrate this type of investigation with research on the word *hynder* for English 'horse'. Every meaning distinction in the dictionary articles is based on and illustrated with citations from two different card index systems that were built up between 1940 and 2011. The oldest card index system was more or less randomly put together, and the latest one was built up more systematically. The lexicographers needed the latter because the random system

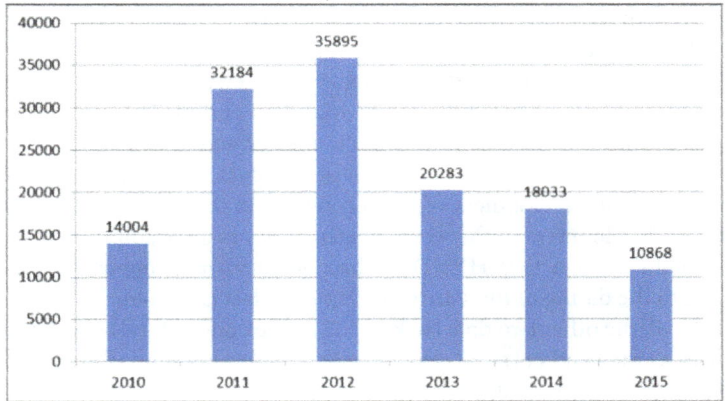

Figure 13.7: Usage (number of queries) through time, WFT-only.

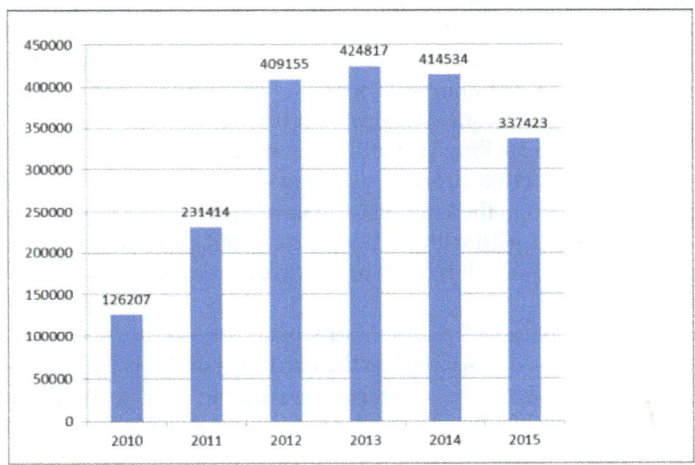

Figure 13.8: Usage through time, WFT-with-other dictionary.

Word	#Queries
gefeliciteerd	20
tot ziens	19
met	18
great	16
jij	16
wie	15
bedankt	13
jullie	13
kleinkind	12
koe	10

is	10
huske	10
jim	10
paard	9
zijn	9
samen	9
z	9
weagen	9
gaat	8
brochje	8
moeilijk	8

fierljeppen	7
groeten	7
froulju	7
meiinoar	7
hie	7
kinderen	7
weze	7
trouwen	7
merel	7

Table 13.4: Frequent lemma searches without result.

did not contain enough function words such as pronouns. In the first half of the 19th century, Frisian was not often written; this was also visible in the first card index system, in which this period was not well represented. When putting the dictionary together, a lot of work was put into collecting citations that would properly represent the entire described period. This means, for example, that if a word form or a collocation with the word form is attested across a period of 150 years, citations with that word form are given across the duration of that period. Because of this, it is possible to make statements about the development of written Frisian in the described 176 years on the basis of the citations. The development of the word *hynder* serves as an example.

In the header of the WFT article HYNDER three form variants appear: *hynder*, *hynsder* and *hynzer*. According to the dating of these three variants the last is the oldest (1808), and, according to the source material, the other two date back to 1851. The editor of the article did not choose the oldest form *hynzer* as the head entry – this is the right choice because in today's standard Frisian *hynder* is the only form that is used (Dykstra et al., 2014).[2] Incidentally, in 20th-century spoken Frisian one still encounters both the forms *hynzer* and *hynsder* (Van der Veen et al., 2001:59). The etymology of the word is best represented in the form *hynsder*, as it is originally a combination of *hynst* ('stallion') and *dier* ('animal').

With the help of avanced search options in the dictionary portal, each of the three word forms of *hynder* that appear in the header of the dictionary article can be selected. We also took into account the written word form *hynser*, which is not attested as a variant form of the lemma in the header of the article, but does occur in dictionary citations.

In the period 1819–1829, five unique citations with the written variant *hijnder* are attested. We have considered that form as a spelling variant of the word form *hynder*. By using the 'extended search' ('uitgebreid zoeken') function with every desired word form filled in in the 'word in citation text' ('woord in citaattekst') field in the 'citations' ('citaten') section, and with a time period selected in 'source data' ('brongegevens'), a list with citations is retrieved. (To select only citations, one needs to select the 'citations' ('citaten') search request in the 'give as results a list of' ('geef als resultaat een lijst met') field.)

In the WFT, not only are citations from literature, magazines and oral records given, but word lists and dictionaries are also used as sources. In the hard copy of the WFT the citations from these last sources are spaced; in the portal, they are tagged as such but are not yet defined as search fields in the extended search functions. The result of this is that the spaced words are missing in the search results.

Because the word *hynder* and its variations can appear as the first part of a construction and derivation and above all can be preceded by one or more parts of words, the wild card function '*' is used before and after the desired root word form when searching. For this example, searches were split into 10-year periods. Only the last period, 1970–1975, is shorter than ten years since the dictionary only includes entries up until 1975.

Searching for occurrences of citations with the four aforementioned forms of *hynder* gives hit totals with a distorted picture of the occurrence of search words, because the same citations can be used in different articles. In order to get a proper picture, unique citations were selected from the total hits. The search functions of the portal do not provide this functionality. For example, compare the next two equivalent citations, presented in two different ways in the dictionary articles SPREKKE (a) and SWAAIE (b):

(a) It fjûrige, krêftútterjende hynder...(hat) altyd folle mear ta it forstân en it herte fen ús foarâlden spritsen, as de slûge kou.

(b) It fjûrige krêftútterjende hynder, mei syn stirt yn 'e biezem, syn swaeijende moannen.

---

[2] http://taalweb.frl/foarkarswurdlist

In Figure 13.9 one can see the development of the use of the variant *hynder*. Up until 1860 there were almost no single unique citations found with this form. Afterwards, numbers increase slightly, but only as of 1930 can we clearly see a rise in numbers.

The form *hynsder* also appears at the beginning of the 19th century, as shown in Figure 13.10. Between around 1900 and 1950 the form appears relatively frequently, but afterwards there are hardly any single hits.

The distributions of the forms *hynzer* (Figure 13.11) and *hynser* (Figure 13.12) developed in the opposite direction to that of *hynder* and *hynsder*; both the *hynzer* and *hynser* word forms actually only appear in the 19th century and disappear completely from the citations after 1950.

Internally, the FA has a database containing all known Middle-Frisian (ca 1550–1800) language material, in which *hynder* and other spelling variations with the consonant <d> do not appear at all, although the form and variations thereof with the consonant <s> do. So, the search results in the online WFT show a clear continuing development in the usage of the word in written Frisian. At the cost of the other three variations, the word form *hynder* is the most used after around 1930, and the forms *hynzer* and *hynser* have now already been out of use for a number of decades.

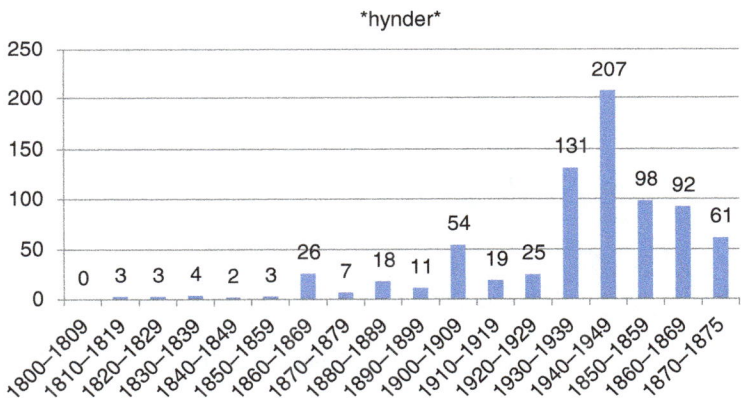

Figure 13.9: WFT *hynder*: number of quotations per decennium.

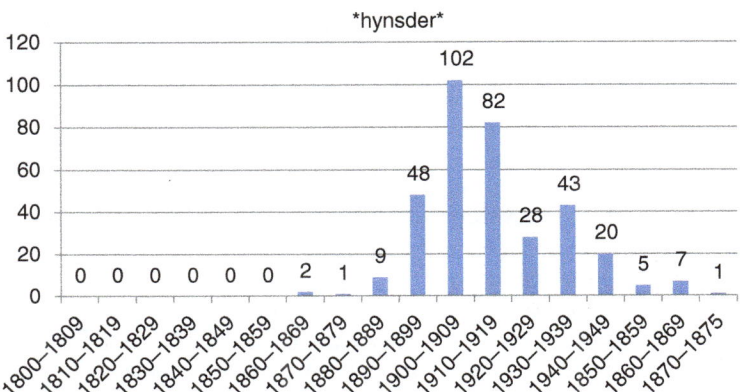

Figure 13.10: WFT *hynsder*: number of quotations per decennium.

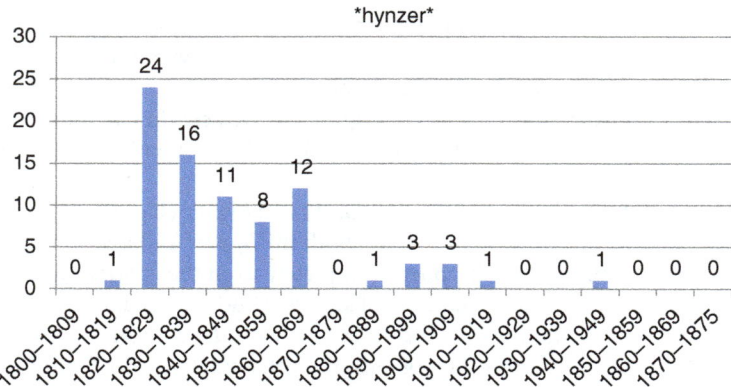

Figure 13.11: WFT *hynzer*: number of quotations per decennium.

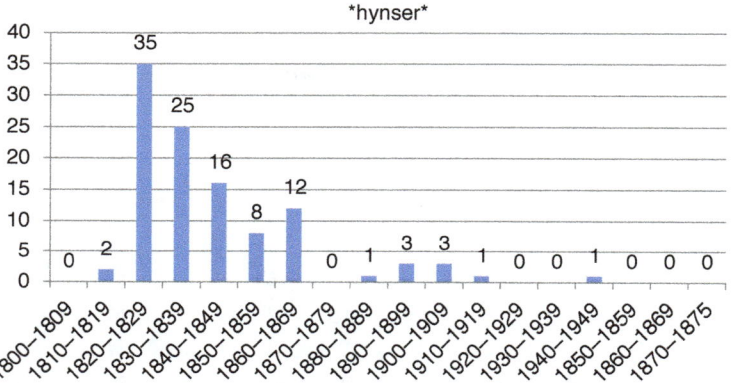

Figure 13.12: WFT *hynser*: number of quotations per decennium.

Apart from providing data on the usage of the Frisian word for 'horse', the 'extended search' function also showed in the article for *hynder* that the dating of the word form *hynder* to 1851 is incorrect, because in six different dictionary articles a source from 1836 is cited in which the simplex word form *hynder* appears, and in four different dictionary articles a source from the year 1819 is cited in which the simplex word form *hijnder* appears. If we accept the form *hijnder* as a written variant of the form *hynder*, the oldest dating of the word in the heading of the article *hynder* is thus 1819 instead of 1851.

13.7   Future Developments: Improvement and Expansion

There are two main ways in which the online WFT can be improved.

On the one hand, the portal application, which dates from 2010, needs to be updated and in some respects redesigned. The current interface uses Adobe Flash, which is rapidly becoming obsolete. Furthermore, in order to enable users to further explore the rich dictionary content, both the query interface, which should provide better guidance, and the general application design ought to be improved.

On the other hand, the WFT data itself can be enhanced. Frisian and Dutch words that are etymologically related are now linked through the same Modern Dutch equivalent. One wish is to enhance the Dutch–Frisian mapping where no plausible 'etymological' equivalent exists.

Furthermore, better tagging of the logical structure of the dictionary is required, especially with respect to the encoding of the field with etymological information in the heading and of the cross-references in the compound and derivation sections.

In order to broaden the possibilities of use, additional information can be added to the dictionary – for instance by linking sources mentioned in the 'literature' field to the relevant pdf files and by implementing links to dialect maps in the 'dialect' field. It should also be possible to link Dutch–Frisian cognates with the Etymological Dictionary of Dutch (Etymologisch woordenboek van het Nederlands, EWN).

Finally, one can imagine various ways in which to use the WFT data as published by means of the REST web service (either as part of the main portal or independent of it), such as the analysis and visualisations of the temporal and regional distribution of search results.

References

Depuydt, K. (2010). 'TEI-structuurcodering van de woordenboeken in de woordenboekencomponent van de Taalbank Nederlands' (internal project document; not published).

Dykstra, A.; P. Duijff; F. Van der Kuip; H. Sijens (2014). *Taalweb Frysk* [on-line] Ljouwert: Fryske Akademy. http://taalweb.frl/foarkarswurdlist [access date 6 June 2016].

Veen van der, K.F.; A. Versloot; W. Rypma (2001). Dialektgeografyske oantekens fan J.J. Hof. Ljouwert: Fryske Akademy.

Wurdboek fan de Fryske Taal/Woordenboek der Friese Taal. Ljouwert/Leeuwarden: Fryske Akademy, 1984-2011.

CHAPTER 14

SLI Diagnostics in Narratives: Exploring the CLARIN-NL VALID Data Archive

Laura Bergmann, Roeland van Hout and Jetske Klatter-Folmer

j.klatter@let.ru.nl

ABSTRACT

In 2014 the Vulnerability in Acquisition: Language Impairments in Dutch (VALID)[1] Data Archive for pathological language data (CLARIN-NL-12-010 grant) was launched. The aim of the VALID Data Archive is to unite various available datasets ranging from metadata, experimental results, and test outcomes to spontaneous speech data, including video recordings, and to develop unambiguous protocols to ascertain the interpretation of research outcomes. In this chapter we report a study that we carried out using the VALID Data Archive. In an earlier project the language development of children with Specific Language Impairment (SLI) had indeed been investigated using a narrative task (retelling of a picture story); the VALID database thus contains transcripts and audio files of the speech of 50 children with SLI and 24 age-matched typically developing (TD) children in the age range between 5;6 to 12;0 years, who all participated in this earlier project. Our study focused on morphosyntactic and lexical accuracy and complexity, in order to determine which language measures are diagnostic indicators of SLI on the basis of this narrative data. Results showed that SLI children performed less well than TD children for morphosyntactic and lexical accuracy and complexity. Interestingly, the results obtained can be compared to results found in three other studies on narratives performed by SLI and TD children. The similarities and differences in the outcomes reveal the urgency to have identical, precise protocols in handling and analysing complex data.

---

[1] http://validdata.org/clarin-project/datasets/

How to cite this book chapter:
Bergmann, L, van Hout, R and Klatter-Folmer, J. 2017. SLI Diagnostics in Narratives: Exploring the CLARIN-NL VALID Data Archive. In: Odijk, J and van Hessen, A. (eds.) *CLARIN in the Low Countries*, Pp. 167–180. London: Ubiquity Press. DOI: https://doi.org/10.5334/bbi.14. License: CC-BY 4.0

14.1   The VALID Data Archive

The Vulnerability in Acquisition: Language Impairments in Dutch (VALID) Data Archive (CLARIN-NL-12-010 grant) that was launched in 2014 is an open multimedia data archive with data from speakers suffering from language impairments. The aim of the VALID Data Archive is to unite various available datasets ranging from metadata, experimental results, and test outcomes to spontaneous speech data, including video recordings, and to develop unambiguous protocols to ascertain the interpretation of research outcomes. In the CLARIN-NL framework five VALID data resources were curated; an overview of the key information on each of these five data resources is provided in the Appendix. For all datasets concerned, written informed consent has been obtained from the participants or their carers. All materials were anonymised. The audio files were converted into wav (linear PCM) files and the transcriptions into CHAT or ELAN format. Research data that consisted of test, SPSS and Excel files were documented and converted into CSV files. All datasets obtained appropriate CMDI metadata files. A new CMDI metadata profile for this type of data resources was established and care was taken that ISOcat metadata categories were used to optimise interoperability. A full overview of VALID metadata categories can be found in Klatter-Folmer et al. (2014). After curation all data were deposited at the Max Planck Institute for Psycholinguistics in Nijmegen, where persistent identifiers are linked to all resources. The content of the transcriptions in CHAT and plain text format can be searched with the TROVA search engine (cf. Klatter-Folmer et al., 2014; van den Heuvel et al., 2014).

The most important difference with the Child Language Data Exchange System (CHILDES[2]) is that VALID is a specialised structured database for all types of data related to pathological language, ranging from metadata, experimental results and test outcomes to spontaneous speech data, including video recordings. CHILDES, on the other hand, covers the spectrum of first-language acquisition research data, focusing in particular on spontaneous speech data, and with fewer datasets from child clinical groups. Moreover, the VALID Data Archive covers all age groups.

The realisation of the data archive was made possible by a CLARIN-NL grant (12-010) for a pilot project. This pilot enabled us to build up experience in conserving different kinds of pathological language data in a searchable and persistent manner. The conserved datasets reflect current research in language pathology rather well, both in the range of designs and in the variety in pathological problems, such as Specific Language Impairment (SLI), deafness, dyslexia and ADHD (Klatter-Folmer et al., 2014; van den Heuvel et al., 2014). The first author of the present contribution carried out the study presented below (Bergmann, 2015), monitored by Roeland van Hout (VALID data provider) and Jetske Klatter (VALID project leader). A main goal of this study was to test the accessibility of the VALID data archive and to signal problems met in extracting the data.

14.2   SLI Diagnostics in Narratives

SLI is a set of speech and language disorders with high co-morbidity with other disorders and impairments. Its definition is based on exclusion criteria and is related to a mix of linguistic, sensory, cognitive, neural-motor, and emotional restrictions. This rather unsatisfactory definition is largely due to the heterogeneous speech and language behaviour of SLI children (Manders, De Bal and Van den Heuvel, 2013), while at the same time no specific causes of SLI have been detected yet (Archibald and Gathercole, 2006). The co-morbidity patterns found do support the idea that SLI is a multi-factorial disorder (Bishop, 2006).

SLI children display a problematic and delayed development in language form, function, and use, where impairments may occur in all language domains, such as phonology, semantics,

---

[2]   http://childes.talkbank.org/

morphosyntax, and pragmatics (Casalini et al., 2007). Bishop (2006) concluded that SLI children obviously have difficulties in adequately processing information that is being offered in a short time span, as is the case in spoken conversations. For the majority of SLI children, grammar is a difficult area, and weak morphosyntactic skills are correlated with poor lexical-semantic skills (Simon-Cereijido and Gutiérrez-Clellen, 2009; Toppelberg and Shapiro, 2000; Bishop, 2013).

Studies focusing on the complexity and accuracy of morphosyntax address a range of features. Smith-Lock (1993) already pointed to differences between SLI and typically developing (TD) children in passive sentence constructions, and Rice performed several investigations into mean length of utterance (MLU), showing that SLI children lag behind in MLU, partly because of the absence of complex morphosyntactic constructions, e.g. subordinate clauses and question clauses (Rice, Redmond and Hoffman, 2006). As for accuracy, research by Vandewalle et al. (2012) showed errors in verb inflection, articles, and word order, when compared to TD children, and Simon-Cereijido and Gutiérrez-Clellen (2009) mentioned deletion of function words. In SLI, the production of complex utterances triggers an increase in morphosyntactic errors, as complex utterances are obviously more demanding (Colozzo et al., 2011).

Considering lexical complexity and accuracy, Bishop (1992) argued that SLI children have difficulties processing linguistic input as a whole, resulting in weak and inefficient connections between words, which in turn leads to longer retrieval time and more errors in word choice (Kambanaros et al., 2014). In a longitudinal study of 500 SLI and TD children, Rice and Hoffman (2015) found that SLI children consistently performed less well than age-matched TD children on lexical tasks.

Gaining more insight into the causes and characteristics of SLI requires a detailed diagnostic procedure. The usual battery of SLI test materials focuses on communication in structured settings, such as inviting participants to select the image that best represents a stimulus word. These experimental settings are unnatural and provide scarce information about linguistic skills in a spontaneous or semi-structured conversation (Peña et al., 2006). This argues for using narrative tests that combine spontaneous quality with a structured content. Retelling a picture story requires quite different competencies to those used in structured settings, such as introducing the characters, explaining the topic and structuring the text. Also, (re)telling a story challenges people to be more explicit and to produce longer linguistic units (Treurniet, 2011; Treurniet and Orgassa, 2011). As in these tasks children tend to show more linguistic variation and produce more utterances, they are an appropriate means for collecting data on morphosyntactic and lexical skills. Several studies confirm that narratives demonstrate the morphosyntactic and lexical problems of SLI children (e.g. Kambanaros et al., 2014; Vandewalle et al., 2012).

The morphosyntactic and/or lexical accuracy and complexity of narratives by SLI children were analysed in three earlier studies in the Netherlands: that of Treurniet (2011); Verhoeven, Steenge and Van Balkom (2011); and Zwitserlood et al. (2015). All three studies mention problems in the morphosyntactic and/or lexical domain for SLI children. Each used a different set of narrative data. The VALID Data Archive contains yet another, new narrative dataset. Departing from the Dutch studies, the following research questions and hypotheses were formulated for our study:

A. How do SLI children perform with regard to morphosyntactic accuracy and complexity in a narrative in comparison to their typically developing peers?

   H1: SLI children use morphosyntactically less complex language

   H2: SLI children are morphosyntactically less accurate

B. How do SLI children perform with regard to lexical accuracy and complexity in a narrative in comparison to their typically developing peers?

   H3: SLI children use lexically less complex language

   H4: SLI children are lexically less accurate

14.3   Method

All the tasks performed by participants in a collective research project led by Radboud University Nijmegen and Kentalis on the expression of spatial relations by SLI children in oral language production were stored in the CLARIN-NL VALID Data Archive; this so-called SLI RU-Kentalis database was one of the five sets that were curated. This database contains narratives by SLI and TD children. In this contribution we discuss a new analysis of the *Frog goes to dinner* narrative. Analysing these data from a perspective that differs from the main aim of the original project (which was to study how SLI children expressed spatial relations in this narrative) was a good test to explore whether the VALID Data Archive is easily accessible and usable for new researchers with new questions.

The Netherlands has special schools for SLI children. To be eligible for special education and extra care, children with SLI have to meet certain criteria that have been acknowledged by the Ministry of Education, Cultural Affairs and Science of the Dutch government. A child's communicative and cognitive abilities are assessed in an examination by a speech therapist, a psychologist and if necessary an audiologist. The SLI diagnosis is made when a child has speech or language impairments that cannot be attributed to limited cognitive abilities. Furthermore, it has to be established that the child has problems in two or more of the following language areas: speech production, auditory processing, and grammatical development or lexical-semantic knowledge. Only the children whose scores on standardised language tests for at least two of these aspects of language are 1.5 standard deviation below average are admitted onto a special form of education.

Only the children with grammatical and lexical-semantic problems were included in the original research project. The selection was made based on the children's achievements on standardised language tests given by the SLI schools: children whose language scores were 1.5 standard deviation or more below average on at least one subtest measuring syntactic and semantic development met the criteria to be included in the research project. The children who participated in the study all have Dutch as a first language.

The sample we used included 74 children out of the total of 93 participants in the original research project: 50 SLI children and 24 TD children, 40 boys and 34 girls. Main reasons for excluding children from the sample were that we constrained the analysis to three age groups or that for some participants less than 30 utterances that could be analysed for the narrative were available (see Bishop and McDonald, 2010). The children came from primary school classes 2 to 7 (Dutch school system), and both the SLI and the TD children were divided into three age groups in order to investigate age effects in the development of their language proficiency (Table 14.1).

The picture book that was used in the narrative was *Frog goes to dinner* (Mayer, 1974). The reason for choosing this book instead of the more famous *Frog, where are you?* (Mayer, 1969) was that the *Frog goes to dinner* book contained a large and varied number of spatial elements and relations which suited the research perspective of the main project much better. In this black-and-white illustrated story, a little boy brings his frog to a fancy restaurant. The frog manages to escape from

	N	Gender		Age group								
		Male	Female	5;6 – 7;5			7;6 – 9;5			9;6 – 12;0		
				N	mean	SD	N	mean	SD	N	mean	SD
TD	24	12	12	10	6.60	0.77	8	8.60	0.62	6	10.27	0.62
SLI	50	28	22	10	6.87	0.39	16	8.13	0.68	24	10.62	0.83
Total	74	40	34		20			24			30	

Table 14.1: Overview of subjects: gender; age group (N, mean age, and SD).

the boy's coat pocket and causes a number of incidents. The plot is worked out in 30 pictures. Before starting the audio recording, the children were invited to leaf through the book. During the actual retelling the researcher, if necessary, asked open questions to motivate the child to continue the narrative. The narrative was recorded using a Sony MZ-NH 700 minidisk recorder. An external microphone was added to enhance the quality of the recordings.

The VALID Data Archive contains not only the audio files, but also the transcripts and TextGrids for the PRAAT analysis tool (Boersma and Weenink, 2004). A TextGrid is a transcript of the audio file that can be made visible simultaneously with the audio file in PRAAT. The transcripts are available in CHAT format (MacWhinney, 2000), which makes calculation of MLU5 and Guiraud's index (CLAN) possible by using CLAN tools.

Before starting the analysis, all transcripts were processed to mark and select the utterances appropriate for the analyses to be performed. Examples of utterances labelled as not appropriate for deeper analyses on the utterance level were 'yes' and 'no' answers and straightforward formulaic utterances (e.g. 'ik weet het niet', 'I don't know'). The steps of analysis are depicted in Figure 14.1. In general, in all three age groups, the TD group produced more appropriate or usable utterances than the SLI group. Both the transcripts and the audio files were used to analyse the data.

Morphosyntactic complexity was measured with MLU5, which stands for the mean length of utterances (in words) of the five longest utterances of a child, using CLAN.

Morphosyntactic accuracy, as the percentage of correct utterances, was measured by marking utterances containing errors in: position/inflection of verbs, noun form, word order, omission of function words, and grammatical gender. Utterances that were rectified by the child (self-correction) were labelled as correct.

For lexical complexity Guiraud's index was calculated. First a list was drawn up of all words in the transcripts, excluding proper names, onomatopoeia, and noninterpretable words. Words like 'ja' ('yes') and 'ok' were also left out, because they are not suitable to establish a child's vocabulary size (Schaerlaekens, 2008). Guiraud's index is computed by dividing the number of types by the square root of the number of tokens, resulting in a measure of richness of the productive lexicon.

Lexical accuracy was again expressed by the percentage of correct utterances. Utterances containing incorrect function words (e.g. prepositions, conjunctions) and neologisms were categorised as incorrect. The same procedure was applied if content words were used with a wrong meaning.

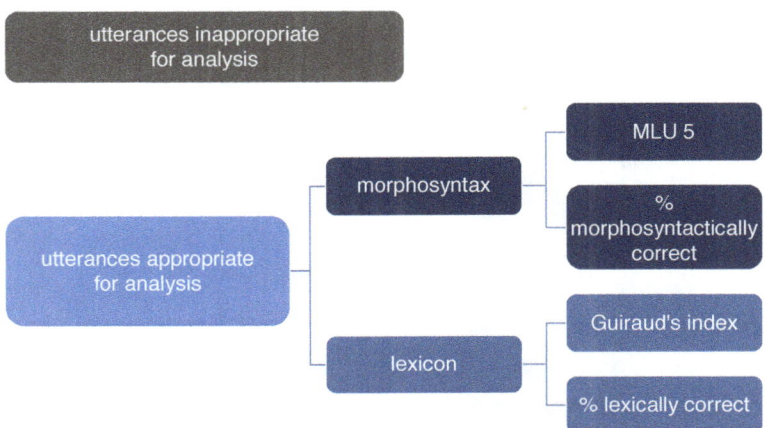

Figure 14.1: Analysis diagram.

14.4   Results

14.4.1   Morphosyntactic Complexity

This variable was investigated by selecting the five longest utterances in words that were lexically and morphosyntactically correct: the MLU5. Figure 14.2 gives the relevant box plots for TD and SLI children.

The (TD vs. SLI) Group (F(1, 68) = 21, 73, $p = 0.000$, $\eta_p^2 = 0, 24$) and Age (F(2, 68) = 9, 42, $p = 0.000$, $\eta_p^2 = 0, 22$) factors turned out to be significant in ANOVA. The interaction effect between these two variables was not significant (F(2, 68) = 0, 37, $p = 0.692$, $\eta_p^2 = 0, 01$). Posthoc tests for age group (Tukey HSD) showed differences between the youngest and the middle group, but not between the middle and oldest group. The TD children reached higher MLU5 values than the SLI group. MLU5 increased with age between the youngest and the two older groups.

14.4.2   Morphosyntactic Accuracy

In Figure 14.3 accuracy in morphosyntax is shown by the box plots of the percentage of correct utterances.

There was a significant effect for Group (F(1, 68) = 15, 79, $p = 0.000$, $\eta_p^2 = 0, 19$) and Age (F(2, 68) = 5, 91, $p = 0.004$, $\eta_p^2 = 0, 15$), but there was again no interaction effect (F(2, 68) = 0, 22, $p = 0.805$, $\eta_p^2 = 0, 01$). Tukey HSD tests pointed again to differences between the youngest and the two older age groups.

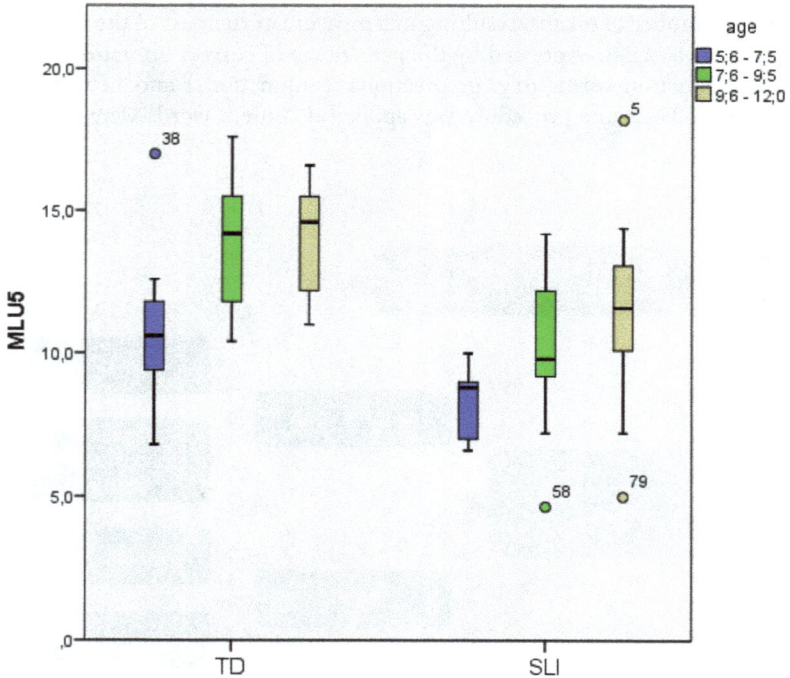

Figure 14.2: Box plots of the mean length in words of the five morphosyntactically longest utterances (MLU5), by child (TD or SLI) and age group.

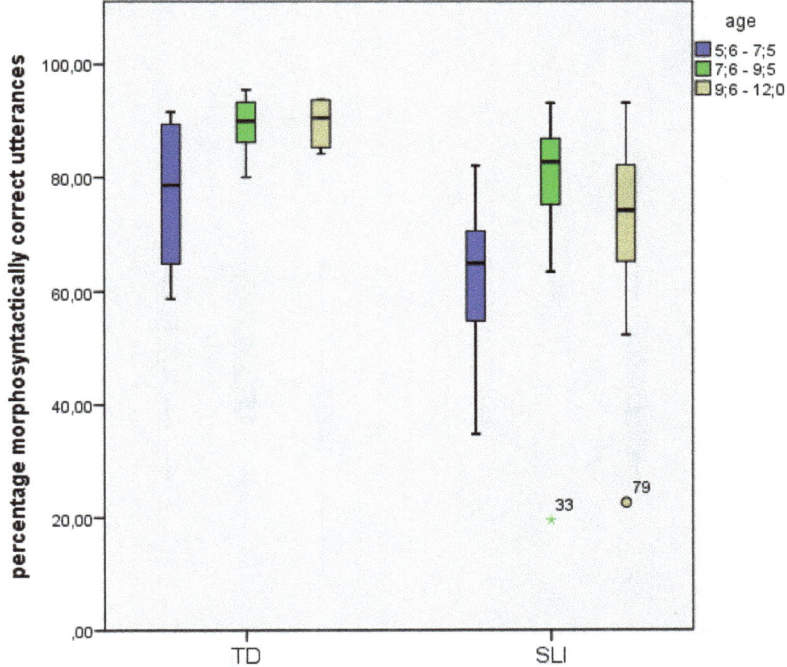

Figure 14.3: Box plots showing the percentage of morphosyntactically correct utterances by child (TD or SLI) and age group.

14.4.3   *Lexical Complexity*

The box plots of the scores on Guiraud's index for lexical richness are shown in Figure 14.4.

Group ($F(1, 68) = 4, 39, p = 0.040, \eta_p^2 = 0, 06$) and Age ($F(2, 68) = 4, 27, p = 0.018, \eta_p^2 = 0, 11$) turned out to be significant, with no significant interaction effect ($F(2, 68) = 1, 68, p = 0.194, \eta_p^2 = 0, 05$). Tukey HSD did not show differences between the age groups, indicating that the age differences are not large.

14.4.4   *Lexical Accuracy*

The box plots of accuracy in vocabulary are given in Figure 14.5.

ANOVA showed that Group caused a significant effect ($F(1, 68) = 0, 16, p = 0.017, \eta_p^2 = 0, 08$), which did not apply to the Age factor ($F(2, 68) = 1, 97, p = 0.854, \eta_p^2 = 0, 01$). An interaction effect between age group and SLI was established ($F(2, 68) = 3, 80, p = 0.027, \eta_p^2 = 0, 10$). Tukey HSD did not point to differences between age groups.

14.5   Discussion

In this section, we first relate the results to our hypotheses. Table 14.2 gives the partial eta squares (η^2) for the effects that turned out to be significant.

Morphosyntactic skills H1: SLI children use morphosyntactically less complex language.

H2: SLI children are morphosyntactically less accurate.

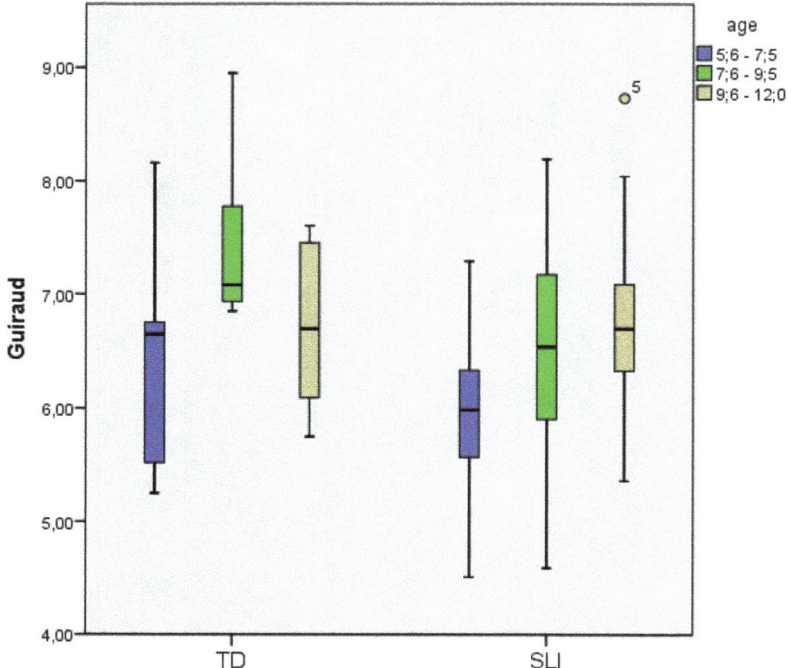

Figure 14.4: Box plots for Guiraud's index, split out by child (TD or SLI) and age group.

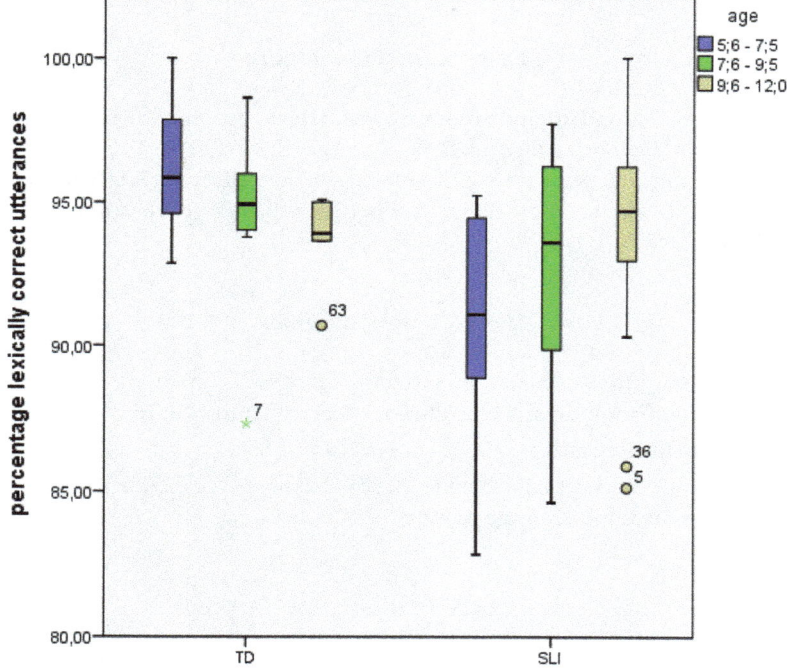

Figure 14.5: Box plots showing the percentage of lexically correct utterances, by child (TD or SLI) and age group.

Language modality	Variable	SLI	Age	SLI × Age
Morphosyntax	MLU5	0.24	0.22	—*
	% correct	0.19	0.15	—
Lexicon	Guiraud	0.06	0.11	—
	% correct	0.08	—	0.10

* No significant effect found

Table 14.2: Overview of significant effects of the ANOVA analyses (η^2).

The results of our study support both hypotheses on morphological skills. In all age groups SLI children produced morphosyntactically less complex and less accurate utterances than age-matched TD children. There is an age effect as well, indicating development over time in both groups. The morphosyntactic skills of SLI children were lower than those of their TD peers. These findings correspond to findings in other studies: Heilmann, Miller and Nockerts (2010) consider MLU a valid diagnostic variable for SLI, and so do Dunn, Flax and Sliwinski (1996). Smith-Lock (1993) has advised to carefully interpret MLU because raw data do not warrant any direct conclusions about the complexity of language, but in combination with other linguistic variables, e.g. the percentage of morphosyntactically correct utterances, MLU is useful in identifying SLI (Moyle et al., 2011; Simon-Cereijido and Gutiérrez-Clellen, 2009). Colozzo et al. (2011) also concluded that SLI children have problems in telling a grammatically accurate story; they therefore investigated the content quality of the story, and observed that children with weak morphosyntactic skills delivered less consistent narratives. In our study an assessment of the content quality was not carried out, but in future research (using the CLARIN-NL VALID Data Archive) content quality could be used to better assess the language production processes in SLI children.

Lexical skills H3: SLI children use lexically less complex language
H4: SLI children are lexically less accurate

The two lexical hypotheses were also corroborated by the data. In comparison to their TD peers, children with SLI produced less lexically complex and less accurate utterances. The age effect was straightforward for complexity: complexity increased with age. There was no main effect of age for accuracy, but an interaction between group and age, indicating that the age difference only affected the SLI group. The TD children already had high lexical accuracy scores in the youngest group, and the mean score does not show a pattern of change over time. The SLI lexical scores are lower than the TD lexical scores, but importantly the SLI lexical accuracy scores are much higher (all above 80%) than the SLI morphosyntactic accuracy scores (with scores as low as 20%). Lexical problems apparently are less strong or surface less strongly than morphosyntactic problems in SLI children, a conclusion supported by the lower partial eta squared values in the lexical outcomes. The morphosyntactic and lexical accuracy scores are marked by outliers, i.e. children who have scores far higher or lower than their age and child group. The variability in scores seems more typical of SLI children, who can have extremely severe impairments in specific linguistic domains. Remarkably, there are high correlations between the lexical and the morphosyntactic accuracy score, i.e. 0.82 for the TD children and 0.92 for the SLI children. This result deviates from the findings in Kambanaros et al. (2014), who investigated lexical proficiency with similar variables: SLI children performed less accurately on the lexical and morphosyntactic level, but contrary to our study no relation between the two skills was observed.

How do our results compare to results found earlier in analyses of narratives of monolingual Dutch TD and SLI children? Treurniet (2011; see also Treurniet and Orgassa, 2011 compared 7-year-old SLI children to 5-year-old TD children. The TD children, although two years younger, turned out to have the same scores as the SLI children for lexical and morphosyntactic accuracy.

As in our study the scores on morphosyntactic accuracy (53%, a score lower than our scores in the same age groups) were much lower than lexical accuracy ones (88%, a score comparable to our scores). Their average Guiraud scores (5.6) seem a bit lower than ours, but they had a different frog story.

A second study including monolingual TD and SLI children is the one performed by Verhoeven et al. (2011), who measured MLU on all usable utterances and grammatical accuracy, with criteria similar to ours. Their MLU returned a significant SLI effect ($\eta^2 = .06$), a significant age effect (two age groups: 7- and 9-year-olds; $\eta^2 = .19$) and no interaction effect. Although they computed the MLU on all usable utterances their effect sizes were lower than ours – this perhaps demonstrates that it is preferable to restrict the MLU to the subset of longest utterances. Their grammatical accuracy scores give an SLI effect ($\eta^2 = .38$), an age effect ($\eta^2 = .06$), and no interaction. The scores (TD with an average of 80% grammatical accuracy and SLI with an average of 46% grammatical accuracy) are lower than we found, and the gap between SLI and TD children seems wider.

A third study on narratives is the longitudinal study by Zwitserlood et al. (2015), which included monolingual SLI and TD children as well, ranging in age from 6.5 to 8.5 years. The authors found an SLI effect ($\eta^2 = .27$), an age effect ($\eta^2 = .16$), and no interaction effect between age and SLI for MLU. They found particular strong effects for grammatical accuracy: the SLI effect was $\eta^2 = .72$, the age effect $\eta^2 = .34$, and there was no interaction effect; the TD scores, with an average of 85%, are similar to ours, while the SLI scores, with an average of 48%, are much lower.

The positive outcome of all studies, including ours, is that the effects found are comparable. The effects all show that our measures, in particular morphosyntactic/grammatical accuracy, proved to be useful in diagnosing SLI children. On the other hand there is an obvious overlap in scores between the TD and SLI groups, restricting the diagnostic value of our measures. At the same time the results of the four studies show substantial variation in effect sizes. Stronger effect sizes are crucial when it comes to powerful diagnostics. The differences in outcomes between the four studies may have multiple sources, e.g. the homogeneity of the groups of participants, the design type (cross-sectional vs. longitudinal), and the coding schemes applied to the complicated, rich narrative data. The data curated in the VALID Data Archive, accessible to all interested researchers, demonstrates the necessity to combine and accumulate data not only in their raw format but also through coding schemes and coded data, to increase the analytic power and to calibrate our research tools. That seems particularly relevant when the data are intricate, as in the case of narratives.

Finally, it is important to observe that precise details on data analysis are often lacking in published articles, including the ones we discussed. One often needs the detailed, original protocols to understand how specific decisions are being taken in defining utterances (or perhaps T-units) and subordination (directly relevant to the MLU). The same applies to the definition of words, morphemes and accuracy measures. These decisions have direct consequences for the outcomes and may obscure the (dis)similarities between different studies.

14.6   Conclusion

As frequently stated in the research literature on language development, narratives are an appropriate and attractive option for gathering rich data on the linguistic, cognitive, and social competencies of SLI children (Befi-Lopes, Bento and Perissinoto, 2008). Gathering, transcribing and coding narratives is laborious and time-consuming, however. Given their richness it seems self-evident to store such data sources in accessible, standardised formats. The CLARIN goals made the VALID Data Archive possible and we see this as a first step in establishing the availability of data sources to improve and widen the research perspectives on language and speech pathology (Rietveld et al., 2005).

We analysed the dataset on SLI children available in the VALID Data Archive and found several small infelicities that could be remedied – the Data Archive is now more easily usable. Using and trying out the Data Archive is an important step not only in improving the database, but also in adding to the data new information that came out of the new analyses. It also shows how important it is to have other research data available. CLARIN also made available the data used in Treurniet (2011) and the Functional Elements in Specific Language Impairment (FESLI)[3] data (Treurniet and Orgassa, 2011); it seems self-evident to link the FESLI corpus (12 bilingual children without SLI, 25 monolingual children with SLI, 20 bilingual children with SLI) more directly to the VALID Data Archive. The Verhoeven et al. (2011) and Zwitserlood et al. (2015) data are unfortunately not accessible. The main goal of the VALID enterprise is to include other databases in the archive. An archive is pivotal in evaluating the robustness of experimental outcomes in terms of reproducibility and replicability. VALID is a proper medium to guarantee the quality and comparability of datasets.

The results of the present investigation motivate more in-depth research on morphosyntactic and lexical variables in order to improve the diagnostics and treatment of SLI children. The effects for morphosyntax were strongest, but in absolute terms were still weak. Morphosyntactic variables are generally considered important indicators for identifying SLI (Dunn, Flax and Sliwinski, 1996). The availability of larger amounts of standardised and enriched data sources might sharpen our analyses by enabling us to focus more on correlational patterns (what is the relation between morphosyntactic and lexical problems, a correlation we found in our analysis but which is not reported in the other Dutch studies) and on actual speech patterns (by applying for instance machine learning techniques on string data). CLARIN and its data formats offer the proper perspective on establishing the rich data sources we need and, hopefully, will motivate researchers to make their data available on the internet.

References

Archibald, L., & Gathercole, S. (2006). Prevalence of SLI in language resource units. *Journal of Research in Special Educational Needs, 6*, 3–10. doi: 10.1111/J.1471-3802.2006.00054.x

Befi-Lopes, D., Bento, A.C.P., & Perissinoto, J. (2008). Narration of stories by children with specific language impairment. *Pró-Fono Revista de Atualização Científica, 2*, 93–8. doi: 10.1590/S1516-18462012005000105

Bergmann, L. (2015). Taalvaardigheden in narratieven van kinderen met SLI. Nijmegen: Radboud University (master thesis).

Bishop, D.V.M. (1992). The underlying nature of specific language impairment. *Journal of Child Psychology and Psychiatry, 33*, 3–66. doi: 10.1111/j.1469-7610.1992.tb00858.x

Bishop, D.V.M. (2006). What causes Specific Language Impairment in children? *Current Directions in Psychological Science, 15(5)*, 217–221. doi: 10.1111/j.1467–8721.2006.00439.x

Bishop, D.V.M. (2013). Neuroscientific studies of intervention for language impairment in children: Interpretive and methodological problems. Emanuel Miller Memorial Lecture 2012. *Journal of Child Psychology and Psychiatry, 54(3)*, 247–259. doi: 10.1111/jcpp.12034

Bishop, D.V.M., & McDonald, D. (2010). Identifying language impairment in children: Combining language test scores with parental report. *International Journal of Language and Communication Disorders, 44*, 600–615. doi: 10.1080/13682820802259662

Boersma, P., & Weenink, D. (2004). *PRAAT*. Amsterdam: Universiteit van Amsterdam.

Casalini, C., Brizzolara, D., Chilosi, A., Cipriani, P., Marcolini, S., Pecini, C., Roncoli, S., & Burani, C. (2007). Non-word repetition in children with specific language impairment: A deficit in phonological working memory or in long-term verbal knowledge? *Cortex, 43*, 769–76.

---

[3]   https://dev.clarin.nl/node/1948

Colozzo, P., Gillam, R.B., Wood, M., Schnell, R.D., & Johnston, J.R. (2011). Content and form in the narratives of children with Specific Language Impairment. *Journal of Speech Language and Hearing Research, 54*, 1609–1627. doi:10.1044/1092-4388(2011/10-0247)

Dunn, M., Flax, J., & Sliwinski, M. (1996). The use of spontaneous language measures as criteria for identifying children with Specific Language Impairment: An attempt to reconcile clinical and research incongruence. *Journal of Speech Language and Hearing Research, 39*, 643–654. doi: 10.1044/jshr.3903.643

Heilmann, J.J., Miller, J.F., & Nockerts, A. (2010). Using language sample databases. *Language, speech, and hearing services, 41*, 84–95. doi: 10.1044/0161-1461(2009/08-0075)

Kambanaros, M., Grohmann, K.K., Theodorou, E., & Michaelides, M. (2014). Can vocabulary size predict narrative abilities in children with SLI? *Language Disorders, 6*, 60–81. doi: 10.1080/14790718.2012.705846

Klatter-Folmer, J., van Hout, R., van den Heuvel, H, Fikkert, P., Baker, A., Jong, J. de, Wijnen, F., Sanders, E. & Trilsbeek, P. (2014). Vulnerability in Acquisition: Language Impairments in Dutch Creating a VALID Data Archive. *Language Resources and Evaluation Conference Proceedings* (LREC), Reykjavik, 26–31 May 2014, 357–364.

MacWhinney, B. (2000). *The CHILDES Project: Tools for Analyzing Talk.* 3rd edition. Mahwah, NJ: Lawrence Erlbaum Associates.

Manders, E., Bal, C. De, & Heuvel, E. Van den (2013). *Taalontwikkelingsstoornissen: fenomenen, onderzoek en behandeling [Language development disorders: phenomena, research, and treatment].* Antwerpen, Belgium: Grant.

Mayer, M. (1969). Frog, where are you? New York: Dial Press.

Mayer, M. (1974). *Frog goes to dinner.* New York: Dial Press.

Moyle, M.J., Karasinski, C., Weismer, S.E., & Gorman, B.K. (2011). Grammatical morphology in school-age children with and without language impairment: A discriminant function analysis. *Journal of Language, Speech and Hearing Service, 42*, 550–560. doi: 10.1044/0161-1461(2011/10-0029)

Peña, E.D., Gillam, R.B., Malek, M., Ruiz-Felter, R., Resendiz, M., Fiestas, C., & Sabel, T. (2006). Dynamic assessment of school-age children's narrative ability: An experimental investigation of classification accuracy. *Journal of Speech, Language, and Hearing Research, 49*, 1037–1057. doi: 10.1044/1092-4388(2006/074)

Rice, M.L., Redmond, S.M., & Hoffman, L. (2006). Mean Length of Utterance in children with Specific Language Impairment and in younger control children shows concurrent validity and stable and parallel growth trajectories. *Journal of Speech, Language and Hearing Research, 49*, 793–808. doi: 1092-4388/06/4904-0793

Rice, M.L., & Hoffman, L. (2015). Predicting vocabulary growth in children with and without Specific Language Impairment (SLI): A longitudinal study from $2\frac{1}{2}$ to 21 years of age. *Journal of Speech Language Hearing Research, 58*, 345–359. doi:10.1044/2015_JSLHR-L-14-0150

Rietveld, T., Stolte, I., van den Heuvel, T., Klatter, J., van Balkom, H., Dupont, J., & Ruiter, M. (2005). *Taal- en spraaktechnologie en communicatieve beperkingen.* 's-Gravenhage: Nederlandse Taalunie.

Schaerlaekens, A. (2008). *De taalontwikkeling van het kind [The language development of the child].* Groningen, The Netherlands: Noordhoff Uitgevers.

Simon-Cereijido, G., & Gutiérrez-Clellen, V. (2009). Spontaneous language markers of Spanish language impairment. *Applied Psycholinguistics, 28*, 317–339. doi: 10.1017.S0142716407070166

Smith-Lock, K.M. (1993). Morphological analysis and the acquisition of morphology and syntax in specifically-language-impaired children. *Status Report on Speech Research, 114*, 113–138.

Toppelberg, C.O., & Shapiro, T. (2000). Language disorders: A 10-year research update review. *Journal of the American Academy of Child & Adolescent Psychiatry, 39*, 143–152. doi: 10.1097/00004583-200002000-00011.

Treurniet, M. (2011). Tweetaligheid en SLI: morfosyntactische en lexicale vaardigheid in narratieven [Bilingualism and SLI: Morphosyntactic and lexical skills in narratives]. Nijmegen, The Netherlands: Radboud University.

Treurniet, M. & Orgassa, A. (2011). 'Kikker, waar ben jij?' Grammaticale en lexicale vaardigheden in SLI en tweetaligheid ['Frog, where are you?' Grammatical and lexical skills in SLI and biligualism]. *Logopedie en Foniartrie, 12*, 392–398.

Van den Heuvel, H., Sanders, E., Klatter-Folmer, J., van Hout, R., Fikkert, P., Baker, A., Jong, J. de, Wijnen, F. & Trilsbeek, P. (2014). Data curation for a VALID Archive of Dutch Language Impairment Data. *Dutch Journal of Applied Linguistics 3(2)*, 127–135, doi: 10.1075/dujal.3.2.02heu

Vandewalle, E., Boets, B., Boons, T., Ghesquière, P., & Zink, I. (2012). Oral language and narrative skills in children with Specific Language Impairment with and without literacy delay: A three-year longitudinal study. *Research in Developmental Disabilities, 33(6)*, 1857–1870. doi: 10.1016/j.ridd.2012.05.004

Verhoeven, L., Steenge, J., & Van Balkom, H. (2011). Verb morphology as clinical marker of specific language impairment: Evidence from first and second language learners. *Research in Developmental Disabilities 32*, 1186–1193. doi: 10.1016/j.ridd.2011.01.001

Zwitserlood, R., van Weerdenburg, M., Verhoeven, L., Wijnen, F. (2015). Development of morphosyntactic accuracy and grammatical complexity in Dutch school-age children with SLI. *Journal of Speech, Language, and Hearing Research 58*, 891–905. doi: 10.1044/2015_ JSLHR-L-14-0015

Appendix

(1) The SLI RU-Kentalis Database

Informants: 63 SLI + 24 controls; Characteristics: 56 boys and 31 girls ; 5 – 12 years old; Specific Language Impairment (SLI); Aim of data collection: investigation of the expression of spatial relations by children with SLI and typically developing children in their spoken language production; Materials available: Tests: Raven, WISC (Block Pattern, Mazes), Peabody: SPSS data files; Photo/Film Task – audio recorded: transcript in Praat; data processed and coded in SPSS; Route Description Task – audio/video recorded: transcript in Praat; data processed and coded in SPSS; TAK Narrative – audio recorded: transcript in Praat; data processed and coded in SPSS; Frog Narrative – audio recorded: transcript in Praat; data processed and coded in SPSS; Size: 1st measure 13.9 GB, 2nd measure +/–13.9 GB (Photo/Film); 18.9 GB (Route Description); 1st measure 1.75GB, 2nd measure 1.46 GB (TAK); 3.10 GB (Frog); 1 MB (test and background data).

(2) The UU SLI-Dyslexia Project Database

Informants: two longitudinal cohorts: (a) babies, from 19 months to approximately 37 months; N ≈ 110. (b) toddlers; 3;2 (years; months) at the onset; about 5;0 at the last test session; N ≈ 140; Characteristics: baby cohort: ~70 children at familial risk (FR) of dyslexia; ~40 controls; toddler cohort: ~70 FR children, ~40 controls, ~30 children (tentatively) diagnosed with Specific Language Impairment (SLI). Children from both cohorts have returned to the lab at age 8 for follow-up tests: toddler cohort: n = 107; baby cohort: n = 65; Aim of data collection: to explore early language development in children at FR of dyslexia; to compare developmental language profiles in FR children and children with SLI. Materials available: preferential listening experiment; measurement of listening times in several trials; categorical perception experiment; tests of productive phonology (elicited naming); various procedures (book reading; card matching); digital recordings of speech, (partly) transcribed in IPA and coded for phonological errors; word–picture matching experiment;

eye gaze to corresponding pictures (one out of two per trial) was recorded; lexical decision experiment: words (presented in combination with pictures) were correctly or incorrectly pronounced (phonemic errors); many speech elicitation experiments (various designs; digital audio recording; partial transcriptions); auditory grammaticality judgement task; all coded responses in Excel / SPSS formats; WISC digit span task; Snijders-Oomen nonverbal intelligence test; N-CDI's: standardised communicative development inventory, completed by participants' parents; Size: raw estimate of 60 GB.

(3) The Bilingual Deaf Children RU-Kentalis Database

Informants: 11 deaf children, longitudinal; Characteristics: 5 boys and 6 girls ; 3 – 6 years old; prelingual deafness (hearing loss of minimally 80dB Fletcher Index on the best ear), no mental restrictions; Aim of data collection: investigation of the bilingual language and communication development of young deaf children in Sign Language of the Netherlands (SLN) and Dutch (D);

Materials available: Tests: Nijmeegse Observatieschaal voor Kleuters (NOK; SLN & D), Reynell Test voor Taalbegrip (SLN & D), Dutch version Assessing British Sign Language Development (SLN): data processed and coded in SPSS; Spider Story (SLN & D): data processed and coded in SPSS; Semi-structured conversations with deaf and hearing adults – video recorded (SLN & D): a selection of five minutes communication per recording has been selected and transcribed in a CHAT-like format (104 recordings); Size: 4 GB complete video recordings; 1 GB selected parts video recordings; 0.1 GB selected parts transcripts; 0.5 GB test and background data.

(4) The ADHD and SLI Corpus UvA Database

Informants: 26 Dutch children with ADHD, 19 Dutch children with SLI, 22 Dutch children controls; Characteristics: ages between 7 and 8 years; 80% male, 20% female; intelligence within normal ranges; Aim of data collection: to compare the language and executive functioning profiles of children with ADHD to that of children with SLI and TD children; Materials available: Tests: Sentence repetition task; Non-Word repetition task; Frog story narratives, processed in SPSS on morphological, syntactic and pragmatic measures; Children's Communicative Check-list II; CANTAB EF tasks for executive functioning; Size: 4 GB (67 recordings).

(5) The Deaf Adults RU Database

Informants: 46 deaf Dutch adults, 38 hearing Turkish adults, 24 hearing Moroccan adults, 10 Dutch controls; Characteristics: males: 22 deaf + 31 Turkish/Moroccan + 5 controls; females: 24 deaf + 31 Turkish/Moroccan + 5 controls; Aim of data collection: investigation of the acquisition of Dutch by deaf Dutch adults (late L1/early L2) and comparison to hearing Turkish and Moroccan-Arabic L2-learners of Dutch (late L2) on morphosyntactic aspects; Materials available: Test: standardised C-test Instaptoets Anderstalige Volwassenen (IAV); coded and processed in SPSS; Writing task The Frog Story: recorded and stored in ScriptLog (Holmquist), data coded and processed in Excel and SPSS; Size: 2 GB.

CHAPTER 15

D-LUCEA: Curation of the UCU Accent Project Data

Rosemary Orr[†] and Hugo Quené

ABSTRACT

The UCU Accent Project was set up in 2010 to collect a wide variety of non-native and native accents of English in an environment where English is the *lingua franca*, namely an international liberal arts and sciences college in Utrecht in the Netherlands. The recordings were made longitudinally over the three years of undergraduate study, and four cohorts of students were recorded in total. This yielded over 1,000 speech recordings over a six-year period in which the development of both native and non-native English accents in a non-native environment can be examined. In order to facilitate sharing the data with the wider research community, the D-LUCEA project undertook to curate the data. For each recording, the relevant concomitant metadata was produced, giving information to users of the database about the speaker, the technical specifications, the kinds of speech material recorded, and so forth. The project was funded by CLARIN, and specific CLARIN tools for curation were made available to us, including the Component Metadata Infrastructure (CMDI). To date, all of the speech data has been processed such that the metadata is available, and research is already running on this corpus, on topics as varied as prosodic convergence, L1 phonetic drift and phone convergence. Further plans include work with speaker recognition, accent recognition and models of language learning such as Flege's Speech Learning Model, the Critical Theory Hypothesis, and the Perceptual Assimilation Model.

15.1 Introduction

This chapter describes the UCU Accent project, and the curation of the resulting D-LUCEA database, making the recorded speech data with its concomitant metadata widely available to the

---

[†] Deceased.

How to cite this book chapter:
Orr, R and Quené, H. 2017. D-LUCEA: Curation of the UCU Accent Project Data. In: Odijk, J and van Hessen, A. (eds.) *CLARIN in the Low Countries*, Pp. 181–193. London: Ubiquity Press. DOI: https://doi.org/10.5334/bbi.15. License: CC-BY 4.0

research community at large. The data-curation project was funded by the Dutch partners in the pan-European CLARIN project, whose goals are to facilitate precisely this kind of work.

We describe some of the research that has been made possible via this project, as well as current plans for employing a similar method for the curation of data in a new speech accent corpus, Sprekend Nederland.

15.1.1   The UCU Accent Project

Evidence from research over the last few decades indicates that when talkers from different language or dialect backgrounds converse with each other, their dialects and accents tend to converge. This phenomenon has been observed for dialects of British English (Evans and Iverson 2007) as well as for dialects of Dutch in the IJsselmeerpolders (Scholtmeijer 1992) and has been observed in phonology, phonetics and stylistics (Pardo 2006).

Such convergence, and its opposite, namely divergence, are described by the Communication Adaptation Theory (Giles et al. 1991). According to this theory, younger talkers are more susceptible to this outside social pressure on their dialect or accent than older talkers are. Hence, university students provide an excellent group for the investigation of this phenomenon. Previous research involving university students has focused on native speakers of Northern and Southern varieties of British English (Evans and Iverson 2007). However, while social context can be important, convergence has also been observed without social context in word shadowing tasks (Goldinger 1998) and Trudgill (2004) suggests that, in line with the general human tendency to act like one's social peers, accommodation can be subconscious and automatic as well as conscious.

It is interesting to consider what happens in this respect when the common language is not a native language for the majority of speakers. When people from native and non-native backgrounds come together, and all speakers use, for example, English as a *lingua franca*, then how do their English accents change over time? Do native speakers drift away from their native pronunciation standards? Do non-native speakers become more native-like, and does interference from their L1 decrease over time? Does increasing proficiency in the L2 cause attrition in the L1? Is the speaker's English accent related to their intelligibility and subjective accentedness? And how stable are the speaker characteristics across L1 and L2?

The international *University College Utrecht* (UCU) in the Netherlands provides an ideal environment to investigate these kinds of adaptation, being an international body of students that includes both native (L1) and non-native speakers (L2) of English. To explore these questions, we set about collecting speech from students at the college at different moments during their three-year undergraduate program, covering four consecutive cohorts over a period of six years. Along with the speech data, we have recorded a rich set of metadata, including technical data about the equipment, speaker and facilitator data, session data, and logbook observations about each recording.

A core hypothesis in this project is that the native and non-native accents of UCU students will gradually converge to a single common international variety of English, which we call the UCU English accent. The convergence of a group of non-native accents to an international non-native variety has implications, both social and linguistic, for the speech of this student group, and is the overarching theme in our work on this project.

We expect that the factors affecting the emergence of a UCU accent of English will include the sort of English spoken by teachers in the classroom setting as well as the social groups formed by the students. Students tend to be very involved in the various campus committees within the Student Association, and their social groups are often formed around these. These observations lend themselves to sociolinguistic research, where the influence of the linguistic environment of the social and academic groups on the emergent accent can be explored. In particular, since the cultural and linguistic profiles of the social groups on campus change with each year, we might expect the UCU accent to be slightly different for each three-year cohort. This is particularly in social groups where a Dutch L1 is not prevalent.

Further opportunities for sociolinguistic research arise in the exploration of attitudes to the development of an accent of English. For example, it has been shown by Garrett (1992) that hyper-accommodation to prestige forms of English may evoke negative reactions from listeners, both native and non-native. Most students have a strong desire to achieve a native-sounding accent (Timmis 2002; Jenkins 2007). It is conceivable that some students will have a prestige accent as their target, while others will not. Listener attitudes to speaker accents, coupled with listener appraisal of accuracy of speaker accents may shed light on the type and degree of accommodation present at UCU, as well as the affective responses and intelligibility scores resulting from such accommodation in listeners from within and outside the campus community.

15.2   D-LUCEA: Sharing the Data in the Research Community

The possibilities for research on this speech data likely extend to a great many areas, including sociolinguistics, sociology, phonetics and phonology, and speech technology.

It has been our intention from the start to make the data freely available for scientific research, so that colleagues from anywhere can use our data to verify our findings or to explore different aspects or themes themselves. This raises the question of how to curate and distribute the speech data and metadata in a way that makes it maximally useful to the broad range of users that we envisage.

In order to be maximally useful, the format of the data and metadata files must facilitate interoperability across different kinds of technological infrastructures and collaboration across different research disciplines. The format should be robust against developments in and variations of software and hardware, and should meet an international standard.

In general terms, the curation of the data consisted of creating a general metadata profile to describe a generic speech recording, and then for each actual speech recording, creating a specific instance of that profile and linking it to the speech recording in question. This information, including the speech data, was then made available for download to the research community at large. The corpus was given the name *D-LUCEA*, for *Database of the Longitudinal Utrecht Collection of English Accents*.

In order to describe the curation process, we first give a description of the procedure for the data collection procedure, and then we describe the process of organising the metadata, and linking the speech recordings to that metadata in order to make it available for general access.

15.2.1   Recording Procedure, Speech Data and Concomitant Metadata

15.2.1.1   Recording Setup

Recording sessions took place in a quiet furnished office, with one or more facilitators and a speaker participant. Recordings were made on eight different channels. Figure 15.1 shows a schematic view of the setup where the positioning of each microphone is clearly marked. Microphone 1 is a close-talking headset microphone.

For each recording session, then, eight speech files were produced. The metadata associated with each recording is specific to the particular microphone channel.

15.2.1.2   Timing of the Recordings

Between August 2011 and June 2016, four cohorts of students took part in the project. For each cohort, between 60 and 80 students took part in at least the first recording. Recordings were made at five moments, or rounds during the students' period of study, namely at the beginning and end of

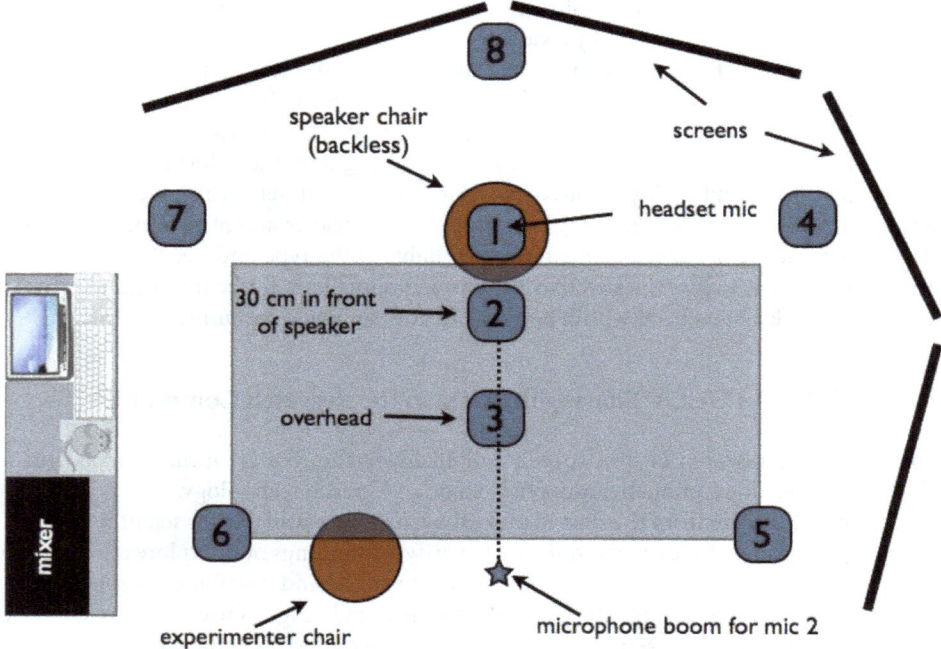

Figure 15.1: Schematic view of the recording setup.

Date	Cohort I	Cohort II	Cohort III	Cohort IV	Total
Sept 2010	79	-	-	-	75
May 2011	67	-	-	-	67
Sept 2011	60	78	-	-	138
May 2012	35	66	-	-	101
Sept 2012	-	61	72	-	122
May 2013	50	47	55	-	152
Sept 2013	-	-	51	58	107
May 2014	-	53	34	37	124
Sept 2014	-	-	-	40	40
May 2015	-	-	47	36	83
Sept 2015	-	-	-		0
May 2016	-	-	-	39	39
Total					1,048

Table 15.1: Six-year schedule of speaker recordings for longitudinal study, showing the number of speakers who participated in each round.

each college year, with the exception of the beginning of the third year, or fifth semester. Table 15.1 shows the recording schedule over the six years of the collection of the corpus.

15.2.1.3   Session Information

For each session, the following information is provided;

- recording ID, incorporating subject number and round number
- recording round, being one of round 1 to 5 for the speaker

- channel number, equivalent to the microphone number in the setup scheme above
- recording date
- whether an audible separator was used, and if so, what kind[1].

15.2.1.4   Speaker Task Information

The speakers were required to perform between 9 and 12 speaking tasks in each round, as outlined in Table 15.2 below. Some explanatory notes are also given for particular tasks, where relevant.

Most of the tasks were present from the very first recording, but others were added in order to produce data for comparison with other accented-speech corpora, in particular, the OSCAAR corpus and the ALLSSTAR corpus.[2] Specifically, the initial design did not include the articles from the Universal Declaration of Human Rights; these were introduced at the second round of recordings of the first cohort.

Task 1 was deleted from the recordings before publishing in order to preserve privacy. It allowed for a double-check on the speaker information per recording.

Task 4, The Boy who Cried Wolf, was initially a long passage with few shibboleths. From the second round of recordings from Cohort I, a second version, shorter and containing shibboleths, replaced the original one. Both versions can be found in Appendix IV, where the texts for tasks 2 to 7 are provided.

The substitution of a text with shibboleths was intended to elicit the different substitutions used by L2 speakers of English, and to examine whether and how these change over time.

Task 5 refers to sentences from Van Wijngaarden et al. (2002) for quantifying intelligibility of speech in noise for non-native listeners. There are 10 sets of 13 sentences, also to be found in Appendix IV. Native speakers of English were generally asked to speak all 10 sets. Non-native speakers were asked to speak between 3 and 4 of these sets. This was done in order to make sure

Task	Task Description
1	Speakers state their name, date and time
2	Short extract from the Rainbow Passage (Fairbanks 1960)
3	'Please Call Stella' (Weinberger 2013)
4	'The Boy who Cried *Wolf*' (Deterding 2006)
5	Balanced sentence sets for intelligibility testing (van Wijngaarden 1999)
6	Five sentences for investigating rhythm (White & Mattys 2007)
7	Extract: Declaration of Human Rights in L1 (Universal Declaration of Human Rights 2013)
8	Extract: Declaration of Human Rights in English (Universal Declaration of Human Rights 2013)
9	2 minute monologue L1, informal free topic
10	2 minute monologue English, informal free topic
11	2 minute monologue English, formal free topic
12	3 minute dialogue English with the facilitator, free topic

Table 15.2: The speaker tasks that could be required in a single recording session.

---

[1] After the first round of recordings, an audible separator was introduced between the tasks. The choice for an audible separator stems from the nature of the recording setup. It is not only a signal for separating tasks, but it is also a prompt for the participant, making clear when they should speak. It varied between the sound of a tap on a glass, a high-pitched recurring ping, or a bell.

[2] OSCAAR corpus: https://oscaar.ci.northwestern.edu/overview.php:
ALLSSTAR corpus: http://groups.linguistics.northwestern.edu/speech_comm_group/allsstar/

that not all non-native participants had read all texts. In this way, the participants could also take part in tests to assess the intelligibility of other speakers in the project. Cohorts I and IV spoke sets 1 to 3; Cohort II spoke sets 4 to 6; Cohort III spoke sets 7 to 10.

The metadata information per recording gives the tasks that were spoken for that recording, the order in which they were spoken, as well as the approximate start and end times for each task. Information included per task is as follows:

- modality (spoken)
- interactivity (whether interactive, semi- or non-interactive)
- whether spontaneous, semi-spontaneous or planned
- whether elicited or spontaneously generated
- whether monologue or dialogue

15.2.1.5   Speakers in the Recordings

The people recorded speaking in the project include the speaker who is producing the speech tasks, as well as the facilitators, who play a role not only in guiding the speaker through the tasks, but also in engaging in dialogue with the speaker during each session.

The speakers are mostly students, plus a few staff or faculty members at University College Utrecht UCU). The facilitators are faculty, staff and graduate or undergraduate students at UCU or at Utrecht University (UU).

15.2.1.6   Speaker Characteristics

For each speaker, a number of aspects of their exposure to different languages, physical characteristics, musicality, hearing ability and language practice are considered relevant to many of the questions that we envisage as applying to this dataset.

The lists below indicate the metadata related to the speaker. Most of the information regarding language usage was gathered from a questionnaire that the students filled in on entry to the project. A second questionnaire was filled in on completion of their degree with new questions which captured information that arose during the three-year period, for example, the student's major or possible minor, or where and when they had gone abroad for a semester.

The questions related to language learning from the first questionnaire were repeated in the exit questionnaire, and if there was a difference in the answers, the second answer was taken as the representative one. The reason for this is that students at UCU are required to learn another language to a good level of proficiency, and after three years they may have become less proficient – either comparatively or actually – in other languages that they spoke on entry to the college.

One of the interesting issues in assessing language exposure and proficiency was that of defining the native language or languages. This particular student population contains members for whom it is difficult to define a native language. Languages which were learned first were not always the dominant languages, and were sometimes either forgotten or underdeveloped.

For example, one participant has a father speaking one language X, a mother speaking language Y. Her father's language X was the first language she learned, albeit poorly, and she could understand but not speak her mother's language Y. She regarded neither X nor Y but English as her native language, although she only learned English via a English-speaking Russian nanny and an English-language day care centre in Beijing.

This was not the only such case, and because of this difficulty in establishing a native language, we opted to ask about languages learned before the speaker was eight years old. The choice of this age is fairly arbitrary, but does allow for childhood development of fluency in a language.

For each speaker, the following general information is available:

- personal information: sex and date of birth
- physiological information: height and weight
- audiometric information: for both ears, the hearing threshold for frequencies between 250 Hz and 8 kHz
- a self-assessment of musical, language and hearing abilities
- languages learned before eight years of age
- all languages spoken by the speaker
- situations in which each language is spoken
- English language information regarding age of learning, years of experience and proficiency

Where the speaker is a student, information is provided on their curriculum. This includes:

- major(s) or main field(s) of study
- minor(s)
- academic disciplines
- whether the student went on an exchange semester abroad, and if so, where, and what language was spoken there
- date of entry to the college
- graduation date

Students were also asked to undergo an audiometric test at the end of their final recording. Hearing threshold values (in dB) were measured for key frequencies[3] for both the left and right ears.

15.2.1.7   Facilitator Characteristics

A recording session could be attended by more than one facilitator. Initially, the facilitators worked in pairs to establish and monitor a standard protocol for recordings.[4] As the project progressed, new facilitators joined and for purposes of monitoring and instructing, a second, more experienced facilitator was present. Many sessions, however, were facilitated by just one person.

Similarly to the speakers, facilitator information includes the general information above, along with the following:

- name
- a liation (UCU or UU)
- whether they were the primary facilitator
- whether they were a student

15.2.1.8   Sound File Information

Information on the sound file itself is provided as follows:

- creation date
- quality of recording – the close-talking headset microphone number 1 was of very high quality, indicated as 2 on a scale of 1 to 7 (where 1 indicates highest quality); the remaining microphones were also of very good quality, but we rated them as having a quality of 3 on this scale

---

[3] at 0.25, 0.50, 1, 2, 3, 4, 6 and 8 kHz.
[4] This protocol is included in the metadata as an accompanying file.

- recording condition (quiet furnished office)
- recording platform software
- recording platform hardware
- size of the file
- sampling frequency (44.1kHz)
- byte order (little endian)
- bit resolution (32)
- speech coding (pcm)
- mime-type (audio/wav)

15.2.1.9   Metadata Structure

A unique feature of the current project is that the data are longitudinal by design. One primary talker or informant is recorded in at least one and at most five rounds, with various interviewers across sessions, and with a variable number of interviewers being present at a single session. All this information is relevant and needs to be accessible. Hence a simple structure of *one session: one talker: one interviewer* does not suffice. Moreover, information may change between sessions: a talker can mention Russian as a native language in session 1, but he or she may no longer mention Russian as a native language in session 5, three years later.

The metadata described above were obtained from various sources. Immediately after the first recording (in the same session), the entry questionnaire was administered. Notes were logged during each recording about any special circumstances and about topics during the monologues. Immediately after the last recording, hearing was measured (the dB threshold values were stored in a spreadsheet) and the exit questionnaire was administred. Technical details of the audio files were also stored in a separate file.

In creating our metadata scheme, we made maximum use of CLARIN's Component Metadata Infrastructure (CMDI). Most of the metadata categories were already in existence, and where necessary, within the CMDI structure, we created new ones.[5]

15.2.2   Linking Speech Recordings and Metadata

The various metadata were combined from all these metadata sources into a single annotation profile named *lucea.xsd*. A custom-built Python script extracted relevant metadata from various sources, checked these metadata for consistency with ISOcat and for internal consistency, and wrote the metadata into an XML file, compatible with the CMDI metadata scheme.[6] These XML files constitute a hierarchy (tree), with multiple metadata files that correspond to multiple audio files in a session, and with multiple sessions nested under a speaker. This meant that relevant information had to be copied to subordinate nodes of this branching hierarchy. Finally, the Python script inserted in each XML metadata file a persistent resource link to the appropriate audio file.

15.3   Current Research Using this Corpus

The collection of the LUCEA speech corpus was completed in May 2016. Some preliminary research has been conducted to explore the potential that the corpus has for answering the questions with which we started out. This initial exploratory research has yielded some interesting results, and the plans for comprehensive work on these questions are taking shape.

---

[5] A list of all 30 new concepts and properties is available from the ISOCat repository of data categories, at http://www.isocat.org/rest/dcs/649.

[6] https://www.clarin.eu/content/component-metadata

15.3.1   Prosodic Convergence

For example, in looking at prosodic patterns over time, Quené and Orr (2014) found that at least one aspect of the speakers' prosodic behaviour seems to converge over time. In this study, the normalised peak frequencies in the spectrum of the intensity envelope were compared for five English sentences, taken from and studied by White & Mattys (2007). Eighteen speakers from the corpus were studied, of whom fifteen talkers declared themselves as native speakers of Dutch, and one talker each as a native speaker of Russian, Vietnamese, and German. Three speakers (one female, two male) also regarded themselves as L1 English speakers, that is, as bilingual Dutch and English.

In Figure 15.2, the peak frequencies in the final recording for these subjects can be seen to converge. In a linear mixed-effects regression analysis of this data, English L1 speakers initially showed significantly higher peak frequencies in the intensity envelope than the Dutch L1 speakers. We interpret this as reflecting the stronger reduction of unstressed syllables in English as compared to Dutch. Over time, the values for the English L1 speakers move towards values in the centre of the range of converged values.

15.3.2   Intelligibility Across Time

The initial investigation of prosodic behaviour supports the results from other research, namely that speakers tend to accommodate to each other while talking. We might expect, then, that

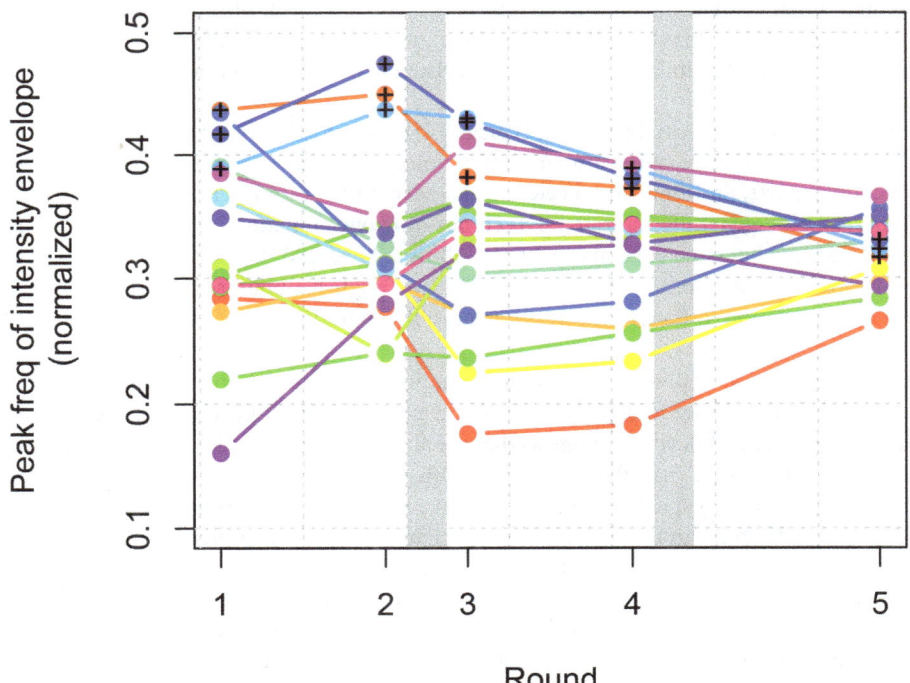

Figure 15.2: Estimates of normalised peak frequencies in the spectrum of intensity envelope, broken down by round of recording (along abscissa, on approximate time scale) and by talker (with plussed symbols representing L1 English speakers). Shaded areas represent 2-month summer breaks during which talkers do not live on the UCU campus. Note that there is a full year gap between round 4 and round 5.

intelligibility – certainly within our student population – increases over time. We would predict that the intelligibility of post-accommodated speech is higher than that of pre-accommodated speech.

In a study of 45 speakers from the corpus, we measured the intelligibility over the first three rounds of recordings, that is, at the beginning of the first semester, the end of the second semester and the beginning of the third semester. The *subjects* were 9 English L1 speakers, 15 Dutch L1 speakers and 6 German L1 speakers. Of the *listeners*, 33 were Dutch L1 speakers, 5 were English L1 speakers and 7 were bilingual in Dutch and English. Intelligibility was measured using the Speech Reception Threshold measure, modeled on work by Van Wijngaarden et al. (2002), and using the sets of 13 test sentences.

The results showed that our subjects were indeed more intelligible in the second round of recordings than in the first round. However, this effect disappeared in the third round, which we attribute to the long two-month break away from the college community during the summer period after the first year. During this period, we suspect that speakers revert to their original ways of talking.

Notably, intelligibility after the third round was measured as poorer than after the first round. This has yet to be investigated, but it is possible that the first-round measurements, which were taken after an intensive introduction week in which incoming first semester students spend every day in activities with more senior students, already showed a small level of convergence.

15.3.3   L1 Phonetic Drift

The results of the initial prosodic investigation support the idea that not only might L2 English speakers' accents change over time, but so might also those of the L1 English speakers. Similarly, it may be that Dutch as L1 exhibits signs of phonetic drift, as a result of immersion in English over a three-year period. For this study (Orr et al. 2015), we looked at possible phonetic drift in word-initial /d/ and /t/, and the sibilant /s/, which are realised with audible phonetic differences in Dutch and English.

In non-clustered word-initial position, typical VOT values for Dutch voiceless stop /t/ and the English voiced stop /d/ are quite similar. Dutch voiced stops have a shorter lag time than their English counterparts, and English voiceless stops have a much longer lag time than their Dutch counterparts, being generally aspirated. Dutch has only one sibilant /s/ whereas English has two, namely /s/ and /ʃ/ (Boersma & Hamann 2008, Collins & Mees 2003). The articulation of the Dutch /s/ is described as being somewhere between the two English sibilants, having a more retracted position of articulation, a flatter tongue, and more lip rounding than the English /s/ (Collins & Mees 2003).

Because these particular phonemes exhibit phonetic, rather than phonemic differences in Dutch and English, it is interesting to explore them in the context of the Speech Learning Model (SLM; Yeni-Komshian et al. 2000), which suggests that the ability to perceive within-phoneme differences between an L1 and an L2 may drive the formation of a new phonetic category within a single phoneme. Conversely, if a speaker does not perceive the difference, this new category may not be formed at all, but both L1 and L2 values will assimilate towards each other.

We compared the two-minute L1 (Dutch) and L2 (English) monologues for 50 Dutch L1 speakers from the first two cohorts. We isolated all instances of /d/, /t/ and /s/ from the first and final rounds of recordings. VOT was measured as the period from stop burst to the onset of voicing, using manual segmentation in Praat (Boersma, 2001). For measuring the Centre of Gravity (COG) for /s/, we used the Kaldi speech recognition system for segmentation, measuring the mean of the spectral energy distribution over the segments. Each candidate for /s/ was listened to and then accepted or rejected, one by one. The COG was calculated for each of the accepted candidates.

We did not find any sign of phonetic drift over time. Interestingly, it seems that the Dutch L1 speakers had already formed different phonetic categories, since the values that they produced in the English language monologues were already clearly different, and more in line with English L1 values, than for the Dutch monologues, even for the recordings in round 1. Figure 15.3 shows this for the /s/ phoneme.

Many of the members of the L1 Dutch group had been educated in English, either at an international school in the Netherlands or abroad. It is possible that, if we isolate L1 Dutch speakers who had never been educated in English before they entered university, we may find evidence of phonetic drift. There is no clear data available on the general range of COG for /s/ in Dutch, and a comparison of this group with a similar counterpart from a regular student group in a Dutch university may provide insights into both standard values for Dutch, and a clearer view of whether this subset of our Dutch L1 group exhibit any phonetic drift for this sibilant.

For VOT values, Lisker and Abramson (1964) suggest lower values than for our group, so again, it may be worth comparing the Dutch L1 speakers from our cohort with members of the Dutch student population at large.

15.3.4 *Further Plans for Analysis of this Corpus*

In terms of models of speech perception and language learning, the corpus will be used to examine in how far the Critical Period Hypothesis (CPH) can be applied to our speaker group. We will also look at Flege's Speech Learning Model, comparing languages of similar and dissimilar prosodic, phonological and phonetic composition, looking for evidence of phonetic category assimilation and dissimilation in this international environment. In contrast to other models, such as the Native

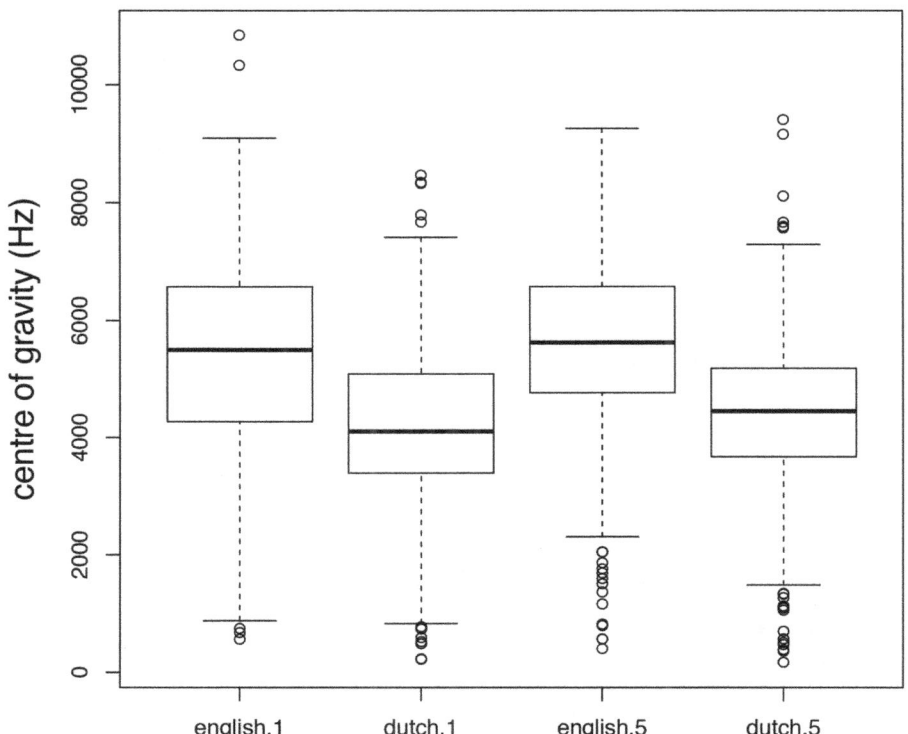

Figure 15.3: Summary of observed Centre of Gravity (COG) values for /s/, for English and Dutch, in rounds 1 and 5 of the recordings, for Dutch L1 male speakers.

Language Magnet Model (NLM; Kuhl 1991) or the Perceptual Assimilation Model (PAM; Best 1994) that have been applied to the perception of non-native sounds, the SLM model is particularly concerned with advanced L2 learners and bilinguals, and so especially applicable to our group.

Analysis of speech from this corpus may also shed light on the nature of speaker characteristics and their dependence on which language, and with what proficiency or accent the speaker is speaking. By building acoustic speaker models using the L1 as training data for automatic speaker recognition, and testing the models on speech data from English as L2 over the three years during which a student has been recorded, we can look at whether and how the performance of the recogniser is affected as the speaker's accent changes over time towards a common variety and accent.

References

Best, C. T. (1994), The emergence of native-language phonological influences in infants: A perceptual assimilation model, MIT Press, chapter 6.

Boersma, P. (2001), 'Praat, a system for doing phonetics by computer', Glot International 5(9/10), 341–345.

Boersma, P. & Hamann, S. (2008), 'The evolution of auditory dispersion in bidirectional constraint grammars', Phonology 25(2), 217–270.

Collins, B. & Mees, I. (2003), The Phonetics of English and Dutch, 5 edn, Brill Academic Publishers.

Deterding, D. (2006), 'The north wind versus a wolf: short texts for the description and measurement of english pronunciation', Journal of the International Phonetic Association 36(2), 187–196.

Evans, B. G. & Iverson, P. (2007), 'Plasticity in vowel perception and production: a study of accent change in young adults', Journal of the Acoustical Society of America 121(6), 3814–3826.

Fairbanks, G. (1960), Voice and Articulation Drillbook, Harper and Row, chapter 5, p. 127.

Garrett, P. (1992), 'Accommodation and hyperaccommodation in foreign language learners: contrasting responses to French and Spanish English speakers by native and non-native recipients', Language and Communication 12(3/4), 295–315.

Giles, H., Coupland, N. & Coupland, J. (1991), Accommodation theory: communication, context and consequence, in J. C. H. Giles & N. Coupland, eds, 'Contexts of Accomodation: Development in Applied Sciolinguistics', Cambridge University Pres, pp. 1–68.

Goldinger, S. D. (1998), 'Signal detection comparisons of phonemic and phonetic priming: The flexible-bias problem', Perception & Psychophysics 60(6), 952–965.

Jenkins, J. (2007), English as a Lingua Franca: attitude and identity, Oxford University Press, Oxford.

Kuhl, P. K. (1991), 'Human adults and human infants show a perceptual magnet effect for the prototypes of speech categories, monkeys do not', Perception & psychophysics 50(2), 93–107.

Lisker, L. & Abramson, A. S. (1964), 'A cross-language study of voicing in initial stops: Acoustical measurements', Word 20(3), 384–422.

Orr, R., van Leeuwen, D., de Rode, J. Z. & Lohfink, G. (2015), 'L1 phonetic drift in Dutch L2 speakers of English', Paper presented at the Satellite Workshop on Phonetic Learner Corpora, Glasgow, 2015.

Pardo, J. S. (2006), 'On phonetic convergence during conversational interaction', Journal of the Acoustical Society of America 119(4), 2382–2393.

Quené, H. & Orr, R. (2014), Long-term convergence of speech rhythm in L1 and L2 English. Paper presented at the 7th Workshop on Speech Prosody, Dublin.

Scholtmeijer, H. (1992), Het Nederlands van de IJsselmeerpolders, Kampen Mondiss.

Timmis, I. (2002), 'Native-speaker norms and international English: a classroom view', ELT Journal 56(3), 240–249.

Trudgill, P. (2004), New-dialect formation: The inevitability of colonial Englishes, Oxford University Press, USA.

Universal Declaration of Human Rights (2013). Retrieved from http://www.un.org/en/documents/udhr/.

van Wijngaarden, S. J. (1999), Speech intelligibility of native and non-native speech, in H. J. M. Steeneken, D. A. van Leeuwen & S. J. van Wijngaarden, eds, 'Multi-lingual Interoperability in Speech Technology', ISCA.

Van Wijngaarden, S. J., Steeneken, H. J. & Houtgast, T. (2002), 'Quantifying the intelligibility of speech in noise for non-native listeners', Journal of the Acoustical Society of America 111(4), 1906–1916.

Weinberger, S. (2013), 'Speech Accent Archive'. Retrieved from URL: http://accent.gmu.edu

White, L. & Mattys, S. (2007), 'Calibrating rhythm: first language and second language studies', Journal of Phonetics 35(4), 501–522.

Yeni-Komshian, G. H., Flege, J. E. & Liu, S. (2000), 'Pronunciation proficiency in the first and second languages of Korean–English bilinguals', Bilingualism: Language and cognition 3(02), 131–149.

CHAPTER 16

Stylene: an Environment for Stylometry and Readability Research for Dutch

Walter Daelemans[a,d], Orphée De Clercq[b] and Véronique Hoste[c]

[a]CLiPS Computational Linguistics Group, University of Antwerp,
walter.daelemans@uantwerpen.be, [b]LT3 Language and Translation Technology Team, Ghent
University, orphee.declercq@ugent.be, [c]LT3 Language and Translation Technology Team, Ghent
University, veronique.hoste@ugent.be,
[d]Corresponding Author: walter.daelemans@uantwerpen.be

ABSTRACT

We describe an educational demonstration interface and tools for stylometry (authorship attribution and profiling) and readability research for Dutch. The Stylene system consists of a popularisation interface for learning about stylometric analysis, and of web-based interfaces to software for readability and stylometry research aimed at researchers from the humanities and social sciences who do not want to develop or install such software themselves.

16.1 Introduction

The last decade has seen a marked increase in research on computational stylometry, the subarea of natural language processing that concerns itself with the categorisation of texts according to the psychological and sociological properties of their authors. Also called text profiling, this research tries to develop systems, mostly based on text analytics techniques, that combine natural language processing and machine learning methods. These systems are trained to determine whether the author of a text is male or female, their education level, region of origin, personality, and even mental health, whether they are a native speaker or not, and many other potentially useful attributes. Of course, authorship attribution research has existed for a long time, and is in a sense the limit case of computational stylometry: supposing that everyone has a unique combination of demographic, psychological and idiosyncratic style properties, this would be their idiolect or 'stylome' (Van Halteren et al, 2005; Coulthard, 2004), and it should be possible to assign texts of unknown authorship to specific authors provided that models of their stylome exist.

How to cite this book chapter:
Daelemans, W, De Clercq, O and Hoste, V. 2017. Stylene: an Environment for Stylometry and Readability Research for Dutch. In: Odijk, J and van Hessen, A. (eds.) *CLARIN in the Low Countries*, Pp. 195–209. London: Ubiquity Press. DOI: https://doi.org/10.5334/bbi.16. License: CC-BY 4.0

Another useful type of information that can be extracted from text using natural language processing and text categorisation is the readability of a text. Readability research and the automatic prediction of readability has a very long and rich tradition (see surveys by Klare 1976; DuBay 2004; Benjamin 2012; and Collins-Thompson, 2014). Whereas superficial text characteristics leading to on-the-spot readability formulas were popular until the 1990s (Flesch 1948; Gunning 1952; Kincaid et al. 1975), recent advances in the field of computer science and natural language processing have triggered the inclusion of more intricate characteristics in present-day readability research (Si and Callan 2001; Schwarm and Ostendorf 2005; Collins-Thompson and Callan 2005; Heilman et al. 2008; Feng et al. 2010).

Current approaches model lexical, syntactic, semantic and discourse complexity, while also considering shallow traditional text characteristics. Furthermore, the focus has shifted from using the formulas to select reading material for children or L2 language learners to assessing the readability of a variety of text types with other user groups or applications in mind.

This chapter introduces the results of a CLARIN Flanders project on the development of practical tools for stylometry and readability.[1] The goal of that project was to implement a robust, modular system for stylometry and readability research on the basis of existing methods, and the development of a web service that would allow researchers in the humanities and social sciences to analyse texts with this system.

The website has three sub-interfaces: (i) a popularisation interface intended to provide basic insight into what stylometry can do; (ii) a readability interface that allows the input of texts and provides elementary and more advanced feedback on the readability of the text; and (iii) a machine learning interface that allows basic experiments in computational stylometry.

In this chapter, we will describe the underlying methods and approaches in the backend of the interfaces. We also developed a stand-alone system for machinelearningbased stylometry that underlies the third interface, but which allows more options and flexibility as a stand-alone system than can be accessed from the interface. The stand-alone system may eventually replace the corresponding interface on the website.

16.2   The Stylometry Popularisation Interface

Computational Stylometry is not yet well-known outside computational linguistics and the specialised digital humanities research community. In order to educate interested lay persons and humanities and social sciences colleagues about the possibilities (and limitations) of the approach, an interface was designed to help a general audience understand computational stylometry in an easy and fun way. An early version was tested out successfully during the 2011 Flemish 'Wetenschapsweek' (Science Week) with secondary school pupils, and afterwards extended. There has been a large interest for the interface (around 50 visitors per month) and some media attention. Figure 16.1 shows the start screen of the interface. Input can be provided either by cut and paste or through file upload. In both cases the input should be raw text (uploaded files should have .txt extension). The demo will only give complete output in browsers that are HTML5compatible and that allow JavaScript. For practical reasons, cutandpaste input is limited to 4000 characters and file upload to 300 sentences.

After the user enters a text and clicks on 'analyse', the software returns a screen with didactic information about the general approach taken in stylometry and information about different stylometric aspects of the text provided. Figure 16.2 shows the introductory information that is

---

[1] The interface and backend software we describe here was developed in the context of the Stylene (Stylometrie en Leesbaarheid voor het Nederlands; An environment for stylometry and readability research for Dutch) project. The project was funded by the Flemish Ministry for Economics, Science, and Innovation (EWI). The system was developed over 2010–2012 in a cooperation between the CLiPS and LT3 research groups. The interface can be found at: http://www.stylene.be.

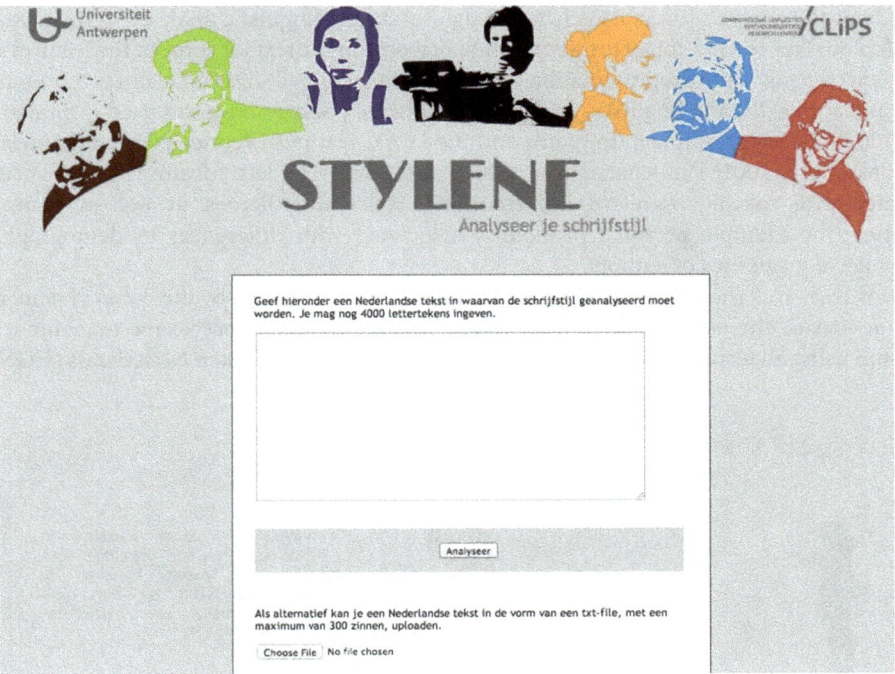

Figure 16.1: Start screen of the stylometry popularisation interface.

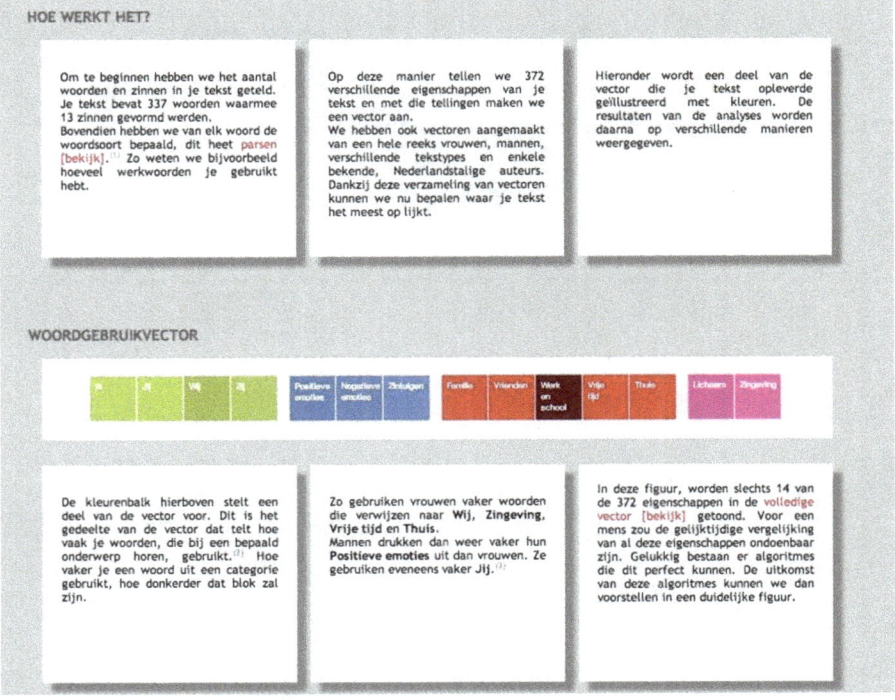

Figure 16.2: Stylometry popularisation interface: output (general).

given about the analysis (users can click through to sample linguistic analyses of the data) and a visual (colour) representation of the distribution of words in the text for some of the features used in the system (the full feature representation can be clicked on as well). Darker features represent more frequent features. For the linguistic analysis, the software package Frog was used (Van den Bosch et al., 2007). As features, token unigrams and the LIWC features (Pennebaker and Francis, 1996; Pennebaker et al 2001; Pennebaker et al, 2007) were used. The latter features group vocabulary associated with specific cognitive and emotional styles and themes, as well as grammatical categories (for example personal pronouns) associated with differences in demographic and psychological properties of authors.

Figures 16.3–16.5 show the additional information that is provided by the demo system: a guess of the gender of the author (based on a model learned by a support vector machine learning algorithm using all features and trained on part of the Corpus Gesproken Nederlands (CGN 2004)

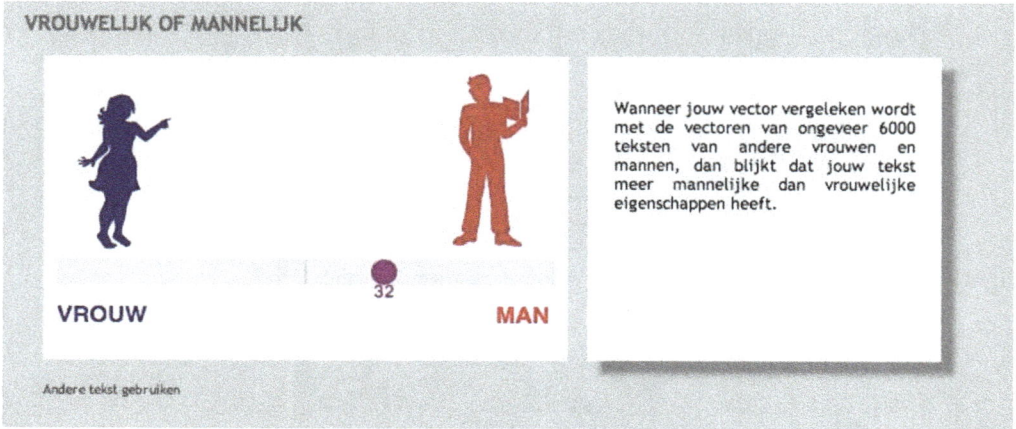

Figure 16.3: Stylometry popularisation interface: output (gender).

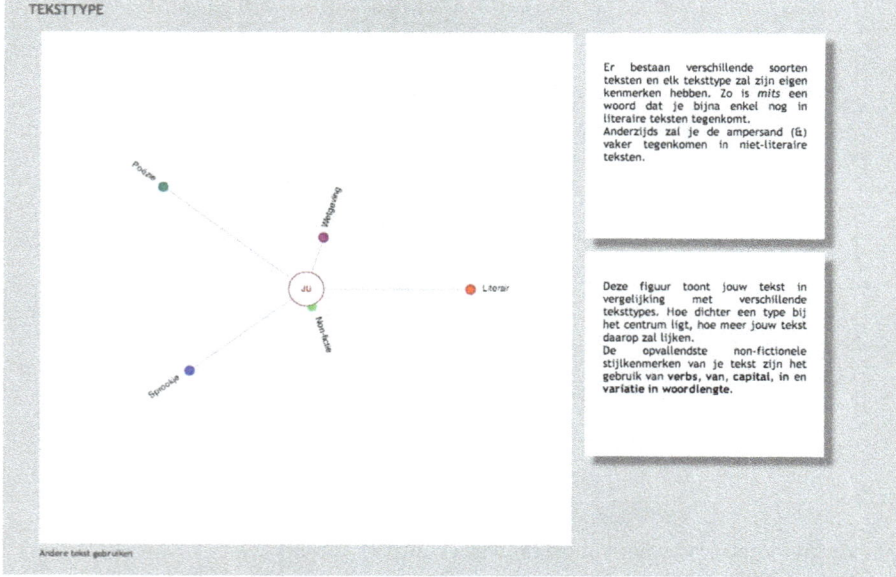

Figure 16.4: Stylometry popularisation interface: output (genre).

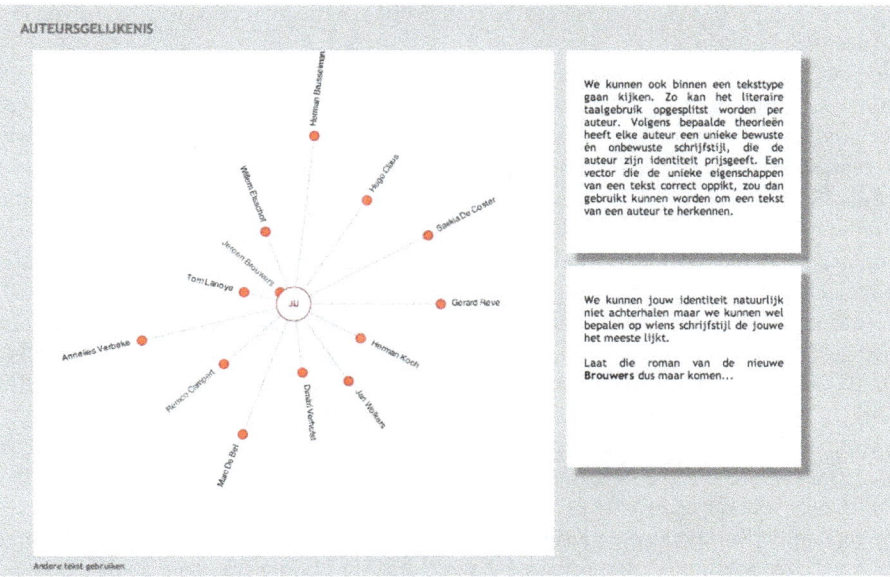

Figure 16.5: Stylometry popularisation interface: output (distance to authors).

data; Figure 16.3); a guess of the genre of the text (based on a small corpus that was collected solely for this demo; Figure 16.4); and a representation of the closeness to samples of the works of a random selection of different Dutch and Flemish authors (based on, on average, the first 11,000 tokens of one of their novels; Figure 16.5). The gender infobox is the result of assessing the proportion of male and female labels of 71 vectors that are in the vicinity of the vector that is based on the input, using cosine similarity. The other two infoboxes are based on the Dice coefficient (a metric that measures similarity) between the different (normalised) vectors that represent the style of the authors.

It should be noted that the models used are simplified, and that we do not make any scientific claims about the selection of genres and authors, or about the meaning of the output of the system. The only goal of this interface is to show what computational stylometry is, and provide a feeling for the type of information it uses and the type of output it produces.

16.3   The Readability Interface

Automatic readability prediction has a long and rich tradition. Research in the 20th century, fuelled especially by educational purposes, has resulted in a large number of readability formulas. Typically, these yield either an absolute score (Flesch, 1948; Brouwer, 1963) or a grade level at which a text is deemed appropriate (Dale and Chall, 1948; Gunning, 1952; Kincaid et al., 1975) and are based on shallow text characteristics such as average word and sentence length and word familiarity.

Over the years, many objections have been raised against these traditional formulas: their lack of absolute value (Bailin and Grafstein 2001), the fact that they are solely based on superficial text characteristics (DuBay 2004; DuBay, 2007; Davison and Kantor 1982; Feng et al. 2009; Kraf and Pander Maat 2009), the underlying assumption of a regression between readability and the modelled text characteristics (Heilman et al. 2008), etc. Furthermore, there seems to be a remarkably strong correspondence between the readability formulas themselves. When evaluating the performance of 12 readability formulas, of which 7 designed for English, 5 for Dutch and one for Swedish, van Oosten et al. (2010) found strong correlations between the formulas, within a given language, but also across languages.

These objections have led to new quantitative approaches for readability prediction which adopt a machine learning perspective for the task. Advancements in these fields have introduced more intricate prediction methods such as Naïve Bayes classifiers (Collins-Thompson and Callan 2004), logistic regression (François 2009) and support vector machines (Schwarm and Ostendorf 2005; Feng et al. 2010; Tanaka-Ishii et al. 2010) – and especially more complex features. Rather than a sole reliance on superficial text characteristics, the added value of features measuring lexical complexity based on n-gram modelling (Schwarm and Ostendorf 2005; Pitler and Nenkova, 2008; Kate et al. 2010) or those relying on deep syntactic parsing (Schwarm and Ostendorf, 2005) have been corroborated repeatedly in the computational approaches to readability prediction that have surfaced in the last decade (Heilman et al. 2007; Petersen and Ostendorf, 2009; Nenkova et al. 2010). Features relating to semantics and discourse processing have proven more difficult to corroborate. While Pitler and Nenkova (2008) have clearly demonstrated the usefulness of discourse relations, the predictive power of these was not corroborated by Feng et al. (2010), for example. Especially for those features requiring deep linguistic processing, a lot still has to be explored (Collins-Thompson 2014).

In the readability interface, we present a re-implementation of several readability formulas and propose a new readability prediction system which does not only take into account these superficial text characteristics, but also relies on features grasping lexical complexity based on n-gram modelling and syntactic complexity based on deep syntactic dependency parsing.

16.3.1   General Text Characteristics

Once a text is provided, either by cut and paste or through file upload, we first present the user with some of the more general characteristics of the text. We include three length-related features that have proven successful in previous work (Nenkova et al. 2010; Feng et al. 2010; François and Miltsakaki 2012): the average word and sentence lengths and the percentage of polysyllabic words (i.e. words containing more than three syllables). We also incorporate two traditional lexical features: on the one hand, we provide the percentage of words also found in a Dutch word list with a cumulative frequency of 77% (or 'freq77').[2] On the other hand we also calculate the type token ratio (TTR) to measure the level of lexical complexity within a text.

All these characteristics are obtained after processing the text with a state-of-the-art Dutch pre-processor, Frog (Van den Bosch et al. 2007) and a designated classification-based syllabifier (van Oosten et al. 2010). Figure 16.6 illustrates how these general characteristics are presented to the user. It should be noticed that we also allow the user to actually highlight those words that contain more than three syllables or that are infrequent in Dutch.

16.3.2   Readability Judgement Based on Classical Formulas

Though many objections have been raised against the classical readability formulas, they remain popular and are still the go-to solution in many disciplines where a reader or author desires a first insight into text readability, e.g. corporate communication (Dempsey et al. 2012) or legislation (van Boom 2014). This is why, in a second step, we apply a number of readability formulas to the text which was entered by the user in the interface.

In essence, a readability formula is a mathematical formula intended for indicating the difficulty of a particular text. The formula typically consists of a number of variables, which are

---

[2] The list is based on a list ordered by descending frequency in a large newspaper corpus, i.e. the '27 Miljoen Woorden Krantencorpus 1995', which is available through the HLT agency at http://tst.inl.nl/en/producten

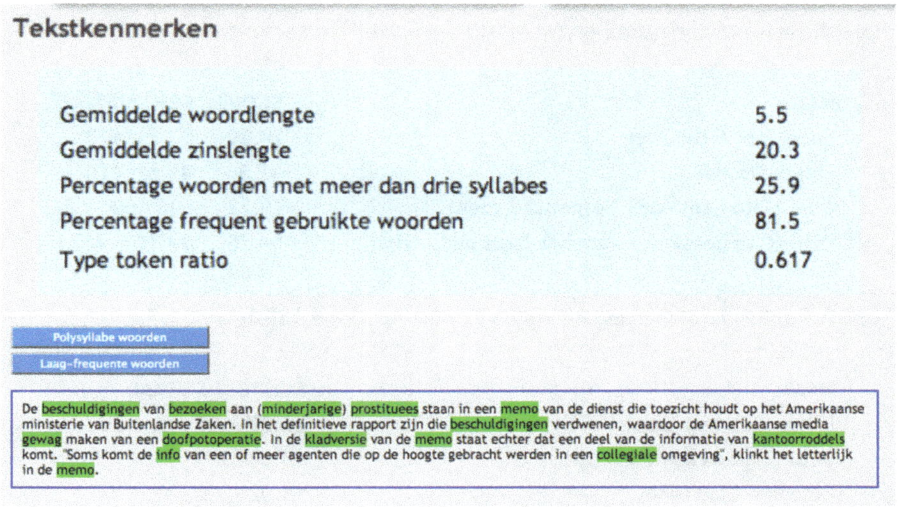

Tekstkenmerken

Gemiddelde woordlengte	5.5
Gemiddelde zinslengte	20.3
Percentage woorden met meer dan drie syllabes	25.9
Percentage frequent gebruikte woorden	81.5
Type token ratio	0.617

Polysyllabe woorden
Laag-frequente woorden

De beschuldigingen van bezoeken aan (minderjarige) prostituees staan in een memo van de dienst die toezicht houdt op het Amerikaanse ministerie van Buitenlandse Zaken. In het definitieve rapport zijn die beschuldigingen verdwenen, waardoor de Amerikaanse media gewag maken van een doofpotoperatie. In de kladversie van de memo staat echter dat een deel van de informatie van kantoorroddels komt. "Soms komt de info van een of meer agenten die op de hoogte gebracht werden in een collegiale omgeving", klinkt het letterlijk in de memo.

Figure 16.6: General text characteristics of the entered text.

characteristics of the text (as displayed in Figure 16.6) and constant weights. Besides the five general text characteristics that were introduced earlier (the average sentence length avgsentencelen; average word length avgwordlen; percentage of polysyllabic words, ppolysylword; freq77; and TTR), five additional variables are required for calculating all of the different formulas presented in the interface. These variables were derived using the same preprocessing toolkits as mentioned above and are listed below:

- avgnumsyl: average word length in number of syllables.
- psw: percentage of sentences per word.
- freq3000: percentage of words not on the Dale-Chall (1948) word list[3]
- avgpolysylsent: average number of words with three or more syllables per sentence.
- ratiolongword: ratio of words with more than six characters

These additional variables are not presented as such to the user. Instead, we display the results of the different formulas for a text which was entered by the user (see Figure 16.7). These formulas have been designed for Dutch (Douma, 1960; Brouwer, 1963; Staphorsius, 1994), English (Dale and Chall 1948; Flesch, 1948; Gunning, 1952; Senter and Smith, 1967; McLaughlin, 1969; Coleman, 1975; Kincaid et al., 1975) or Swedish (Björnsson, 1968). As van Oosten et al. (2010) have shown that there is a strong correspondence between the readability formulas intended for different languages, all readability formulas are displayed in the interface independently of the language they aim to model. The following readability formulas are displayed in the interface:
Dutch-language formula:

- Leesindex Brouwer (195 − 2 × avgsentencelen − 67 × avgnumsyl)
- Flesch-Douma (207 − 0.93 × avgsentencelen − 77 × avgnumsyl)
- CILT: Cito leesindex technisch lezen (114 + 0.28 × freq77 − 12 × avgwordlen)
- CLIB: Cito leesbaarheidsindex voor het basisonderwijs (46 + 0.47 × freq77 − 6.6 × avgwordlen − 0.37 × TTR + 1.4 × psw)

---

[3] The Dale-Chall word list contains 3,000 of the most frequent words in the English language.

Leesbaarheidsformules ontwikkeld voor het Nederlands

NAAM	SCORE	SCHAAL
Leesindex A Brouwer	24.39	0 - ca. 120
Flesch-Douma	37.8	0 - ca. 120
CILT (Cito Leesindex Technisch Lezen)	69.72	50 - 100
CLIB (Cito Leesindex voor het Basis onderwijs)	54.75	0 - 100

Leesbaarheidsformules ontwikkeld voor andere talen

NAAM	SCORE	SCHAAL
Flesch Reading Ease	21.26	0 - ca. 120
Dale-Chall Reading Grade Score	18.68	0 - 16
Coleman-Liau Index	15.02	0 - 15
Flesch-Kincaid Grade Level	15.32	1 - 15
Gunning Fog Index	18.47	0 - 15
ARI (Automated Readability Index	14.51	1 - 15
SMOG (Simple Measure of Gobbledygook	16.22	1 - 15
LIX (Lasbarhetsindex Bjornsson)	49.88	0 - 100

Figure 16.7: Readability scores for entered text.

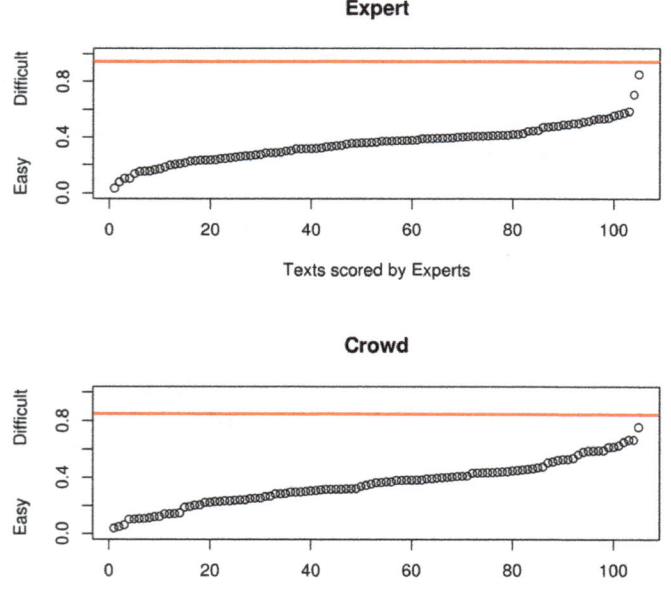

Figure 16.8: Hendi readability score of the text under consideration in comparison to the expert and crowd readability assessments of all texts in the training corpus.

English-language formula:

- Flesch Reading Ease (207 − avgsentencelen − 85 × avgnumsyl)
- Dale-Chall Reading Grade Score (0.16 × freq3000 + 0.05 × avgsentencelen + 3.6)
- Coleman-Liau Index (5.9 × avgwordlen − 0.3 × avgsentencelen − 16)
- Flesch-Kincaid Grade Level (0.39 × avgsentencelen + 12 × avgnumsyl − 16)
- Gunning Fog Index (0.4 × (avgsentencelen + ppolysylword))
- ARI: Automated Readability Index (4.7 × avgwordlen + 0.5 × avgsentencelen − 21)
- SMOG: Simple Measure of Gobbledygook: $\sqrt{(30 \times avgpolysylsent)} + 3.1$

Swedish-language formula:

- Läsbarhetsindex Björnsson: avgsentencelen + ratiolongword

The last column in Figure 16.7 gives information on the scale on which the formulas are calculated. For some formulas (all English formulas except for Flesch Reading Ease; the Swedish formula; and the Dutch CLIB and CILT), a higher score applies to a more difficult text and a lower score to a more readable text; their slope is considered positive. For the other formulas, viz. Flesch Reading Ease, Flesch-Douma and Leesindex Brouwer, the situation is exactly opposite and the slope is considered negative.

16.3.3   *Readability Prediction Based on Supervised Machine Learning*

Given the many objections raised against the classical formulas, we also judge the readability of the entered text using the corpus-based readability prediction system developed by De Clercq et al. (2014). In order to compile the gold standard underlying this system, first a general-purpose corpus consisting of a large variety of text genres was compiled which was then assessed on readability. For the actual assessments, two web applications were designed to collect readability assessments for Dutch and English texts: one that is intended exclusively for language experts and one that is open to the general public. Both applications are available under the following link: http://www.lt3.ugent.be/en/tools/

Figure 16.8 gives an overview of these text scores assigned to texts by the experts and the crowd. The red line in both figures shows how our corpus-based readability prediction system scores the text compared to the other texts in the corpus.

Two flavours of the Hendi system have been integrated in this interface: a system which mainly relies on traditional and lexical text characteristics, and a second system which also integrates information representing the syntactic complexity of the text.

The former readability prediction system relies on a feature space of the traditional features mentioned above and lexical n-gram features which have proven to be good predictors of readability in previous work. Since we tried not to have presuppositions about the various levels of complexity in our corpus, a generic language model for Dutch was built based on a subset of the SoNaR corpus (Oostdijk et al. 2013). This subset contains only newspaper, magazine and Wikipedia material and should qualify as a generic representation of standard written Dutch. The language model was built up to an order of 5 (n = 5) with Kneser-Ney smoothing using the SRILM toolkit (Stolcke 2002). As features we calculated the perplexity of a given text when compared to this reference data and also normalised this score by including the document length, as seen in Kate et al. (2010). For more information on this system we refer the reader to De Clercq et al. (2014) and De Clercq and Hoste (2016).

In the latter system, syntactic information as displayed in Figure 16.9 is also taken into account. To this purpose we incorporated the parse tree features as first introduced by Schwarm and Ostendorf (2005) and that have proven successful in many other readability prediction studies

Name	Value
Average dependency tree depth	9.5
Average number of subordinating conjunctions	1.5
Average number of passive constructions	0.5
Average number of noun phrases	9.0
Average number of prepositional phrases	7.5
Average number of verb phrases	4.0

1.2. Other Formulas

Name	Value
Sentences with subordinating conjunctions	2
Sentences with passive constructions	2
Sentences with deep syntactic trees	0

Figure 16.9: Syntactic information calculated on the basis of the dependency tree of the sentence under consideration.

(Pitler and Nenkova 2008; Petersen and Ostendorf 2009; Nenkova et al. 2010; Feng et al. 2010). We calculate the parse tree height, the number of subordinating conjunctions and the ratios of the noun, verb and prepositional phrases. As an additional feature, we also include the average number of passive constructions in a text. The parser underlying these features is the Alpino parser (van Noord et al. 2013), a state-of-the-art dependency parser for Dutch.

As the parsing of the text may take some time, this calculation is performed offline and a pdf report is sent to the user as soon as the text is fully processed.

16.4   The Stylometry Interface

The Stylometry Machine Learning (ML) interface makes possible experiments following the full textcategorisation approach to stylometry: it allows the linguistic analysis of Dutch language documents, the extraction of features used regularly in the research literature, the creation of instances for ML experiments using these features, and the ML experiments themselves. We will describe here the different steps to use it in turn. The interface itself contains helpful hints, examples, and information as well. The system available through the interface has reduced functionality compared to the full stand-alone system, which is also available from the authors.

To use the interface on their data, users must first provide an email address in the appropriate field of the interface so that results can be sent to that address. Then the following procedure must be applied.

16.4.1   Step 1. Preparing and Uploading Data for Training

The goal of a supervised ML experiment is to use examples of some mapping to learn a model that generalises to independent similar data. For example, on the basis of a number of texts we know to have been written by Willem Elsschot and other texts written by other authors, we train a machine learning method to learn a model of the style of Elsschot. Afterwards we can test the accuracy of this model by applying it to texts that we did not use for training. The interface therefore makes a distinction between a Training run and a Testing run, and the user starts by uploading data for training.

Suppose we want to do a stylometry experiment predicting the gender of the author of tweets. We create a directory with two subdirectories (one for male, one for female), and put the 'train' tweets each in a separate file in their corresponding subdirectory. All files should be .txt files with utf8 encoding. After creating a .zip file by compressing this directory (a directory that has as many subdirectories as classes – here, two – and with the texts belonging to each class in their corresponding subdirectory), this archive can be uploaded for training. After uploading, a result screen is presented indicating successful uploading and providing an identity number for further use.

16.4.2   Step 2. Defining the Experimental Parameters

To set up the way the uploaded data will be treated in building a model about style, several types of information have to be provided. First of all, a name has to be provided for the corpus (i.e. the data) that has been uploaded – e.g., 'Elsschot-1', or 'Gender-twitter', etc. This could for example be the name of the top directory in which you provided subdirectories with training texts.

Next, up to three 'analyses' can be provided. An 'analysis' in this context is a specific definition of the information that will be used to represent the text for the ML algorithm (the so-called document representation or instance definition). To define an analysis, the user selects a type, n-gram size, and frequency counting method. Analysis types supported are token (the tokenised words occurring in the text), character (the characters occurring in the text), lemma (the lemmatised tokens in the text), and pos (the part of speech, or grammatical category, of the words in the text). The n-gram size refers to the length of the sequences that we take into account; e.g. for characters, 'n' set to 3 would select all the character trigrams occurring in the text. A sentence such as 'Give me a break!' would result in the following character trigrams: '=Gi, Giv, iv=, =me, me=, =a=, =br, bre, rea, eak, ak=, =!='. Analogously, selecting n = 2 with tokens would result for the same sentence in the token bigrams '= Give, Give me, me a, a break, break !, ! ='. Additional information to be provided for each analysis is the frequency count type which can be absolute (how many times does a particular feature, for example the character trigram '=!=' occur in the document) or relative (what is the proportion of the occurrences of this feature in all the occurrences of all features in the document).

For each analysis specified, two datasets will be generated: one where document representations consist of binary vectors, and one where they consist of numeric vectors (where the numeric values are absolute or relative as selected by the user). In addition a dictionary is provided with the selected features for that experiment, their position in the document vector, and their frequency.

16.4.3   Step 3. Selecting the Features

The document representation defined in the previous step can be very large. In the 'filter' step, this set of features can be reduced to a manageable number on the basis of frequency, informativeness or a combination of both.

There are three filters that can optionally be selected. If none is selected, all features will be used. The total set filter allows the defining of a frequency band. For example, we might be interested in selecting the 10% most frequent features (set upper percentage to ten and leave lower percentage at 0), the 50% least frequent features (set upper percentage to 0 and set lower percentage to 50), or the middle band (in case one wants the features that are neither very frequent nor infrequent) – in this last case both thresholds could be set to 20, for example. (It is worth reminding that the term 'features' in this context refers to the items generated for the document representation, such as character trigrams or lemma bigrams.)

Not all features are equally relevant for distinguishing between classes. Statistical and information-theoretic methods such as chi-squared and information entropy can be used to analyse the degree to which a particular feature (e.g. the character trigram '=!=') can differentiate between the classes. The two remaining filters order the features according to relevance as defined by these methods and allow the selection of a percentage of these most relevant features.

All that remains to be done at this stage is indicating whether one wants document features (average word length, average sentence length, average number of syllables, number of hapax legomena, number of hapax dis legomena and readability) to be computed, which Machine Learning algorithm one wants to use, and which document representation (binary or numeric). By clicking start, the whole process will be activated and an ID generated.

The user will receive by email a zip file that contains all instance vectors for the analyses and filters chosen for the current training run. The email will also contain a unique identifier that is used as a link between the training run and any test run the user may want to perform in relation to this training run.

16.4.4   Step 4. Testing

With the identifier provided, the user can enter the Stylene machine learning interface again, this time with a test dataset submitted in the same format as the training data. The trained model will be applied on the test data provided and an analysis will be returned.

The user will receive by email a zip file that contains all the instance vectors that have been generated for this test run.

16.4.5   Using the Interface for Text Analysis Only (Optional)

In case the user is interested only in parsing their text(s), it is possible to go to the Frog parser interface, and submit an archive of texts (again following a zip archive format now with one directory of files to be analysed) that will then only be parsed. No ML models will be built in that case and with each input file in the archive a Frog output file will appear with the parsed input text. The Frog parser is also accessible from the Readability interface. The Frog parser used for this project is frozen at version 0.12.15 (c) ILK 1998 - 2012 to prevent compatibility issues in the future.

16.5   Conclusion

The Stylene project, funded by the Department of Economy, Science, and Innovation of the Flemish government, and executed by the department of Economy, Science and Innovation of the Flemish government (EWI), and executed by the CLiPS[4] and LT3[5] research groups, resulted in several resources, collected behind a single interface, that we hope will prove useful for different categories of users. People interested in the computational linguistics applications of stylometry and readability can analyse texts and be educated about the types of analysis that these research fields apply. Users in the digital humanities can test the automatic text categorisation approach to stylometry in a userfriendly interface suited for exploratory research. Whereas the first stylometry interface is based on simplified models, the readability interface and the machine learning of stylometry interfaces rely on stateoftheart software for Dutch. In addition, the interface provides an easy access to the stateoftheart Dutch text analysis software package Frog.

Acknowledgements

Apart from the authors, several people participated in the development of the Stylene system components and implementation. We gratefully acknowledge the contributions of Philip van

---

[4] http://www.clips.uantwerpen.be
[5] http://www.lt3.ugent.be

Oosten, Dries Tanghe, Peter Velaerts, Koen Vereeken, Guy De Pauw, and Vincent Van Asch. Herwig De Smet implemented most of the interface and the stand-alone stylometry system underlying the machine learning for the stylometry interface.

More information about the Stylene project can be obtained from
Prof. Dr. Walter Daelemans
CLiPS, Department of Linguistics, University of Antwerp
walter.daelemans@uantwerpen.be

References

Bailin, A. and Grafstein, A. (2001). The linguistic assumptions underlying readability formulae: a critique. Language & Communication 21(3):285–301.

Benjamin, Rebekah George. (2012). Reconstructing Readability: Recent Developments and Recommendations in the Analysis of Text Difficulty. Educational Psychology Review, 24(1):63–88.

Björnsson, C-H. (1968). Läsbarhet. Almqvist and Wiksell, Stockholm.

Brouwer, R. H. M. (1963). Onderzoek naar de leesmoeilijkheden van Nederlands proza. Pedagogische Studiën, 40:454–464.

Coleman, M. and Liau, T. L. (1975). A computer readability formula designed for machine scoring. Journal of Applied Psychology, 60:283–284.

Collins-Thompson, K. and Callan, J. (2004). A language modeling approach to predicting reading difficulty. Proceedings of the Human Language Technology Conference and the North American chapter of the Association for Computational Linguistics annual meeting (HLT - NAACL-2004), pp. 193–200.

Collins-Thompson, Kevyn and Jamie Callan. (2005). Predicting reading difficulty with statistical language models. Journal of the American Society for Information Science and Technology, 56:1448–1462.

Corpus Gesproken Nederlands (CGN) (2004). Nederlandse Taalunie. http://tst-centrale.org/images/stories/producten/documentatie/cgn_website/doc_Dutch/start.htm (Last accessed: June 2013).

Coulthard, Malcolm (2004). 'Author identification, idiolect, and linguistic uniqueness.' Applied linguistics 25.4: pp. 431–447.

Dale, E. and Chall, J. S. (1948). A formula for predicting readability. Educational research bulletin, 27:11–20.

Davison, A. and Kantor, R. (1982). On the failure of readability formulas to define readable texts: a case study from adaptations. Reading Research Quarterly 17(2):187–209.

De Clercq, O., Hoste, V., Desmet, B., van Oosten, P., De Cock, M., & Macken, L. (2014). Using the Crowd for Readability Prediction. Natural Language Engineering 20(3):293–335.

De Clercq, O. and Hoste, V. (2016). All mixed up? Finding the optimal feature set for general readability prediction and its application to English and Dutch. Computational Linguistics, 42:3.

Dempsey, S. J., Harrison, D. M., Luchtenberg, K. F., & Seiler, M. J. (2012). Financial Opacity and Firm Performance: The Readability of REIT Annual Reports. The Journal of Real Estate Finance and Economics, 45(2):450–470.

Douma, W. (1960). De leesbaarheid van landbouwbladen: een onderzoek naar en een toepassing van leesbaarheidsformules. Bulletin, 17.

DuBay, W. H. (2004). The Principles of Readability. Impact Information.

DuBay, W. H. (ed.) (2007). Unlocking Language: the Classic Readability Studies. BookSurge.

Feng, L., Elhadad, N. and Huenerfauth, M. (2009). Cognitively motivated features for readability assessment. Proceedings of the 12th Conference of the European Chapter of the Association for Computational Linguistics (EACL-2009), pp. 229–237.

Feng, L., Jansche, M., Huenerfauth, M. and Elhadad, N. (2010). A comparison of features for automatic readability assessment, Proceedings of the 23rd International Conference on Computational Linguistics Poster Volume (COLING-2010), pp. 276–284.

Flesch, R. (1948). A new readability yardstick. Journal of Applied Psychology, 32(3):221–233.

François, T. (2009). Combining a statistical language model with logistic regression to predict the lexical and syntactic difficulty of texts for FFL. Proceedings of the 12th Conference of the European Chapter of the Association for Computational Linguistics: Student Research Workshop (EACL-2009), pp. 19–27.

François, T. and Miltsakaki, E. (2012). Do NLP and machine learning improve traditional readability formulas? Proceedings of the 1st Workshop on Predicting and Improving Text Readability for Target Reader Populations(PITR2012), pp. 49–57.

Gunning, R. (1952). The technique of clear writing. McGraw-Hill, New York.

Heilman, M. J., Collins-Thompson, K., Callan, J. and Eskenazi, M. (2007). Combining lexical and grammatical features to improve readability measures for first and second language texts. Proceedings of the Human Language Technology Conference and the North American chapter of the Association for Computational Linguistics annual meeting (HLT - NAACL 2007), pp. 460–467.

Heilman, M., Collins-Thompson, K. and Eskenazi, M. (2008). An analysis of statistical models and features for reading difficulty prediction. Proceedings of the 3rd ACL Workshop on Innovative Use of NLP for Building Educational Applications (EANL-2008), pp. 71–79.

Kate, R. J., Luo, X., Patwardhan, S., Franz, M., Florian, R., Mooney, R. J., Roukos, S. and Welty, C. (2010). Learning to predict readability using diverse linguistic features. Proceedings of the 23rd International Conference on Computational Linguistics (COLING-2010), pp. 546–554.

Kincaid, J. P., Jr., R. P. F., Rogers, R. L., and Chissom., B. S. (1975). Derivation of New Readability Formulas (Automated Readability Index, Fog Count and Flesch Reading Ease Formula) for Navy Enlisted Personnel. Research branch report RBR-8-75, Naval Technical Training Command Millington Tenn Research Branch, Springfield, Virginia.

Klare, George. (1976). A second look at the validity of the readability formulas. Journal of reading behavior 8:159–152.

Kraf, R. and Pander Maat, H. (2009). Leesbaarheidsonderzoek: oude problemen, nieuwe kansen, Tijdschrift voor Taalbeheersing 31(2):97–123.

McLaughlin, G.H. (1969). SMOG grading - a new readability formula. Journal of Reading, pp. 639–646.

Nenkova, A., Chae, J., Louis, A. and Pitler, E. (2010). Structural features for predicting the linguistic quality of text: Applications to machine translation, automatic summarization and human-authored text. Empirical Methods in NLG, Lecture Notes in Articial Intelligence 5790, pp. 222–241.

Oostdijk, N., Reynaert, M., Hoste, V. and Schuurman, I. (2013). The construction of a 500-million-word reference corpus of contemporary written Dutch. Essential Speech and Language Technology for Dutch, Theory and Applications of Natural Language Processing, Springer, pp. 219–247.

Pennebaker, J. W. and Francis, M.E. (1996). Cognitive, emotional, and language processes in disclosure. Cognition and Emotion 10(6):601–626.

Pennebaker, J. W., Francis M.E., and Booth R.J. (2001). Linguistic Inquiry and Word Count (LIWC): LIWC2001. Mahwah: Lawrence Erlbaum Associates.

Pennebaker, J. W., Francis M.E., and Booth R.J. (2007). Linguistic Inquiry and Word Count (LIWC): LIWC2007. http://www.liwc.net.

Petersen, S. and Ostendorf, M. (2009). A machine learning approach to reading level assessment, Computer Speech & Language 23(1):89–106.

Pitler, E. and Nenkova, A. (2008). Revisiting readability: A unified framework for predicting text quality. Proceedings of the 2008 Conference on Empirical Methods in Natural Language Processing (EMNLP-2008), ACL, pp. 186–195.

Schwarm, S. E. and Ostendorf, M. (2005). Reading level assessment using support vector machines and statistical language models. Proceedings of the 43rd Annual Meeting of the Association for Computational Linguistics (ACL-2005), pp. 523–530.

Senter, R. J. and Smith, E. A. (1967). Automated readability index. Technical Report AMRLTR-66-220, University of Cincinnati, Cincinnati, Ohio.

Si, Luo and Jamie Callan. (2001). A Statistical Model for Scientific Readability. In Proceedings of the tenth international Conference on Information Knowledge Management, pages 574–576.

Staphorsius, G. (1994). Leesbaarheid en leesvaardigheid. De ontwikkeling van een domeingericht meetinstrument. Cito, Arnhem.

Stolcke, A. (2002). SRILM - an extensible language modeling toolkit, Proceedings of the 7th International Conference on Spoken Language Processing (ICSLP-2002), pp. 901–904.

Tanaka-Ishii, K., Tezuka, S. and Terada, H. (2010). Sorting texts by readability, Computational Linguistics 36(2):203–227.

van Boom, W. (2014). Begrijpelijke hypotheekvoorwaarden en consumentengedrag, in T. B. en A.A. van Velten (ed.), Perspectieven voor vastgoedfinanciering (Congresbundel Stichting Fundatie Bachiene), Stichting Fundatie Bachiene, pp. 45–80.

Van den Bosch, A., Busser, G.J., Daelemans, W., and Canisius, S. (2007). An efficient memory-based morphosyntactic tagger and parser for Dutch, In F. van Eynde, P. Dirix, I. Schuurman, and V. Vandeghinste (Eds.), Selected Papers of the 17th Computational Linguistics in the Netherlands Meeting, Leuven, Belgium, pp. 99–114.

Van Halteren, H., Baayen, R.H., Tweedie, F., Haverkort, M. and Neijt, A. (2005). New Machine Learning Methods Demonstrate the Existence of a Human Stylome. In Proceedings of Journal of Quantitative Linguistics. pp. 65–77.

van Noord, G. J., Bouma, G., van Eynde, F., de Kok, D., van der Linde, J., Schuurman, I., Sang, E. T. K. and Vandeghinste, V. (2013). Large scale syntactic annotation of written Dutch: LASSY, Essential Speech and Language Technology for Dutch, Theory and Applications of Natural Language Processing, Springer, pp. 231–254.

van Oosten, P., Tanghe, D., and Hoste, V. (2010). Towards an Improved Methodology for Automated Readability Prediction. In Calzolari, N., Choukri, K., Maegaard, B., Mariani, J., Odijk, J., Piperidis, S., and Tapias, D., editors, Proceedings of the seventh International Conference on Language Resources and Evaluation (LREC'10), Valletta, Malta. European Language Resources Association.

PART III

Infrastructure for Syntax

CHAPTER 17

Infrastructure for Syntax: Introduction

Jan Odijk

UiL-OTS, Utrecht University, j.odijk@uu.nl

17.1   Introduction

A lot of work has been done by CLARIN-LC to fill CLARIN with data and applications to support syntactic research. For this reason, a separate part of this book is dedicated to this topic.

The chapters in this part only partially cover the work done in CLARIN-LC to support syntactic research. I will first briefly describe the work done that is not covered by the chapters in this part (section 17.2), and then introduce the chapters (section 17.3).

17.2   Work on Syntax

Some data and applications have a broader scope than syntax but are nevertheless highly relevant for syntactic research. The Typological Database System (TDS, described in chapter 11), provides the user with integrated access to a collection of independently developed typological databases which also contain syntactic properties. The TTNWW application, described in chapter 7, provides a wide range of workflows for enriching text corpora, but some of these workflows are highly relevant for syntactic research, such as the workflows for tokenization, lemmatization, part-of-speech tagging, and parsing of modern Dutch texts. Tools for tokenising, lemmatising, part of speech tagging and parsing mediaeval Dutch have been made available through Adelheid and INPOLDER.

Most applications for syntactic research focus on search for syntactic properties. The DuELME (Odijk, 2013a;b) data and associated search application enable a user to search for syntactic properties of Dutch multiword expressions. FESLI has provided a corpus with monolingual and bilingual children (Dutch - Turkish) with and without Specific Language Impairment, enriched with part of speech annotations on tokens, and an application for searching for morpho-syntactic properties in this corpus.

How to cite this book chapter:

Odijk, J. 2017. Infrastructure for Syntax: Introduction. In: Odijk, J and van Hessen, A. (eds.) *CLARIN in the Low Countries*, Pp. 213–215. London: Ubiquity Press. DOI: https://doi.org/10.5334/bbi.17. License: CC-BY 4.0

AutoSearch enables a user to search in one's own corpora once they have been enriched with part of speech tags using TTNWW (see chapter 7), and Nederlab enables a user to search in all digitised texts relevant for the Dutch national heritage and the history of Dutch language and culture (ca 800 - present).

The MIMORE application enables combined searching in and analysis of three databases on dialect variation (see Barbiers et al. (2016) for an example of research that crucially used this application).

Finally, the LASSY Word Relations Search application (Tjong Kim Sang et al., 2010) enables a user to search for syntactic dependency triples in specific Dutch treebanks.

17.3   Contents of Part III: Infrastructure for Syntax

All chapters focus on applications for search in and analysis of syntactically annotated corpora.

Some applications enable search in corpora with linguistic annotations on tokens, e.g. part of speech codes. Chapter 18 describes the SHEBANQ application, which enables search in the WIVU Hebrew Bible Text Database. It illustrates a typical project in which certain data, originally stored in an idiosyncratic format, have been curated and converted to a CLARIN-supported format based on the Linguistic Annotation Framework (LAF; Ide and Suderman, 2014), and a web application has been built for searching in these data, either by creating queries oneself, or by reusing queries created by others and stored here.

Chapter 19 describes the application interface (front-end) of the OpenSoNaR application, which enables search in the large scale Dutch reference corpora SoNaR and SoNaR New Media (Oostdijk et al., 2013), while chapter 20 describes the search engine (back-end) of this application. The second version of this application also provides access to the Spoken Dutch Corpus (Corpus Gesproken Nederlands, CGN; Oostdijk et al., 2002). The OpenSoNaR web application, with multiple interfaces varying in complexity, opens up the SoNaR corpora for research by humanities scholars, who until recently could access these data only with great difficulty. For the CGN data an exploration application existed already (called COREX; Hellwig and Weijers, 2004), but it was developed more than 12 years ago, is a desktop application, and is not being maintained anymore.

Another set of applications enable search in text corpora in which each sentence has been assigned a syntactic structure (treebanks). One example is CorpusStudioWeb, which not only enables searching in treebanks, but offers additional important functionality for researchers, in particular keeping a number of related searches together in a search 'project' and annotating search results automatically or semi-automatically. This is described in chapter 21.

GrETEL is a web application for search in treebanks in which a user can create queries on the basis of an example sentence (example-based search) and does not have to know all annotation guidelines of the treebank or even a formal query language. It is described in chapter 22.

Chapter 23 describes PaQu and a small case study using PaQu. PaQu is an extension of the LASSY Word Relations Search application (Tjong Kim Sang et al., 2010), and offers searching for grammatical dependency triples in the user's own corpora.

The Taalportaal is a comprehensive and authoritative digital scientific grammar for Dutch, Frisian, and Afrikaans. In the Taalportaal, links to several search applications were made to provide concrete evidence related to specific constructions described in the Taalportaal. The links cover morphology and phonology, but the links to stored queries in treebanks are most prominent. This is the topic of chapter 24.

Acknowledgements

This work was financed by CLARIN-NL and CLARIAH.

References

Barbiers, Sjef, Marjo van Koppen, Hans Bennis, and Norbert Corver (2016), MIcrocomparative MOrphosyntactic REsearch (MIMORE): Mapping partial grammars of Flemish, Brabantish and Dutch, *Lingua* **178**, pp. 5–31. Linguistic Research in the CLARIN Infrastructure. http://www.sciencedirect.com/science/article/pii/S0024384115002211.

Hellwig, Birgit and Erik Weijers (2004), COREX: A tool for exploiting the Corpus Gesproken Nederlands (CGN), *Manual*, Max Planck Institute for Psycholinguistics, Nijmegen, the Netherlands. 2nd version. http://www.mpi.nl/corpus/manuals/manual-corex.pdf.

Ide, Nancy and Keith Suderman (2014), The linguistic annotation framework: A standard for annotation interchange and merging, *Language Resources and Evaluation* **48** (3), pp. 395–418.

Odijk, Jan (2013a), DUELME: Dutch electronic lexicon of multiword expressions, *in* Francopoulo, G., editor, *LMF - Lexical Markup Framework*, ISTE / Wiley, London, UK / Hoboken, US, pp. 133–144.

Odijk, Jan (2013b), Identification and lexical representation of multiword expressions, *in* Spyns, P. and J.E.J.M Odijk, editors, *Essential Speech and Language Technology for Dutch. Results by the STEVIN-programme*, Theory and Applications of Natural Language Processing, Springer, Berlin/Heidelberg, pp. 201–217. http://link.springer.com/content/pdf/10.1007%2F978-3-642-30910-6_12.

Oostdijk, N., M. Reynaert, V. Hoste, and I. Schuurman (2013), The construction of a 500 million word reference corpus of contemporary written Dutch, *in* Spyns, Peter and Jan Odijk, editors, *Essential Speech and Language Technology for Dutch: Results by the STEVIN-programme*, Springer, Berlin, pp. 219–247. http://link.springer.com/book/10.1007/978-3-642-30910-6/page/1.

Oostdijk, N., W. Goedertier, F. Van Eynde, L. Boves, J.P. Martens, M. Moortgat, and H. Baayen (2002), Experiences from the Spoken Dutch Corpus project, *in* González Rodriguez, M. and C. Paz Suárez Araujo, editors, *Proceedings of the third International Conference on Language Resources and Evaluation (LREC-2002)*, ELRA, Las Palmas, pp. 340–347.

Tjong Kim Sang, Erik, Gosse Bouma, and Gertjan van Noord (2010), LASSY for beginners, Presentation at CLIN 2010, Utrecht, http://ifarm.nl/erikt/talks/clin2010.pdf. http://ifarm.nl/erikt/talks/clin2010.pdf.

CHAPTER 18

The Hebrew Bible as Data: Laboratory - Sharing - Experiences

Dirk Roorda*,**

*Data Archiving and Networked Services - Royal Netherlands Academy of Arts and Sciences, Anna van Saksenlaan 10; 2593 HT Den Haag, Netherlands, **The Language Archive - Max Planck Institute for Psycholinguistics, Wundtlaan 1; 6525 XD Nijmegen, Netherlands, dirk.roorda@dans.knaw.nl

ABSTRACT

The systematic study of ancient texts including their production, transmission and interpretation is greatly aided by the digital methods that started taking off in the 1970s. But how is that research in turn transmitted to new generations of researchers? We tell a story of Bible and computer across the decades and then point out the current challenges: (1) finding a stable data representation for changing methods of computation; (2) sharing results in inter- and intra-disciplinary ways, for reproducibility and cross-fertilisation. We report recent developments in meeting these challenges. The scene is the text database of the Hebrew Bible, constructed by the Eep Talstra Centre for Bible and Computer (ETCBC), which is still growing in detail and sophistication. We show how a subtle mix of computational ingredients enable scholars to research the transmission and interpretation of the Hebrew Bible in new ways: (1) a standard data format, Linguistic Annotation Framework (LAF); (2) the methods of scientific computing, made accessible by (interactive) Python and its associated ecosystem. Additionally, we show how these efforts have culminated in the construction of a new, publicly accessible search engine SHEBANQ, where the text of the Hebrew Bible and its underlying data can be queried in a simple, yet powerful query language MQL, and where those queries can be saved and shared.

18.1 Introduction

The Hebrew Bible is a collection of ancient texts resulting from a ten-centuries long tradition. It is one of the most studied texts in human culture. Information processing by machines is only two centuries old, but since its inception its capabilities have evolved in an exponential manner

How to cite this book chapter:
Roorda, D. 2017. The Hebrew Bible as Data: Laboratory - Sharing - Experiences. In: Odijk, J and van Hessen, A. (eds.) *CLARIN in the Low Countries*, Pp. 217–229. London: Ubiquity Press. DOI: https://doi.org/10.5334/bbi.18. License: CC-BY 4.0

up till now (Gleick, 2011). We are interested in what happens when the Hebrew Bible as an object of study is brought under the scope of the current methods of information processing. The Eep Talstra Centre for Bible and Computing (ETCBC) formerly known as Werkgroep Informatica Vrije Universiteit (WIVU), has been involved in just this since the 1970s and their members are dedicated to this approach. The combination of a relatively stable set of data and a rapidly evolving set of methods urges for reflection. Add to that a growing set of ambitious research questions, and it becomes clear that not only reflection is needed but also action. Methods from computational linguistics and the wider digital humanities are to be used, hence people from different disciplines have to be involved. How can the ETCBC share its data and way of working productively with people that are used to a wide variety of computational ways?

In this article we tell a story of reflection and action, and the characters are databases, data formats, query languages, annotations, computer languages, archives, repositories and social media. This story has a beginning in February 2012, when a group of biblical scholars convened at the Lorentz center at Leiden for the workshop Biblical Scholarship and Humanities Computing: Data Types, Text, Language and Interpretation (Roorda et al., 2012). They searched for new ways to obtain computational tools that matched their research interests. The author was part of that meeting and had prepared a demo application: a query saver. It was an attempt to improve the sharing of knowledge. It is a craft to write successful queries for the ETCBC Hebrew Text database, and by publishing their queries, researchers might teach each other how to do it.

In the years that followed, this idea has materialised as the result of the SHEBANQ project (System for HEBrew text: ANnotations for Queries and markup), a curation and demonstrator project funded by CLARIN-NL, the Dutch department of the Common LAnguage Resource INfrastructure in Europe CLARIN. We have chosen a modern standard format for the data: Linguistic Annotation Framework (LAF), and have built a web-application for saving queries. During the execution of this project we also have built LAF-Fabric, a tool to analyze and manipulate LAF resources. At the time of writing the first version of this chapter, late 2014, we can say that we have a modern data laboratory for historico-linguistic data, plus ways to share results, not only among a small circle of theological experts, but also among computational linguists on the one hand and students and interested lay people on the other.

Of course, every beginning of such a story is arbitrary. There is always so much more that happened before. In order to provide the reader with enough context, we shall also relate key moments of that greater story. But we cannot tell the whole story: our perspective is biased to the computational side. We shall not delve into the intricacies of manuscript research, but focus on the data models and computational methods that help analyze a rather fixed body of transcribed text. Yet, we believe that this simplified context is rich enough material for a good story. Whereas this chapter deliberately scratches only the surface of the computational methods, a more technical account can be found in (Roorda et al., 2014b), which also relates how researchers have already made use of them.

18.2   Ground Work: WIVU and ETCBC

Since the 1970s, Eep Talstra, Constantijn Sikkel and a group of researchers at the VU University Amsterdam have been compiling a text database of the Hebrew Bible. This database started as a set of files, containing the transliterated Hebrew text of the Bible according to the Biblia Hebraica Stuttgartensia edition (Elliger and Rudolph, 1997). To this text, they added files with their observations of linguistic patterns in it as coded annotations, anchored to the individual words, phrases, clauses, and sentences. They tested tentative patterns against the data, refined them, and added manual exceptions. This led to a complex web of files, containing the base text and a set of semi-automatically generated annotations. They refrained from shaping these annotations in a hierarchical, linguistic model, because they wanted to represent observations, not theory

(Talstra and Sikkel, 2000). The result of this work is a database in the sense of being observational data on which theories can be based. It is not a database in the sense of a modern relational database system.

The advantages of a proper (in the sense of computer science) database are obvious indeed, but the relational model does not represent textual data in a natural way, and does not facilitate queries that are linguistically meaningful. In the 1990s there have been promising efforts to define the notion of a text database. In his Ph.D. thesis, Crist-Jan Doedens (Doedens, 1994) defined a data model for texts and the notion of a topographic query language (QL) to retrieve linguistic results. He identified the relations of sequence and embedding as the key structures to store and retrieve texts. A query is topographic if its internal structure exhibits the same sequence and embedding relations as the results it is meant to retrieve. Interestingly, he did not postulate that a text is one hierarchy. In his data model, textual data may be organised by means of multiple, overlapping hierarchies.

The definition of a data model and a query language are not yet a working database system. In the 2000s, Ulrik Petersen undertook to create an implementation of Doedens's ideas. This led to the Emdros database system with the MQL (Mini-QL) query language Petersen (2004; 2006; 2002-2014). Emdros consists of a front-end, which is an MQL interpreter, and a back-end, which is an existing production class relational database system such as PostgreSQL or MySQL. Despite the fact that MQL is a concession to practicality, it is still a topographic query language and very convenient to express real-life textual queries without invoking programming skills. Since then, an Emdros export of the current Hebrew text database is being maintained by the ETCBC team. Emdros is open source software, the data model is very clear, so this export is a *communication device*: the intricacies of the internal annotation-creation of the ETCBC workflow are largely left behind, and users of the export have a well-defined dataset at their disposal.

18.3   Idea: Queries As Annotations

During the aforementioned Lorentz workshop (Roorda et al., 2012), an international group of experts reflected on how to bring biblical data resources to better fruition in the digital age. The ETCBC database had been incorporated in Bible study software, but developments there were not being driven by agendas set by academic research. Yet those bible study applications offered attractive interfaces to browse the text, look up words and more. The problem was: how can theologians, with limited ICT resources, regain control over the development of software that works with their data? The workshop offered no concrete solutions, but some ingredients of potential long-term solutions did get mentioned: open up the data and develop open source tools. Theologians can only hope to keep up with ICT developments if they allow people building on each others' accomplishments. A very concrete articulation of this statement was made by Eep Talstra himself, when he deposited the ETCBC database into EASY, the research archive of DANS (Talstra et al., 2012). It must be admitted that there remained barriers: the data was not Open Access and the format in which it was deposited was MQL, which is not a very well-known format, so the experimenting theological programmer still has a hard time to do some meaningful work with this data. But it was definitely a step towards increased sharing of resources.

In that same workshop, the author showed a demo application (Roorda, 2012) (see Figure 18.1) by which the user could browse the Hebrew text and highlight a number of linguistic features. The idea to highlight features, which are essentially annotations to the text, triggered another idea: to view queries as annotations to the passages that contain their results (Roorda and van den Heuvel, 2012). If researchers can save their carefully crafted queries as annotations, and if those annotations are centrally stored, then other researchers have access to them and may encounter them when they are reading a passage. Just as readers encounter ordinary annotations by other scholars in

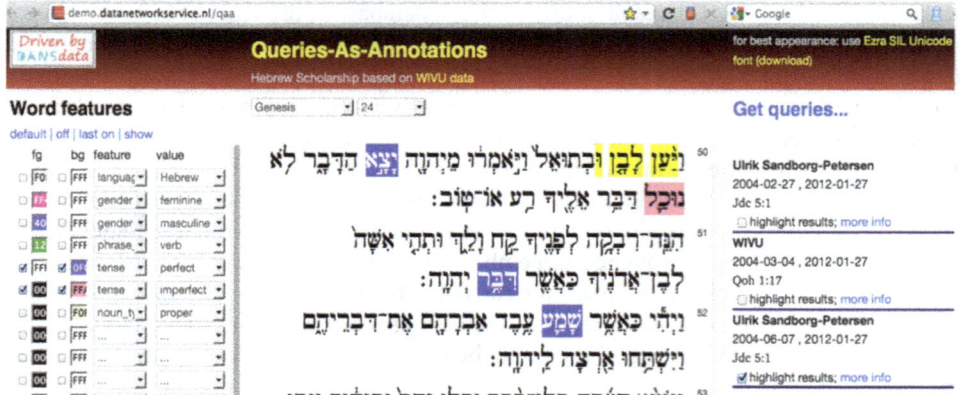

Figure 18.1: Queries/Features as Annotations.

formalism	web app	data prep tool
sql	90	80
python	250	
perl		650
javascript	300	
html	50	
css	60	
shell script		280

Table 18.1: Amount of lines of code per formalism per application.

printed books, they will encounter results of queries of others when they are browsing a chapter of the Hebrew Bible in their web browser. With a single click they are led to not only the query instruction itself but also a description of the provenance and motivation of the query. This could be the basis of interesting scenarios for cross-fertilisation.

It is interesting to note the stack of computational tools needed to write this demo. Its construction involved a data preparation tool for transforming the contents of the ETCBC database into a relational database for driving a website. The web app itself was based on Web2py, a lightweight python based web-application framework (Di Pierro, 2015).

Table 18.1 is a list of languages used to implement both the data-preparation tool and the website, together with the amount of code needed in each formalism. There are several things to note:

1. The numbers of lines of code are very small.

2. The formalisms, while considerable in number, are utterly commonplace.

3. The number of formalisms may be reduced by one by dropping Perl in favor of Python

It can be concluded that mastering commonplace ICT techniques may generate a good return on investment, in the form of a web application that expose data on the web in rich interfaces.

18.4   Realisation: LAF-Fabric and SHEBANQ

In 2013-2014, ETCBC together with DANS has carried out the CLARIN-NL project SHEBANQ. We seized the opportunity to implement the idea of queries-as-annotations, but to make it possible at all more work had to be done.

18.4.1   LAF

First of all, a new representation of the data had to be selected, one that conformed to a standard used in linguistics. Linguistic Annotation Framework, an ISO standard (Ide and Romary, 2012), was chosen. LAF defines a data model in which an immutable stream of primary data is annotated by feature structures. The data stream is addressed by means of a graph of nodes and edges, where the nodes may be linked to regions of the primary data, and where edges serve to connect smaller parts to bigger wholes. Both nodes and edges can act as targets of annotations, which contain the feature structures. Finally, all entities, except the primary data, are serialised in XML.

In concrete terms, we have extracted the complete text of the Hebrew Bible as a plain Unicode text file. As far as LAF is concerned, this is our primary data. For the books, chapters and verses we have created nodes that are linked to the stretches of text that they correspond to. For every individual word there is a node, linked to a region defined by the character positions of the first and last character of that word. For the phrases, clauses and sentences there are nodes, linked to the regions corresponding to the words they contain. Relationships between constituents correspond to edges. The properties of sectional units, words, and constituents are key-value pairs targeted at the corresponding nodes.

For a graphic representation of how this model works, Figure 1 of (Roorda et al., 2014b) is just one tap away.

18.4.1.1   LAF Versus FoLiA

Another approach for linguistic annotations is provided by FoLiA (see chapter 6). LAF, however, is more abstract and conceptually simpler, which gave us the freedom to translate the existing data model of the ETCBC database in a straightforward way, including its more idiosyncratic data features.

18.4.1.2   From EMDROS to LAF

The LAF data model shares a lot of structure with the Emdros data model of text, objects and features. We only had to map objects to nodes and features to key-value pairs inside annotations targeting the proper nodes, so this conversion has been a straightforward process with only a few devilish details.

The result is a good example of stand-off markup. The primary data is left untouched, and around it is a graph of annotations. It is perfectly possible to add new annotations without interfering with the primary data or the other annotations. The annotations are like a fabric, into which new threads can be woven, and that can be stitched to other fabrics. In this way, the stand-off way of adding information to sources facilitates cooperation and sharing much better than adding markup inline, such as TEI prescribes. This bold assertion must be qualified by two considerations, however:

1. Stand-off markup works best in those cases where the primary sources are immutable. As easy as it is to add new annotations, so difficult it is to insert new primary data.

2. Stand-off markup flourishes in cases where the main access mode to the sources is by programmatic means. Manual inspection of stand-off data and their annotations becomes quickly overwhelming.

In our case, the first condition holds for years in a row, but updates do occur. We have dealt with that by having several copies of the database co-existing, and the website SHEBANQ exposes them all.

Table 18.2 indicates some quantities of the ETCBC data, both in their Emdros form and in their LAF form. These numbers suggest that manual inspection of individual files is so cumbersome that it pays off to invest in programmatic access of the data.

quantity	Emdros	LAF
words	426,555	426,555
linguistic objects resp. nodes	945,726	945,726
total number of features	22,622,100	25,504,388
serialised size (MQL resp. XML)	455 MB in 1 file	1640 MB in 14 files
compiled size (SQLite3 resp. binary)	126 MB	260 MB

Table 18.2: Quantities in the ETCBC data.

The LAF version of the Hebrew text database has been archived at Data Archiving and Networked Services (DANS), the research archive for the humanities and social sciences in the Netherlands by Peursen and Roorda (2014; 2015).

18.4.2   LAF-Fabric

As LAF is a relatively new standard, there are few LAF-compatible tools. A LAF resource is represented in XML, but the nature and size of this XML make it difficult to be handled by ordinary XML tools. Looking through the surface syntax, a LAF resource is neither a relational database, nor a document, but a graph. XML processing works well when the underlying data structure is a single hierarchy, no matter how deep, or a table of records, no matter how large, but it grinds to a halt when the data is a large and intricate web of nodes and edges, i.e. a graph.

In order to facilitate productive work with the freshly created LAF representation of the Hebrew Bible, we have developed LAF-Fabric (Roorda, 2013-2014b), which is a LAF compiler and loader. In a typical workflow, a researcher wants to inspect the LAF data, focus on some aspects, sort, collate, link and transform selected data, and finally export results. Without LAF-Fabric, the obvious way to do so is read the XML data, apply XPATH, XSLT or XQUERY scripts and collect the results. Reading the XML data means parsing it and building an internal representation in memory, and this alone takes an annoying 15 minutes on a average laptop and uses a prohibitive amount of memory. This is not conducive to an interactive, explorative, agile use of the data, and LAF-Fabric remedies this. When first invoked on a LAF-resource, it compiles it into efficient data structures and writes those to disk, in such a way that this data can be loaded fast. This one-time compilation process takes roughly 15 minutes, but then the data loads in a matter of seconds every time you want to work with it. Furthermore, LAF-Fabric offers a programmers interface (API) to the LAF data, by which the programmer can walk over the nodes and edges and collect feature information on the fly. These walks are fast, and can be programmed easily.

The idea to create LAF-Fabric arose after we tried to use a library called graf-python (Bouda, 2013-2014), part of POIO (Bouda et al., 2012), for the biblical LAF data. Unfortunately, the way graf-python was programmed made it unsuitable for dealing with our LAF resource because of its size. Python is a scripting language with a clean syntax and a good performance if used judiciously, hence we undertook to write LAF-Fabric in Python as well. We use those parts of Python that perform best for the heavy data lifting, and those parts that are most user friendly for the programmers interface. LAF-Fabric is a package that can be imported in any Python script, and it behaves particularly well when invoked in an IPython notebook. It is available on the Python Package Index (Roorda, 2013-2014b), so that a user can get it by just typing on the command line.

```
pip3 install laf-fabric
```

IPython Notebook is an interactive way of writing Python scripts and documentation (Pérez and Granger, 2007). A notebook is a document in which the data analyst writes cells with Python code and other cells with documentation. Code cells can be run individually, in any order, while the results of the execution remain in memory. The notebook has powerful capabilities of formatting

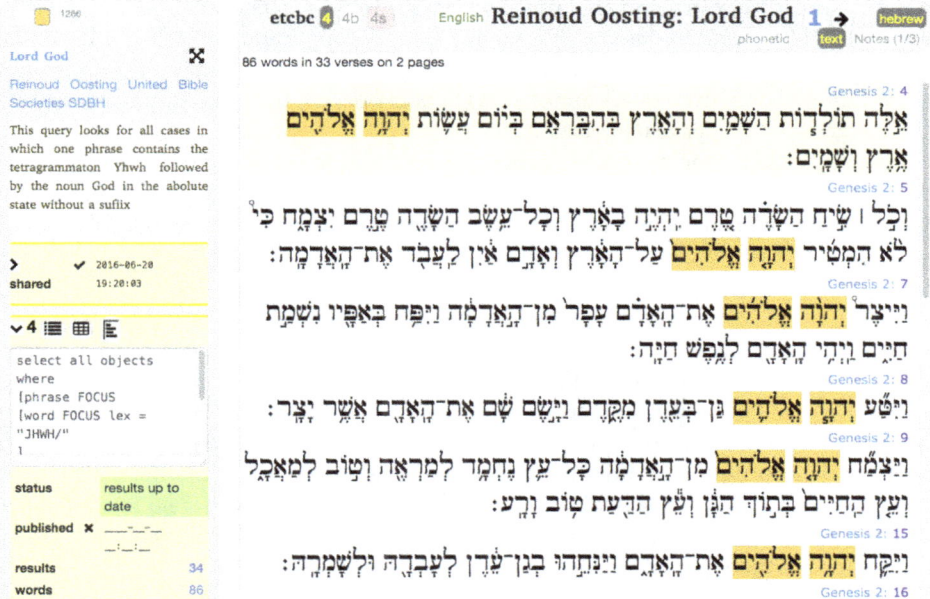

Figure 18.2: A saved query in SHEBANQ.

results. A notebook can be published easily on the web, so that others can download it and execute it as well, provided they have the same data and packages installed. IPython notebook belongs to a branch of computer programming called scientific computing. It is about explorative data analysis by means of computing power. The scientific programmer produces analyses, charts, and documents that account for his data and results. By contrast, the typical software engineer produces applications that perform well-defined tasks for end users. The scientific programmer works close to the researchers, and writes special purpose code fast, and reacts to changing demands in an agile way. The software engineer works at a greater distance from the actual use cases. He uses programming languages that support good software organisation at the cost of a much slower development process. He is less prepared to accomodate fast-changing requirements.

When LAF-Fabric runs in an IPython notebook, even the few seconds it needs to load data are required only once. The programmer can experiment with his code cells at will, without the need to reload the data all the time.

LAF-Fabric has already been used for some significant data extractions. There is a varied and growing set of notebooks (Roorda, 2014a) on Github that is testimony to the extent of use cases that can be served. Not only data analysis, but also adding new annotations is supported. One of the use cases is the query saver itself.

18.4.2.1   Text-Fabric

From the start of 2017 onwards, I have deprecated LAF-Fabric in favour of a new format and tool: Text-Fabric. The data fits now easily in a Github repository: BHSA.

18.4.3   SHEBANQ: Demonstrator

The actual goal of the SHEBANQ project was to create a demonstrator query saver for the ETCBC data. This has been achieved, and the resulting web application is called SHEBANQ (van Peursen et al., 2014).

It went live on 2014-08-01, and contains now, on 2016-06-24, 609 shared queries, saved by 84 users of a total of 293 registered users. The public part of the application offers users the options to read the Hebrew Bible chapter by chapter, to see query results of public queries as annotations in the margin, and to jump from query annotations to query descriptions and result lists. Figure 18.2 shows a screenshot of the page of a saved query.

When a user clicks on the passage indicator of a result, he is led to the relevant chapter, where other queries show up and can be navigated to, see Figure 18.3.

When users register and log in, they can write their own queries, have them executed, save them, including the query results, and make them public.

18.4.4   SHEBANQ: Research Environment

If the demonstrator shows one thing, then it is the fact that there are many additional desiderata. Whereas SHEBANQ has been designed to fulfill the sharing function, researchers also want to use it as a research tool. It is not easy to write a good MQL query, because many of the linguistic aspects of the data are not shown on the interface. If, for instance, a user wants to use the dictionary entries of the words or the syntactic features of clauses and phrases, he has no immediate, visual clues. So we added linguistic information in layers below the plain text, accessible by a tap on the verse number, see Figure 18.4.

Other additions we have made are:

• easy access to lexical information by clicking on words;
• clickable charts for query results and word occurrences, Figure 18.5);
• CSV exports of data;
• support for multiple versions of the data;
• manual annotation, also with images; bulk-uploadable annotations, e.g. cross-references;
• corpus-driven phonetic transcription;
• user manual, query manual, and feature documentation one tap away;
• generation of citable links of page views, and published queries.

One particular addition is a consequence of the success of SHEBANQ: more and more users leave their queries in SHEBANQ, and the need is felt to suppress queries from the margin. For this *muting* has been added.

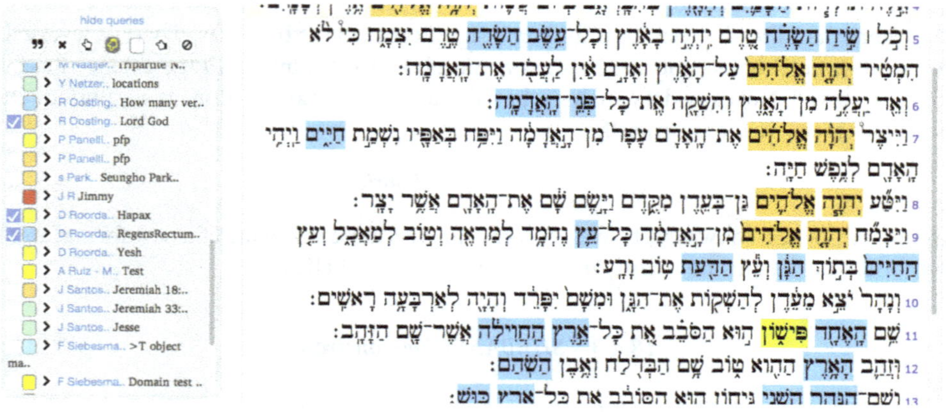

Figure 18.3: Reading a passage and seeing the results of various queries.

Figure 18.4: Text and underlying data.

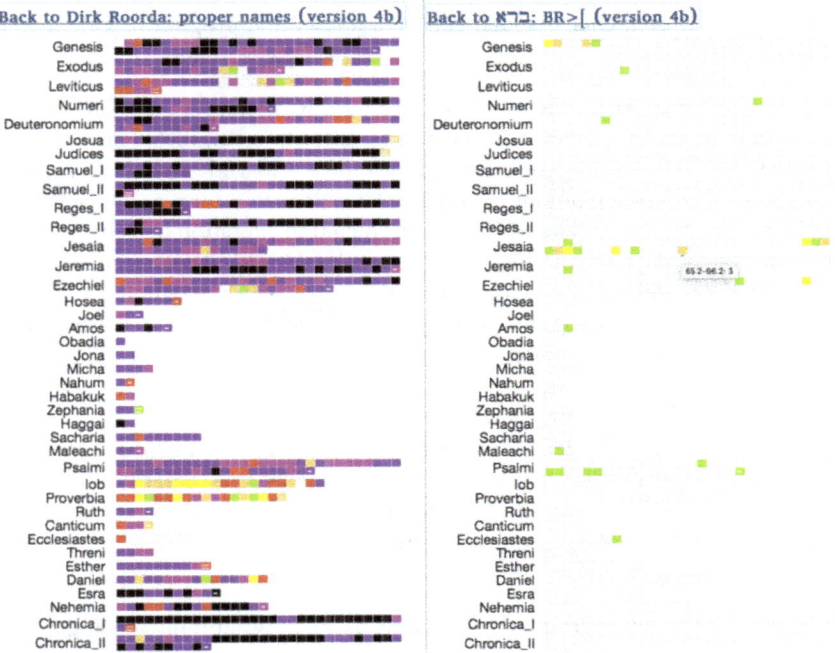

Figure 18.5: Clickable charts; left: proper name occurrences; right: the verb create.

18.5   Reflection

Back in 2012 we faced the challenge to provide better data models and better programs for biblical scholars. It had become clear that the software companies that were developing the bible study applications were not interested in building software for researchers. The researchers did not have access to programmers' time. There seemed to be only one way out: researchers should take their fate in their own hands and write the software themselves, which looked like a daunting proposition at best and an impossible one at worst. Yet, in 2014, we have created a publicly accessible tool for querying the linguistic data of the Hebrew Bible, with a means to share those queries. We also have a data laboratory where the programming theologian can take control over her data. Collectively, biblical scholars can use the data laboratory to help the query tool evolve according to their needs. Several factors have contributed to this achievement.

1. The existence of the LAF standard, which turned out to be a natural fit for this kind of data.

2. The realisation that the plain text of the Hebrew Bible is not subject to copyright, and hence that the ETCBC database of text and annotations can be made available as Open Source.

3. The existence of a research archive, DANS, acting as a data-hub; the intellectual heritage of many years of ETCBC work lays deposited there and is open to scrutiny by anyone at any time.

4. The existence of a social medium for program code, Github; all software for LAF-Fabric and SHEBANQ (and even some of the supporting software) lies there ready to be cloned and re-used.

5. The rise of scientific computing and its paraphernalia, such as (interactive) Python and auxiliary packages; it offers an unprecedented level of user-friendliness to novice programmers; it has the potential to draw a much wider range of humanities scholars into the enticing world of computing. A researcher is much closer to a scientific programmer than to a software engineer.

Yet, this is not sufficient to get the job done. The ETCBC is steeped in its own ways, it has an efficient internal data workflow, run with the best tools that were available in the late 1980s. The internet existed then, but had not yet morphed into the world-wide web. Data sharing is not in the genes of the ETCBC. Doing unique things in relative isolation for a prolonged stretch of time tends to make you idiosyncratic. The ETCBC has its own transliteration of Hebrew, its own, locally documented way of coding data into forms that are optimal for local data processing.

Opening up to the world poses new requirements on the ways the data is coded and how it is documented. Along with archiving the existing ETCBC documentation at DANS, we have published a new kind of feature documentation on the web (Roorda et al., 2014a). There we document not only the intended meaning of features, but we also provide frequency lists of their complete value sets, things that are easily computed by means of LAF-Fabric.

Can we say that we have succeeded in meeting the challenges posed in 2012? The big question is: will there be enough programming theologians to make this a viable route? Proof of success would be the adoption of LAF-Fabric by at least some theological researchers, interest in the Hebrew data from the side of computational linguistics and artificial intelligence.

Here are some indicators:

• there is a small but growing group of LAF-Fabric users: programming theologians;
• works using LAF-Fabric and/or citing queries in SHEBANQ: (Roorda et al., 2014b), Kalkman 2013; 2015, (de Vree, 2016);
• several courses on MQL queries have been given, in the US and the Netherlands;
• SHEBANQ interlinks with Bible Online Learner (Winther-Nielsen and Tøndering, 2013).

Because all these activities occur in the open, people interested in these techniques find each other through Github, Academia.edu, Twitter, and keep in touch through media such as Slack. Time will tell if the pull exerted by the digital methods will be enough to keep this nascent community together.

Acknowledgements

The following people contributed significantly to the work described in this chapter, in very different ways:

Ulrik Petersen for creating EMDROS, providing it as Open Source software and maintaining it all those years.

The ETCBC people: Eep Talstra and Constantijn Sikkel for creating and maintaining the ETCBC database and sharing so much knowledge about it; Wido van Peursen for paving the way for increased sharing of data. Oliver Glanz (now Andrews University Michigan) for showing order in the forest of features of the database; Gino Kalkman and Martijn Naaijer for using the new tools and challenging me. Grietje en Johan Commelin for their efforts to get LAF-Fabric working in the cloud. Reinoud Oosting for finding subtle bugs in SHEBANQ and Janet Dyk introducing new use cases.

Wider Digital Humanities: Joris van Zundert (HuygensING) for leading an inspiring Interedition bootcamp (van Zundert, 2012) which set me on the track of rapid development for the humanities; Rens Bod (Univ. of Amsterdam) and Andreas van Cranenburgh (Univ. of Amsterdam and HuygensING) who asked for the Hebrew data as tree structures in order to try out Data Oriented Parsing for classical Hebrew.

Last but not least: my colleagues at DANS: Henk Harmsen and Andrea Scharnhorst for granting additional time for research in these topics; Henk van den Berg and Heleen van de Schraaf for developing fundamental portions of the web-service and web application of SHEBANQ.

References

Bouda, Peter (2013-2014), graf-python. Python software on Github. https://github.com/cidles/graf-python.

Bouda, Peter, Vera Ferreira, and António Lopes (2012), Poio API - an annotation framework to bridge language documentation and natural language processing., *Proceedings of The Second Workshop on Annotation of Corpora for Research in the Humanities, Lisbon, 2012*, Lisbon, Portugal. ISBN: 978-989-689-273-9, http://alfclul.clul.ul.pt/crpc/acrh2/ACRH-2_papers/Bouda-Ferreira-Lopes.pdf.

de Vree, Frederik (2016), Using social co-occurrencenetworks to analyze biblicalnarrative. Master Thesis, VU Amsterdam. https://github.com/Fred-Erik/social-biblical-networks, https://www.academia.edu/26149493/Using_social_co-occurrence_networks_to_analyze_Biblical_narrative.

Di Pierro, Massimo (2015), Web2py. full stack web framework, 6th edition. Online book. http://web2py.com/book.

Doedens, Crist-Jan (1994), *Text Databases. One Database Model and Several Retrieval Languages*, number 14 in *Language and Computers*, Editions Rodopi, Amsterdam, Netherlands and Atlanta, USA. ISBN: 90-5183-729-1, http://books.google.nl/books?id=9ggOBRz1dO4C.

Elliger, Karl and Wilhelm Rudolf Rudolph, editors (1997), *Biblia Hebraica Stuttgartensia*, 5th corrected ed., Deutsche Bibelgesellschaft, Stuttgart, Germany. http://www.bibelwissenschaft.de/startseite/wissenschaftliche-bibelausgaben/biblia-hebraica/bhs/.

Gleick, James, editor (2011), *The Information: a History, a Theory, a Flood*, HarperCollins. ISBN: 0007225741, http://en.wikipedia.org/wiki/The_Information:_A_History,_a_Theory,_a_Flood.

Ide, Nancy and Laurent Romary (2012), Linguistic Annotation Framework. ISO standard 24612:2012. Edition 1, 2012-06-15. http://www.iso.org/iso/home/store/catalogue_tc/catalogue_detail.htm?csnumber=37326.

Kalkman, Gino J. (2013), Functions of asyndetic clause relations in biblical Hebrew. IPython Notebook. `http://nbviewer.ipython.org/github/ETCBC/Biblical_Hebrew_Analysis/blob/master/Miscellaneous/AsyndeticClauseFunctions.ipynb`.

Kalkman, Gino J. (2015), *Verbal Forms in Biblical Hebrew Poetry: Poetical Freedom or Linguistic System?*, PhD thesis, VU University, Amsterdam. `https://shebanq.ancient-data.org/tools?goto=verbsystem`.

Pérez, Fernando and Brian E. Granger (2007), IPython: a system for interactive scientific computing, *Computing in Science and Engineering* **9** (3), pp. 21–29, IEEE Computer Society. `http://ipython.org`, ISSN: 1521-9615, DOI: `http://dx.doi.org/10.1109/MCSE.2007.53`.

Petersen, Ulrik (2002-2014), Emdros. text database engine for analyzed or annotated text. Open Source software. `http://emdros.org`.

Petersen, Ulrik (2004), Emdros - a text database engine for analyzed or annotated text, *Proceedings of COLING 2004*, p. 1190–1193. `http://emdros.org/petersen-emdros-COLING-2004.pdf`.

Petersen, Ulrik (2006), *Principles, Implementation Strategies, and Evaluation of a Corpus Query System*, Vol. 4002, Springer, p. 215–226. `http://link.springer.com/chapter/10.1007%2F11780885_21`.

Peursen, Wido Th. and Dirk Roorda (2014), Hebrew text database ETCBC4. Dataset available online at Data Archiving and Networked services, Den Haag, Netherlands. DOI: `http://dx.doi.org/10.17026/dans-2z3-arxf`.

Peursen, Wido Th. and Dirk Roorda (2015), Hebrew text database ETCBC4b. Dataset available online at Data Archiving and Networked services, Den Haag, Netherlands. DOI: `http://dx.doi.org/10.17026/dans-z6y-skyh`.

Roorda, Dirk (2012), Queries-as-annotations. Github repository. `https://github.com/Dans-labs/annotation-paradigm`.

Roorda, Dirk (2013-2014b), LAF-Fabric. workbench for analysing LAF resources. Python software on the Python Package Index with source on Github. `https://github.com/Dans-labs/laf-fabric`, `https://pypi.python.org/pypi/laf-fabric`.

Roorda, Dirk (2014a), LAF-Fabric notebooks. examples of data processing for the hebrew bible. Python software on Github. `https://shebanq.ancient-data.org/tools`, `https://github.com/ETCBC/laf-fabric-nbs`.

Roorda, Dirk and Charles M.J.M. van den Heuvel (2012), Annotation as a new paradigm in research archiving, *Proceedings of ASIS&T 2012 Annual Meeting. Final Papers, Panels and Posters*. `https://www.asis.org/asist2012/proceedings/Submissions/84.pdf` (author's version: `http://arxiv.org/abs/1412.6069`).

Roorda, Dirk, Constantijn Sikkel, and Wido Th van Peursen (2014a), Feature documentation of shebanq. Github repository published on readthedocs. `https://etcbc.github.io/bhsa/`.

Roorda, Dirk, Gino Kalkman, Martijn Naaijer, and Andreas van Cranenburgh (2014b), Laf-fabric: a data analysis tool for linguistic annotation framework with an application to the hebrew bible, *Computational Linguistics in the Netherlands Journal* **4**, pp. 105–120, CLIN. `http://www.clinjournal.org/sites/clinjournal.org/files/08-Roorda-etal-CLIN2014.pdf`.

Roorda, Dirk, Jan Krans, Bert-Jan Lietaert-Peerbolte, Wido Th. van Peursen, Ulrik Sandborg-Petersen, and Eep Talstra (2012), Scientific report of the workshop biblical scholarship and humanities computing: Data types, text, language and interpretation, held at the lorentz centre leiden from 6 feb 2012 through 10 feb 2012, *Technical report*, Lorentz Center, Leiden. `http://www.lorentzcenter.nl/lc/web/2012/480/report.php3?wsid=480&venue=Oort`.

Talstra, Eep and Constantijn J. Sikkel (2000), Genese und kategorienentwicklung der wivu-datenbank, *in* Hardmeier, C. et al, editor, *Ad Fontes! Quellen erfassen - lesen - deuten. Wat ist Computerphilologie? Ansatzpunkte und Methodologie - Instrument und Praxis*, VU University Press, Amsterdam, Netherlands, pp. 33–68.

Talstra, Eep, Constantijn J. Sikkel, Oliver Glanz, Reinoud Oosting, and Janet W. Dyk (2012), Text database of the hebrew bible. Dataset available online after permission of the depositor at Data Archiving and Networked services, Den Haag, Netherlands. DOI: http://dx.doi.org/ 10.17026/dans-x8h-y2bv.

van Peursen, Wido Th., Dirk Roorda, Henk van den Berg, and Heleen van de Schraaf (2014), SHE-BANQ, a search engine and query saver for the etcbc text database of the hebrew bible. web application. https://shebanq.ancient-data.org.

van Zundert, Joris et al. (2012), Proceedings of the leuven2012 interedition workshop. Wiki page. http://interedition.eu/wiki/index.php/Leuven2012_Proceedings.

Winther-Nielsen, Nicolai and Claus Tøndering (2013), Bible online learner. Website, learning system for Hebrew students. http://bibleol.3bmoodle.dk/.

CHAPTER 19

WhiteLab 2.0: A Web Interface for Corpus Exploitation

Matje van de Camp[c,a], Martin Reynaert[b,a] and Nelleke Oostdijk[a]

[a]CLS / Radboud University Nijmegen, [b]TiCC / Tilburg University,
[c]De Taalmonsters, The Netherlands

ABSTRACT

The OpenSoNaR-CGN project set out to develop WhiteLab 2.0 for the online exploitation of the SoNaR-500 and CGN corpora. Important changes in comparison to the first version of WhiteLab are the addition of audio support and support for multiple corpora. The web interface has been redeveloped and adapted to accommodate these changes. At the backend, WhiteLab 2.0 comes with a new data importer and plugin for Neo4j, while also remaining compatible with BlackLab. Although performance of the new backend is not yet up to par with BlackLab, the investment in new technology that will likely be further developed is expected to make the application more future-proof and a great addition to the set of tools available to the humanities.

19.1 Introduction

Since the Spoken Dutch Corpus (Corpus Gesproken Nederlands, CGN (Oostdijk 2000)) project set out in 1998 to compile a corpus of standard Dutch, the landscape of Dutch language resources has changed dramatically. At the turn of the century Strik et al. (2002) reported in a survey they conducted of Dutch language resources that they found the Human Language Technologies (HLT) infrastructure to be "scattered, incomplete, and not sufficiently accessible". Thanks to substantial investments by the Dutch and Flemish governments and research foundations in the STEVIN programme[1] (D'Halleweyn et al. 2006; Spyns and Odijk 2013) and the CLARIN-NL project (Odijk 2010) most of what are generally considered to be basic language resources are now in place and can be accessed in a common infrastructure.

---

[1] STEVIN was a five-year (2004-2009) joint Dutch-Flemish programme for Language and Speech Technology.

How to cite this book chapter:
van de Camp, M, Reynaert, M and Oostdijk, N. 2017. WhiteLab 2.0: A Web Interface for Corpus Exploitation. In: Odijk, J and van Hessen, A. (eds.) *CLARIN in the Low Countries*, Pp. 231–243. London: Ubiquity Press. DOI: https://doi.org/10.5334/bbi.19. License: CC-BY 4.0

Since the focus of the STEVIN programme was on settling the pressing needs as they existed in the HLT community, its orientation was first and foremost towards users that had the necessary skills to handle the tools and the data. The CLARIN project, however, aimed to develop an interoperable research infrastructure for humanities researchers that work with language data and tools. The infrastructure should make it possible for them to find and access data and tools relevant for their research. Importantly, researchers should be able to apply available tools to their data in such a way that no technical background is needed or ad-hoc adaptations to the tools or the data are necessary.[2]

As the opportunity arose within CLARIN-NL to address the need for a corpus exploitation tool that would make it possible for users to access the large (500+ million-word) reference corpus of written standard Dutch (SoNaR-500 for short; Oostdijk et al., 2013), the OpenSoNaR project (Reynaert et al., 2014) was initiated[3]. It took its lead from other projects concerned with large national corpora, which successfully employed the latest online web-based technology, and developed WhiteLab as a frontend to the then new corpus indexer BlackLab[4] which had been developed by the former Institute for Dutch Lexicology (INL), now Institute for the Dutch Language (INT). Then, in 2015, as WhiteLab had proved its usability and user-friendliness through OpenSoNaR, with additional funding from CLARIN-NL through the OpenSoNaR-CGN project it was extended to add support for spoken language corpora. The resulting system, WhiteLab 2.0, makes it possible for users to access and exploit both SoNaR and CGN, either independently of each other or in combination. The combined corpora are now online under the new name OpenSoNaR+[5].

In this chapter we describe WhiteLab 2.0 and the interface to SoNaR and CGN. The structure of the chapter is as follows: in the next section, we introduce the two corpora in some more detail. In Section 19.3 we describe WhiteLab 2.0's architecture and provide a preliminary comparison of its newly developed backend with the existing BlackLab. Then, in Section 19.4 we turn to the user-functionality that it offers by describing the OpenSoNaR+ interface. In Section 19.5 attention is given to the performance and availability. Section 19.6 concludes this chapter.

19.2   The Corpora

The Spoken Dutch Corpus (Oostdijk, 2000) is a corpus of some 800 hours of speech, comprising a large number of samples recorded from adult speakers in the Netherlands and Flanders speaking standard Dutch. All data have been orthographically transcribed, annotated for parts-of-speech, and lemmatised. For a subset of the data phonetic transcriptions and syntactic annotations are also available. The metadata provide information about the speakers (e.g. age, sex, place of birth, educational background) and the recordings (e.g. duration, recording conditions, number of speakers). In order to allow for less technically savvy researchers to use the corpus without having to call upon the assistance of someone with programming skills, the COREX (CORpus EXploitation) software was developed (Oostdijk and Broeder 2003). It enables users to browse and search the corpus, and to view and export the results. Exploitation in COREX is limited to the transcriptions and annotations that are available for the full corpus. For the other annotation layers users are expected to make use of dedicated software, such as Praat[6] for phonetic transcriptions or Dact[7] for the

---

[2] http://www.clarin.nl/

[3] It was apparent that the dedicated software developed for exploitation of the Spoken Dutch Corpus would not be able to handle the amounts of data found in the SoNaR corpus.

[4] https://github.com/INL/BlackLab

[5] http://opensonar-cgn.science.ru.nl

[6] http://www.fon.hum.uva.nl/praat/

[7] http://rug-compling.github.io/dact/

exploitation of the syntactic annotations. Since all transcriptions and annotations are directly or indirectly aligned with the audio, the user can access the recordings from any point in the corpus. Searches can be conducted involving information from different annotation layers. The metadata may be used to further restrict a search to a specific subset. Results are presented in the form of concordance lines or, in the case multiple where content searches are executed on different subcorpora, frequency lists.

SoNaR-500 (Oostdijk et al., 2013) is a 540-million-word reference corpus of contemporary written Dutch. It includes a balanced collection of full texts representing a broad range of genres and text types, such as books (fiction and non-fiction), newspaper articles, and brochures, but also from the new and social media, such as discussion fora, chats, and tweets. The texts are original Dutch texts from the Dutch-speaking language area in the Netherlands and Flanders, or Dutch translations published in and targeted at this area. All texts have been tokenized, identifying paragraphs, sentences, and (word) tokens. In view of its size, the corpus has been tagged and lemmatized automatically, using Frog[8] (Van den Bosch et al., 2007). Unlike the Spoken Dutch Corpus, SoNaR came without exploitation software that would support users with limited or non-existent programming skills.

In the OpenSoNaR-CGN project, the texts of the Spoken Dutch Corpus or CGN have been curated and brought in line with the SoNaR-500 corpus by converting them to the FoLiA XML[9] format (van Gompel and Reynaert 2013).[10]

19.3   WhiteLab 2.0: Architecture

19.3.1   Design Considerations

Given the limitations in the functionality and scalability of existing tools, there clearly existed a great need for a new corpus exploitation suite in the Dutch language community. Since the development of COREX in 2003, technologies for web-based exploitation of large-scale datasets have also become more readily available and the use of these for linguistic research has been widely reported (Hoffmann and Evert, 2006; McEnery and Hardie, 2011; Hardie, 2012; Evert and Hardie, 2015). The need was partly met with the development of WhiteLab in the OpenSoNaR project (Reynaert et al., 2014). WhiteLab version 1.0 is a Java-based web application for the search and exploration of large-scale, linguistically annotated corpora. It caters to users of all skill levels by providing interfaces ranging from simple string querying to tools for advanced query composition, and even plain CQL entry using the Corpus Query Language, first introduced by Christ (1994). Metadata can be explored and queried in a comprehensive way. At the backend, WhiteLab relies on BlackLab and BlackLab-server[11] for corpus indexing and querying.

Nevertheless, the application was developed specifically for the SoNaR-500 corpus and, as such, does not provide support for speech-related annotations or audio. Furthermore, it can host only a single corpus, which limits its flexibility as a research tool. To overcome these issues, the

---

[8]   In some of the data named identities have also been labeled.

[9]   See Chapter 6 on FoLiA in this volume.

[10] As for the POS tagging, we observe that the tagset originally developed for tagging the Spoken Dutch Corpus Van Eynde et al. (2000) was later extended to account for tokens typically found in written texts Van Eynde (2005), and what was conceived as the CGN tagger-lemmatizer was reincarnated in Frog (http://languagemachines.github.io/frog/). Thus the POS tagging of CGN and SoNaR was already fully compatible.

[11] https://github.com/INL/BlackLab-server

OpenSoNaR-CGN project set out to develop WhiteLab 2.0 with the following considerations, which are in line with the recommendations made by Hoffmann and Evert (2006):

1. Users of different skill levels should be able to use the interface without problem, and continued use of the application should contribute to increasing a user's skill level.

2. The application needs to provide support for multiple corpora out of the box. Users should be able to query the corpora simultaneously, or separately.

3. The system should not be restricted to just the CGN and SoNaR-500 corpora, by providing support for widely used formats for content and metadata.

4. The manager of the application should have control over the metadata and how they are displayed in the interface. Since multiple corpora are now supported with multiple metadata formats, the manager should be able to group together fields with different labels under the same moniker in the interface.

5. Before querying the corpora, the user should be able to explore the data to get a sense of what is available.

6. Besides types, lemmata, and part-of-speech (POS) tags, phonetic transcriptions need to be indexed and made available for search.

7. Audio playback should be enabled for both recordings or parts thereof (hits).

8. All results should be exportable at least in CSV format for post-processing.

9. The application should be future-proof by investing in technologies that are particularly suited to the growing needs of the research community and are expected to stand the test of time to a reasonable degree.

Considering the previous version of WhiteLab, some of these criteria (1, 5, 8) had already been met in OpenSoNaR. The original application has been successfully applied in educational settings, proving its ability as a teaching tool. It also provides interfaces for both exploration and search, each with its own unique purpose and export functionality. Extensions made upon the interface are described in Section 19.4. Regarding the technical implementation, some choices have been made that really distinguish WhiteLab 2.0 from its predecessor, as we discuss in the remainder of this section.

19.3.2   System Design

A complete WhiteLab 2.0 setup consists of three components: an importer module to add corpora to the corpus index, a plugin to enable CQL searches on the index, and a web application that allows access to the index in an online context. For the first version of WhiteLab, the indexing and querying was handled by BlackLab and BlackLab-server. WhiteLab 2.0 also supports BlackLab, but by default it comes with its own newly developed WhiteLab 2.0 Importer and Plugin.

The most innovative aspect of WhiteLab 2.0 as opposed to WhiteLab is its use of the NoSQL graph database Neo4j (Neo Database AB, 2006). NoSQL databases have gained a lot of momentum over the last few years as a promising alternative to relational SQL databases for storing huge datasets. The main advantage of NoSQL over SQL[12] in general is its possibility to easily scale horizontally, meaning data may be spread over different servers, and its suitability for dynamic datasets. For the purpose of searching large collections of linguistically annotated data, two types of NoSQL databases are appropriate: document stores and graph databases. Document stores encapsulate data in structured documents, such as XML, which seems a perfect fit for linguistic corpora. However,

---

[12] Structured Query Language, standardized in ISO/IEC 9075-1:2011.

the specific structure of the FoLiA format that our corpora are encoded in makes it an arduous task to implement and optimise the arbitrary complex queries that can be produced by WhiteLab directly on the source documents. Therefore, a complete remapping of the data would likely be required when using a document store. Moreover, document stores are inherently document-centric, providing a strictly hierarchical view on the data.

Graph databases are similar to document stores, but incorporate the concept of relations between documents and other elements by modeling the data as a network. In contrast to document stores, this network is not necessarily hierarchical. It allows for references between (parts of) documents that would not be possible in a tree, which in turn provides a more expressive and easily navigable model of the data. Linguistic data encode networks of different natures, both syntactic and seman-tic, and both hierarchical and (seemingly) random, which would essentially be captured in a single database. Graph databases therefore seem a logical choice for our data and purpose, resulting in our choice for Neo4j. Neo4j stores data as nodes that are interconnected through relationships. Labels and properties may be defined on both nodes and relationships.

The web application itself has been redeveloped in Ruby on Rails (RoR).[13] RoR was chosen based on its transparent division of model, view, and controller, which increases speed of development and allows for easy extension of the application and reuse of its parts in other applications.

19.3.3   Data Model

Figure 19.1 displays the WhiteLab 2.0 data model implemented in Neo4j for linguistically anno-tated corpora. When designing a data model for Neo4j, it is important to consider the sizes of nodes, relationships, and their properties as they are stored in the database, which are respectively 15, 34, and 64 bytes.[14] A combination of two nodes and a relationship requires less storage space than a single node with one property (64 versus 79 bytes). Therefore, it is always more efficient to store an element attribute as a new node rather than a property, and connect the element node to it (Figure 19.2, red and black lines). In this scenario, the extra property node would not require its own property, since Neo4j allows nodes to be identified or typed using labels. However, at the time of development of WhiteLab 2.0, it was not possible to efficiently query labels using regular expres-sions, which is a base requirement for the target audience. Properties can be indexed for improved

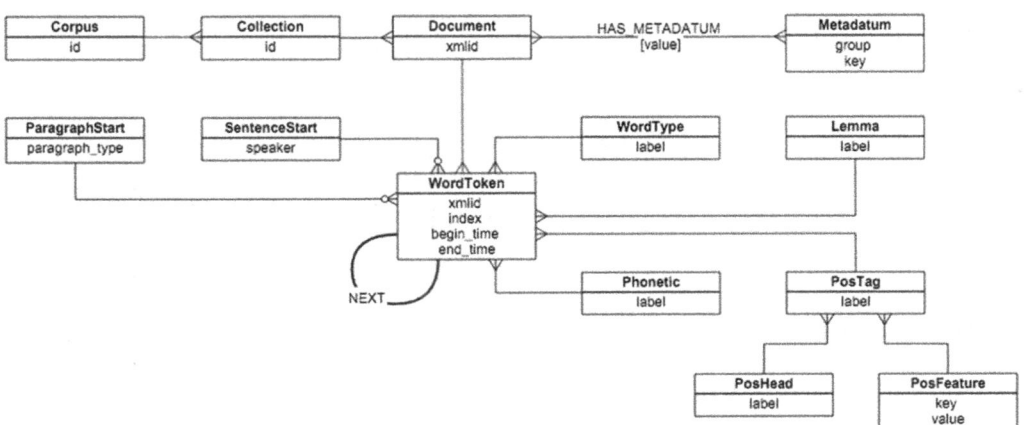

Figure 19.1: The WhiteLab 2.0 data model for the Neo4j backend.

---

[13] http://api.rubyonrails.org/
[14] http://neo4j.com/docs/stable/configuration-io-examples.html

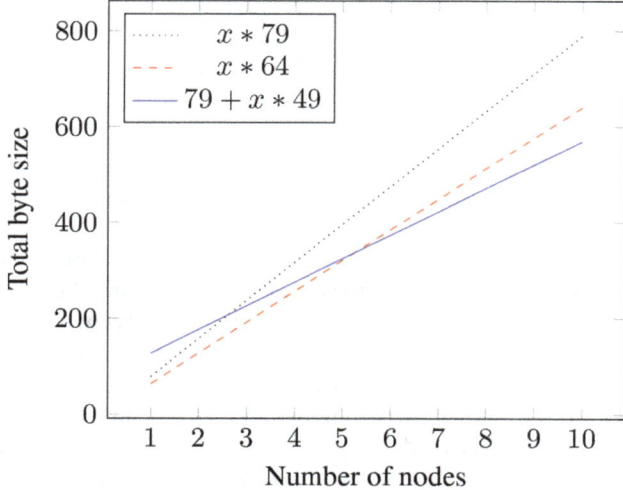

Figure 19.2: The WhiteLab 2.0 data model for the Neo4j backend.

search and do allow for regular expression queries, but the total size of two nodes, a relationship and one property (128 bytes) is larger than a single node with one property. Nevertheless, if more elements have the same attribute and their nodes connect to the same property node, the total size quickly becomes less than when storing each element node with its own property (Figure 19.2, blue, full line). In practice this means that attribute values with a frequency lower than 3 are most efficiently stored as properties of the element node they describe, whereas higher frequency attribute values should be placed in their own node, which is then connected to the appropriate element nodes.

Compared to WhiteLab, the set of annotations in WhiteLab 2.0 has been extended to include phonetics. This includes the addition of token attributes regarding the token's position in the audio, as well as identification of the speaker at sentence level. Also, the Part-of-Speech attributes (head and features) are separated from the complete tag, allowing for more fine-grained analysis of these annotations.

In order to retain support for BlackLab, a new index tool has been added to BlackLab[15] that enables indexing of multiple corpora, and a set of new BlackLab indexers has been developed specifically for use with WhiteLab 2.0. With the current indexers and Importer, the size of the Neo4j database is approximately twice that of the equivalent BlackLab index.

19.3.4   *Administration*

A new feature in WhiteLab 2.0 is the Admin interface. It allows the application manager to inspect and manage the metadata and Part-of-Speech tags across corpora. This functionality was added in light of known differences in the tagsets used for SoNaR-500 and CGN, which can now be easily inspected. The Admin interface also allows control over the interface language and info page content (Section 19.4).

The types of corpora that WhiteLab 2.0 is designed to make accessible are mostly of a static nature, certainly so at the document level. Therefore, result sets for queries are not expected to change after deployment. We have taken advantage of this fact by including an SQL database in the web application for user and query logging. The query logging is set up in such a way that no

---

[15] https://github.com/Taalmonsters/BlackLab

duplicate queries are sent to the Neo4j database. For instance, if two users enter the same query within a short timeframe, the query is sent to the database only upon first request. The second request will simply wait for the first to finish and then access its results. Another request for the same data at a later time will also quickly return the previously stored result to the user. To keep a handle on the resources used, the web application includes some easy-to-set-up scheduled tasks, so-called Cron jobs, that run daily to remove queries that have timed out or have not been accessed in a while. A further advantage are the insights that the application manager may gather from the query statistics.

19.3.5 Performance

We test the performance of the WhiteLab 2.0 plugin for Neo4j compared to that of BlackLab-server 1.3 on the same dataset. Due to limitations of available hardware, the tests are performed on a sub-set of the complete OpenSoNaR+ data, namely, the entire CGN, plus the following SoNaR-500 collections: WR-P-E-E Newsletters, WR-P-E-F Press releases, WR-P-E-H Teletext pages, WR-P-E-J Wikipedia, WR-P-E-K Blogs, WR-P-P-B Books, WR-P-P-D Newsletters, WR-P-P-I Policy documents, WR-P-P-K Reports, and WR-U-E-A Chats[16]. The total size is around 83 million tokens. Tests are performed in a single dedicated server setup on a 12-core system with 64 Gb of RAM.

We test the response time of both backends to five queries with increasing absolute hit counts ranging from approximately 7,500 to 250,000 hits. Each query is sent to the server 51 times over the command line. By bypassing the GUI, we disable the WhiteLab query caching for these tests. The first call is discarded for both backends, as this warms up the index and takes considerably more time to complete. Figure 19.3 shows the average response time over the remaining 50 calls for each query. As is shown, BlackLab's performance is unhindered by increasing hit counts, where WhiteLab 2.0's response time increases almost linearly to the hit count. When we inspect the logs, we see that Neo4j spends most time on collecting the nodes that match the first token in the CQL query, and on grouping results where necessary. Similar tests on queries of increasing complexity

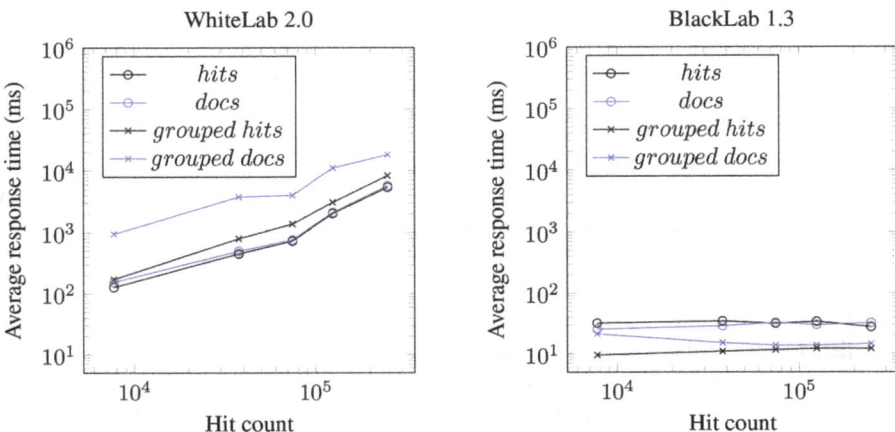

Figure 19.3: Performance of WhiteLab 2.0 compared to BlackLab 1.3. Five queries with increasing result counts (in absolute hits) are each performed 51 times. The first call is discarded, as this warms up the indexes. We report the average response time over the remaining 50 calls.

---

[16] The SoNaR User Manual (available from `http://ticclops.uvt.nl/SoNaR_end-user_documentation_v.1.0.4.pdf`) explains these codes.

as measured in n-gram size confirm that the initial node selection is the crux; the n-gram size has little to no effect on the response time. The delay in the grouping is particularly detrimental to queries for grouped documents, as these require two groupings: first from hits to documents, and then into groups of documents. Overall, the tests show that there is still a lot to be done in terms of optimization of the WhiteLab 2.0 Neo4j plugin.

19.4   OpenSoNaR+: User Functionality[17]

We describe the WhiteLab 2.0 web interface as it is designed for OpenSoNaR+. It largely resembles the WhiteLab interface for OpenSoNaR, with added support for audio. A major advantage over the previous version is the addition of easy-to-configure interface translations. By default, the application comes with Dutch and English translations, but these may be extended by the application manager through the Admin interface. This interface also provides functionality to streamline metadata over different corpora. The metadata labels and values are listed including their coverage of indexed corpora, which provides a quick overview of possible similarities and discrepancies between corpus metadata. Different labels that refer to the same type of information can be grouped together under the same label. The translation functionality used for the interface components is also applied to the metadata labels.

The WhiteLab user by default lands on the **Search** page of OpenSoNaR+ when logging in. Next to this page we have the **Explore** page and the **Info** page. The Admin interface is hidden behind a login page and thus not available to regular users.

19.4.1   Info Page

The Info page provides information about the system. It provides a first-user manual which gives an overview of the main functionalities that OpenSoNaR+ offers. It also provides the user manuals of the SoNaR and CGN corpora, which offer in-depth information on the composition of both the contemporary written Dutch corpus and the spoken Dutch corpus. The system also provides a guided tour to its users, which gives the user a quick introduction to each page's uses and possibilities. Access to the guided tour is through the question mark button to the left in the top bar of the interface.

19.4.2   Explore

The Explore page gives statistical and visual information about the corpus contents. It provides insight into the distribution of the texts available per genre and according to their provenance, which is basically whether they were collected in the Netherlands or in Flanders or are of unidentified or unidentifiable provenance. The latter is the case for example with text materials obtained from the European Union or Wikipedia.

On the basis of metadata selections under the 'statistics' tab, the user can obtain custom frequency lists for particular subselections of the corpora. These are further discussed under Subsection 19.4.5. This page also affords access to n-gram (where n is 1 to 5) frequency lists derived from subcorpora for word forms, lemmata, POS tags and phonetic transcriptions.

Finally, the page affords direct access to a particular document in the incorporated collections on the basis of its file name. This should be a useful feature for possible research verification or replication when the particular document has been referred to in a research paper.

---

[17] This section is an adaptation and extension of the initial description in Reynaert et al. 2014.

19.4.3 *Search*

The Search environment is to date the most elaborate. It provides four levels of access to the contents: Simple, Extended, Advanced and Expert.

The **Simple search** option provides Google-style, single query box access. Entering a search term here will instantiate a search over the full contents of the corpus. The search is for word forms, which may be phrases (*n*-grams), in which case insensitive matches are sought that respect the actual sequence of words. This latter functionality is also provided by the Extended and Advanced search environments.

The **Extended search** environment allows one to impose selection filters on the search effected. These filters are of two kinds. First, there are filters on the metadata. Second, there are filters on the lexical level, allowing one to search for either word forms, lemmata, POS tags and phonetic transcriptions for the spoken Dutch data.

The metadata filters are at first hidden behind a bar visible above the actual lexical query fields. When the user wants to impose metadata filters the bar is expanded by a simple mouse click and the user is presented with a row consisting of three drop-down boxes. The middle box has just two options: 'is' or 'is not'. The left box gives access to all the metadata fields available in the corpus CMDI metadata files. The right box, upon selection of a particular metadata field in the left box, dynamically expands with the list of available metadata contents, where applicable. Metadata filters can be stacked. Through a 'plus' button to the right of the query row, one may obtain further rows in each of which further restrictions on the query may be imposed. The metadata view shows the proportional and absolute (i.e. number of tokens) size of the dataset matching the currently selected filters. When a metadata filter is selected or updated, these numbers are automatically updated, allowing the user to quickly inspect subcorpus size prior to searching.

The metadata selection interface additionally provides the option of grouping the query results obtained by a range of features. For example, if one here selects the option of having the results presented by country of origin of the hit texts, one is not presented directly with the Key Words in Context (KWIC) list of results, but rather with a bar representation of the number of hits per country. One may then click on one of these bars and be presented with the KWIC list. This then gives the user the possibility to select one of these subsets and to further work on these as a new, independent query.

The lexical filters allow one to optionally perform case-sensitive searches for word forms, lemmata and/or phonetic transcriptions. POS tags can of course be searched too. When the search is for lemmata, all the word forms sharing the same lemma will be retrieved. For POS tag searches the user is presented with a drop-down list which presents a layperson's translation in plain language for the actual POS tags involved. Combinations of, for instance, word forms and POS searches are possible to direct the search for the word 'drink' (ibidem in English) towards the first person singular of the present tense verb form, rather than its use as a noun.

For the **Advanced search** option we fully acknowledge to have emulated the elegant interface to CQL-query building as provided by the Swedish Språkbanken[18]. Users are first presented with a single box containing three query fields. By horizontally or vertically adding further boxes they may build quite complex queries without the need to know the query language behind them. Vertical boxes may be stacked with 'and' or 'or' conditions. These boxes give access not only to queries on full word forms (word 'is' or word 'is not') but also to words beginning with or containing or ending with a specific character string. Regular expressions are a further option. Users get to see the query they have built and have the option of further extending it, manually.

---

[18] See 'Korp' at https://spraakbanken.gu.se/korp/#?lang=en&search_tab=1

The **Expert search** requires knowledge of the query language incorporated in the system. It is CQL, the Corpus Query Language[19]. In its essence, this search option's limitations are defined mainly by the user's CQL proficiency. However, to support the educational requirements of White-Lab 2.0, queries can be entered in one interface (e.g. Simple search) and viewed in another, more complex interface (e.g. Expert search) without first having to execute the query. Using this functionality, students and laypeople can directly see the CQL query generated from their string query and actually increase their familiarity with the Corpus Query Language.

19.4.4   Presentation of the Results

Regardless of the search option one has chosen, by default, eventually a KWIC list of results is presented. A red button for each of the text snippets gives direct access to the full-text view of the document. There, moving the cursor over any of the words in the text, one gets to see a small window with the word form's unique ID, lemma and POS tag. Documents retrieved from CGN have a button for the whole text and buttons per sentence for calling up the appropriate sound recording. New tabs give access to the particular document's full metadata, to document specific statistics on size in terms of word tokens and types and derived measures. Finally, the user is presented with a visualisation of the token to POS tag distribution and the vocabulary growth curve.

A feature of the Extended and Advanced search options we have not seen in other corpus exploration environments is that multiple queries can be performed in one operation. This is facilitated by the fact that by clicking on the 'list' button to the right of the query boxes the user may effortlessly upload a pre-prepared list of query terms. After uploading, these query terms are converted by the system into actual, separate CQL queries which are visible in the query history. The user then has the option of having the output presented separately, per query, or mixed. If in the Advanced search environment a user uploads more than one query list, the system makes a combination of all the query terms in the lists. Given x terms in list A and y terms in list B, this results in x times y queries. If this is not what the user intended, then the user has the option of uploading a list of, for instance, word bigrams to be searched for in the Extended search environment.

19.4.5   Export of the Results

Both the Explore and Search pages allow the users to export the results of their queries. This would be the frequency list built on the basis of the selections made, whether metadata-based, lexical, or indeed both. Or else, one may export the list of documents that were selected. What WhiteLab by design does not provide, is export of the full documents. This facility exceeds for the best part the IPR-agreements that were achieved with the text providers. However, the full corpora containing the full texts are freely obtainable for research purposes from the INT.

The query results are exported in various formats, including comma-separated lists suitable for loading in a spreadsheet. The format should be easily convertible to the specific formats required by statistical packages such as R[20] or SPSS[21].

19.4.6   Query History

An important new feature of the updated WhiteLab is that a user's query history is stored and is accessible to the user through an unobtrusive sea-green button in the lower left corner of the window.

---

[19] A nice tutorial is at: http://cwb.sourceforge.net/files/CQP_Tutorial/.
[20] https://www.r-project.org/
[21] https://www.ibm.com/marketplace/cloud/statistical-analysis-and-reporting/

The results of one's export actions are to be found here as part of the summary of each query one has undertaken.

19.5   Performance and Availability

19.5.1   Performance

As far as technologies go, Neo4j is relatively young and still in active development. Since the start of the OpenSoNaR-CGN project, many new versions have already been released, including updates that will likely increase performance for WhiteLab 2.0 once implemented. This trend is expected to continue over the coming years. WhiteLab 2.0 is already set up to reap the benefits of these advancements, while also being able to function with established technologies through BlackLab.

Currently, the query caching of the interface is resolved using an SQL database. We recognize that this can also be solved using a key-value store such as Redis. At the time of development of the current version of WhiteLab, use of Redis still imposed a lot of security risks and was not advised in production systems. However, recent developments have greatly improved Redis's security[22], making it a feasible alternative that we will definitely consider. Moreover, BlackLab-server provides its own query caching.

Independent from external developments, we see a number of possibilities for improving performance of the Neo4j backend. Certainly, the application itself can be further optimized and streamlined. But most benefit would likely be gained from decreasing the size of the Neo4j database, either through simplification of the data model, or separation of structure and content. The latter could be achieved, for instance, through a dual-database setup, where one database holds the document structures and the other the linguistic network. Another possibility we intend to investigate is storage of the annotations in an optimized string index such as the one used by word2vec (Mikolov et al., 2013), which reaches great speeds on huge collections of strings.

19.5.2   Availability

All WhiteLab 2.0 components are released under the GNU Affero General Public License and are currently available at https://github.com/Taalmonsters/WhiteLab2.0. An installation manual for use with either the BlackLab or the Neo4j backend is provided.

19.6   Conclusion

The distribution version of CGN requires 115GB in archived form and SoNaR-500 takes up 62.6GB. Unwieldy at best, and to all intents and purposes practically inaccessible to the average researcher. Though freely available for research, some unwary researchers were nastily surprised when trying to unpack SoNaR on common laptops running everyday software. Reports of these mishaps prompted the original OpenSoNaR project proposal to be written.

Results of the first project being well-received, OpenSoNaR-CGN followed suit. In relatively little time and on a modest budget with a small, but dedicated, team, we have managed to put OpenSoNaR+ – both corpora, text and sound – at everyone's fingertips.

We hope WhiteLab may serve researchers well. We definitely hope it will find favour with new and existing corpus endeavours in the Low Countries and far beyond.

---

[22] https://www.reddit.com/r/redis/comments/3zv85m/new_security_feature_redis_protected_mode/

Acknowledgements

We gratefully acknowledge the feedback we received from our user group and the funding provided by CLARIN-NL under grant numbers CLARIN-NL-12-013 and CLARIN-NL-15-005. Martin Reynaert further acknowledges being funded by the new Dutch national CLARIN project CLARIAH and by NWO in project Nederlab. Finally we would like to thank the two anonymous reviewers of the prefinal version of this chapter for their constructive feedback.

References

Christ, Oliver (1994) A modular and flexible architecture for an integrated corpus query system. *Proceedings of COMPLEX'94: 3rd Conference on Computational Lexicography and Text Research.* Budapest, Hungary. pp. 23–32.

Elisabeth D'Halleweyn, Jan Odijk, Lisanne Teunissen, and Catia Cucchiarini. 2006. The Dutch-Flemish HLT Programme STEVIN: Essential Speech and Language Technology Resources. In Nicoletta Calzolari et al., editor, *Proceedings of the Fifth international conference on Language Resources and Evaluation (LREC-2006)*, pages 761–766, Genoa, Italy. European Language Resources Association (ELRA).

Stefan Evert and Andrew Hardie. 2015. Ziggurat: A new data model and indexing format for large annotated text corpora. In Piotr Bański, Hanno Biber, Evelyn Breiteneder, Marc Kupietz, Harald Lüngen, and Andreas Witt, editors, *Proceedings of the 3rd Workshop on Challenges in the Management of Large Corpora (CMLC-3), Lancaster, 20 July 2015*, pages 21–27.

Andrew Hardie. 2012. CQPweb - combining power, flexibility and usability in a corpus analysis tool. *International Journal of Corpus Linguistics*, 17(3):380–409.

Sebastian Hoffmann and Stefan Evert, 2006. *BNCweb (CQP edition) - the marriage of two corpus tools*, pages 177–195. Peter Lang.

Tony McEnery and Andrew Hardie. 2011. *Corpus Linguistics: Method, Theory and Practice.* Cambridge Textbooks in Linguistics. Cambridge University Press.

Tomas Mikolov, Ilya Sutskever, Kai Chen, Greg S. Corrado, and Jeff Dean. 2013. Distributed representations of words and phrases and their compositionality. In *Advances in Neural Information Processing Systems*, pages 3111–3119.

Neo Database AB. 2006. The Neo Database – A Technology Introduction. http://dist.neo4j.org/neo-technology-introduction.pdf.

Jan Odijk. 2010. The CLARIN-NL project. In *Proceedings of the Seventh International Conference on Language Resources and Evaluation, LREC-2010*, pages 48–53, Valletta, Malta.

Nelleke Oostdijk and Daan Broeder. 2003. The Spoken Dutch Corpus and its exploitation environment. In A. Abeille, S. Hansen-Schirra, and H. Uszkoreit, editors, *Proceedings of the 4th International Workshop on linguistically interpreted corpora (LINC-03)*, pages 93–101.

Nelleke Oostdijk, Martin Reynaert, Véronique Hoste, and Ineke Schuurman. 2013. The construction of a 500-million-word reference corpus of contemporary written Dutch. In *Essential Speech and Language Technology for Dutch: Results by the STEVIN-programme*, chapter 13, pages 219–247. Springer Verlag.

Nelleke Oostdijk. 2000. The Spoken Dutch Corpus. Overview and first evaluation. In Nicoletta Calzolari et al., editor, *Proceedings of the Second international conference on Language Resources and Evaluation (LREC-2000)*, pages 887–894, Athens, Greece. European Language Resources Association (ELRA).

Martin Reynaert, Matje van de Camp, and Menno van Zaanen. 2014. OpenSoNaR: user-driven development of the SoNaR corpus interfaces. In *Proceedings of COLING 2014: System*

Demonstrations, pages 124–128, Dublin, Ireland. Dublin City University and Association for Computational Linguistics.

Peter Spyns and Jan Odijk, editors. 2013. *Essential Speech and Language Technology for Dutch. Results by the STEVIN-programme.* Theory and Applications of Natural Language Processing. Springer-Verlag, Berlin.

Helmer Strik, Walter Daelemans, Diana Binnenpoorte, Janienke Sturm, Folkert De Vriend, and Catia Cucchiarini. 2002. Dutch HLT resources: from BLARK to priority lists. In *Proceedings of ICSLP-2002*, pages 1549–1552, Denver.

Antal Van den Bosch, Gertjan Busser, Sander Canisius, and Walter Daelemans. 2007. An efficient memory-based morpho-syntactic tagger and parser for Dutch. In P. Dirix et al., editor, *Computational Linguistics in the Netherlands: Selected Papers from the Seventeenth CLIN Meeting*, pages 99–114, Leuven, Belgium.

Frank Van Eynde, Jakub Zavrel, and Walter Daelemans. 2000. Part of speech tagging and lemmatisation for the Spoken Dutch Corpus. In *Proceedings of the Second international conference on Language Resources and Evaluation (LREC-2000)*, pages 1427–1433, Athens, Greece.

Frank Van Eynde. 2005. Part of speech tagging en lemmatisering. Protocol voor annotatoren in D-Coi. Technical report, Centrum voor Computerlinguïstiek, K.U. Leuven.

Maarten van Gompel and Martin Reynaert. 2013. FoLiA: A practical XML Format for Linguistic Annotation - a descriptive and comparative study. *Computational Linguistics in the Netherlands Journal*, 3.

CHAPTER 20

Creating Research Environments with BlackLab

J. de Does[a], J. Niestadt[b] and K. Depuydt[c]

[a]INT, Leiden, Netherlands, jesse.dedoes@ivdnt.org, [b]INT, Leiden, Netherlands, jan.niestadt@ivdnt.org, [c]INT, Leiden, Netherlands, katrien.depuydt@ivdnt.org

ABSTRACT

The *BlackLab* search engine for linguistically annotated corpora is a recurring element in several CLARIN and other recent search and retrieval projects. Besides the core search library, we have developed the *BlackLab Server* REST web service which makes it easy for computational linguists and programmers to write anything from quick analysis scripts to full-fledged search interfaces, and the *AutoSearch* application which allows nontechnical linguistic researchers to index and search their own data.

This chapter describes the motivation for developing the BlackLab platform, how it has been used in actual research, and sketches future developments which will make it a more powerful tool for the creation of research environments.

20.1   Introduction: Why BlackLab and BlackLab Server?

There are several excellent linguistic corpus search engines that support the creation of corpus retrieval systems: the Sketch Engine (Kilgarriff et al., 2004) is a superb product, the Corpus Work-bench (Evert and Hardie, 2011) is widely used to create search interfaces for corpora, cf. for instance (Borin et al., 2012; Nygaard et al., 2008), and there are more recent alternatives like Corpuscle (Meurer, 2012), and Poliqarp (Janus and Przepiórkowski, 2007).

Nevertheless, there were reasons to look for alternatives. In the context of the CLARIN and CLARIAH research infrastuctures, we need a versatile platform that supports the creation of research environments that can be either generic or tailored to specific needs. Of course, the search engine at the heart of such a platform should still be powerful, scalable, efficient and feature-rich, but other requirements are just as important: the core components should be easy to maintain and

How to cite this book chapter:

de Does, J, Niestadt, J and Depuydt, K. 2017. Creating Research Environments with BlackLab. In: Odijk, J and van Hessen, A. (eds.) *CLARIN in the Low Countries*, Pp. 245–257. London: Ubiquity Press. DOI: https://doi.org/10.5334/bbi.20. License: CC-BY 4.0

extend because of clear APIs and modular design, and, because of the simplicity of both the library and the server API, it should be easy to develop custom front ends and extensions.

Our choice to develop a new corpus retrieval platform that uses Lucene as the underlying search engine has the advantage that we can profit not only from the active development of the Lucene core, but also from Lucene-based products like Solr and Elasticsearch to implement new features.

20.2   BlackLab, BlackLab Server and AutoSearch

20.2.1   The Design of BlackLab

We had the following objectives in mind while designing BlackLab:

1. Modularity and flexibility, enabling, for instance, easy implementation of new document formats (for instance, a FoLiA[1] indexer has been added in less than a day)
2. Strict separation of front end and back end
3. Scalability of the indexing core only bounded by the excellent Lucene scalability
4. Incremental indexing
5. Support for Corpus Query Language (CQL),[2] a widely-used linguistic query language
6. Development in a modern, mainstream language (Java) enabling fast and robust development of the engine itself and of retrieval applications that use the engine
7. Open source

Extending the Basic Lucene Indexing and Retrieval Model

Lucene is at the heart of BlackLab. Each indexed document becomes a Lucene document, and metadata fields such as title and author become Lucene fields. The document content is indexed in a more sophisticated way: token and character positions are stored. This enables highlighting of search results in the original content.

BlackLab extends this basic mechanism in several ways:

Multiple token attributes   Multiple properties can be stored for each word. A common use case is to store the word form, lemma and part of speech, but any other type of information is possible. Each of these properties is stored in a separate Lucene field, and BlackLab transparently combines these fields while searching.

Querying   BlackLab uses Lucene's SpanQuery classes for querying. This allows the most flexibility in matching complex patterns. The SpanQuery classes included with Lucene were not enough to support the more advanced features of Corpus Query Language, so we had to extend them. The extension of the Span query mechanism supports features like the repetition operator (e.g. for finding a sequence of two or more adjectives) and searching inside XML tags. Besides the Corpus Query Language (abbreviated as CQL or CQP), BlackLab also supports the (basic) Contextual Query Language (SRU/CQL).

Content store   Retrieving and (optionally) highlighting the original content is made possible by efficiently storing the original indexed (XML) content in the 'content store'. The data is stored using gzip compression, which saves a lot of disk space.

---

[1]   http://proycon.github.io/folia/

[2]   The Corpus Workbench site has a great introduction to CQL: http://cwb.sourceforge.net/files/CQP_Tutorial/ Note that BlackLab supports the most important features, but not yet all of the features.

Forward index For quickly displaying keyword-in-context (KWIC) views, sorting and grouping hits on context, and counting occurrences of terms in whole documents or in the vicinity of a set of hits, a specialized data structure called a forward index has been implemented. The forward index is really the complement to Lucene's reverse index: whereas Lucene answers questions of the form 'where in my documents does the word X occur?', the forward index is optimized to answer questions of the form 'what word occurs in document Y at position Z?'

20.2.2   Features of BlackLab Server

BlackLab Server was developed for two reasons: to provide a clean back end for the corpus front end, a large part of which is written in JavaScript, and to make it as easy as possible to carry out quick corpus analyses from any scripting language without compromising the speed of the Black-Lab Java code. BlackLab Server is a REST web service: it responds to URL requests in either JSON or XML format. It is implemented as a Java servlet that will run, for instance, in Apache Tomcat. It provides several different search modes, such as: search for occurrences of a word, search for documents containing a word, show a snippet of text from a document, or retrieve the full original document. In addition to sorting results, it also allows you to group results by many criteria, including the context of the hits found (e.g. the word to the left of the hit). Some important aspects of its design are:

- Smart caching of search results
- The user can decide to use blocking or nonblocking request mode
- Protection against overtaxing the server. BlackLab Server tries to prevent (intentional or unintentional) server abuse by monitoring searches and terminating ones that are taking too long or consuming too many resources.

20.2.3   AutoSearch

For researchers who are not computational linguists or programmers, but would like to be able to quickly search their annotated texts, we have developed BlackLab AutoSearch. This application allows end users to simply upload text data in a supported format (today, FoLiA or TEI). It is then indexed on our servers, after which it may be searched using Corpus Query Language.

If the user does not have FoLiA or TEI data yet, but rather text data in another format (e.g. Word, PDF, HTML or ePub), we have also developed OpenConvert[3], which allows users to convert their plain text data into FoLiA or TEI, and run it through a (simple) tagger/lemmatiser for Dutch. In the future, we would like to incorporate this functionality into AutoSearch, to streamline the process as much as possible.

20.2.4   Performance

An elaborate comparison to other corpus retrieval systems is outside the scope of this chapter. Benchmarking would be easier if standard query and datasets were available for this purpose. Nevertheless, to obtain an indication of the performance level, we tagged and lemmatized the *DUTCH PARLIAMENTARY PROCEEDINGS 1814-2012* dataset, consisting of about 700 million tokens,

---

[3]   Both AutoSearch and OpenConvert can be found in our CLARIN portal at https://portal.clarin.inl.nl/. OpenConvert is also available on GitHub: https://github.com/INL/OpenConvert. AutoSearch should soon be available under https://github.com/INL/ as well; send us a message if you are interested.

query	hits	CWB	BlackLab
[pos="AA.*"] [lemma="krokodil"]	73	13s	**48ms**
"beslissing" "om" "niet" "te" [pos="VRB.*"]	8	**60ms**	273ms
[pos="NOU.*"] "om" "te" [pos="VRB.*"]	76660	50s	**22s**
[pos="VRB.*"]{7}	1672	38s	**17s**
[pos="AA.*"]+ [pos="NOU.*"] [pos="VRB.*=fin.*" & lemma='doen'] [pos="AA.*"]+ [pos="NOU.*"]	95	**24s**	25s

Table 20.1: Query times on Parliamentary Proceedings Corpus.

available from the Dutch Data Archiving and Networked Services (DANS)[4], and indexed the data with BlackLab and with CWB[5].

The performance on some example queries is illustrated in Table 20.1. We found the systems to be roughly comparable in performance, with some queries running faster in BlackLack (command line query tool) and others in CWB (command line tool cqp).

20.3   Using BlackLab and BlackLab Server to build your own research environment

This hands-on section explains how to use BlackLab and BlackLab server to build simple applications.

20.3.1   Indexing Data with BlackLab

BlackLab can index any textual data, but we have focused on using it with XML. Several XML formats (including popular corpus formats FoLiA and TEI[6]) are supported out-of-the-box, and it is easy to create custom versions of indexers or add support for a new XML format.

XML corpus formats generally have an XML tag for each word, with tags or attributes for the different properties of the word (such as lemma and part of speech). BlackLab indexes each property in its own Lucene field, and automatically combines these fields while searching, so you can construct complex queries that specify constraints on different properties as needed.

20.3.2   Using BlackLab Directly from Java

Before introducing the web service, we start with the BlackLab Java API, so that we can compare the two. Here is some example code that uses the BlackLab API directly to search for a Corpus Query Language query:

```
// Convert word array to string
String words(List<String> words) {
    return StringUtil.join(words, " ");
}

final static File PATH_TO_MY_CORPUS = new File("/tmp/bla/");

// Search and show hits
public void search(String cqlQuery) {
```

---

4   https://easy.dans.knaw.nl/ui/datasets/id/easy-dataset:51640
5   BlackLab 1.3.1, cwb 3.0.0, 12-core Intel(R) Xeon(R) CPU E5-2630 0 @ 2.30GHz, 128G ram.
6   http://www.tei-c.org/

```
        try (Searcher searcher = Searcher.open(PATH_TO_MY_CORPUS)) {
            TextPattern tp = CorpusQueryLanguageParser.parse(cqlQuery);
            Hits hits = searcher.find(tp);
            for (Hit hit: hits) {
                Kwic kwic = hits.getKwic(hit);
                Document document = searcher.document(hit.doc);
                String title = document.get("title");
                System.out.println(words(kwic.getLeft("word")) + " ["
                        + words(kwic.getMatch("word")) + "] "
                        + words(kwic.getRight("word")) + " (" + title + ")");
            }
        } catch (Exception e) {
            throw new RuntimeException(e);
        }
}
```

As we shall see below, using BlackLab Server results in very similar code.[7]

20.3.3   BlackLab Server

As stated, BlackLab Server allows you to use BlackLab from any programming language, and we will give two examples of this here.

20.3.3.1   A Simple Example

Here is a simple Python example of searching a corpus for a CQL pattern ([pos="a.*"] "fox"), i.e. the word 'fox' preceded by an adjective and displaying a simple textual KWIC view with document titles.

```
import urllib
import json

def words(context):
    """ Convert word array to string. """
    return " ".join(context['word'])

def search(cqlQuery):
    """ Search and show hits. """
    url = "http://example.com/blacklab/mycorpus/hits?patt="
        + urllib.quote_plus(cqlQuery)
    with (urllib.open(url)) as f:
        response = json.loads(f.read())
    hits = response['hits']
    docs = response['doc-infos']
    for hit in hits:
        # Show the document title and hit information
        doc = docs[hit['doc-pid']]
        print words(hit['left']) + " [" + words(hit['match']) + "] " +
                words(hit['right']) + " (" + doc['title'] + ")"

# "Main program"
search('[pos="a.*"] "fox"')
```

We have translated this basic example into other languages as well (including JavaScript, R, PHP, Perl, C# and Ruby). These may be found online[8].

---

[7]   The complete Java BlackLab API documentation can be found at http://inl.github.io/BlackLab/apidocs/.

[8]   http://github.com/INL/BlackLab-server/wiki/Using-BlackLab-Server-from-different-languages

20.3.3.2   Slightly More Complex BlackLab Server Example

This example draws bar charts of the collocations of certain words in some author's works.

To start, here is a simple HTML page: just a search form and a div to render our chart to. It includes jQuery (for convenience), Google Charts (for drawing the chart) and our own JavaScript file, blacklab-server.js.

```html
<html>
  <head>
    <script type="text/javascript" src="jquery.js"></script>
    <script type="text/javascript" src="https://www.google.com/jsapi"></script>
    <script type="text/javascript" src="blacklab-server.js"></script>
  </head>
  <body>
    <h1>Zen and the Art of Collocations</h1>
    <form onsubmit="search(); return false;">
      Show words that occur within 5 words of <input id='word' type='text' />
      <input type='submit' value='Update' />
    </form>
    <div id="chart" style="width: 900px; height: 500px;"></div>
  </body>
</html>
```

The next example, blacklab-server.js, sends a request to the server, counts context words in the response, and draws the chart. To be precise, when the form is submitted, the search function is called, which builds a CQL query, glues it to a URL, and retrieves that URL. When the server responds, the handleResults function iterates over the hits in the response object, counting words in the left and right contexts, and renders the resulting word frequency data using Google Charts.

```javascript
google.load("visualization", "1", {packages:["corechart"]});

var whichContext = "word"; // which collocations? e.g. word/lemma/pos/..

function search() {
    var cqlQuery = '"' + jQuery("#word").val() + '"';
    var url = "http://example.com/blacklab/mycorpus/hits?filter=author:pirsig&"
            + "context=5&patt=" + encodeURIComponent(cqlQuery);
    jQuery.get(url, handleResponse);   // AJAX call to BlackLab Server
}

function handleResponse(response) {
    // Count context words for each hit
    var wordFreq = {};
    jQuery.each(response['hits'], function (index, hit) {
        countWords(hit['left'], wordFreq);   // left context
        countWords(hit['right'], wordFreq); // right context
    });

    // Draw Google Chart
    var data = new google.visualization.DataTable();
    data.addColumn('string', 'Word');
    data.addColumn('number', 'Frequency');
    jQuery.each(wordFreq, function (word, freq) {
        data.addRows([[word, freq]]);
    });
    data.sort([{column: 1, desc: true}]);
    var chart = new google.visualization.BarChart(jQuery('#chart').get(0));
    chart.draw(data);
}

function countWords(context, wordFreq) {
    jQuery.each(context[whichContext], function (index, word) {
```

```
        if (!wordFreq[word]) wordFreq[word] = 0;
        wordFreq[word]++;
    });
}
```

20.4   Using BlackLab and BlackLab Server for Linguistic Research

We summarize how BlackLab has been used for research, and analyze the requirements that can be deduced from these experiences. Finally, a use case based on the *Letters as Loot* corpus illustrates how a (small) research environment created with BlackLab server can support historical linguistic research.

20.4.1   Projects Using BlackLab

IMPACT The IMPACT[9] project was about enhancing the accessibility of historical documents in library collections. To demonstrate the potential of using linguistic resources for this purpose, INL developed a Lucene-based search engine, intended to exploit linguistic data in full text retrieval of library collections.

CLARIN search and develop An SRU endpoint implementation for BlackLab was developed to integrate the search engine in the CLARIN-NL research infrastructure.

Corpus Gysseling The Corpus Gysseling[10] contains almost all known 13th-century Dutch text. It is the principal source for the Dictionary of Early Middle Dutch.

Corpus Hedendaags Nederlands (Corpus of contemporary Dutch) The Corpus Hedendaags Nederlands (CHN) is a first step towards a monitor corpus for contemporary Dutch, intergrating corpora gathered by INL in the 1990s with more recent material. The corpus is available to the research community as part of the CLARIN-NL research infrastucture[11].

OpenSoNaR OpenSoNaR is an online system that allows for analyzing and searching the large scale Dutch reference corpus SoNaR. SoNaR is a 500-million-word reference corpus of contemporary written Dutch for use in different types of linguistic (including lexicographic) and language technology research and the development of applications. In this CLARIN-NL project, a powerful corpus exploration user interface was developed for the SONAR-500 corpus, using BlackLab server as a back end[12].

Letters as Loot The *Letters as Loot* corpus is a corpus of 1,033 Dutch letters from the 17th and 18th century. They were sent home from abroad by sailors and others, but also abroad by those staying behind who needed to keep in touch with their loved ones. Many letters did not reach their destinations: they were taken as loot by privateers and confiscated by the High Court of Admiralty during the wars fought between the Netherlands and England.

   This corpus, to which metadata from the research programme's database were added, was lemmatised, PoS-tagged and provided with elaborate search facilities by the Institute for Dutch Lexicology[13].

Early Modern English corpora at Northwestern University Phil Burns of Northwestern University has created an experimental corpus search site[14] that is powered by BlackLab. At

---

[9] http://www.impact-project.eu/, http://www.digitisation.eu

[10] http://gysseling.corpus.taalbanknederlands.inl.nl/

[11] http://corpushedendaagsnederlands.inl.nl/

[12] http://opensonar.clarin.inl.nl

[13] http://brievenalsbuit.inl.nl

[14] http://devadorner.northwestern.edu/corpussearch/

present the corpus of Shakespeare's plays, the TCP ECCO corpus (Eighteenth Century Collections Online), the TCP Evans corpus (Evans Early American Imprints), and the Shakespeare His Contemporaries corpus (Early Modern English Drama) are publicly searchable. Martin Mueller (Professor of English & Classics) has written about his experiences with the application (Mueller, 2013).

20.4.2   Research and education based on BlackLab corpora

The following research uses the BlackLab query engine:

- OpenSoNaR and CHN have been used in teaching corpus linguistics in courses at Leiden university and Utrecht university
- Marc van Oostendorp and Nicoline van der Sijs had a very interesting presentation[15] on the history of *na* vs. *naar* at the LUCL workshop *Effects of Prescriptivism in Language History, 21-22 January 2016*[16], using (among others) the *Letters as Loot* corpus
- Den Ouden (2014) looks for transitive verbs in intransitive contexts
- Kiers (2014) investigated periphrastic versus synthetic comparatives in Dutch and Polak (2015) made an analysis of the influence of phonetical context on the distributions of the suffixes -ig, -erig, -achtig, respectively, a Master's Thesis and a Bachelor's thesis relying on data obtained from the Corpus Hedendaags Nederlands.

We also mention some research that makes use of the corpora mentioned in another way, sometimes simply because the research was performed before the corpus was online. We list this type of research because of the requirements it poses:

- The *Letters as Loot* corpus has been used as the main source of information for a groundbreaking study in historical sociolinguistics (Rutten and Van der Wal, 2014). Most analyses are based on careful manual work, which remains indispensable in many cases. In many cases the analysis requires comparing frequencies of different phonological and grammatical phenomena.
- Nobel (2013) investigates diminutives in the *Letters as Loot* corpus.

20.4.2.1   Requirements emerging from these experiences

Teaching sessions   Elaborate corpus retrieval sessions with the OpenSoNaR user interface at Utrecht University in courses given by Jan Odijk yielded, among others, the following requirements:

Querying 1. Define variables, or at least equality restrictions that can for instance query for word repetitions[17]; 2. Improve part-of-speech querying, so regular expression matching is not needed to select a part-of-speech feature[18]; and 3. Enable parametrized queries from input list
Grouping and sorting 1. Grouping and filtering by arbitrary combinations of metadata, and arbitrary functions of hit text, e.g case-insensitive grouping of word forms; 2. Relative frequencies of groups with respect to subcorpus size; and 3. Custom sorting criteria.
User data and annotation 1. Persistent query history per user; 2. Metadata upload (in CMDI format); and 3. Support for categorization of results, subsequently usable for grouping, sorting, etc.

---

[15] https://prezi.com/ofiy5m-a6vbe/na-and-naar/?utm_campaign=share&utm_medium=copy
[16] http://nederl.blogspot.nl/2015/11/21-22-january-2016-effects-of.html?m=1
[17] This refers to a CQL feature not yet implemented by BlackLab.
[18] This can be solved easily by a different indexing scheme.

Export of query results 1. Tab-separated export format: separate all fields by tabs; options for simple and extended part-of-speech export; options to export metadata; and 2. Export of CMDI metadata describing the result export: including query, filters, grouping criteria, number of documents/hits/groups in results. This should be uploadable to the application to reproduce the result.

Research experiences Out of the above-mentioned research, the following requirements can be deduced:

- Many would have benefited from flexible options to export data in the user interface.
- In several cases, some elementary statistics incorporated in the user interface could have been helpful in the course of investigation, although the complete investigation requires types of analysis that cannot be foreseen in a generic interface. In (Kiers, 2014), a simple option to analyze the distribution over time (in the style of Google n-grams) would have helped the researcher; in (Polak, 2015), analyses are more complex, but direct data export to R from BlackLab Server[19] would have helped
- Relative frequencies instead of absolute counts in grouping results
- Grouping by arbitrary combination of metadata attributes, and custom criteria defined by user
- Cleaning result data, adding information to it both on a document level and on a token-by-token basis (this is in agreement with the desideratum of result categorization by users, mentioned above) would benefit many researchers. Nobel (2013), for instance, discards results from letters where spelling does not give her enough information to deduce the phonological realisation of the diminutive suffix in a reliable way
- Comparison of number of results from two (or more) queries, distributed over metadata properties, would also have benefited Van Oostendorp and Van der Sijs
- An option to involve lexical data often seems called for, enabling options like 'give me intransitive occurrences of verbs that normally require a direct object'. This corresponds roughly to the parametrized queries mentioned before.

In most of these cases, we can argue that the use of BlackLab Server could make it very easy to implement the requested features. For some features, extensions to BlackLab server are necessary, but mostly of a rather simple nature, e.g. an option to return all relevant subcorpus sizes corresponding to metadata grouping criteria.

20.4.3   Use case: signs and sounds in the Letters as Loot corpus

For this case study, we have developed a small research environment to start exploring how we can support the kind of research that has been conducted in (Rutten and Van der Wal, 2014), most of it before the corpus appeared online. To this end, we compare some results from chapter 2 ('Sounds and signs - From local to supralocal usage') of (Rutten and Van der Wal, 2014) to results obtained from querying the corpus and analyzing the query results.

It is obvious that automatic retrieval from corpora cannot replace careful manual analysis in many cases. For instance, the analysis of the orthographical representation of etymologically distinct long *e*'s[20] requires information which is simply not present in the annotated corpus.

---

[19] `https://github.com/INL/BlackLab-server/wiki/Using-BlackLab-Server-from-different-languages#r`

[20] Cf. section 2.4.5 in (Rutten and Van der Wal, 2014): 'Many Dutch dialects, the southern ones in particular, maintain the phonological difference between lengthened *ē* out of originally short vowels in open syllables, and *ê* out of the West Germanic diphtong **ai*'.

20.4.3.1   H-Dropping in the 17th Century: First Case Study

Many dialects from the south and the south-west of the Dutch language area are characterised by the absence of the phoneme *h*, as in, *and* instead of *hand*. In the texts, this may result in deletion or prothesis of *h*.

As we have seen, contrasting two result sets is a desideratum emerging from corpus research. As a test case, we have used the BlackLab Server API and Google Charts (in a similar vein to the simple concordance example (section 20.3.3.1) to implement this functionality in a simple way (cf. Figure 20.1). Our environment will consist of a search and grouping form, a bar chart, and a simple concordance view.

In the example, we contrast the number of hits of the corpus query

```
[lemma != "h.*"] [lemma="h.*" & word = "[aeo].*"]
```

(indicating *h*-dropping[21]) to the query specifying orthographic expression of *h*:

```
[lemma != "h.*"] [lemma="h.*" & word = "h.*"]
```

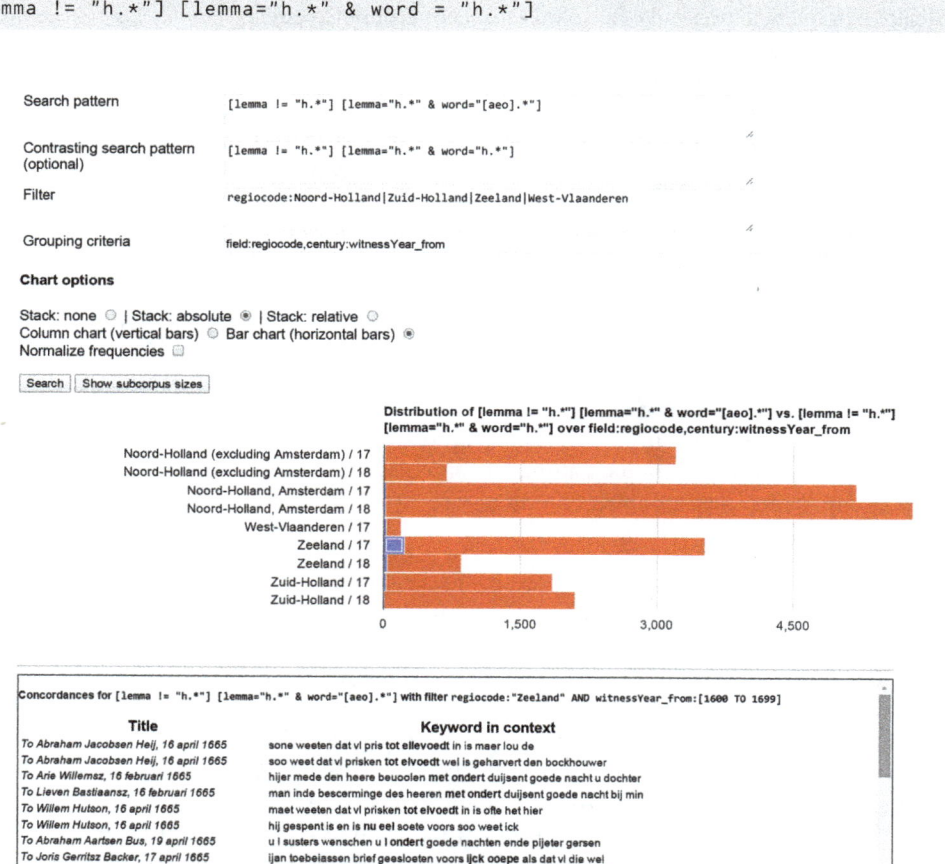

Figure 20.1: H-dropping 1: absolute frequencies.

---

[21] The restriction on the previous word is there to avoid situations like 'hier om', where both word parts have the lemma 'hierom'.

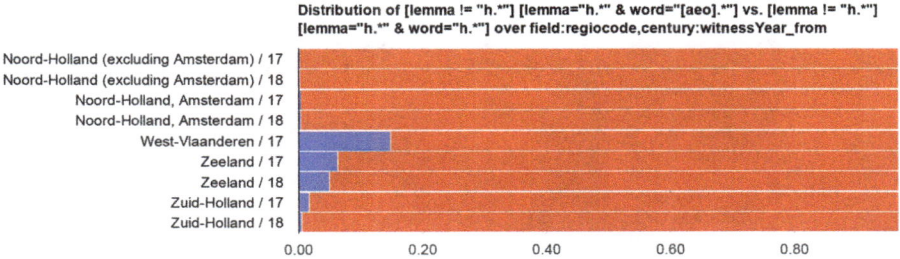

Figure 20.2: H-dropping 2: relative frequencies.

The result (cf. also Figure 20.2) indicates clearly that *h*-dropping is a southern (Zeeland and Western Flanders) phenomenon, and is more predominant in the 17th than in the 18th century. Comparing to the manual results (133 cases of *h*-dropping in the 17th-century Zeeland corpus), we should note that counts are not identical because we are using a larger corpus and the selection criteria are different, but the observed tendency is in agreement with the Rutten-Van der Wal results.

Summarizing, we are able to reproduce this type of analysis comparatively easily. The fact that our query results are, with respect to the phenomenon we are looking for, neither complete nor quite clean, does not impair their usefulness as a quick way to analyze a tendency. For more thorough analysis, one would need the result categorization feature discussed above.

20.4.3.2   Loss of Final -e

One of the most salient changes in the history of Dutch is apocope of final schwa, a linguistic phenomenon that also occurred in English and to a lesser extent in German. By the 17th century, many dialects and particularly Holland dialects had a high proportion of schwa-less forms.

The change shows prominently in first person singular forms of verbs. In nouns, forms with final -*e* are hard to distinguish from plurals with loss of final *n*.

Hence:

```
[lemma="ik" & word=".*[ck].*"]
[pos="VRB" & word=".*e" & word != ".*[td]e"
            & lemma != "doen|gaan|staan|slaan|zien|zijn"]
[pos != "VRB"]
```

is a way to find word forms with final *e*, and

```
[lemma="ik" & word=".*[ck].*"]
[pos="VRB" & word!=".*e"
            & lemma != "doen|gaan|staan|slaan|zien|zijn"]
[pos != "VRB"]
```

finds their *e*-less counterparts, cf. Figure 20.3.

20.5   Conclusions and Future Plans

We are still improving BlackLab and its related projects: scaling BlackLab up to ever larger corpora, making sure even complex searches remain fast, and adding useful features. We are interested in looking at distributed search and multi-corpus search, both for speeding things up and keeping larger datasets manageable. We are considering to integrate BlackLab with Solr or Elasticsearch to enable this functionality. Another feature on our wishlist is the ability to search tree- and graph-like

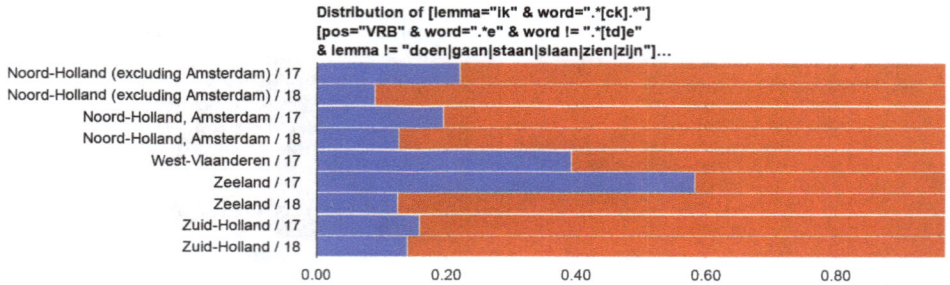

Figure 20.3: Dropping of final *e* in first person singular.

structures (e.g. treebanks). We will look at both of these desirable features as part of CLARIAH. Other CLARIAH objectives that fit in very well with the requirements that emerge from the research discussed in this chapter are so-called 'Chaining Search' (serial combination of searches in heterogeneous datasets, e.g. a corpus and a lexicon) and adding comprehensive support for dealing with subcorpora, included those defined by document metadata uploaded by researchers.

In the near future, we would like to create a library for talking to BlackLab Server from one or more popular programming languages, which could abstract away the last few technical details, making things even easier. Support for statistical explorations and visualizations should be enhanced, cf. for instance (Speelman, 2014). As has been discussed before, the aim is not to develop a monolithic application that satisfies all requirements, but rather the development of a platform that supports quick development of the analysis scripts and user interface elements that are necessary for a research use case.

References

Borin, L., Forsberg, M. and Roxendal, J. (2012). Korp – the corpus infrastructure of språkbanken, *Proceedings of LREC 2012. Istanbul: ELRA*, pp. 474–478.

Den Ouden, M. (2014). *Theta rollen en argument drop*, B.S. Thesis, Universiteit van Amsterdam, the Netherlands.

Evert, S. and Hardie, A. (2011). Twenty-first century corpus workbench: Updating a query architecture for the new millennium, *Proceedings of the Corpus Linguistics 2011 Conference*, Birmingham, UK.

Janus, D. and Przepiórkowski, A. (2007). Poliqarp: an open source corpus indexer and search engine with syntactic extensions, *Proceedings of the 45th Annual Meeting of the ACL*, Strouds-burg, PA, USA, pp. 85–88.

Kiers, F. (2014). *Frequenter of meer frequent - Een corpusonderzoek naar de invloed van het Engels op de trappen van vergelijking in het Nederlands*, Master's thesis, Universiteit Utrecht, the Netherlands.

Kilgarriff, A., Rychly, P., Smrz, P. and Tugwell, D. (2004). The sketch engine, *Proc EURALEX 2004*, Lorient, France, pp. 105–116.

Meurer, P. (2012). Corpuscle - a new corpus management platform for annotated corpora, *in* G. Andersen (ed.), *Exploring Newspaper Language: Using the web to create and investigate a large corpus of modern Norwegian*, Benjamins.

Mueller, M. (2013). Blacklab: searching a tcp corpus by linguistic and structural criteria.
URL: *https://scalablereading.northwestern.edu/?p=296*

Nobel, J. (2013). Small but tough – Diminutive suffixes in seventeenth-century Dutch private letters, *Taal en tongval* **65**.

Nygaard, L., Priestley, J., Nøklestad, A. and Johannessen, J. B. (2008).   Glossa: a multilingual, multimodal, configurable user interface., *LREC*, European Language Resources Association.

Polak, W. (2015). *In welke fonologische context komt afleiding met de achtervoegsels -ig, -erig en -achtig voor?*, B.S. Thesis, Universiteit van Amsterdam, the Netherlands.

Rutten, G. and Van der Wal, M. (2014). *Letters as Loot. A sociolinguistic approach to seventeenth- and eighteenth-century Dutch*, John Benjamins, Amsterdam & Philadelphia.
  URL: *http://www.jbe-platform.com/content/books/9789027269577*

Speelman, D. (2014). Logistic regression: A confirmatory technique for comparisons in corpus linguistics, *Corpus Methods for Semantics: Quantitative studies in polysemy and synonymy* , Vol. 43 of *Human Cognitive Processing*, John Benjamins, pp. 487–533.

CHAPTER 21

Beyond Counting Syntactic Hits

Erwin R. Komen

Radboud University Nijmegen, SIL-International, E.Komen@ru.nl

ABSTRACT

Linguists who would like to make use of the increasing number of syntactically annotated text corpora in their research can use existing tools to find and count instances of the syntactic constructions they are interested in. Software supporting linguists in their work should also make it possible to build databases of search results where each hit is accompanied by a number of calculated (or manually addable) features. The stand-alone CorpusStudio program is able to provide this help, since it allows queries and feature calculations to be defined in the XQuery language. The web application of CorpusStudio, which is still under development, aims to have comparable functionality but with an easier accessibility. The main aim of this chapter is to demonstrate why software should go beyond counting syntactic hits.

Keywords: syntax, corpus research, XQuery

21.1   Introduction

A linguist who is interested in studying a particular syntactic construction in a language can do so by manually or programmatically looking through a number of texts in that language. It is the availability of syntactically annotated texts that makes this latter programmatic approach possible.

There are quite a number of programs and even web applications linguists can use to find instances of the syntactic construction they are interested in.[1] Studies conducted by linguists, however, involve more than locating constructions that satisfy particular conditions. Two other important aspects of a study are: (a) keeping a number of related searches together in a search

---

[1] Some of these programs are mentioned later on in this article.

How to cite this book chapter:
Komen, E. R. 2017. Beyond Counting Syntactic Hits. In: Odijk, J and van Hessen, A. (eds.) *CLARIN in the Low Countries*, Pp. 259–268. London: Ubiquity Press. DOI: https://doi.org/10.5334/bbi.21. License: CC-BY 4.0

'project' that can be stored and retrieved to improve replicability, and (b) annotating search results automatically or semi-automatically with information that can be gleaned from the search hits. While the latter activity is an integral part of corpus linguists' everyday research, little support in terms of software is available.

This chapter discusses and exemplifies the kind of facilities beyond those for counting syntactic hits that linguists would greatly appreciate in syntactic corpus research programs. The observations discussed are based on experience with the CorpusStudio and Cesax programs, which have so far been used in historical linguistics, second language acquisition and information structure research for Indo-European (Dutch, English, Welsh) as well as Caucasian (Chechen, Lak, Lezgi) languages (Komen 2014; Komen et al. 2014; Los and Dreschler 2012; van Vuuren 2013). The CorpusStudio application allows researchers to formulate and execute syntactic searches, store them in a 'Corpus Research Project', and annotate the search results with features that are determined programmatically.

21.2   The Linguist

I would like to underscore the idea that linguists want to do more than finding syntactic constructions by considering what kinds of questions linguists ask when studying the syntax of a particular language. Linguistics is a broad research area, but I would like to focus on the research on syntax and information structure where annotated corpora are used. The important questions that researchers in this area ask are summarised in (1):

(1) a. Under what circumstances does construction 'x' occur, and, coupled with this question, what are the distinguishing properties of this construction?[2]

    b. How does the occurrence of construction 'x' depend on genre, dialect or author, and how did the construction develop over time?

Finding instances of construction 'x' and counting them in a particular corpus is a good first step towards answering these questions, but more should and could be done. Let me illustrate this with a real-life research question. Consider the examples from the 'standard' conditional construction in Dutch in (2a) and the alternative conditional inversion in (2b).

(2) a. Nou **als** je   niet kijkt op een paar miljoen
        well if   you not look on a   few million
        dan kun je   dus   stellen dat de eerste drie kernactiviteiten
        then could you therefore posit   that the first   three nuclear.activities
        nagenoeg evenveel budget ter beschikking hebben.
        almost   equal   budget to disposal   have
        'If a few million aren't too important, then one could say that the first three activities have
        more or less the same budget.'   **[fn000056:0047]**
    b. **Heeft** u   de partners gevonden **dan** begint het eigenlijk pas
        have   you the partners found   then starts it   actually only
        want   dan moet er   een projectvoorstel geschreven worden.
        because then must there a   project.proposal written   become

---

2   I use the term 'construction' here to denote a constellation of syntactic units. Any construction in this sense can be defined by making use of hierarchy and linear order of units that are identified by syntactic labels, possibly together with limitations on the content of these units.

'It is only when the partners have been found, that the matter actually starts. That's when the project proposal needs to be written.'   **[fn000056:0147]**

Suppose that linguists want to investigate the occurrence of the conditional inversion as opposed to the standard if-then conditional: they would at least want to know the numbers, so that they can figure out whether one of the two constructions is more or less exceptional. The numbers can be found by searching through syntactically annotated texts. Tools that facilitate syntactic searches are, for instance, the web applications PaQu[3] (Parse and Query; see chapter 23) and GrETEL[4] (see chapter 22) as well as the Windows version of CorpusStudio.[5] All three search engines handle the corpus of Dutch texts in which the examples above occur: the Corpus of spoken Dutch (Oostdijk et al., 2002).[6]

It should be obvious from the examples in (2) that the two conditional syntactic constructions differ.[7] If linguists want to find all relevant results, they would probably need to write two different queries. Even if the researchers' focus is not on the 'standard' conditional, they would want to have the number of their occurrences for the sake of comparison. The two different queries do, however, belong to the same 'research project', which is why it would be of great help for linguist-users of the search software to have these queries stored together – and they could do with some metadata too, identifying what the goal of the queries is, for instance. One possibility to reach this goal would be to keep searches and documentation in different files, but store them in a single project directory. This is a good approach, but keeping all relevant information together in one structured file (e.g. in XML format) makes it even more transparent, prevents potential errors and promotes clarity.

In line with the general research question in (1), linguists would like to know under which circumstances the conditional inversion occurs. They want to know whether its occurrence depends on linguistic factors, as in (1a), extra-linguistic factors, as in (1b), or a combination of the two. Table 21.1 identifies a number of linguistic and extra-linguistic features that linguists would probably want to have for each hit.

How do linguists investigating the conditional inversion enrich their list of hits with the information they need? They could look through all the hits identified by a syntactic search program, and then find all the relevant information for each of the hits manually, by checking the texts. But such an approach is error-prone, and, if there are no other reasons to check the texts manually, should be avoided. As for a programmatic approach, a few authors have suggested that XQuery could be used to extract the information that is required (Bouma, 2008; Bouma and Kloosterman, 2007; Yao and Bouma, 2010). The XQuery language is well suited to this task, since it allows the user to work with variables and functions (Boag et al., 2010). The language would, however, form an obstacle for linguists who are less familiar with computer languages. Applications that support XQuery, then, should consider supporting easier query definition methods for some, while allowing the use of XQuery's fuller capabilities for others.

Suppose, now, that the features mentioned in Table 21.1 have been determined for each of the hits. This gives the linguists basic data to do their research. They would be much helped if it were possible to divide the results into groups, the categories of which depend on the features that are

---

[3] http://portal.clarin.nl/node/4182

[4] http://nederbooms.ccl.kuleuven.be/eng/

[5] http://erwinkomen.ruhosting.nl/software/CorpusStudio

[6] Other systems that facilitate syntactic search queries are outside the scope of this chapter. Among them is the CLARIN-developed PML Tree Query web application, which aims for dependency treebanks and makes use of the PML query language (Mírovský et al., 2010)

[7] No numerical results of the searches discussed here are given, since the focus of this chapter is not on this particular syntactic phenomenon, but on the question of how best to help a linguist wanting to research this and similar phenomena.

Type	Feature	Value
Linguistic	TenseType	Is this a periphrastic ('*heeft ... gevonden*') or a simple tense?
	FirstSize	The size of the first part of the condition (the protasis).
	Pre	The kind of element (if any) preceding the conditional (e.g. the *nou* 'well' in (2a)).
	ParaPosition	The position within the paragraph (start, middle, end).
	FirstStatus	The information status of the first part of the condition: does it link back to the preceding context or is it new?
Extra-linguistic	AuthorName	Who is the author (perhaps the use of the conditional inversion is linked to a limited number of authors?)?
	AuthorAge	Would the conditional inversion be an innovation (young authors) or a remnant from the past (old authors)?
	AuthorDialect	Is the conditional inversion linked to particular dialects?
	TextType	Is it linked to a particular type of text?
	TextDate	The publication date of the text.

Table 21.1: Features that could be relevant for choosing a conditional inversion.

calculated. That would give them a fast way to check the hypotheses that underlie the determination of the features in the first place.

It would also be nice if they could divide their search into two parts. In a first step, they could first look for instances of the conditional inversion and the standard conditional, enrich them with the features listed in Table 21.1, and store them in some kind of database. They could manually check and adapt features such as 'ParaPosition' and 'FirstStatus', since these may not be determinable automatically with enough accuracy. They would need to have access to the hits in their context at this point.

The next step would be to formulate and test hypotheses that determine the choice between a standard conditional and a conditional inversion. This step would require to take the data in the result database from the previous step as input. It would be quite natural to implement this step by using the same machinery as in the previous step.

Once all of this has been done, the linguists have quite likely reached a point where they want to make use of programs such as R or SPSS to test statistical models of their hypotheses. The corpus research software should allow the data to be exported in such a way that it can be used by statistics programs.

The facilities that corpus research software should provide to help linguists address the kind of research questions in (1) are summed up in (3).

(3) a. Find and count instances of syntactic constructions.

   b. Provide figures that allow for the calculation of relative frequencies: the number of words, clauses, and texts that have been searched.[8]

   c. Store the search results separately, so that features can be added to them.

   d. Calculate required features automatically as much as possible.

---

[8]   Calculation of relative frequencies is left to the linguist, since the point of reference by which absolute frequencies should be divided may be taken differently depending on the purpose.

e. Allow for researchers to adjust or add features manually.

f. Allow results to be divided into categories that are data-dependent.

g. Allow results to be divided into groups that are metadata-dependent.

h. Allow using a collection of (annotated) results as input for one or more other queries.

i. Have the queries and the feature calculations that belong to one research project together in one place, allowing interchange and replicability.

j. Allow users to enrich texts with features.

k. Allow exporting the data for use in statistics programs and for publications.

Facility (3a) looks for and finds instances of the construction, and (3b) adds information to allow for a good quantitative study. The facilities in (3c–e) allow researchers to equip each 'hit' with as many features as are needed to help answer the research question. Facilities (3f–g) help provide more insight into how the results are divided in terms of aspects of the data itself or the metadata. Facility (3i) promotes the exchange of research projects and contributes to replicability. Facility (3c) allows for the process in (3a–h) to be divided into two parts: one where a database with hit-feature combinations is created, and one where the results in this database are divided into adjustable groups. Facility (3k) provides the connection with a possible next step: a statistical analysis.

21.3   Current Software

Software that addresses points (3a,g) partly or completely has been made or continues to be made. The programs produced or enhanced for CLARIN-NL and CLARIN Flanders are no exception. A consortium of organisations and universities developed the Corpus Hedendaags Nederlands tool and later the OpenSONAR tool (Oostdijk et al., 2002; Reynaert et al., 2014).[9] The Nederlab web application provides access to a huge (and growing) amount of Dutch texts (Brugman et al., 2016).[10] All interfaces address (3a,g), some address (3f) partly, but none of these currently feature syntactic searches.

21.3.1   Web-based CLARIN Tools for Syntactic Research

Two tools that have been supported by CLARIN that do allow for some kind of syntactic search are PaQu and GrETEL. PaQu has been developed by the University of Groningen.[11] It not only incorporates online access to the Alpino parser of Dutch, but also provides search interfaces that allow the user to define queries in XPath. Satisfying facility (3a), search results can be downloaded and are accompanied by some metadata.

The GrETEL tool allows searches in a number of different Dutch corpora as well as in Afrikaans corpora.[12] Its user interface vastly differs from that of PaQu: searches are formed on the basis of a real-life example provided by the linguist. This means that researchers do not need to have in-depth knowledge of what goes on inside the search engine. Augustinus et al. (2012) explain that their search engine uses XPath for the actual searches. The XPath code produced by GrETEL can, in fact, be used without changes in the PaQu web interface. The GrETEL application addresses point (3a), it allows the downloading of all the hits, and it has an option that provides a table with the counts divided per treebank; this table partly addresses facilities (3b,g).

---

[9]   opensonar.clarin.inl.nl and opensonar-cgn.science.ru.nl

[10]   http://www.nederlab.nl

[11]   http://www.let.rug.nl/alfa/paqu

[12]   http://nederbooms.ccl.kuleuven.be/eng/gretel

21.3.2   Windows-based CorpusStudio and Cesax

Two Windows-based programs combine into a set of tools that address most of the ambitious goals defined in (3): CorpusStudio and Cesax (Komen et al., 2013). Figure 21.1 shows how the programs cooperate.

The CorpusStudio program works with Corpus Research Projects (CRPs), XML definitions of queries, and metadata that together describe a research project. It allows the defining of searches in XQuery, which means that users can define variables and functions and use these in their queries. CorpusStudio works on XML text corpora that are located on the user's computer, addressing (3a) fully. The search results it provides contain the total number of words and sentences of the texts being searched, allowing for (3b), the calculation of relative frequencies. Dividing the results in a data-dependent way – (3f) – is possible through a CorpusStudio-specific built-in XQuery function. Division of the results on the basis of metadata is only possible to a limited extent, so point (3g) is addressed only partly. The results can be turned into a separate XML database, and each 'hit' can be accompanied by user-definable features, addressing (3c). The extensive capabilities of the XQuery language, and the fact that it allows for user-defined functions in particular, facilitate calculation of such hit-dependent features in a comprehensive but relatively user-friendly way, as per (3d). The Cesax program allows for working with the kinds of result databases produced by CorpusStudio, so that the features can be adapted manually as per (3e). Points (3h) and (3j) are also taken care of by CorpusStudio and Cesax respectively. And where GrETEL offers an example-based definition of queries, Cesax and CorpusStudio contain a 'query wizard' that allows users to base a query on key elements of an example sentence in the corpus. Keeping queries, feature calculations, and metadata together in one research project, as indicated by (3i), is addressed fully by CorpusStudio (this was actually one of the main reasons to write the program in the first place).

The stand-alone version of CorpusStudio does, unfortunately, come with a number of shortcomings. It is platform-dependent, since it only works on Windows. Its speed depends very much on the characteristics of the computer on which it is running, but it is not very fast. And while CorpusStudio could be adapted to work with XML texts in the FoLiA format, this is not facilitated

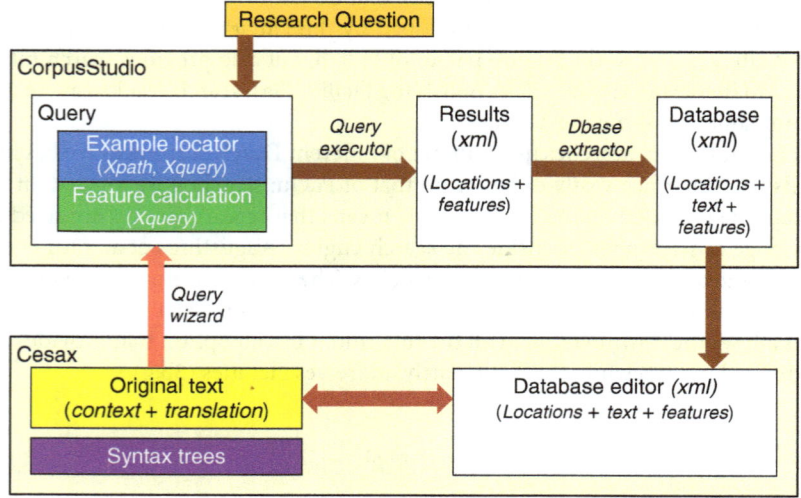

Figure 21.1: Cooperation between CorpusStudio and Cesax.

directly.[13] A disadvantage related to its nature as a stand-alone program is the fact that a copy of the corpus to be researched needs to be held on each user's own machine.[14] Where text corpora are being adapted, one may quickly lose track of where the most up-to-date version is located. Most of these disadvantages are alleviated in the web-version of CorpusStudio.

21.4   The Web Application

The stand-alone CorpusStudio Windows program has partly been re-written as a web application.[15] The key components of the web application are shown in Figure 21.2.[16]

The core of the application is the 'Query Executor', a Java application that accepts a Corpus Research Project and executes the XQuery code from that project on a corpus of XML texts (in the FoLiA or the TEI-Psdx format).[17] The CrpxProcessor divides the query execution workload over the available processors; the more processors, the faster the query execution. The CrpxProcessor can be run as a stand-alone application, but it is used as part of a web service within the CorpusStudio web application: the /crpp search service.

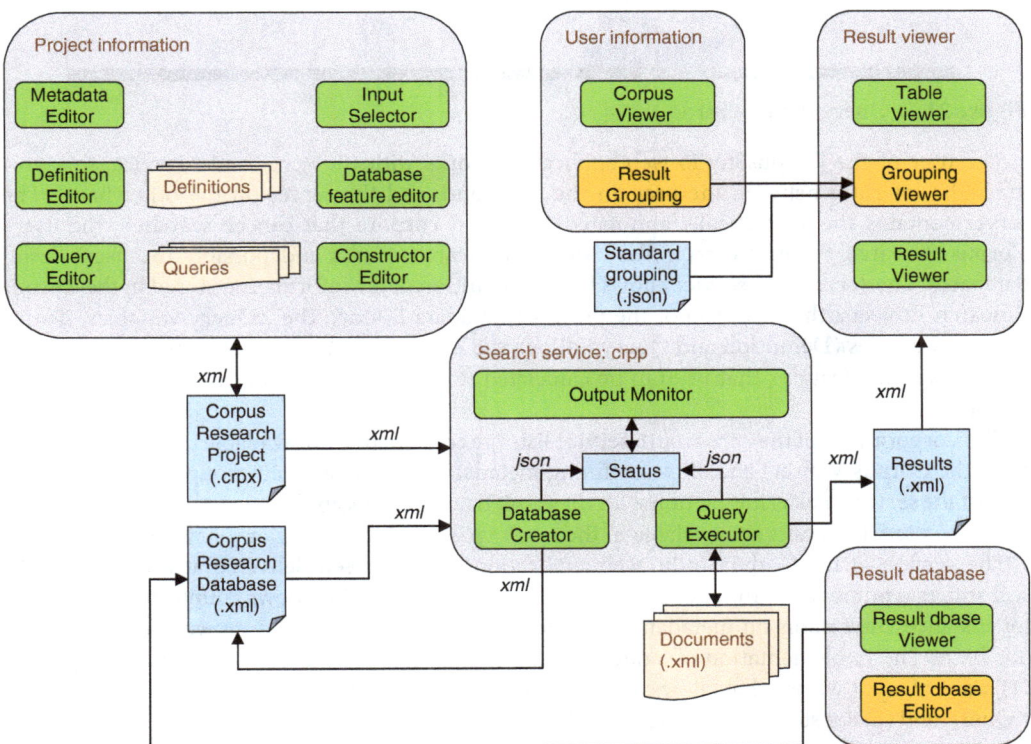

Figure 21.2: Principal components of the CorpusStudio web application.

---

¹³ Texts in the FoLiA format can be converted to the TEI-Psdx format in Cesax and then processed.

¹⁴ This is a particular shortcoming of CorpusStudio, not of stand-alone programmes as such. A reviewer pointed out that the Dact programme, for instance, is a stand-alone cross-platform application that supports working on remote corpora with remote parsing servers (van Noord et al., 2013). See http://rug-compling.github.io/dact/

¹⁵ http://www.clarin.nl/node/2095

¹⁶ The source code of the application is available at https://github.com/ErwinKomen.

¹⁷ A number of other formats can be converted into FoLiA or Psdx through the Cesax programme.

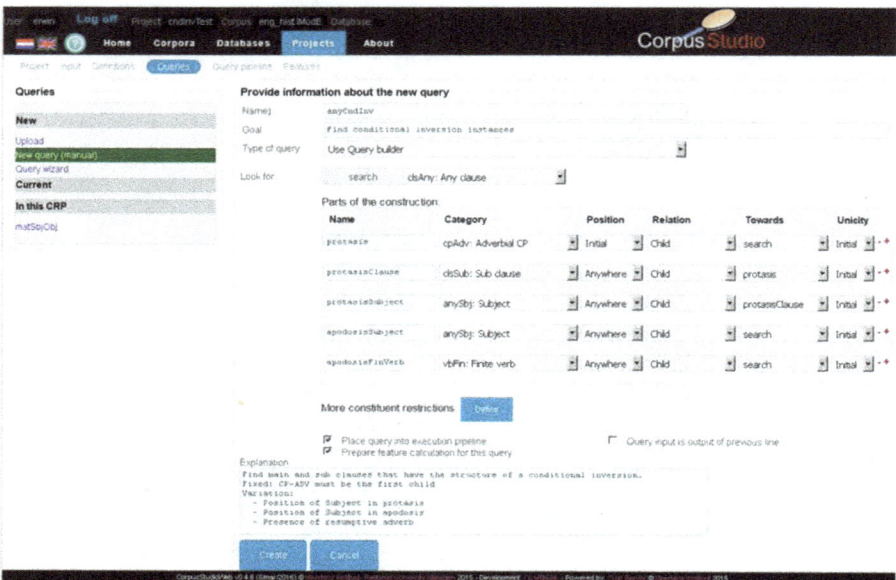

Figure 21.3: Query input wizard.

The user of the CorpusStudio web application works with the /crpstudio service; this provides the interface between the user on the one hand, and the server on the other hand. The server contains the syntactically annotated XML text corpora that can be searched, the user's Corpus Research Projects (.crpx files), the user's search results and possibly the user's result databases. The /crpstudio service allows for the definition of the information stored in the Corpus Research Projects: the metadata of the project (Metadata Editor); the XQuery variables, definitions and queries (Definition and Query Editor); the hierarchy between the queries (Constructor Editor); and the features that need to be calculated if the output is a database (Database feature editor).

The 'corpora' part of the /crpstudio service lists the corpora that are available in the web application (the Corpus Viewer) and allows defining metadata-dependent result groupings. The 'dbases' part of the service makes interaction with the result databases possible. Once a research project has been executed, its results are available in the result viewer, which also allows downloading them.

The version of the CorpusStudio web application that has been delivered at the end of 2015 still suffers a number of limitations compared to its stand-alone Windows counterpart; there are, for instance, limitations on metadata-dependent grouping of results and on working with result databases The implementation of a query wizard has started in 2016 and consists of two phases: (1) a query input wizard that allows easy input of queries, which are subsequently translated into XQuery, and (2) a system level that forms a shell around XQuery, allowing users to define and adapt queries without the need for them to know any XQuery (queries are translated into XQuery only just before execution).

The query input wizard is currently being implemented, and Figure 21.3 gives an idea of its intermediate state. The main idea is that the user can: (1) name and identify constituents and their relations towards one another, (2) stipulate additional relations between the named constituents, and (3) formulate feature definitions on top of the standard ones (the latter of which are the labels of each of the identified constituents, and the text of these constituents). More information on the current status of the program, including the second phase (of easy access to XQuery), will be made available online.[18]

---

[18] See the 'About' section of the web application: http://www.clarin.nl/node/2095.

Most importantly, the program has extended the CLARIN infrastructure with a syntactic research tool that allows interested linguists to make use of points (3a–i) in their research[19]

21.5   Discussion and Conclusions

Current tools available to linguists who are interested in doing syntactic research on annotated corpora allow finding and counting syntactic constructions. This chapter takes the conditional inversion as an example, and shows that more software help can be given to address the kinds of questions a linguist asks. This chapter argues that a researcher would want to annotate all the instances of constructions like the standard conditionals and the conditional inversion with features, taking the research beyond counting syntactic hits.

Users of the stand-alone CorpusStudio have already shown that the availability of this kind of sofware influences the research process itself: instead of focusing on finding one particular syntactic construction, the creation of feature databases that can again serve as the input to the search process leads to initially broader searches that make use of quite specific feature calculation functions.

Software that facilitates the intended process could make use of the query language XQuery, since it not only allows searching through syntactically annotated corpora, but also allows calculating the values of the features a linguist may be interested in. The existing CorpusStudio stand-alone Windows program makes use of this query language but has the drawbacks of most stand-alone applications. It is platform-dependent and does not easily help other linguists to work with the same corpus. This chapter mentions the first version of the CorpusStudio web application, a web-based version of the Windows program. While it does not yet offer all the facilities a researcher would like to make use of, it brings the kind of corpus-based syntactic research advocated in this chapter a step closer to users of the CLARIN infrastructure.

Acknowledgements

I am grateful to CLARIN-NL, who shared my vision and financed the development of the web application. My Radboud colleagues Meta Links and Sanne van Vuuren have provided useful comments on CorpusStudio and shared their ideas about the web application with me. I owe a lot of thanks for fruitful discussions on technical aspects to my Meertens Institute colleagues Matthijs Brouwer, Erik Tjong Kim San, Hennie Brugman, and Jan Pieter Kunst.

References

Augustinus, Liesbeth, Vandeghinste, Vincent & van Eynde, Frank. 2012. 'Example-based tree-bank querying'. Paper presented at *Eighth international conference of language resources and evaluation (LREC2012)*, Istanbul, Turkey.

Boag, Scott, Chamberlin, Don, Fernández, Mary F., Florescu, Daniela, Robie, Jonathan & Siméon, Jérôme. 2010. *XQuery 1.0: An XML Query Language (Second Edition)*: W3C Recommendation, <http://www.w3.org/XML/Query/#specs>.

---

[19] I leave a detailed discussion of the CorpusStudio web application to another platform, since the main goal of this chapter is to show that syntactic research would be served by software that goes beyond counting hits. Much of the information one would be interested in is available in the CorpusStudio manual. The application is not a typical database application: it searches through physical texts. The search speed of the web application is proportional to the number of processor cores the server it runs on makes available, since the search of each text takes place in a separate thread. Eight cores give a speed improvement of 7.8 compared to one core. The speed of the benchmark project ('V2_test_versie11') running on the Old English YCOE corpus (1.5 million words) is 18 min, 49 sec on the Windows stand-alone application (2 GHz processor), while it takes 22.64 sec on the web application that makes use of 20 cores.

Bouma, Gosse. 2008. XML information extraction with Xquery: processing wikipedia and Alpino trees. Groningen: Information science, university of Groningen.

Bouma, Gosse & Kloosterman, Geert. 2007. Mining syntactically annotated corpora with XQuery. In *Proceedings of the Linguistic Annotation Workshop*. Prague, Czech Republic: Association for Computational Linguistics.

Brugman, Hennie, Reynaert, Martin, Sijs, Nicoline van der, Stipriaan, René van, Tjong Kim Sang, Erik, Bosch, Antal van den, Kunst, Jan Pieter, Zeeman, Rob, Kooij, Dieuwertje, Brussee, Ineke, Brouwer, Matthijs, Kemps-Snijders, Marc & Bennis, Hans. to appear. Nederlab: towards a single portal and research environment for diachronic Dutch text corpora. In *Language resources and evaluation conference (LREC 2016)*. Portorož (Slovenia).

Komen, Erwin R. 2013. Corpus databases with feature pre-calculation. In *Proceedings of the twelfth workshop on treebanks and linguistic theories (TLT12)*. Sandra Kübler, Petya Osenova & Martin Volk (eds), 85–96. Sofia, Bulgaria: The institute of information and communication technologies, Bulgarian academy of sciences, <http://www.bultreebank.org/TLT12/TLT12Proceedings.pdf>.

Komen, Erwin R. 2014. Chechen extraposition as an information ordering strategy. In *Information structure and reference tracking in complex sentences*. Rik van Gijn, Dejan Matić, Jeremy Hammond, Saskia van Putten & Ana Vilacy Galucio (eds), 99–126. Amsterdam: John Benjamins.

Komen, Erwin R., Hebing, Rosanne G. A., van Kemenade, Ans & Los, Bettelou. 2014. Quantifying information structure changes in English. In *Information Structure and Syntactic Change in Germanic and Romance Languages*. Kristine Gunn Eide & Kristin Bech (eds), 81–110. Amsterdam, New York: John Benjamins.

Los, Bettelou & Dreschler, Gea. 2012. The loss of local anchoring: From adverbial local anchors to permissive subjects. In *Rethinking Approaches to the History of English*. Terttu Nevalainen & Elizabeth Closs Traugott (eds), 859–872. New York: Oxford University Press.

Mírovský, Jiří, Mladová, Lucie & Žabokrtský, Zdeněk. 2010. 'Annotation tool for discourse in PDT'. Paper presented at *Proceedings of the 23rd International Conference on Computational Linguistics: Demonstrations*.

Oostdijk, Nelleke, Goedertier, W. , Eynde, F. van, Boves, Lou , Martens, J.-P. , Moortgat, M. & Baayen, Harald. 2002. 'Experiences from the Spoken Dutch Corpus Project'. Paper presented at *Proceedings of the 3rd international conference on language resources and evaluation (lrec2002)*, Las Palmas.

Reynaert, Martin, Camp, Matje van de & Zaanen, Menno van. 2014. 'OpenSoNaR: user-driven development of the SoNaR corpus interfaces'. Paper presented at *Proceedings of the 25th International Conference on Computational Linguistics (Coling 2014)*, Dublin, Ireland.

van Noord, Gertjan, Bouma, Gosse, Van Eynde, Frank, de Kok, Daniël, van der Linde, Jelmer, Schuurman, Ineke, Tjong Kim Sang, Erik & Vandeghinste, Vincent. 2013. Large Scale Syntactic Annotation of Written Dutch: Lassy. In *Essential Speech and Language Technology for Dutch*. P. Spyns & J. Odijk (eds), 147–164.

van Vuuren, Sanne. 2013. Information structural transfer in advanced Dutch EFL writing: a crosslinguistic longitudinal study. In *Linguistics in the Netherlands 2011 [AVT30]*. Suzanne Aalberse & Anita Auer (eds), 173–187. Amsterdam: John Benjamins.

Yao, Xuchen & Bouma, Gosse. 2010. 'Mining Discourse Treebanks with XQuery'. Paper presented at *Ninth international workshop on treebanks and linguistic theories (TLT9)*, Tartu, Estonia.

CHAPTER 22

GrETEL
A Tool for Example-Based Treebank Mining

Liesbeth Augustinus, Vincent Vandeghinste, Ineke Schuurman and
Frank Van Eynde

Centre for Computational Linguistics, KU Leuven

ABSTRACT

This chapter describes the use of GrETEL for linguistic research. GrETEL is a linguistic
search tool that enables users to look up constructions in syntactically annotated corpora
or *treebanks*. It provides online access to the data, allowing users to query a treebank using
either an example sentence or an XPath expression in order to look for similar constructions. A major asset of GrETEL is that it enables non-technical users to consult treebanks in
a user-friendly way, which is also in line with the main CLARIN goal of applying the results
of speech and language technology to research in the humanities and the social sciences.
Besides a description of the querying procedure in GrETEL, this chapter presents a selection of research in Dutch syntax and semantics that has been carried out using GrETEL.
Furthermore, an overview is given of further developments.

22.1 Introduction

The construction of syntactically annotated corpora or *treebanks* has created exciting opportunities
for the empirical investigation of syntax.[1] For Dutch, several treebanks are available, e.g. the CGN
treebank (van der Wouden et al., 2002) for spoken Dutch, and LASSY (van Noord et al., 2013)
and SoNaR (Oostdijk et al., 2013) for written Dutch. While treebanks have the potential to be an
added value for descriptive and theoretical linguistics, the exploitation of such treebanks usually
requires that the user have in-depth knowledge of the annotation guidelines and master a formal

---

[1] We use the term *treebank* to refer to both manually constructed syntactically annotated corpora and automatically
parsed corpora.

How to cite this book chapter:
Augustinus, L, Vandeghinste, V, Schuurman, I and Van Eynde, F. 2017. GrETEL: A Tool for Example-Based
Treebank Mining. In: Odijk, J and van Hessen, A. (eds.) *CLARIN in the Low Countries*, Pp. 269–280.
London: Ubiquity Press. DOI: https://doi.org/10.5334/bbi.22. License: CC-BY 4.0

query language. Some users are not deterred by this, but many are, so that the potential of the treebanks will not be realised. To make the treebanks useful for the computationally less inclined we have developed GrETEL, a user-friendly search engine for treebanks (Augustinus et al., 2012; Augustinus et al., 2013). It offers the possibility to provide the system with an example sentence in order to collect relevant corpus data. Therefore, the development of GrETEL paves the way for combining treebank mining with descriptive and theoretical linguistics.

22.2   What is GrETEL?

GrETEL stands for *Greedy Extraction of Trees for Empirical Linguistics*. It is a linguistic search engine that enables users to extract information from treebanks in a user-friendly way. Instead of a formal search instruction, it takes a natural language example as input. This provides a convenient way for novice and non-technical users to use treebanks with a limited knowledge of the underlying syntax and formal query languages.

Since linguists tend to start their research from example sentences, example-based querying allows them to use those examples as a starting point for treebank search. Work related to our approach is the Linguist's Search Engine (Resnik and Elkiss, 2005), a tool that also made use of example-based querying, but is no longer available, and the TIGER Corpus Navigator (Hellmann et al., 2010), which is a Semantic Web system used to classify and retrieve sentences from the TIGER corpus on the basis of abstract linguistic concepts.

The system we present here is an online system,[2] which shares the advantages of tools like TüNDRA (Martens, 2013) and INESS-Search (Meurer, 2012): they are platform-independent and no local installation of the treebanks is needed. This is especially attractive for (very) large parsed corpora which require a lot of disk space. Another related tool is the more recently constructed PaQu application (Odijk, 2015, see chapter 23). In addition to an online search interface, PaQu also offers the possibility to upload and parse a locally installed corpus.

For a presentation of the way in which GrETEL works we first focus on the basic search mode of example-based querying (section 22.2.1) and then we turn to more advanced modes of querying (section 22.2.2).

22.2.1   Example-Based Querying

The example-based querying procedure consists of six steps.

1. Example   The user provides an example sentence, containing the syntactic construction (s)he is looking for. For instance, in colloquial Dutch the complementizer *van* 'of' is sometimes used in constructions reflecting direct speech (Coppen, 2010; Hoekstra, 2010). An example is given in (1).

(1)   Hij dacht   van ik zal dat morgen   wel   doen.
       he thought of   I will that tomorrow rather do
       'He thought: I will do that tomorrow'.

2. Parse   GrETEL automatically parses the input construction using the Alpino parser (van Noord, 2006), and returns it as a syntax tree (see Figure 22.1). The user can verify the parse tree. If Alpino returns an erroneous parse, the user is advised to choose another input example.

3. Selection matrix   In the selection matrix, shown in Figure 22.2, the user indicates which parts of the entered example are relevant for the construction under investigation, as well as their level of abstraction. We have indicated lemma for *van* 'of', and word class of the verbs *dacht* 'thought' and

---

[2]   http://gretel.ccl.kuleuven.be

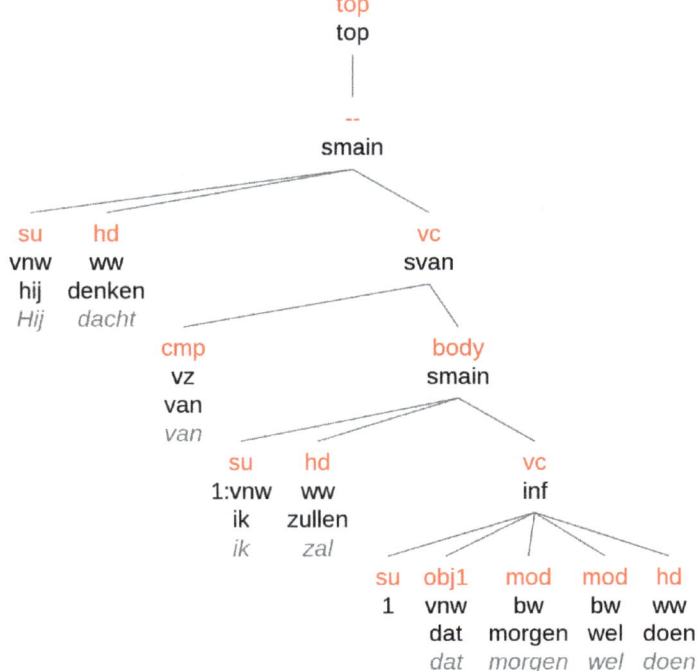

Figure 22.1: Parse tree of the input construction.

sentence	Hij	dacht	van	ik	zal	dat	morgen	wel	doen
word	○	○	○	○	○	○	○	○	○
lemma	○	○	●	○	○	○	○	○	○
word class	○	●	○	○	●	○	○	○	○
optional in search	●	○	○	●	○	●	●	●	●

Figure 22.2: Selection matrix.

zal 'will', as we want to abstract over verb forms.[3] The other words in the example are not relevant for the construction under investigation, so those words are indicated as 'optional in search'.

The dependency relation and the word class (POS tag) of all selected items are automatically included in the search instruction. For instance, it will be taken into account that the word *van* is a preposition (tagged as vz) functioning as a complementizer (cmp).

4. Treebank selection   In the next step the user can choose which treebank(s) to query. Currently one can choose between the CGN treebank for spoken Dutch, and LASSY Small and the SoNaR-500 treebank for written Dutch.[4] It is possible to query the CGN and LASSY Small treebanks as a whole, or one can select one or more treebank components, for instance to compare data from different genres. Because of its size (500 million words, ca 41 million sentences), it is

---

[3] The embedded verb is indicated in order to avoid constructions without an embedded sentence, such as *Hij dacht van wel* 'He thought so'.

[4] The SoNaR-500 treebank is a subset of the LASSY Large treebank.

only possible to query SoNaR per component. For this example we have chosen the part of SoNaR containing discussion lists (WR-P-E-A, 50 million words, ca 4.5 million sentences).

5. Query   Based on the information provided in the selection matrix, GrETEL extracts a query tree from the parse tree (Figure 22.3). Besides the lexical information indicated in the selection matrix, the dependency relation (rel) and the phrasal category (cat) of the relevant nodes are included in the query tree, see (5). GrETEL automatically converts the query tree into an XPath expression,[5] which is used to search the treebank.

6. Results   The results of the query are presented to the user as a list of sentences, with the matching part emphasised. The user can click on any of these sentences in order to visualise the results as syntax trees. For the query in Figure 22.3 GrETEL finds 175 results in the WR-P-E-A component of SoNaR. Some are presented in (2-4).

(2)   Dat filmpje   zegt bijna   van: dit is de nieuwe norm.
      That video.DIM says almost of   this is the new   norm

      'That video almost says: this is the new norm.' (SoNaR,
      WR-P-E-A-0000850955.p.5.s.3)

(3)   Na   het voorprogramma had ik zoiets   van IK BEN HIER WEG.
      after the opening act   had I something of   I   am   here   away

      'After the opening act I was like I AM OUT OF HERE.' (SoNaR,
      WR-P-E-A-0000295207.p.1.s.1)

(4)   ... maar ik dacht   van, ik ga wachten voor da   liedje.
      ... but I thought of   I go wait   for that song

      '... but I thought, I'll wait for that song.' (SoNaR, WR-P-E-A-0000258967.p.1.s.1)

The results show the *greedy* nature of GrETEL: it not only returns constructions in which the parts of the construction indicated in the matrix are adjacent, but also returns examples in which those elements are discontinuous.[6] For instance, the finite verb *zegt* 'says' in (2) is not adjacent to *van* 'of'. Because of this discontinuity, looking for similar constructions in a *flat* (raw or POS-tagged) corpus would be much harder.

If we run the same query on less informal data, such as the component of SoNaR containing periodicals and magazines (WR-P-P-H), we only find 42 hits even though the corpus is larger

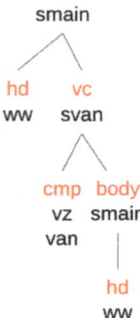

Figure 22.3: Query tree based on the input example.

---

[5]   http://www.w3.org/TR/xpath
[6]   In addition, the XPath expressions that are used (by default) in GrETEL ignore word order. This also gives rise to more general queries compared to queries used in string-based methods.

in size (ca 5.5 million sentences) than WR-P-E-A (ca 4.5 million sentences). This confirms the colloquial nature of the construction.

Example-based querying has the advantage that the user does not need to be familiar with XPath, nor with the exact syntactic structure of the XML in which the trees are represented, nor with the exact grammar implementation that is used by the parser or the annotators.

22.2.2   XPath Search

In the advanced mode of example-based search, users can inspect not only the query tree (Figure 22.3), but also the corresponding XPath expression, spelled out in (5).

(5)   //node[@cat="smain"   and   node[@rel="hd"   and   @pt="ww"]   and   node[@rel="vc"
       and   @cat="svan"   and   node[@rel="cmp"   and   @pt="vz"   and   @lemma="van"]   and
       node[@rel="body"   and   @cat="smain"   and   node[@rel="hd"   and   @pt="ww"]]]]

Moreover, they can make modifications to this query. For instance, one can use an or-statement to construct more general queries; e.g. node[@cat="smain" or @cat="ssub"] looks for constructions in both main and subordinate clauses. This approach allows more flexibility in the type of patterns that are searched.

For users who are thoroughly familiar with XPath and with the details of the annotation there is also the possibility to directly formulate an XPath query describing the syntactic pattern the user is looking for. This query is then processed in the same way as the automatically generated query in the first approach.

22.3   Using GrETEL for Research and Education

GrETEL has been used for linguistic research on various topics within Dutch syntax and semantics (section 22.3.1). In addition, it has been used for teaching, and it has been presented at several conferences and guest lectures (section 22.3.2).

22.3.1   Research on Dutch Syntax and Semantics

While GrETEL has been used to investigate several linguistic topics, two strands of research received considerable attention, i.e. the investigation of verb clusters and of copular constructions.

22.3.1.1   Verb Clusters

Augustinus (2015) provides both a theoretical and a treebank-based account of Dutch verb clusters, i.e. constructions in which multiple verbs group together. She shows how such constructions can be extracted from the treebanks using GrETEL, and how the treebank observations serve as an empirical basis to verify the claims made by the theory. She conducted several case studies, such as word order variation in verb clusters, the occurrence of *Infinitivus pro Participio* (a.k.a. the IPP effect), and interruption of the cluster by nonverbal elements.

Dutch verb clusters are characterised by an unusual type of word order variation, i.e. one that does not entail a change of meaning, as shown by the examples in (6).

(6)   a.   ... dan denk ik ook dat die man 't heeft gedaan.
             ... then think I also that that man it has   done
             '... in that case I also think that that man has done it.' (CGN, fna000458_166)

       b.   ah dan hoop ik dat Ivo dat gedaan heeft.
             ah then hope I that Ivo that done   has
             'ah in that case I hope that Ivo has done that.' (CGN, fva400092_136)

Augustinus (2015) investigates which types of word order variation occur in non-dialectal varieties of Dutch, i.e. in the CGN and LASSY Small treebanks included in GrETEL. Barbiers and Schuurman (2015) compare the word order variation in three-verb clusters encountered in those treebanks to data obtained from MIMORE, a tool for investigating morphosyntactic variation in Dutch dialects.[7]

Infinitivus pro Participio or IPP refers to constructions in which an infinitive occurs instead of a past participle, as in (7).

(7) a. Ik heb 't twee keer   zien   gebeuren.
        I   have it two   times see.IPP happen

        'I have seen it happen twice.' (CGN, fna000773_212)

    b. * Ik heb 't twee keer   gezien gebeuren.
        I   have it two   times seen   happen

IPP appears in a subset of the Germanic languages, such as Dutch, German and Afrikaans. These languages differ, however, with respect to the set of verbs that can appear as IPP verbs, and with respect to whether the phenomenon occurs obligatorily or optionally. For some verbs, the literature is not conclusive on whether they can occur in IPP constructions or not. Augustinus and Van Eynde (2012) and Augustinus (2015) describe how a treebank-supported investigation of Dutch IPP verbs using GrETEL results in a more exhaustive and empirically valid typology of Dutch IPP verbs than the lists available in the literature.

Augustinus and Van Eynde (2017) compare the set of Dutch IPP verbs to the German IPP verbs. In order to add this cross-linguistic perspective, they queried two German treebanks using the TüNDRA treebank search tool (Martens, 2013). The case study not only illustrates how the results obtained by GrETEL can be complemented by using additional resources, but also shows how the treebank data can be employed to evaluate theoretical accounts of IPP.

A third case study on IPP using GrETEL investigates the choice of the auxiliary of the perfect in Dutch IPP constructions, i.e. the choice between *hebben* 'have' and *zijn* 'be'. Canonically the choice for the auxiliary in IPP constructions is determined by the IPP verb, as in (8a). However, one also encounters constructions in which the auxiliary is determined by the main verb, as in (8b).

(8) a. en Erwin Jans die is er   weer bij   komen   zitten want   …
        and Erwin Jans who is there again with come.IPP sit   because …

        'and Erwin Jans, he has come to join us because …' (CGN, fvl600281_1)

    b. heeft er   niemand dat komen   zeggen tegen jullie?
        has   there no one   that come.IPP say   to   you

        'Did nobody come to tell you that?' (CGN, fva400386_18)

While this variation has been reported in the literature, no large-scale corpus study was available pointing out the frequency and the distribution of the phenomenon. Van Eynde et al. (2016a) investigate the choice between *hebben* 'have' and *zijn* 'be' in IPP constructions by means of GrETEL and OpenSoNaR.[8] The corpus study provides insight in the set of verbs that allow this alternation. For the verbs *moeten* 'must' and *kunnen* 'can' the distribution of the canonical and the alternative construction is investigated in more detail.

Besides word order variation and the IPP effect, Augustinus and Van Eynde (2014) and Augustinus (2015) investigate the occurrence of cluster interruption. Canonical verb clusters

---

[7] http://www.meertens.knaw.nl/mimore/

[8] OpenSoNaR provides string search of the flat SoNaR-500 corpus. (http://opensonar.clarin.inl.nl)

cannot be interrupted by nonverbal elements (9). There are some exceptions though, such as *cluster creeping* by separable verb particles, predicative adjectives, and stranded adpositions (10).

(9)   a.   ... de voorstellen die de NS vandaag heeft gedaan ...
          ... the proposals that the NS today   has done   ...
          '... the proposal that the NS has made today ...' (CGN, fnk001631_2)

      b.   * ... de voorstellen die de NS heeft vandaag gedaan ...
           ... the proposals that the NS has   today   done   ...

(10) De plicht die hem nu   roept, kan hem straks de mooiste   baan kosten waar   een
      the duty than him now calls   can him later the most-beautiful job   cost   where a
      Beier   kan *van* dromen.
      Bavarian can of   dream

      'The duty that calls him now can cost him the most beautiful job a Bavarian can dream of.'
      (LASSY, WR-P-P-I-0000000033.p.21.s.4)

The treebank investigations conducted in Augustinus and Van Eynde (2014) and Augustinus (2015) show that the set of cluster creepers is larger than the literature suggests. This illustrates once more how a treebank-based investigation can provide additional insights into syntactic phenomena.

22.3.1.2   *Copular Constructions*

In addition to the research on verb clusters, GrETEL is used for research on copular constructions. Van Eynde et al. (2014) illustrate that the set of copular verbs discussed in traditional grammars is incomplete. Typically those grammars mention a set of 10 to 15 verbs, adding, as an afterthought, that the list is not complete. By means of GrETEL treebank data were collected in order to get a more complete and empirically motivated typology of Dutch copular constructions, which consists of at least 40 verbs. As the typology is based on linguistically motivated criteria, it can be used to complete the list of verbs by investigating a larger dataset.

Van Eynde et al. (2016b) deal with number agreement in copular constructions. Canonically, there is number agreement between the subject and the predicate nominal in Dutch copular constructions, as in (11). Mismatches are not excluded, however, as shown in (12).

(11) De volgende figuur is een eenvoudig voorbeeld ...
      the next   figure is a simple   example   ...
      'The next figure is a simple example...' (LASSY, dpc-bmm-001092-nl-sen.p.5.s.1)

(12) Beide aftredende bestuurders blijven wel aandeelhouder.
      both resigning directors   remain POL shareholder
      'Both resigning directors remain shareholder.' (LASSY, WR-P-E-I-0000 049645.p.1.s.68.2)

This research demonstrates how the data obtained from the treebanks not only provide information with respect to the frequency and the distribution of number agreement in copular constructions, but also serve as an empirical basis for a theoretical analysis. In addition, the treebank data were employed to define under which circumstances mismatches between the subject and the predicate nominal are allowed.

22.3.2   *Dissemination*

GrETEL is currently used in courses on descriptive linguistics, syntax and semantics, corpus analysis, and computational linguistics in order to teach students how to look up syntactic constructions and their frequencies in a treebank without requiring them to familiarise themselves with the specifics of XPath or the specific syntax of the treebank. It teaches students about syntactic parses and treebanks by providing them easy online access to large amounts of data.

As GrETEL has a focus on user-friendliness and is freely available online, it is an example of how *Digital Humanities* applications disclose datasets and computational tools, without requiring the user to have a technical background.

GrETEL was presented to a technical audience at several conferences within the field of computational linguistics and to an audience of potential users at general linguistic conferences and doctoral schools in Flanders and the Netherlands. Those lectures typically include a tutorial demonstrating the functionality and use of GrETEL, followed by a hands-on session. In addition, some case studies are discussed, showing how the results obtained from the treebanks in GrETEL can serve as an empirical basis for research in linguistics. One of the case studies includes the combined use case of GrETEL and MIMORE (Barbiers and Schuurman, 2015). It illustrates how GrETEL and MIMORE can be used as complementary tools for studies on Dutch syntax.

22.4   Further Developments

GrETEL has been designed in such a way that it can also be used for treebanks in other languages, even if they have different annotation schemes compared to the Dutch treebanks. In the Afri-Booms project (Augustinus et al., 2016a), a treebank for Afrikaans has been developed, which is also included in GrETEL (section 22.4.1). In the context of the SCATE project (Vandeghinste et al., 2016), GrETEL was adapted to query parallel treebanks (section 22.4.2). The tool is also included in Taalportaal (Landsbergen et al., 2014), an online descriptive grammar of Dutch (section 22.4.3).

22.4.1   GrETEL for Afrikaans

In comparison to Dutch, Afrikaans is a low-resource language, so until recently no treebanks for Afrikaans were available. In the AfriBooms project a (small) treebank containing ca 50K words has been developed, based on the corpus of the South African National Centre for Human Language Technologies (NCHLT). The annotations of the treebank are manually corrected, which makes it a reliable resource for linguistic research. In addition, a first parser for Afrikaans was developed. Both the treebank and the parser are included in a version of GrETEL for Afrikaans (Augustinus et al., 2016a).[9]

22.4.2   Querying Parallel Treebanks with Poly-GrETEL

In the context of the SCATE project, large-scale parallel treebanks are constructed which are used for syntax-based machine translation. Since parallel treebanks are a valuable resource for translators and linguists as well, Poly-GrETEL was developed, i.e. an extension of GrETEL for querying parallel treebanks (Augustinus et al., 2016b).[10] Currently it contains the (automatically annotated) Europarl parallel treebank for Dutch and English.

The Europarl parallel treebank   We have made an update of the treebank described in Kotzé et al. (2016): we used the data from Europarl version 7 (Koehn, 2005) and extracted the Dutch and English sentence-aligned data from www.statmt.org. The Dutch side was parsed with the

---

[9] http://gretel.ccl.kuleuven.be/afribooms
[10] http://gretel.ccl.kuleuven.be/poly-gretel

Alpino parser and the English side with the Stanford parser (Klein and Manning, 2003) with added dependencies (de Marneffe et al., 2006). The phrase structure output of the Stanford parser is converted into an XML-tree,[11] analogous to the XML-output of Alpino, as shown in Figure 22.4. Besides the syntactic annotations the parallel treebank contains node alignments.[12]

Poly-GrETEL   In combination with the example-based query functionality, Poly-GrETEL avoids the need for users to be familiar with the query language and the structure of the trees in the source and target language, thus facilitating the use of parallel corpora for comparative linguistics and translation studies.

The user can query the treebanks in a similar way as in the monolingual GrETEL environment, i.e. example-based or by means of an XPath query. The main difference is that the user can choose between a bilingual and a monolingual input. In the bilingual search option the user provides two input constructions: one in English and one in Dutch. Poly-GrETEL returns two parses, and the user can indicate the relevant parts of both the English and the Dutch input examples. Poly-GrETEL automatically extracts a search instruction in a similar fashion as the monolingual GrETEL, but provides the option to return only the constructions in which the English and the Dutch query trees are aligned. It is a syntactic concordancer for parallel treebanks, as it shows how a Dutch syntactic construction is translated in English (or vice versa). One could, for instance, investigate how the Dutch *van*-construction presented in section 22.2.1 is translated in English. This makes the tool interesting not only for research in (comparative) linguistics and translation studies, but also to serve as a tool for computer-aided translation for translators and language learners.

Adding the parallel English-Dutch treebank furthermore implies that GrETEL also includes English data. Since it is possible to query the English side of the parallel treebank in a monolingual way, one can use these data for a monolingual treebank investigation of syntactic phenomena in English.

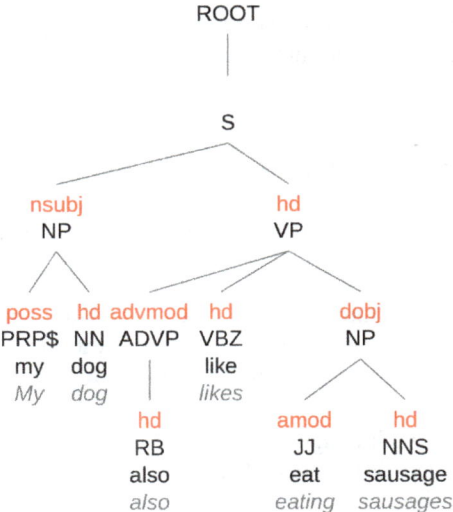

Figure 22.4: Stanford parse with added dependencies, converted into Alpino-XML.

---

[11] The bracketed tree and the XML tree are isomorphous.
[12] In future versions alignments resulting from several different alignment algorithms will be made available. In the current version, only alignment according to Zhechev (2009) is available.

22.4.3   Link with Taalportaal

Recently, GrETEL was linked to *Taalportaal*, a website that contains online descriptive grammars for Dutch, Frisian and Afrikaans (Landsbergen et al., 2014, see chapter 24).[13] By means of intelligent links, users can look up linguistic phenomena described in Taalportaal in a variety of online corpora, amongst others the treebanks included in GrETEL (van der Wouden et al., 2015).

The link with Taalportaal enhances the visibility of GrETEL, and encourages its use, alone or in combination with other corpus tools. Bouma et al. (2015) mention how they have used the example-based input method of GrETEL to facilitate query formulation. It turns out to be particularly useful if one does not know exactly how certain phenomena are annotated in the treebanks. In addition, the authors mention how they have used GrETEL's example-based querying functionality to become aware of differences between the treebank annotations and the analyses of the descriptive grammar included in Taalportaal (Bouma et al., 2015: 18).

22.5   Conclusion and Future Work

We have described GrETEL, a user-friendly search tool for treebanks. It originated in the context of a CLARIN-Flanders project, which aimed at the creation of tools for the exploitation of Dutch treebanks. In follow-up research, GrETEL was extended to other languages (Afrikaans and English), and other types of treebanks, i.e. parallel ones. The extensions make the tool also useful for a larger (CLARIN) audience, i.e. researchers who are not (only) working on Dutch.

Future work includes adding more languages to GrETEL, such as German and French, as for those languages we also have high-quality parsers and treebanks available.

In the framework of the Dutch CLARIAH infrastructure project and the Anncor project (University of Utrecht), there are plans to further extend the functionality of GrETEL. An upload function will be added, enabling researchers to upload their own corpus and metadata, supporting multiple formats. Another extension concerns adding options for data analysis, and creating possibilities to sort, group, and filter search results and metadata.

Acknowledgements

The work on GrETEL was carried out in the framework of the following projects:

- Nederbooms: Exploitation of Dutch treebanks for research in linguistics (2010–2012) Flemish government, Department of Economy, Science and Innovation.
- Complement Raising and Cluster Formation in Dutch. A Treebank-supported Investigation (2011–2015) FWO (G.0.559.11.N.10).
- GrETEL2.0 (2013–2014) Dutch Language Union.
- AfriBooms (2013–2014) Dutch Language Union and Department of Arts and Culture of the Government of South Africa.
- CLARIN Educational Module GrETEL (2014) CLARIN-NL 14-008.
- SCATE (2014–2018) IWT SBO-130041.

---

[13] http://taalportaal.org

References

Liesbeth Augustinus and Frank Van Eynde. 2012. A Treebank-based Investigation of IPP-triggering Verbs in Dutch. In *Proceedings of the 11th International Workshop on Treebanks and Linguistic Theories (TLT11)*, pages 7–12, Lisbon. Edições Colibri.

Liesbeth Augustinus and Frank Van Eynde. 2014. Looking for Cluster Creepers in Dutch Treebanks. Dat we ons daar nog kunnen mee bezig houden. *Computational Linguistics in the Netherlands Journal*, 4:149–170.

Liesbeth Augustinus and Frank Van Eynde. 2017. A Usage-based Typology of Dutch and German IPP verbs. *Leuvense Bijdragen*, 101:101–122.

Liesbeth Augustinus, Vincent Vandeghinste, and Frank Van Eynde. 2012. Example-Based Treebank Querying. In *Proceedings of the 8th International Conference on Language Resources and Evaluation (LREC 2012)*, pages 3161–3167, Istanbul.

Liesbeth Augustinus, Vincent Vandeghinste, Ineke Schuurman, and Frank Van Eynde. 2013. Example-Based Treebank Querying with GrETEL - now also for Spoken Dutch. In *Proceedings of the 19th Nordic Conference of Computational Linguistics (NODALIDA 2013)*, pages 423–428, Oslo. NEALT Proceedings Series 16.

Liesbeth Augustinus, Peter Dirix, Daniel van Niekerk, Ineke Schuurman, Vincent Vandeghinste, Frank Van Eynde, and Gerhard van Huyssteen. 2016a. AfriBooms: An Online Treebank for Afrikaans. In *Proceedings of the 10th International Conference on Language Resources and Evaluation (LREC 2016)*, pages 677–682, Portorož.

Liesbeth Augustinus, Vincent Vandeghinste, and Tom Vanallemeersch. 2016b. Poly-GrETEL: Cross-Lingual Example-based Querying of Syntactic Constructions. In *Proceedings of the 10th International Conference on Language Resources and Evaluation (LREC 2016)*, pages 3549–3554, Portorož.

Liesbeth Augustinus. 2015. *Complement Raising and Cluster Formation in Dutch. A Treebank-supported Investigation*. LOT Dissertation Series 413. LOT, Utrecht.

Sjef Barbiers and Ineke Schuurman. 2015. Combined Case Study MIMORE - GrETEL. http://www.meertens.knaw.nl/mimore/educational_module/case_study_mimore_gretel.html.

Gosse Bouma, Marjo van Koppen, Frank Landsbergen, Jan Odijk, Ton van der Wouden, and Matje van de Camp. 2015. Enriching a Descriptive Grammar with Treebank Queries. In *Proceedings of the 14th International Workshop on Treebanks and Linguistic Theories (TLT14)*, pages 13–25, Warsaw.

Peter-Arno Coppen. 2010. Bericht van de innerlijke stem. Synchronie en diachronie van de *heb-zoiets-van*-constructie. *Nederlandse Taalkunde*, 15(1):33–53.

Marie-Catherine de Marneffe, Bill MacCartney, and Christopher D. Manning. 2006. Generating typed dependency parses from phrase structure parses. In *Proceedings of the 5th International Conference on Language Resources and Evaluation (LREC 2006)*, pages 449–454, Genoa.

Sebastian Hellmann, Jörg Unbehauen, Christian Chiarcos, and Axel-Cyrille Ngonga Ngomo. 2010. The TIGER Corpus Navigator. In *Proceedings of the The 9th Workshop on Treebanks and Linguistic Theories (TLT9)*, pages 91–102, Tartu.

Eric Hoekstra. 2010. *Van* als markeerder van zinnen in de directe en indirecte rede in het Fries en het Nederlands. *Leuvense Bijdragen*, 96:169–188.

Dan Klein and Christopher D. Manning. 2003. Fast Exact Inference with a Factored Model for Natural Language Parsing. In *Advances in Neural Information Processing Systems 15 (NIPS 2002)*, pages 3–10, Cambridge, MA. MIT Press.

Philipp Koehn. 2005. Europarl: A Parallel Corpus for Statistical Machine Translation. In *Proceedings of MT Summit X*, pages 79–86, Phuket.

Gideon Kotzé, Vincent Vandeghinste, Scott Martens, and Jörg Tiedemann. 2016. Large Aligned Treebanks for Syntax-based Machine Translation. *Language Resources and Evaluation*. Vol. 51: 249–282.

Frank Landsbergen, Carole Tiberius, and Roderik Dernison. 2014. Taalportaal: an online grammar of Dutch and Frisian. In *Proceedings of the 9th International Conference on Language Resources and Evaluation (LREC 2014)*, pages 2206–2210, Reykjavik.

Scott Martens. 2013. TüNDRA: A Web Application for Treebank Search and Visualisation. In *Proceedings of the 12th International Workshop on Treebanks and Linguistic Theories (TLT12)*, pages 133–144, Sofia.

Paul Meurer. 2012. INESS-Search: A search system for LFG (and other) treebanks. In *Proceedings of the LFG'12 Conference. LFG Online Proceedings*, pages 404–421, Stanford.

Jan Odijk. 2015. Linguistic Research with PaQu. *Computational Linguistics in the Netherlands Journal*, 5:3–14.

Nelleke Oostdijk, Martin Reynaert, Véronique Hoste, and Ineke Schuurman. 2013. The Construction of a 500-Million-Word Reference Corpus of Contemporary Written Dutch. In Peter Spyns and Jan Odijk, editors, *Essential Speech and Language Technology for Dutch. Results by the STEVIN programme*, pages 219–247. Springer.

Philip Resnik and Aaron Elkiss. 2005. The Linguist's Search Engine: An Overview. In *Proceedings of the ACL Interactive Poster and Demonstration Sessions*, pages 33–36, Ann Arbor.

Ton van der Wouden, Heleen Hoekstra, Michael Moortgat, Bram Renmans, and Ineke Schuurman. 2002. Syntactic Analysis in the Spoken Dutch Corpus (CGN). In *Proceedings of the 3rd International Conference on Language Resources and Evaluation (LREC 2002)*, pages 768–773, Las Palmas.

Ton van der Wouden, Gosse Bouma, Matje van de Kamp, Marjo van Koppen, Frank Landsbergen, and Jan Odijk. 2015. Enriching a grammatical database with intelligent links to linguistic resources. In *CLARIN Annual Conference 2015 Book of Abstracts*, pages 89–92, Wroclaw.

Frank Van Eynde, Liesbeth Augustinus, Ineke Schuurman, and Vincent Vandeghinste. 2014. Het verrassende resultaat van een copulativiteitspeiling. In Freek Van de Velde, Hans Smessaert, Frank Van Eynde, and Sara Verbrugge, editors, *Patroon en Argument. Een dubbelfeestbundel bij het emeritaat van William Van Belle en Joop van der Horst*, pages 47–62. Universitaire Pers, Leuven.

Frank Van Eynde, Liesbeth Augustinus, Ineke Schuurman, and Vincent Vandeghinste. 2016a. *Hebben* of *zijn* bij IPP's. *Leuvense Bijdragen*, 99-100:11–28.

Frank Van Eynde, Liesbeth Augustinus, and Vincent Vandeghinste. 2016b. Number agreement in copular constructions. A treebank-based investigation. *Lingua*, 178:104–126.

Gertjan van Noord, Gosse Bouma, Frank Van Eynde, Daniël de Kok, Jelmer van der Linde, Ineke Schuurman, Erik Tjong Kim Sang, and Vincent Vandeghinste. 2013. Large Scale Syntactic Annotation of Written Dutch: Lassy. In Peter Spyns and Jan Odijk, editors, *Essential Speech and Language Technology for Dutch. Results by the STEVIN programme*, pages 147–164. Springer.

Gertjan van Noord. 2006. At Last Parsing Is Now Operational. In *Proceedings of TALN*, pages 20–42.

Vincent Vandeghinste, Tom Vanallemeersch, Liesbeth Augustinus, Joris Pelemans, Geert Heyman, Iulianna van der Lek-Ciudin, Arda Tezcan, Donald Degraen, Jan Van den Bergh, Lieve Macken, Els Lefever, Marie-Francine Moens, Patrick Wambacq, Frieda Steurs, Karin Coninx, and Frank Van Eynde. 2016. Smart Computer Aided Translation Environment. In *Baltic Journal of Modern Computing. Proceedings of the 19th Annual Conference of the European Association for Machine Translation (EAMT 2015)*, volume 4 (2), page 382, Riga.

Ventislav Zhechev. 2009. *Automatic Generation of Parallel Treebanks: An Efficient Unsupervised System*. Dublin City University.

CHAPTER 23

The Parse and Query (PaQu) Application

Jan Odijk, Gertjan van Noord, Peter Kleiweg and Erik Tjong Kim Sang

Utrecht University – RU Groningen – Meertens Institute, j.odijk@uu.nl

ABSTRACT

In this chapter we describe the web application PaQu (Parse and Query), and carry out a small case study to illustrate its use. PaQu is an application for searching in Dutch treebanks and for analysing the search results. One can search in the LASSY and CGN treebanks, or upload one's own Dutch corpus, which is then parsed and made available for search and analysis. PaQu offers, next to an interface to formulate Xpath queries, a dedicated interface for searching for dependency triples. This makes it easy to search in treebanks for grammatical dependencies, which would otherwise require very complex queries. It offers extensive functionality for analysing the search results. The dedicated search interface makes PaQu a prime example of the kind of applications that CLARIN promotes. The case study provides an analysis of the syntactic selectional differences between two near-synonymous verbs.

23.1   Introduction

In this chapter we describe the web application PaQu[1] (Parse and Query), and carry out a small case study to illustrate its use. PaQu is an application for searching in treebanks (i.e. text corpora in which each sentence has been assigned a syntactic structure) and for analysing the search results. PaQu was developed by the University of Groningen in the CLARIN-NL project and is an extension of the LASSY Dependency Relations Search application originally developed by Tjong Kim Sang et al. (2010). Here is a direct link to the application and its documentation.

---

[1]   This chapter contains many hyperlinks. In electronic versions they are easily visible by special marking (blue colour). In the printed black and white version the hyperlinks may be visible as grey text. The relevant URLs are explicitly listed in the appendix.

How to cite this book chapter:

Odijk, J, van Noord, G, Kleiweg, P and Tjong Kim Sang, E. 2017. The Parse and Query (PaQu) Application. In: Odijk, J and van Hessen, A. (eds.) *CLARIN in the Low Countries*, Pp. 281–297. London: Ubiquity Press. DOI: https://doi.org/10.5334/bbi.23. License: CC-BY 4.0

PaQu has been used for carrying out research, inter alia for an analysis of the Dutch intensifiers *heel, erg, zeer* (each meaning 'very') by Odijk (2015a) and Odijk (2016), and for an analysis of normative and non-normative variants of Dutch constructions by Odijk (2015b) and Van Noord and Odijk (2016). It is also heavily used in the Taalportaal, a digital grammar for Dutch (Van der Wouden et al., 2016), where many of the links with queries for corpus examples use the PaQu interface (see Bouma et al. (2015), Van der Wouden et al. (2015) and chapter 24).

PaQu offers three types of functionality: corpus management (described in section 23.2), search (described in section 23.3), and analysis (described in section 23.4). Section 23.5 contains an analysis of the predicative complements of the near-synonymous copular verbs *worden* 'become' and *raken* 'get' as a small case study. Section 23.6 summarises our conclusions and sketches future work. The appendix contains a list of all hyperlinks.

23.2   Corpus Management

PaQu enables one to select a treebank to search in from the publicly available Dutch treebanks in PaQu. These include LASSY-Small, the Wikipedia part of LASSY-Large (Van Noord et al., 2013), and the treebank of the Spoken Dutch Corpus (Oostdijk et al., 2002). One can also upload one's own Dutch text corpus.[2] One's own corpora can be kept private or shared with others. Login is required for managing one's corpora, since the user wants to see his/her own corpora but not someone else's (unless they are shared).

PaQu accepts as input plain text (in multiple varieties), which it then parses using Alpino (Van der Beek et al., 2002), or a text corpus already parsed by Alpino in the LASSY XML format. After this, the treebank is available for search and analysis. New input formats are being added (see section 23.6).

PaQu offers full parses of sentences in one's own corpus, but these parses are generated in a fully automatic manner, so they inevitably will contain errors. It is therefore required to evaluate the quality of the automatically generated parses.[3] Odijk (2015a) describes the results of such an evaluation for the words *heel, erg* and *zeer* in the CHILDES Van Kampen subcorpus, and he concludes that PaQu is excellent for carrying research on these phenomena, since the accuracy of Alpino for these data is in part very high (accuracy well over 90%), and the part where the accuracy is low is easily identifiable with PaQu. Though these results cannot be automatically generalised to other cases, they show that PaQu can be very useful even in cases where Alpino's accuracy is low, provided that the problematic cases can be automatically identified with PaQu.

Finally, PaQu enables the user to store the results of a query in a new corpus.

23.3   Search

PaQu enables search for utterances in the treebank by selecting for properties in the syntactic structures of these utterances. Before discussing this in more detail in section 23.3.2, we will say some words on the nature of the syntactic structures in the treebanks that PaQu deals with (section 23.3.1). We conclude with a description of the search results in section 23.3.3.

---

[2]   This raises the question of how long these user corpora are retained, as one of the anonymous reviewers noted. On 18 May 2016, PaQu hosted 47 user corpora for 34 different users, and so far there are no problems in hosting these. Ultimately, the retention policy will be determined by the CLARIN Centre that will host PaQu.

[3]   See Bloem (2016) for general strategies to evaluate automatically generated parses in the absence of a gold standard.

23.3.1 *Syntactic Structures in Dutch Treebanks*

The character of the syntactic structures in the treebanks in PaQu is in accordance with the *de facto* standard for syntactic structures in treebanks for the Dutch language (Hoekstra et al., 2003; Van Noord et al., 2011), defined in projects for the construction of Dutch treebanks such as CGN (for spoken Dutch; Oostdijk et al., 2002) and LASSY (for written Dutch; Van Noord et al., 2013). They are tree structures of a particular kind.[4] They differ from pure constituent structures (as used e.g. in Chomskyan generative grammar (Chomsky, 1965) and LFG's c-structures (Bresnan, 1982)) in two respects: they explicitly label grammatical relations, and order in the tree is not significant and need not correspond to the surface order.[5] They differ from dependency structures (on the analytical layer) as used in the Prague Dependency Treebank (Hajič and Hajičová, 1997) in explicitly allowing grouping of nodes under non-word nodes. The following simple (English) example illustrates the differences between a constituent structure (1a), a dependency structure (1b) and a CGN/LASSY-structure (2) for the sentence *The man saw a boy*:[6]

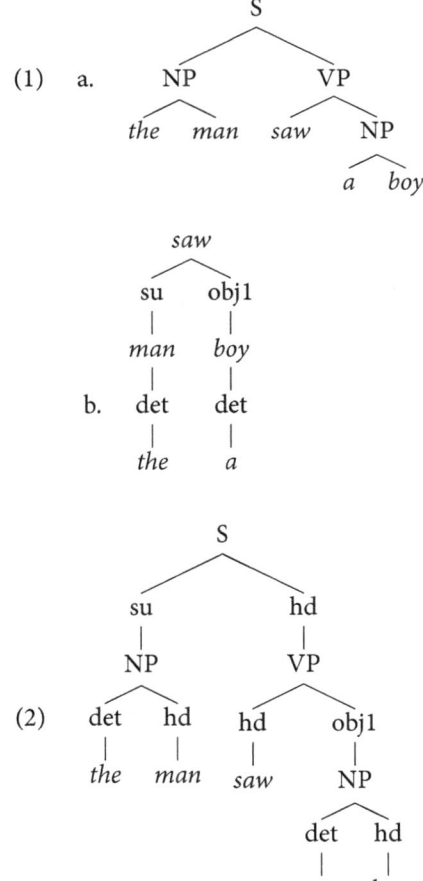

---

4   There is no generally accepted name for these tree structures. Van Noord et al. (2011) call them 'dependentiestructuren' (dependency structures), but that is not a very fortunate choice.

5   The surface order is specified in attributes on nodes for words.

6   The nonsignificance of order in the CGN/LASSY tree is not visible in these trees.

The syntactic structure for the Dutch sentence *De man zal dat boek niet willen lezen* 'The man will not want to read that book' in (3) clearly shows that order in the tree does not necessarily correspond to surface order:[7]

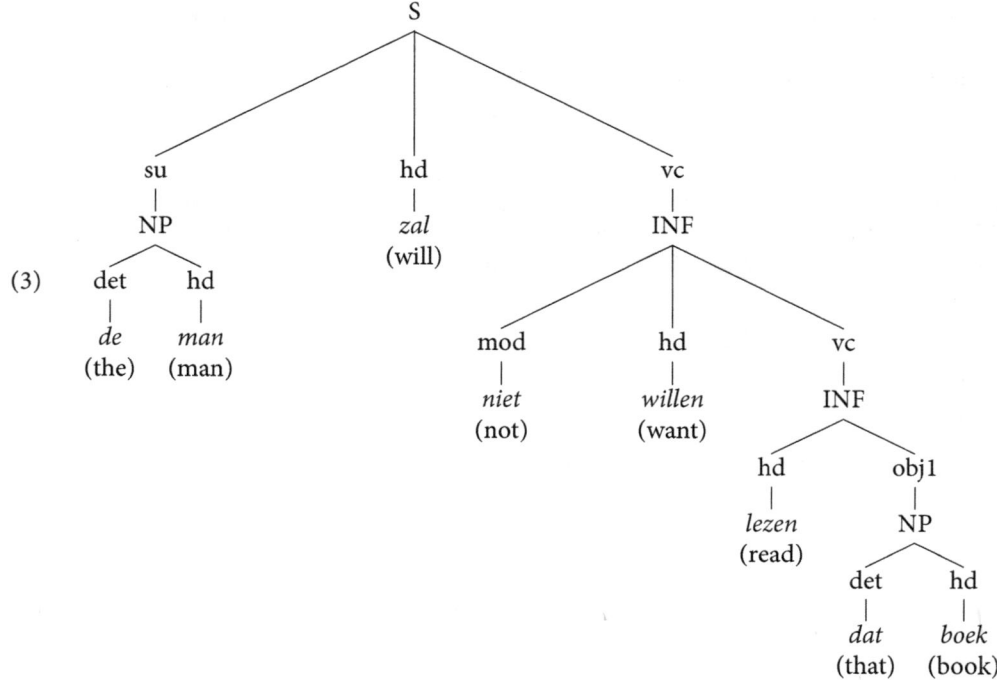

Another characteristic of the syntactic structures that is in accordance with the Dutch *de facto* standard for syntactic structures in treebanks is that a structure cannot contain nodes that dominate a single node. So, e.g., if the subject of a sentence consists of a single pronoun (e.g. a pronoun such as 'he'), then the structure is not like in (4), since that structure contains a node (NP) that dominates a single node (*he*):

but is instead as in (5):

---

7   Thus enabling the representation of discontinuous dependencies or what are called *non-projective structures* in Dependency Grammar.

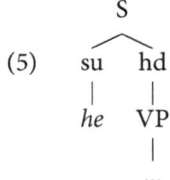

(5)

Syntactic structures can also contain nodes that have no content except for an index attribute ('empty categories'). These are always co-indexed with some node with content. This mechanism is used to express constructions in which a single word or phrase plays multiple syntactic roles. We will see several examples of this in section 23.3.2.

23.3.2   Queries in PaQu

PaQu offers two interfaces for formulating queries to search in the treebanks. The first one enables one to formulate queries in the Xpath query language. This requires expert knowledge of the query language Xpath. Learning Xpath, or at least the most common elements required in PaQu, is easy, so this actually poses no problems. A more serious problem is that Xpath queries tend to become quite complex very quickly. Here PaQu aids the user by providing a syntax check: is the Xpath query well-formed (white background colour), or not (red background colour), and are valid elements and attributes used in the query or not (yellow background)?. It also provides suggestions for completing the Xpath expression that is being constructed. In addition, extensions of Xpath originally developed for the desktop Alpino corpus tool DACT (Van Noord et al., 2013) can be used: macros, which can be used for abbreviating often occurring complex Xpath expressions, and query pipelines, which are useful for improving performance.

Most problematic for constructing Xpath queries is that the user must know, in every fine detail, what the syntactic structures for a variety of constructions actually look like in the treebank. The GrETEL application ((Augustinus et al., 2012) and chapter 22) avoids this problem through a dedicated user interface that makes example-based querying possible. This imposes restrictions on the types of queries that can be made, but many often used query types can be constructed in this way on the basis of an example without actually having to formulate a query in a formal query language or to know in great detail what the syntactic structures look like.

The second query interface that PaQu offers is, like GrETEL's interface, a highly user-friendly dedicated interface, but it is user-friendly in a completely different way than GrETEL's interface. PaQu enables searching for dependency triples (see Figure 23.1). Such triples are of the form '(dependent word, relation, head word)'. PaQu's dedicated interface enables one to formulate queries in terms of these three elements. One can query for the head word and the dependent word by specifying some of their properties, in particular, their lemma, their word form, and their part of speech. The *relation* element is an attribute that takes atomic labels for grammatical relations such as subject (su), direct object (obj1), modifier (mod), etc. The query can basically be formulated in terms of the seven attributes *lemma, word, postag* (for the dependent word), *hlemma, hword, hpostag* (for the headword) and *rel* for the relation. One has to specify minimally one of these elements in the query. If one does not specify anything at all for any of these elements, it effectively acts as a variable and matches with anything. Some examples may illustrate this:[8]

(6)   a.   Yield sentences from CGN that contain the lemma *heel* as a modifier: (lemma='heel', rel='mod').

---

[8]   Clicking on the queries executes them.

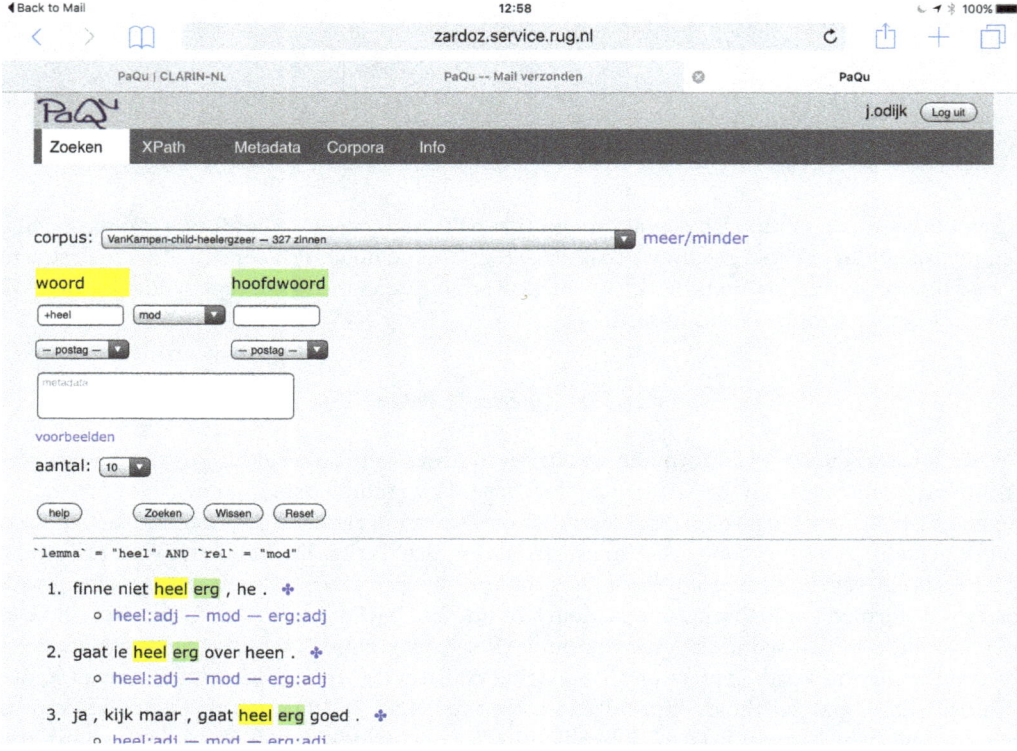

Figure 23.1: PaQu web interface with a query for occurrences of the lemma *heel* as modifier.

b. Yield sentences from CGN that contain the lemma *heel* as a modifier of an adjective: (lemma='heel', rel='mod', hpostag='adj')

c. Yield sentences from LASSY-Small that contain a predicative complement to the verb *raken*: (rel='predc', hlemma='raken')

Searching for dependency triples is very often needed in linguistic research, so having a simple and very user-friendly way of formulating such queries is one of PaQu's greatest benefits. Obviously, the simple and user-friendly way in which this can be done also restricts the kind of queries one can pose, but it does so in a completely different way than GrETEL does. In this way PaQu is complementary to GrETEL.

The relevant queries for dependencies triples are not easily expressed in Xpath. Such a query has to take into account not only headed structures but also coordinated structures and co-indexed nodes in the syntactic structure. In addition, the dependent word can be contained in a phrase that is a dependent of the head word. We will elaborate a little bit on this.

A word *w* that modifies some other word *h* can be modified itself. In that case *w* is the head of a constituent, and *h* is actually modified by the constituent dominating *w*. For example, the result of the query (word='erg', rel='mod') in LASSY-Small contains such examples, in particular the resulting sentences 1, 18, 71, 77.[9] The relevant part of the structure of 18 (*heel erg zwaar*, lit. very awfully heavy, 'really very heavy') is given in (7):

---

[9]   The order of the query output is not always guaranteed to be the same, so one might find these examples under other numbers in a different instantiation of the query. The links should work, however.

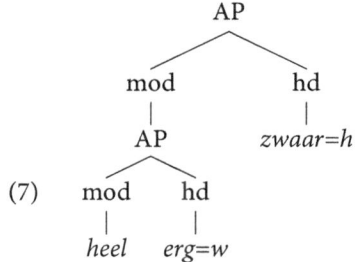

(7)

In (7) *erg* 'awfully' is the head of the AP (*heel erg*) 'very awfully', which modifies *zwaar* 'heavy': in such cases we want the dependency triple (*erg*, mod, *zwaar*) in the results, which is what PaQu's dedicated interface achieves.

Suppose that one is interested in subjects of the verb *lopen*. This word, as almost any word in natural language, is highly ambiguous: the online Van Dale lists nine senses (and De Boer (2007) even lists eleven), and possible translations into English include 'walk', 'run', 'stream', 'last', 'move', 'work', and others). The ambiguity is often reduced and occasionally even resolved by combining it with its arguments. For investigating combinations of the verb *lopen* with subjects, one can use the query (rel=su, hword='lopen') in LASSY-Small. But a subject of a verb can be a conjunction of multiple words, e.g. *droom en werkelijkheid* (dream and reality) in the sentence *Droom en werkelijkheid lopen door elkaar*[10] (example 10), as well as in many other examples, among them 21, 65 and 90 of the result set. PaQu counts each conjunct and the conjunction itself as a subject of the verb in such cases, which is a reasonable and very useful strategy.

Another pecularity of the syntactic trees is that they can contain nodes that are co-indexed with other nodes (as described above). If a node *a* is co-indexed with node *b*, and *b* is a dependent of some head *h*, then we want to consider *a* to be a dependent of *h* as well. Co-indexed nodes are used for a range of linguistic phenomena. Ellipsis is one: in the query (word='heel', rel='mod') examples 2 and 4 have been analysed as containing ellipsis; in an informal notation, for example 2, the part *heel afwisselende en rijke* is analysed as *heel afwisselende en ~~heel~~ rijke*, in which the striked-out *heel* is an 'empty category' co-indexed with the first occurrence of *heel*.

Coindexation is also used for control, for subject and object raising, and for long distance movements (e.g., preposed relative and interrogative pronouns). In the query (rel=su, hword='lopen') we find subject raising in examples 15 (subject of *was* and subject of *gelopen*), 16 (subject of *blijkt* and *lopen*) and 32 (subject of *leken* and *lopen*); ellipsis and subject control in example 17 (subject of *wil* and *lopen*); object raising in 21 (object of *laat* and *lopen*), subject raising twice in 22 (subject of *hebben*, *kunnen*, and *lopen*); and object raising in 28 (direct object of *zagen* and subject of *lopen*); etc. etc. An example of wh-movement can be found in example 15 (preposing of the relative pronoun *die*) .

Making queries that take into account all these different aspects is very difficult, and these queries are not easily expressed in Xpath (see the DACT Cookbook, section *Antecedents of co-indexed nodes* for an implementation of including indexed nodes in Xpath). PaQu's dedicated search interface, however, does it all automatically without the user having to worry about these cases: when searching for any relation, PaQu not only searches for nodes with that relation, but also searches for nodes that are the head of a phrase with that relation, or that are a conjunct in coordinated phrases; and when it finds a node searched for, it also searches for nodes co-indexed with the found node.

Each executed query in PaQu yields a URL that can be used to replicate the query. The URL encodes the server that PaQu runs on and parameters of the query to be performed. Any web

---

[10] 'Dream and reality intermingle'.

browser can interpret these URLs (as HTTP GET requests), so that it is easy to replicate the query exactly. We have used many of these URLs in this document in hyperlinks to queries. They have also been used extensively in the Taalportaal (Van der Wouden et al., 2016) to provide the links from descriptions of constructions to examples in text corpora (see Bouma et al. (2015), Van der Wouden et al. (2015) and chapter 24).

23.3.3   Search Results

The output of a PaQu query is a list of utterances that match the query. They are preceded by a specification of the query (for example `word` = "heel" AND `rel` = "mod" for the query (word='heel', rel='mod')).

PaQu shows the results on different web pages, with by default 10 utterances per page, though one can have up to 500 utterances per page. To see more results, one has to browse to the next results page. Representing only a limited number of utterances per page, and initially only one results page, enables users to experiment with a query, to quickly inspect the initial results, and, if needed, to adapt the query, while at the same time saving computing time and avoiding unnecessary waiting time on the user side. If one is interested in all results, one can compute and analyse them in the analysis part.

Each utterance in the results is assigned a number, and the syntactic structure of the utterance can be viewed by clicking on the clover button to the right of the utterance. In the dependency relations search interface the head and the dependent words are marked by colour: green for the head word(s), yellow for the dependent word(s). Each utterance is followed by the dependency triple(s) found in the utterance, and each of these triples is a query itself, automatically generated by PaQu. For example, in the query (word='heel', rel='mod'), result 3 is followed by the triple hele:adj – mod – land:n, which itself is a link containing a query *(word='hele', postag='adj', rel='mod', hword='land', hpostag='n')* that searches for utterances containing the adjective *hele* as a modifier of the noun *land*. Clicking on it executes this query.

23.4   Analysis

The results page of a query shows not only the resulting utterances, but also several options for analysing the search results. The button *Tellingen algemeen* (General Counts) provides counts of the occurrences of each of the seven attributes that define a dependency relation query: *word, lemma, postag, rel, hword, hlemma, hpostag*. The resulting statistics can be downloaded as a tab-separated text file.

One can also compute counts of combinations of these attributes, using the button *Tellingen van Combinaties* (Combination Counts; see Figure 23.2). The result is a table with counts of the examples that meet the criteria, with instantiation of the unspecified attributes by the values occurring in the search results (i.e. they are acting as variables). The counts in the table are hyperlinks with automatically generated queries for exploring specific subcases in more detail. Clicking on the column header sorts the table by the values in this column (the header is then represented in italics).

PaQu already enables analysis of search results in combination with metadata, at least for some corpora, e.g. the Spoken Dutch Corpus. This result was achieved in the CLARIAH project, the successor of CLARIN-NL. This aspect has been heavily used in Van Noord and Odijk (2016), where it is shown that certain non-normative variants of Dutch construction only occur in a specific region, e.g. *hun* 'them' as a subject only occurs in the Netherlands part of the corpus, while *'m* 'him' as a subject only occurs in the Flanders part of the corpus.

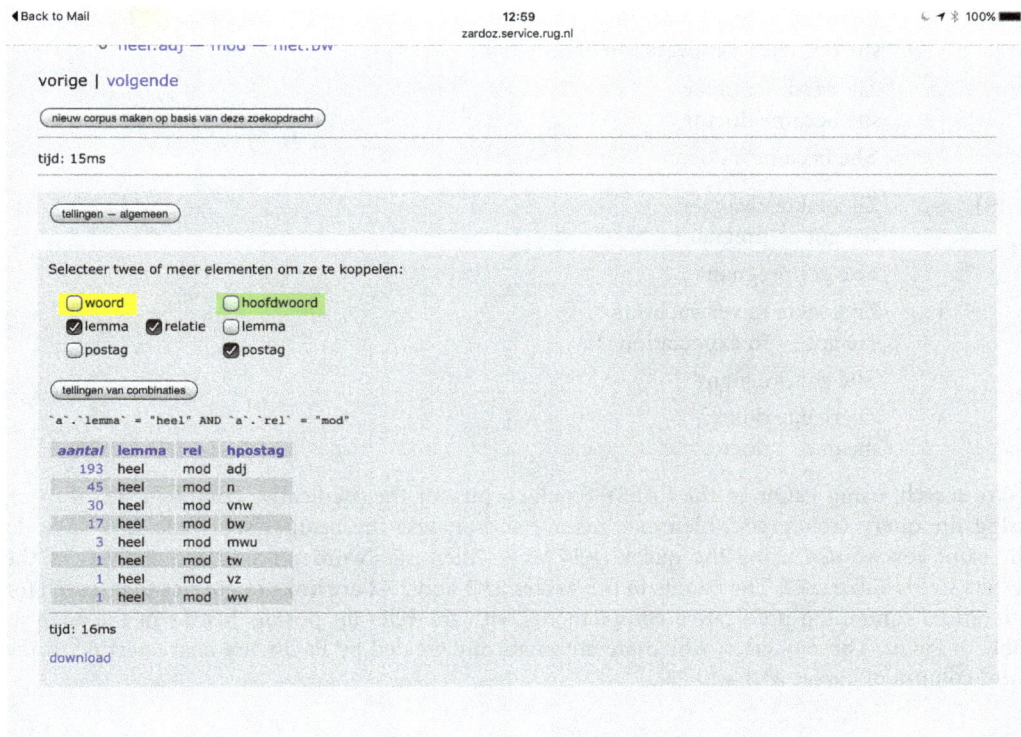

Figure 23.2: PaQu analysis: count of occurrences of the lemma *heel* as modifier by part of speech of the modifiee.

23.5   Case Study

Odijk (2011) sketched a research problem concerning the acquisition of syntactic selectional properties of words. Odijk (2015a) and Odijk (2016) investigate this problem for the words *heel*, *zeer* and *erg* (all meaning 'very'): *heel* (under this reading) only selects adjectival predicates while *erg* and *zeer* select adjectival, verbal and adpositional predicates.

Here we illustrate an initial step in an investigation of this problem for a similar but different case: on the basis of initial data, we assume that the verb *worden* 'become' selects only adjectival and nominal predicates (8), while the almost synonymous[11] verb *raken* 'get' selects only adjectival and adpositional[12] predicates (9):[13]

(8)   a.   Zij werd   zwanger
             she became pregnant
             'She became pregnant'

---

[11] The only semantic difference, as far as we can see, is that *raken* implies accidentality of the state or property change, while *worden* is neutral in this respect.

[12] This includes words that are traditionally called locational and directional 'adverbs'.

[13] Of course, these verbs, like almost all natural language words, have multiple uses: *worden* is also used to form passive constructions, and *raken* is also a transitive verb meaning 'hit'. We will ignore these uses here, which is easy since PaQu enables us to separate them from the copular use of these verbs.

b.   * Zij werd   in verwachting
       she became in expectation

c.   Zij werd   dokter
       she became doctor

       'She became a doctor'

(9) a.   Zij raakte zwanger
            she got   pregnant

            'She got pregnant'

     b.   Zij raakte in verwachting
            she got   in expectation

            'She got pregnant'

     c.   * Zij raakte dokter
            she got   doctor

We search, using PaQu, in the LASSY-Small corpus for the predicative complements of *raken* using the query (rel='predc', hlemma='raken') and analyse the results (see Table 23.1). We do the same for *worden* using the query (rel='predc', hlemma='worden'), and the analysis of the results yields Table 23.2. The counts in the Tables 23.1 and 23.2 are links to queries that search for utterances containing predicative complements with the relevant postag, just as in the analysis table of PaQu. These queries, which are automatically created by PaQu, are characterised in the third column of Tables 23.1 and 23.2.[14]

Count	postag	Query
112	adj	(rel='predc', hlemma='raken', postag='adj')
67	ww	(rel='predc', hlemma='raken', postag='ww')
33	vz	(rel='predc', hlemma='raken', postag='vz')
3	vg	(rel='predc', hlemma='raken', postag='vg')
2	mwu	(rel='predc', hlemma='raken', postag='mwu')
1	n	(rel='predc', hlemma='raken', postag='n')

Table 23.1: Counts of predicative complements to *raken* grouped by postag.

Count	postag	Query
693	n	(rel='predc', hlemma='worden', postag='n')
665	adj	(rel='predc', hlemma='worden', postag='adj')
59	vg	(rel='predc', hlemma='worden', postag='vg')
54	ww	(rel='predc', hlemma='worden', postag='ww')
49	tw	(rel='predc', hlemma='worden', postag='tw')
40	mwu	(rel='predc', hlemma='worden', postag='mwu')
32	vnw	(rel='predc', hlemma='worden', postag='vnw')
13	bw	(rel='predc', hlemma='worden', postag='bw')
8	spec	(rel='predc', hlemma='worden', postag='spec')
4	vz	(rel='predc', hlemma='worden', postag='vz')

Table 23.2: Counts of predicative complements to *worden* grouped by postag.

---

[14] The relevant part of speech codes used in the LASSY-Small treebank are:adj (adjective), ww (verb), vz (adposition), vg (conjunction), mwu (multiword unit), n (noun), tw (numeral), vnw (pronoun), bw (adverb), and spec (special).

For *raken*, we find, as expected, adjectival predicative complements (*adj*) and adpositional predicative complements (*vz*). PaQu also lists verbal predicative complements (*ww*), but many of these are adjectives that happen to be identical in form to passive participles of verbs: such adjectives are always analysed in the Dutch treebanks as verbs, but in reality they are adjectives, as can be shown with standard tests to distinguish verbal participles from homophonous adjectives. An example is *besmet* 'contaminated' in this example, also represented in (10):

(10)   In China zijn varkens besmet   geraakt met de vogelpest
       in China are pigs   contaminated got   with the fowl pest

       'In China, pigs got contaminated with the fowl pest'

It is not fully clear to me that all examples can be analysed as adjectives, though many researchers claim this (e.g. Broekhuis and Corver (2015:section 6.2.3, I, p. 989)). This requires further research. If not, we must allow verbal participial complements to the verb *raken* as well. Examples with the part of speech tag *vg* concern conjoined structures (in all cases with adjectival conjuncts). The code *mwu* stands for *multiword unit*: the treebank identifies certain word combinations as multiword units without assigning them any part of speech tag other than *mwu*. The two examples are the expressions *in de war* and *door de war*, both meaning 'mixed up' or 'confused'. They are clearly adpositional phrases, even though the treebank does not explicitly state this (probably because the expressions have an idiosyncratic meaning and the word *war* only occurs in these expressions).

Finally, PaQu lists one example with a nominal predicate (*n*), which is not expected. Closer inspection shows that the syntactic structure for this example contains an error: the example contains the transitive verb *raken* and the nominal complement should have been assigned the grammatical relation *obj1*. Even in treebanks that are claimed to have been manually verified some errors will occur. The fact that this error occurs is actually good, because it shows that the grammar behind the treebank does not exclude nominal predicative complements to the verb *raken*. If it did, there would be a danger of circularity: we would then not find any nominal complements because the grammar behind the treebank cannot create such structures. But this example shows that there is no circularity here.

Of course, the presence of such errors raises the question of how reliable the data underlying the analysis given here are. Van Noord et al. (2013) mention an independent validation which reports a sentence accuracy, i.e. sentences without any error in the syntactic analysis divided by all sentences, of 97.8% for LASSY-Small. To assess the accuracy for dependency triples with *raken* or *worden* as hlemma, we manually annotated all 1,039 dependency triples with hlemma=*raken* (yielding an accuracy of over 96.1%) and a sample of 866 out of the 27,697 dependency triples with hlemma=*worden* (yielding an accuracy of over 98.8%). These high accuracy figures clearly indicate that the data that the analysis given here is based on are reliable.

It makes sense to also look at examples where *raken* has a complement marked with the grammatical relation *ld*. The label *ld* is intended for marking locative and directional complements, but it is not obvious that a syntactic distinction with *predc* must or can be made. The distinction between *ld* and *predc* might just be semantic in nature. This distinction is especially difficult to make in many cases because many predicates are expressed by locative phrases in some metaphorical abstract form of space, and many expressions that are literally locative have an idiomatic or metaphorical reading as a state (e.g. *aan lager wal raken*, lit. 'end up at the lee shore', fig. 'come down in the world', as in this example). All *ld*-complements to *raken* are adpositional (*vz*), except for one (this example), in which the complement has postag *bw* (adverb) and is a locative adverb that falls under adpositions.[15] Furthermore, there is one example with an *ld* complement in

---

[15] The relevant adverb is *waarin*, lit. where-in', for which an analysis as two separate syntactic formatives, *waar* and *in*, that form an adpositional phrase and that happen to be a single word phonologically and orthographically is very plausible.

which the verb *raken* is actually the (passivised) transitive verb (with meaning 'hit'). It is not obvious that the phrase marked as a complement here is indeed a complement.[16]

Finally, we should consider elements with the grammatical relation *svp*, which is for separated verbal particles. Such particles can be adpositional, nominal or adjectival, and single word predicative complements can often behave as such particles. A concrete example is *opraken* 'run out', which is composed of the (intransitive) adposition *op* 'exhausted' and the verb *raken* 'get'. But often the combination of a particle and a verb leads to an unpredictable meaning and unpredictable syntactic selectional properties. There are 19 occurrences of an *svp*-complement to *raken* in LASSY-Small, and in 12 cases it indeed involves *svp*-complements, for the idiosyncratic verbs *aanraken* 'touch', transitive *kwijtraken* 'lose' (which are irrelevant for our analysis), and for *opraken*. In 7 cases, the analysis as an *svp*-complement is dubious. The examples all involve idiosyncratic expressions such as *in de vergetelheid raken* 'become forgotten' and *in zwang raken* 'get fashionable', *slaags raken* 'start fighting' and *(ergens) verzeild raken* 'get (somewhere)'. Even when they are analysed as predicative complements (which is a more plausible analysis and is also adopted in traditional grammars), they conform to our assumptions on the syntactic selectional properties of the copular verb *raken*.

To summarise, these data fully confirm our assumptions about the syntactic selectional properties of the copular verb *raken*, though perhaps participial complements should be added as an option.

For *worden*, we find many nominal (*n*) and adjectival (*adj*) predicative complements, as expected. The examples labelled with *vg* involve nominal and adjectival conjoined structures. The examples labelled with *ww* concern true verbal participles incorrectly labelled as *predc* instead of as *vc* (verbal complement), or adjectives that are identical to participles, e.g. *opgewonden* 'excited' as an adjective, 'wound up' as a participle, in this example, the relevant part of which is in (11):

(11) Je overschat   jezelf en wordt   opgewonden
      one overestimates oneself and becomes excited

      'One overrates oneself and becomes excited'

The examples labelled with *tw* concern numerals, both cardinals and ordinals. Many researchers analyse these as nouns (cardinals) and adjectives (ordinals), but if a separate syntactic category *tw* can be justified, we should add it to the syntactic selectional specification of *worden*. The *mwu* examples mostly involve names, titles and citations (all nominal in character). There is one example of an adpositional expression, but here the syntactic structure is incorrect (this example). However, there are also examples with the adpositional expression *van kracht*, lit. 'of power', fig. 'valid, in force', and these are real counterexamples to our original assumptions about the syntactic selectional properties of copular *worden*. We will come back to them below.

The examples labelled with *vnw* concern pronouns, and these are all nominal or adjectival. The examples labelled *bw* concern adverbs: under our grammatical assumptions, all these examples (*zo* 'so, this way', *het eens* 'agreeing', *anders* 'different') are considered adjectives. The examples labelled with *spec* concern unknown (often foreign) words: the complements to *worden* here clearly are all nominal. Finally, there are 4 cases with adpositional predicative complements, which we do not expect. They come in two classes: first, expressions introduced by the word *als* 'as', which is traditionally analysed as a subordinate conjunction, as in (12):

(12) Het zou   nooit meer worden als vroeger
      it   would never more become as in-the-past

      'It would never be as before'

---

[16] It involves a locative PP containing an inalienable body part related to the (surface) subject, just as in the English example *he was hit in the head.*

We must either allow phrases introduced by the conjunction *als* as complements to the verb *worden* or assume that a covert adjective comparable to *zo* 'in the way' is present with the *als*-phrase as its modifier. The second class involves genuine adpositional phrases such as *van belang* 'of importance' and *van het grootste belang* 'of the greatest importance'. These are very similar to the example *van kracht* we saw earlier. We must conclude that *worden* does allow some adpositional predicative complements, though not all (see (8)), and we need to find properties that distinguish these two types of adpositional phrases. The adpositional phrases here are all introduced by the adposition *van*, but that cannot be the distinguishing factor since expressions such as *van streek* 'worried' and *van slag* 'confused' cannot combine with *worden* and must be combined with *raken*. It is also worth noting that the adpositional phrases that occur with *worden* cannot occur as complements to *raken*, which is also not expected.

For the grammatical relation *ld*, only one example is found with *worden*, and it has the wrong grammatical relation: it should be *mod* instead of *ld*.

We conclude, based on our search for relevant examples and the analysis of the search results in PaQu, that our initial assumptions about the selectional properties for *worden* must be adapted. This example thus shows that systematic search of linguistic phenomena in corpora can be used to find evidence to support or falsify hypotheses, and may lead to adaptations of proposed hypotheses. The exact nature of the adaptation that is needed here, however, requires further research, for which PaQu again can be fruitfully used.

23.6   Conclusions and Future Work

We have described the functionality that PaQu offers: corpus management, in particular uploading one's own corpora to have them parsed and make them searchable as a treebank; searching in the treebank; and analysis of the search results. We have shown that queries that are pretty difficult to formulate in a query language such as Xpath are very easy to formulate using PaQu's dedicated search interface. PaQu is a prime example of what CLARIN aims to achieve: it is a web application with a user interface dedicated to researchers (mainly linguists) that supports them in their research. We have illustrated the use of PaQu with one small case study, which could be a first step in a full investigation on the syntactic selectional properties of the near-synonyms *worden* and *raken* and their acquisition. This small case study with PaQu forced us to modify our initial assumptions about the properties of these verbs.

We conclude that the functionality and interface of the PaQu application make it an effective and practical tool for supporting syntactic research of the Dutch language, and this claim is supported by the fact that PaQu has already been used in several research projects and for linking descriptions of grammatical constructions in the Taalportaal to corpus examples.

The development of PaQu was initiated independently of CLARIN with the Lassy Dependency Relations search application, though it was clearly inspired by the goal of CLARIN to make large, richly annotated corpora accessible and easily usable by linguists through dedicated interfaces. CLARIN-NL later ensured the continued existence of the Lassy Dependency Relations application, and requested extensions of its functionality, which resulted in PaQu. PaQu's development is being continued in the CLARIAH-CORE project, and some results of this work are already visible and can already be used, in particular analysis in terms of metadata and support for more input formats than just plain text, among them FoLiA (Van Gompel and Reynaert, 2013 and chapter 6) and TEI.

Acknowledgements

This work crucially uses data and/or tools made available through the CLARIN infrastructure. The work was financed by CLARIN-NL and CLARIAH-CORE, NWO projects in the Netherlands. We thank the anonymous reviewers for valuable comments on an earlier version of this chapter.

References

Augustinus, Liesbeth, Vincent Vandeghinste, and Frank Van Eynde (2012), Example-based tree-bank querying, *in* Calzolari, Nicoletta, Khalid Choukri, Thierry Declerck, Mehmet Uğur Doğan, Bente Maegaard, Joseph Mariani, Asunción Moreno, Jan Odijk, and Stelios Piperidis, editors, *Proceedings of the Eight International Conference on Language Resources and Evaluation (LREC 2012)*, European Language Resources Association (ELRA), Istanbul, Turkey.

Bloem, Jelke (2016), Evaluating automatically annotated treebanks for linguistic research, *in* Bański, Piotr, Marc Kupietz, Harald Lüngen, Andreas Witt, Adrien Barbaresi, Hanno Biber, Evelyn Breiteneder, and Simon Clematide, editors, *Proceedings of the 4th Workshop on Challenges in the Management of Large Corpora (CMLC 4)*, ELRA, Paris, pp. 8–14. http://www.lrec-conf.org/proceedings/lrec2016/workshops/LREC2016Workshop-CMLC_Proceedings.pdf.

Bouma, Gosse, Marjo van Koppen, Frank Landsbergen, Jan Odijk, Ton van der Wouden, and Matje van de Camp (2015), Enriching a descriptive grammar with treebank queries, *Proceedings of the Fourteenth International Workshop on Treebanks and Linguistic Theories (TLT14)*, Vol. 14, pp. 13–25. http://tlt14.ipipan.waw.pl/files/4614/5063/3858/TLT14_proceedings.pdf.

Bresnan, Joan, editor (1982), *The Mental Representation of Grammatical Relations*, MIT Press Series on Cognitive Theory and Mental Representation, The MIT Press, Cambridge, Massachusetts /London, England.

Broekhuis, Hans and Norbert Corver (2015), *Syntax of Dutch: Verbs and Verb Phrases*, Vol. II of *Comprehensive Grammar Resources*, Amsterdam University Press, Amsterdam. http://www.oapen.org/download?type=document&docid=555749.

Chomsky, Noam (1965), *Aspects of the Theory of Syntax*, MIT.

de Boer, Theo, editor (2007), *Groot Woordenboek Hedendaags Nederlands, digitale versie 6.10*, Van Dale, Utrecht.

Hajič, Jan and Eva Hajičová (1997), Syntactic tagging in the Prague Dependency Treebank, *in* Marcinkeviciene, R. and N. Volz, editors, *Proceedings of the Second European Seminar "Language Applications for a Multilingual Europe"*, TELRI, Kaunas, Lithuania, pp. 55–68.

Hoekstra, H., M. Moortgat, B. Renmans, M. Schouppe, I. Schuurman, and T. van der Wouden (2003), CGN syntactische annotatie, *CGN report*, Utrecht University, Utrecht, the Netherlands. http://lands.let.kun.nl/cgn/doc_Dutch/topics/version_1.0/annot/syntax/syn_prot.pdf.

Odijk, Jan (2011), User scenario search, internal CLARIN-NL document, http://www.clarin.nl/node/166. http://www.clarin.nl/sites/default/files/User%20scenario%20Serach%20110413.docx.

Odijk, Jan (2015a), Linguistic research with PaQu, *Computational Linguistics in the Netherlands Journal* 5, pp. 3–14. http://www.clinjournal.org/sites/clinjournal.org/files/odijk2015.pdf.

Odijk, Jan (2015b), Zoeken naar constructies, Presentation and demo held at the DRONGO Language Festival 2015, Utrecht.

Odijk, Jan (2016), A Use case for Linguistic Research on Dutch with CLARIN, *in* De Smedt, Koenraad, editor, *Selected Papers from the CLARIN Annual Conference 2015, October 14-16, 2015, Wrocław, Poland*, number 123 in *Linköping Electronic Conference Proceedings*, CLARIN, Linköping University Electronic Press, Linköping, Sweden, pp. 45–61. http://www.ep.liu.se/ecp/article.asp?issue=123&article=004.

Oostdijk, N., W. Goedertier, F. Van Eynde, L. Boves, J.P. Martens, M. Moortgat, and H. Baayen (2002), Experiences from the Spoken Dutch Corpus project, *in* González Rodriguez, M. and C. Paz Suárez Araujo, editors, *Proceedings of the third International Conference on Language Resources and Evaluation (LREC-2002)*, ELRA, Las Palmas, pp. 340–347.

Tjong Kim Sang, Erik, Gosse Bouma, and Gertjan van Noord (2010), LASSY for beginners, Presentation at CLIN 2010, Utrecht. http://ifarm.nl/erikt/talks/clin2010.pdf.

van der Beek, Leonoor, Gosse Bouma, and Gertjan van Noord (2002), Een brede computationele grammatica voor het Nederlands, *Nederlandse Taalkunde* 7, pp. 353–374.

van der Wouden, Ton, Gosse Bouma, Matje van de Camp, Marjo van Koppen, Frank Landsbergen, and Jan Odijk (2015), Enriching a grammatical database with intelligent links to linguistic resources, *in* De Smedt, Koenraad, editor, *Selected Papers from the CLARIN Annual Conference 2015*, Linköping Electronic Conference Proceedings, CLARIN, Linköping University Electronic Press, Linköping, Sweden, pp. 108–117. `http://www.ep.liu.se/ecp/article.asp?issue=123&article=009`.

van der Wouden, Ton, Jenny Audring, Hans Bennis, Frits Beukema, Geert Booij, Hans Broekhuis, Norbert Corver, Crit Cremers, Roderik Dernison, Marcel den Dikken, Siebren Dyk, Carlos Gussenhoven, Ger de Haan, Vincent van Heuven, Eric Hoekstra, Jarich Hoekstra, Bart Hoogeveen, Gerbrich de Jong, Evelien Keizer, Anna Kirstein, Björn Köhnlein, Frank Landsbergen, Kathrin Linke, Marc van Oostendorp, Nina Ouddeken, Koen Sebregts, Carole Tiberius, Arjen Versloot, Willem Visser, Riet Vos, Truus de Vries, and Joke Weening (2016), Het Taalportaal, *Nederlandse Taalkunde* **21** (1), pp. 157–168. `http://dx.doi.org/10.5117/NEDTAA2016.1.WOUD`.

van Gompel, Maarten and Martin Reynaert (2013), FoLiA: A practical XML format for linguistic annotation - a descriptive and comparative study, *Computational Linguistics in the Netherlands Journal* **3**, pp. 63–81. `http://www.clinjournal.org/sites/clinjournal.org/files/05-vanGompel-Reynaert-CLIN2013.pdf`.

van Noord, Gertjan and Jan Odijk (2016), Goed of fout? Wat gebruikt men feitelijk?, Presentation held at Grote Taaldag 2016, Utrecht.

van Noord, Gertjan, Gosse Bouma, Frank Van Eynde, Daniël de Kok, Jelmer van der Linde, Ineke Schuurman, Erik Tjong Kim Sang, and Vincent Vandeghinste (2013), Large scale syntactic annotation of written Dutch: Lassy, *in* Spyns, Peter and Jan Odijk, editors, *Essential Speech and Language Technology for Dutch*, Theory and Applications of Natural Language Processing, Springer Berlin Heidelberg, pp. 147–164. `http://dx.doi.org/10.1007/978-3-642-30910-6_9`. http://dx.doi.org/10.1007/978-3-642-30910-6_9.

van Noord, Gertjan, Ineke Schuurman, and Gosse Bouma (2011), Lassy syntactische annotatie (revision 19455), *Lassy report*, RU Groningen, Groningen. `https://www.let.rug.nl/vannoord/Lassy/sa-man_lassy.pdf`.

Appendix: List of Hyperlinks

(lemma='heel', rel='mod') in CGN `http://www.let.rug.nl/alfa/paqu/?db=cgn&word=%2Bheel&rel=mod&hword=&postag=&hpostag=&meta=&sn=10`

(lemma='heel', rel='mod', hpostag='adj') in CGN `http://www.let.rug.nl/alfa/paqu/?db=cgn&word=%2Bheel&rel=mod&hword=&postag=&hpostag=adj&meta=&sn=10`

(rel='predc', hlemma='raken') in LASSY-Small `http://www.let.rug.nl/alfa/paqu/?db=lassysmall&word=&rel=predc&hword=%2Braken&postag=&hpostag=&meta=&sn=10`

(rel='predc', hlemma='raken', postag='adj') in LASSY-Small `http://www.let.rug.nl/alfa/paqu/?db=lassysmall&word=&postag=adj&rel=predc&hword=%2braken&hpostag=&meta=`

(rel='predc', hlemma='raken', postag='mwu') in LASSY-Small `http://www.let.rug.nl/alfa/paqu/?db=lassysmall&word=&postag=mwu&rel=predc&hword=%2braken&hpostag=&meta=`

(rel='predc', hlemma='raken', postag='n') in LASSY-Small `http://www.let.rug.nl/alfa/paqu/?db=lassysmall&word=&postag=n&rel=predc&hword=%2braken&hpostag=&meta=`

(rel='predc', hlemma='raken', postag='vg') in LASSY-Small `http://www.let.rug.nl/alfa/paqu/?db=lassysmall&word=&postag=vg&rel=predc&hword=%2braken&hpostag=&meta=`

(rel='predc', hlemma='raken', postag='vz') in LASSY-Small `http://www.let.rug.nl/alfa/paqu/`
`?db=lassysmall&word=&postag=vz&rel=predc&hword=%2braken&hpostag=&meta=`
(rel='predc', hlemma='raken', postag='ww') in LASSY-Small `http://www.let.rug.nl/alfa/paqu/`
`?db=lassysmall&word=&postag=ww&rel=predc&hword=%2braken&hpostag=&meta=`
(rel='predc', hlemma='worden') in LASSY-Small `http://www.let.rug.nl/alfa/paqu/?db=`
`lassysmall&word=&rel=predc&hword=%2Bworden&postag=&hpostag=&meta=&sn=10`
(rel='predc', hlemma='worden', postag='adj') in LASSY-Small `http://www.let.rug.nl/alfa/`
`paqu/?db=lassysmall&word=&postag=adj&rel=predc&hword=%2bworden&hpostag=&meta=`
(rel='predc', hlemma='worden', postag='bw') in LASSY-Small `http://www.let.rug.nl/alfa/`
`paqu/?db=lassysmall&word=&postag=bw&rel=predc&hword=%2bworden&hpostag=&meta=`
(rel='predc', hlemma='worden', postag='mwu') in LASSY-Small `http://www.let.rug.nl/alfa/`
`paqu/?db=lassysmall&word=&postag=mwu&rel=predc&hword=%2bworden&hpostag=&meta=`
(rel='predc', hlemma='worden', postag='n') in LASSY-Small `http://www.let.rug.nl/alfa/paqu/`
`?db=lassysmall&word=&postag=n&rel=predc&hword=%2bworden&hpostag=&meta=`
(rel='predc', hlemma='worden', postag='spec') in LASSY-Small `http://www.let.rug.nl/alfa/`
`paqu/?db=lassysmall&word=&postag=spec&rel=predc&hword=%2bworden&hpostag=&meta=`
(rel='predc', hlemma='worden', postag='tw') in LASSY-Small `http://www.let.rug.nl/alfa/`
`paqu/?db=lassysmall&word=&postag=tw&rel=predc&hword=%2bworden&hpostag=&meta=`
(rel='predc', hlemma='worden', postag='vg') in LASSY-Small `http://www.let.rug.nl/alfa/`
`paqu/?db=lassysmall&word=&postag=vg&rel=predc&hword=%2bworden&hpostag=&meta=`
(rel='predc', hlemma='worden', postag='vnw') in LASSY-Small `http://www.let.rug.nl/alfa/`
`paqu/?db=lassysmall&word=&postag=vnw&rel=predc&hword=%2bworden&hpostag=&meta=`
(rel='predc', hlemma='worden', postag='vz') in LASSY-Small `http://www.let.rug.nl/alfa/`
`paqu/?db=lassysmall&word=&postag=vz&rel=predc&hword=%2bworden&hpostag=&meta=`
(rel='predc', hlemma='worden', postag='ww') in LASSY-Small `http://www.let.rug.nl/alfa/`
`paqu/?db=lassysmall&word=&postag=ww&rel=predc&hword=%2bworden&hpostag=&meta=`
(rel=su, hword='lopen') in LASSY-Small `http://www.let.rug.nl/alfa/paqu/?db=lassysmall&`
`word=&rel=su&hword=%2Blopen&postag=&hpostag=&meta=&sn=100`
(rel=su, hword='lopen') in LASSY-Small, sent. 10 `http://www.let.rug.nl/alfa/paqu/tree?db=`
`lassysmall&arch=0&file=4671&yl=0,1,2&gr=3&ms=5,2,3,6,4`
(rel=su, hword='lopen') in LASSY-Small, sent. 15) `http://www.let.rug.nl/alfa/paqu/tree?db=`
`lassysmall&arch=0&file=4815&yl=23&gr=31&ms=49,58`
(rel=su, hword='lopen') in LASSY-Small, sent. 16 `http://www.let.rug.nl/alfa/paqu/tree?db=`
`lassysmall&arch=0&file=4845&yl=1&gr=15&ms=19,30,4`
(rel=su, hword='lopen') in LASSY-Small, sent. 17 `http://www.let.rug.nl/alfa/paqu/tree?db=`
`lassysmall&arch=0&file=4868&yl=0&gr=13&ms=16,24`
(rel=su, hword='lopen') in LASSY-Small, sent. 21 `http://www.let.rug.nl/alfa/paqu/tree?db=`
`lassysmall&arch=0&file=5109&yl=23,24,25&gr=27&ms=41,45,47,42,43`
(rel=su, hword='lopen') in LASSY-Small, sent. 21 `http://www.let.rug.nl/alfa/paqu/tree?db=`
`lassysmall&arch=0&file=5109&yl=23,24,25&gr=27&ms=43,41,45,47,42`
(rel=su, hword='lopen') in LASSY-Small, sent. 22 `http://www.let.rug.nl/alfa/paqu/tree?db=`
`lassysmall&arch=0&file=5606&yl=2&gr=8&ms=19,7,12`
(rel=su, hword='lopen') in LASSY-Small, sent. 28 `http://www.let.rug.nl/alfa/paqu/tree?db=`
`lassysmall&arch=0&file=6506&yl=31&gr=37&ms=57,58`
(rel=su, hword='lopen') in LASSY-Small, sent. 32 `http://www.let.rug.nl/alfa/paqu/tree?db=`
`lassysmall&arch=0&file=7602&yl=6&gr=11&ms=6,15,20`
(rel=su, hword='lopen') in LASSY-Small, sent. 65 `http://www.let.rug.nl/alfa/paqu/tree?db=`
`lassysmall&arch=0&file=11901&yl=1,5,7&gr=10&ms=18,2,3,5,11,12,14`
(rel=su, hword='lopen') in LASSY-Small, sent. 90 `http://www.let.rug.nl/alfa/paqu/tree?db=`
`lassysmall&arch=0&file=15812&yl=3,5,7&gr=9&ms=14,10,15,6,7,11,12`

CHAPTER 24

Enriching a Scientific Grammar with Links to Linguistic Resources: The Taalportaal

Ton van der Wouden[a,f], Gosse Bouma[b], Matje van de Camp[c], Marjo van Koppen[d], Frank Landsbergen[e] and Jan Odijk[d]

[a]Meertens Instituut Amsterdam, [b]Groningen University, [c]Taalmonsters, [d]Utrecht University, [e]Institute for Dutch Lexicology INL.
[f]Corresponding Author: ton.van.der.wouden@meertens.knaw.nl

ABSTRACT

Scientific research within the humanities is different from what it was a few decades ago. For instance, new sources of information, such as digital grammars, lexical databases and large corpora of real-language data offer new opportunities for linguistics. The Taalportaal grammatical database, with its links to other linguistic resources via the CLARIN infrastructure, is a prime example of a new type of tool for linguistic research.

24.1   Introduction

This chapter focuses on the ways that the digital Taalportaal grammar is enriched with links to language corpora and other digital linguistic resources. We first give an introduction to the goals and architecture of the Taalportaal, a new type of online scientific grammar that covers the syntax, the morphology, as well as the phonology, of Dutch and Frisian, the two official languages of the Netherlands. In the second part, we elaborate on why and how the Taalportaal's grammatical information is enriched with links to corpora and other linguistic resources.

24.2   The Taalportaal

Language is everywhere. The working linguist is confronted with linguistic data any moment they read a newspaper, talk to their neighbour, watch television, or switch on the computer. To overcome the volatility of many of these data, digitised corpora have been compiled for languages all around the globe since the 1960s. These days, there is therefore no lack of natural language resources, at

How to cite this book chapter:
van der Wouden, T, Bouma, G, van de Camp, M, van Koppen, M, Landsbergen, F and Odijk, J. 2017. Enriching a Scientific Grammar with Links to Linguistic Resources: The Taalportaal. In: Odijk, J and van Hessen, A. (eds.) *CLARIN in the Low Countries*, Pp. 299–310. London: Ubiquity Press. DOI: https://doi.org/10.5334/bbi.24. License: CC-BY 4.0

least not for commonly studied languages like English and Dutch. Large corpora and databases of linguistic data are amply available, both in raw form and enriched with various types of annotation, and often free of charge or for a very modest fee.

There is no lack of linguistic descriptions either: linguistics is a very lively science area, producing tens of dissertations and thousands of scholarly articles in such a small country as the Netherlands alone. An enormous body of linguistic knowledge, however, is stored in paper form only: in grammars, dissertations and other publications, be they aimed at scholarly or lay audiences. The digitisation of linguistic knowledge is only beginning, and online grammatical knowledge is relatively scarce in comparison with all the treasures that are hidden in the bookshelves of libraries and studies.

Of course, there are notable exceptions. One such exception is the Taalportaal (Language Portal) project, an online portal containing a comprehensive and fully searchable digitised reference grammar, i.e. an electronic reference of Dutch and Frisian phonology, morphology and syntax. Information about the Afrikaans language is currently being added as well. With English as its meta-language, the Taalportaal aims at serving the international scientific community by organising, integrating and completing the grammatical knowledge of the Dutch and Frisian languages, as well as of Afrikaans.

The Taalportaal (www.taalportaal.org) is a collaboration project of the Meertens Institute, the Fryske Akademy, the Institute of Dutch Lexicology and Leiden University, funded, to a large extent, by the Netherlands Organisation for Scientific Research (NWO). The project is aimed at the development of a comprehensive and authoritative scientific grammar for Dutch and Frisian in the form of a virtual language institute (cf. Landsbergen et al., 2014).

The Taalportaal is built around an interactive knowledge base of the current grammatical knowledge of Dutch and Frisian. Its prime intended audience is the international scientific community, which is why English is chosen as the language used to describe the language facts. The Taalportaal aims to provide an exhaustive collection of the currently known data relevant for grammatical research, as well as an overview of the currently established insights about these data. This is an important step forward compared to presenting the same material in the traditional form of (paper) handbooks. For example, the three sub-disciplines of syntax, morphology and phonology are often traditionally studied in isolation, but, by presenting the results of these sub-disciplines on a single digital platform and internally linking these results, the Taalportaal contributes to the integration of the results reached within these disciplines.

This can be illustrated by means of a simple example concerning diminutive formation in Dutch. At first sight, this may look like a strictly morphological phenomenon, but upon closer inspection there are certainly also phonological and syntactic aspects to it. For example, the form of the diminutive morpheme depends on the phonological structure of the preceding noun: *hond-je* 'dog.dim', *kam-metje* 'comb.dim', *konin-kje* 'king.dim', etc. There is also a syntactic effect of diminutive formation in that it changes the gender of the input noun; diminutives are all neuter and thus select the definite singular article *het* 'the' (cf. *de hond* 'the dog' versus *het hondje* 'the dog.dim') and may also trigger different forms of agreement (cf. *een oude hond* 'an old dog' versus *een oud hondje* 'an old dog.dim'). Semantically, many morphological diminutives carry a (positive or negative) emotional load. Thus, the usage possibilities of *hondje* '(cute) doggy' are different from those of *kleine hond* 'small dog'. The Taalportaal makes visible these and less obvious cases of grammatical phenomena that are not restricted to one of the traditional sub-disciplines, to the benefit of each of the three disciplines and thus to the study of grammar in general.

The Netherlands are not the only country considering a linguistic knowledge base like the Taalportaal. Recently, South Africa has started building a virtual language institute called VivA (http://viva-afrikaans.org/) that aims at developing a digital infrastructure for the Afrikaans language. Among its goals are the study and description of Afrikaans, as well as the development of tools and resources for written and spoken Afrikaans, including digital dictionaries and corpora; language advice is also supplied. The cornerstone of the VivA portal is a comprehensive grammar of Afrikaans, which is inspired by and based on the Taalportaal architecture, and is currently being added to the Taalportaal infrastructure.

As of January 2016, the first release of the Taalportaal is online. Figure 24.1 below shows an instance of the portal's opening screen.

Technically, the Taalportaal is built as a number of XML files, organised as DITA-topics.[1] It is freely accessible via the Internet via any standard internet browser. The organisation and structure of much of the linguistic information is reminiscent of, and to a certain extent inspired by, Wikipedia and comparable online information sources. An important difference, however, is that Wikipedia's democratic (anarchistic) model is avoided by restricting the right to edit the Taalportaal information to authorised experts.

Figure 24.2 shows a small, introductory fragment of the portal concerning Dutch phonology:[2]

Figure 24.1: the opening page of the taalportaal site.

---

[1] DITA, the Darwin Information Typing Architecture, is an XML data model for authoring and publishing. According to https://en.wikipedia.org/wiki/Darwin_Information_Typing_Architecture (as of 17 June 2016), 'the name derives from the following components:

Darwin: it uses the principles of specialization and inheritance, which is in some ways analogous to the naturalist Charles Darwin's concept of evolutionary adaptation,

Information typing, which means each topic has a defined primary objective (procedure, glossary entry, troubleshooting information) and structure,

Architecture: DITA is an extensible set of structures'.

[2] A-class vowels are known as 'long vowels' or 'tense vowels' in other frameworks; cf. http://www.taalportaal.org/taalportaal/topic/pid/topic-13998813314542255#a_vowel.

The rounded high front-central vowel /y/

The rounded, high, front-central A-CLASS VOWEL /y/ is found in words such as:

Example 1

a. nu /ny/ 'now'

b. humor /hy.mɔr/ [ˈhymɔr] 'comedy, humour'

c. bruto /bry.to/ [ˈbryto] 'gross amount, bruto'

d. puur /pyr/ 'pure'

e. kostuum /kɔs.tym/ [kɔsˈtym] 'suit, dress'

It is spelled with a single letter <u> in open syllables (see (1a)-(1c)); this letter is doubled (<uu>) in closed syllables (see (1d)-(1e)).

Figure 1 (cf. Gussenhoven 1992) depicts the (Dutch) vowel's position within the vowel chart.

Figure 1

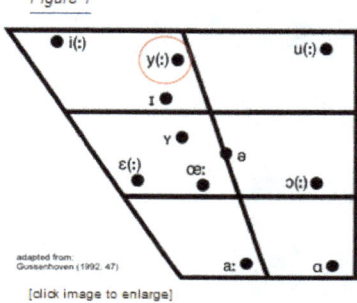

[click image to enlarge]

Articulation

/y/ is a rounded, high, front-central, A-class vowel. The tongue body is fronted, the tongue tip is down. Articulation is like that of /i/ except with rounded lips: the front cavity is enlarged because of pursing of the lips (Collins and Mees 2003; Eijkman 1937).

Figure 24.2: Dutch phonology example.

Among other things, the information about the vowels contains data about their distribution, phonetic details, and links to sound files exemplifying the realisation of the sound in several positions within the word. This is illustrated in figure 24.3:

The Taalportaal grammars were not built from scratch. One of their main components is an online version of the *Syntax of Dutch* (*SoD*; Broekhuis et al., 2012–2016), a descriptive grammar that goes well beyond the level of detail provided by other sources, including reference grammars. Although the *SoD* grammar is descriptive in nature, the emphasis in the selection and presentation of the phenomena discussed is clearly guided by discussions in the (generative) theoretical literature (Broekhuis, 2013; Hoeksema, 2013; Bouma et al., 2015); by implication, the same holds for the Taalportaal's treatment of Dutch syntax. For Dutch morphology, the Taalportaal has been built, among many other sources, upon the first volume of Haeseryn et al. (1997), as well as on morphological handbooks such as those of De Haas and Trommelen (1993), Booij (2002) and Smessaert (2013). The parts on Dutch phonology are indebted to Booij (1995) and Kooij and van Oostendorp (2003). For Frisian there was no lack of studies that could be profited from either, for instance Visser (1997), Hoekstra (1998), Tiersma (1999), Popkema (2006), and De Haan et al. (2010).

Table 3: Soundfiles, waveforms and spectrograms of the above sound files, with indications of the relevant acoustic parameters of Northern Standard Dutch /y/

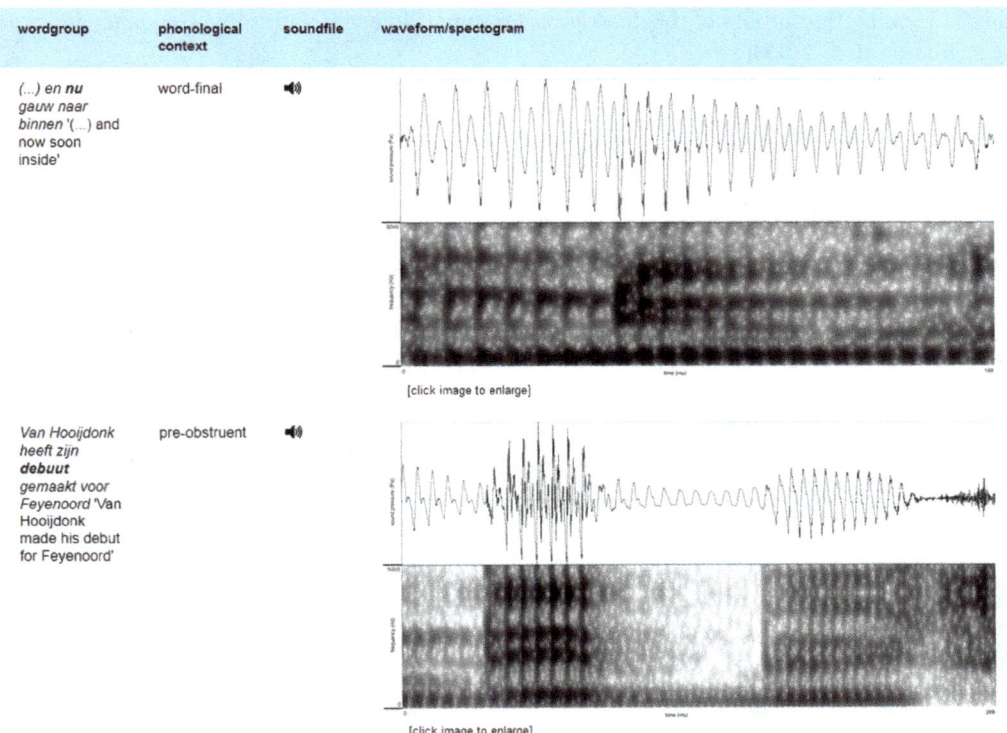

wordgroup	phonological context	soundfile	waveform/spectogram
*(...) en **nu** gauw naar binnen* '(...) and now soon inside'	word-final	🔊	[click image to enlarge]
*Van Hooijdonk heeft zijn **debuut** gemaakt voor Feyenoord* 'Van Hooijdonk made his debut for Feyenoord'	pre-obstruent	🔊	[click image to enlarge]

Figure 24.3: Dutch phonetics example.

As an internet grammar portal, the Taalportaal is somewhat comparable to the grammis portal of the German Language Institute (IDS; http://hypermedia.ids-mannheim.de/call/public/sysgram.ansicht). grammis, however, covers only one language (German) and is not aimed at the international scientific community but primarily at a German audience. These differences explain both the choice of the metalanguage (English for Taalportaal, German for grammis) and the differences in depth of analysis. grammis moreover is far less connected to other data sources than Taalportaal.

Besides the grammar modules, the Taalportaal contains an extensive ontology of linguistic terms (recently recast in the CLARIN Concept Registry; cf. Schuurman, 2015) and a large bibliography. Many of the words and phrases in the texts are marked: they can be clicked on, which results in sounds being played, definitions popping up and/or related topics being opened, a feature that will be elaborated upon in the following sections.

24.3   Enriching the Taalportaal

It is becoming more and more common for 21st-century linguists to want to check whether and to what extent the linguistic facts as they are presented in the linguistics literature correspond to the linguistic reality. In this context, '[c]reating a link between a descriptive grammar and a syntactically annotated corpus can be valuable for various reasons. Illustrating a given construction with corpus examples may help to get a better understanding of the variation of the construction and the frequency of these variants. Corpus data may also convince a reader that a given variant actually occurs in (well-formed) text, or in some cases may illustrate that examples judged un-grammatical by the authors of the descriptive grammar do occur with some frequency in actual text' (Bouma et al., 2015).

Searching for realistic language data becomes easier by the day, thanks to joint efforts such as CLARIN (www.clarin.eu) that seek to enhance the scientific research infrastructure by, among many other things, linking and making available large existing corpora and other linguistic resources under a single user licence.

The (syntactically annotated part of the) Spoken Dutch Corpus (manually verified, speech from various situations, 1M words; Oostdijk, 2000; van der Wouden et al., 2003), the Lassy Small treebank (manually verified, written material from various genres, 1M words, 65,200 sentences) and the Lassy Large treebank (automatically created, written material from various genres, 700M words, 8.6M sentences; van Noord et al., 2013) are all suitable corpora for this kind of applica-tion. The first two resources provide high-quality data for a limited amount of text, while the last resource provides wide-coverage, but noisy, data. All treebanks follow (with minor modifications) the same annotation standard (Van Eynde, 2003 for lemmatisation and POS tagging; Schuurman et al., 2003 for syntax), which has become a *de facto* standard for Dutch corpus annotation, allowing for the re-use of the queries on these new data.

Taalportaal has been enriched with a range of queries that search for relevant constructions in these corpora. Queries are linked to:

• Linguistic examples;
• Linguistic terms; or
• Names or descriptions of constructions.

The queries are embedded in the Taalportaal texts as standard hyperlinks. Clicking these links brings the user to a corpus query interface where the specified query is executed – or, if it can be foreseen that the execution of a query takes a lot of time, the link may also connect to an internet page containing the stored result of the query.

Syntactic annotations are a complex type of data, usually formally encoded in accordance with a well-defined schema in XML at present. Sometimes these syntactically annotated corpora come with a search interface, but to search these complex data efficiently and optimally, one needs a command of an XML search language such as XPath.[3] Many researchers in linguistics lack these skills. Although the basics of the XPath language are not difficult, interesting queries often become very complex. Moreover, one has to know every particular detail of the encoding of constructions in a particular treebank.

24.3.1   Automatic Links

Many of the links have been generated automatically: all examples in the Taalportaal can be clicked on, which will open a 'pop-up' window like the one in figure 24.4:

By clicking the links, the example sentence *Jan is niet boos (over die opmerking)* can be searched in a number of resources, as is illustrated in the screen dump above: in this case the choices are Google, DBNL, GrETEL, CHN, OpenSoNar, and TaalPortaal. Suppose we choose the third option, the GrETEL web application (http://portal.clarin.nl/node/1967; cf. Augustinus et al., 2013 and chapter 22 in this volume); we can then search for linguistic structures in the most user-friendly

---

[3]   Cf. https://en.wikipedia.org/wiki/XPath.

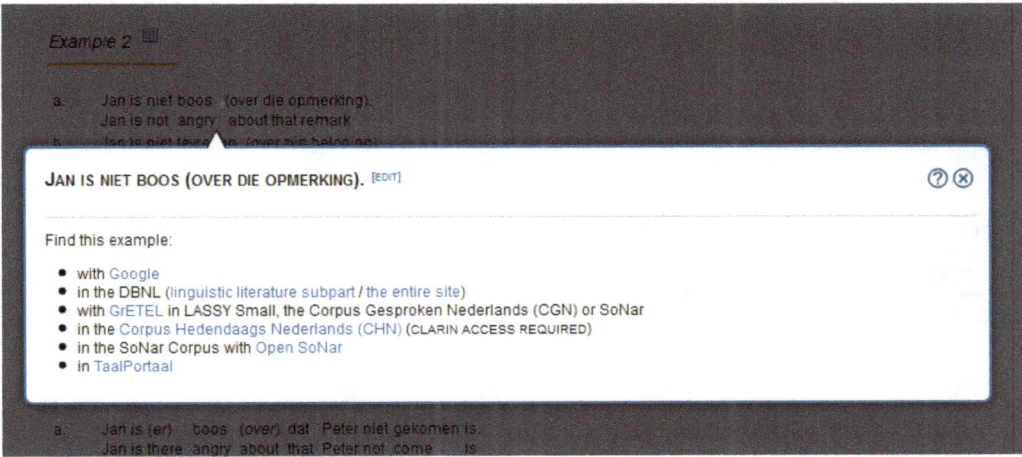

Figure 24.4: Taalportaal pop-up example.

Step 2: Input Parse

The structure of the **tagged** [?] and **parsed** [?] sentence: *Jan is niet boos (over die opmerking)*

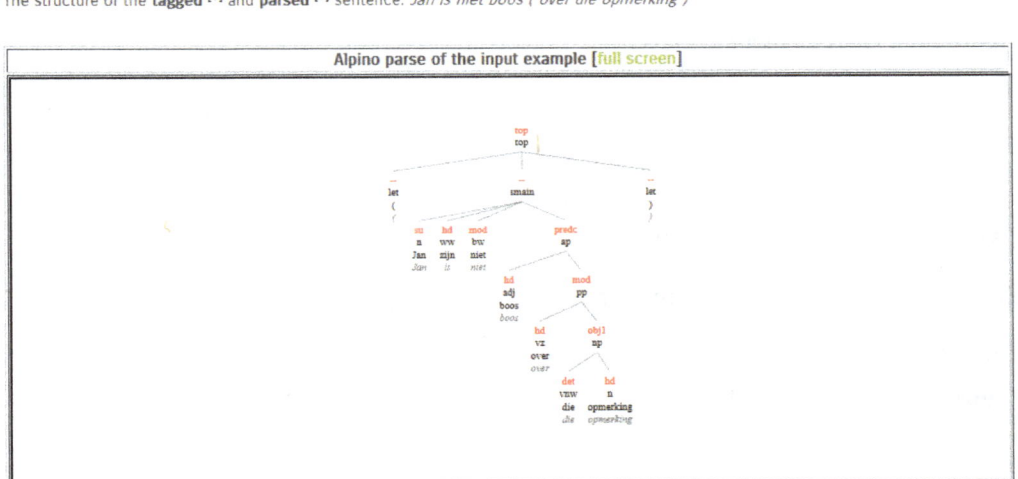

Figure 24.5: Taalportaal syntactic analysis example.

way – that is, without having to learn a corpus query language – in a number of large annotated corpora of Dutch (cf. Augustinus et al., 2012). The sentence is parsed using the Alpino parser (cf. van Noord, 2006). The resulting parse is shown in figure 24.5.

The query can be edited via a menu, for example by replacing specific lexical items by syntactic categories, as illustrated in figure 24.6:

If the user has made their choices, the structure can be searched for. Part of the result is given in figure 24.7:

The example sentences show copula sentences with an adjective that has a prepositional comple-ment: *Peking is niet tevreden met zijn groeiende economische macht* 'Beijing is not satisfied with its growing economic power' and *Rotterdam is ook bezig met zo'n plan* 'Rotterdam is busy with such a plan as well'.

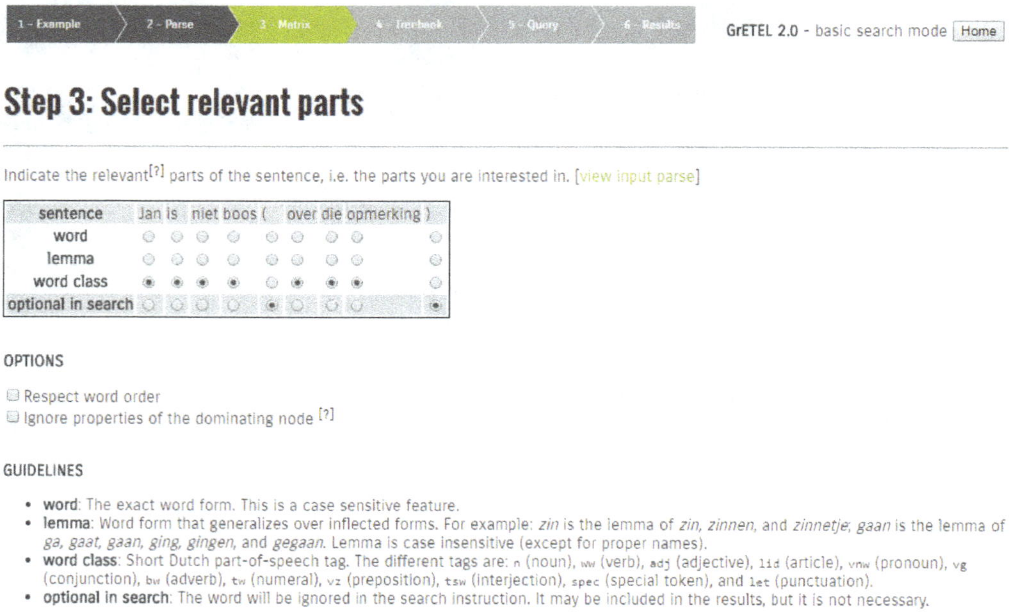

| 1 - Example | 2 - Parse | 3 - Matrix | 4 - Treebank | 5 - Query | 6 - Results | GrETEL 2.0 - basic search mode Home |

Step 3: Select relevant parts

Indicate the relevant[?] parts of the sentence, i.e. the parts you are interested in. [view input parse]

sentence	Jan is niet boos (over die opmerking)
word	⊙ ⊙ ⊙ ⊙ ⊙ ⊙ ⊙ ⊙ ⊙
lemma	⊙ ⊙ ⊙ ⊙ ⊙ ⊙ ⊙ ⊙ ⊙
word class	● ● ● ● ⊙ ● ● ● ⊙
optional in search	⊙ ⊙ ⊙ ⊙ ● ⊙ ⊙ ⊙ ●

OPTIONS

☐ Respect word order
☐ Ignore properties of the dominating node [?]

GUIDELINES

- **word**: The exact word form. This is a case sensitive feature.
- **lemma**: Word form that generalizes over inflected forms. For example: *zin* is the lemma of *zin, zinnen,* and *zinnetje; gaan* is the lemma of *ga, gaat, gaan, ging, gingen,* and *gegaan.* Lemma is case insensitive (except for proper names).
- **word class**: Short Dutch part-of-speech tag. The different tags are: n (noun), ww (verb), adj (adjective), lid (article), vnw (pronoun), vg (conjunction), bw (adverb), tw (numeral), vz (preposition), tsw (interjection), spec (special token), and let (punctuation).
- **optional in search**: The word will be ignored in the search instruction. It may be included in the results, but it is not necessary.

Figure 24.6: GrETEL input example.

dpc-ind-001645-nl-sen.p.35.s.1	**Peking is niet tevreden met zijn groeiende economische macht** , maar wil ook politieke en diplomatieke invloed verwerven in Azië .
WS-U-E-A-0000000216.p.11.s.10	**Rotterdam is ook bezig met zo'n plan** .

Figure 24.7: GrETEL output example.

2.1. Prepositional complements

The examples in (2) show that complements of adjectives are normally PPs, which are often optional.

Figure 24.8: Taalportaal PP example.

24.3.2   *Manually Prepared Queries*

Whereas it is relatively easy to automatically translate example words or sentences into corpus queries, this usually does not hold for grammatical descriptions meant for human readers. Still, these readers might be interested to check the grammarian's claims in corpus data.

CLARIN-NL made it possible to enrich Taalportaal fragments, most of them dealing with Dutch syntax, with more sophisticated queries in annotated corpora (cf. Bouma et al., 2015).

The translation of a linguistic example, a linguistic term, or a name or description of a construction is not a task that is easy or that even has deterministic results that could be implemented in an algorithm (cf. Bouma et al., 2015). Therefore, the queries were formulated by experts, who got selections of the Taalportaal texts to read, interpret, and enrich with queries where appropriate. The queries were amply annotated with explanations concerning the choices made in translating the grammatical term or description or linguistic example into the corpus query. When necessary, warnings about possible false hits, etc., were added as well. The results were checked by senior linguists. Consider the small section from Dutch syntax depicted in figure 24.8:

1. Met cd-rom voor Windows en Mac , 15.000 Nederlandse trefwoorden afkomstig uit andere talen , 684 blz. , EUR 55 ; ISBN 90-6648-0270 . ✣
2. Zo is het woord japon bijvoorbeeld afkomstig uit Japan , werd het woord sauna geleend van de Finnen en is bazaar een woord dat uit het Perzisch komt . ✣
3. De cd-rom maakt gebruik van standaardbrowsertechniek en is daardoor geschikt voor zowel Windows als Mac . ✣

Figure 24.9: first Lassy output example.

1. Maar hoe dat precies komt is niet zo duidelijk . ✣
2. In het Frans zijn buitenlandse woorden officieel niet welkom en op IJsland wordt voor elk nieuw begrip een IJslands woord bedacht . ✣
3. Hij studeerde medicijnen en filosofie aan de Universiteit van Leiden (1685 - 1690) en emigreerde vervolgens naar Engeland , waar hij als arts werkzaam was en een aantal politieke en geschriften in het Engels vervaardigde . ✣

Figure 24.10: second Lassy output example.

The result of the annotation process is as follows:

QUERY/QUERIES:

DESCRIPTION:
Adjectives with a prepositional complement (**@rel="pc"**) as sister.

XPATH:
```
//node[@rel="hd" and @pt="adj" and ../node[@rel="pc" and @cat="pp"]]
```

Show results of this query in lassysmall with PaQu

DESCRIPTION:
Modified adjectives without a PP-complement.

XPATH:
```
//node[@rel="predc" and @cat="ap" and node[@rel="mod"] and node[@rel="hd" and @pt="adj"] and not(node[@cat="pp"])]
```

Show results of this query in lassysmall with PaQu

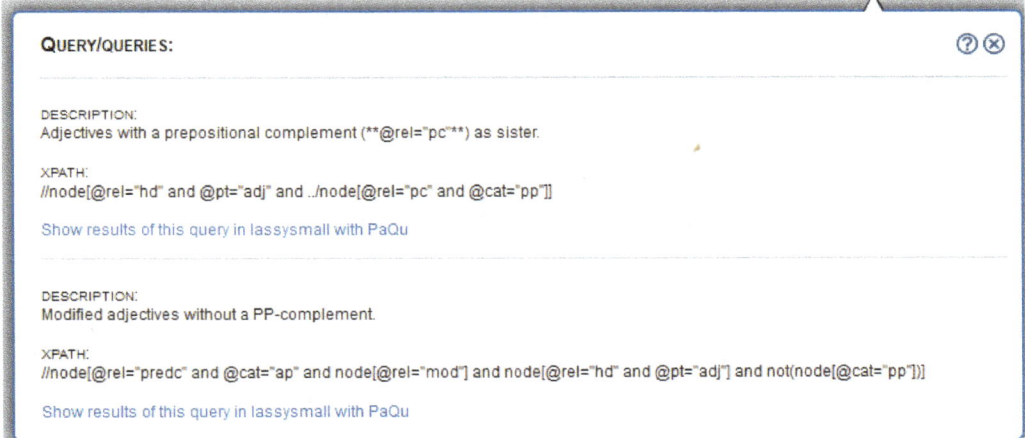

Figure 24.11: result of the annotation process.

The sentence about adjectives has been translated into two, radically different queries: the first one searches for adjectives with a prepositional complement as sister, the second one for predicatively used modified adjectives without a PP-complement or any kind of modifier. Clicking the (blue) link 'Show results of this query in lassysmall with PaQu' will open a new browser window to the PaQu interface (`http://portal.clarin.nl/node/4182`; cf. Odijk, 2015). The first query results in a number of hits from the Lassy Small corpus; the first ones are given in figure 24.9:

We twice see the adjective *afkomstig* 'originating' followed by a prepositional phrase headed by *uit* 'from', and once the adjective *geschikt* suitable with a prepositional phrase with *voor* 'for'.

The second query results in the sentences, among many others, given in figure 24.10:

Here we see the three adjectives *duidelijk* 'clear', *welkom* 'welcome', and *werkzaam* 'active', modified with *niet zo* 'not so', *niet* 'not', and *als arts* 'as a doctor', respectively.

If the user clicks the small plus ign following the result sentence, a parse tree is shown. (PaQu offers corpus statistics as well, but that is beyond the scope of this chapter.)

As the corpora dealt with so far offer little or no morphological or phonological annotation, they cannot be used for the formulation of queries to accompany the Taalportaal texts on morphology and phonology. There is, however, a linguistic resource that is in principle extremely useful for precisely these types of queries, namely the CELEX lexical database (cf. Baayen et al., 1995), which offers morphological and phonological analyses for more than 100,000 Dutch lexical items. This database is currently being transferred from the Nijmegen Max Planck Institute for Psycholinguistics (MPI) to the Leiden Institute for Dutch Lexicology (INL). It has its own query language, which implies that Taalportaal queries that address CELEX have to have another format – but again, the Taalportaal user will not be bothered with the small details.

As was mentioned above, the Frisian language – the other official language of the Netherlands, with Dutch – is described in the Taalportaal as well, in parallel to Dutch. Although there is no lack of digital linguistic resources for Frisian, internet accessibility of these resources is lagging behind. This makes it difficult at this point to enrich the Frisian parts of the Taalportaal with queries. It is to be hoped that this CLARIN project will stimulate further efforts to integrate Frisian language data in the research infrastructure.

24.4   Concluding Remarks

In the first part of this chapter, we have introduced the Taalportaal grammar portal, a digital scientific grammar of Frisian and Dutch, covering the syntax, morphology and phonology of the two official languages of the Netherlands. In the second part of the chapter, we focused on the dynamic links from the grammatical descriptions to other linguistic resources of various sorts – something that is of course impossible in traditional paper grammars. By this extension, the Taalportaal functions as a hub within the scientific infrastructure supplied by CLARIN. This is relevant for the Taalportaal users in at least two ways:

- it increases the value of the Taalportaal as a research tool; and
- it lowers the threshold to use the linguistic resources involved.

The Taalportaal's open architecture allows for extension with new languages (Afrikaans is well under way), but also with new language varieties (dialectal data, historical data, etc.). Moreover, the CLARIN network allows for extension with links to new and so far largely unexplored linguistic resources, such as the huge digital dictionaries of the INL and semantically organised lexical databases such as Open Dutch WordNet (http://wordpress.let.vupr.nl/odwn/; cf. Postma et al., 2016), which may make linguists' practical work even easier and, at the same time, even more exciting.

It is to be foreseen that future corpora of Dutch (and hopefully of Frisian as well) will be embedded in the very same CLARIN infrastructure, using the same architecture, the same type of interface, and the same kind of linguistic annotation.

Acknowledgements

The Taalportaal project was a joint effort of the Meertens Institute, the Fryske Akademy, the Institute of Dutch Lexicology, and Leiden University. It was made possible by a grant from the Netherlands Organisation for Scientific Research (NWO Grant 175.010.2009.003).

Parts of the Taalportaal were enriched with queries to corpora in a separate project, CLARIN TPC, which was a collaboration of the Meertens Institute, the Institute of Dutch Lexicology, the Universities of Groningen and Utrecht, and De Taalmonsters. CLARIN TPC was made possible by a grant from CLARIN-NL (CLARIN-NL-15-001).

Previous Publications

Earlier publications that cover parts of the Taalportaal project or linguistic resources mentioned in this chapter are the following: Landsbergen et al. (2014), Bouma et al. (2015), and Van der Wouden et al. (2015, 2016).

References

Augustinus, Liesbeth, Vincent Vandeghinste, & Frank Van Eynde (2012). Example-Based Tree-bank Querying. In: *Proceedings of the 8th International Conference on Language Resources and Evaluation (LREC-2012)*. Istanbul, Turkey: European Language Resources Association (ELRA), 3161–3167.

Augustinus, Liesbeth, Vincent Vandeghinste, Ineke Schuurman, & Frank Van Eynde (2013). Example-Based Treebank Querying with GrETEL – now also for Spoken Dutch. *In: Proceedings of the 19th Nordic Conference of Computational Linguistics (NODALIDA 2013)*. NEALT Proceedings Series 16. Oslo, Norway. 423–428.

Baayen, R. Harald, Richard Piepenbrock, & L. Gulikers (1995). *The CELEX Lexical Database* (CD-ROM). Philadelphia, PA: Linguistic Data Consortium, University of Pennsylvania.

Booij, Geert (1995). *The Phonology of Dutch*. Oxford: Oxford University Press.

Booij, Geert (2002). *The Morphology of Dutch*. Oxford: Oxford University Press.

Bouma, Gosse, Marjo van Koppen, Frank Landsbergen, Jan Odijk, Ton van der Wouden, & Matje van de Camp (2015). Enriching a Descriptive Grammar with Treebank Queries. In Markus Dickinson, Erhard Hinrichs, Agnieszka Patejuk and Adam Przepiórkowski (eds.), *Proceedings of the Fourteenth International Workshop on Treebanks and Linguistic Theories (TLT14)*. Warsaw: Institute of Computer Science, Polish Academy of Sciences, 13–25.

Broekhuis, Hans (2013). De Syntax of Dutch: nieuw gereedschap voor de internationale neerlandistiek. *Internationale Neerlandistiek*, 51, 3, 243–260.

Broekhuis, Hans, Norbert Corver, Marcel den Dikken, Evelien Keizer, & Riet Vos (2012–16). *Syntax of Dutch*. Amsterdam: Amsterdam University Press (7 volumes).

Van Eynde, Frank (2003). Part of speech tagging en lemmatisering van het Corpus Gesproken Nederlands. Centrum voor Computerlinguïstiek K.U.Leuven.

de Haan, Germen, Jarich Hoekstra, Willem Visser, & Goffe Jensma (red.) (2010). *Studies in West Frisian Grammar: Selected Papers by Germen J. de Haan*. Amsterdam: John Benjamins Publishing Company.

de Haas, Wim, & Mieke Trommelen (1993). *Morfologisch Handboek van het Nederlands*. Den Haag: SDU uitgeverij.

Haeseryn, Walter, Kirsten Romijn, Guido Geerts, Jaap de Rooij, & Maarten C. van den Toorn (1997). *Algemene Nederlandse Spraakkunst*, 2e, geheel herz. dr. Groningen en Deurne: Martinus Nijhoff and Wolters Plantijn.

Hoeksema, Jack (2013). Review of: Syntax of Dutch. Noun and Noun Phrases vols. 1 and 2. *Lingua*, 133, 385–390.

Hoekstra, Jarich (1998). *Fryske Wurdfoarming*. Ljouwert: Fryske Akademy.

Kooij, Jan, & Marc van Oostendorp (2003). *Fonologie, uitnodiging tot de klankleer van het Nederlands*. Amsterdam: University Press.

Landsbergen, Frank, Carole Tiberius, & Roderik Dernison (2014). Taalportaal: an online grammar of Dutch and Frisian. *Proceedings of the Ninth International Conference on Language Resources and Evaluation (LREC '14)*. Reykjavik, Iceland: European Language Resources Association (ELRA), 2206–2210.

van Noord, Gertjan (2006). At Last Parsing Is Now Operational. In Piet Mertens, Cedrick Fairon, Anne Dister, and Patrick Watrin, editors: *TALN06. Verbum Ex Machina. Actes de la 13e conference sur le traitement automatique des langues naturelles*, 20–42.

van Noord, Gertjan, Gosse Bouma, Frank van Eynde, Daniel de Kok, Jelmer van der Linde, Ineke Schuurman, Erik Tjong Kim Sang, & Vincent Vandeghinste (2013). Large scale syntactic annotation of written Dutch: Lassy. In Peter Spyns and Jan Odijk (red.), *Essential Speech and Language Technology for Dutch: the STEVIN Programme*, Springer, 147–164.

Odijk, Jan (2015). Linguistic Research with PaQU. *Computational Linguistics in The Netherlands journal* 5, 3–14.

Oostdijk, Nelleke (2000). The Spoken Dutch Corpus: Overview and first evaluation. In *Proceedings of LREC 2000*, 887–894.

Popkema, Jan (2006). *Grammatica Fries: de regels van het Fries*. Utrecht: Prisma.

Postma, Marten, Emiel van Miltenburg, Roxane Segers, Anneleen Schoen, & Piek Vossen (2016): Open Dutch WordNet. In *Proceedings of the Eight Global Wordnet Conference*, Bucharest, Romania.

Schuurman, Ineke, Machteld Schouppe, Heleen Hoekstra, & Ton van der Wouden (2003). CGN, an annotated corpus of spoken Dutch. In Anne Abeillé, Silvia Hansen-Schirra, and Hans Uszkoreit (eds.): *Proceedings of 4th International Workshop on Language Resources and Evaluation*, Budapest: European Language Resources Association (ELRA), 340–347.

Schuurman, Ineke (2015). Concept revival: from ISOcat to CLARIN Concept Registry. *CLARIN News* 7 January 2015 https://www.clarin.eu/news/concept-revival-isocat-clarin-concept-registry.

Smessaert, Hans (2013). *Basisbegrippen morfologie*. Leuven/Den Haag: ACCO.

Tiersma, Piter Meijes (1999). *Frisian Reference Grammar*, 2e ed. Ljouwert: Fryske Akademy.

Visser, Willem (1997). *The Syllable in Frisian*. Dissertation Vrije Universiteit Amsterdam (Holland Academic Graphics).

van der Wouden, Ton, Ineke Schuurman, Machteld Schouppe, & Heleen Hoekstra (2003). Harvesting Dutch trees: Syntactic properties of spoken Dutch. In Tanja Gaustad (ed.): *Computational Linguistics in the Netherlands 2002. Selected Papers from the Thirteenth CLIN Meeting*. Amsterdam/New York: Rodopi, 129–141.

van der Wouden, Ton, Gosse Bouma, Matje van de Kamp, Marjo van Koppen, Frank Landsbergen, & Jan Odijk (2015). Enriching a grammatical database with intelligent links to linguistic resources. In Koenraad De Smedt (ed.): *Selected Papers from the CLARIN Annual Conference 2015, October 14–16, 2015, Wroclaw, Poland*. Linköping University Electronic Press, Linköpings Universitet.

van der Wouden, Ton, Jenny Audring, Hans Bennis, Frits Beukema, Geert Booij, Hans Broekhuis, Norbert Corver, Crit Cremers, Roderik Dernison, Marcel den Dikken, Siebren Dyk, Carlos Gussenhoven, Ger de Haan, Vincent van Heuven, Eric Hoekstra, Jarich Hoekstra, Bart Hoogeveen, Gerbrich de Jong, Evelien Keizer, Anna Kirstein, Björn Köhnlein, Frank Landsbergen, Kathrin Linke, Marc van Oostendorp, Nina Ouddeken, Koen Sebregts, Carole Tiberius, Arjen Versloot, Willem Visser, Riet Vos, Truus de Vries, & Joke Weening (2016). Het Taalportaal: Een nieuwe wetenschappelijke grammatica voor het Nederlands en het Fries (en het Afrikaans). *Nederlandse Taalkunde* 21, 1 2016, 157–168.

PART IV

Infrastructure for Other Humanities Disciplines

CHAPTER 25

Infrastructure for Other Humanities Disciplines: Introduction

Jan Odijk and Arjan van Hessen

UiL-OTS, Utrecht University, j.odijk@uu.nl, a.j.vanhessen@uu.nl

25.1 Introduction

Though CLARIN originated in the linguistics and computational linguistics communities, CLARIN-LC (in particular CLARIN-NL) covers a lot of other Humanities disciplines. This is in part due to the bottom-up approach for subprojects for data curation and software demonstrators, and in part to the active policy to include these other disciplines, implemented with an interactive user survey and active 'evangelising' among researchers of all Humanities disciplines.

We will first provide a brief overall overview of the relevant data and software that resulted from CLARIN-LC (section 25.2), and then summarise the topics of the chapters of this part (section 25.3).

25.2 Work on Other Humanities Disciplines

Subdisciplines from the Humanities other than linguistics that were covered in CLARIN-LC include historical research, literary research, religion research, media research, social research, and philosophy:

Historical research The INTER-VIEWS application enables search in the IPNV interviews with war veterans, in part data curated in the INTER-VIEWS project. The WIP application enables search in parliamentary debates. WAHSP / BILAND[1] enables search in textual data of news media from the period 1863-1940 of the *Koninklijke Bibliotheek* and *Staatsbibliothek*

---

[1] These applications have in the meantime been superseded by Texcavator.

How to cite this book chapter:

Odijk, J and van Hessen, A. 2017. Infrastructure for Other Humanities Disciplines: Introduction. In: Odijk, J and van Hessen, A. (eds.) *CLARIN in the Low Countries*, Pp. 313–316. London: Ubiquity Press. DOI: https://doi.org/10.5334/bbi.25. License: CC-BY 4.0

zu Berlin (see chapter 27). The VK application enables search in the collected works of Loe de Jong on the Netherlands in the Second World War (VK data). The ePistolarium application enables search in a corpus of 20,000 letters of scholars who lived in the 17th-century Dutch Republic (see chapter 26). The RemBench application enables searching and browsing for works of art, artists, primary sources and library sources related to Rembrandt (Rembench data, see chapter 28). DSS provides a tool chain and methodology for converting legacy datasets in the area of maritime history and a search application that enables search in maritime history, in particular in datasets related to recruitment and shipping in the East-India trade and in the shipping of the northern provinces of the Netherlands (DSS data). Nederlab, which is still under development, enables searching and analysing data from digitised texts spanning the full recorded history of the Netherlands, its language and culture. The Dutch Song Database (DSD) integrates four different datasets into a single database. It contains (meta-)data on 140,000 songs and their 15,000 sources (songbooks, pamphlets, field recordings, etc.) from the Middle Ages to the present day. The literary data also include EMIT-X: data and metadata from the Emblem Project Utrecht (EPU), which created a digital collection of 27 books of love emblems.

Literary research The Arthurian Fiction web application enables searching and browsing in data on mediaeval Arthurian narratives and the manuscripts in which they are transmitted throughout Europe (Arthurian Fiction data). COBWWWEB enables search in the Women-Writers Database and connected databases in women's literature, while NameScape enables searching for names and analysing their use in literary works (see chapter 30). BNM-I enables searching in a collection of textual, codicological and historical information about thousands of Middle Dutch manuscripts.

Religion research The PILNAR application enables search in a corpus of PILNAR pilgrims' narratives with Dutch texts written after 2000 (see chapter 31). The SHEBANQ application, already described in chapter 18, enables search in the SHEBANQ curated WIVU database containing the Bible text in Hebrew.

Media research Polimedia provides search in the minutes of the debates in the Dutch Parliament (Dutch Hansard) in combination with the databases of historical newspapers and ANP radio bulletins to allow cross-media analysis of coverage. AVResearcherXL enables the combined exploration of radio and television programme descriptions, television subtitles and general newspaper articles.

Social research MIGMAP enables searching and analysing data on migration flow between Dutch municipalities (see chapter 29).

Philosophy @PhilosTEI is a workflow for converting digital images into textual resources in TEI[2] format, and has specifically been applied to philosophical works (see chapter 32)

In addition, there are data from CLARIN data providers covering a wide number of disciplines. These data include the NISV Academia Collection and digital publications from Utrecht University Library, as well as digital publications from the National Library (KB).

25.3   Contents of Part IV: Infrastructure for Other Humanities Disciplines

The current book's part IV on infrastructure for other Humanities disciplines contains chapters for only a small sample of the resources described in section 25.2. We already referred to the chapters

---

2   TEI (Text Encoding Initiative) is a widely used standard for encoding textual resources supported by CLARIN.

that describe these resources. For the reader's convenience, we summarise the contents of part IV on infrastructure for other Humanities disciplines here and briefly describe the contents of each chapter:

Chapter 26 describes the *ePistolarium*, a virtual research environment for browsing and analysing a corpus of letters written by and sent to 17th-century scholars who lived in the Dutch Republic. It was developed in an independently financed project named *Circulation of Knowledge: A Web-based Humanities' Collaboratory on Correspondences and Learned Practices in the 17th century Dutch Republic (CKCC)*. The authors describe this project and provide an overview of the analysis methods that are available to the users of the ePistolarium, emphasising the role of Natural Language Processing techniques.

Chapter 27 claims that the human language technology that has been developed and used in the CLARIN demonstrator projects WAHSP and BILAND supports advanced forms of (multilingual) text mining in large datasets of newspapers. The authors argue that it is the massive processing of sources (pre-processed and offering a reliable critical text) – rather than the exhaustive analysis of a limited number of records – that will offer an added value to the historical sciences. The authors describe the development, use, and challenges of the WAHSP and BILAND text mining tools and their successor, Texcavator, to support distant reading in historical newspaper collections. They show how semantic text mining enables new and advanced forms of historical analysis based on case-studies focusing on the circulation of ideas and notions regarding drugs and eugenics during the first four decades of the 20th century.

Chapter 28 presents *RemBench*, a search engine for research into the life and works of Rembrandt van Rijn. RemBench combines the data from four different databases behind one interface using federated search technology. Metadata filtering is enabled through faceted search. RemBench enables art historians and other professionals interested in Rembrandt's period to find all information on Rembrandt that is available in online repositories in one application. The authors describe the user interface and results of its evaluation and claim that RemBench sets an example for search engines in the digital humanities.

Chapter 29 presents MIGMAP, software for the interactive mapping of socio-cultural phenomena in the Netherlands on the web. It demonstrates the possibilities that MIGMAP offers for the mapping of migration in the Netherlands across four generations. Both origin and dispersion of the population can be explored at the geographic levels of municipality, region, dialect area and province.

Chapter 30 presents NameScape, which enables researchers to carry out comparative literary onomastics on a large corpus of literary works. In comparative literary onomastics it is assumed that patterns and trends can be discovered in the way in which literary authors make use of proper names in their work. The NameScape project created a large corpus of literary works, made available tools to perform high-quality named entity recognition on literary material and tried to perform named entity resolution so as to determine whether names in literary works are plot internal or plot external. The data were made available in an environment in which the researcher can search and visualise search results.

Chapter 31 describes PILNAR, which created and opened up a corpus of Dutch pilgrim narratives for interested researchers. The growing number of narratives were collected and structured in a meaningful manner, providing a research tool that enables academics to work with this fascinating set of stories. The contribution takes a retrospective look at the construction of the PILNAR database and looks ahead to the possibilities of its results.

Chapter 32 addresses the problem of corpus building by developing an open source, web-based, user-friendly workflow from textual images to TEI, based on state-of-the-art open source OCR software and a powerful OCR post-correction tool developed earlier in

CLARIN-LC (TICCLops). The authors demonstrate the utility of the tool by applying it to a multilingual, multi-script corpus of important 18th- to 20th-century European philosophical texts, thus satisfying a basic pre-condition for the step towards e-research in philosophy.

Acknowledgements

This work was financed by CLARIN-NL and CLARIAH.

CHAPTER 26

The ePistolarium: Origins and Techniques

Walter Ravenek, Charles van den Heuvel and Guido Gerritsen

Huygens ING, Postbus 10855, 1001 EW Amsterdam, The Netherlands

ABSTRACT

The *Circulation of Knowledge: A Web-based Humanities' Collaboratory on Correspondences and Learned Practices in the 17th-century Dutch Republic* (CKCC) project was an NWO project aimed at developing an infrastructure for researchers. Its main goal was to gain insight into the Dutch share of the circulation of knowledge in the 17th-century 'Republic of letters' by means of analysis and visualisation tools. A database of 20,000 letters in TEI-format offered the possibility to falsify hypotheses that were often based on extrapolations from limited numbers of letters. The complexity of this collection of data – caused by the presence of multilingual letters, often with several languages within a letter, extensive spelling variation, and early modern language variants – was a challenge for the researchers and IT specialists. With the support of CLARIN-NL and the EU, however, we were able to overcome these linguistic problems.

26.1 Introduction

This chapter deals with various aspects of the *ePistolarium*, a virtual research environment for browsing and analysing a corpus of letters written by and sent to 17th-century scholars who lived in the Dutch Republic. Firstly, we describe the project from which the ePistolarium arose, named *Circulation of Knowledge: A Web-based Humanities' Collaboratory on Correspondences and Learned Practices in the 17th-century Dutch Republic* (CKCC; ePistolarium, 2013). Secondly, we give an overview of the analysis methods that are available to the users of the ePistolarium, emphasising the role of Natural Language Processing techniques.

How to cite this book chapter:

Ravenek, W, van den Heuvel, C and Gerritsen, G. 2017. The ePistolarium: Origins and Techniques. In: Odijk, J and van Hessen, A. (eds.) *CLARIN in the Low Countries*, Pp. 317–323. London: Ubiquity Press. DOI: https://doi.org/10.5334/bbi.26. License: CC-BY 4.0

26.2   Project

Whereas internationally renowned projects such as *Cultures of Knowledge* (CofK; 2016) and *Mapping the Republic of Letters* (RofL; 2013) which both more or less started at the same time as the CKCC project focused on metadata to get insight into the circulation of knowledge, the CKCC project focused on analysing the content of the letters themselves. The project aimed at providing researchers with tools for answering questions related to the dissemination and appropriation of knowledge:

1. How did knowledge circulate in the 17th-century Dutch Republic? How were elements of knowledge – generated in workshops, at sea, in the colonies overseas, on the battlefield and in libraries – picked up and used by the learned community? How was this new knowledge processed, disseminated, theorised and ultimately accepted, or, for that matter, rejected?

2. How can we combine and structure various sets of letters of 17th-century scholars and their correspondents in such a way that we can analyse the circulation and appropriation of knowledge production in a wider international context and recognise the development of themes of interest and scholarly debates in space and time?

3. How can we search and contextualise this information on knowledge production and its appropriation to make it accessible to interdisciplinary research in the Humanities?

As will be discussed in Section 26.5, researchers also use the ePistolarium to answer their own research questions, which are more specific than the general questions formulated at the start of the project.

Wijnand Mijnhardt (Descartes Centre University of Utrecht) was the principal investigator of the CKCC project, while Huygens ING was responsible for the technical development and implementation of its infrastructure, its analytical and visualisation tools and its user interface. CKCC was funded from November 2008 to February 2013 by the Netherlands Organisation for Scientific Research (NWO) as part of the Investment Grant NWO Medium programme to provide a large group of researchers with suitable tools to analyse and visualise the circulation of knowledge in the Dutch Republic. CLARIN-EU selected the CKCC project as a 'flagship' demonstrator to show the potential of the CLARIN infrastructure, not only for linguistics but for other humanities disciplines as well. CLARIN-NL provided extra funding for the adaptation of language and knowledge representation technologies for keyword extraction and concept extraction. Finally, after its completion in 2013, CKCC was one of the projects selected by CLARIN-NL for the development of an educational module. In June 2013, the ePistolarium was officially launched and made public. Its web location is ckcc.huygens.knaw.nl/epistolarium.

26.3   Corpus

The CKCC corpus currently contains 20,020 letters, ignoring duplicates. It consists of the correspondence of the 17th-century scholars Caspar Barlaeus, Isaac Beeckman, René Descartes, Hugo Grotius, Christiaan Huygens, Constantijn Huygens, Antoni van Leeuwenhoek, Dirck Rembrantsz van Nierop, and Jan Swammerdam. Most of this correspondence was already digitised at the start of the project, but the formats of the letters differed widely, requiring us to convert the letter texts to a standardised format, for which we chose TEI. In addition, the metadata of the letters needed to be standardised, and concordances of person and place lists to an aggregated dataset needed to be prepared. Even though we use a limited number of metadata tags (date, correspondents and sender/recipient locations) considerable effort was needed to standardise and enrich the metadata.

From a language perspective our corpus has a number of characteristics that are important when it comes to processing the letters:

- The corpus contains letters in various languages, the most important ones being Dutch, French and Latin. As can be seen from Table 26.1, these three languages account for almost 95% of the text.
- Many letters are multilingual. In order to apply language resources and technology we have to segment the letters to at least the paragraph level.
- The letters often contain elaborate opening and closing phrases that contribute little to the subject matter of the letters. Currently we have some 10,000 opening and 17,500 closing sections marked up. It is worthwhile to exclude such sections from content extraction.
- Finally, 17th-century writing exhibits a large degree of spelling variation, which has a negative effect on the performance of analysis techniques.

26.4   Analysis Techniques

The ePistolarium offers its users a range of analysis techniques, the most advanced ones being topic modelling and cocitation analysis, both of which depend on natural language processing. In this section we give a concise overview of the techniques employed in the ePistolarium.

26.4.1   Language Identification

For language identification – applied at the paragraph level – we used the N-gram based cumulative frequency addition algorithm (Ahmed, Cha and Tappert, 2004). The text is preprocessed by removing punctuation, quotes, mathematical symbols, digits and Roman numerals. The algorithm requires language profiles which are constructed using a selected set of monolingual letters from the corpus.

26.4.2   Spelling Normalisation

Of the three major languages in the corpus, Dutch exhibits most spelling variation; it is also the language that differs most from its modern counterpart. In addition it is the language of the lesser educated correspondents, e.g. Antoni van Leeuwenhoek.

Language	Paragraphs	Tokens	Rel. size
Dutch	37,570	2,491,730	30.33%
English	865	85,290	1.04%
French	26,747	2,810,484	34.21%
German	2,728	106,180	1.29%
Greek	46	709	0.01%
Italian	2,011	63,203	0.77%
Latin	38,331	2,458,403	29.92%
Portuguese	2	614	0.01%
Spanish	26	2,110	0.03%
Not Assigned	27,202	196,672	2.39%
CKCC corpus	135,528	8,215,395	

Table 26.1: Corpus size by language.

Correspondence	Recognised	Identified
Barlaeus	3,073	1,460
Beeckman	139	120
Descartes	4,096	3,917
Grotius	76,790	57,286
Chr. Huygens	21,647	17,411
Const. Huygens	17,354	12,632
Van Leeuwenhoek	899	869
Van Nierop	394	326
Swammerdam	567	532
CKCC corpus	124,959	94,553

Table 26.2: Results of NER for person references. *Recognised* names are annotated in the letter texts; *identified* names are used in cocitation analysis.

We decided to use the sophisticated spelling normalisation application VARD 2 (Baron and Rayson, 2008) for Dutch, and handled spelling variation in French and Latin with a rule-based approach. The basic philosophy of VARD 2 is to normalise text to modern spelling, allowing existing linguistic tools to be used unmodified. It was developed and trained to deal with spelling variation in Early Modern English, but can also be trained to deal with spelling variation in other languages. We used a version of VARD 2 that was adapted by its author Alistair Baron to allow integration in our text-processing pipeline.

26.4.3   Named Entity Recognition

We used Named Entity Recognition (NER) to label person names in the letter texts – the availability of identified names is a prerequisite for cocitation analysis.

We used an iterative, rule-based approach to build gazetteers (lookup lists of names), which were extended with hand-annotated names and names from indexes of book editions. More names were generated by applying rules to Latinised names (for instance, if 'Grotius' and 'Grotio' occur the names 'Grotium' and 'Grotii' are also generated). For the actual matching the well-known Aho-Corasick (1975) algorithm is used on a normalised representation of the gazetteers and the letter texts. The normalisation involves removing diacritical marks and applying the character mappings j → i, y → i, v → u, and w → u; this normalisation is language-independent and works well for 17th-century texts. (See Table 26.2 for NER statistics.)

26.4.4   Keyword Analysis

We performed a keyword analysis for the three main languages in the corpus, following an approach similar to the one implemented by Rayson in the Wmatrix corpus analysis tool (Rayson, 2008). The analysis is based on frequency profiling of the individual letters and comparing the obtained profiles with the corresponding profile of the full letter collection as a reference corpus. Keywords are determined with a log-likelihood estimator, using a threshold of 99% confidence of significance. We thus obtained keywords for 82% of the letters; these results are displayed in the ePistolarium.

26.4.5   Topic Modelling

Topic modelling constitutes a statistical approach to content extraction. The major approaches to topic modelling are able to identify hidden variables that can be interpreted as 'topics'. We tested three topic modelling methods: Latent Dirichlet Allocation (LDA), Latent Semantic Analysis (LSA), and Random Indexing (RI). We found that RI performed best in the task of reproducing topic labels assigned by human experts for a randomly selected subset of letters (Wittek and Ravenek 2011). From a computational point of view RI has the benefit that it does not rely on computationally intensive matrix operations as, for example, LSA does. Instead, RI builds an incremental word space model that scales very well with increasing corpus size. For these reasons we employed RI as the topic modelling method in the ePistolarium.

Preprocessing for the actual calculation of the topic model involves some general processing (e.g., elimination of opening and closing phrases, of formulas, and of words with a length smaller than three characters) and some languagespecific processing (e.g., removal of stop words, spelling normalisation). We calculated a single topic model for all languages combined.

In the ePistolarium the topic model is used for calculating similarities between letters and between words. To illustrate the latter we describe the query term suggestion feature (see Figure 26.1): the ePistolarium offers a fulltext search, implemented with the *Lucene* search library. The user enters search terms and can request query terms that have the largest cosine similarity with the terms entered. These new, suggested terms can be transferred to and used in the regular fulltext search. Two examples of such query term suggestions are:

- construction → bernoulli, bernoully, calcul, …, courbes, egale, hyperbole, logarithmique, probleme, quadrature; and
- roi de france → affaires, angleterre, espagne, espagnols, gens, guerre, paix, reine

Based on the qualitative judgement of users (see Section 26.5) we find that the best results are obtained for terms that pertain to a topic that has a specific terminology.

26.4.6   *Cocitation Analysis*

One of the visualisations offered by the ePistolarium is a cocitation network graph. It shows individuals that play a role in an intellectual debate and their connections. The graph is constructed using references to individuals in the same *paragraph* of a letter: the more often individuals are mentioned together, the stronger their connection.

In our analysis we excluded the opening and closing phrases of the letters. Obviously, only identified person names can be taken into account. The analysis is performed by combining data for the selection of letters made by the user with the faceted search and/or the fulltext search (see Figure 26.2 for an example of a cocitation graph).

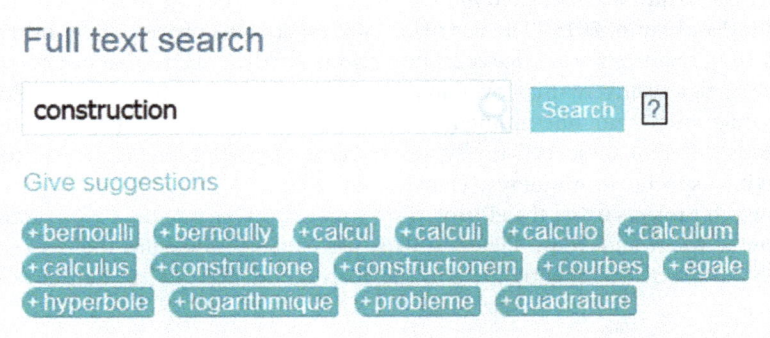

Figure 26.1: Example of query terms suggested with topic modelling.

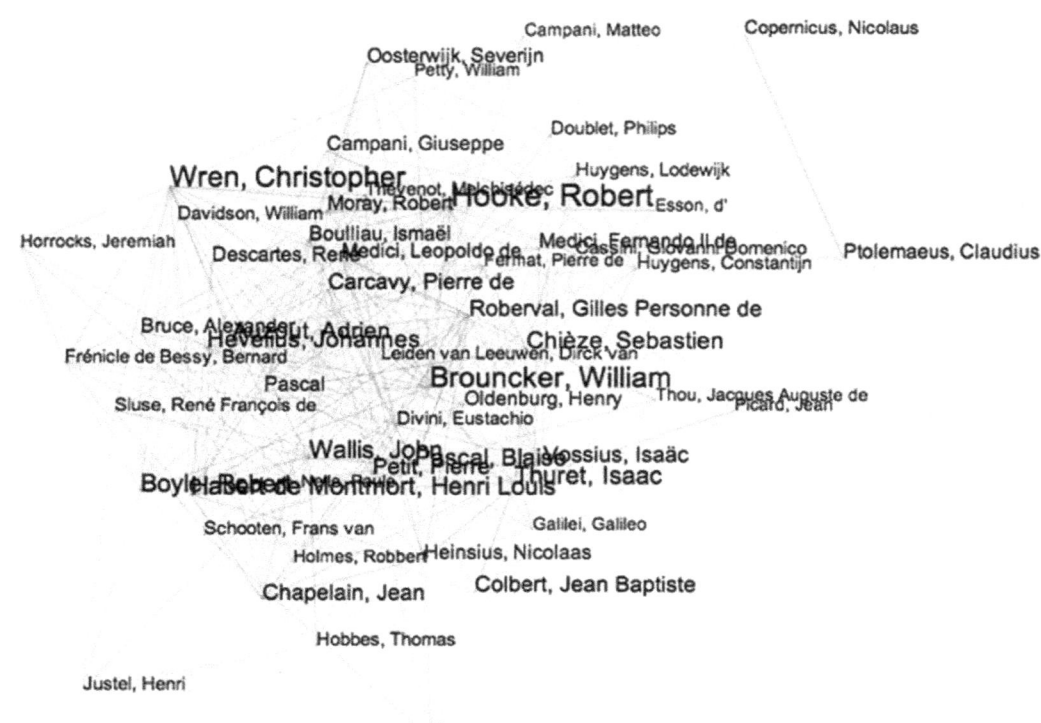

Figure 26.2: Example of a co-citation graph.

26.5   Usability Tests

During the development of the ePistolarium we organised various usability tests by historians of science, both with researchers involved in the project and with participants of the NIAS-Lorentz workshop *Mathematical Life in the Dutch Republic* (Leiden, 2010) The feedback led to improved versions of the faceted search and to a shift of focus in the application of topic modelling. The interpretation of the 'topics' proved hard and ambiguous; therefore we decided to use topic modelling to calculate similarities between (paragraphs of) letters and for search term suggestions.

When the ePistolarium was launched in June 2013, new experiments were set up that are all fully documented (ePistolarium, 2013) The use of co-citation analysis proved quite succesful. The use of topic modelling requires knowledge of its limitations: firstly, it seems that our corpus is still too limited in size, with a relatively small overlap in subject matters. Secondly, it seems that the unit of modelling (paragraphs) is not fine-grained enough, as paragraphs in the letters tend to be long and to cover various different subjects. Thirdly, search term suggestion yields the mostusable results for subjects with a specific terminology (Heuvel et al., 2016).

Several research projects using the ePistolarium were set up outside the CKCC consortium. For instance, Wouter Klein and Toine Pieters (2016) used the ePistolarium tool to reveal the hidden history of an exotic therapeutic drug in the correspondence of Constantijn and Christiaan Huygens.

26.6   Outlook

To remedy the problem of the small size and imbalance in the composition of the corpus we intend to include more data in the CKCC corpus with the last three volumes of the Van Leeuwenhoek correspondence and the correspondence of Pierre Bayle and Carolus Clusius to be added; other correspondence will follow. In order to obtain more data the CKCC project plays an active role in the European project *Reassembling the Republic of Letters* (RROL; 2015).

One of the major disadvantages in our current approach to topic modelling is that the texts in the various languages each 'live' in their own subspace of the overall word space. Using a translation to a common language, preferably English, would allow us to build a unified topic model covering the bulk of the text in the corpus.

Although the analysis methods in the ePistolarium are dynamic in the sense that they are applied to selections made by the user, the texts themselves and the annotations made on them (e.g. person identifications) are static. We intend to extend the ePistolarium by allowing user annotations to be made. This will be accommodated by using the storage mechanism provided by Alexandria, an annotation environment that is currently being developed at the Huygens ING. Alexandria will be compliant with the CLARIAH infrastructure, the largest digital infrastructure for the humanities in the Netherlands.

References

Ahmed, B, Cha, S, and Tappert, C 2004 *Language identification from text using n-gram based cumulative frequency addition.* In: *Proceedings of Student/Faculty Research Day*, CSIS, Pace University.

Aho, A V and Corasick, M 1975 Efficient string matching: An aid to bibliographic search. *Communications of the ACM* 18, 333–340.

Baron, A and Rayson, P 2008 *VARD 2: A tool for dealing with spelling variation in historical corpora.* In: Proceedings of the Postgraduate Conference in Corpus Linguistics, Birmingham, UK.

CofK 2016. Available at http://www.culturesofknowledge.org.

ePistolarium 2013. Available at http://ckcc.huygens.knaw.nl.

Heuvel, C van den, Weingart, S, Spelt, N and Nellen, H 2016 Circles of Confidence in Correspondences Confidentiality in seventeenth-century knowledge exchange in networks of letters and drawings. *Nuncius* 31, 78–106.

Klein, W and Pieters, T 2016, The Hidden History of a Famous Drug: Tracing the Medical and Public Acculturation of Peruvian Bark in Early Modern Western Europe (c. 1650–1720). *Journal of the History of Medicine and Allied Sciences*, DOI: http://dx.doi.org/10.1093/jhmas/jrw004.

Rayson, P 2008 From key words to key semantic domains. *International Journal of Corpus Linguistics* 13, 519–549.

RofL 2013. Available at http://republicofletters.stanford.edu.

RROL 2015. RROL- ISCH - COST-action IS1310 *Reassembling the Republic of Letters*. Available at http://www.republicofletters.net.

Wittek, P and Ravenek, W 2011 *Supporting the Exploration of a Corpus of 17th-Century Scholarly Correspondences by Topic Modeling.* In: B. Maegaard (Ed.), *Supporting Digital Humanities 2011: Answering the unaskable.* Copenhagen, Denmark.

CHAPTER 27

A Digital Humanities Approach to the History of Culture and Science
Drugs and Eugenics Revisited in Early 20th-Century Dutch Newspapers, Using Semantic Text Mining

Stephen Snelders[a], Pim Huijnen[a,b], Jaap Verheul[b],
Maarten de Rijke[c] and Toine Pieters[a]

[a]Descartes Centre for the History and Philosophy of the Sciences and the Arts, Freudenthal Institute, Utrecht University(UU), The Netherlands {s.snelders, t.pieters@uu.nl},
[b]Research Institute for History and Art History, UU {p.huijnen, j.verheul@uu.nl}
[c]ISLA, University of Amsterdam, The Netherlands {m.derijke@uva.nl}

ABSTRACT

Human language technology developed and used in CLARIN demonstrator projects WAHSP and BILAND supports advanced forms of (multi-lingual) text mining of large datasets of newspapers. We argue that the combination of exploratory search and text mining offers an innovative research approach to systematically set up search trails in the historical sciences. We describe the development, use, and methodological challenges of the WAHSP and BILAND text-mining tools and the successor tool, Texcavator, to support alternating forms of distant reading and close reading in newspaper collections. We will show how semantic text mining speeds up the heuristic process and thus helped to provide new and challenging perspectives on the circulation of ideas and notions regarding drugs and eugenics in Dutch newspapers in the first four decades of the 20th century.

27.1 Introduction

Historical scholars are increasingly applying computational tools and methods to all phases of their research. Digital tools are used to open, present, and curate textual and multi-media sources in semantic text mining, for integration of geospatial information data, for various forms of visualisation, and for enhanced and multi-media publication of research results, blogs, and wikis. Digital history is a methodological approach that is framed by these digital tools' ability to make, define,

How to cite this book chapter:
Snelders, S, Huijnen, P, Verheul, J, de Rijke, M and Pieters. T. 2017. A Digital Humanities Approach to the History of Culture and Science: Drugs and Eugenics Revisited in Early 20th-Century Dutch Newspapers, Using Semantic Text Mining. In: Odijk, J and van Hessen, A. (eds.) *CLARIN in the Low Countries*, Pp. 325–336. London: Ubiquity Press. DOI: https://doi.org/10.5334/bbi.27. License: CC-BY 4.0

query, and annotate associations and explore long-term patterns of economic, technological, and cultural change in past human records. Digital history touches on all aspects and forms of historical scholarship that come together around digitised data and digital tools (Graham et al., 2013; Van Eijnatten et al., 2013). There have been inspiring examples of good digital historical scholarship, like the use of N-grams to mine the Google Books archive (Michel, 2010), the engagement in creative visual analysis of historical geography,[1] or the study of the 'circulation of knowledge and learned practices' by means of a virtual research environment (VRE).[2] However, historians are still in the process of learning how to incorporate and implement data-mining technology in methodologically sound and reproducible ways (Seefeldt and Thomas, 2009; Bingham, 2010; Earheart and Jewell, 2011; Berry, 2012; Burdick et al., 2012; Van Eijnatten et al., 2013; Van Eijnatten et al., 2014).[3]

Semantic text analytics is a particularly promising form of text mining that can be applied to 'big data' sets. Text analytics, or text mining, is an umbrella term for the incorporation and implemention of a wide range of tools or techniques (algorithms, statistics), including data mining, machine learning, natural language processing, and artificial intelligence (Jackson and Moulinier, 2007). The goal of text mining is to reduce the effort required to obtain meaningful information from large digitised text data sources. In principle, text-mining tools can process large numbers of texts reasonably quickly and support researchers in tracing sentiments, potentially meaningful events, and context-related concepts. However, being able to retrieve historically meaningful information requires that historians as domain users have a prominent role in the development of text- and data-mining technology.

Research programmes such as Digging into Data,[4] CLARIN-NL[5] and CLARIAH[6] demonstrate the feasibility of performing interdisciplinary humanities research facilitated by digital research tools. These programmes also show that collaborative, interdisciplinary and integrative strategies such as common group learning (where all knowledge is necessarily pooled, and learning is both shared and cumulative), modelling, and iterative and incremental approaches are central to the function, and, therefore, success, of digital humanities. It is therefore important to include articulating and aligning user needs, in our case historians, with technological options. For instance, incorporation of regular feedback loops allows for an iterative refinement of text-mining algorithms (e.g. identifying polarities and named entity recognition, etc.) and the development of a user-friendly interface (Warwick et al., 2012; Huijnen et al., 2014).

The combination of exploratory search and text mining has supported our research team to set up systematic search trails. Our thesis is that this approach enables fruitful alternating modes of distant reading and close reading. We will demonstrate our thesis by presenting case studies of debates about drugs and eugenics. Both topics represent a meeting ground between science and society with shifting cultural and political connotations. Drug use and eugenics as controversial social practices represent not only an important component of our cultural heritage, but also key elements of European modernisation (Hahn, 2000; Lombardo, 2001; Snelders et al., 2006; Reulecke, 2007; Levine and Bashford, 2010; Turda, 2010).

How can we use digitised newspaper collections to analyse the public's perceptions, opinions, and sentiments about eugenics and drugs? One approach suggests perusing lead and opinion articles about drugs or specific eugenic policy measures. The digital history projects discussed here have not limited their searches to this obvious choice. Rather, public debates are perceived as part

---

[1] http://web.stanford.edu/group/spatialhistory/cgi-bin/site/index.php (accessed 03-02-2017)
[2] http://ckcc.huygens.knaw.nl/ (accessed 25-01-2016)
[3] For an overview of more recent trends and discussions in digital humanities see http://dh2016.adho.org/ (accessed 03-02-2017).
[4] http://diggingintodata.org/ (accessed 03-02-2017)
[5] http://clarin.nl/ (accessed 05-02-2016)
[6] http://clariah.nl/ (accessed 05-02-2016)

of a public sphere in which perceptions, opinions, and sentiments are constructed and structured. The conceptual developments in the history of culture and science and their related disciplines after Foucault's discourse analysis suggest that implicit assumptions and perceptions of drugs and eugenics are pervasive throughout Western culture, and can be found in detective stories, advertisements, visual representations, journalistic reports and a wide range of other cultural texts. Implicit assumptions are a powerful expression of public perceptions and notions. For uninformed or biased readers, these 'hidden' discourses can construct and reinforce a range of associations of drug use as dangerous, criminal, anti-social and exotic, and the same is true for implicit associations with eugenics, in terms of deviant, weak and depraved social groups. We will show that the identification and analysis of these 'hidden' discourses and the possible overlap between discourses on drugs and eugenics generate potentially transformative insights into the construction and shift of meaning around science-related social practices such as drugs and eugenics.

27.2   Towards Historical Text Mining of Public Media

27.2.1   WAHSP Tool Features

The development of an open-source mining technology that historians without specific computer skills can and will use requires a user-friendly and user-informed interface. This was the basis requirement for developing the CLARIN-supported web application for historical-sentiment mining (a form of semantic text analytics that focuses on historical opinions, attitudes, and value judgements) of public media known as WAHSP. WAHSP was specifically designed for text mining the digital newspaper archive of the National Library of the Netherlands (Delpher collection). At present, this repository includes over 11 million pages from more than 200 newspapers and periodicals published between 1618 and 1995, which adds up to over 100 million articles.[7] WAHSP's technical basis is an ElasticSearch instance combined with the xTAS text analytics platform developed by the ISLA Informatics Institute of the University of Amsterdam.[8] xTAS includes modules for online and offline processing, and provides essential text pre-processing modules (morphological normalisation, format and encoding reconciliation, named-entity recognition and normalisation; Meij et al., 2009). It also incorporates algorithms and tools for the identification of polarity (positive/support or negative/criticism), sources (opinion-holders), frequency of items, and specific targets of discourses (Jijkoun et al., 2010). WAHSP comes with visualisation modules built in D3.js (interactive word clouds and timelines). WAHSP has been developed in a specific research context, but is generic and usable in other domains for which topic, context and attitude analysis is needed for large volumes of text.

The main added value of the WAHSP tool lies in exploratory readings of historical patterns in public debates. The WAHSP research team has found that in terms of methodology, semi-automatic document selection fits rather well with historical research as an alternative to manual or random sampling. This approach speeds up the heuristic process considerably. Word clouds that depict a linguistic context within which keywords occur are instrumental for helping an historian (with expert knowledge of the domain) to combine and compare various historical periods in a free associative manner on the basis of a large number of historical documents. Each query immediately yields a document selection without laborious sampling. Exploring word associations and metadata, as well as visualisations of the original newspaper articles over time, can lead to improved queries and allow the historian to alternate between distant and close reading and to systematically explore search trails.

---

[7]   http://www.delpher.nl/nl/platform/pages/helpitems?nid=385 (accessed 03-02-2017)
[8]   http://xtas.net/ (accessed 05-02-2016)

27.2.2   *Exploring the Construction of Public Images of Drugs and Drug Users*

Our aim was to analyse how Dutch newspapers represented debates on drugs, drug trafficking, and drug users in the early 20th century (1900–1940). We wanted to determine whether these early media debates on drugs were predominantly based on medical aspects (addiction, therapeutic benefit) or social aspects (crime, stigmatised groups of drug users).

How did we use WAHSP? First, we created a lexicon of terms related to drugs to capture all possible relevant terms for high document recall. We used our drug history domain knowledge to create a list of words, and WAHSP provided query-guided word (frequency) clouds based on all retrieved documents from the Delpher collection (see Figure 27.1). The word clouds enabled us to gradually expand the original query with terms we recognised as drug-related terms. We kept lab logs of all our queries and word cloud visualisation results.

Our point of departure was marking key events, such as the Shanghai Opium Conference (1909) and additional treaties, and the introduction and subsequent tightening of the Dutch Opium laws (1920 and 1928). We looked for word associations with drugs targeted by the Opium Law of 1919: opium, morphine, heroin and cocaine. We split these associations in four time periods: (I) before The Hague conference of 1912; (II) from 1912 to the enforcement of the Opium Law in 1920; (III) between 1920 and 1928, at which latter date the law was changed to make opium possession an offence; and (IV) from 1928 to the Second World War, when war-related issues took precedence in the mind of the public. It is significant to note that *after* 1920, the public's ideas about drugs seemed to change. The generic term *drugs* did not exist in the language of Dutch newspapers during the interwar period, but rather the terms were *narcotica* or *verdovende* or *verdoovende middelen* [all translated as 'narcotics']. Before 1920, newspapers used these Dutch words to refer to opium or cocaine (or chloroform, which had an important role as a narcotic in medicine). The number of articles addressing narcotics in this early period was quite limited compared to 1920–1928 and 1928–1940. After 1920, the number of articles increased by a factor of 16. The associations with these three words changed as well, from 'medicines', 'poisons', 'science', 'pharmacies', 'sleep' or 'narcosis' to 'police', 'contraband trade', 'arrested', and 'confiscated'. Not only are there increasing associations between the generic terms for narcotics and crime, but also for individual drugs and crime (Snelders and Pieters, 2012).

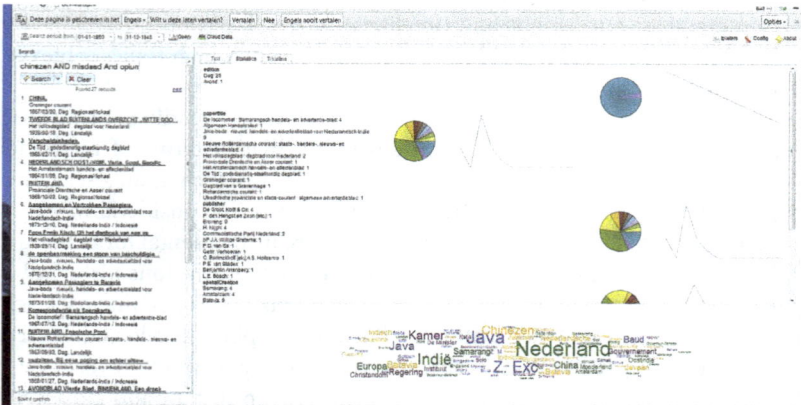

Figure 27.1: WAHSP search result plus word cloud based on the National Library of the Netherlands newspaper repository using the query 'chinezen' AND 'misdaad' AND 'opium' for 1900–1945. (6 September 2013).

By carefully inspecting word counts, we found exciting quantitative evidence for a historical caesura indicating that there was a criminalisation of the drug debate in approximately 1924 (Odijk et al., 2012). At that time, opium became associated with Chinese, China, or with the Dutch East Indies (see Figure 27.1). Even *Opiumregie*, the opium distribution and control regime of the colonial state in the Dutch East Indies, was initially associated with Chinese (and 'pathetic') users, and with Chinese crime syndicates that tried to evade the *Opiumregie* by smuggling illicit opiates into the East Indies. These opiates were smoked opium with a different quality than standard government-issued opium. In the 1930s, smugglers also attempted to bring morphine and heroin into the East Indies.

The negative and alienating ('othering') images of Chinese drug users and traders were found in the so-called 'hidden discourses' we mentioned above, which can also be associated with deviant groups and eugenics. We subsequently alternated from distant reading by means of exploratory search and text mining to conventional close reading of *Dick Bos*, a popular Dutch pulp comic series in the early 1940s, the first five parts of which were published in instalments in weekly papers from 1940–1942. The character Dick Bos was a detective who was an expert in an Asian fighting art (jiu jitsu). In his first appearance, he was immediately caught up in a drug case. Bos went on the trail of a gang smuggling cocaine on a Chinese ship. When the gang captured him, he was sent to China and put to work as a slave on a plantation. Of course, he escaped and ultimately helped to capture the gang.[9] That the actual relationship between cocaine and China was more complicated did not matter in this story; many (young) readers would have become firmly convinced of a connection between China, cocaine and deviancy. In *Dick Bos*, opium and cocaine were clearly and visually associated with a dark underworld, low-life taverns, and exotic and criminal Chinese groups. As such the alternation between distant and close reading provides evidence of a meaningful overlap and interference between drugs and eugenics discourses that deserves further research.

27.2.3   *Mining Ambiguities in the Meaning of Eugenics*

The WAHSP tool enables, as we have seen in the previous drugs case history, searches in the Delpher collection with combinations of keywords that do not necessarily refer specifically to eugenics, but rather imply eugenic thinking, such as in the case of the combination of 'Chinese' and crime. 'Eugenics' is a term loaded with historical meanings and polarities. Its literal meaning – 'good birth' – suggests a suitable goal for all prospective parents, yet its historical connotations tie it to a rather wide range of beliefs and practices, from good nutrition and education, pre-natal care for mothers, and birth-control to the extremes of selective breeding programmes, forced sterilisation, and euthanasia (Klausen and Bashford, 2010). Possible linguistic associations with eugenics include: 'ancestry', 'lineage', 'descent', 'reproduction', 'selection', 'unhealthy', 'pure'/'purity', 'weak', and 'deviant'.

By combining these words with keywords from social or cultural domains like sports, entertainment, economy and religion, one can obtain explicit discussions not only about eugenics, but also about implicit notions influenced by hereditary and eugenic thinking within certain debates. At the same time, one has to be aware that keyword searching is in itself not without problems – it is a rather 'blunt' instrument in the words of Adrian Bingham (Bingham, 2010: 229). Finding the right keywords demands expert knowledge of the field of study and significant perseverance and creativity (Nicholson, 2013: 67).

The hints of eugenic notions in pre-war Dutch economic debates can serve as yet another example that is highly suitable to illustrate what we mean by exploratory search methods. The economic

---

[9]   Alfred Mazure, 'Het geval "Kleyn" in: *Dick Bos. Alle avonturen*, I. ('s-Gravenhage: Panda, 2005).

historian Thomas C. Leonard argues that economists in the Progressive Era (ca 1890–1920s) of the United States advocated for a minimum wage as a eugenic tool: a minimum wage would cause job losses and thus discourage prospective immigrants from coming to the US, as well as remove the more unfit (the so-called 'low wage races') from employment (Leonard, 2005: 213). It is an interesting question to consider whether similar arguments were used in Dutch debates on minimum wage, since although the Netherlands did not adopt a general minimum wage before 1968 the introduction of a minimum wage was debated from as early as the turn of the 20th century. The WAHSP tool generated almost 10,000 hits on 'minimum wage' before 1945.

The words *Amerika* and *Amerikaansche* [America and American] both form part of the resulting word cloud, indicating that the Dutch debate on the minimum wage might be informed by eugenic arguments from abroad – notably from the US. There are several exploratory angles to follow this trail. For instance, one can query (combinations of) relevant keywords that characterise this particular debate ('race', '(minimum) wage', 'immigration' and the like) or look for a possible link with the US. The combination 'race AND immigration' (see Figure 27.2), for example, hints at a connection with the US. Moreover, both the combinations 'wage AND race' and 'wage AND immigration' yielded a relatively high number of hits (more than 9,000 and almost 2,500, respectively; Huijnen et al., 2014: 78)

We operationalised the combination of exploratory search and text-mining as the ongoing process of refining and expanding queries with the help of text-mining techniques. Word clouds are an important part of this digital search method, because striking words can trigger the historian who has a profound knowledge of the subject matter to incorporate them in new queries after close reading of a particular subset of newspaper articles. The key question derived from this method is: what do the word cloud results tell us? The results seem to indicate a meaningful connection between the concepts of race, wage and immigration in the Netherlands before the Second World War. The relatively large numbers of hits resulting from queries with combinations from these keywords are tempting clues to investigate this particular topic further. After all, it is obvious that the results from these queries alone do not demonstrate how these concepts were meaningfully connected; the researcher has to assess this connection by further alternating between query-guided distant reading and 'traditional' close reading of relevant texts (Huijnen et al., 2014: 79).

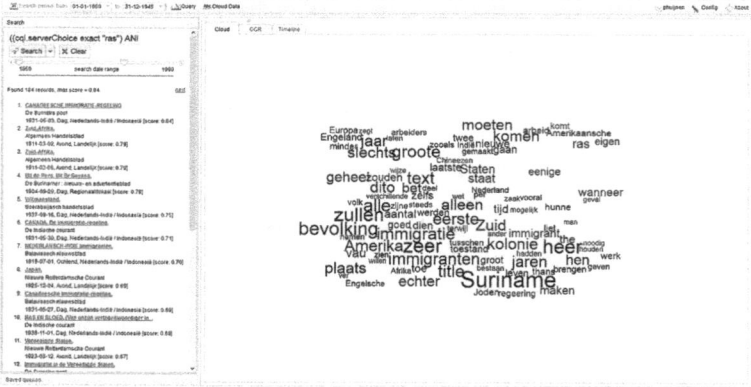

Figure 27.2: WAHSP search result plus word cloud based on the National Library of the Netherlands newspaper repository using the query 'race' AND 'immigration' ('ras' AND 'immigratie') for 1860–1945. (13 June 2013).

27.3   New Horizons: Historical Text Mining for Comparative Research as Part of The bilingual Text-Mining Tool Biland

An interdisciplinary team of researchers have tailored WAHSP to the language-specific needs of comparative historical research, with a particular focus on the identity, intensity, and location of discourses about heredity, genetics, and eugenics in Dutch and German newspapers between 1863 and 1940. The challenge has been to incorporate the semantics of the two languages (Dutch and German). A statistical machine translation service was included and used to translate existing lexicons and documents from Dutch and German (in both directions). xTAS's functionalities are used to leverage interactive creation, and the expansion and refinement of lexicons that are specific to the user's research questions and needs. xTAS feeds' visualisations allow users to examine the research domain along the aforementioned dimensions of time, context, and the identity and frequency of the discourse. As in WAHSP, BILAND employs a user-oriented, iterative model of collaboration between humanities scholars and ICT developers. Comparative, bilingual historical text mining raises a range of challenges. An important question is that of the linguistic comparability of the research topic as it is formulated in a specific query. The national vocabularies may not be literally translatable, for example, in the case of 'eugenics'. Whereas the Dutch terminology follows the English – *eugenetica, eugeniek* – in the German language the most common translation for eugenics is *Rassenhygiene* [racial hygiene]. The more literal translation *Eugenik* existed and was used in the same sense, but was not a sufficient keyword to explore eugenic notions in German newspapers. In this specific historical text mining, it is of utmost importance to be aware of the specifics of comparisons – a word or a concept, i.e., the idea behind that word (Huijnen et al., 2014: 81).

In addition to the comparability of historical concepts, the possibility of a comparison between given datasets should be tested. Do given datasets represent a similar historical entity – the public, the public debate (in an ideal situation)? In our media history case study the question is: is an equal range and coverage of newspapers represented in the dataset in a given period? Is there a comparable balance between national and regional newspapers, or newspapers representing urban and rural regions, etc.?

In BILAND, comparability is not yet possible. Because of IPR problems and the lack of useful digitised newspaper archives, the only digitised newspaper archive from Germany that this project was able to use was the *Amtspresse Preussens*. This dataset includes three 19th-century newspapers, with a total of less than 20,000 digitised pages.[10] These are hardly comparable to the Dutch dataset of 10 million pages, since the German dataset has neither the quantity, nor the wide time period or national scope of the Dutch dataset. However, German national libraries are rapidly catching up. They have initiated several digitising projects, e.g. within the Europeana community[11] or the *Deutsche Digitale Bibliothek*.[12]

Despite these IPR and digitisation challenges, the use of text-mining techniques holds promise as an innovative and exciting method for comparative international historical research. It can point to transnational concurrences or transfers of ideas, beliefs or knowledge in a far more time-efficient and validated way than traditional historical research has been able to do. Figure 27.3, for example, shows the concurrence of the word 'hygiene' in Dutch and German datasets.

---

[10] http://zefys.staatsbibliothek-berlin.de/ (accessed 03-02-2017)
[11] http://www.europeana.eu/portal/ (accessed 10-02-2016)
[12] https://www.deutsche-digitale-bibliothek.de/ (accessed 10-02-2016)

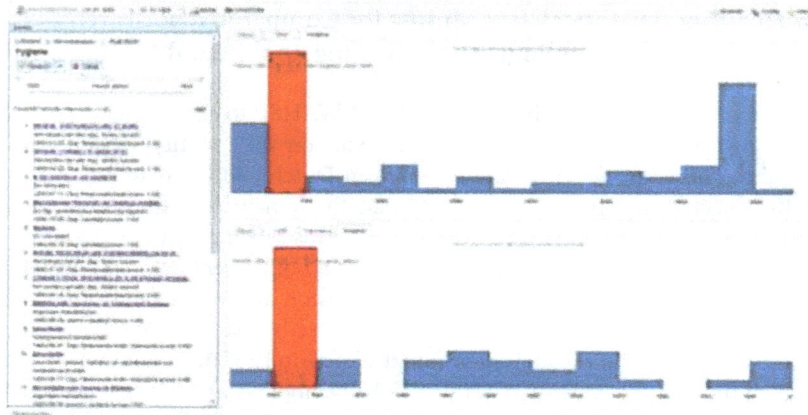

Figure 27.3: concurrence of the word 'hygiene' in Dutch and German datasets. Without ignoring the usual problems of historical comparison, the burst in 1863 in both sets of historical newspapers is significant enough to continue this line of research. (17 June 2013).

27.4   Up-Scaling WAHSP and BILAND for Larger Groups of Users: The Challenges

In 2013, the WAHSP and BILAND CLARIN-NL demonstrator projects were used as bases for two digital humanities projects in which historians and computer scientists cooperated. First, WAHSP modules were implemented and further developed in the open-source text-mining application Texcavator, which was developed as the supporting tool in the NWO-funded programme 'Translantis: Digital Humanities Approaches to Reference Cultures'.[13] One of the aims of the Translantis programme is to test and further develop Texcavator for historical research using 'big data' sets.[14] This allows a team of about ten historians to address conceptual historical questions on the role of reference cultures in 20th-century debates about social issues and collective identities, looking specifically at the emergence of the United States in public discourse in the Netherlands. The research team combines exploratory search and text mining to dig into the Delpher corpus of digitised historical newspapers and journals provided by the National Library of the Netherlands. Initially Texcavator combined xTAS with Elasticsearch as a natural follow-up of the WAHSP and BILAND tools.[15] However, from the beginning there were stability and scalability issues. In particular, the uptake of the tool was greater than foreseen, as were the underlying dynamically generated datasets, and the required high performance computing was underestimated. This resulted in a lack of responsiveness of the tool and user frustration. With the help of the eScience Center and SURF-sara, and by eliminating the xTAS-supported tool functionalities, the stability and scalability were significantly improved. However, these performance gains came at the expense of the functionality profile of the tool.

The stable and scalable Texcavator tool is able to provide four main services: (1) allow researchers to carry out full-text searches and save queries, (2) produce normalised timelines showing how often (a combination of) keywords are produced in a specific period, (3) create word clouds

---

[13] http://translantis.wp.hum.uu.nl/ (accessed 03-02-2017)
[14] http://texcavator.hum.uu.nl/ (accessed 03-02-2017)
[15] https://github.com/elastic/elasticsearch (accessed 11-02-2016)

displaying the words used most often in the articles containing the entered keyword(s) (including the removal of stop words) and (4) export the query results to other text-analytics tools. The tool's main benefits are that it enables historians to trace specific words and changes in the contextualised word use over time and to keep systematic data logs. For named-entity recognition and sentiment mining (functionalities that were part of the original WAHSP tool), however, researchers now rely on other available open-source tools.

Second, the set of BILAND modules were implemented and further developed in the open-source multi-lingual text-mining application Asino, which is an integral part of the HERA-funded programme 'AsymEnc: Asymmetrical Encounters: Digital Humanities Approaches to Reference Cultures in Europe, 1815–1992'.[16] The AsymEnc Asino application was meant to be used as a multi-lingual text-mining tool to map the dynamics, intensity, and direction of intercultural references within European public discourse as represented in newspaper collections such as those of the British Library, the National Library of the Netherlands, and the Bibliothèque Nationale de Luxembourg. The AsymEnc research group developed this tool in order to trace and analyse regional, national, and European dimensions of cultural encounters, such as references to European urban centres, mass media, and consumer products. However, from the beginning, stability and scalability issues also became manifest, as had been the case for WAHSP. The computational expert group in Trier also chose Solr as an alternative to Elasticsearch and xTAS, and underestimated the time needed to integrate a machine translation service for Dutch, English, and German.[17] Moreover, the IPR rules for the cross-border exchange of digitised newspaper collections proved to be significantly stricter, due to commercial interests, than could have been foreseen at the beginning of the project. The historians involved have sought to overcome these limitations by using alternative open-source tools to perform named-entity recognition, topic modelling and GIS mapping of the locally available digitised newspaper collections, such as the *Pall Mall Gazette*,[18] while the Asino tool is being further developed by the Institute of Computer Science at the University of Göttingen (Coll Ardanuy et al., 2016).

27.5   Conclusion

Digital tools will enable historians to analyse massive volumes of texts and other big data sets and to integrate (socio-)linguistics, statistics, and geo-informatics in historical research. However, the technical and infrastructural requirements to meet those promises have not yet been fully realised. A crucial prerequisite for a productive digital research platform is the availability of high-performance computing facilities comparable with those used in physics and the life sciences in combination with a transdisciplinary working programme aimed at articulating and aligning the needs of the users. If these conditions are met, techniques of big data analytics will stimulate historians to set up new forms of systematic search trails that can, as we have shown, provide challenging perspectives on the circulation of ideas and notions in the public sphere. The evidence of a meaningful overlap and interference between drugs and eugenics as well as between wage and eugenics discourses certainly deserve further research.

Exploratory search methods that can provide a quick overview combined with tools to zoom into details on a predefined timeline are particularly useful for alternating effectively between distant reading and close reading. Our proposed integration of interactive exploratory search and text mining will support historians to set up systematic search trails. The tooling will help them interpret and contrast the returned result sets by exploring word associations for a result set, inspecting

---

[16] http://asymenc.wp.hum.uu.nl/ (accessed 11-02-2016)
[17] http://www.opensemanticsearch.org/ (accessed 11-02-2016)
[18] http://dhbenelux.org/wp-content/uploads/2015/04/42.pdf (accessed 11-02-2016)

the temporal distribution of documents and comparing selections so that more informed and principled document selection for close reading is possible. Obviously, this is no substitute for historical craftsmanship. WAHSP, BILAND, Texcavator and other open-source semantic text-mining tools are meant to be exploratory tools that ideally inspire new ideas and insights that would not have been generated through reading a small number of articles and can only be brought forth through the analysis of hundreds of articles. Insights gained by means of distant reading may help to frame new research questions, thus catalysing historical research. Digitally produced results often lead to unexpected associations that turn out to be promising for further research, but, in order to be meaningful, these require further conventional close reading.

There are a number of prerequisites that have to be met before digital tools can become standard procedure in historical research. First, it is essential that historians working with digital tools and building their arguments on digitally obtained research results be aware of what they are doing and keep meticulous lab logs of all their queries and visualisation results. This may sound obvious, but it does not always happen. Historians should have a clear understanding of the realities and causalities that word clouds, normalised time lines, or word vector approaches represent. They must also understand how to generate meaningful queries based on linguistic expertise. Historians should be able to interpret and explain text-mining research results in formulations such as, 'within the given digitized source material, in all articles containing word x and word y, word z also appears with a significant and normalized frequency'. This makes their arguments transparent and thus reproducible. Digital tools should not be treated as black boxes, with queries only going in and multiple visualisations mysteriously coming out and being used as evidence-based results. As Gibbs and Owens (2012) argue, '[t]he processes for working with the vast amounts of easily accessible and diverse large sets of data suggest a need for historians to formulate, articulate, and propagate ideas about how data should be approached in historical research'.

Demonstrator tools like WAHSP, BILAND and Texcavator offer explorative hints for certain lines of arguments, but do not automatically generate strong evidence or explanations for the arguments. The use of the aforementioned research tools indicates that in the public debate in the Netherlands at the start of the 20th century, drugs and inheritance were predominantly framed as medical, but the results of the text mining do not prove that this was true or explain why it was so.

In sum, open-source text-mining tools are not built to make historical scholarship obsolete, but rather to strengthen expertise through iteratively alternating distant and close reading, thus broadening heuristic capacities, and offering new analytical tools for data interpretation. These tools are meant to provide historians with new perspectives, and draw their attention through distant reading to potentially interesting cases that need further close reading. In this sense, it is evident that text mining can form a relevant addition to the historian's toolbox, and this outside the topics of drug and eugenic debates as well: text mining can be used to analyse cultural trends and patterns found in newspaper publications on a much broader scale.

Acknowledgements

This research was supported by the European Community's Seventh Framework Programme (FP7/2007–2013) under grant agreement nr 288024 (LiMo- SINe project); by the Netherlands Organisation for Scientific Research (NWO) under project nrs 640.004.802, 727.011.005, 612.001.116, 317-52-010, HOR-11-10, Hor-11-19; by the Center for Creation, Content and Technology (CCCT), the WAHSP, BILAND and QuaMerdes projects funded by the CLARIN-nl program, the TROVe project funded by the CLARIAH program, Hera JRP Cultural Encounters 12-HERA-JRP-CE-FP-045 project, the Dutch national program COMMIT, the ESF Research Network Program ELIAS, the Elite Network Shifts project funded by the Royal Dutch Academy of Sciences (KNAW), the Netherlands eScience Center under project number 027.012.105 and the Yahoo! Faculty.

References

Berry, D.M. (ed.): Understanding Digital Humanities. Palgrave Macmillan (2012)

Bingham, A.: The digitization of newspaper archives: Opportunities and challenges for historians. Twentieth Century British History 21(2), 225–231 (2010)

Burdick et al., A.: Digital Humanities. MIT Press (2012)

Coll Ardanuy M, Knauth, J. Beliankou A., Bos van den M., Sporleder C. Person-centric mining of historical newspaper collections. In. Volume 9819 of the series Lecture Notes in Computer Science (Springer, 2016), pp. 320–331.

Earheart, A.E., Jewell, A. (eds.): The American Literature Scholar in the Digital Age. University of Michigan Press (2011)

van Eijnatten, J., Pieters, T., Verheul, J.: Big data for global history: The transformative promise of digital humanities. Low Countries Historical Review 128, no.4, 55–77 (2013)

van Eijnatten J., Verheul J., Pieters T.: TS Tools: Using Texcavator to Map Public Discourse: TS: Tijdschrift voor Tijdschriftstudies 35, 59–65 (2014)

Gibbs, F., Owens, T.: The hermeneutics of data and historical writing. http://writinghistory.trincoll.edu/data/gibbs-owens-2012-spring/ (2012)

Graham, S., Milligan, I., Weingart, S.: The hermeneutics of data and historical writing. In: The Historian's Macroscope: Big Digital History. Imperial College Press (2013)

Hahn, D.: Modernisierung und Biopolitik: Sterilisation und Schwangerschaftsabbruch in Deutschland nach 1945. Campus (2000)

Huijnen P., Laan F., de Rijke M., Pieters T.: A digital humanities approach to the history of science; eugenics revisited in hidden debates by means of semantic text mining. In. A. Nadamoto et al (Eds): Soc Info 2013 Workshops, LNCS 8359 (Springer, New York), pp.71–85 (2014)

Huurnink, B., Hollink, L., van den Heuvel, W., de Rijke, M.: Search behavior of media professionals at an audiovisual archive: A transaction log analysis. Journal of the American Society for Information Science and Technology 61(6), 1180–1197 (June 2010)

Jackson, P., Moulinier, I.: Natural Language Processing for Online Applications: Text Retrieval, Extraction and Categorization. John Benjamins, 2nd edn. (2007)

Jijkoun, V., de Rijke, M., Weerkamp, W.: Generating focused topic-specific sentiment lexicons. In: ACL '10 (2010)

Klausen, S., Bashford, A.: Fertility control: Eugenics, neo-malthusianism, and feminism. In: Bashford, A., Levine, S. (eds.) The Oxford Handbook of the History of Eugenics, pp. 98–115. Oxford University Press (2010)

Leonard, T.C.: Eugenics and economics in the progressive era. Journal of Economic Perspectives 19, 207–224 (2005)

Levine, P., Bashford, A.: Introduction: Eugenics and the modern world. In: Levine, P., Bashford, A. (eds.) The Oxford Handbook of the History of Eugenics, pp. 3–24. Oxford (2010)

Lombardo, P. (ed.): A Century of Eugenics in America: from the Indiana Experiment to the Human Genome Era. Indiana University Press (2001)

Meij, E., Bron, M., Huurnink, B., Hollink, L., de Rijke, M.: Learning semantic query suggestions. In: ISWC '09. Springer (2009)

Michel, J.B.: Quantitative analysis of culture using millions of digitized books. Science 6014, 176–183 (2010)

Nicholson, B.: The digital turn. Media History 19(1), 59–73 (2013)

Odijk D., de Rooij O., Peetz M-H., Pieters T., de Rijke M., Snelders S.: 'Semantic Document Selection', TPDL 2012: Theory and Practice of Digital Libraries: Springer. (2012)

Reulecke, J. (ed.): Herausforderung Bevölkerung: zu Entwicklungen des modernen Denkens über die Bevölkerung vor, im und nach dem 'Dritten Reich'. VS Verslag für Sozialwissenschaften (2007)

Seefeldt, D., Thomas III, W.G.: What is digital history? a look at some exemplar projects. Faculty Publications, Department of History. Paper 98. http://digitalcommons.unl.edu/historyfacpub/9 (2009)

Snelders, S., Pieters, T.: Van degeneratie tot individuele gezondheidsopties: Het maatschappelijk gebruik van erfelijkheidsconcepten in de twintigste eeuw. Gewina 26(4), 203–215 (2003)

Snelders S., Pieters T.: The blue lotus revisited: Public perceptions of drug use in the Dutch Empire, c. 1900-1942. Paper held at Drugs and drink in Asia: New perspectives from history. Conference of June 22–23, Shanghai. (2012)

Snelders S. Kaplan C. Pieters T.: On cannabis, chloral hydrate, and career cycles of psychotropic drugs in medicine. Bulletin of the History of Medicine 80, 95–114. (2006)

Turda, M.: Modernism and Eugenics. Palgrave MacMillan (2010)

Warwick, C., Terras, M.M., Nyhan, J.: Digital Humanities in Practice. Facet (2012)

CHAPTER 28

RemBench: A Digital Workbench for Rembrandt Research

Suzan Verberne[a,d], Rudie van Leeuwen[b], Guido Gerritsen[c] and Lou Boves[a]

[a]Centre for Language Studies, Radboud University
[b]Centre for Historical, Literary and Cultural Studies, Radboud University
[c]Huygens Institute for the History of the Netherlands
[d]Leiden Institute for Advanced Computer Science, Leiden University
Corresponding author: s.verberne@liacs.leidenuniv.nl

ABSTRACT

In this chapter, we present RemBench, a search engine for research into the life and works of Rembrandt van Rijn. RemBench combines the data from four different databases behind one interface using federated search technology. Metadata filtering is enabled through faceted search. RemBench enables art historians and other professionals interested in Rembrandt's time to find all the information on Rembrandt that is available in online repositories through one application. The functionality and user interface of RemBench were developed in close collaboration with domain experts, and evaluated in a user study with nine students of history and art history. We found that the users were positive about the usability of RemBench, especially about its user interface and interaction design. We think that RemBench sets an example for search engines in the digital humanities. Our most important recommendation is the use of federated search (with different types of results in different verticals) and faceted search in the art history domain. In addition, we recommend evaluation through a user observation study, which is already possible with a small number of participants.

28.1 Introduction

Art historians typically study different types of sources: works of art, primary and secondary sources describing these works of art, the life of the artist, the provenance of the work, and the social and economic context in which the artist worked. The relevant information can be found in independent digital (and, non-digital) resources, developed by museums, archives and libraries.

How to cite this book chapter:
Verberne, S, van Leeuwen, R, Gerritsen, G and Boves, L. 2017. RemBench: A Digital Workbench for Rembrandt Research. In: Odijk, J and van Hessen, A. (eds.) *CLARIN in the Low Countries*, Pp. 337–350. London: Ubiquity Press. DOI: https://doi.org/10.5334/bbi.28. License: CC-BY 4.0

More and more sources are being digitised and made accessible online (Rodríguez Ortega, 2013). However, with each source type residing in its own database, art historians have to use a number of independent digital applications in parallel, each with their idiosyncratic interface. In the worst case, their research even requires visiting several museums, libraries or archives in different cities.

In this chapter we describe the development and evaluation of a specialised search engine in the art history domain that integrates multiple databases behind one interface: RemBench.[1] RemBench stands for 'a Digital Workbench for Rembrandt Research'. The overall goals of the RemBench project were (1) to develop a working environment in which researchers have easy access to all the information about the 17th-century Dutch artist Rembrandt van Rijn and his environment and (2) to show the value of online digital data for art history research.

RemBench was developed in the context of CLARIN-NL, a large national project in the Netherlands (2009–2015) which aimed to improve the research infrastructure for humanities researchers who work with language data and tools. Data and tools developed in the context of CLARIN-NL are available to outside researchers via the CLARIN infrastructure, thereby making humanities research that requires language resources 'easier, faster, better, and in some cases even possible for the first time'.[2] Within CLARIN-NL, RemBench was the only project directed at the art history domain. The art history domain is an interesting case for search engines tailored to digital humanities, because relevant information is typically contained in diverse sources (primary sources as well as secondary ones), and the data can be in textual as well as in graphical form.

RemBench is a *faceted search* engine: free text search is combined with filtering functionality for metadata values (Tunkelang, 2009). Access to four different databases is realised through *federated search*. Federated search (sometimes called distributed information retrieval) is a technique for searching multiple collections simultaneously for one single query; the results returned by selected collections are integrated into a single result page (Jacsó, 2004; Shokouhi and Si, 2011). In the context of CLARIN, a federated search infrastructure was developed for enabling the search for suitable language resources (Stehouwer et al., 2012): researchers can use the infrastructure to search through the content of multiple language resources (corpora) that potentially contain useful information for answering their research question. This type of federated search makes high demands on the unification of metadata.

Art historians who study the life and works of Rembrandt van Rijn are the primary target group of RemBench. We identified several additional target groups, such as historians with questions related to 16th–18th century life, literary scholars, linguists studying 17th-century Dutch, genealogists, and economists studying the art market in the Golden Age.

The contributions of this project are threefold: (1) the integration of the metadata of four Rembrandt-related databases; (2) the development of a user-friendly search engine for Rembrandt research that gives access to distributed resources; and (3) recommendations for the evaluation of search engines in the art history domain.

28.2   About RemBench

RemBench connects four existing databases. The first two are RKDartists and RKDimages,[3] two art historical databases maintained by the Netherlands Institute for Art History (RKD). RKDartists is a database of biographical information about Dutch and foreign artists from the Middle Ages to the present day. RKDimages is a database with descriptions and images of mainly Dutch paintings, drawings, prints and original photos from before the Second World War.

---

[1]   http://rembench.huygens.knaw.nl/
[2]   http://www.clarin.nl/
[3]   http://explore.rkd.nl/

The third database connected to RemBench is RemDoc,[4] a digital collection of primary documents that relate to the life and works of Rembrandt van Rijn. In the RemDoc project, all known documents that relate to Rembrandt, as a person and as an artist, as well as to his ancestors, family, and business partners, from the 15th to the 18th century have been collected and published. The database contains 1,667 documents.

The fourth database in RemBench is a university library catalogue, digitised and made available through the RUQuest[5] system, a library search system that provides access to the full collection of the Radboud University Library and to the full-text articles of all journals that Radboud University has subscribed to.

The project consisted of two phases: first, the metadata of the four different databases were connected by mapping them onto one common metadata scheme. Second, a search engine was developed to disclose the data in these databases. The RemBench user interface was designed by a professional designer, in interaction with art historians, who added their specific wishes.

The architecture of RemBench is shown in Figure 28.1; its user interface in Figure 28.2. The URL of RemBench is http://rembench.huygens.knaw.nl/.

28.3 Challenges

In this section, we summarise the challenges that we faced in the RemBench project: (1) selecting the relevant data and metadata fields from four different databases; (2) the interoperability of the resources; (3) developing the search engine; and (4) designing the user interface. The following four subsections address these challenges.

28.3.1 Selecting Data and Metadata Fields

For the integration of the four databases, the following three questions needed to be answered: (a) which subset of the data from each database should be made searchable? (b) which metadata fields should be shown as facets in the faceted search? and (c) which fields should be searched with free text search?

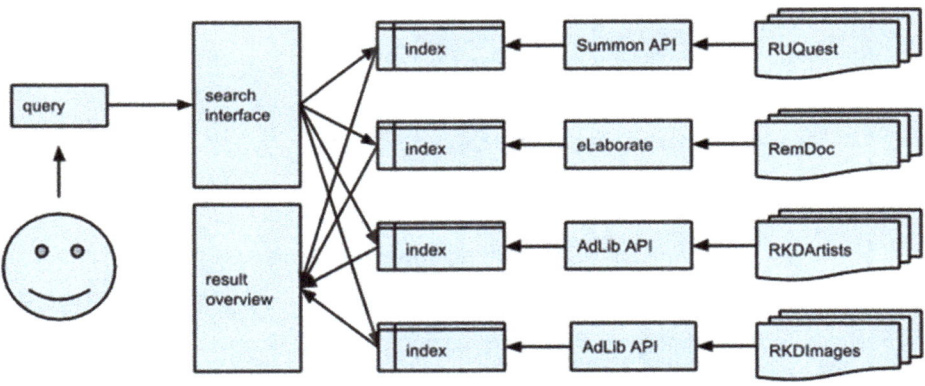

Figure 28.1: The architecture of RemBench

4 http://www.remdoc.org/
5 https://ru.on.worldcat.org/discovery

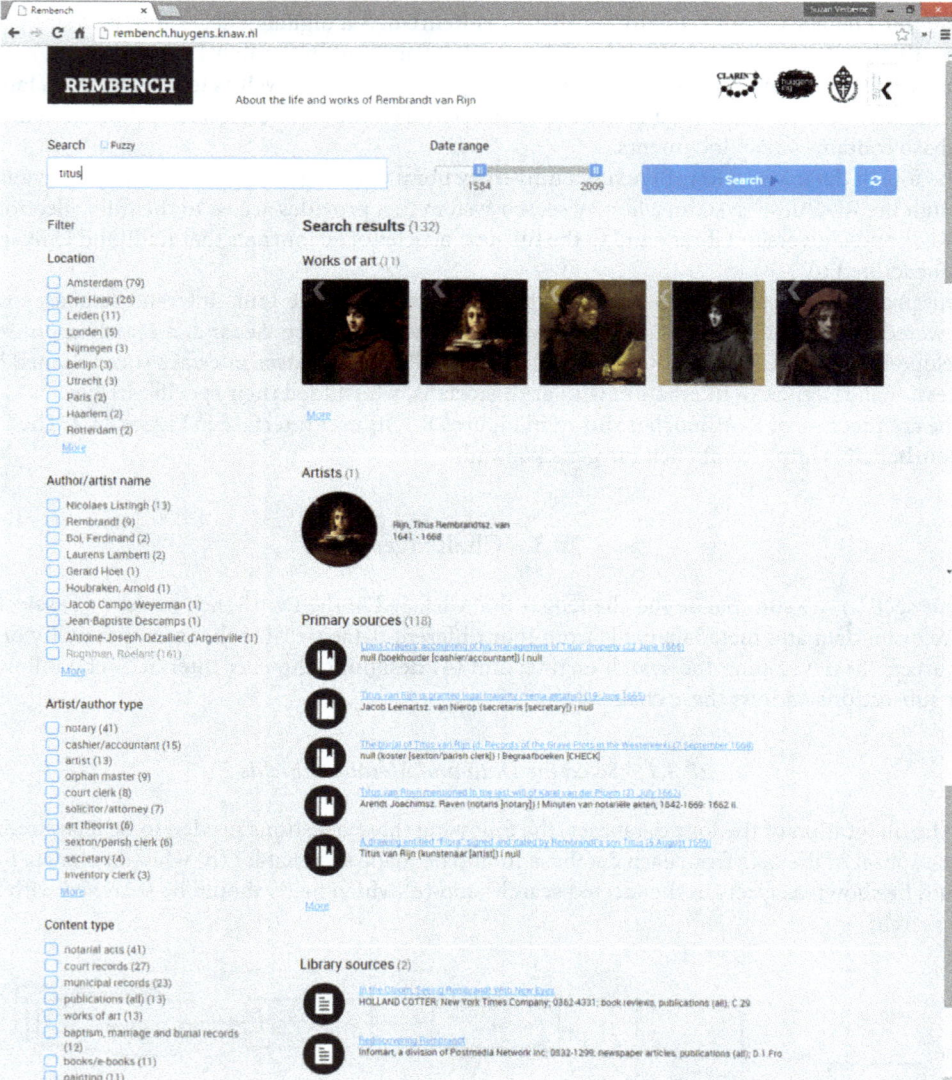

Figure 28.2: The user interface of RemBench

28.3.1.1   Data Selection from the Databases

We made a selection of records from the RKD databases by including only artists and images that are were related to Rembrandt van Rijn. The starting point for this selection was the record of Rembrandt himself in RKDartists. In the selection of artists, all artists that are mentioned in the Rembrandt record (either under 'pupil of', 'teacher of', 'followed by', 'influenced by' or 'had influence on') were included. In the selection of images, all works of art from RKDimages that have been attributed to one of the artists in the artist selection were included. The resulting selection consists of 1,857 works of art and 59 artists.

No selection needed to be performed in RemDoc, because all content in RemDoc is related to Rembrandt.

In RUQuest, we planned to harvest all items that were returned from the collection for the search term 'Rembrandt' (84,081 results). This would ensure a filtering for the domain, so that RemBench queries will only give results that are relevant to the Rembrandt domain of research. (Without filtering, a query such as 'saskia' would give many results that are not about Rembrandt's wife Saskia van Uylenburgh.) However, the API that gave access to RUQuest could only return a maximum of 1,000 records. Consequently, not all records relevant to Rembrandt could be harvested at index time. As an alternative to pre-fetching all 84,081 records, we retrieved the maximum of 1,000 results through the API for each query at query time, and stored the results in a local index. The local index was searched again for every following query, together with a call to the API for another 1,000 results.

28.3.1.2   Field Selection for Faceted Search

In the RemBench interface, free text search is combined with faceted search (filtering for metadata values, see Section 28.3.2). We initially chose three metadata fields for faceted search: Content type, Artist/author type, and Location, and included Publication date as an additional filter. Later, we added Author/Artist name, to allow filtering by one specific artist or author. For each of these fields, we mapped the values for the different databases onto each other. For example, for content type, we defined a value 'articles in magazines/journals', which corresponds to six different content type values in RUQuest ('Journal article', 'Newsletter article', etc.) and one value for Document type in RemDoc: 'periodical/magazine'. Not all facets have a corresponding metadata field in all databases. For example, when the user selects a value for the Content Type facet, RKDartists does not return any results.

28.3.1.3   Field Selection for Free Text Search

In the original databases there is a distinction between free text fields and restricted metadata fields. In the local index, we indexed all fields with textual content as free text fields. Table 28.1 shows the fields that were indexed for free text search.

28.3.2   Interoperability of the Resources

After selecting the data and metadata field from the databases that are used for faceted search, we needed to map the metadata categories onto each other. The central step was to map the resource-specific metadata categories to ISOcat data categories (DCs). ISOcat distinguishes between *Complex DCs*, which are (meta)data fields that can have a value, and *Simple DCs*, which are the values themselves. For example, the RemBench Facet 'Context type' (a complex DC) can have as values 'altar piece', 'articles in magazines/journals', 'baptism, marriage and burial records' etc. (simple DCs). Table 28.2 shows an overview of the complex DCs that we defined in ISOcat. The first two, date and author, already existed as DCs with the same meaning in ISOcat.

The majority of the complex DCs are open categories: they can get any value (either a string or a date). When harmonising the contents of multiple databases, the content of these fields needed to be standardised, especially in the case of names. For example, one database might use 'Paris' as name, while another uses 'Parijs' (the Dutch word for Paris) and a third one 'Paris, France'. For the standardisation of geographical names, we used the controlled vocabularies by Getty.[6] Note that disciplines unrelated to art might have preferred a different vocabulary, for example the UNGEGN World Geographical Names database.[7]

---

[6]   https://www.getty.edu/research/tools/vocabularies/tgn/
[7]   http://unstats.un.org/unsd/geoinfo/geonames/

Database	Field	Explanation/comments
RemDoc	Entry Name	
	Translation	
	Diplomatic	This field contains the transcription
	Comments	
RUQuest	SubjectTerms	
	Title	
	PublicationTitle	
	Author	
	Abstract	
RKDimages	i2 'benaming_kunstwerk' i3 'andere_benaming' i4 'titel_engels'	Title of work of art, alternative title and English title
	i8 'naam'	Artist
	i75 'RKD_algemene_trefwoorden'	General keywords. Example value: 'oude testament & apocriefen' (old testament & apocryphals)
	i50 'collectienaam'	Collection
	i96 'inbrenger'	Contributor
	i97 'naam_koper'	Buyer's name
	i29 'opdrachtgever'	Patron
	i123 'persoonsnummer'	Person number (portrayed person)
	i102 'veilinghuis'	Auction house
	i122 opmerking_algemeen	General comment
RKDartists	a1 'kunstenaarsnaam'	Name of artist
	a7 'spelling_variant'	Spelling variant of name
	a29 'plaats_van_werkzaamheid'	Place of activity
	a34 'kwalificatie'	Qualification ('role'/profession)
	i122 opmerking_algemeen	General comment

Table 28.1: Fields from each of the databases that were indexed for free text search

Three DCs are closed with respect to the values they can get: 'Content Type', 'Archive Main Type' and 'Person Type'. The values that the closed categories can take have been defined in the simple DCs in ISOcat. An example of a simple DC is 'articlesInMagazinesJournals', which is a possible value for the complex DC 'Content Type'. All data categories (complex and simple) that are used in a project are defined in the Data Category Selection (DCS). We delivered the RemBench-DCS to CLARIN-NL as an XML file in the Data Category Interchange Format (DCIF).

In addition, we defined the RemBench metadata on the level of resources in the Component MetaData Infrastructure (CMDI), which provides a framework to describe and reuse metadata formats. We submitted three entries to CMDI for each of the three resources contained in RemBench: RemDoc, RKDexplore and RUQuest; these entries can be found in CLARIN's Virtual Language Observatory.[8]

---

[8]   https://vlo.clarin.eu/

DC name	Field in RemDoc	Field in RKD
date (existing DC-4335)	Date	i13 datering
author (existing DC-4115)	Author	
English Translation	Translation	
Name of Object	Name of object	i2 benaming kunstwerk
Location of Object	Location	
Content Type	Document Main Type	i18 objectcategorie
Archive Main Type	Archive Main Type	
Person Type	Role	a34 kwalificatie persoon
name of artist		a1 kunstenaarsnaam=i8 naam
date of birth		a17-a18 geboortedatum_begin en geboortedatum_eind
date of death		a22-a23 sterftedatum_begin en steftedatum_eind
period of activity		a26-a27 werkzame_periode_begin en werkzame_periode_eind
place of activity		plaats_van_werkzaamheid
text transcription	Diplomatic	
secondary document	Comments	

Table 28.2: List of complex data categories defined for RemBench in ISOcat.

28.3.3 Developing the Search Engine

The effectiveness of faceted search for research in the art history domain has been shown by Yee et al. (2003), who present the results of a usability study in which art history students explored a collection of 35,000 fine arts images using a faceted interface for metadata filtering. They found that for these data 90% of the participants preferred the metadata approach over a free-text search functionality, despite the fact that the latter was more familiar to them.

The technology for faceted[9] search and free text search that allows the user to search all databases at once was developed by the Huygens Institute for the History of the Netherlands using Apache Solr.[10] With Solr, it is possible to search in multiple fields from multiple databases at the same time (federated search). The user's query is forwarded from the RemBench interface to each of the database-specific indexes (see Figure 28.1), and its content is matched to each of the text fields listed in Table 28.1. The results are returned from each of the databases in order of relevance.

28.3.4 Designing the User Interface

The four databases were treated as four separate verticals in the interface, which did not merge the results in one result list. The main reason for that decision came from the art historians in the research team: they argued that four different groups of results would be clearer to the user. Keeping verticals separate avoids the challenge of ranking the results from the different verticals relative to each other (Ponnuswami et al., 2011). In the user interface, the verticals are labelled 'Works of art' (group of results from RKDimages), 'Artists' (group of results from RKDartists), 'Primary Sources' (group of results from RemDoc), and 'Library Sources' (group of results from RUQuest). In every

---

[9] https://github.com/HuygensING/faceted-search
[10] http://lucene.apache.org/solr/

vertical, a maximum of five results are shown on the front page. To see more results (in an overlay screen), the user has to click on 'More' (cf. Figure 28.2).

28.4   Evaluation

In order to evaluate the beta version of RemBench and improve it for the final version, we set up a user observation study. In this section, we describe the study and the results.

28.4.1   Design, Materials and Procedure

Students of history and art history (bachelor's and master's level) from Radboud University were recruited to participate in the user study; there were nine participants (two male, seven female; median age: 20.5) in total. We expected that nine participants would be sufficient, because Nielsen and Landauer (1993) show that for most usability tests, the proportion of additional usability problems found when adding test users quickly decreases beyond five users. The participants were paid a volunteer fee of €10.

The common way of evaluating the usability of search engines is to give users a series of information problems and ask them to find the answers using the search engine at hand; afterwards, the users are presented with a questionnaire in order to assess their satisfaction with the system (Spink, 2002). This method of usability testing is adopted in the current chapter. In addition, we combine screen capturing with thinking-aloud, as suggested by Van Waes (2000), to collect the user interactions.

The task for the students was to find the best possible answers to a series of questions related to Rembrandt, using RemBench. Each participant was given 10 questions (see Section 28.4.2), one question at a time. Some of the questions required a single answer (yes/no, name, title, or place), others a list of items. The participants were asked to use all the functionalities of RemBench they needed to find the answers and to stop their search when they felt that they had tried everything they could to find the answers.

The participants were working on a Windows 7 PC with Firefox. A researcher loaded the Rem-Bench homepage for them and gave them the list of questions to work on. User-system interaction was observed using a thinking-aloud set-up (Gerjets et al., 2011): the participants were asked to voice aloud their thinking process, what actions they took in the search process and why they took them. A researcher was sitting next to the participant and took extensive notes of what the participant did and said. Desktop activity was recorded using screen capture software.[11] After 45 minutes, the researcher asked the participant to finish the current question and skip the remaining ones.

After each question, the participants were asked to write down the answer they found on paper, and give two evaluative judgements:

• How satisfied are you with the answer found? (5-point rating scale)
• How satisfied are you with the use of RemBench for answering the question? (5-point rating scale)

After finishing the task, the participants were given a post-task questionnaire with two evaluative questions:

• Please list the positive aspects of RemBench
• Please list the negative aspects of RemBench

---

[11]   BB FlashBack Express: http://www.bbsoftware.co.uk/BBFlashBack_FreePlayer.aspx

28.4.2   Questions about Rembrandt

Two art historians from our research team (who are working on the topic of Rembrandt themselves) phrased a number of questions about Rembrandt that are likely to be addressed by Rembrandt researchers. They provided 61 questions. Some examples of questions are listed in Table 28.3. Each participant was assigned 10 of the 61 questions.

28.4.3   Results

Out of the 61 questions, 54 were addressed by at least one participant. The remaining seven were all skipped, because not all participants succeeded in answering all 10 questions assigned to them in the 45-minute time slot. Fifteen questions were answered by two participants. In this section, we report (a) the measured user satisfaction, (b) the outcomes of the post-task questionnaire and (c) which features of RemBench were used by the participants and which were not.

28.4.3.1   User Satisfaction

The participants answered the questions 'How satisfied are you with the answer(s) found?' (*answer satisfaction*) and 'How satisfied are you with the use of RemBench for answering the question?' (*usability satisfaction*). Scores were given on a rating scale of 1–5, 5 being the highest satisfaction score. The mean score that was obtained for answer satisfaction was 2.90, with a standard deviation of 1.46. The mean score that was obtained for usability satisfaction was 2.84, with a standard deviation of 1.27. We found a strong positive relationship between answer satisfaction and usability satisfaction (Pearson's $r = 0.91$, N = 54). This indicates that usability satisfaction was dependent on answer satisfaction: if the user was not able to find the answer with RemBench, then both the satisfaction with the answer and with RemBench were likely to be low.

28.4.3.2   Outcome of Post-Task Questionnaire

All participants wrote down positive and negative points about RemBench. The eighth and ninth participant did not bring up any new points, which confirms that there were enough users to reach saturation in the reported usability issues. The lists of positive aspects and the lists of negative aspects provided by the participants in the post-task questionnaire were merged, and sorted by topic.

   We found that the users were predominantly positive about the graphical user interface, the interaction design, and the content of the underlying databases, and that they were most critical about the search functionalities. We made the following adaptations to the final version of RemBench in order to follow the advice given by the participants in their comments:

• How old was Titus when he died?
• How many works by Rembrandt are in private collections?
• Where is Rembrandt's *Storm on the Sea of Galilee*?
• Was Rembrandt's *Reading Woman* in the Rijksmuseum painted on canvas or panel?
• Did Rembrandt know any Jews?
• Did Rembrandt paint dogs?
• Which paintings by Rembrandt have been in the collections of the House of Orange-Nassau?
• Which works by Rembrandt are in St. Petersburg?
• Find etchings after Rembrandt's self-portraits

Table 28.3: A few examples of questions in our dataset (translated from Dutch)

- Functionality was added for searching works by one specific artist, by adding an 'Author/artist name' facet;
- Discounting of the term weight for the query term 'Rembrandt' was implemented, in order to ensure that for queries with the word 'Rembrandt' and some other word(s), results that contain only the other word(s), e.g. 'dog', are ranked higher than results that contain only the word 'Rembrandt'.

A few other issues identified in the comments could not be solved because they require expansion of the content of the (external) databases. One example is the comment that it is sometimes difficult to find works of art with specific topics (e.g. dogs, snow). Since works of art can only be found through the topics that are included in the metadata, it might be valuable to expand the topical annotation of works of art in future work, for example through crowd sourcing (Trant, 2009). The value of topic annotations for image search in the historical domain has also been pointed out by Choi and Rasmussen (2003), who found that topic descriptors that represent the image content were very important for user satisfaction.

28.4.3.3   Which Features were Used by the Participants and Which were Not?

All functionalities were used by the participants, except for the Refresh button (Clear everything) and the advanced query options of fuzzy search and Boolean query operators. Instead of the Refresh button, the users manually cleared the fields when starting a new query. This sometimes led to mistakes, because they forgot to clear a facet value and then entered a new query, getting fewer results than they expected.

Fuzzy search is an option that allows the user to find non-exact matches of their search term. This can be very useful for finding spelling variants or in case the user is not sure of a specific spelling. With the fuzzy search option selected (via a checkbox above the search field), the search system can return primary documents containing the string *Rembrant* for the query 'Rembrandt' (in the 17th century, Dutch spelling was not normalised yet), or the painting *Storm on the Sea of Galilea* for the query 'Galilee'. The students participating in the study either did not know the purpose of the fuzzy search option or overlooked the option in the interface.

Boolean query operators are useful to force a specific term to be presented in the result list. For example, to answer the question 'Did Saskia have brothers?' it might be profitable to require both terms 'Saskia' and 'brothers' to be present in the results, because there are many sources containing either one of the two. The Boolean query 'Saskia AND brothers' would accomplish this. Similarly, to answer the question 'Did Rembrandt paint dogs?' a user might want to require that the term 'dog(s)' be in any result, because there are many results returned for the term 'Rembrandt'.[12]

In the final version of RemBench, some user guidance for these unused functionalities was added in the form of mouse-over tooltips.

28.5   Discussion

In this section, we make a number of recommendations based on the challenges that we faced in the RemBench project.

---

[12]   It should be noted here that if a search system provides good ranking of the results, the Boolean 'AND' operator should not be necessary, because results with both terms present should be ranked higher in the result list than results with only one of the two terms. In addition to this, query terms that occur in few documents ('dogs') should be weighted heavier than query terms that occur in many documents ('Rembrandt'). Although this term characteristic ('inverted document frequency') is a component of the ranking algorithm in Solr (see http://www.solrtutorial.com/solr-search-relevancy.html), it was sometimes difficult for the participants to get the results they wanted for queries with one or more highly frequent terms.

28.5.1   Recommendations for Data Management in Digital Humanities Projects

28.5.1.1   Increasing the Scope of Metadata from Linguistics to Humanities

When we started RemBench, the CLARIN-NL metadata infrastructure was fully directed at language resources with linguistic metadata. To make the CLARIN infrastructure useful for the humanities as a whole, this scope must be broadened. We made a start with RemBench, introducing the ISOcat-profile 'Historical objects'. We were able to reuse the data categories DC-4335 date (from profile Terminology) and DC-4115 author (from profile Metadata) in ISOcat, but we had to create new data categories for the other (meta)data fields in RemBench. Interestingly, for a number of them, seemingly similar data categories existed in other profiles, such as for 'transcription', but these always had a different meaning. This is not a problem, and is inevitable if you create a repository across multiple domains, but in many cases it was clear from the definitions of the data categories that the creator was not aware of possible reuse outside the scope of linguistics. For example, the definition for DC-6037 translation is 'representation in another language (of a motto)'.

In the meantime, CLARIN-EU has abandoned ISOcat in favour of the less complex CLARIN Concept Registry (CCR) and the Component MetaData Infrastructure (CMDI). This holds the promise of making the CLARIN infrastructure attractive for a broader range of humanities researchers.

28.5.1.2   Distinction between Data and Metadata

A clear distinction between data and metadata on the record level does not exist in all domains and for all data types. For example, if we have a collection of 18th-century hand-written documents that is stored physically in a city archive and electronically in a database, then we could consider the documents themselves, the scan of the documents, and perhaps also their transcription (computer-readable representation of the text on the scan) to be the data, and all other information (translation, comments, annotations, author, date, location) to be the metadata. But when we are indexing these fields for searching and filtering, we often consider all fields that we use for free-text search (transcription, translation, comments) as data – perhaps secondary data is a good term here. The same situation occurs for spoken language, where the written transcription can be considered as data and as metadata. This matters for the documentation of requirements for descriptive metadata, and for other locations where CLARIN-NL speaks of 'metadata' in documentation.

28.5.1.3   Access to Library Data

In the linking of library sources to RemBench, we ran into technical and IPR issues. The original plan was to use Picarta as library source. Unfortunately, there was no API for direct access to Picarta. Alternatives were WorldCat and RUQuest (implemented as Summon database by Serial Solutions). After testing both, we concluded that the WorldCat API returns very limited metadata, and is less flexible for implementations. The Summon API that gave access to the RUQuest library database was much more complete, was more flexible to work with and retrieves very extensive metadata. One disadvantage, as mentioned in section 28.3.1.1, is that the Summon API could only return a maximum of 1,000 records. The same problem may also occur in future projects, which limits the use of library data. This should be taken into account when writing project plans for future projects using library data. It also shows that CLARIN needs a facility for tracking changes in all external resources and applications that CLARIN services link to.

28.5.2   Recommendations for the Evaluation of Search Engines in the Humanities

Based on our experiences, we encourage researchers to conduct user observation studies to evaluate the usability of domain-specific search engines. In our user study, nine participants were enough to discover all usability issues. The thinking-aloud protocol has proven to be successful. When a researcher makes extensive notes, no microphone recordings are necessary.

There is one caveat that should be taken into account in the design of usability studies for search engines: there is a strong correlation between answer satisfaction and usability satisfaction. In other words: the more difficult the questions that the participants try to answer with the search engine, the lower their judgements of its usability.

One limitation of our study is that all participants were students. One risk of this is that the information-seeking behaviour of students differs from the behaviour of (older) researchers (Weiler, 2005). According to Rowlands et al. 2008 (2008:290), the generation who grew up with Google-style search relies 'heavily on search engines, view rather than read and do not possess the critical and analytical skills to assess the information that they find on the web.' On the other hand, the authors state that the impact of ICT on this generation should not be overestimated, and that 'we are all the Google generation, the young and old, the professor and the student and the teacher and the child' (Rowlands et al., 2008). Future research should address the differences between students and researchers in their information-seeking behaviour.

28.6   Conclusions

In the RemBench project, we integrated the data and metadata from four different databases behind one search interface, to facilitate online research on the topic of Rembrandt van Rijn, his works and his relatives. The usability of RemBench was evaluated by nine users. We found that the users were positive about the usability of RemBench, especially its user interface and interaction design. They were moderately satisfied with the use of RemBench for answering Rembrandt-related questions. It appeared to be possible to develop a workable combination of faceted and federated search with an acceptable amount of effort needed for mapping and standardising metadata values.

In its current version, RemBench serves as a portal for further research. Its main value for scholars is that multiple sources are brought together at one location ('as a single bookmark in the browser', according to an art historian who studies iconography by Rembrandt; personal communication). This allows the user to immediately find the secondary literature that relates to the works of art that are the focus of study. In addition, RemBench serves an exploratory purpose: using topical queries, the user can quickly see whether a specific topic (or iconographical subject) is frequently addressed in works of art and primary documents such as inventories. If it is, the topic is potentially relevant; this a starting point for further research.

From the (art) history perspective there are three directions in which RemBench can (and should) be developed: (a) extending and integrating the metadata content of RemBench with other resources, such as the Montias Database[13]and ECARTICO[14]; (b) the integration of data that provide insight into (business) relationships in the 17th century, including those of Rembrandt's students and followers in the Amsterdam art community; and (c) the development of a publication platform for newly written commentaries and other secondary literature. Access to new book and journal publications is handled via the live interface with RUQuest, but that is not the case for new commentaries.

---

[13] http://research.frick.org/montias/
[14] http://www.vondel.humanities.uva.nl/ecartico/

We think that RemBench sets an example for search engines in the digital humanities. Our most important recommendation is the use of federated search and faceted search in the art history domain: with federated search, it is possible to search multiple databases at once, while faceted search enables filtering for metadata. We also set an example for usability studies of search engines in the digital humanities, using a thinking-aloud set-up and desktop activity recording.

Our recommendations for the future development of search engines in the art history domain are: (1) to involve users in the target groups, both for formulating search questions and for evaluating the application; (2) to study the information-seeking behaviour of diverse target groups (researchers, students, tourists) in more detail and investigate the possibility of tailoring search interfaces to the specific target groups; and (3) to extend the topical labelling of images in art history databases, for example through crowd sourcing.

Acknowledgements

The research for this chapter was funded by CLARIN-NL under grant CLARIN-NL-12-022. We thank our colleagues from Huygens ING, the Netherlands Institute for Art History (RKD), and the Art History department of Radboud University for their collaboration.

References

Choi, Y., & Rasmussen, E. M. (2003). Searching for images: the analysis of users' queries for image retrieval in American history. *Journal of the American society for information science and technology, 54*(6), 498–511.

Gerjets, P., Kammerer, Y., & Werner, B. (2011). Measuring spontaneous and instructed evaluation processes during Web search: Integrating concurrent thinking-aloud protocols and eye-tracking data. *Learning and Instruction, 21*(2), 220–231.

Jacsó, Péter (2004). Thoughts about federated searching. *Information Today:* 21(9).

Nielsen, J., & Landauer, T. K. (1993, May). A mathematical model of the finding of usability problems. In *Proceedings of the INTERACT'93 and CHI'93 conference on Human factors in computing systems* (pp. 206–213). ACM.

Ponnuswami, A. K., Pattabiraman, K., Wu, Q., Gilad-Bachrach, R., & Kanungo, T. (2011, February). On composition of a federated web search result page: using online users to provide pairwise preference for heterogeneous verticals. In *Proceedings of the fourth ACM international conference on Web search and data mining* (pp. 715–724). ACM.

Rodríguez Ortega, N. (2013). It's Time to Rethink and Expand Art History for the Digital Age. *The Getty Iris.* Retrieved from http://blogs.getty.edu/iris/its-time-to-rethink-and-expand-art-history-for-the-digital-age

Rowlands, I., Nicholas, D., Williams, P., Huntington, P., Fieldhouse, M., Gunter, B., ... & Tenopir, C. (2008, July). The Google generation: the information behaviour of the researcher of the future. In *Aslib Proceedings* (Vol. 60, No. 4, pp. 290–310). Emerald Group Publishing Limited.

Shokouhi, M., & Si, L. (2011). Federated search. *Foundations and Trends in Information Retrieval, 5*(1), 1–102.

Spink, A. (2002). A user-centered approach to evaluating human interaction with web search engines: an exploratory study. *Information processing & management, 38*(3), 401–426.

Stehouwer, H., Durco, M., Auer, E., & Broeder, D. (2012). Federated search: Towards a common search infrastructure. In *LREC 2012: 8th International Conference on Language Resources and Evaluation* (pp. 3255–3259). European Language Resources Association (ELRA).

Trant, J. (2009). Tagging, folksonomy and art museums: Early experiments and ongoing research. *Journal of Digital Information.*

Tunkelang, D. (2009). Faceted search. *Synthesis lectures on information concepts, retrieval, and services, 1*(1), 1–80.

Van Waes, L. (2000). Thinking aloud as a method for testing the usability of websites: the influence of task variation on the evaluation of hypertext. *Professional Communication, IEEE Transactions on, 43*(3), 279–291.

Weiler, A. (2005). Information-seeking behavior in Generation Y students: Motivation, critical thinking, and learning theory. *The Journal of Academic Librarianship, 31*(1), 46–53.

Yee, K. P., Swearingen, K., Li, K., & Hearst, M. (2003, April). Faceted metadata for image search and browsing. In *Proceedings of the SIGCHI conference on Human factors in computing systems* (pp. 401–408). ACM.

CHAPTER 29

Mapping Migration across Generations

Gerrit Bloothooft[a], David Onland[a] and Jan Pieter Kunst[b]

[a]Utrecht institute of Linguistics – OTS, Utrecht University,
[b]Meertens Institute KNAW, Amsterdam,
Corresponding author: g.bloothooft@uu.nl

ABSTRACT

Flexible software has been developed for the interactive mapping of socio-cultural phenomena in the Netherlands on the web. The possibilities of such software are demonstrated for the mapping of migration in the Netherlands across four generations. Both the origin and dispersion of the population can be explored at the geographic levels of municipality, region, dialect area and province.

29.1   Introduction

Most people leave their parental home as adolescents, taking with them their cultural capital, including language. If they remain close to their parents, family and social networks, local and regional traditions may endure. However, when there is a significant amount of long-distance migration, intercultural interactions may result in changes in their behaviour and identification. To understand such socio-cultural changes, including for instance dialectal variation, it is of interest to know how the composition of a population in a place or region varies over time and to visualise this complex process in an insightful way. Such a presentation requires both migration data and mapping software.

For the description of migration, full population data for the Netherlands was available, including place and year of birth, place of residence in 2006 and, most importantly and uniquely, family relations across four generations. These data can be used to show the roots of the inhabitants of any municipality (or a larger geographical entity) and their ancestors for up to four generations (great-grandparents) by means of place of birth (origin maps). Conversely, we can start with the inhabitants who were born in a municipality between 1880 and 1900 and trace the dispersion of their descendants over the following three generations both by means of the birthplace and place

How to cite this book chapter:

Bloothooft, G, Onland, D and Kunst, J.P. 2017. Mapping Migration across Generations. In: Odijk, J and van Hessen, A. (eds.) *CLARIN in the Low Countries*, Pp. 351–360. London: Ubiquity Press. DOI: https://doi.org/10.5334/bbi.29. License: CC-BY 4.0

of residence in 2006 – these are the dispersion maps. For the visualisation of migration processes, mapping software has been developed., The software was designed for flexible online visualisation of linguistic-cultural phenomena in general, including an easy selection interface. The current application on migration is a demonstration of the possibilities of this software, and is available at www.meertens.knaw.nl/migmap. In the following sections, the properties of the underlying data are described, as well as the presentation options for migration maps, including some examples. A technical description of the mapping software is given in the appendix.

29.2   Data

29.2.1   Population Data

We investigated and mapped migration on the basis of the date and place of birth as well as the postal code of Dutch nationals in 2006. These data were a subset of the information which was made available to the Meertens Institute KNAW and Utrecht University from the Civil Registration (GBA, municipal personal records database) for onomastic research.[1] The full corpus encompasses 22,274,761 individuals, including all 15.6 million Dutch nationals who lived in the Netherlands in 2006, and 6.6 million of their ancestors. For each individual alive in or after 1994 (the start of GBA digitisation; see Prins and Kuijper, 2007) information on both parents was also available (including their date and place of birth). On this basis, and through linking across generations, relations between up to four generations could be established in so far as the ancestors or descendants were part of the corpus.

As the first generation of interest we chose the 4.6 million individuals who were between 30 and 50 years of age in 2006. This is the age when families are usually settled, children are raised and most people stay in the same place. For this generation, 3.8 million parents, 3 million grandparents and 1.2 million great-grandparents are known. Because people share ancestors, it cannot be determined what part of the total number of ancestors are covered by the data. But, at the level of parents, the coverage should be fairly complete since in most cases the person–parent relationship is known through identifiers. Parents that died before 1994 have no personal record, which means that their parents (i.e. the grandparents of the first generation) will in turn be unknown. We estimate that a coverage of 95% at the grandparent level is realistic. Great-grandparents are only known for grandparents alive in 1994, and we estimate that the coverage at this level is around 50%. In all, these figures suggest a sample that is sufficiently large to map migration. A comparison of the total number of births since 1880 as provided by Netherlands Statistics (CBS) and those reconstructed from the Civil Registration is presented in Figure 29.1.

Conversely, we started with 1.4 million individuals born in the Netherlands between 1880 and 1900. Based on birth figures from Netherlands Statistics we estimate this to be 60% of all births during this period, after correction for infant mortality. As the Civil Registration is fairly complete for births after around 1945, we assume that most descendants living in 2006 are present in our corpus: the result is 3.8 million children, 4.9 million grandchildren and 5.5 million great-grandchildren.

29.2.2   Geographic Levels of Presentation

The mapping of migration is always done at the level of municipalities, with the administrative situation in January 2007, when there were 443 municipalities, as a baseline. However, different geographic areas may be chosen as the basis for the search question. The largest of these is that of

---

[1]   See the Dutch corpus of first names at www.meertens.knaw.nl/nvb and the Dutch corpus of family names at www.cbgfamilienamen.nl/nfb

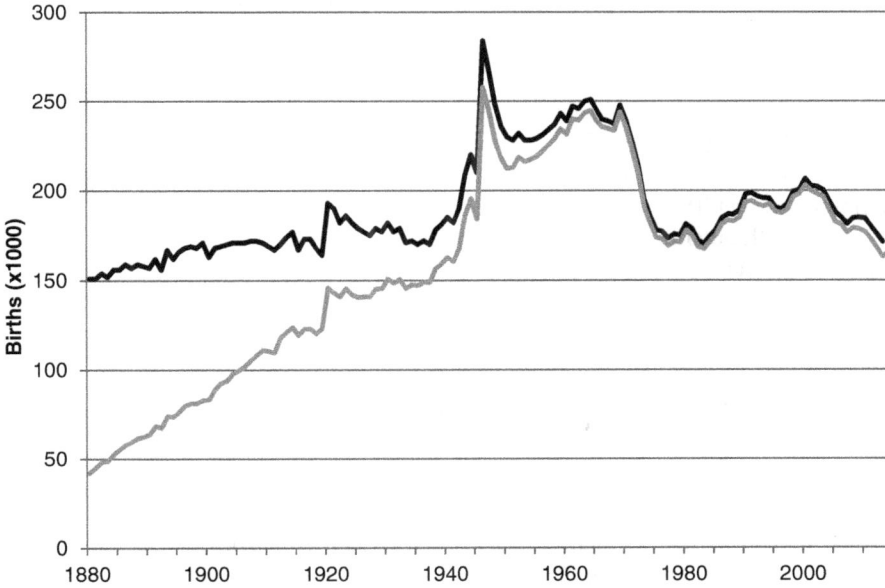

Figure 29.1: Number of births in the Netherlands according to Netherlands Statistics (black line) and number of births of individuals derived from the digitised Civil Registration (grey line). Differences in recent years (about 3%) result from the requirement of Dutch nationality in our data selection.

the 12 provinces of the Netherlands. At a more detailed level, we have the 40, so-called COROP regions,[2] which are defined on the basis of a central core and a certain homogeneity of their population. Another option is the presentation at the level of 24 dialect areas, as defined by Daan and Blok (1969), projected on the municipalities of 2007. For example, it is possible to see where the grandparents of current inhabitants (the latter of whom are 30–50 years old) of the province of Drenthe were born. The result will be presented at the municipal level, including within the province of Drenthe itself.

The choice to use the level of 443 municipalities in 2007 as a reference meant that we had to map places of birth to the corresponding 2007 municipalities.[3] Fortunately almost all changes in municipal boundaries have been reductions of the number of municipalities through mergers and annexations, and therefore did not pose a problem. In a few cases, however, municipalities were split up or only partially annexed by a neighbouring municipality; as specific birth addresses were not known this could not be repaired.[4]

Another complication are hospital births. These accounted for 30% of all deliveries in 1968 (De Haas-Posthuma and De Haas, 1968), increasing to 77% in 2002 (Anthony et al., 2005). When the hospital is not in the municipality of the parental home, this confounds the results. No statistics of this effect are available, although it is likely to be small for the older generations, for which delivery at home was the standard. For the youngest generations (especially the

---

[2] COROP refers to *Coördinatie Commissie Regionaal OnderzoeksProgramma*. The COROP areas correspond to the level 3 of the European Nomenclature of Territorial Units for Statistics (NUTS3).

[3] See www.bprbzk.nl/BRP/Informatiebank/publicaties.rvig.nl/Landelijke_tabellen/Landelijke_tabellen_32_t_m_60_excl_tabel_35/Landelijke_Tabellen_32_t_m_60_in_csv_formaat.

[4] Only in the case of Ermelo (split into Ermelo and Nunspeet in 1972) did we keep the original undivided municipality.

great-grandchildren) it is advisable to consider the place of residence during childhood, as this may give a better indication of the parental home at the time of birth. An example is the traditional village of Bunschoten, of which 44.3% of the great-grandchildren were born in the village itself and 23.6% in the nearby city of Amersfoort, while 62.6% live in Bunschoten and only 5.3% in Amersfoort. Not surprisingly Bunschoten has no hospital within its boundaries, while the nearest large hospital is in Amersfoort. In this case the figures for residence are likely more representative of the parental home during birth.

For places of birth outside the Netherlands (relevant for origins) we give percentages for major immigration countries in a separate list presented on the map. These are Belgium, Germany, Turkey, Morocco, Surinam, Netherlands Antilles, Dutch East Indies or Indonesia, Other (Europe), and Other (World).

29.3   Migration Maps Per Generation

Migration is visualised in maps by generation. Starting with a target group, the maps show the spread across the country for each generation of ancestors or descendants in a percentage per municipality, represented by a colour gradient on a (partly) logarithmic scale with ranges of 0, 0.001, 0.01, 0.5, 1, 2, 4, 8, 16, >32 %. By using mouse-over the actual percentage per municipality is shown.

By choosing to represent time through generation the family relation becomes clear, but the disadvantage is that the time periods may become increasingly longer for earlier (or later) generations or even overlap. This could imply that the same motives for migration may apply for different generations when they share, for instance, the same socio-economic conditions in some period of time. For the map showing origins (places of birth), the initial generation is born between 1957 and 1977 (a period of 20 years), the parents were born roughly between 1922 and 1952 (30 years), the grandparents between 1887 and 1927 (40 years), and the great-grandparents between 1852 and 1902 (50 years). Conversely, dispersion maps show the places of birth or residence of descendants, for an initial generation born between 1880 and 1900 (which is not shown in maps as most of them were deceased in 2006), children between 1905 and 1935, grandchildren between 1930 and 1970, and great-grandchildren between 1955 and 2007.

Percentages are calculated relative to the current number of inhabitants of a municipality (or any other available geographic entity) or the number of known ancestors per generation. It is assumed that the geographical distribution of the known individuals is representative of that of the larger population. While the coverage of generations is high enough in the Netherlands to consider this assumption to be valid, deviations will occur when parents are born in foreign countries. In that case the coverage of older generations is poor and their share will be underestimated. For example, in 2006 in Amsterdam 8.8% of the inhabitants between 30 and 50 years of age were born in Surinam. For their parents this is a still somewhat realistic 7.8%, but for their grandparents – who most likely lived in Surinam as well – the percentage drops to 2.6%, because information about most of them is not available in the Dutch Civil Registration; for great-grandparents this is an even lower 0.47%.

The migration maps are based on average figures per place of birth or residence in 2006. No individual migration history can be deducted from them. But at an aggregate level, a comparison of maps can illustrate moving patterns over time. For place of birth it should be kept in mind that this is an indication of the place of residence of the parents. A comparison of two subsequent origin maps (from older to younger generation) therefore shows – at an aggregate level – the migration between the parents' own birth place and their place of residence at the time children were born. This type of migration (leaving the parental home and starting a family) is among the most dominant in the life-course of individuals (see for example Kley, 2011). In addition, a comparison between the dispersion maps on the basis of place of birth and place of residence gives an indication of the move pattern during the (later) lifetime of people. For the older generations, especially, the place of residence in 2006 will be the final in life.

As a summary of how far people move between generations, the average distance between the places of birth or residence and the target area is calculated per generation. Because the distribution of these movements is positively skewed to higher distances, the median distance is used. This figure is only calculated for those individuals who do not live in the target area anymore. In addition the percentage of the population that did stay is shown for each generation.

It would be too complicated to include every possible gender combination for different generations. Nevertheless we provide results for the full female and male family lines, that is: mothers, grandmothers and great-grandmothers for women; and fathers, grandfathers and great-grandfathers for men. By comparing male and female lines the effect of gender on migration can be studied.

29.4   Implementation and Examples

In this section we present some typical examples of the results which show the rich possibilities for exploration of migration, and the options for presentation and output. The examples stem from the border municipality of Emmen; the very traditional, religious village of Bunschoten-Spakenburg; and the town of Almere in the newly reclaimed polder of South-West Flevoland. At a larger geographic scale the migration patterns for the province of Friesland and for the area of the Limburgish dialect are shown. Finally, the level of migration across the Netherlands can be made visible by the percentage of great-grandparents and great-grandchildren that were born in the same municipality: the lower this percentage, the more migration has taken place.

Figure 29.2 shows a screenshot with the origin maps of the grandparents of those inhabitants of the municipality of Emmen that are between 30 and 50 years old. In the main map the origin percentages for foreign countries are shown as well, while the percentage per municipality is given as a mouse-over effect. The maps for the other generations are shown in a smaller size on the side which, when clicked, switch places with the main map. The simultaneous presentation of maps for four generations facilitates the understanding of migration patterns over roughly a century. By clicking a municipality the corresponding map will be shown, which allows for a fast comparison of migration patterns between different municipalities. On the right-hand side is the menu with options to choose one of the 443 municipalities, 40 COROP regions, 24 dialect areas or 12 provinces. The generation, gender line and type of map (origin or dispersion) can also be chosen. In the right lower corner, some overall statistics are presented.

We can see a typical dispersal pattern in Figure 29.2, with the largest group of grandparents born in Emmen itself (32.1%) and a rapidly decreasing share the further a municipality lies from the town. The four nearest municipalities together account for 18.5%, indicating that moving houses in the region itself is highly preferred. The big cities in the west of the country together account for 4.8% while the northern city of Groningen has a share of 1.3%. Of interest in this border town are the grandparents born in Germany, constituting a relatively low cross-border migration of 2.7%. Figure 29.3 demonstrates the origin and dispersion of the traditional and religious village of Bunschoten-Spakenburg, where over two-thirds of the fourth generation were born or still live. The visualisation allows us to quickly see that this is a municipality with little movement in or out over the last century, with the exception of the population concentration in the four major cities in the west of the country.

The opposite effect can be found in Figure 29.4, which presents the roots of inhabitants of the newly developed town of Almere (founded in 1976). This town was intended to house the quickly increasing population, especially from the nearby capital of Amsterdam, in which city 28% of

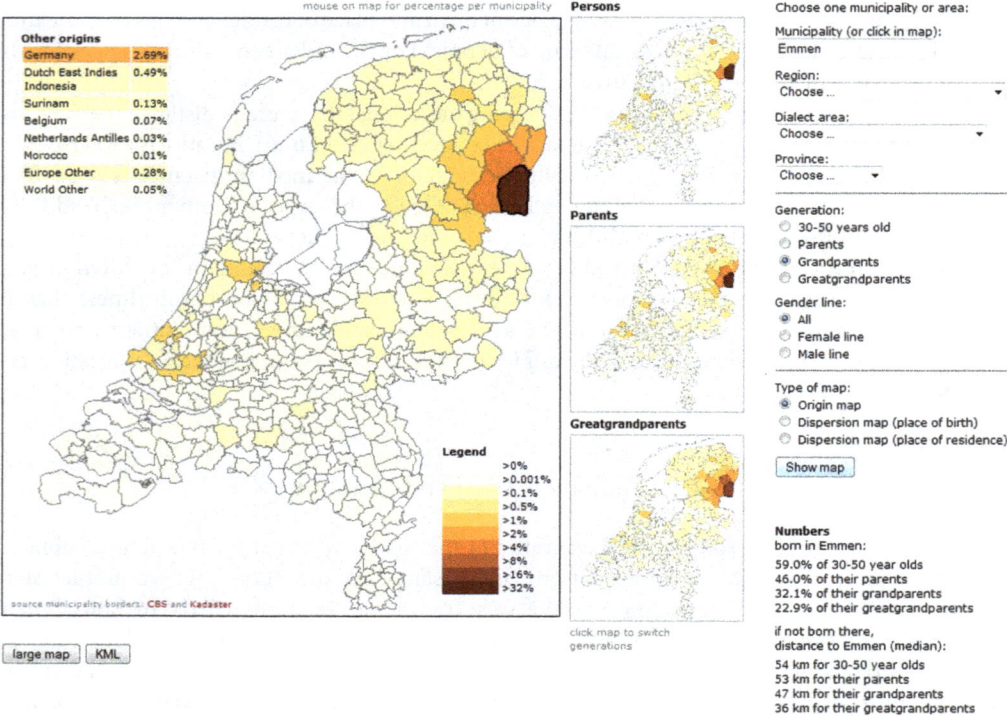

Figure 29.2: Screenshot of the origin maps of the grandparents of the inhabitants of the municipality of Emmen who are 30–50 years of age. Note that the central polders were not yet reclaimed at the birth of this grandparent generation. (The colour legend is valid for all figures.)

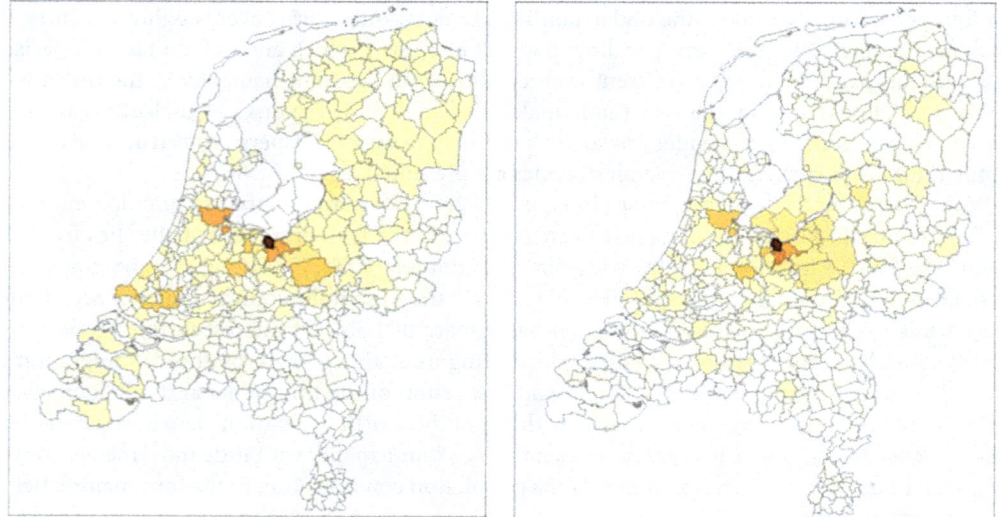

Figure 29.3: Origin and dispersion for the traditional village of Bunschoten-Spakenburg. Left-hand panel: birth place of great-grandparents (50% in the village); right-hand panel: places of residence of great-grandchildren (63% in the village).

Figure 29.4: Birth places of parents of citizens of Almere, created in 1976 in the newly reclaimed polder of South-West Flevoland.

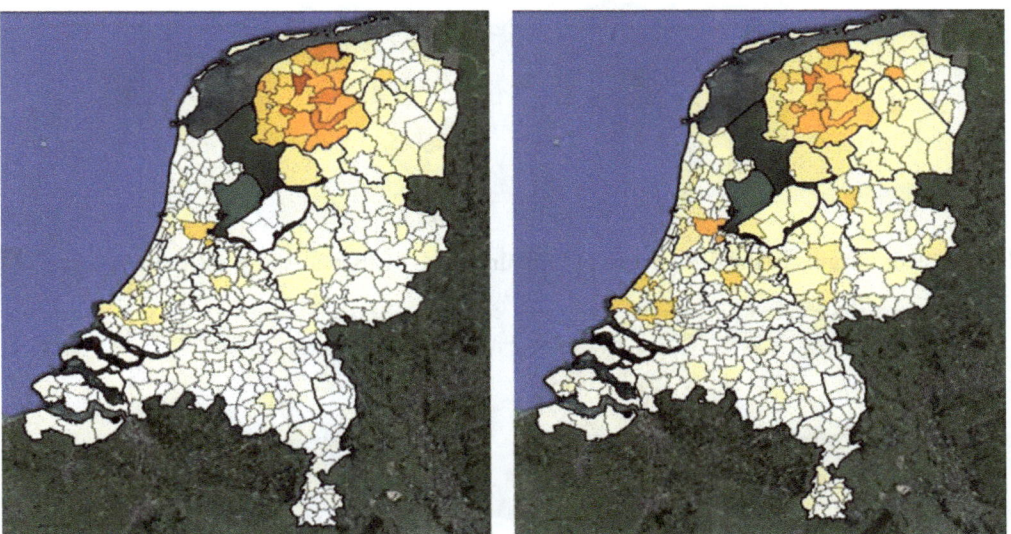

Figure 29.5: Origin and dispersion of inhabitants for the province of Friesland, projected on Google Earth. Left-hand panel: birth place of inhabitants who are 30–50 years of age (in 2006); right-hand panel: places of residence of great-grandchildren of inhabitants born 1880–1900.

the inhabitants of Almere were born. Another significant portion of the inhabitants were born in Surinam (10%) and in other foreign countries (13.9%).

Maps can be exported in KML format and projected on Google Earth. Figure 29.5 gives an example for origins and dispersion of inhabitants of the province of Friesland. This province has a strong identity, expressed by its own language. For all ancestral generations about 70% of the generation were born in Friesland itself, which is the highest percentage in the Netherlands. For descendants, 70% of the great-grandchildren were born in Friesland as well.

Another approach, which is of linguistic interest, is a look into the origins of the population of a dialect area. This is shown in Figure 29.6 for the area of Limburgish, where 57% of the great-grandparents of the current population were born in the area. A strong border effect is noticeable as well, with the share of German ancestors at 6.5%, several times higher than in other border regions.

A special option is the possibility to show the percentage of a generation that were born in the same municipality as their furthest ancestors or descendants. By choosing 'alle gemeenten' ('all municipalities') the site gives an overview of the extent to which people stay in the same municipality over multiple generations. This is shown for the fourth generation in Figure 29.7. Places

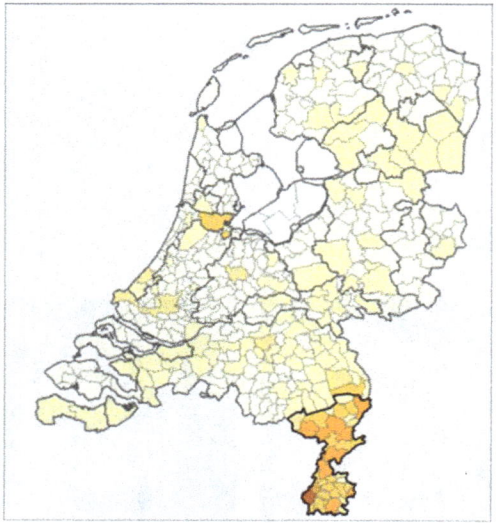

Figure 29.6: Origins in the dialect area of Limburgish, as birth places of great-grandparents.

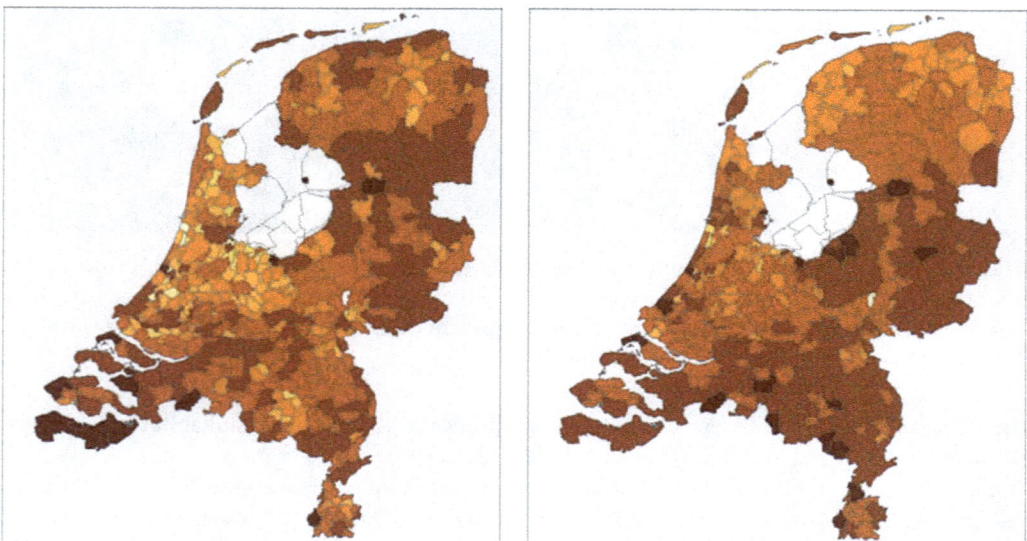

Figure 29.7: Percentage of great-grandparents that were born in the same municipality as their great-grandchildren (left-hand panel), and, conversely, percentage of great-grandchildren that still live in the same municipality as their great-grandparents (right-hand panel).

that are dark in both panels have the least migration and the most stable population, notably Urk, Staphorst, Bunschoten-Spakenburg, Volendam, Katwijk and to a lesser extent Goedereede, Zundert and Maastricht – the first five of which are among the most orthodox Protestant municipalities. The areas in the west have had a significant influx from the rest of the country, resulting in a lighter shade.

29.5   Conclusion

The map tool allows for quick analysis of complex data with a geographical and time component. The current demonstrator on migration across generations can be helpful for the study of linguistic and social phenomena, by enhancing an understanding of the origins of the current population, which could serve as an inspiration for further research. An example of a demographic study of the distance between places of birth of great-grandparents and great-grandchildren is presented in Ekamper (2013).

Appendix: Technical Background

Maps are produced with the open source (GPLv2) mapping module *Kaart*, which can be found at www.meertens.knaw.nl/kaart/. A REST service, which powers the migration maps, is available and documented at www.meertens.knaw.nl/kaart/v3/rest/. Maps can be downloaded as KML files (via a button under each map) for presentation in Google Earth and for combination with other types of maps; downloading of maps as 1200 * 1320 pixel PNG files for e.g. embedding in publications or presentations is also possible.

Information about municipalities, COROP areas, dialect areas and provinces, as well as all migration data underlying the maps, are available under the Creative Commons Attribution-NonCommercial-ShareAlike 3.0 licence at www.meertens.knaw.nl/migmap/migrationdata/. This is also the source for migration data used by the Migmap application itself.

Acknowledgements

The MIGMAP (migration mapping) project, as part of the CLARIN-NL programme, was realised in 2012, with the website launched in January 2013. We wish to thank Peter Ekamper and Frans van Poppel from the Netherlands Interdisciplinary Demographic Institute (KNAW) for their helpful comments, and Folkert de Vriend for the integration of the results of the project in the CLARIN infrastructure.

References

Anthony, S, Amelink-Verburg, M P, Jacobusse, G W and Van der Pal-de Bruin, K M 2005 *De Thuisbevalling in Nederland 1995–2002, rapportage over de jaren 2001–2002.* Leiden: TNO Kwaliteit van Leven Jeugd.

Daan, J and Blok, D 1969 *Van Randstad tot Landrand; toelichting bij de kaart: Dialecten en Naamkunde.* Volume XXXVII, Bijdragen en mededelingen der Dialectencommissie van de Koninklijke Nederlandse Akademie van Wetenschappen te Amsterdam. Amsterdam: Noord-Hollandsche Uitgevers Maatschappij.

De Haas-Posthuma, J H and De Haas, J H 1968 Infant loss in the Netherlands. In: *Vital and health statistics. Analytical studies* 3. Washington D.C.: National Center for Health statistics. pp. 3–11.

Ekamper, P and Bloothooft, G 2013 Weg van je wortels. De afstand tussen overgrootouders en achterkleinkinderen. *DEMOS* 29(2): 8.

Kley, S 2011 Explaining the Stages of Migration within a Life-Course Framework. *European Sociological Review,* 27(4): 469–86.

Prins, C J M and Kuijper, H 2007 Bevolkingsstatistieken onder het persoonskaartenstelsel en het GBA-stelsel: overeenkomsten en verschillen. *Bevolkingstrends*, 55: 14–33.

CHAPTER 30

Namescape: Named Entity Recognition from a Literary Perspective

Jesse de Does[a], Katrien Depuydt[a], Karina van Dalen-Oskam[b,c] and Maarten Marx[c]

[a]Dutch Language Institute, Leiden, jesse.dedoes@ivdnt.org, katrien.depuydt@ivdnt.org;
[b]Huygens Institute for the History of the Netherlands, The Hague,
karina.van.dalen@huygens.knaw.nl;
[c]Universiteit van Amsterdam, Amsterdam, maartenmarx@uva.nl

ABSTRACT

The project Namescape: Mapping the Landscape of Names in Modern Dutch Literature (2012–2013) was a demonstrator project granted in the third CLARIN-NL call. Partners in the project were the Huygens Institute for the History of the Netherlands, the University of Amsterdam, and the Dutch Language Institute (CLARIN centre). The project dealt with Named Entity Recognition (NER) for modern Dutch fiction and delivered two new NER tools for this purpose. It also addressed Named Entity Resolution and focused on a set of visualisations of names in individual texts from the corpus. This chapter gives an overview of the results of the project, starting with a description of the background of the research questions in the discipline of comparative literary onomastics. It then goes on to describe the tools that were delivered, and which can be found on the project website, http://www.namescape.nl/.

30.1 Introduction

The research discipline dealing with name studies – onomastics – includes a subdiscipline in which scholars aim to analyse and compare the usage and the function of names in literary works. In this kind of research, which can be called comparative literary onomastics, the scholar assumes that patterns and trends can be discovered in the way in which literary authors make use of proper names in their work (van Dalen-Oskam, 2005, van Dalen-Oskam, 2016). The comparative literary onomastics analysis not only deals with quantitative issues, such as the amount of names in a work, but also with a more qualitative evaluation of the functions of the names that have been

How to cite this book chapter:
de Does, J, Depuydt, K, van Dalen-Oskam, K and Marx, M. 2017. Namescape: Named Entity Recognition from a Literary Perspective. In: Odijk, J and van Hessen, A. (eds.) *CLARIN in the Low Countries*, Pp. 361–370. London: Ubiquity Press. DOI: https://doi.org/10.5334/bbi.30. License: CC-BY 4.0

used. Names almost always have an identifying function, to discriminate one place or person from another, but in some literary cases names are also used to do the opposite, that is to hide a person's identity or the location of a place. And, to give just a few examples of other functions, personal names may also be used to describe the personality of a certain character, and place names clearly help to situate a story in a specific geographical area or to emphasise that area as imaginary.

The problem that the Namescape project wanted to address is that this type of literary onomastics until now could deal with only one text or a very small corpus, due to a lack of specialised tools for named entity recognition and classification in literary texts. The most efficient approach available was to privately scan texts and manually annotate them, whereas the need clearly was to be able to compare name usage and name functions in much larger corpora of literary works. Direct incentive for the Namescape project was a pilot performed by literary onomastician van Dalen-Oskam on a collection of 22 Dutch and 22 English novels, in which the use of proper names was analysed (van Dalen-Oskam, 2013). Tagging this corpus, using a combination of semi-automatic and manual tagging, took around 12 months. The literary named entity recognition applied in the pilot differs from usual named entity recognition in two respects: (1) personal names, place names, and other names were tagged. Personal names were also tagged as being a first name, a family name, or a nickname. This was necessary from the perspective of literary onomastic analysis to be able to test the hypothesis that first names and family names may be used with different effects and different functions. Furthermore, the literary onomastician needs to view these as separate instances of separate names and not lumped together as one name. References to a character with only a first name, only a family name, or a combination of both may each have a different stylistic effect and a different (set of) function(s). (2) All names were further labelled with information on whether they were purely fictional, referring to 'plot internal' entities (e.g. Harry Potter), or referred to 'plot external', really existing, named entities (e.g. Churchill, London).[1] This was done to be able to test the hypothesis that 'plot internal names' and 'plot external names' have a different set of functions.

The conclusion of the pilot was that a much larger corpus of literary works was needed to confirm or correct the observations that were made in the pilot project, helping the scholar to perform statistically significant quantitative analysis of the use of names, and so was a set of tools for the researcher to tag, search and analyse the corpus, including insightful visualisations. The Namescape project set out to do just that.

30.2   Namescape Research Environment Components

The main tasks for the Namescape project were: to create a larger corpus, to perform good quality Named Entity (NE) recognition on literary material and try to perform NE resolution so as to determine whether names in literary works are plot internal or plot external, and finally to make the data available in an environment in which the researcher can search and visualise search results (technical details can be found in van Dalen-Oskam et al., 2014).

30.2.1   Backend: Corpora and Annotation Tools

30.2.1.1   Namescape Corpora and Annotation Scheme

For the core NE corpus, the project took the Dutch part of the corpus that van Dalen-Oskam used (the 'Huygens corpus') in the above mentioned pilot, consisting of 22 Dutch novels and containing ca 1.5 million tokens, and extended it with a collection of 550 OCRed Dutch books from the period 1970–2009 and containing ca 28 million tokens.

---

[1] When real, existing persons are acting characters in a novel, their names were tagged as plot-internal.

Random paragraphs were selected from that extended core corpus in order to create a manually annotated gold standard corpus for NE recognition, consisting of about 1 million tokens. There were two reasons to compose the gold standard corpus in this way. First, annotating a limited selection of complete works would have severely limited the amount and variety of name mentions in the training corpus.[2] Furthermore, by choosing snippets of annotated texts instead of complete texts as training material we hoped to circumvent IPR issues, so as to be able to distribute the training corpus for research purposes.[3] For evaluation of NER performance, we used a fixed random split of the corpus in a training and a testing partition.

In the course of the project, three additional corpora were collected and curated: a corpus of eBooks (over 7,000 books and ca 500 million tokens), a subselection of the SoNaR Corpus[4] (over 100 books and ca 11 million tokens) and a corpus with the Dutch books from the Gutenberg project (530 books and ca 30 million tokens). The last corpus contains books from the 17th to 20th century, which is a challenge for NE recognition because of the historical Dutch spelling.

The XML encoding was done in TEI P5. We made a simple extension to TEI (Text Encoding Initiative) to tag the named entity properties. We also chose to use a single tag for named entities and a different tag for entity parts to avoid nested name tags. For the basic principles for NE recognition, we have followed the 1999 Named Entity Recognition Task Definition Chinchor et al., 1999. The basic definitions (quoted from section 30.3 of the Task Definition) are:

> PERSON: named person, family, or certain designated non-human individuals
> ORGANIZATION: named corporate, governmental, or other organizational entity
> LOCATION: name of politically or geographically defined location (cities, provinces, countries, international regions, bodies of water, mountains, etc.) and astronomical locations (Chinchor et al., 1999).

We refer to the Task Definition document for further details.

We added a MISC category for name occurrences which did not clearly fit in any of the three basic types.

30.2.1.2   Named Entity Recognition

We have used our Namescape training corpus and trained two named entity taggers: the Namescape-trained instance of the Conditional Random Field-based Stanford tagger[5] (with the default settings), and a Support Vector Machine-based (SVM) tagger,[6] which has been designed to improve performance by making use of information derived in an unsupervised way from a corpus (in this case the extended core Namescape corpus). Both taggers are fairly standard supervised machine learning applications with slightly different, but similar, feature sets, consisting of a set of context features and a set of word shape features. The SVM tagger had a slightly better performance (cf. van Dalen-Oskam et al., 2014). Table 30.1 gives an evaluation of NER performance, using a fixed random split of the gold standard corpus. The application of NER to the other corpora has not been evaluated in a strict way; manual inspection shows a roughly similar accuracy on the

---

[2] Cf. also Landsbergen (2012), where the two approaches are compared, and better performance is shown for the snippet approach.

[3] We hope to make the training corpus available from http://www.inl.nl/taalmaterialen.

[4] Oostdijk et. al. (2008), Oostdijk et. al. (2013).

[5] The Stanford NER tagger is described in Finkel et al. (2005) and is available from http://wwwnlp.stanford.edu/ner/ We have used version 1.2.6, from 2012-07-09.

[6] The Namescape Support Vector Machine-based tagger has been developed at the INL using SVM[light] (http://svmlight.joachims.org/) by way of the Java native interface JNI SVM-light-6.01 (http://adrem.ua.ac.be/~tmartin/).

Tagger	NE type	precision	recall	F1
Stanford	location	0.802	0.712	0.754
	misc	0	0	0
	organisation	0.433	0.228	0.299
	person	0.876	0.895	0.881
	overall	0.853	0.824	**0.838**
Namescape	location	0.83	0.729	0.776
	misc	0	0	0
	organisation	0.516	0.251	0.339
	person	0.867	0.917	0.896
	overall	0.853	0.838	**0.845**

Table 30.1: Tagging accuracies obtained on the Namescape gold standard corpus.

eBooks and SoNaR corpora, and, as was to be expected given the differences in language, a much worse accuracy on the historical Gutenberg data.

It should also be mentioned that, taking advantage of the annotation of the pilot corpus, we endeavoured to go beyond the standard NER annotation categories by distinguishing between first names, family names and nicknames, thus accommodating the wish of the literary name scholar to compare, for example, the usage and functions of first names with that of family names, instead of heaping them all together as personal names.

Web Service and Application   Since we wanted to enable non-technical users to do named entity recognition on their own texts, we created a small lab environment which has both NE taggers implemented as a web service and is easy to use (http://ner.namescape.nl/namescape/tagger). Text can be uploaded in several formats (plain text, HTML, EPUB, Word, TEI) from the user's own computer or directly from the web by supplying a URL. The result of the tagging process is a TEI file with the inline annotation, delivered to the user either as is ('raw output') or formatted and displayed with NEs highlighted. The formatted display also includes overviews of names per category, snippets per name and a co-occurrence graph allowing the user to explore the relations between the named entity mentions.

30.2.1.3   Named Entity Resolution

To establish whether a name is plot internal or plot external, NE resolution has been performed by means of the ILPS semanticiser (Odijk et al., 2013; cf. http://semanticize.uva.nl/doc/). The tool tries to link named entities in the texts to entries in Wikipedia (a process also known as wikification). A name is considered to be plot-external when the entry in Wikipedia describes a non-fictitious entity.[7]

The application of the method does not require a manually annotated training corpus. For evaluation, the pilot corpus was used, in which plot-internality and plot-externality is manually tagged. For the 3862 distinct name types and 35852 name tokens, we have obtained a type accuracy of 74.5% and a token accuracy of 79.8%. The most prominent type of error is perhaps over-resolution: plot-internal entity mentions are often resolved to an apparently unconnected Wikipedia entry. This is understandable when we take into account that most proper names in a novel are expected to be plot-internal, and that the semanticiser has been designed to optimise the choice between

---

[7] The fictitiousness features we used were whether the article title or category contained any variant of 'legend', 'mythological' or 'fictional'.

different possible resolutions, rather than the decision between resolution and non-resolution (for more details see van Dalen-Oskam et al., 2014).

30.2.2   Front End: Search Interface and Visualisations

30.2.2.1   Search Interface

To enable the user to search and browse the texts, a search interface was built using XQuery on an eXist XML database (http://search.namescape.nl; see Figure 30.1). Unfortunately, IPR restrictions forced us to limit access to the full texts for part of the corpus.

30.2.2.2   Visualisations

Visualisations of NEs in a single text are enabled through the Namescape visualiser. Visualisation of NEs in a corpus is done via the barcode browser.

Namescape Visualiser   The Namescape Visualizer[8] (http://visualizer.namescape.nl/) gives an overview of the names in a text and shows the co-occurrence of names in paragraphs. To create a picture of the onymic landscape of proper names in the novel *De vergaderzaal* by A. Alberts, you may select the novel in the tool, and then an overview is given of the top twenty most frequent

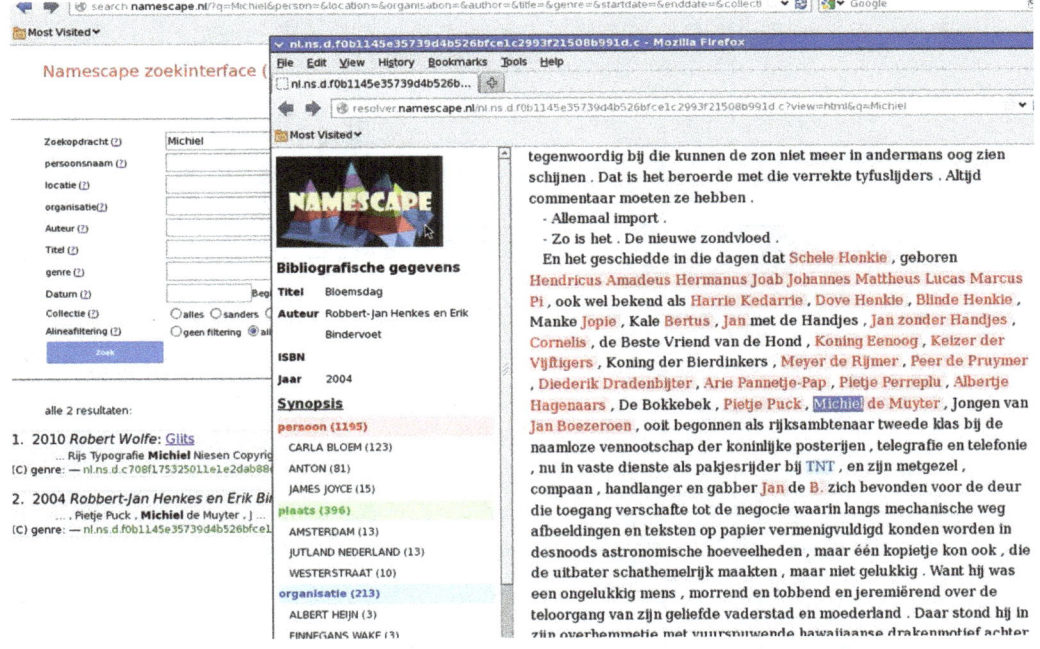

Figure 30.1: Components of the Namescape search interface. Left: search form (above) and hits (texts in which the name 'Michiel' occurs). Right: detailed view of the second hit, with an overview of all names (left) and part of the text with names highlighted (right). The three colours represent the three main name types: personal names (pink), place names (green, no example in the paragraphs shown), and names of organisations (blue). The example also shows that the tagger does not yield complete accuracy.

---

[8]   Developed by Max Grim and Floris den Heijer under the supervision of Maarten Marx.

names (as recognised by an earlier tagger), with an automatically generated link to Wikipedia. The network of named entities in the novels is visualised in three ways: two different representations of the co-occurrence network, and a dispersion plot (see Figure 30.2).

Network of Characters   Each book contains a network of named entities, usually characters. Two named entities are considered connected if they are both mentioned in the same paragraph. Clustering is performed according to the Louvain method (Blondel et al., 2008) for finding communities in social networks.

This is a fast algorithm that optimises a *modularity* criterion (the modularity of a partition is a measure that compares the density of links inside a cluster to links between clusters).[9]

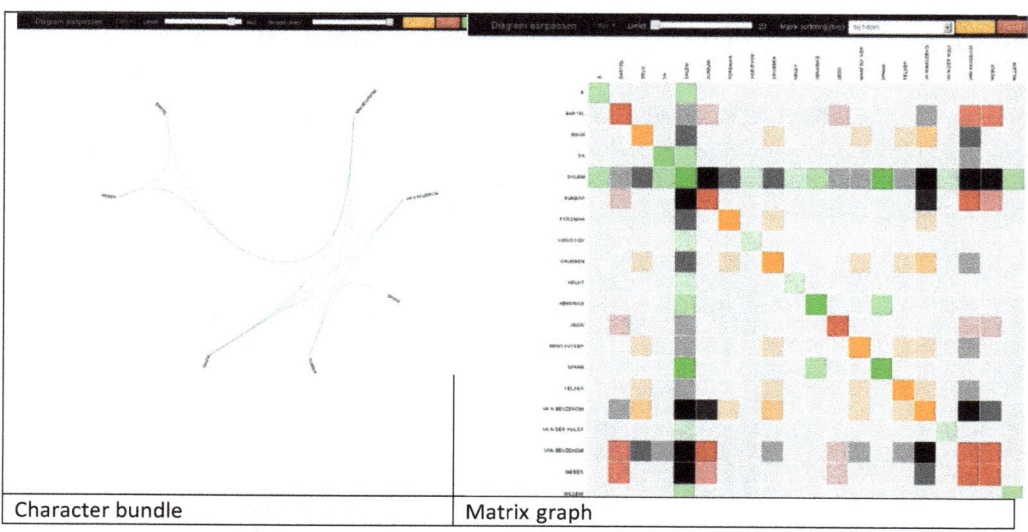

Character bundle   Matrix graph

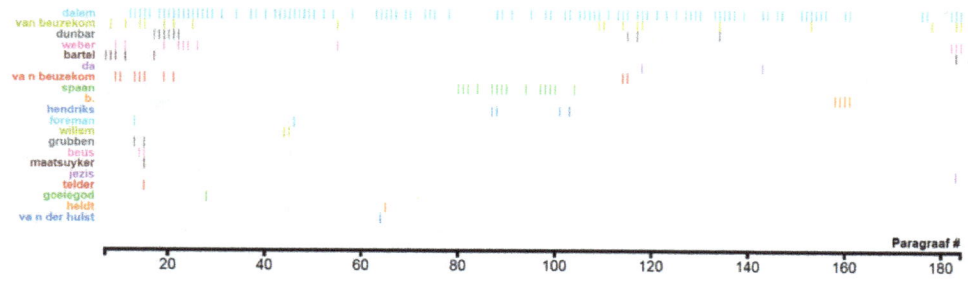

Dispersion graph

Figure 30.2: Examples of the visualisation options in Namescape for A. Alberts' *De vergaderzaal*. The Character bundle and Matrix graph are different visualisations of co-occurrence of names in the same paragraphs; the more co-occurrences, the thicker the lines (Character bundle) or the darker the colour (Matrix graph). The Dispersion graph shows in which paragraphs the names occur, linearly through the text from left to right.

---

[9] The algorithm proceeds by iterative application of two phases: a *modularity optimisation phase* which improves modularity by movement of nodes between clusters, and a *community aggregation phase* which builds a new network consisting of clusters resulting from the optimisation phase.

The character bundle and the matrix graph are different ways of displaying the network. The colours in the matrix graph correspond to the clusters, and the intensity of the colour indicates the frequency of the name co-occurrence in the book.

Dispersion Graph (Barcode Graph)   The dispersion graph shows which character is mentioned in which paragraph. The horizontal axis represents paragraphs in the book, from the first on the left to the last on the right; the vertical axis represents characters. A coloured bar at (x, y) means that character y is mentioned in paragraph x. The dispersion measure (cf. Juilland et al., 1970), based on the frequency and the distribution of occurrences, is believed to be a good indicator for the prominence of a character in a novel (cf. Karsdorp et al., 2012 for this point in the context of folk tales).

Barcode Browser   The Barcode Browser (http://barcode-browser.namescape.nl/index.xql) gives an overview of the search results for a collection of documents (see Figure 30.3). Each document in the search result is a column; the lines represent the paragraphs in the document. Paragraphs matching the search query are highlighted with a colour ranging from yellow (low relevance) to red (highly relevant).

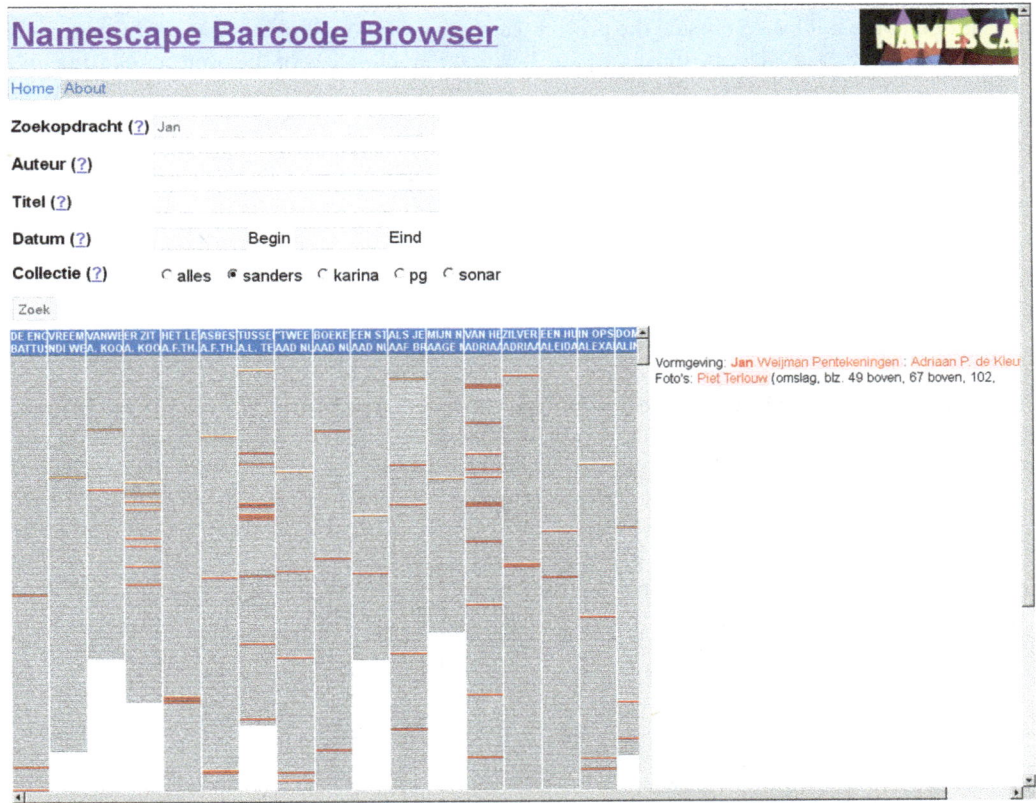

Figure 30.3: The Namescape Barcode Browser (part of the search interface). The example shows a search for the name 'Jan' in one of the subcorpora, with the search form above, and part of the results below. Each text in which the name was found is shown as a vertical column, with a bar for each paragraph. The paragraphs containing the name Jan are highlighted, from yellow (low relevance) to red (high relevance). Hovering over a coloured bar shows the text of the paragraph with all names in red and the search query in red and bold.

30.3   Evaluation

The most important results of the Namescape project are the specialised tagger for Dutch literary texts, and the visualisation tools to explore the landscape of names in individual texts. The search option is a great help to check the occurrence of certain names in a large corpus. Of course the corpus is still too small for really ambitious overviews, and it is unfortunate that we cannot make the full text of many works available, but it still gives a much broader view than ever before. Furthermore, although the scholar can get a nice overview on screen, it is not possible yet to download statistical reports or to view them in more detail. Another wish for the future is the option to submit privately owned texts to the tagger and download the results.

The Visualizer is a great tool to help explore the data. This is truly inspirational and may lead to many new hypotheses that could be tested in future projects. A drawback of the current Visualizer is that it does not have an upload function and only works on a static set of annotated novels which, furthermore, have been annotated with an older version of the NER tagger. There is therefore a need to update the tagging in the files underlying the Visualizer to make the explorations more reliable as well as more detailed (recall that the final Namescape NER distinguishes first names, family names and nicknames).

New onomastic research was not part of the Namescape project, but is in preparation. The new possibilities were not tested outside the project team. In a paper for the International Congress of Onomastic Sciences in Glasgow in August 2014, we gave an overview of the project, focusing on a problem many mainstream literary onomasticians still have when looking at the results of software. For the human eye, the results still show a lot of mistakes. Even now, many scholars conclude that it is therefore better not to use the tools at all. We think it would be better to find ways to deal with all this noise, and we described a couple of these potential solutions in an earlier paper (van Dalen-Oskam and de Does, 2016). Still, one of the ways we do not mention and which would certainly be useful is to try to improve the new tagger of literary texts.

30.4   What Came After

After the Namescape project, we have been able to enhance the performance of the SVM NER tagger by adding distributional word vectors (cf. Turian et al., 2010), produced by the word2vec program (Mikolov et al., 2013), as features to the classifier. This has yielded a significant improvement of tagging accuracy on the Namescape training corpus (cf. Table 30.2).

tagger	NE type	precision	recall	F1
Namescape SVM	location	0.83	0.729	0.776
	misc	0	0	0
	organisation	0.516	0.251	0.339
	person	0.867	0.917	0.896
	overall	0.853	0.838	**0.845**
Namescape SVM (+wv)	location	0.858	0.830	0.844
	misc	0.4	0.154	0.222
	organisation	0.656	0.459	0.54
	person	0.932	0.941	0.936
	overall	0.904	0.881	**0.893**

Table 30.2: Results of the enhancement of the Namescape tagger with distributional word embedding features.

The project also inspired a project called Beyond the Book; the ultimate aim of the researchers in this project was to examine if knowledge of names in a novel could contribute to a book being found interesting for readers in another language. They assumed that a novel that mentions a lot of culture-specific information may be less interesting for readers from other cultures, unless there is a special hype of literature focusing on the exotic. They thought that a tool that can show how exotic a novel is could be useful for publishers in helping them decide which novels to push for translation in which languages. To make a very first step towards this possible goal, Beyond the Book focused on names and applied the Semanticizer for named entity resolution. Names were linked to the most probable Wikipedia entry. For each of these Wikipedia entries the researchers calculated the number of contributors and their background (country of origin) and the number of edits. Then they compared these with the mean number of contributions from a certain country to the whole of Wikipedia. The difference between the outcome per entry then showed if the editors from certain countries made more changes than average to this entry, or less. If they made more, the scholars assumed that in the country of origin of these editors, the named entity was well-known and found culturally relevant. They explored several ways of visualising the results of such analysis for individual names and individual novels (Martinez-Ortiz et al., 2015). A tool that could be used by publishers and translators to get suggestions for the selection of novels for translation is still far away, however.

30.5   Future Work

Apart from finding more ways of dealing with noise, we have several other wishes for next steps in this research. Obviously, one would want to optimise the tools for automatic tagging. As we have seen, progress in the field of NE recognition is possible; for NE resolution, a first step is to develop more gold standard data. Furthermore, to truly turn the Namescape interactive environment into a virtual research environment that enables researchers to tag, explore, refine, and publish their data, we need to implement additional functionality.

After uploading documents to the NE tagger, researchers should be able to use the exploration and visualisation tools on their own data. To be able to deal with the noise problem described above, scholars should have the option to correct the markup after automatic tagging in a user-friendly way. Finally, we would like to have options to publish tagged material: users should at least be able to download not only their tagged texts (and, if there are no IPR issues at stake, to make them available to other users), but also statistical overviews of names and name co-occurrences.

References

Blondel, Vincent D, Jean-Loup Guillaume, Renaud Lambiotte, and Etienne Lefebvre 2008 Fast unfolding of communities in large networks, Journal of Statistical Mechanics: Theory and Experiment 2008 (10), pp. P10008. http://stacks.iop.org/1742-5468/2008/i=10/a=P10008.

Chinchor, Nancy, Erica Brown, Lisa Ferro, and Patty Robinson 1999 1999 named entity recognition task definition, *Technical report* MITRE. ftp://ftp3.nist.gov/ace/phase1/ne99_taskdef_v1_4.ps.

Finkel, Jenny Rose, Trond Grenager, and Christopher Manning 2005 Incorporating Non-local Information into Information Extraction Systems by Gibbs Sampling, *Proceedings of the 43rd Annual Meeting on Association for Computational Linguistics*, ACL '05, Association for Computational Linguistics, Stroudsburg, PA, USA, pp. 363–370. http://dx.doi.org/10.3115/1219840.1219885.

Juilland, Alphonse, Dorothy Brodin, and Catherine Davidovitch [and Others] 1970 *Frequency Dictionary of French Words* Mouton.

Karsdorp, Folgert, Peter Van Kranenburg, Theo Meder, and Antal Van den Bosch 2012 Casting a spell: Identification and ranking of actors in folktales, *The Second Workshop on Annotation of Corpora for Research in the Humanities*, Lisbon, Portugal.

Landsbergen, Frank 2012 Evaluation of named entity work in IMPACT: NE Recognition and matching, *Technical report.*

Martinez-Ortiz, Carlos, Marijn Koolen, Floor Buschenhenke, Karina van Dalen-Oskam 2015 Beyond the Book: Linking Books to Wikipedia. 2015 IEEE 11th International Conference on eScience, Munich, Germany, p. 12–21.

Mikolov, Tomas, Kai Chen, Greg Corrado, and Jeffrey Dean 2013 Efficient Estimation of Word Representations in Vector Space, *Proceedings of Workshop at ICLR* Vol. abs/1301.3781.

Odijk, Daan, Edgar Meij, and Maarten de Rijke 2013 Feeding the second screen: Semantic linking based on subtitles, *Open research Areas in Information Retrieval (OAIR 2013)* Lisbon, Portugal.

Oostdijk, Nelleke, Martin Reynaert, Paola Monachesi, Gertjan Van Noord, Roeland Ordelman, Ineke Schuurman, and Vincent Vandeghinste 2008 From d-coi to sonar: a reference corpus for dutch., *LREC.*

Oostdijk, Nelleke, Martin Reynaert, Véronique Hoste, and Ineke Schuurman 2013 The Construction of a 500-Million-Word Reference Corpus of Contemporary Written Dutch, *in* Spyns, Peter and Jan Odijk, editors, *Essential Speech and Language Technology for Dutch* Theory and Applications of Natural Language Processing, Springer Berlin Heidelberg, pp. 219–247. http://dx.doi.org/10.1007/978-3-642-30910-6.

Turian, Joseph, Lev Ratinov, and Yoshua Bengio 2010 Word representations: A simple and general method for semi-supervised learning, *Proceedings of the 48th Annual Meeting of the Association for Computational Linguistics* ACL '10, Association for Computational Linguistics, Stroudsburg, PA, USA, pp. 384–394. http://dl.acm.org/citation.cfm?id=1858681.1858721.

van Dalen-Oskam, Karina 2005 Vergleichende literarische Onomastik, *in* Brendler, A. and S. Brendler, editors, *Namenforschung morgen: Ideen, Perspektiven, Visionen* Baar, Hamburg, pp. 183–191. (An English translation 'Comparative Literary Onomastics', is available at https://www.huygens.knaw.nl/wp-content/bestanden/pdf_vandalenoskam_2005_Comparative_Literary_Onomastics.pdf)

van Dalen-Oskam, Karina 2013 Names in novels: an experiment in computational stylistics, *LLC: The journal of digital scholarship in the Humanities* 28 pp. 359–370. http://dx.doi.org/10.1093/llc/fqs007.

van Dalen-Oskam, Karina, Jesse de Does, Maarten Marx, Isaac Sijaranamual, Katrien Depuydt, Boukje Verheij, Valentijn Geirnaert 2014 Named entity recognition and resolution for literary studies. *Computational Linguistics in the Netherlands Journal* 4 (2014), 121–136. 20 December 2014, http://www.clinjournal.org/sites/clinjournal.org/files/09-VanDalenOskam-etal-CLIN2014.pdf.

van Dalen-Oskam, Karina 2016 Corpus-based approaches to names in literature. Carole Hough (Ed.), *The Oxford Handbook of Names and Naming.* Oxford University Press, 2016, 344–354.

van Dalen-Oskam, Karina and Jesse de Does 2016 Namescape, or how to deal with noise. *Names and Their Environment' Proceedings of the 25th International Congress of Onomastic Sciences, Glasgow, 25–29 August 2014.* Eds. Carole Hough & Daria Izdebska, 5 Vols. Vol. 5, 57–64, http://www.icos2014.com/congress-proceedings/.

CHAPTER 31

Creating a Corpus of Pilgrim Narratives: Experiences and Perspectives from the PILNAR Project

Suzanne van der Beek, Paul Post and Marc Kemps-Snijders

Tilburg University, Tilburg School of Humanities, Department of Culture Studies, research group Ritual in Society & Meertens Institute

ABSTRACT

The PILNAR project was set up in order to prepare large sets of pilgrim narratives for analysis and interpretation. The narratives that pilgrims create on the Camino de Santiago give us a good insight in the dynamics of a changing ritual in a late-modern and superdiverse society. In this project, specialists from different backgrounds contributed to create a database that brings together narratives from a variety of different online and offline platforms. This chapter presents a retrospective on the process that led to the PILNAR database and the accompanying mobile application, and sketches possible directions in which the project could develop in the future.

31.1   Introduction

The pilgrimage to Santiago de Compostela, lovingly called the 'Camino' by its pilgrims, is an interesting site of research for a number of reasons. As its origins date back to the 10th century, its routes are spread across Europe and it is widely seen as one of the three major European pilgrimages, its opportunities for academic exploration are wide-ranging. Its significance has again become apparent in the last 20 to 30 years, when, after a period of relative quiet, pilgrims started to flock to Santiago once more. According to reports issued by the official pilgrim office in Santiago the amount of pilgrims that register at the Cathedral have grown from 2,491 in 1986 to 215,880 in 2013 (Informe estadístico, 2016). These new pilgrims have not just stepped into a traditional Catholic ritual. Rather, they have brought onto the Camino a contemporary take on what it means to be a

How to cite this book chapter:
van der Beek, S, Post, P and Kemps-Snijders, M. 2017. Creating a Corpus of Pilgrim Narratives: Experiences and Perspectives from the PILNAR Project. In: Odijk, J and van Hessen, A. (eds.) *CLARIN in the Low Countries*, Pp. 371–378. London: Ubiquity Press. DOI: https://doi.org/10.5334/bbi.31. License: CC-BY 4.0

pilgrim in a late-modern, superdiverse society. This means that the Camino is now a site where pilgrims explore the many different repertoires and traditions of ritual and seek for encounters with the sacred in a myriad of different fields including religion, local architecture, conversations with strangers, physical endurance, and reflections on their personal past (Post, Pieper and Van Uden, 1998). Contemporary pilgrim profiles reflect the diversity of the current ritual and religious dynamics in the Netherlands, and pilgrim narratives can be explored as a unique point of entry in studying these dynamics.

There are different approaches to exploring the pilgrim identity that emerged at the end of the last century. One of the most productive approaches has proven to be based upon the narrative dimension of the pilgrim profile. For the pilgrim is a highly enthusiastic storyteller. S/he tells stories about the pilgrimage s/he has planned, informs family and friends about the pilgrimage while s/he is on the Camino, and will not miss an opportunity to recount the adventures for some time after the journey has been completed. These stories can take many forms and have many functions: they might be serious expressions of expectation, amusing anecdotes about eccentric pilgrims met along the way, personal contemplations upon life decisions, or modern reflections upon canonical Camino legends. This narrative inclination of the pilgrim opens up an opportunity for academic exploration of the contemporary pilgrim identity. It has nourished a long tradition of academic interest that stems from the stories pilgrims engage with in order to better understand what drives the pilgrims on their journey, how their experience shape them, and what transformation or affirmation they find on the Camino (Post, 2015; Van der Beek, 2015; Post, 1994).

As we entered the 21st century, however, both the character of the pilgrim profile and the creation and distribution of narratives have changed. Not only has the great increase of pilgrims on the Camino led to an increase of pilgrim narratives, but the popularisation of online platforms has provided the opportunity for the creation of a potentially endless amount of pilgrim narratives. As pilgrims took to the internet, their narratives became as diversified as their ritual identity had become. This growing collection of pilgrim narratives therefore became an interesting and fruitful site for academic inquiry. However, as we will see in this contribution, the emerged complexity and diversity of the genre of the pilgrim narrative complicates any initiative to take stock and create a corpus.

To dig into the potential described, what was needed was an infrastructure that prepared pilgrim narratives for analyses and interpretation. This meant gathering pilgrim narratives from the different platforms on which they were created and distributed and curating them in a manner that would highlight their complexity and diversity. Preferably, this database would have the potential to grow along with the narratives that would keep being created by pilgrims in future years. With these goals in mind, the PILNAR ('PILgrim NARratives') project was set up (PILNAR, 2016).

In this contribution we sketch our experiences in the PILNAR project. Although we also give some perspectives for the future, the focus is retrospective.

31.2   Team PILNAR

The initiative for the PILNAR project came from researchers at the Tilburg School of Humanities (Tilburg University), where the study of ritual in general, and pilgrimage in particular, has been a key interest. They also provided the coordinator of the project, in the person of Paul Post. However, different Dutch parties were also found to be interested in the goals of the PILNAR project. One partner was found in the Meertens Institute (KNAW), the research institute for the study of Dutch language and culture. The Meertens Institute had formerly provided academic study into Dutch religiosity and ritual via a large-scale documentation project on Dutch places of pilgrimages (BiN, 2016; Margry and Caspers, 2004), and had experience in gathering and curating large collections of narratives (Collections on meertens.knaw.nl 2016). Therefore, it was decided that the PILNAR database would be developed and curated within the infrastructure of the Meertens Institute.

A third obvious partner in the PILNAR project was the Dutch Society of Saint James. As the main Dutch society of Camino pilgrims (with nearly 14,000 members), they shared an interest in the creation of a database of pilgrim narratives, as well as in the academic study that would emerge from this collection (Het Genootschap van Sint Jacob, 2014). A last partner that contributed to PILNAR would be the Museum Catharijneconvent, the Utrecht national museum for Christian art and culture. In 2008, the Catharijneconvent started collecting personal narratives of its visitors and creating online datasets which made them accessible to all interested parties. After an exhibition on the Camino in 2010, inspired by the 25th anniversary of the Society of Saint James, the museum started a collection of online pilgrim narratives (Pelgrims vertellen over hun tocht on catharijneverhalen.nl 2016).

In order to shape the proposed setup, an online infrastructure was needed that would support the complex wishes of the PILNAR team. To this end, CLARIN was approached. The funding for the start of a digital corpus of Dutch pilgrim narratives was awarded in 2011, and a year later the PILNAR project was started as a one-year CLARIN enterprise.

31.3   Creating the Corpus

From the start, the PILNAR team sought to create a corpus of pilgrim narratives from various sources, thereby mirroring the wide-ranging platforms and reflections that shape these stories. PILNAR aimed at including narratives in different forms and characters: written accounts in (offline) journals, individually created booklets, articles in periodicals, personal weblogs, discussions in magazines. The different PILNAR partners could contribute to this collection of narratives. For example, the Society of Saint James had access to the archive of their monthly magazine *De Jacobsstaf* as well as their monthly online newsletter *Ultreia*. Together, this collection would render a great number of pilgrim stories, ranging from personal accounts to practical information, and from spiritual reflections to historical background. The Catharijneconvent had available to them the set of stories uploaded by pilgrims onto their website (pelgrimsverhalen.nl).

Additionally, a website was created on which pilgrims themselves could upload any narrative that they deemed interesting for the PILNAR dataset (PILNAR, 2016). Pilgrims were approached to participate in the creation of the PILNAR dataset via different channels: the Society of Saint James placed calls for stories in their newsletter and their website, the Catharijneconvent addressed the visitors of their website, and individual pilgrim bloggers were individually asked for their narratives to be included. All of these channels would provide a solid base for the PILNAR database and allow for expansion in the future. In the last phases of the PILNAR project, Tilburg University took the initiative to develop a PILNAR app. This app would function as a mobile tool with which pilgrims could upload their narratives (directly) into the PILNAR database.

31.4   Using the Corpus

After the gathering of these narratives, the database needed some initial perspectives for structuring and using the corpus. To prepare the dataset for academics seeking to trace meaningful categories in the multiplicity of the contemporary pilgrim identity the heuristic instrument of the 'Fields of the sacred' was used. This heuristic frame was developed in the 'Religion and Ritual' research group at Tilburg University (Post, 2010a; Post, 2010b; Post, 2010c; Post, 2011a; Post, 2011b; Post, 2011c). As a tool, these fields are used to locate sacred practices in the Netherlands; rather than explicitly demarked areas, these fields should be understood as spheres or domains with a certain coherence in ideas, outlook, cultural practice, and ritual repertoire. The four fields of the sacred are the religious field, the field of marking and remembering, the cultural field (art, culture), and the field of leisure culture (sport, tourism). These four domains help to map the diversity in possibilities for engaging with the sacred when analysing contemporary ritual. Their use will be apparent with regard to the modern Camino pilgrim, whose diverse and layered appropriation of the ritual of pilgrimage calls for an approach that is similarly open. The implementation of the fields of the sacred in PILNAR took place mainly at the level of the choice of metadata. Narratives are manually labelled with keywords that implicate different fields (Figure 31.1). The religious field is indicated by keywords like 'God' or 'Ritual', the field of marking and remembering by keywords like 'diseased' or 'history', the cultural field by keywords like 'art' or 'culture', and the field of leisure by keywords like 'nature' or 'food'. These fields also play an important role in the development of the PILNAR app mentioned earlier.

31.5   Technical Implementation

The PILNAR application takes advantage of the flexibility of CLARIN's CMDI specification. In total six profiles were used to describe the different types of PILNAR submissions to the project: JacobsstafVerhaal, Website, Pelgrimsverhaal, UserSubmission, VirtualCollection and Image. Each profile captures specific information, such as title, author, description or participant information, related to the type of material submitted to the project. As indicated above, keywords provide an important distinguishing feature to the PILNAR researchers and are represented across almost all profiles.

The PILNAR application provides a workspace to the project members where they can interact with metadata profiles. Depending upon the type of material, the user interface supports selection of profile-specific editors, i.e. each profile is associated with its own editor. Each of these editors is dynamically loaded when a user selects to create or modify a specific type of resource. The resulting metadata and data files are stored on the server and automatically indexed to support search across all metadata files. This also allows for the displaying of distributions across facets in customised user interface components, such as the keyword pie chart shown in Figure 31.1.

For those interested in the implementation details of PILNAR, it is worth noting that the user interface is implemented in Flash, the workspace backend is implemented in Java and is delivered through a Tomcat server, and the indexing and search procedures take advantage of SOLR.

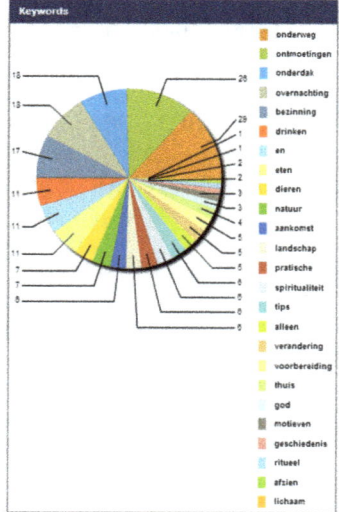

Figure 31.1: PILNAR keywords.

31.6   Bumps in the Road

As the project took shape, different issues started to rear their head. These difficulties can be clustered in three categories: the variety of the source material (including their different property rights); difficulties in the communication between more content-oriented partners and the technical infrastructure; and challenges in the curation process and other unforeseen dynamics during the process of the project itself (cf. the development of the PILNAR app). A short elaboration on these 'bumps on the road' may illustrate the clusters.

First, the variety in sources created complications in the construction of a single structure to include all desired narratives. For example, the archive of *De Jacobsstaf*, although digitally available, posed difficulties, because it contains many forms of narratives. It proved difficult to select the texts included in the magazine that would be eligible for inclusion in PILNAR – personal accounts and thematic reflections were obviously wanted, but should discussions of movies and books be included? Or editorial pieces? Or experiences on Spanish language courses? Another problem that relates to the character of the narratives' source came from the upload website. Pilgrims that uploaded their own stories via this specially created website used the fields provided in a way that was not expected by the PILNAR team. This resulted in a lot of material that had to be converted manually before it could be included in the final dataset. Yet another type of difficulty was presented by the set of texts collected on the Catharijneconvent website, which used a different set of privacy regulations than the PILNAR project. This means that before the collection of the Catharijneconvent could be imported, every single author that contributed to this collection had to be approached individually – this has proven a task too extensive to perform within the PILNAR project.

A different cluster of problems were related to the cooperation between 'Tilburg' as the centre for content and project coordination and 'Amsterdam', with the Meertens Institute as the centre for the computational infrastructure (with in the background a critical CLARIN representative keeping track of time and financial planning). A first issue is well-known and broadly recognised in multidisciplinary projects like this one: communication often proves complicated between partners with such different backgrounds and outlooks. During the project, it proved difficult to explain the possibilities and limitations of the chosen technical setup of the database to the Tilburg sub-team, while, on the other end, the specific character of the different sources and deliverables were hard to communicate to the team that would structure and present the data in the database. A second issue in this cluster was very practical. Although there were a set of milestones and work packages agreed upon in the initial project description, the variety of chosen materials (as described above) made it impossible to plan in detail the stages of the project. Choices needed to be made, and, in the end, only a part of the sources was incorporated. Also, the curation of the material in the database was preliminary. However, the project staff underlined the pioneering character of the project: it was all about making a start on a narratives corpus.

A third cluster of problems revolved around the method of structuring the collected texts for the end user. As discussed above, the inspiration for the PILNAR heuristics was the structure of the four fields of the sacred. Due to the somewhat flexible nature of these fields and to the complex character of the data, the fields proved more difficult to apply to specific texts than was foreseen. These and other internal dynamics of the project played their role in difficulties faced by PILNAR. In different phases of the project, new insights came to the fore. Some of these could be incorporated into the project, while others could no longer be included. Inspired by the PhD project of Suzanne van der Beek on online pilgrim narratives, the PILNAR app was initiated in one of the last stages of the project. As this was not a foreseen development, PILNAR could not support the implementation of the stories gathered by this app directly into the database.

31.7   Results and the Future of PILNAR

Despite the difficulties encountered by PILNAR, the project resulted in a functioning database with potential for growth and expansion (CLARIN – PILNAR, 2015). As it stands, pilgrims are still sending in their narratives, a new *Jacobsstaf* and *Ultreia* appear monthly, and we are exploring the possibilities for importing narratives from popular platforms like Facebook and Twitter. Since 2013, Suzanne van der Beek has become one of the main users of the database as an academic tool. Her PhD project on the narrative identity construction of contemporary pilgrims benefits from a central collection of pilgrim stories that explores the width and depth of the complex pilgrim identity.

Perhaps the most interesting development in the PILNAR project, and the most concrete opportunity to guarantee continuity for the PILNAR database, is the creation of the PILNAR app (PILNAR Pelgrimsdagboek, 2014): in 2014, a mobile application was created that was supposed to give pilgrims the possibility to upload their narratives directly onto the database as they walked or cycled to Santiago de Compostela. The idea for this extension came from our colleague Dr Suleman Shahid, who also designed the structure of the app. Shahid's main interest lies in creating technologies that respond to the specific needs of marginal groups of users. In the case of the Camino pilgrims, we decided to respond to the pilgrims' need for a platform on which they could exchange stories exclusively about their pilgrimages. Rather than letting pilgrims become distracted by unrelated stories on platforms like Facebook or Twitter, the *PILNAR Pilgrim Diary* (Figure 31.2) provides an environment that invites reflection upon the pilgrim's journey via different categories and inspirational questions. The keywords that can be added by users are the same as the ones used in the PILNAR database. The app would thus combine the continuation of the PILNAR database and the media-specific needs of its pilgrim users.

In an early phase of creating the app, it became apparent that a structural connection to the PILNAR infrastructure would not be possible within the time and budget we had for the PILNAR app. This direct connection remains a wish, but is not currently an urgent issue. Pilgrims using it see the app and the database as part of the same project. The two are connected by their name, and in our communication the two are mentioned in the same breath. In this way, PILNAR travels not only different platforms, but also different countries in the pockets of pilgrims to Santiago de Compostela.

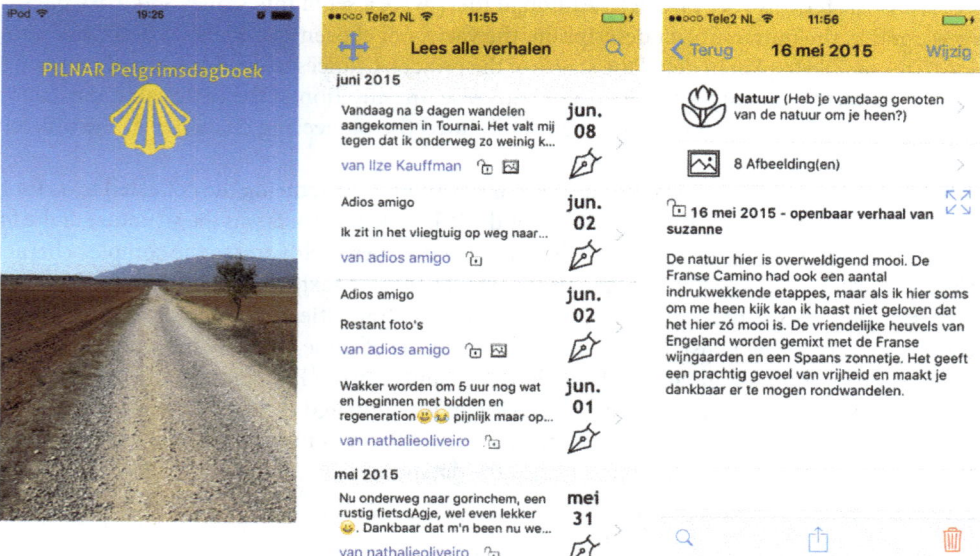

Figure 31.2: Screen captures from the PILNAR app.

About the Authors

Suzanne van der Beek is a PhD researcher at the Department of Culture Studies of Tilburg University (NL), and underwent undergraduate training at the universities of Amsterdam, Leiden, and Lille. Her research is on the identity construction of Dutch pilgrims on the Camino to Santiago de Compostela. In particular, she studies the dynamics of online narratives in relation to the appropriation of a contemporary pilgrim profile.

Paul Post studied theology and liturgical studies in Utrecht and Christian art and archaeology in Rome. He is professor of Ritual Studies at Tilburg University (NL; School of Humanities, Department of Culture Studies). He is vice dean for research and director of the Graduate School of Humanities. His main interests are in the fields of ritual, popular religion and (post)modern developments in ritual, on which he published books and articles. In recent years the focus of his research has been on ritual space and place, and cyber ritual.

Marc Kemps-Snijders is Head of Technical Development at the Meertens Institute. He has been involved in infrastructure development right from the start of the CLARIN project at both the European and the national level in areas such as semantic interoperability, services and workflows, information retrieval, and research data management.

References

Books

Margry, PJ and Caspers, Ch (eds.) 2004 *Bedevaartplaatsen in Nederland. Deel 4: Addenda – Index – Bijlagen*. Amsterdam: Meertens Insituut.

Post, P 2010a *Voorbij het kerkgebouw. De speelruimte van een ander sacraal domein*. Heeswijk: Abdij van Berne. pp. 69–198 (part III en IV).

Post, P 2010b Place of Action: Exploring the Study of Space, Ritual and Religion. In: Post, P and Molendijk, A L (eds.) *Holy Ground. Re-inventing Ritual Space in Modern Western Culture.* (Liturgia condenda 24) Leuven: Peeters. pp. 17–54

Post, P 2011a Der moderne Pilger: Die Perspektive aktueller sakraler Felder. In: Böntert, S (ed.) *Objektive Feier und subjektiver Glaube? Beiträge zum Verhältnis von Liturgie und Spiritualität.* (Studien zur Pastoralliturgie 32) Regensburg: Pustet. pp. 275–298

Post, P 2011b Fields of the sacred. Reframing identities of sacred places. In: Post, P and Molendijk, AL and Kroesen, J (eds.) *Sacred Places in Modern Western Culture.* Leuven: Peeters. pp. 13–59.

Post, P and Pieper J and van Uden, M (eds.) 1998 *The modern pilgrim. Multidisciplinary explorations of Christian pilgrimage.* (Liturgia condenda 8), Leuven: Peeters.

Articles

Post, P 1994 The modern pilgrim: a study of contemporary pilgrim's accounts. *Ethnologia Europaea* 24(2): 85–100.

Post, P 2010c Heilige velden. Panorama van ritueel-religieuze presenties in het publieke domein. *Tijdschrift voor Religie, Recht en Beleid* 1(3): 70–91.

Post, P 2011c Profiles of pilgrimage: on identities of religion and ritual in the European public domain. *Studia Liturgica* 41: 129–155.

Post, P 2015 Pelgrimsverhalen – pelgrims verhalen. Mapping the field. *Jaarboek voor liturgieonderzoek/Yearbook for Liturgical and Ritual Studies,* 31: 63–76. http://rjh.ub.rug.nl/index.php/jvlo/article/view/19536/17014 [Last accessed 07-07-2017]

Van der Beek, S 2015 Als pelgrims online gaan: De invloed van nieuwe media op de Camino. *Jaarboek voor liturgieonderzoek/Yearbook for Liturgical and Ritual Studies,* 31: 77–91. http://rjh.ub.rug.nl/index.php/jvlo/article/view/19537/17015 [Last accessed 07-07-2017]

Webpages/PDFs

CLARIN – PILNAR. 2015. Available at https://vimeo.com/100788014, or http://www.youtube.com/watch?v=iMWhO3D_n_Q [Last accessed 25-01-2016].

Collections. Available at http://www.meertens.knaw.nl/cms/en/collections [Last accessed 25-01-2016].

Databank Bedevaart en Bedevaartsplaatsen in Nederland (BiN). Available at http://www.meertens.knaw.nl/bedevaart/ [Last accessed 25-01-2016].

Het Genootschap van Sint Jacob. 2014. Available at https://www.santiago.nl/het-genootschap [Last accessed 25-01-2016].

Informe estadístico. Año 2013 (report from the Oficina del Peregrino, Santiago de Compostela). Available at http://www.peregrinossantiago.es/esp/wp-content/uploads/informes/peregrinaciones2013.pdf [Last accessed 25-01-2016].

Pelgrims vertellen over hun tocht naar Santiago de Compostela. Available at http://www.catharijneverhalen.nl/3482/nl/pelgrims-vertellen [Last accessed 25-01-2016].

PILNAR. Available at http://yago.meertens.knaw.nl/apache/pilnar_web/ [Last accessed 25-01-2016].

PILNAR Pelgrimsdagboek. 2014. Available at https://itunes.apple.com/nl/app/pilnar-pelgrimsdagboek/id897587238?mt=8 [Last accessed 25-01-2016].

PILNAR: Pilgrimage Narratives: Creating a Corpus for Studying the Profile of the Modern Pilgrim. Available at http://www.clarin.nl/node/278 [Last accessed 25-01-2016].

CHAPTER 32

@PhilosTEI: Building Corpora for Philosophers

Arianna Betti[a], Martin Reynaert[c,d] and Hein van den Berg[a,b]

[a]Axiom Group/University of Amsterdam, [b]Vrije Universiteit Amsterdam, [c]TiCC/Tilburg University, [d]CLST/Radboud University Nijmegen, The Netherlands

ABSTRACT

For philosophers to be able to take a computational turn in their field, especially if that field relies heavily on historical material, it is crucial to be able to build high-quality, easily and freely accessible corpora in a sustainable format composed from multi-language, multi-script books from different historical periods. At the moment, corpora matching these needs are virtually non-existent. Within the CLARIN-NL project @PhilosTEI, we have addressed the problem of building this kind of corpora by developing an open-source, web-based, user-friendly workflow from textual images to TEI, based on state-of-the-art open-source OCR software Tesseract, and a multi-language version of TICCL, a powerful OCR post-correction tool. We have demonstrated the utility of the @PhilosTEI tool by applying it to a multilingual, multi-script corpus of important 18th to 20th century European philosophical texts.

32.1 Introduction

The main objective of the CLARIN-NL project @PhilosTEI was to develop a web-based, user-friendly workflow from scanned images of text to TEI (Text Encoding Initiative) (Betti and van den Berg, 2014b).[1] The workflow in question integrates state-of-the-art open-source OCR (Optical Character Recogniton) software Tesseract and a multi-language version of TICCL, a powerful OCR post-correction tool developed by Martin Reynaert at Tilburg University (Reynaert, 2010). Through building @PhilosTEI, we address a major challenge faced by researchers in philosophy and the digital humanities today: the lack of existing high-quality, easily accessible corpora.

---

[1] In this chapter, we sometimes lift text from the (unpublished) (Betti and van den Berg, 2014b).

How to cite this book chapter:

Betti, A, Reynaert, M and van den Berg, H. 2017. @PhilosTEI: Building Corpora for Philosophers. In: Odijk, J and van Hessen, A. (eds.) *CLARIN in the Low Countries*, Pp. 379–392. London: Ubiquity Press. DOI: https://doi.org/10.5334/bbi.32. License: CC-BY 4.0

@PhilosTEI is meant to offer a user-friendly way to transform images of texts into a machine-readable format, and thus provides researchers with an easy way to build exactly the kind of corpora they need. In particular, the machine-readable format delivered by @PhilosTEI, TEI XML[2] (Burnard and Bauman, 2007), is today's standard for digital editions, and is also a most suitable format to make texts ready for further digital exploration.

In Section 32.2 we describe related work and discuss the problems researchers in philosophy and history of ideas face when building philosophical corpora. In Section 32.3 we describe currently available solutions for building the corpora in question, while also highlighting some of the shortcomings of these solutions. Section 32.4 describes @PhilosTEI, the tool we have developed in order to help philosophers to build the corpora they need. An evaluation of @PhilosTEI is given in Section 32.5, and we discuss future work and challenges in Section 32.6.

32.2   The Problem: Building Philosophical Corpora

Computational tools and methods have significantly impacted philosophical research (van den Berg et al., 2014; Ess, 2004).[3] Many different computing technologies have been applied within the field of logic (Barwise and Etchemendy, 1998); philosophers have been involved in the field of computer ethics (Bynum, 2001), and computing technologies have influenced and changed specific philosophical disciplines, such as epistemology, philosophy of science, and metaphysics (Bynum and Moor, 1998). Finally, the last few years have seen a discipline called 'philosophy of information' blossom - which comprises the study of the application of computing technologies to philosophy (Floridi, 2011; van den Berg et al., 2014; Ess, 2004).

A number of philosophers are involved in computational methods in a somewhat different way, that is, they apply computational tools to study (large amounts of) textual material. For example, Overton (2012) has applied text mining techniques to scientific articles in order to philosophically explore the phrase 'explain', while Herbelot et al. (2012) have analysed phrases such as 'man' and 'woman' from the perspective of gender theory by applying distributional techniques to Wikipedia. Formal ontologies aiding philosophical research have been constructed on the basis of the *Stanford Encyclopedia of Philosophy* and writings of Wittgenstein (Buckner et al., 2011; Pichler and Zöllner-Weber, 2013; Pasin et al., 2008).[4] There are also examples of applications of ontologies to the history of philosophy (e.g. to texts by Kierkegaard and Schelling (McKinnon, 1977; Ziche et al., 2014), the field on which we focus in the present chapter.

A crucial prerequisite to apply computational tools and methods to textual material in the way just mentioned is access to high-quality corpora (van den Berg et al., 2014). The work cited in the previous paragraph is produced by researchers who have access to suitable corpora, but the vast majority of researchers do not have such access. A particularly disadvantaged group are historians of philosophical ideas, i. e. researchers working with (massive amounts of) philosophical texts stretching across centuries, written by many different authors in multiple languages and printed in a variety of scripts. Philosophers working with a history-of-ideas approach face harder challenges than historians of philosophy concentrating on works by only one author, one language, one short period, or even one work.

---

[2]   http://www.tei-c.org/

[3]   We here partly follow (van den Berg et al., 2014): the reader can consult this article for more information on the methods and tools used by historians of ideas. On these topics, see also (Betti and van den Berg, 2014a).

[4]   Another ontology aiding philosophical research is given by (Grenon and Smith, 2009).

The humanities researchers within @PhilosTEI (the 'Axiom group/Concepts in Motion' at the University of Amsterdam[5]) trace shifts of meaning of philosophical concepts such as *truth, explanation*, and *life* by studying texts in multiple languages published from the 17th up to the 20th century (Betti and van den Berg, 2014a,b). These researchers are keenly aware that their work would benefit significantly from the use of computational methods, especially natural language processing, text-mining, and machine learning. However, currently these methods can only be applied in an extremely limited way due to the lack of high-quality philosophical corpora in a sustainable and suitable open format.[6]

32.2.1 Availability of Historical Texts and Use Restrictions

In the last decades there have been several attempts to create high-quality digital editions of historical texts. For example, the Thesaurus Linguae Graecae (TLG)[7] is a digital library of Greek literature, providing access to all extant Greek texts from Homer to AD 600, thus including many ancient philosophers. Similarly, the Perseus Project[8] provides online access to works of ancient philosophers such as Plato and Aristotle. The famous Index Thomisticus provides a complete lemmatization of the works of Saint Thomas Aquinas.[9] The Bonner Kant-Korpus[10] provides an online and searchable digital edition of the complete works of Immanuel Kant, whereas the project Transcribe Bentham[11] provides digital images and transcriptions of the writings of Jeremy Bentham. Other historical works, including those of Nietzsche and Wittgenstein, have been made available within the PhiloSource federation.[12] There are, moreover, commercial companies that sell CD-ROMs or downloads of the works of famous philosophers such as Spinoza, Leibniz, Husserl, and others.[13]

Importantly, many among these editions are not in open access, so their use within digital philosophy projects is severely limited. This applies to e.g. commercial electronic editions, and to the content provided by the TLG. The TLG materials are copyrighted: users can browse and search the TLG but are not allowed to download material. Similarly, users can browse but not download the contents of the Bonner Kant-Korpus. Obtaining a licence for scholarly use of materials is sometimes possible, but one should keep in mind that the threshold for endeavouring to obtain appropriate licences might be too high for many users, and certain publishers will not give any licences.

32.2.2 Multilinguality, Minor Authors and Machine-Unreadability

Historians of ideas need to be able to build corpora of texts written in diverse languages such as Latin, German, French, Dutch, Polish, and English; they also need suitable editions of many works written by relatively unknown or 'minor' philosophers, whose works are not digitally available (Betti et al., 2014); finally, and most importantly, even many texts by known and important thinkers are not yet digitized in a way suitable for computational exploration. Our Axiom Group/Concepts

---

[5] http://www.axiom.humanities.uva.nl/

[6] For an example of what this group achieved by constructing and applying a simple text-mining tool on a single, albeit long (2,000 pages) text of reasonable quality, see (van Wierst et al., 2016).

[7] http://stephanus.tlg.uci.edu/index.php

[8] http://www.perseus.tufts.edu/hopper/

[9] http://www.corpusthomisticum.org/

[10] https://korpora.zim.uni-duisburg-essen.de/kant/

[11] http://blogs.ucl.ac.uk/transcribe-bentham/

[12] http://www.discovery-project.eu/philosource.html

[13] https://www.infosoftware.de/index.htm

in Motion philosophers study the works of e. g. Bernard Bolzano (1781–1848) and Gottlob Frege (1848–1925). Digitizations of a number of these philosophers' works are scattered across different repositories, such as Google Books, Hathi Trust, and Europeana, and researchers can often only download low-quality, scanned PDF images of original printings in Gothic typefaces (Betti and van den Berg, 2014b; van den Berg et al., 2014). Texts of this kind are unsuitable for minimally sophisticated computational exploration.

The challenges above are faced by historians of ideas and other researchers working in text-based digital humanities alike. For printed texts, Gothic typefaces – also known as Fraktur or blackletter – emerged in the 16th century and have been widely used up into the 20th century.[14] Hence, many historians work with material of this kind. Researchers working with texts published in different languages, typefaces, and formats would also profit from having a simple tool that allows them to create high-quality, easily and freely accessible corpora in a sustainable format. The purpose of @PhilosTEI was to develop such a tool.

32.3   Existing OCR Solutions to Building Corpora, and their Shortcomings

The main challenge faced by historians of philosophical ideas who wish to build corpora is how to transform scanned PDFs of texts printed in historical typefaces such as Gothic into a machine-readable format. In other words, the main challenge is how to perform automatic image-to-text conversion or OCR on images of texts written in a Gothic typeface (Furrer and Volk, 2011), such as depicted in Figure 32.1.

Historians who wish to OCR images of texts typeset in Gothic currently have a limited number of options. The first option is to use the OCR software developed by ABBYY (Fuchs, 2016). The downside to using ABBYY is that the software is not open-source and that users have to pay a specified amount of money for OCRing volumes of texts. At the time of writing of this chapter, the pricing for ABBYY Recognition Server 4 with Gothic/Fraktur was 999 euros for 50,000 pages, which equals approximately 160 digitised books, and might be considered a corpus of acceptable size for a single-researcher project in the history of ideas. Though not prohibitive, this is still a significant cost as it equals two thirds of the travel money for an entire year for a senior researcher in a Humanities Faculty in the Netherlands.

A second option for historians is to use the open source OCR engine Tesseract. The advantage of using Tesseract is that it is free. In addition, the quality of the OCR output seems to be comparable to that of the output of the ABBYY software. In a 2012 report conducted within the IMPACT project, the quality of the output of ABBYY Finereader and the quality of Tesseract were deemed to be relatively similar (Heliński et al., 2012). However, Tesseract also has its downsides. Setting up Tesseract properly is highly challenging. Tesseract would benefit from proper documentation as it comes with over 2,000 option settings that are impenetrable to researchers in the humanities who lack a strong technical background. Without appropriate setup and training, the quality of Tesseract OCR on diverse historical material (different languages, periods, and scripts) remains unsatisfactory (Betti and van den Berg, 2014b).

At the time of drafting our @PhilosTEI proposal (September 2012) an open-source alternative to Tesseract, namely OCRopus (Breuel, 2008) seemed set to help overcome Tesseract's drawbacks, while in fact it incorporated the system. In the following section we explain why in the end we did not follow this path.

---

[14] https://en.wikipedia.org/wiki/Fraktur

Figure 32.1: Cover of philosopher Bolzano's work *Wisschenschaftslehre*, printed in Fraktur.

32.4   The Solution: @PhilosTEI

In order to provide philosophers with an easy way to build philosophical corpora, and thus to solve some of the problems mentioned in the previous section, we have developed the web-based demonstrator tool @PhilosTEI.[15] This tool provides researchers with a free, open-source workflow from (scanned) images of texts to TEI, which is today's standard for digital editions. The system is easy to use and was developed in such a way that users with little technical knowledge can use the workflow. The system performs automatic OCR error post-correction on output delivered by the OCR software built in the workflow, namely Tesseract, in order to improve the quality of the output. It comes with at least basic lexica and provisions for 18 languages and diachronic language varieties.

---

[15] In this section, we draw on (and occasionally lift sentences from) the description of the TICCLops system given in (Reynaert, 2014c) and on the description of the @PhilosTEI system in (Betti and van den Berg, 2014b).

The tool is currently hosted by the Institute for the Dutch Language (INT).[16] When visiting the online system, the user sees the main interface page (Figure 32.2). There, the user can upload input files for a transcription project. These can be e.g. scanned images in PDF, TIFF or DjVu (Betti and van den Berg, 2014b; Reynaert, 2014c). The user needs to specify the language of the original text (necessary for having Tesseract load the appropriate training files for the language) and needs to provide the project with a name (to help the user locate the output for their own project). Advanced users can select a number of further options, which allows them, for example, to choose to modernise spelling to contemporary or to the original diachronic spelling on the basis of the specific lexicon selected or to select how many ranked post-correction variants TICCL will return (Figure 32.3).

When the user presses the 'Process files' button, the system runs and eventually provides different kinds of output. These include, most importantly, the OCR output and the OCR output as corrected by the OCR post-correction system that is an integral part of @PhilosTEI (Betti and van den Berg, 2014b). Users are provided with a reader that allows them to visually compare the original image files with the fully-automatically corrected OCR output (Figure 32.4).

Of necessity, the @PhilosTEI is internally far more complex than will ever be apparent to its users. Tesseract, to start with, delivers its output in hOCR HTML format (Breuel, 2007). This is converted to FoLiA XML (van Gompel and Reynaert, 2013) before being delivered to the OCR post-correction system we describe next.

The CLARIN-NL Call 1 project TICCLops delivered the Text-Induced Corpus Clean-up system (or TICCL) as a web application and service thanks to the development of the Computational Linguistics Application Mediator (or CLAM) (van Gompel and Reynaert, 2014), a generic solution for turning linguistic applications with a command-line interface into web applications and RESTful services.

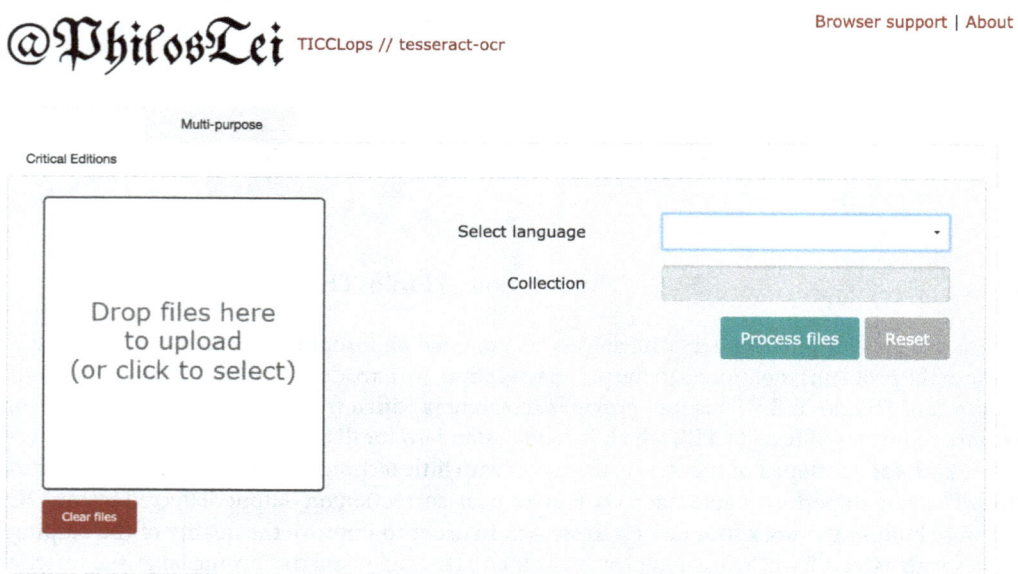

Figure 32.2: Main interface page.

---

[16] http://ticclops.clarin.inl.nl/philostei/

Collection	
File type	Plain text ▾

**Drop files here
to upload
(or click to select)**

[Process files] [Reset]

Hide advanced options   [Clear files]

Transcription
Transcribe to old or new spelling | Old spelling OCR post-correction ▾ |

How many ranked variants?
Return N best-first ranked variants | Up to three N-best ranked ▾ |

How many edits?
Search a distance of N characters for variants | Up to two edits ▾ |

Minimum Word Length
Integer between zero and one hundred | 5 |

Maximum Word Length
Integer between zero and one hundred | 100 |

Figure 32.3: Interface page for advanced users.

TICCLops // tesseract-ocr

Collection: demo1449839759854

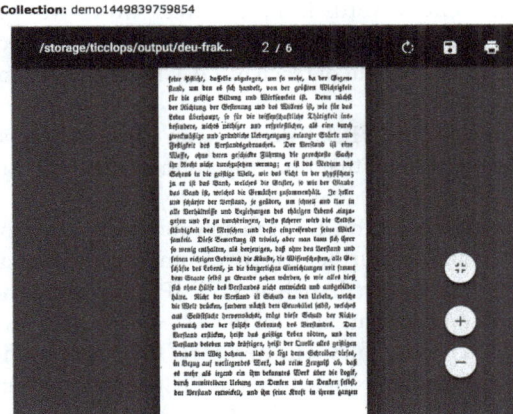

seine Pflicht, dasselbe abzulegen, um so mehr, da der Gegen-
stand, um den es sich handelt, von der größten Wichtigkeit für
die geistige Bildung und Wirksamkeit ist. Denn nächst der
Richtung der Gesinnung und des Willens ist, wie für das Leben
überhaupt, so für die wissenschaftliche Tätigkeit ins- besondere,
nichts nötiger und ersprießlicher, als- eine durch zweckmäßige
und gründliche Überzeugung erlangte Stärke und Festigkeit des
Verstandsgebrauches. Der Verstand ist eine Waffe, ohne deren
geschickte Führung die gerechteste Sache ihr Recht nicht
durchzusetzen vermag; er ist das Medium des sehen in die
geistige Welt, wie das Licht in der physischen; ja er ist das Band,
welches die Geister, so wie der Glaube das Band ist, welches die
Gemüter zusammenhält. Je heller und schärfer der Verstand, je
geübter, um schnell und klar in alle Verhältnisse und
Beziehungen des tätigen Lebens hinzu gehen und sie zu
durchdringen, desto sicherer wird die Selbst- Beständigkeit des
Menschenkind desto eingreifender seine Wirk- sankest Diese
Bemerkung ist trivial, aber man kann sich ihrer so wenig

Figure 32.4: Original page image and corrected text output.

One of the great advantages of using a system such as CLAM is that developers get the opportunity to select the linguistic application's features and parameters they choose to confront the web application's users with or to shield users from.

TICCL's availability as a web application and service made it the natural OCR post-correction system of choice. In the @PhilosTEI project we set out to expand the existing TICCLops system (Reynaert, 2014c) with OCR facilities. Our first ideas for the OCR-engine went to OCRopus (Breuel, 2008), but preliminary tests did not deliver the necessary results. In fact, the latest version of OCRopus no longer incorporated Tesseract, and very few trained models for its new OCR-engine were as yet available. This meant that our workflow building project might get side-tracked into an OCR-engine training project, and this we could not afford. We soon found out that the Andrew W. Mellon Foundation-funded Early Modern OCR Project[17] had project plans very similar to our own and much the same experience with the system. In consultation with eMOPS at the Dutch National Library KB, we too redirected our attention to the open source OCR solution Tesseract and co-opted it for our own pipeline. Tesseract's broad range of pre-trained languages made it perfectly suited for our purposes.

In @PhilosTEI we incorporated a totally new implementation of TICCL. This now consists of a series of C++ modules which are wrapped in a Perl script which takes care of a large part of the file handling peculiarities. TICCL emphatically does not handle a single page of text of a single document at a time; rather it derives the unigram frequency list of the full batch of documents to be corrected, uses a range of derived statistics to rank its list of correction candidates for the focus words and delivers a list of focus words paired with their ranked correction candidates.

TICCL was further made multilingual in the sense that it was equipped with available open source spelling dictionaries for 18 languages. From these, per language, a language-specific alphabet is first derived on the basis of the dictionary's character frequency list. In order to restrain the spelling variation search space, the characters below an ad-hoc frequency threshold are in essence disregarded. The alphabet is next used to precalculate the anagram hash values for the character confusions possible up to a particular Levenshtein distance (LD) (Levenshtein, 1966), in practice LD 2, given the characters available. Given the 25 characters in the smallest alphabet in our language selection, that for Latin, this gives 72,009 character confusion values. For the largest alphabet, i.e. Classical Greek with 100 characters, this amounts to 13,802,616 values. It should be noted that the actual alphabet is supplemented with two extra wildcard values, one encoding for any punctuation mark, another for all the characters not deemed to belong to the particular language. This has the handy result that if - say - a Latin text has Greek words in it, the Greek words will get an anagram value which is equal to the wildcard value times its length in characters. This in effect puts foreign words in another script automatically and neatly out of reach of TICCL's lexical variant retrieval mechanism for the given language.

On the basis of the character confusion anagram value list, TICCL performs an efficient exhaustive search for all the word string pairs in the corpus at hand that differ by no more than the LD threshold set.

The two main components of @PhilosTEI are integrated into CLAM in an extended Perl wrapper which encompasses both Tesseract and TICCL and the further assistive components such as convertors for the diverse page image formats that are supported, such as TIFF, JPG and PDF. The wrapper allows for flexible handling of numbers of input/output files, taking e.g. x PDF input files for separate book chapters apart into y (where $y \geq x$) image files, one per page, to be sent to the OCR engine Tesseract, then presenting the y OCRed files as a single batch to TICCL, which eventually corrects the y FoLiA XML page files to be collated into a single output FoLiA XML book and also, as the philosopher-user desires, a TEI XML output e-book, using TEI Lite.

32.5   Evaluation

Within @PhilosTEI, we have conducted two types of evaluation: (a) a quantitative evaluation of the OCR post-correction tool TICCL, and (b) a qualitative user evaluation of the web-based workflow from textual images to TEI. Below we present the main results of these evaluations.

---

[17] http://emop.tamu.edu/

32.5.1   Quantitative Evaluation of TICCL

The @PhilosTEI project benefitted from a large-scale quantitative evaluation of TICCL undertaken in part in the framework of the NWO 'Groot' project Nederlab as described in (Reynaert, 2014b). As was described in its companion paper (Reynaert, 2014a), undertaking an evaluation of an OCR-post-correction system on the scale of even a single OCRed book is an extremely expensive and labour-intensive undertaking. The scale and scope of @PhilosTEI did not permit for this to be undertaken on a full philosophical work.

The evaluation on the Gold Standard book reported that TICCL improved the accuracy of the OCRed historical text by 5.5%, from 88.94% to 94.51%.

A new evaluation (Reynaert, 2016) on 1,000 randomly chosen word strings of the same post-correction of 10,333 Dutch mostly late-18th-century books has shown that the extremely high correction precision scores of over 99% reported on the single history book written for children are, as was to be expected, not obtained throughout the whole collection. However, at over 84% for fully automatic correction on the random sample of the whole collection, precision remains good. The score on recall, 35%, means one in three errors are fully-automatically corrected. Almost half of the errors are corrected when one takes into account the ten best-ranked correction candidates. This new evaluation points clearly towards necessary and possible future extensions of TICCL. These should finally allow for meaningful noisy-text improvement to be achieved fully automatically.

32.5.2   Qualitative User Evaluation of the @PhilosTEI Workflow

The qualitative user evaluation of the workflow from textual images focused on two main criteria: (i) user-friendliness, and (ii) quality of the output.[18]

Ad (i): Humanities users often have little experience with using computational tools for research purposes, and have little or no technical background knowledge. It is thus vital that the workflow be intuitive and very easy to use, and presupposes as little technical knowledge as possible.

During the development of the workflow, six users have provided evaluations by using a Google document template prepared by the user with the most extensive experience with this kind of testing (Hein van den Berg). The evaluations were collected at three different phases of development: after the development of the first user interface (July 2014, three researchers), after the development of the second user interface (October 2014, two researchers, one student), and after completion of the project (October 2015, students). The first batch of evaluations led to the development of a new interface. The first – classical CLAM – interface that was developed provided users with a lot of configuration options. Inexperienced users felt there were too many configuration options, which made the interface unintuitive to use. Based on this feedback, we built a new interface, presented in Section 32.4, enabling the user to select one out of two configuration methods. With this interface, novice users have no configuration options, and expert users have a fair range of configuration options.

The new interface has been evaluated very positively by the users within the project who had performed the first batch of evaluations. The experience of these users with many research tools produced within computational projects is that such tools are unappealing to use. By contrast, the new interface resembles the design of online tools for a large public that is typically found attractive and pleasant to interact with.

The evaluation of the two students who tested the new interface after completion of the project was less positive. Importantly, the students had no knowledge of the previous interface, and

---

[18]   In this section, we draw on the description in (Betti and van den Berg, 2014b), which provides a more comprehensive qualitative evaluation than can be given in the current chapter.

had a different goal, namely identifying as quickly as possible the best tool available for building a highest-quality corpus for a text-mining project,[19] consisting, crucially, of modern English texts containing a huge amount of logico-mathematical formulas. With respect to other OCR tools available on the market, the main shortcoming was deemed to be usability (including e.g. the lack of an interactive correction panel). The choice of the students fell on ABBYY Finereader, a choice that posed additional institutional challenges with commercial licensing for the students involved, resulting in a great amount of institutional red tape.

Ad (ii): The two more experienced users from the project team have also evaluated the quality of the output. They converted scanned images of the texts mentioned in Table 32.1 below and evaluated both the OCR output and the TICCL output on how well the output matches the original text. What counts as 'good performance' has been evaluated on the basis of an intuitive measure of what our colleagues would consider useful results.

In general, the quality of the OCR and TICCL output was evaluated as having reasonably high quality, with ample opportunity for improvement. The OCR output for samples of the German texts (Bolzano, 1837; Frege, 1879) contains several spelling mistakes, and the OCR engine cannot handle end-of-line splits. TICCL also cannot yet handle end-of-line splits. In addition, TICCL currently does not correct words that contain multiple OCR-induced errors beyond the edit distance limit of 2 edits imposed and sometimes introduces incorrect changes by itself. The quality of the Polish OCR and TICCL output (Tarski, 1936) is comparable to that of the German. The quality of the Latin OCR output (Wolff, 1740) was not as good as that of the German or Polish. In general, each line of text contained multiple mistakes. TICCL corrects several of these mistakes, but, again, not all of them, and it also introduced errors of its own.

32.5.3   Discussion of the Evaluations

There is a major drawback of TICCL's incorporation in the @PhilosTEI web application that was insufficiently addressed during its development. This is that the online system on the whole is geared towards processing only a single book at a time. As TICCL's evaluations described in Reynaert (2014b) clearly show on the basis of comparison of the correction of a single book in isolation versus the correction of the same book within a batch of 10,333 books of the same era, the tool's performance on the isolated single book is far inferior to that on the full batch. This is due to the far poorer and sparser word string statistics obtainable from just a single book.

This is to be remedied in the current follow-up project PICCL (Reynaert et al., 2015) within the CLARIAH programme. We describe this future work in the next section.

The users in the project find it crucial to stress that improving TICCL's usability and performance would have important advantages over commercial solutions, namely cutting users' costs and institutional red tape to zero.

	Language	Typeface	Period	Format	Location
Wolff (1740)	Latin	Roman	middle 18th century	PDF	archive.org
Bolzano (1837)	German	Gothic	middle 19th century	PDF	dml.cz
Frege (1879)	German	Roman	last third 19th century	PDF	Gallica
Tarski (1936)	Polish	Roman	middle of 20th century	DjVu	TEL/Europeana

Table 32.1: Overview of philosophers' works, dates, print typefaces, languages, periods and source locations used in the @PhilosTEI system evaluations.

---

[19] https://quine1960.wordpress.com/the-quine-in-context-project/

32.6   Future Work and Challenges

In 2016–2017 in the PICCL or 'Philosophical Integrator of Computational and Corpus Libraries' project we build further on the foundations laid in the @PhilosTEI project and expand the work flow into a full-fledged corpus building pipeline.

Next to the image input already catered for, we are to incorporate the necessary convertors for all manner of electronic text formats. We will revisit the current OCR and OCR-post-processing scene and see whether OCRopus or perhaps new approaches to OCR are now contenders for the Tesseract engine. In emulation of Volk et al. (2010), we will strive towards combining multiple OCR versions for the same works and let TICCL sort out statistically which of close but divergent renderings of the same word tokens – the assumption being that different OCR engines will produce differing results – best fit the actual text.

For TICCL, one pathway we will obviously follow is to allow the user to also provide the system with the frequency list obtained from contemporary and where possible comparable works, whether well-edited hand-keyed transcriptions or noisy OCRed versions. Users will likewise be able to furnish the system with domain-specific lexicons and name lists at their disposal. In the short run, TICCL is to be extended with word bigram information to allow for addressing split and run-on word errors and short word forms.

In order to allow the digital humanities scholar to obtain the best possible text result, we will provide solutions geared at manual and interactive text correction. This will be based on FLAT,[20] the 'FoLiA Linguistic Annotation Tool', which is a modern web application that offers an interface for the visualisation and editing of FoLiA documents. We will also see if some of the tools developed in the Impact[21] project – Aletheia[22] for text segmentation and PoCoTo[23] for OCR post-correction are interesting prospects, for example – may likely be enlisted.

The pipeline will next provide linguistic enrichments in the form of annotations for lemmata, part-of-speech and named entities towards more fine-grained exploration and analysis of the texts. To this end, the memory-based tool Frog[24] will be made part of the pipeline. In fact, we aim towards integrating all the available FoLiA XML tools[25] in PICCL.

Finally, indexing towards online availability in a corpus exploration and exploitation environment[26] will be provided.

In short, PICCL is about choosing the best possible tools currently available, wrapping them all in an environment that allows non-experts to nevertheless harness their contribution and making this environment freely and openly available to all.

32.7   Conclusion

The @PhilosTEI project has been successfully completed and has managed to bring its philosopher-users and its more technically directed developers closer together and more aware of each other's needs and limitations. While the system we built does not to-date allow for unfettered, fully-automatic corpus building, it does allow non-technical people to convert mere text images into electronic text presented in state-of-the-art corpus formats ready for further manual editing.

---

[20] https://github.com/proycon/flat
[21] http://www.digitisation.eu
[22] http://www.primaresearch.org/tools
[23] https://github.com/cisocrgroup/PoCoTo
[24] https://languagemachines.github.io/frog
[25] See Chapter 6 on FoLiA in this volume.
[26] See Chapter 19 on WhiteLab in this volume.

Some of the hurdles which have not been overcome yet are hoped to be overcome by follow-up project PICCL, which is currently underway in CLARIAH.

Acknowledgements

The authors acknowledge having been funded by CLARIN-NL project @PhilosTEI. Martin Reynaert further acknowledges being funded by the new Dutch national CLARIN project CLARIAH and by NWO in project Nederlab. Hein van den Berg further acknowledges being funded by Europeana eCloud (325091).

References

Jon Barwise and John Etchemendy. 1998. *Computers, Visualization, and the Nature of Reasoning.* Blackwell Publishers: Oxford.

Arianna Betti and Hein van den Berg. 2014a. Modelling the History of Ideas. *British Journal for the History of Philosophy*, 22(4): 812–835.

Arianna Betti and Hein van den Berg. 2014b. @PhilosTEI: Final user evaluation report. Technical report, Amsterdam, November.

Arianna Betti, Dirk Gerrits, Bettina Speckmann, and Hein van den Berg. 2014. Glammap: visualising library metadata. In *Proceedings of VALA* 2014 – Libraries, Technologies, and the Future: Melbourne, Australia.

Bernard Bolzano. 1837. *Wissenschaftslehre. Versuch einer ausführlichen und größtentheils neuen Darstellung der Logik mit steter Rücksicht auf deren bisherige Bearbeiter.* J.E. v Seidel, Sulzbach.

Thomas Breuel. 2007. The hOCR microformat for OCR workflow and results. In ICDAR '07 - *Proceedings of the Ninth International Conference on Document Analysis and Recognition* 2: 1063–1067. IEEE Computer Society: Washington, DC, USA.

Thomas Breuel. 2008. The OCRopus Open Source OCR System. In B.A. Yanikoglu and K. Berkner, editors, *Proceedings of SPIE 6815, Document Recognition and Retrieval XV, 68150F.* SPIE: San Jose, California, USA.

Cameron Buckner, Mathias Niepert, and Colin Allen. 2011. From encyclopedia to ontology: Toward dynamic representation of the discipline of philosophy. *Synthese*, 182(2): 205–233.

Lou Burnard and Syd Bauman, editors, 2007. *TEI P5: Guidelines for Electronic Text Encoding and Interchange.* Text Encoding Initiative Consortium.

Terrell Ward Bynum and James Moor, editors. 1998. *The Digital Phoenix: How Computers Are Changing Philosophy.* Blackwell Publishers: Oxford.

Terrell Ward Bynum. 2001. Computer ethics: Its birth and its future. *Ethics and Information Technology*, 3(2): 109–112.

Charles Ess. 2004. "Revolution? What Revolution?" Successes and Limits of Computing Technologies in Philosophy and Religion. In S. Schreibman, R. Siemens, and J. Unsworth, editors, *A companion to Digital Humanities*: 132–142. Blackwell Publishers: Oxford.

Luciano Floridi. 2011. *The philosophy of information.* Oxford University Press: Oxford.

Gottlob Frege. 1879. *Begriffsschrift, eine der arithmetischen nachgebildete Formelsprache des reinen Denkens.* Louis Nebert: Halle.

Michael Fuchs. 2016. White paper. ABBYY historic OCR: the use of Gothic OCR in processing historical documents. http://www.frakturschrift.com/_media/en:white_paper_gothic-fraktur_ocr_e.pdf

Lenz Furrer and Martin Volk. 2011. Reducing OCR errors in Gothic-script documents. In Vertan et al., editor, *Proceedings of the RANLP 2011 workshop on Language Technologies for Digital Humanities and Cultural Heritage*: 97–103. Incoma, Shoumen, Bulgaria.

Pierre Grenon and Barry Smith. 2009. Foundations of an ontology of philosophy. *Synthese*, 182(2): 185–204.

Marcin Heliński, Miłosz Kmieciak, and Tomasz Parkoła. 2012. Report on the comparison of Tesseract and ABBYY Finereader OCR engines. PCSS, Poznań.

Aurélie Herbelot, Eva Von Redecker, and Johanna Müller. 2012. Distributional techniques for philosophical enquiry. In LaTeCH '12 - *Proceedings of the 6th Workshop on Language Technology for Cultural Heritage, Social Sciences, and Humanities*: 45–54. Association for Computational Linguistics Stroudsburg, PA, USA.

Vladimir I. Levenshtein. 1966. Binary codes capable of correcting deletions, insertions, and reversals. *Cybernetics and Control Theory*, 10(8): 707–710.

Alastair McKinnon. 1977. From co-occurrences to concepts. *Computers and the Humanities*, 11(3): 147–156.

James A. Overton. 2012. "Explain" in scientific discourse. *Synthese*, 190(8): 1383–1405.

Michele Pasin, Milton Keynes, and Enrico Motta. 2008. PhiloSURFical: Browse Wittgenstein's World with the Semantic Web. In A. Pichler and H. Hrachovec, editors, *Wittgenstein and the Philosophy of Information: Proceedings of the 30th International Ludwig Wittgenstein-Symposium in Kirchberg, 2007*: 319–331. De Gruyter: Berlin.

Alois Pichler and Amélie Zöllner-Weber. 2013. Sharing and debating Wittgenstein by using an ontology. *Literary and Linguistic Computing*, 28(4): 700–707.

Martin Reynaert, Maarten van Gompel, Ko van der Sloot, and Antal van den Bosch. 2015. PICCL: Philosophical Integrator of Computational and Corpus Libraries. In *CLARIN Annual Conference 2015 – Book of Abstracts*: 75–79 CLARIN ERIC: Wrocław, Poland.

Martin Reynaert. 2010. Character confusion versus focus word-based correction of spelling and OCR variants in corpora. *International Journal on Document Analysis and Recognition*, 14: 173–187.

Martin Reynaert. 2014a. On OCR ground truths and OCR post-correction gold standards, tools and formats. In A. Antonacopoulos and K.U. Schulz, editors, DATeCH 2014 - *Proceedings of Digital Access to Textual Cultural Heritage*: 159–166. ACM: New York, NY, USA.

Martin Reynaert. 2014b. Synergy of Nederlab and @PhilosTEI: diachronic and multilingual Text-Induced Corpus Clean-up. In N. Calzolari et al. *Proceedings of the Ninth International Conference on Language Resources and Evaluation (LREC-2014)*. ELRA: Reykjavik, Iceland.

Martin Reynaert. 2014c. TICCLops: Text-Induced Corpus Clean-up as online processing system. In L. Tounsi and R. Rak, *Proceedings of COLING 2014, the 25th International Conference on Computational Linguistics System Demonstrations*: 52–56. Dublin City University and Association for Computational Linguistics: Dublin, Ireland.

Martin Reynaert. 2016. OCR post-correction evaluation of Early Dutch Books Online – revisited. In N. Calzolari et al., editor, *Proceedings of the Tenth International Conference on Language Resources and Evaluation (LREC-2016)*. ELRA: Portorož, Slovenia.

Alfred Tarski. 1936. O pojęciu wynikania logicznego. *Przegląd filozoficzny*, 39: 58–68.

Hein van den Berg, Gonzalo Parra, Anja Jentzsch, Andreas Drakos, and Erik Duval. 2014. Studying the History of Philosophical Ideas: Supporting Research Discovery, Navigation, and Awareness. In i-KNOW '14 - *Proceedings of the 14th International Conference on Knowledge Technologies and Data-driven Business*, 12:1–8. ACM: New York, NY, USA.

Maarten van Gompel and Martin Reynaert. 2013. FoLiA: A practical XML Format for Linguistic Annotation - a descriptive and comparative study. *Computational Linguistics in the Netherlands Journal*, 3: 63–81.

Maarten van Gompel and Martin Reynaert. 2014. CLAM: Quickly deploy NLP command-line tools on the web. In *Proceedings of COLING 2014, the 25th International Conference on Computational Linguistics: System Demonstrations*: 71–75. Dublin City University and Association for Computational Linguistics: Dublin, Ireland.

Pauline van Wierst, Sanne Vrijenhoek, Stefan Schlobach, and Arianna Betti. 2016. Phil@Scale: Computational Methods within Philosophy. In *Proceedings of the Third Conference on Digital Humanities in Luxembourg with a Special Focus on Reading Historical Sources in the Digital Age*, 1681. Aachen: CEUR-WS.org.

Martin Volk, Torsten Marek, and Rico Sennrich. 2010. Reducing OCR errors by combining two OCR systems. In C. Sporleder and K. Zervanou, editors, *Proceedings of the Workshop on Language Technology for Cultural Heritage, Social Sciences, and Humanities (LaTeCH 2010)*: 61–65. Faculty of Science, University of Lisbon: Lisbon, Portugal.

Christian Wolff. 1740. *Philosophia rationalis sive logica*. Officina libraria Rengeriana: Frankfurt and Leipzig.

Paul Ziche, Dirk van Miert, Peter Sperber, Timmy de Goeij, Tom Giesbers, Daniel Meijer, et al. 2014. Mining for associated words in philosophical texts. *Schelling Studien: Internationale Zeitschrift zur Klassischen Deutschen Philosophie*, 2(1): 215–231.